The Basic Survival Kit

Small flashlight

Hex nut driver

Offset screwdrivers (to take out PC/XT drives without removing circuit boards)

Tweezers or hemostats

Multimeter

Digital temperature probe

Compressed air

Hair dryer or heat gun

Tweaker screwdriver to pull chips

AC circuit wiring tester

Tasco AC monitor (reports voltage delivered by the power company and power spikes)

Breakout box

PARA Systems AC power meter (measures how many watts your system uses)

Software: Mace Utilities Gold or Norton Utilities Advanced Edition version 4.5.1 or later; Kolod hTEST/hFORMAT; and a toolkit disk with the following:

> DOS bootable (include any device drivers, like OnTrack Disk Manager's DMDRVR.BIN)
>
> DOS FDISK
>
> DOS FORMAT
>
> DOS SYS
>
> HDAT or some other low-level format
>
> HFORMAT, GETSEC, PUTSEC, and XFDISK from hTEST/hFORMAT
>
> DOS DEBUG
>
> Some disk head–parking program
>
> Mace REMEDY or Norton's DISKTEST (DT) or DISKDOCTOR (NDD)
>
> SETUP, if you're working on an AT or 386

For every kind of computer user, there is a SYBEX book.

All computer users learn in their own way. Some need straightforward and methodical explanations. Others are just too busy for this approach. But no matter what camp you fall into, SYBEX has a book that can help you get the most out of your computer and computer software while learning at your own pace.

Beginners generally want to start at the beginning. The **ABC's** series, with its step-by-step lessons in plain language, helps you build basic skills quickly. Or you might try our **Quick & Easy** series, the friendly, full-color guide.

The **Mastering** and **Understanding** series will tell you everything you need to know about a subject. They're perfect for intermediate and advanced computer users, yet they don't make the mistake of leaving beginners behind.

If you're a busy person and are already comfortable with computers, you can choose from two SYBEX series—**Up & Running** and **Running Start**. The **Up & Running** series gets you started in just 20 lessons. Or you can get two books in one, a step-by-step tutorial and an alphabetical reference, with our **Running Start** series.

Everyone who uses computer software can also use a computer software reference. SYBEX offers the gamut—from portable **Instant References** to comprehensive **Encyclopedias, Desktop References**, and **Bibles**.

SYBEX even offers special titles on subjects that don't neatly fit a category—like **Tips & Tricks**, the **Shareware Treasure Chests**, and a wide range of books for Macintosh computers and software.

SYBEX books are written by authors who are expert in their subjects. In fact, many make their living as professionals, consultants or teachers in the field of computer software. And their manuscripts are thoroughly reviewed by our technical and editorial staff for accuracy and ease-of-use.

So when you want answers about computers or any popular software package, just help yourself to SYBEX.

For a complete catalog of our publications, please write:

SYBEX Inc.
2021 Challenger Drive
Alameda, CA 94501
Tel: (510) 523-8233/(800) 227-2346 Telex: 336311
Fax: (510) 523-2373

SYBEX is committed to using natural resources wisely to preserve and improve our environment. As a leader in the computer book publishing industry, we are aware that over 40% of America's solid waste is paper. This is why we have been printing the text of books like this one on recycled paper since 1982.

This year our use of recycled paper will result in the saving of more than 15,300 trees. We will lower air pollution effluents by 54,000 pounds, save 6,300,000 gallons of water, and reduce landfill by 2,700 cubic yards.

In choosing a SYBEX book you are not only making a choice for the best in skills and information, you are also choosing to enhance the quality of life for all of us.

This Book Is Only the Beginning.

The Complete PC Upgrade and Maintenance Guide

THIRD EDITION

MARK MINASI

SYBEX®

• *San Francisco* • *Paris* • *Düsseldorf* • *Soest*

DEVELOPMENTAL EDITOR: Gary Masters
EDITOR: Guy Hart-Davis
TECHNICAL EDITOR: Dan Tauber
BOOK DESIGNER: Suzanne Albertson
PRODUCTION ARTIST: Claudia Smelser
TYPESETTER: Ann Dunn
PROOFREADER/PRODUCTION ASSISTANT: Stephen Kullmann
INDEXER: Ted Laux
COVER DESIGN: Ingalls + Associates
COVER PHOTOGRAPHER: Michael Lamotte

Library of Congress Card Number: 93-87698
ISBN: 0-7821-1498-9

Manufactured in the United States of America

10 9 8 7 6 5 4 3 2 1

To Kris Ashton, my MacSweetie.
(I'll do the "how to fix the Mac" book next, Kris.)

ACKNOWLEDGMENTS

THIS was a big task. I couldn't have done it without some essential help. I'd like to thank several people in particular.

For the Third Edition: Thanks go, of course, to everyone mentioned in the acknowledgments for the previous editions. I'd also like to thank the staff at *Compute* who edit my monthly Hardware Clinic column—Dave English and Cliff Karnes in particular. Gary Masters is, as always, an invaluable natural resource for ideas and support. And, again, Christa Anderson has endured a lot of scutwork to get this edition out.

Sheila Walsh read everything I wrote to make sure that it would make sense to normal humans. She calmly insisted that obscure parts be rewritten, even when I was at my most ursine. She even tactfully ignored me when I was fed up with rewriting and just yelled "if they're too dumb to understand *that*, they're not *allowed* to read the book!" Such comments were only the product of late nights and long hours, however, and I eventually saw things her way. (One might say I was then at my most "ursinine.") The text is much better for her suggestions, and I appreciate her tenacity. She also pointed out stylistic errors in pictures and tables, and cleaned up nearly fifty tables in this book. On top of that, she ran errands for me and made me eat when I forgot to. Rarely have I worked with an assistant who assists so well.

Rob Oreglia, a seminar-teaching buddy of many years (we were once partners in a four-partner firm), patiently explained the details of electrical ground, do's and don'ts about surge protectors, and has in general kept me on the straight-and-narrow about facts that I otherwise might have let slip. Rob's insistence on actually *reading the documentation* (an obsession that I lack, sadly) when he sets out on a project has taught me a few things and gotten me out of a few corners. Rob advised me heavily on the *Power Supplies and Power Protection* chapter, and designed the AT memory error message maps in the *Semiconductor Memory* chapter. Rob also took the pictures in this book, and did a very nice job, I think you'll agree. Rob still teaches with me at Mark Minasi & Company; if you ever get a chance to see him in action leading a class, don't miss it.

Pete Moulton and I worked for years as managing partners in a seminar/consulting firm. As a sideline to his teaching and consulting, he installed PC systems for big and small companies. He's got more war stories than you can hear in the time it takes to drink *several* pints of your favorite ale, and they have enriched this class. (Don't order Pete a beer, however—he drinks red wine.) The "Rules of Troubleshooting Almost Anything" in the beginning of the chapter on *Troubleshooting Problems* are derived from one of Pete's lectures. Pete was one of the seminal forces in helping me get set up in business. Had Pete not shown me that it's actually possible to make a living at this stuff, I'd still be an economist.

Terry Keaton not only teaches some of our classes, he is also staggeringly good at technical illustrations. You'll notice that there are good illustrations in this book and not-so-good illustrations. The good illustrations are Terry's; I've placed a "TK" in the lower-right corner of his pictures. The not-so-good illustrations are mine.

Scott Foerster, another former partner, has shared dozens of troubleshooting tips over the past few years with the rest of us who teach the troubleshooting classes, and we're all grateful for his suggestions. Scott knows this stuff right down to the soldering irons. When I write stupid things at 4 A.M. like "set your voltmeter to AC current and test to see if you're getting 120 volts," Scott catches it. Thanks, Scott.

Christa Anderson did the running around and scutwork essential to getting the second edition out in some kind of reasonable time. Assistance of this quality is a real productivity-enhancer.

Thanks to the other MM&Co "Next Generation" staff that I haven't yet mentioned: Bob "Big Bad Bobby" Deyo, Donna "Marketing Animal" Cook, Kris "Ms. Mac" Ashton, Jim "Cap'n Jim" Booth, Pat "Commander"

Campbell, Andy "The Lieutenant" Broyles, Doug "Mr. Doug" Zimmer, Truman "Trusty Ted" Deyo, Katie Barrett, Ben "The Benster" Okopnik, Sharon "The Mayor of Northern Virginia" Weaver, Elizabeth "Maeve" Creegan, Erin Malone, and Pam Sullivan.

There are now quite a number of companies offering PC Troubleshooting seminars, but ours was the first. So when I looked for a seminar house to sponsor a PC Troubleshooting seminar, the only folks who would take a chance on it were John and Doug at Data-Tech Institute. They were brave enough to give it a shot and savvy enough to market it so that it became a success. To the DTI folks, thanks very much. Similarly, in the overseas market, it was Maureen Quinn who saw to it that the course made it to London and points east. If this hadn't been a seminar workbook, I would probably never have found the time to amass this much information about fixing PCs.

Thanks also to the following companies for allowing me to reproduce some of their materials in this book:

Hewlett-Packard Printer Division (for LaserJet inserts)

Hewlett-Packard Office Automation (for ScanJet inserts)

Iomega Corporation (for Bernoulli Host Adapter inserts)

Finally, I want to give a big "thank you very much!" to all of you who've purchased this book, the seminar, and/or the videotapes. Seeing the book sales numbers is great, but it's not nearly as great as hearing from people like Cheryl Stewart. Cheryl found me at a conference and stopped me just to tell me that she'd looked high and low for a textbook for a community college course that she teaches on PC repair, and she picked mine out of the bunch of them. Thanks, Cheryl!

Contents
AT A GLANCE

CONTENTS

INTRODUCTION TO THE THIRD EDITION

SINCE this book first appeared in 1990, I'm told that it's become the best-selling PC upgrade and repair book on the market. I'm very grateful to my readers for that, and I know that they need the most up-to-date information possible—that's why SYBEX and I have prepared this Third Edition.

If you're already an owner of an earlier edition, a new buyer, or perhaps an owner of a (ahem!) competing volume, then I thought you'd like an overview of what's new in this edition.

- The CPU section has been expanded, with up-to-the minute coverage of the Pentium and clock triplers.

- Likewise, the section on buses now includes PCI, more information on VLB, and PCMCIA bus slots. You'll also find (in Chapter 6, the chapter on installing new circuit boards) an overview of the new Plug and Play standard being pushed by Microsoft, Intel, and Compaq.

- The section on SCSI has been greatly expanded. I was able to do extensive SCSI research this year, and that's covered in a new and separate chapter on SCSI technology, as well as a bunch of tips on how to troubleshoot it and keep it working. SCSI's time has come, so start considering SCSI peripherals when buying drives, tape drives, and CD-ROMs! (Before you do, however, read the SCSI chapter—Chapter 11.)

- A few vendors have begun surreptitiously reducing the reliability of their motherboards by using 8-bit memory modules. Read about this in Chapter 8.

- CD-ROMs are changing from "power user" items to "gotta have 'em" peripherals. NT can't load without them, OS/2 loads more easily with them, and a number of applications are now available on CD-ROM. As a result, the CD-ROM coverage has been expanded in this edition, including a discussion of triple-spin and quadruple-spin drives.

- Local bus video brings with it a new installation headache, the configuration of something called the *video aperture*. The video chapter explains what it is and how to solve the problems that it may cause.

- Increased interest in multimedia means that many of us must go out and get sound boards. The Second Edition's coverage of sound boards is updated and expanded, and now includes a discussion of sound boards that plug into laptop parallel ports.

- Technology references have been updated to reflect current market realities.

I hope you find this book an invaluable resource when fixing, upgrading, or buying PCs. Even if you never fix a PC, it's always nice to know how a machine that you depend so much upon works.

And if you come upon a tip that I can share with the rest of the world in our next edition, or if you have a question that the book doesn't cover, then you can e-mail me at either **71571,264** (CompuServe), or **mminasi@access.digex.net** (Internet). Thanks for reading, and happy upgrading!

INTRODUCTION

Why This Book?

I wrote this book because I've always wanted to teach a five-day PC troubleshooting class. But that's not why I got *started* writing this, so let me start at the beginning.

Imagine you're using your PC one day. All of a sudden, the floppy drive light goes on for no apparent reason, the system reboots itself, and "601" appears on the screen. Nothing else happens—the machine refuses to do any more. You turn it off and on again, and it does the same thing. What now? Call the serviceman? The local PC expert? Open the yellow pages?

The above disk disaster happened to me in 1982, shortly after PCs arrived on the scene but after the warranty on my PC ran out. I had an all-IBM machine, but since some of the parts came from a dealer who wasn't an authorized IBM dealer, IBM wouldn't even talk to me. So I went to the service department of a large computer-store chain seeking help. I looked at their hourly rates and *knew* from their high prices that they must have known what they were doing, so I confidently left my machine with them. They kept the machine for two months, said they couldn't find anything wrong with it, and charged me $800.

The problem, of course, persisted. I was scared. I had just spent some big bucks for this computer, plus $800 on some nonrepairs, and it still didn't work. So I figured, "What the heck, I can't make it any worse," and took off the top.

What I saw was that the drive was connected with a ribbon cable to a circuit board that I later found was called the "floppy controller board." The controller board was new, the drive was new (the repair shop had already replaced them)—but what about the cable? You guessed it. For $35 I bought a new cable from a local computer-supply place, and the problem went away forever.

I found out that I wasn't the only person with PC repair needs. In 1987, seven out of ten PCs suffered a breakdown of some kind. Each problem took an average of five days to fix, and the fix cost an average of $257. (This is according to a survey from the Business Products Consulting Group of Centerport, NY, as reported in *PC Week* on 12 January 1988. The results were based on a survey of 500 business users. Besides, it was about time for a statistic.) Even if you pay a maintenance company lots of money to keep your machine in shape, you should still do whatever repairs you can. That's because the high cost of machine failures isn't the cost of the machine—it's the cost of the lost work time. You might have to wait four hours for a serviceperson, only to find that the fix is a simple five-minute operation. Result: four hours of lost time.

Emboldened by my success, I read what few references existed about microcomputer repair, and I tried fixing a lot of things. Some things got fixed, some got "smoked." I asked a lot of questions, made a lot of mistakes, and finally got to the point where at the worst I didn't do any damage, and usually I met with success.

I'd like to accelerate you to that point with this book (although you'll still smoke the occasional device—everybody does). Once I figured out how simple it is to fix PCs, I developed a series of seminars on PC repair that my coworkers and I conduct in the U.S., Canada, and Europe. These two- to three-day seminars have been popular because of the significance of the topic and the fine work of the marketing companies handling them, Data-Tech Institute and Frost & Sullivan, Ltd.

But I've always wanted to teach a five-day class.

You see, a five-day professional seminar really doesn't sell. The seminar would cost too much to run, we would have to charge too much for it, and no one would come because companies can't afford to let their people (particularly their PC support staff) stay away five consecutive days. So we trim the less important stuff, do fewer exercises, and rush like crazy to get out in two or three days. It drives me crazy not to be able to cover the topics with the thoroughness they deserve. Worse, the classes unanimously say they've had a great time and learned a lot, but that they desperately needed an extra day or two.

So, welcome to the five-day class.

This book won't teach you to fix all problems. Not all problems can be fixed—for instance, leaving a hard disk out in the rain will probably render that erstwhile data storage medium usable for little more than a paperweight. Nevertheless, even if you've never opened up a PC or installed an expansion board, this book can help.

I'll also help with terminology. If you provide technical support or if you are working on your own computer, you might need to talk to technical types. Some of those folks are good at talking to ordinary mortals, but there are some (and I'm sure you know a few of them) who can't seem to speak a single sentence without a liberal sprinkling of TLAs (Three-Letter Acronyms). A thorough reading of this book will enable you to speak fluent "PC-ese."

You'll also see a fair amount about installation in this book. Installation of new equipment often brings headaches: how to do it, why it doesn't work once installed, testing the new equipment, ensuring that it doesn't adversely affect equipment already installed. You'll also learn how to take a tired old PC and soup it up for better performance.

Who Is This Book For?

I'm writing this for the needy and the curious. Some of you need to understand the machines you depend upon so much so that you can better keep them in top shape. Others might just wonder what's going on under the hood. Whoever you are, dig in and try something!

Don't let that useful little gray box on your desk control you when it goes down—take control of it. (Remember who's supposed to be boss.) Even if you never take the machine apart, you'll still learn a lot from this book about what goes on under the hood of your machine, and how to make it work faster and live longer. This will help both the home do-it-yourselfer and the professional technical support person.

Terminology

There are so many machines, it's hard to know how to refer generically to PCs. Here are the informal conventions used in this book: *PC* in this text includes all PC-compatible machines—the XT, XT clones, the AT, AT clones, and the 386 and 486 machines, unless otherwise specified. *XT* refers to XTs and XT clones—8088-based machines. *AT* refers to 286, 386, or 486 machines in general. I don't refer to IBM machines in particular unless specified otherwise. *PS/2* refers to the Micro Channel PS/2s (the 50 through the 80) and does not include the 25 and 30.

My goal in developing this book is to include material of use to "techies" as well as to those who have never even opened up a PC. I'm not going to try to make an electrical engineer out of you; I'm not one myself. All it takes to do most PC maintenance is a screwdriver and some patience. I've made every effort to keep the jargon to a minimum and to define unusual PC terms as they're used.

The Structure of This Book

In Chapter 1, we'll discuss tools that you'll find useful, and quickly survey the kinds of machines that you're likely to encounter. Chapter 2 shows you how to disassemble your machine, with particular attention to disassembling it so that you can reassemble it without any trouble. Once you've gotten it open, Chapter 3 leads you through it: You'll find it a valuable chapter, as it will enable you to open up a strange machine and identify "RAM," "ROM," "CPU," and dozens of other components in a flash. After all, if you can't find it, you can't fix it.

Preventive maintenance—simple things that you can do to make your PC last a long time—is covered in Chapter 4. That's followed by a chapter about approaches to troubleshooting: When something goes wrong, how do you methodically approach repair? Repair is discussed in greater detail in Chapters 6 and 7, which show how to identify and repair bad circuit boards. Chapter 6 also shows you how to install new circuit boards, grappling with the mysteries of DMA, IRQs, and I/O addresses, ending with tips on general system setup. Chapter 8 then discusses aspects of memory: how it's organized, how to identify memory chips, and how to diagnose memory errors—often right down to the chip. Chapter 9 discusses power supplies and power protection.

Chapters 10, 11, 12, 13, and 14 examine hard disks in detail— disk terminology, installation, preventive maintenance, hardware failure recovery, and software failure recovery. Chapter 15 is all about floppies: how they work, how to install them, and how to test them. Chapters 16 and 17 examine printer software and hardware troubleshooting, with a particular emphasis on laser printers. Chapter 18 explains serial ports and RS-232 cabling. Chapters 19 and 20 are brief treatments of keyboard and video fundamentals, maintenance, and repair. All of the hardware items that have been explored so far are wrapped up in Chapter 21 on how to upgrade an existing system, or how to choose the best system for the least money. Chapter 22 discusses multimedia.

Appendix A lists various suppliers and products that may be useful to you. Appendix B provides an introduction to reading hexadecimal. Finally, Appendix C presents some detailed information about hard disks.

What's New in the Second Edition?

If you follow the world of PCs at all—and if you don't, what are you doing reading this?—you'll know that huge changes have taken place in the last couple of years. Prices have fallen through the floor (long may *that* continue!), 486s are getting faster and faster, and everyone needs more RAM than a sheep rancher. The Second Edition contains updated information on these topics and many more: You'll learn what kind of PC to get or how to upgrade your old system, what to put in it, and what to expect to pay for the components.

The Second Edition also deals with the newest technology, such as overdrive chips and clock doubling, new CPUs, local bus, SCSI, and multimedia.

What *is* clock doubling? Chapter 3 will tell you. How is all that memory laid out? Take a look at Chapter 8 and find out. What is SCSI, and what are you going to do with it? Go into Chapter 11 and investigate. And what about multimedia? Do you want your WordPerfect file to mutter cryptic asides at the click of a button, or dazzle your superiors with a slide-show of soaring sales and the skyrocketing salary that should accompany them? Chapter 22 discusses how and why to add *son et lumière* to your applications.

Safety Notes and Cautions

Before we get started, a few disclaimers:

This text mentions many products. I'm not endorsing these products. Where they are noted, they've been of value. However, manufacturing quality can vary, and goods can be redesigned.

In general, it's pretty hard to hurt yourself with the PC, short of dropping it on your toe. But there are a few exceptions:

There's a silver or black box with a fan in it in the back of your machine. It's the *power supply;* it converts AC from the wall socket into DC for the PC's use. You can't miss the label that says in five languages, "If you open me, I'll kill you." Don't open it. In fact, let me reiterate:

> ***Don't open the power supply or the monitor. Under the wrong circumstances it could kill you.***

There's always somebody who doesn't pay attention to the important stuff, but **PAY ATTENTION TO THIS.** If you open the top of the power supply while the machine is plugged in, even if the power is off, you could get a full 120 volts through you if you touch the wrong things. Even if it's not plugged in, there are power-storing devices called *capacitors* that can give you a good shock even after the machine has been unplugged and turned off. The same, by the way, goes for monitors.

Why go into the power supply in the first place? The only possible user repair imaginable is replacement of the fuse in the box; don't even think of trying that unless you know how to discharge large capacitors safely. It's certainly safe to *replace* a power supply, although when doing such a replacement, you should double-check that it's unplugged before removing the original one.

Another power supply precaution: Never connect a power supply to the wall socket and turn it on *when it isn't connected to a PC motherboard.* Only turn on a power supply when the motherboard power connectors are in place. This is called running without a load; some power supplies will literally explode if you run them like this.

Unless it's an emergency procedure, you should back up your data before doing anything drastic. What if something goes wrong and the machine never comes back on?

Be aware that you can damage circuit boards by removing them while the power's on. Don't do it. Turn the machine off before removing a circuit board.

The rest of the things you'll find in the PC are safe, but don't ignore the above warnings.

CHAPTER 1

Getting Started

BEFORE you can start digging into your PC's innards, you need to know what tools you'll need and roughly what kind of machine you'll be working on—that is, "XT" versus "AT" versus "Micro Channel," and the like.

Basic Tools

Despite the seemingly endless number of tools that you could buy for use on your PC, you can start your toolkit with a fairly inexpensive inventory. As your interest in PC maintenance and upgrading grows, you may desire to augment your toolkit, so I'll present recommendations on more advanced tools later on in this chapter.

Start off your toolkit with the basics—screwdrivers. Most PC troubleshooting requires no more than a few screwdrivers:

- Full-size straight-slot screwdriver
- Phillips number one screwdriver
- Small "tweaker" straight-slot screwdriver
- Phillips number zero (small) screwdriver

You'll need the large straight-slot and Phillips screwdrivers to open the case and remove boards, drives, and power supplies. The smaller screwdrivers loosen screws that secure interface cables: You'll find that before you can open the PC, you must first disconnect the cables attaching the monitor, printer, and any other peripherals to the system unit.

The small straight-slot screwdriver also serves as a chip remover. As we'll see in Chapter 7, the easiest way to remove a chip is by gently prying it from its socket with a small screwdriver. There are chip-remover tongs, but it's very easy to destroy a chip with them, rendering the tool virtually useless.

While I'm on the subject of screwdrivers, you might want to supplement your screwdriver collection with *nut* drivers, *Torx* screwdrivers, and *offset* screwdrivers.

Nut drivers (sounds like what MADD wants to keep off the road, eh?) turn hex-head screws by gripping the six-sided head of the screw, not the slot cut through the head. It's a better method of manipulating screws—you're less likely to accidentally strip the screw's head than you would be to strip the slot—but you need *lots* of them, because there are a lot of sizes of hex heads. Buying and keeping track of all those head sizes gets cumbersome. An offset screwdriver's handle is bent 90 degrees, allowing the screwdriver access to tight places.

If you're working on a Compaq computer, you'll need two Torx screwdrivers, sizes T-10 and T-15. These fit an odd screw that has a star-shaped slot atop it. If you own a car made by GM, you may already have these screwdrivers, as you'd use them to change the headlights on those cars.

A small flashlight can be a real blessing to have around when poking inside a dark case. You'll find that as the years go on, the insides of the cases get darker and the little lettering on top of the chips gets smaller.

Screwdrivers and flashlights are the basic troubleshooting hardware—although there's more hardware I'll discuss in a minute. And keep this software handy:

- A bootable DOS floppy
- Drive setup software
- Data recovery software

"Bootable" means that it includes whatever device drivers you use to start up your system—look at your hard disk's CONFIG.SYS and

AUTOEXEC.BAT, and be sure that you've got all the files mentioned there on your floppy. If you load network drivers, make sure there are copies of the network drivers on your boot floppy. If you use a disk device driver like Stacker or OnTrack Disk Manager, make sure there's a copy of that on the floppy. Test the bootable floppy *before* you need it.

As you'll often find yourself rebuilding dead hard drives, you should make sure your disk contains the basic DOS setup utilities: FDISK, FORMAT, SYS, DEBUG, and CHKDSK. In case your PC's internal battery has run down—leading the computer to forget its configuration—make sure you've got the SETUP utility for your computer around. Whatever program will low-level format the disk (see Chapter 12 about formatting hard disks if you don't know what "low-level format" means), ensure that it's on the floppy. You'll also need a utility to park your hard disk's heads, as you shouldn't remove a hard disk without first parking it. Finally, keep your favorite disk maintenance program—the Norton Utilities, PC Tools, or the Mace Utilities—handy on a floppy.

In roughly descending order of usefulness, here are some other devices you may find useful.

Hemostats (you may know them as forceps) are just as useful for doing PC surgery as doctors find them for doing human surgery. In medical supply catalogs, these run $50 and up, but you can find them in electronics houses like Radio Shack for $8. Cans of compressed gas are terrific for cleaning dust out of the insides of dusty machines. An electronic multimeter will test voltage, amperage, and resistance of electrical circuits, something often of some value. Getting the most out of a multimeter requires some reading in a beginning electronics text, but there are some simple "cookbook" usages of a multimeter that we'll cover in this text. You may find a digital thermometer useful in measuring a PC's inside temperature: too hot and the system fails.

Working with power protection can be easier with a few tools. I will describe them in greater detail in Chapter 9 (which discusses power supplies and power protection), but briefly, an AC power meter allows you to measure the wattage used by your PC; an AC monitor will easily—just plug it into a socket—and inexpensively monitor line surges and voltage fluctuations; and an AC circuit–wiring tester will quickly test an outlet, warning you of any hazards due to miswiring, *before* you plug a precious PC into the outlet.

More and more vital PC chips come in a square package known as a Plastic Leadless Chip Carrier (PLCC). The only way to safely remove these chips is with a device designed for that purpose. Pick up a PLCC extractor, and you'll complete your toolkit.

Well, that's quite a list. Here it all is, summarized:

- Large and small straight-slot and Phillips screwdrivers
- Torx T-10 and T-15 screwdrivers
- Hex-head nut drivers
- Offset screwdrivers
- Flashlight
- Hemostats
- Cans of compressed gas
- Multimeter
- Digital thermometer
- AC power meter
- AC line monitor
- AC circuit–wiring tester
- Software to boot from and to set up or recover disks with

Top-Level PC Taxonomy: Chips and Buses

This book has already referred to *XT-type machines* versus *AT-type machines,* not a fair thing to do to the troubleshooting novice. Here's where I make amends. In some ways, all PC-compatibles are the same. From the lowliest 256K floppy-only PC to the mighty Ambra Pentium, they all run DOS. Lotus 1-2-3 Release 2.1 runs on just about everything. But look closer, and soon they start to appear pretty different.

Let's start out differentiating machines by two things: their *software compatibility* and their *hardware compatibility*. Software compatibility is determined by the kind of processor chip used. We'll discuss processors in some more detail a bit later in the book, but for now just understand that you'll see either the 8088/8086/80188/80186 family, composed of a number of very similar chips; the 80286, which is a newer and more powerful chip that constitutes a family in itself; or the 80386/80386SX/80486 Pentium family, the newest and most powerful part of the Intel *x*86 (and compatible) lineup of central processing unit chips.

Hardware compatibility encompasses the question, "Can I take a circuit board, put it in the computer, and make it work?" The XT, PC, and AT share a common *bus*—the connector used to attach expansion boards to the computer's main circuit board (called a *motherboard*). Expansion boards, like memory or I/O boards, that work in a PC will generally work just fine in an AT. The PS/2 line, however, uses a newer and completely incompatible bus called the *Micro Channel Architecture*. PS/2 expansion boards don't work in PCs, and vice versa. Please note that when I say *PS/2*, I'm referring to the *real* PS/2s—the models 50 through 80. The 25s and 30s aren't completely PS/2 machines.

Many vendors today support a third standard, EISA (Extended Industry Standard Architecture). ISA, EISA, and Micro Channel are the traditional buses nowadays, but many new computers now incorporate one of three new bus standards: VESA Local Bus (VLB), Peripheral Connect Interface (PCI), or Personal Computer Memory Card Industry Association (PCMCIA) slots. These buses are important, and they're discussed in some detail in Chapter 3; but for now, if you've got VLB, PCI, or PCMCIA, just consider your bus temporarily to be an EISA bus for the purposes of this discussion.

So there are three basic processor chip families and three basic bus types (there are variations within each group, but you'll see them later). There are, then, nine potential PC types. You can see some examples in Table 1.1.

Most PCs nowadays are variations on the old 1984-model AT. Even Pentium systems are quite AT-like in their design. Hence, I will say "AT-type" throughout the book, but I'm referring to all kinds of computers.

TABLE 1.1: Types and Examples of PC Compatible Computers

PROCESSOR CHIP	PC (ISA) BUS	MICRO CHANNEL ARCHITECTURE (MCA)	EXTENDED INDUSTRY STANDARD ARCHITECTURE (EISA)
Intel 8088, 8086, 80188, 80186	IBM PC, XT, Portable, PC Jr, XT/370, PC/3270, PS/2 Model 30 and Model 25	None in category	None in category
NEC V20, V30	Compaq Deskpro, Portable		
	Toshiba T1000, T1100+, T1200		
	Zenith Z171, 181, 183, 151, 158, 159, Eazy PC		
	AT&T 6300		
	Leading Edge Model D		
	Hyundai Blue Chip		
Intel 80286	IBM AT, XT286, AT/370, AT/3270, PS/2 Model 30-286	IBM PS/2 Model 50	None in category
	Compaq Deskpro 286	IBM PS/2 Model 50Z	
	Zenith Z248, LP286, SuperSport 286	IBM PS/2 Model 60	
	AT&T 6300+		
	Toshiba 1600, 3100, 3200		
	AST Premium/286		

TABLE 1.1: Types and Examples of PC Compatible Computers (continued)

PROCESSOR CHIP	PC (ISA) BUS	MICRO CHANNEL ARCHITECTURE (MCA)	EXTENDED INDUSTRY STANDARD ARCHITECTURE (EISA)
Intel 80386, 80486, and Pentium families	Compaq Deskpro 386, 386S	IBM PS/2 Model 55	ALR Business VEISA
	Zenith Z-386	IBM PS/2 Model 70	Compaq Deskpro 486/33
	AT&T 6386	IBM PS/2 Model 70	
	AST Premium/386	IBM PS/2 Model 80	
	ALR FlexCache 20	IBM PS/2 Model 95	
		Tandy MC5000	

The Next Step: PC Features

Buses and chips are the big stuff, but you might be saying, "That's not all there is to it—I've heard of megahertz, BIOS type, video boards, and other things. Just what are they, and how do they fit in?"

The answer is that they're indeed important; we'll get to them in various parts of the book. Not to leave you hanging, however, there's a brief mention of the big PC features in Table 1.2.

I don't want to minimize the importance of, say, the video board, but you don't commit yourself to a long-term decision about video when you buy most machines. Virtually any video board can be added to most machines later, as a nice stereo system can be added to virtually any car. (Why the weasel wording about "most" machines? A few machines—the AT&T 6300, the Leading Edge PC, and Zenith's LP286 and Eazy PC come to mind—

incorporate the video function right on the main circuit board, or *motherboard,* which makes video upgrade difficult or impossible.)

TABLE 1.2: Features That Make PCs Different

FEATURE	BRIEF DESCRIPTION	TYPICAL EXAMPLES
CPU	The CPU determines how much memory the system can address, what kind of software it can run, and how fast it can go.	8088, 80286, 80386, 80486
Bus	The bus determines what kind of expansion circuit boards will work in the machine. All of the common buses here are compatible in varying degrees with each other except Micro Channel, which is not compatible. ISA (Industry Standard Architecture) is the new name given to the old bus most machines use. Micro Channel was introduced in 1987 by IBM for their PS/2 machines. EISA (Extended Industry Standard Architecture) is the non-IBM manufacturer's answer to Micro Channel.	PC Bus (8-bit ISA), AT Bus (16-bit ISA), Proprietary 32-bit, 16-bit Micro Channel, 32-bit Micro Channel, EISA, local bus, or "VESA" bus, Personal Computer Memory Card Industry Association (PCMCIA), Peripheral Component Interconnect (PCI)
BIOS	BIOS (Basic Input/Output System) is the low-level system software that determines your machine's compatibility.	IBM, Compaq, Phoenix, Award
CPU speed	Megahertz (MHz) roughly measures system speed. If all other things were equal, a 10-MHz machine would be faster than a 5-MHz machine. (All other things usually aren't equal.)	4.77 MHz (PC speed) up to 99 MHz
Video board	The video board affects what kind of software you can run and how quickly data gets onto the screen. You can easily change it, and the oldest PC can use anything from a monochrome board up to a VGA or 8514. Video boards get better by offering more colors, by being able to show more dots on the screen, and by being faster.	Monochrome Adapter (MDA), Color/Graphics Adapter (CGA), Enhanced Graphics Adapter (EGA), Professional Graphics Controller (PGC), Video Graphics Array (VGA), 8514 High Resolution Adapter, Super VGA, Extended Graphics Array (XGA)

TABLE 1.2: Features That Make PCs Different (continued)

FEATURE	BRIEF DESCRIPTION	TYPICAL EXAMPLES
Parallel port	The parallel (printer) port can serve as a high-speed bidirectional interface on some computers. Some manufacturers tout this feature, but it isn't very important.	Unidirectional, Bidirectional, EPP (Enhanced Parallel Port)
Serial port UART	The Universal Asynchronous Receiver/ Transmitter is the main chip around which a serial port or internal modem is built. You need a 16450 to run OS/2. The PS/2 Models 50Z and 70 have a chip slightly different from either the 8250 or the 16450, a difference which will keep some communications software from running. UART can be changed on many systems.	8250, 16450
Memory	There are several kinds of memory: conventional, extended, and expanded. They all solve different problems. Some software won't run without a particular amount and/or kind of memory.	640K, and so forth
System Clock/Calendar	Again, not terribly important. Machines with built-in clocks usually have DOS support to read or modify the time and date directly. Some must run a separate program.	Built-in on motherboard, added on expansion board
Hard disk interface	The method that the *hard disk controller* (a circuit card in the system) uses to talk to the hard disk. Affects speed. Can be easily changed in most systems.	ST506/412, ESDI, SCSI, IDE
Hard disk– encoding scheme	Method used to squeeze more data onto a *track* (an area on a hard disk). Can easily be changed.	MFM, RLL, ARLL

TABLE 1.2: Features That Make PCs Different (continued)

FEATURE	BRIEF DESCRIPTION	TYPICAL EXAMPLES
Keyboard	IBM originally put a keyboard control chip in the keyboard for the PC and XT. They moved it to the motherboard for the AT, so you must know which kind of keyboard interface you have. Most clone keyboards have a switch allowing them to swing both ways.	XT type, AT type
Floppies supported	The kind of floppies your machine supports. Can be changed fairly easily.	5¼" 360K, 5¼" 1.2M, 5¼" 720K (unusual), 3½" 720K, 3½" 1.44M
Expansion slots		3 to 10
Configuration method	Computers won't work until you tell them about themselves, or *configure* them. It's done either with physical switches or with software.	Switches, configuration (CMOS) memory
Interrupts (IRQ levels) supported	Affects the number and type of expansion boards in a system.	8 or 16
DMA (Direct Memory Access) channels supported	Affects the number and type of expansion boards in a system.	4 or 8
Printer control language	Tells your printer how to underline words, put pictures on the page, and change typefaces.	Epson codes, HPPCL (LaserJet commands), PostScript, others

Don't let Table 1.2 make your head spin and convince you to go back to simpler work, like high-energy physics. All those things are included in the table because you'll hear about them if you set about repairing a PC. All these issues (and much more, as they used to say in the great days of radio announcing) are covered later on.

That's half of PC identification. There's more, but it will make more sense to you after we've gotten under the hood, so I'll leave that for Chapter 2. Now that you have some idea of the kind of machine you have and where it fits into the PC universe, let's open it up and take a look inside.

CHAPTER

2

Disassembling the PC

NEVER been inside your PC? Step inside.... Maintenance, upgrades, and troubleshooting sometimes require disassembly of the PC. That's sometimes—as you'll see in the chapters that follow, most problems can be solved without taking the hood off the machine, so avoid becoming trigger-happy with your electric screwdriver. Here's some advice to take your machine apart safely so you can get it back together again.

General PC Disassembly Advice

1. **If possible, let cowardice and practicality form a marriage of convenience.** If the machine is still in the warranty period, take a look at the warranty to see if you void it by disassembling the computer. If you can make the problem an SEP (Somebody Else's Problem), then by all means do. If you're sure a printer is dead right out of the box, don't try to fix it—just send it back.

2. **Make sure you have adequate workspace.** You'll need a lot of room—most of a tabletop would be good. To reduce the potential for static electricity, raise the air humidity to 50 percent or so, use a commercial antistatic remedy, or just touch something metal before you touch any PC component. (See Chapter 4, "Avoiding Service: Preventive Maintenance" for more ideas on handling static electricity.)

3. **Keep the small parts organized.** Get a cup to store screws and small pieces of hardware. If you just leave the screws on the table, you'll eventually end up accidentally sweeping the screws off the table and onto the floor, where they'll roll down a vent or under the heaviest object around. I knew a guy who kept the screws in the vent atop the power supply, the one just above the fan. One day he forgot they were there and turned the machine on. Power supply fans can *really* sling screws around!

    As there will be at least two kinds of screws (the ones that secure the case tend to be a different size from the rest of the screws in the system, and Seagate 200-series hard disks generally require short screws), it's not a bad idea to steal a page from car mechanics' books and use an egg carton. It has a bunch of compartments, and you can label each one. Remember, the plan here is to end up without any spare parts.

4. **Back up the configuration.** If you're disassembling an AT-type machine (386s and 486s are included here), your machine stores a small bit of vital configuration information in a special memory chip—sometimes called the *configuration chip*, sometimes called the *CMOS chip*—that's backed up with a battery. You're probably going to end up removing the battery, so the system will complain about not being configured when you reassemble it. That means you'll have to run your machine's SETUP program to reconfigure the system once it's back together. SETUP will be covered later, but it's basically going to ask you how much memory you have, what kind of floppies you use, and it'll want a number from 1 to 47 to describe your hard disk type. You can figure out all this for yourself, but why go to the trouble? Just run the SETUP program before disassembly. It'll tell you what your current configuration is. Write that down and then remember to park your hard disk before shutdown. When you reassemble the computer, run the SETUP program and type in the CMOS information. Set the DATE and TIME with DOS, reboot, and the system will be fine.

    This is important; you never know when you'll need this information. DOS 6's MemMaker accidentally erased my CMOS. Without a backup, things would have been difficult to get right.

5. **Protect the hard disk.** Does your machine have a hard disk? Your computer should have come with a program to park the

heads of the hard disk. Parking the heads protects the drive, and we'll talk more about it in the hard disk chapters. Run that program to park the heads. If your drive was an expensive one, it might be an auto-park model that doesn't require parking. Check the documentation, if it's available. By the way, you can't hurt an auto-park drive by running a parking utility, so if you're unsure, go ahead and run a parking utility.

6. Turn the PC and associated peripherals off.

7. Remove the monitor from atop the PC and set it aside. If you don't have much workspace, it's not a bad idea to put the monitor on the floor, with the tube facing the wall so you don't kick in the tube accidentally.

8. Remove the top carefully. On the back of most PCs and compatibles there are five screws (two on ancient pre-1983 PCs)—see Figures 2.1 and 2.2. Remove them and put them in the cup. Don't knock the cup on the floor yet; wait for more, smaller screws and hardware. Slide the cover forward and set it aside carefully— don't rip the thin ribbon cables when you remove the top. Also, it's very easy to break one of the little wires. Just a nick can make your floppy or hard disk (the peripherals that use these cables) misbehave. I once saw a cable that had received the "rip the top open and scratch the cable" treatment cause floppies to read and write fine, but refuse to format.

If you've never done it before, take this opportunity to put your name on the inside of the case. This is a small extra bit of security. By the way, the most important screw in the back is the top center screw—it holds the weight of the monitor. In normal usage, it's best to ensure that all five screws are in place. However, if you're going to be lazy, the one screw you must have in place is the center screw. Incidentally, should you need to replace the case screws on most PC-type systems, they're type 6-32, $\frac{3}{8}$-inch screws. The circuit boards and drives are secured with type 4-40, $\frac{3}{8}$-inch screws.

FIGURE 2.1

IBM XT with cover removed

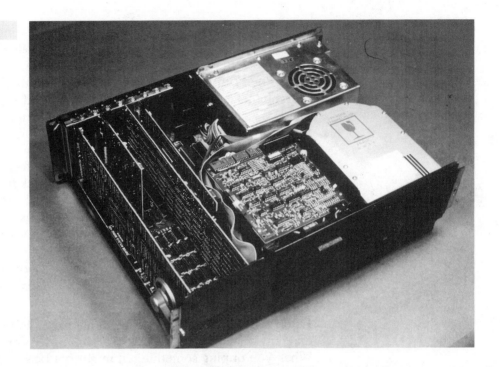

FIGURE 2.2

Removing a PC's cover (rear view)

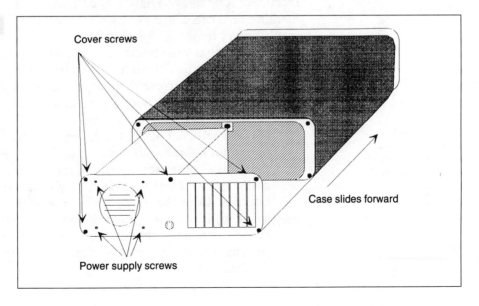

Here's a piece of advice you weren't expecting: keep the PC plugged in. The reason why is simple: to help you avoid problems with static electricity.

When I'm teaching my PC troubleshooting class, I make everyone take the "power supply pledge." "Raise your right hands," I say. "Then put them on the power supply." The idea is that if the PC is plugged in, then the case of the power supply is grounded, and so touching the case of the power supply drains away any built-up static charges. It's not a perfect answer, but it will often do in a pinch. You will *not* get a shock from touching the case of the power supply, or at least you *should* not get a shock. It's possible to get a shock only if a lot of things are wired very wrongly... and if that's the case, I don't imagine that the PC will be working very well.

By the way, the *best* answer to the static problem is to get an anti-static wrist strap. They're discussed in Chapter 4, on preventive maintenance.

9. Diagram! Ensure that you have some paper and a pen so you can diagram what you disassemble. In what order were the boards? When you unplug something, it might not be simple to see how to reconnect it unless you have a good diagram. If there's no distinct marking on a cable, use a marker to make one. These machines aren't library books; it's okay to write on them. Remember, the game plan is that you should leave the machine the way you found it. You might not be able to fix the system, but you certainly don't want to leave it any worse than you found it. If you're new to computers, pay special attention to these items (see Figure 2.3):

- Ribbon cables. They're flat cables connected to upright pins on circuit boards, and there's a definite "correct" way to put them on a connector. Put them on backwards, and your PC could smoke. Note that the ribbon cables have a dark line on one side. Does that go up on the board? Down? Toward the speaker? Toward the power supply? (Note that I don't say *left* or *right*—those directions can get you into trouble.) Make sure to note the current position of the cables in your diagram.

FIGURE 2.3

Where things are in
an XT- or AT-type
chassis (front view)

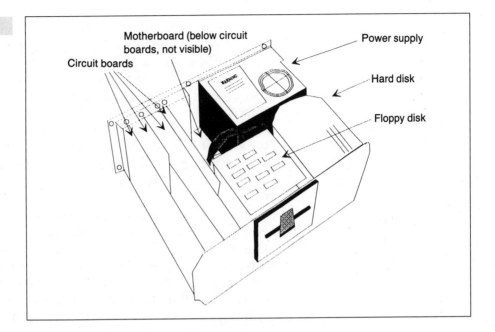

- Board and cable placement. In general, it doesn't matter to the computer in which slot you put a board. But certain boards might be in particular places to ease routing cables. You should be able to tuck cables out of the way when reassembling; take note of how it's done on your diagram before you take the machine apart.

- DIP switches. After you remove a board, it never hurts to make a note of the DIP switch settings. I've spent 20 minutes setting a DIP switch bank only to find that I've set the wrong bank, messing up a perfectly good configuration and making my reassembly task all the more difficult. Besides, there are "DIP switch gremlins" who move the switches when you're not looking. (Honest, there *are*—I don't have kids or cats, and I can think of no other explanation.)

- Motherboard connections. Once you've gotten the box open, you'll see the main circuit board or motherboard. It will have a number of things connected to it: *a)* Power supply connections. They're often two white plastic connectors labeled P8 and P9. Mix them up when you reassemble the machine, and poof! goes the system. *b)* Speaker connection. This connects the *timer* (which generates the sound signal) to the speaker. It's generally a connector with yellow and black wires. *c)* Keylock connection. On systems with front panel keylocks, a set of wires (two on some systems, four on others) connects the motherboard to the keylock. Fail to reconnect it, and the keylock feature won't work. *d)*Turbo switch/light. Many "turbo" clones have a front panel switch to speed up or slow down the computer. There might also be a light to indicate whether the machine is operating at high speed (turbo mode) or not.

- Brackets and braces. On an AT-type desktop case, you'll see small metal tabs screwed into the case to hold the drives in place. Before you remove them, notice if they're identical or if they vary in size. Ensure that you can return them where you found them. Newer AT-type desktop cases have a *keeper bar* across the front of the drive. Diagram it, or you'll play "how does this fit?" when trying to reassemble.

Another problem child is the later (1986–87) XT with IBM-supplied half-height drives. An upright steel clip holds the two drives together so they can be supported adequately by the older XT case, which features screw holes for a single full-height drive. You might think when you disassemble it that it's obvious where it goes back in place, but you won't think that when you put the machine back together.

10. **Use caution when removing boards and drives.** If you're going to remove a circuit board or drive, detach all connectors to it. Be very careful about forcing anything open or off. Remove the board's retaining screw (put the screw in the cup, remember) and grasp the board front and back with two hands (Figure 2.4). Rock the board back and forth (not side to side!) and it will come out. Don't touch the gold edge connectors on the bottom part of the board—keep finger gunk off the edge connectors.

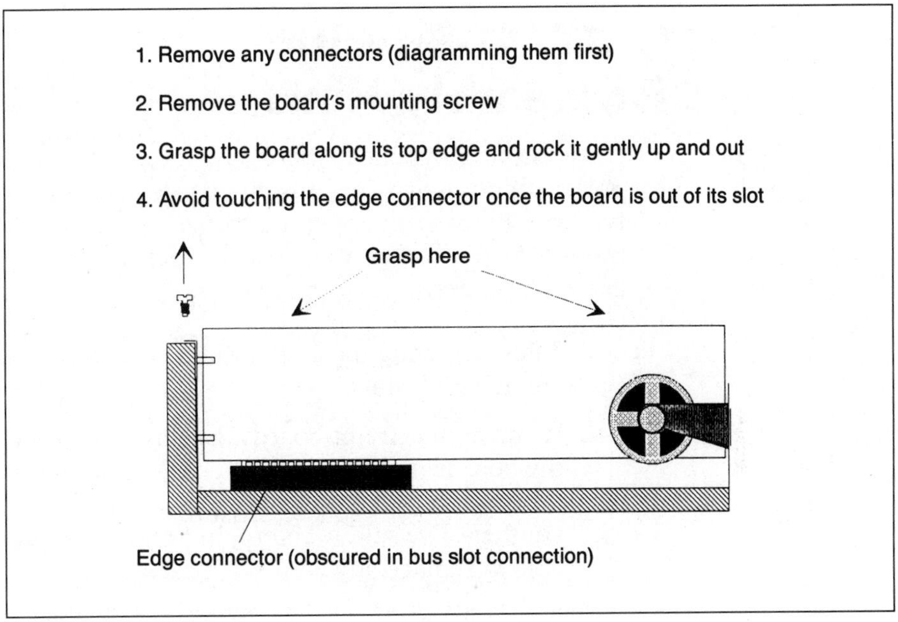

FIGURE 2.4

Removing a circuit
board

1. Remove any connectors (diagramming them first)

2. Remove the board's mounting screw

3. Grasp the board along its top edge and rock it gently up and out

4. Avoid touching the edge connector once the board is out of its slot

Grasp here

Edge connector (obscured in bus slot connection)

Summary: Disassembly Hints

- Always ask yourself first: "Is this procedure necessary?"
- Park the hard disk.
- Back up the configuration or document DIP switch settings.
- Work with sufficient space.
- Don't force things. Stop and look.
- Be careful when removing the top that you don't rip cables.
- Diagram!
- Keep screws and other small things organized.
- Detach cables and connectors before removing devices or boards.

PC/XT/AT-Specific Disassembly Hints

Most desktop machines these days look fairly similar inside. They have a power supply, drives, expansion boards, and a motherboard. XT- and AT-type machines are very similar here except for the way their drives are mounted. You can vary these steps, but here's one basic approach to disassembling these specific machines.

1. After removing the cover, again note in a diagram which boards are in which slots.

2. Remove the circuit boards. Ensure that you can differentiate the boards (see Figure 2.5)—is there a marking, a connector, an unusual chip that will allow you to distinguish one board from another? I've said it before, but remember that you must be able to replace any connector cable.

FIGURE 2.5

Hints for differentiating circuit boards

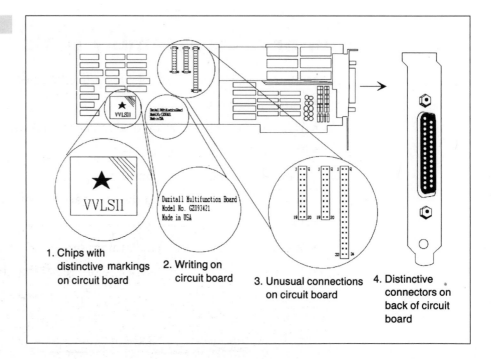

1. Chips with distinctive markings on circuit board

2. Writing on circuit board

3. Unusual connections on circuit board

4. Distinctive connectors on back of circuit board

This means you should also note what connectors are not attached to anything. For example, if you have a hard disk in your machine (not a hardcard), you'll have a board in your machine called a hard disk controller. It's easy to pick out— it's the circuit board with ribbon cables running from it to the hard disk. Your hard disk controller will have between two and four cables coming from it, extending to your hard disk and, possibly, your floppy disk. Each cable will have 20, 34, or 40 wires in it. Put one of them on backwards, and you could permanently damage something.

The point I'm trying to make here is that one of the top two or three mistakes that troubleshooting tyros make is to blithely remove cables without noting where they should go on reassembly, or in what configuration—red line up, red line down, or whatever. Every cable's layout looks obvious when it's removed, I know. But it's often *not* obvious when the time comes to replace it. (End of sermon.)

3.   Once the boards are out, it's easier to get to the drives. Drive mounting is one of the few places where the XT-type and AT-type machines differ. With both drives, however, you'll see the same cable connections: separate power and data/control cables for floppies, and separate power, data, and control connections for hard disks.

Let's consider these cables first, and then look at XT- and AT-specific removal problems. The power cable is a four-wire, milky-white plastic connector running from the power supply to the floppy. On IBM machines, it's generally labeled P10, P11, or P12 (see Figure 2.6). Remove it from the drive's circuit board carefully, as the connector tends to be a bit balky about coming loose from some drives; now and then I see some would-be Hercules breaking the connector right off the floppy altogether. Just grasp the power connector and gently rock it from side to side. It will come loose.

P10 power connector
on floppy disk

DISASSEMBLING THE PC

Next, you'll see a ribbon cable or two on the backs of the drives—one ribbon for floppies, and one or two for hard disks (see Figures 2.7 and 2.8).

FIGURE 2.7

Floppy data and power connection for an AT-type machine

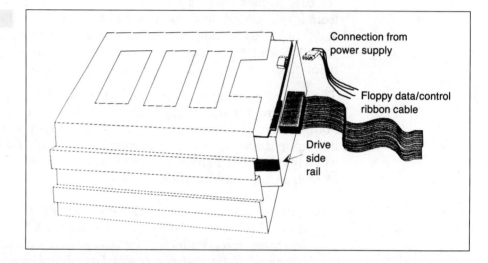

FIGURE 2.8

Data and control cables for ST506 or ESDI hard disk (note *two* cables—IDE or SCSI use only one cable)

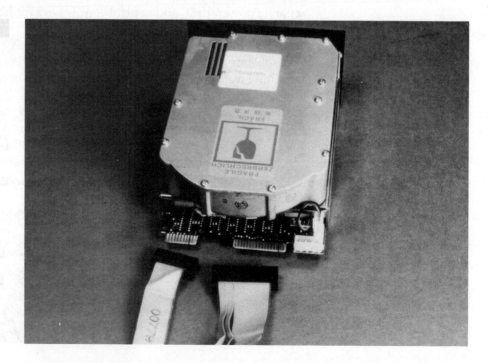

Diagram and remove them. Older drives use an interface called ST506 or its successor, ESDI. ST506 and ESDI drives use two cables to connect the hard disk to the controller. Other drives use either the SCSI or IDE interfaces, which use a single cable to link controller and drive. Now you're ready to remove the drives.

XT-type machines generally secure drives with holes predrilled in the chassis. The XT chassis was designed for two full-height drives (floppy and hard), but half-heights have been popular for years. Some XT-type manufacturers have responded by drilling holes that can accommodate either half-height *or* full-height drives. Others have kludged up a solution wherein two half-heights are joined with a bracket to form a single unit; then the (full-height) unit is screwed into the chassis that only accommodates full-height drives.

Most XTs only secure their drives with screws on one side of the chassis, as shown in Figure 2.9. That's not wonderful, but nearly all XT-type

FIGURE 2.9

Removing mounting screws from the XT hard disk

manufacturers do it. IBM tried to shore up drives on the last batch (1986–87) of their XTs with an extra screw in *the bottom.* (Imagine my surprise after spending ten minutes trying to figure out why the drive didn't come out like all the others I'd taken apart over the previous five years.)

Once you've removed the screws, pull the drives out through the front of the chassis, as shown in Figure 2.10. Be careful not to "behead" any of the little components on top of the floppy drive's circuit board.

The exception to the "pull it out through the front" rule comes from IBM. I just mentioned the 1986–87 XTs: Be careful if you come across one of these machines. They're IBM XTs with two IBM-supplied half-height floppy drives. Your first clue is that there are two half-height floppy drives with asterisks (*) embossed on the front bezel, or face plate. Now pick up the chassis and look underneath the drives. Are there two screws (or screw holes, if someone disassembled it previously but was too lazy to put them back)? Take these bottom screws out. These drives won't come out the

FIGURE 2.10

Pulling floppy drive
from computer chassis

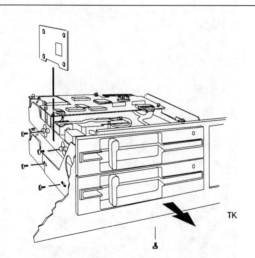

TK

Drives are removed from XT-style cases by removing retaining screws (sometimes found *underneath* the drive) and pulling drives out the front. Some systems use a bracket plate to hold the two drives together. Floppy drives on late-model IBM XTs must be removed from the *back.*

front. Instead, locate and remove a thin rectangular piece of plastic fitted around the front plates of the drives. Now the two drives come out of the system together *from the back.*

Some AT-type machines use a somewhat more elegant approach to drive mounting. Plastic rails mount on the side of the drive, sort of like the rails on the sides of desk drawers. The chassis includes "drive bays" that mate to the rails. The drive then slides in and out of the chassis like a drawer out of a desk.

Now, having the drives slide around like drawers might not be the neatest thing around, so the drives are secured with metal tabs and screws. Once you've unscrewed the tabs (see Figure 2.11), the drives come right out (see Figure 2.12). Some systems vary the design of each tab slightly, to make it easier to return tabs to their proper locations without mixing them up.

FIGURE 2.11

Removing AT drive tabs

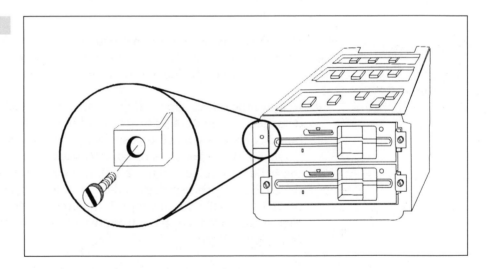

FIGURE 2.12

Removing AT drives

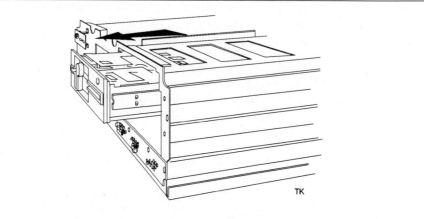

Drives are removed from AT-style cases by first removing their retaining tabs (previous diagram), then sliding them out the front of the case, like a drawer from a desk.

Many tower-type cases require that you bolt the drive directly into the PC case, somewhat like the XT did. In such cases, you must remove four screws—two from each side—to remove the drive.

4. Remove the power supply. By now its drive connections are detached, so you needn't worry about them. There are two motherboard connectors, however, usually labeled P8 and P9, that must be detached. Note that P8 is toward the back of the machine, and P9 toward the front (see Figure 2.13). Next, remove the four screws in the back of the chassis that hold the power supply in place (see Figure 2.14). Finally, you must push the power supply forward (as in Figure 2.15) to disengage it from two clips built into the chassis (see Figure 2.16).

Many modern PCs do not use a power switch mounted on the right rear, as did older PCs with IBM AT-type cases. Instead, newer PCs bring in the 110-volt line current right up to the PC front panel, through a thick black cable. There are four wires inside that cable: a black, a blue, a white, and a brown cable. Now, AC power doesn't include "positive" and "negative" wires—there's a "hot" and a "return" wire instead. Ordinarily, the white is the hot, and the black is the return; older power supplies just run a white

FIGURE 2.13

Power supply
connections

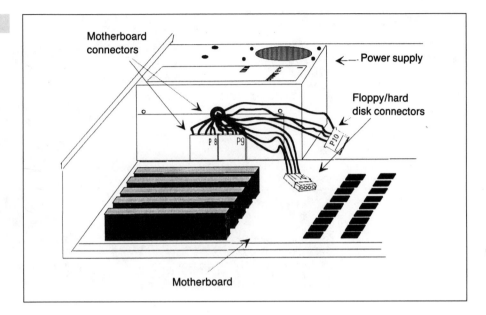

FIGURE 2.14

Removing power
supply mounting
screws

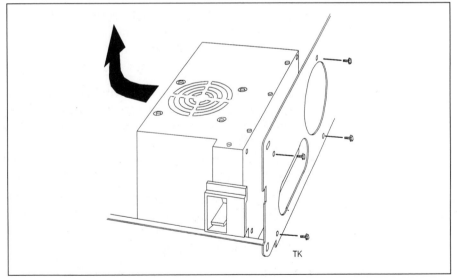

FIGURE 2.15

Pushing a power supply forward

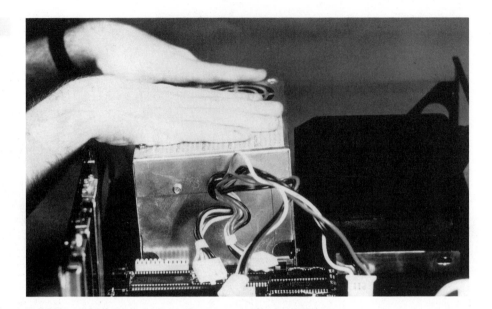

and black into the power supply from the wall socket, and that was all that was needed—but the needs of the new power supply's front panel switches change all that. (Actually, old power supplies also included a third wire, a green one, for ground—but it's not important for this discussion.)

In order to build a front-panel switch, power supply/case makers decided to drag both the hot *and* the return out to the front of the case, and then send the hot and return back into the power supply.

- The *white* wire connects the "hot" side of the wall outlet to the power switch.

- The *brown* wire connects the "hot" side of the power supply's power input to the power switch. When you push the switch "on," you connect white and brown, providing a "hot" AC connection for the power supply.

- The *black* wire connects the "return" side of the wall to the power switch.

- The *blue* wire connects the "return" side of the power supply's power input to the power switch. When you push the switch "on," you connect black and blue, providing a "return" AC connection for the power supply.

FIGURE 2.16

A power supply with
mounting clips

If you disconnect the black, blue, white, and brown wires from the front panel switch, you should be able to see from the previous discussion how important it is to diagram your connections. This is one case where if you reconnect things backwards, then you could end up directly connecting "hot" from the wall socket right into "return" from the wall socket. That would cause a short circuit that could make your computer catch *fire!*

If you look at the front panel switch, then you'll see four flat connection points called *spade lugs* where you can connect or disconnect the white, black, brown, or blue wires. You'll notice a <u>very low ridge</u> on the connector, and that there are <u>two spade lugs on either side of the ridge</u>. Before disconnecting the wires from the switch, notice that the black and the blue are on one side of the ridge, and white and the brown are on the other side. The ridge is just a "reminder" about which wires go with which other wires. Just keep the white and the brown on one side, and the black and the blue on the other side, and all will be well. The way I remember it is that one side is "black and blue."

If you have any doubts, however, it might be best to enlist the aid of a friend who's knowledgable in AC power and voltmeters. You really can do some damage if you wire these switches wrong.

Again, be *sure* to diagram the power connectors! They look exactly the same… but put them on the motherboard backwards, and you'll smoke that motherboard!

5. Finally, the motherboard comes out. Again, the motherboard is the circuit board lying flat in the bottom of the case. It's about the only thing left in the system by now, so you need only remove the speaker and keylock connections and take out a couple of screws.

   You'll see from one to five (depending, again, on whether it's an IBM or a clone PC, XT, or AT) small plastic connectors with a few wires attached to them on the motherboard (see Figures 2.17 and 2.18). Most systems have a speaker cable with yellow and black wires. On IBM ATs, the speaker connection has the black wire to the front of the case, yellow toward the back. AT-type systems generally have a keylock connector. The keylock has four wires: two blacks, a green, and an orange. The orange wire goes toward the front of the box, the black one toward the back.

FIGURE 2.17

XT motherboard view
with detail showing
connection points

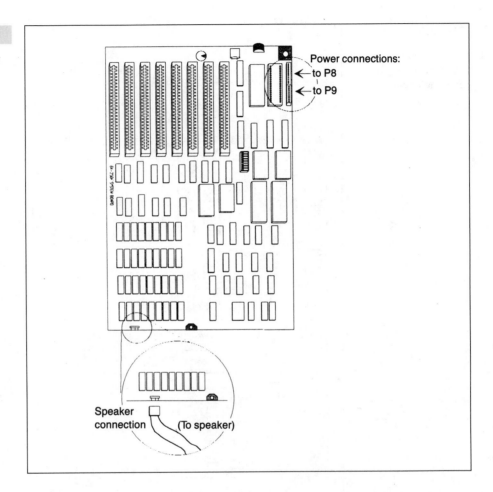

You can remove the battery from the motherboard (assuming it
has one), but if possible try to remove the motherboard with the battery attached. This saves you the trouble of reconfiguring the system
when you reassemble it.

6. The motherboard is now held down only by two screws. Remove
   them, as shown in Figure 2.19. They're held off the metal case
   with some plastic spacers. *Remove only the screws*—not the spacers.
   The board slides over and out of the case (see Figure 2.20).

FIGURE 2.18

AT motherboard view with detail showing connection points

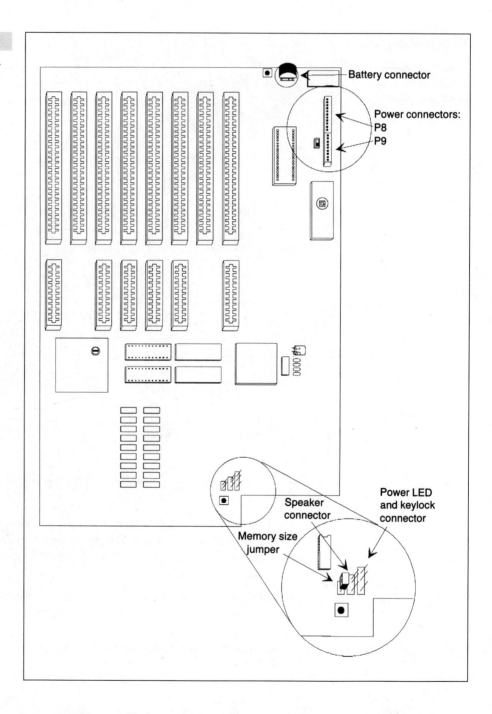

FIGURE 2.19

Removing
motherboard
mounting screws

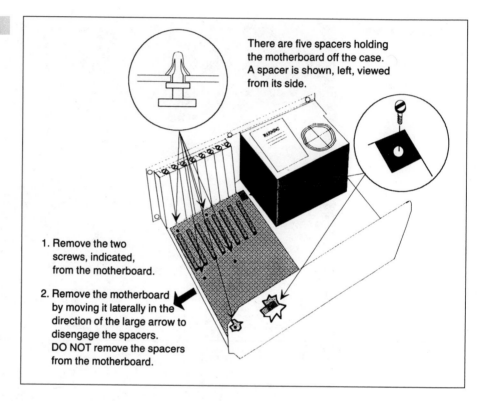

FIGURE 2.20

How to remove a motherboard

There are five spacers holding the motherboard off the case. A spacer is shown, left, viewed from its side.

1. Remove the two screws, indicated, from the motherboard.

2. Remove the motherboard by moving it laterally in the direction of the large arrow to disengage the spacers. DO NOT remove the spacers from the motherboard.

Disassembling the PS/2s

Each model in the PS/2 line is disassembled differently, but here's how to take apart the most common ones: Model 50, Model 50Z, and Model 70.

1. Take the cover off (see Figures 2.21 and 2.22). Note the lack of cables—less diagramming to do. The Model 50 is organized into a "two-story" arrangement with the drives and the fan on the top floor, and the speaker, power supply, and motherboard on the bottom floor. We'll remove the speaker, clean off the second floor, and then remove the second floor altogether.

FIGURE 2.21

Opening a desktop PS/2

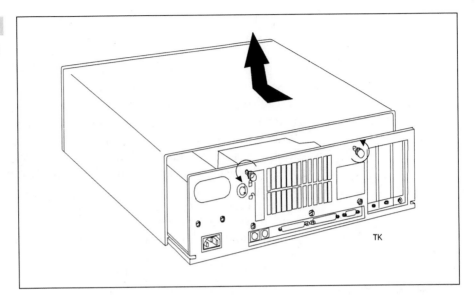

FIGURE 2.22

Opening a tower PS/2

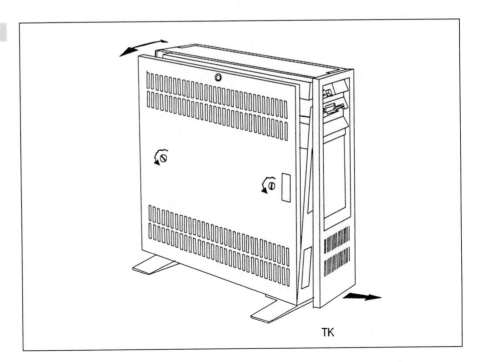

2. Find the speaker/battery module. It will pull up and off, but there's a catch on the bottom of the module that holds it in place. Push in the catch, then pull up. (See Figure 2.23.) On other PS/2 models there's a four-wire connection to the side of the speaker; remove it. While you have the speaker off, notice two pins sticking out of the side. If you have a PS/2 password you want to get rid of, just turn the machine off, short the two pins, and turn it back on. The password goes away. You short the two pins by putting a jumper on them and squeezing them so they touch, or else putting a metal object like a screwdriver between them so there's an electrical connection. (Why remove a password? Someone might have maliciously *put* a password on a machine that didn't have one, or you might have been asked to fix a machine with a password. You can't run diagnostic software without the password.)

FIGURE 2.23

Removing a PS/2 speaker

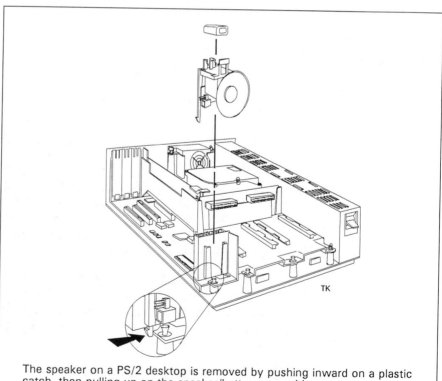

The speaker on a PS/2 desktop is removed by pushing inward on a plastic catch, then pulling up on the speaker/battery assembly.

Unfortunately, some of the newer PS/2s don't have the two pins. Instead, on those models there's a multiwire connector that goes from the speaker assembly to the motherboard. Remove the motherboard connection and reconnect it backwards. This will eliminate the password. Figure 2.24 shows both methods of disabling the password.

FIGURE 2.24

Disabling a PS/2 password

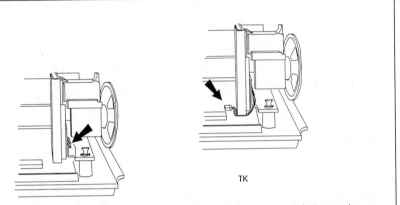

A password on a PS/2 can be disabled either by shorting two jumper pins on the side of the speaker, or (as the pins are not always present) momentarily reversing the connection between the speaker/battery assembly and the motherboard.

3. Remove the floppies. (See Figures 2.25 and 2.26.) Each one has a catch on the bottom. Just pull it up and the drives slide out. On the 60, 80, and 95 there is, in addition, a black spring lever you must pop up; you'll hear a "click." Then remove the drive by pulling up on its catch and sliding it out.

4. Remove the hard disk. (See Figures 2.27 and 2.28.) The Model 50's hard disk slides left and right like a sled on skids. It's held in place with two plastic stays. Press the stays down with one hand, and push the drive over the stays while they're flattened. The drive will come right out.

FIGURE 2.26

Removing a desktop
PS/2's floppies

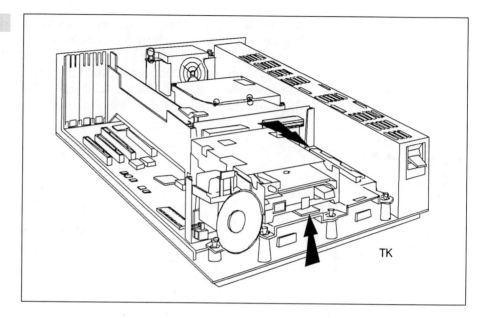

FIGURE 2.25

Removing a tower
PS/2's floppies

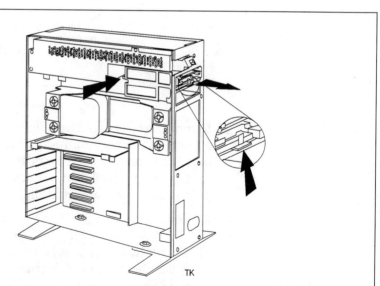

PS/2 tower-model floppy drives are removed by lifting up on the plastic tab under the front of the floppy drive, and pushing on the black plastic tab in the back of floppy. The tab in the back may require some fiddling.

FIGURE 2.28

Removing a desktop
PS/2's hard disk

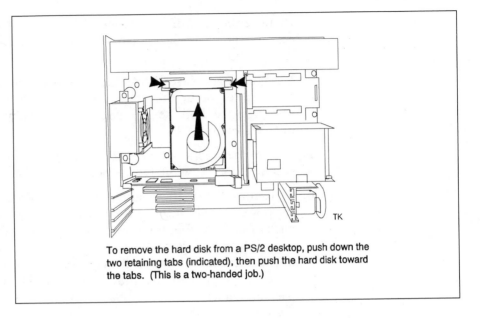

To remove the hard disk from a PS/2 desktop, push down the
two retaining tabs (indicated), then push the hard disk toward
the tabs. (This is a two-handed job.)

FIGURE 2.27

Removing a tower
PS/2's hard disk

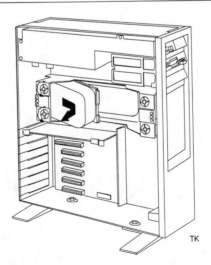

A PS/2 tower-model hard disk can be removed by loosening the two large plastic nuts atop the
hard disk, then sliding the drive backward out of its cradle. If a second hard disk is present, it
can be removed through a cutout in the front panel.

5. Remove the hard disk controller. It's the board where the hard disk was attached. Just grasp it by the big blue handles, and rock it up and out.

6. Find the small plastic "crowbar" tool near the speaker in the case. It's used to pop up the white plastic snaps that hold the second floor in place. Pop the two snaps up on the fan, and the fan comes out. See Figure 2.29.

7. Pop up the several snaps on the second floor, and remove the second floor. Now the motherboard is exposed.

8. To remove the motherboard on a desktop PS/2, you must remove the power supply at the same time. There are several screws in back of the case that hold the power supply to the case; a few that secure the interface connections to the case; and several that hold the motherboard down on the case. Remove them, and remove the power supply and the motherboard at the same time. Then you can detach the motherboard from the power supply. See Figures 2.30 and 2.31.

FIGURE 2.29

Removing a desktop PS/2's fan

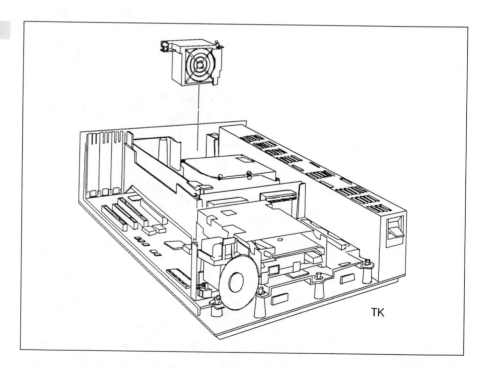

FIGURE 2.31

Removing a tower
PS/2's power supply

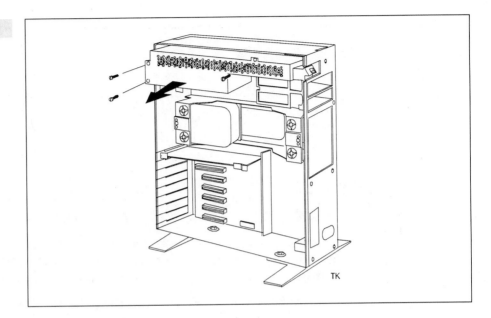

FIGURE 2.30

Removing a tower
PS/2's motherboard

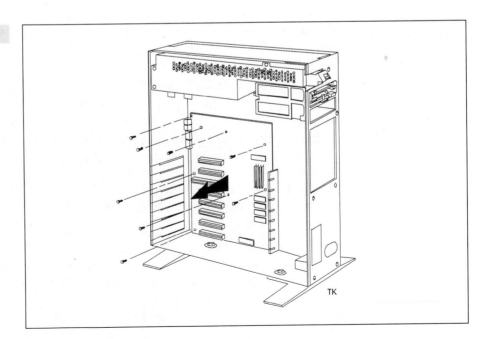

Reassembly Hints

When reassembling machines, just reverse the order of disassembly. Plan ahead. Don't be afraid to pull some things out and start over if you're in a corner. The important thing is to *take your time.* Here are a few tips on putting your computer back together.

Connecting Cables and Edge Connectors: The Pin 1 Rule

Expansion boards in the PC are often controller boards for external devices like disk drives or displays. Cables connect the boards to the drives or displays. A common short cable type is a ribbon cable.

Most ribbon connectors are symmetrical with respect to one or more axes. They could plug in one or two ways. Plugging in a connector upside-down will usually damage the device, or the controller board, or both. Most cables are *keyed*—a connector is modified so it cannot be plugged in incorrectly. However, some are not, and so the following bit of information is valuable.

A ribbon cable consists of many small wires laid out flat in parallel to form a flat cable, hence the "ribbon" name. One of the wires on the extreme outside of the cable will be colored differently from the others. For instance, ribbon cables are usually blue, white, or gray. The edge wire's color is often darker, like dark blue or red. This wire connects to pin 1 of the connector. This information has saved me more times than I care to recount. I learned it after incinerating a hard disk. (If you're going to make mistakes, you might as well learn from them.)

How do you find pin 1 on the circuit board? Many are stenciled right onto the board, which is very nice. Others only label pin 2, as pin 1 is on the back of the board. So look for a 1, and if you can't find it, use 2. If you can't find either, turn the circuit board over. Notice the round blobs of solder where chips are secured to the circuit board. These are called *solder pads.* On some circuit boards, all of the solder pads are round except for pin 1's—it's square. Take a look at Figure 2.32, which illustrates two ways of finding pin 1.

FIGURE 2.32

How to find pin 1 on a
circuit board

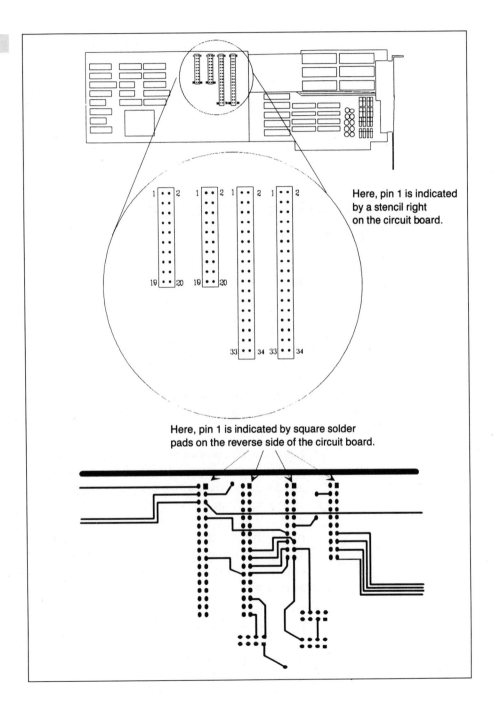

Here, pin 1 is indicated
by a stencil right
on the circuit board.

Here, pin 1 is indicated by square solder
pads on the reverse side of the circuit board.

You'll find pin 1 on the circuit board of a hard or floppy disk, on disk controllers, or anywhere a ribbon cable connects to a circuit board.

On the ribbon cables on the back of a CD-ROM, floppy, hard disk, and tape drives, you'll usually find that pin 1 goes towards the power connection.

Like most other convenient rules, there are exceptions. You might not find any indication of pin 1. Not all boards are labeled. Sadly, there are no Pin 1 Police. That's why diagrams are so important.

Common Reassembly Mistakes

In general, all you need to do a good reassembly is patience and a good diagram. But here's where people tend to go wrong. Most of this stuff isn't fatal to your system in the long term, but it'll make you sweat until you figure it out. And if you take it to a repair shop to get it "fixed," the repair people will know who caused the problem.

- **Forgetting to reconnect P8 and P9.** This isn't actually common (thank goodness), but it's important. If you forget to connect the motherboard power connectors P8 and P9 to the motherboard, the power supply may actually explode when you turn the machine on.

- **Bad motherboard seating.** Pay special attention when reseating the motherboard on its plastic spacers. Notice that the spacers are designed with a top disk and a bottom disk, and a bit of space between. Then notice that the motherboard has raised metal slots with a V shape. The spacers are supposed to sit so that the V is between the upper and lower disk. Get a flashlight and check the spacers. Another way to test motherboard seating is to insert a circuit board; if it doesn't fit right, your motherboard is probably seated wrong.

- **Reversed data or control cables.** "Let's see, which side *does* this blue line go on?" Very common. If you don't diagram carefully, you could find yourself having trouble trying to figure out how a ribbon cable connects to a drive. If you didn't diagram carefully, use the Pin 1 Rule to help you.

- **Mishandled boards.** Don't stack boards; lay them out separately. Occasionally, rough handling can scratch and remove a circuit board trace. This can be repaired by soldering a short wire (as short as possible!) across the cut in the trace. If you're unsure, since traces can be faint or thin to begin with, use your ohmmeter. Set it to low ohms (Rx1 on the dial), and then put the probes on either side of the suspected cut. The meter should read 0 if everything's okay.

- **Forgetting to attach power.** This one's good for a heart attack. You forget to attach that milky-white four-wire P10, P11, or P12 power connector to the hard disk, and—auggh!—you get "disk boot failure."

- **Neglecting to plan cabling.** Amateur troubleshooters stuff the cables any which way to get them in the box. Then, the next time they open the box, the cables pop up and get caught on the tab for the center screw. Cables rip and bend, teardrops flow—you get the picture. Stuffed cables also impede airflow in the case and heat up the inside of the machine.

Put the drives partway in, attach their cables, and then look and ask: How can I route these cables so they'll be out of the way? Sometimes the best way is to move the drives around, so don't hesitate to be creative. For example, most XTs with one full-height floppy drive and one full-height hard drive would be better configured with the floppy on the outside (that is, to the right of the hard disk, as seen from the front) rather than vice versa, which is the norm. You can sometimes rearrange the boards to facilitate cable placement.

- **Forgetting the speaker connection, keylock connection,** or battery. The first two are minor, the last annoying. Forget to reconnect the battery, and you won't be able to configure the system.

- **Panicking when it doesn't power up immediately.** I've seen students do this sometimes. They can't get the computer to boot up, so they tear it apart again, ripping cables and forcing boards out before removing their screws. Stay calm. No matter how important the machine is, you cannot fix it by rushing.

Peculiarities of Particular Models

The above material provides useful advice in general, but here are some strangenesses you'll see in particular computers:

- **Backplane design.** Many (but not all) compatible computers don't have a motherboard per se but put the CPU on expansion boards. In fact, that's all there is on one of these machines—expansion slots. For example, when you open a Z-248, Zenith's popular 286-based system, you find only a board with slots and a battery after you've removed the expansion board. What *would* be the motherboard is divided, like the old kingdom of Gaul, into three parts: the *backplane board,* with the battery; the *CPU/memory* board, with the CPU, memory, ROM, and some other chips; and the *I/O card* with the keyboard controller, diagnostic LEDs, and more chips. Zenith's not the only one to use the backplane approach. Kaypro, Wyse, and Telex have all used it at one point.

  The reason for this seems to have been flexibility. You could change from a 286 to a 386 CPU by just replacing the CPU/memory and I/O boards. A nice idea, but what's so hard about replacing a motherboard? Besides, for what Zenith charges for the upgrade kit you can buy a brand-new AST 386 computer. It's also annoying in that it forces you to buy parts from Zenith, rather than allowing use of generic motherboards for replacements. Zenith and Kaypro seem to concur. Their most recent computers have a more traditional motherboard.

- **Hidden motherboards.** Open up an AT&T 6300 or 6386, and at first glance you seem to have stumbled on a backplane machine: no motherboard, and only slots. But look further—none of the expansion boards has a CPU. The trick is to turn the box over and remove a bottom panel. You'll see a large motherboard, one that includes a few extra functions. The 6300 motherboard includes serial and parallel ports and the floppy controller right on the motherboard, rather than on separate boards as in other machines. This is both a blessing and a curse. It's a blessing because it saves you slots. It's a curse because it means that when the floppy controller fails you, you must buy a whole new motherboard rather than changing a $29.95 floppy controller board (as you can do in an XT clone).

- **Workaholic motherboards.** Some compatible machines incorporate several functions that ordinarily would be found on expansion boards, like video, parallel and serial ports, and floppy controllers right on the motherboard. My personal preference is toward less motherboard integration, as that means there are several cheap boards in a system rather than one expensive board. In fairness, I should say on the positive side that integration can reduce chip count and increase reliability. The devil's deal, then, is that you get a computer that's more reliable but will cost more money to fix when it does fail.

   The most prominent offenders in this category are the PS/2 machines (more about them later). Another is the Zenith LP286: It puts an entire computer on the motherboard, including hard disk controller, video, parallel, serial, and floppy. You want 8514 video or SCSI disk controllers? No can do, unless you can figure out how to disable the on-board resources. In defense of Zenith, though, they picked Cadillac components—1:1 hard disk controller and VGA video paired up with a 0-wait–state 10-MHz 286 make it a computer with a nice response. Just don't try to fix it.

- **Kooky keyboards.** The AT&T machines all use a keyboard with a D-shell connector rather than the more common round five-pin DIN connector.

- **Strange video.** The old AT&T machines insist on a nonstandard graphic board. In text mode, they respond like a normal PC, but they support a graphic standard used only by AT&T. Thankfully, the 386 machines (the 6386s) also support EGA. Some of the video monitors use a female 25-pin connector just like the parallel port. Plug the printer into the video or vice versa, and you can literally smoke either the port or the peripheral.

Most compatibles, like Compaqs and ASTs, follow the IBM structure pretty closely. There are, however, some that are a bit off the beaten path. Here, then, is some extra advice on two common compatibles, the AT&T 6300 (an XT-type machine) and the Zenith Z-248 (an AT-type machine).

AT&T Disassembly Steps

The 6300's not bad, once you know what to expect.

1. Remove the top. Take out the circuit boards in the usual way, except for the large board on the outside edge of the motherboard. It's the video board and requires some extra work (it's usually the last thing you remove from the system).

2. Remove the two large power cables that connect to the video board. Make sure you know which cable goes to which connector.

3. Disconnect the drives from power (white cables) and data (ribbons). Then look under the bottom drive. You'll see a metal tongue. Pull up the end of the tongue with a screwdriver. Then a cradle containing both drives can be pulled forward and out.

4. Turn the machine upside down. Remove the bottom panel to expose the motherboard. Remove its retaining screws. Remove and note the ribbon connections from the upper part of the computer. The motherboard will now only be secured with the edge connectors from the video board. Slide the motherboard away from the connectors, and set it aside.

5. Turn the machine back right side up. Remove the backplane board, the one with the slots. Again, you'll do this with the video board still in place.

6. Remove the metal panel protecting the video board. It's held in place with several screws.

7. You can now remove a few screws and the video board comes off.

Zenith Z-248 Disassembly Hints

The Zenith is pretty close to most AT-like machines, with a couple of exceptions.

• The power supply has only one connection line, not two as in most compatibles.

- The drives are contained in a *cradle* that must be removed before the drives can be serviced or replaced. Note a black Phillips screw on the outside front of the chassis, just below the drives. Remove this. You'll also notice a horizontal metal tab sticking out of the chassis right below where the screw was. Tap that with the back of a screwdriver to loosen the cradle. Now notice the metal box—the cradle—containing the drives. Pull it toward the back of the Z-248, and it'll come right out. Then the drives can be removed by taking out the side screws.

Two very important words of caution about the Zenith hard disks:

- Notice that the hard drives are secured with short screws. Keep them. If you put regular ⅜-inch screws into the side of the common Seagate ST225, ST238, or ST251, you'll damage the drive.

- With these Seagate drives, *do not* install all four screws, as many drive chassis mountings have holes that don't line up exactly. The drive will be twisted slightly, and won't work. Only use three—any three of the four will do.

Now you're ready for open-PC surgery. Chapter 3 shows you what you can expect to see inside.

CHAPTER

3

Inside the PC:
Pieces of the Picture

NOW that it's in pieces, let's see what you've got... The PC is a modular device. This modularity makes problem determination and repair much more tractable than, say, repairing your TV. Also, your PC lacks the large *capacitors* that make the TV dangerous to fool around with even when unplugged; but remember not to open the power supply. Even if the problem's so bad that you have to open the machine to fix it (remember that most PC problems involve broken software or "broken" users, not hardware), many repairs just involve finding and replacing the faulty component. Also, if you are a PC support person, being able to go to a strange machine and identify the components impresses the heck out of a skeptical audience, such as those folks who question your troubleshooting abilities. So Step 1 is to identify what's in the box.

A PC is composed of just a few components:

- System board or motherboard, containing:

    CPU (Central Processing Unit) Bus

    Expansion slots

    Planar memory (main memory on the system board)

    System clock

    Numeric coprocessor

    Keyboard adapter (interface)

- Power supply
- Keyboard
- Display and display adapter
- Floppy disk controller and floppy disk drives
- Hard disk controller and hard disk drive(s)

- Multifunction board, containing:
    Printer port
    System clock/calendar
    Serial port (RS-232C port)

The System Board/Motherboard

Since their creation in 1974, microcomputers have usually included most of their essential electronics on a single printed circuit board called the *motherboard,* shown in Figures 3.1–3.3. The IBM PC and compatibles are no exception (save those that put the CPU on an expansion board, like Kaypro, Zenith, and Wyse), but IBM chose to use a different term. Rather than calling this main circuit board a motherboard, Big Blue calls it the *system board,* shown in Figure 3.4. I'll use both terms interchangeably in this text. The PC compatibles are no exception, but, again, some models (Kaypro PC, Telex 12xx, Zenith Z-15x, and old Zenith Z-248 computers) use the backplane approach.

The Z-248 backplane is a pain, but Zenith included a neat diagnostic feature: six LEDs labeled *CPU, ROM, RAM, INT, DSK,* and *RDY.* Turn the machine on, and all six LEDs light up. The CPU does a quick self-test, and its LED goes out. The system then checks and extinguishes LEDs for ROM, RAM, interrupts, and the disk controller. Finally RDY goes out once DOS has loaded correctly.

The newer PS/2 machines have yet another name for the motherboard: the *planar board.* Some PS/2s use the backplane method, like the model 95.

Several "big-name" vendors have used the backplane approach in recent times, claiming that it makes their PCs "modular." By that, they mean that you'd upgrade your PC's CPU simply by removing the circuit board

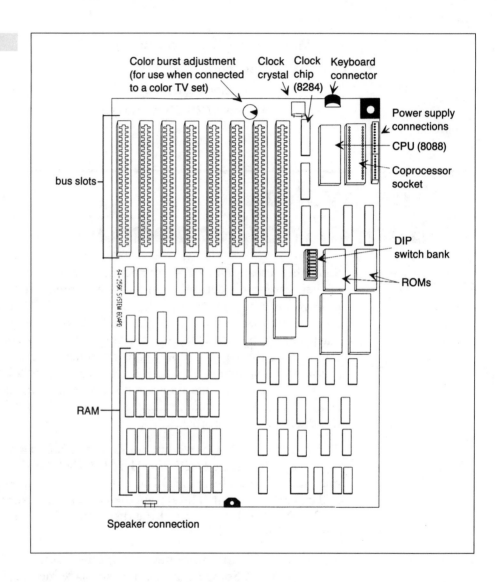

that contains the PC and replacing it with a new CPU board—a five-minute bit of brain surgery that instantly transforms your PC from, say, a 286 to a 486DX computer.

That's a neat idea on the face of it, but when you look more closely, there's really no reason to buy one of these "upgradable" PCs. The reason that

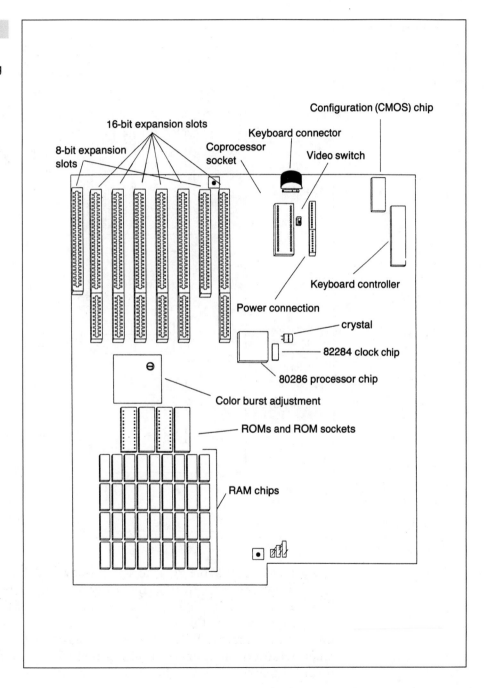

FIGURE 3.2

Original AT
motherboard detailing
significant areas

FIGURE 3.3

AT model 339 motherboard detailing significant areas

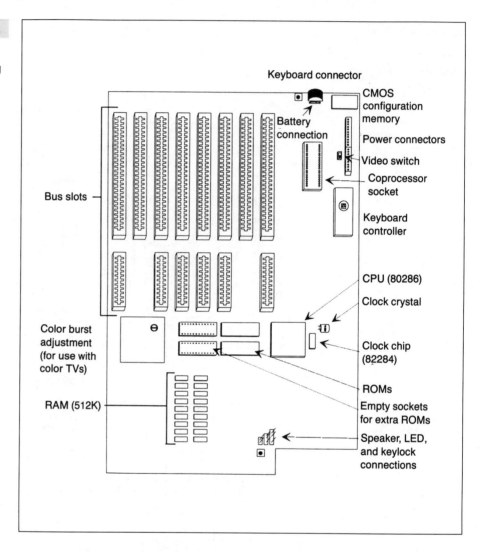

you want an upgradable PC is to save money, and that's the *only* reason—you can always buy a new PC; you just don't want to spend a lot of money. Having said that, take a look at some of the costs of the upgrade kits offered by Compaq, Tandon, ALR, and the other companies offering modular, upgradable PCs. The upgrade costs that *I've* seen for (for example) 486 upgrades are generally quite high—often costing more than if you'd gone out and bought a whole new 486-based clone computer!

IBM PC system board outline

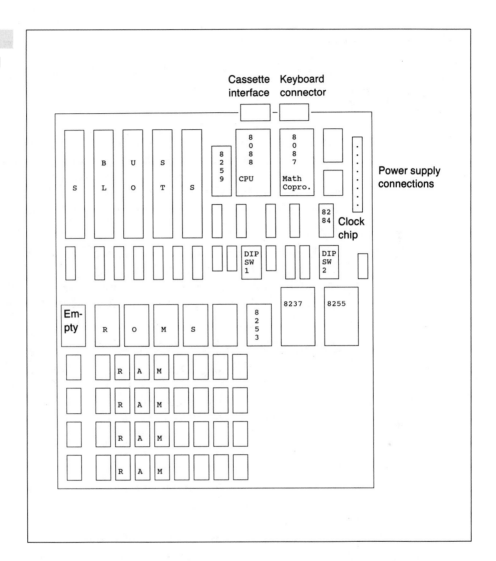

My idea of an "upgradable" computer is a generic clone. It's based on a standard-sized motherboard that fits in a standard-sized case and takes standard boards and drives. When I want to upgrade it, all I do is buy a new motherboard and swap it out for the old one. For example, I recently upgraded a 10-MHz 286 computer to a 40-MHz 386DX computer for $200—all I needed was a new motherboard. (I'll have more to say on the whole idea of buying generic throughout the book.)

Central Processing Unit (CPU)

The "heart" of the PC is a microprocessor chip created by Intel Corporation or some other company that they have licensed. Intel has designed and created many microprocessors over the years, but the ones that interest us are the 8088, 80286, 80386, 80486, and Pentium. Many of those chips have been cloned by other manufacturers, but they're still Intel x86 compatible.

CPU performance determines, in part, computer performance. CPUs vary in several ways that affect their performance. These ways are introduced in Table 3.1. Take a minute now and look over this section so you'll understand where a lot of PC limitations come from later.

TABLE 3.1: CPU Properties

PROPERTY	DESCRIBES	UNITS	RANGE
CPU speed	The number of operations that can be done per second	MHz	4.77 MHz–99 MHz
Microcode efficiency	The number of steps required, for example, to multiply two numbers	clocks	varies
Word size	The largest number that can be handled in one operation	bits	16 bits–32 bits
Data path	The largest number that can be transported into the chip in one operation	bits	8 bits–64 bits
Maximum memory	How much memory the chip can use	MB	1 MB–4,096 MB

CPU Speeds (Megahertz)

Computers run to the beat of a clock, as a beginning piano player plays to the beat of a metronome. If you set the metronome too fast, the beginner will become confused and the music won't come out right. Similarly, if you set the clock rate of a CPU too high, it will malfunction. You won't damage the chip; the computer just won't function properly. Part of the design of a computer like the PC includes determining a clock rate.

CPU clocks generally "tick" more than a million times per second. A clock that ticks at exactly one million times per second is said to be a one-megahertz clock, abbreviated 1 MHz. The Apple II used a 2-MHz clock. The original PC and XT use a 4.77-MHz clock. The AT originally used a 6-MHz clock, and later IBM offered a version that ran at 8-MHz. Clone makers offer computers with clock speeds up to 33 MHz. All other things being equal, a faster clock means faster execution and better performance. Table 3.2 lists some clock rates for some true Blue models.

TABLE 3.2: Typical Computer Speeds for IBM Computers

COMPUTER	SPEED (MHZ)
PC	4.77
XT	4.77
AT	6 or 8
Model 25/30	8
Model 30-286	10
Model 50, 60, 50Z	10
Model 55	16
Model 70	16 to 25
Model 80	16 to 20
Model 95	33 to 66

Word Size

Any computer can be programmed to manipulate any size number, but the bigger the number, the longer it takes. The largest number the computer can manipulate in one operation is determined by its *word size*. This is either 8, 16, or 32 bits.

Think of it this way: If I asked you, "What is 5 times 6?" you would answer, "30" immediately—you did it in one operation. If I asked, "What is 55 times 66?" you would do a series of steps to arrive at the answer. Fifty-five is larger than your word size. So you took a too-complex problem—55×66—and broke it down to tractable subproblems—50×60, 50×6, 5×60, 5×6—and then summed the results.

Computers do the same thing. Even though a 16-bit computer cannot *directly* manipulate any number larger than 2^{16}, or 65,536, it can compute much larger problems when programmed to break down a large problem into smaller ones. The advantage of a 32-bit computer over a 16-bit computer is that it can handle a larger number all in one "gulp"—a number of up to four billion for a 32-bit computer. A larger word means fewer sub-operations, and therefore faster throughput (the amount of work the system performs). That's one reason why a 386, with 32-bit registers, is faster than a 286, with 16-bit registers.

Data Path

No matter how large the computer's word size, the data must be transported into the CPU. This is the width of the computer's "loading door." It can be 8, 16, or 32 bits. Obviously, a wider door will allow more data to be transported in less time than will a narrower door.

Consider, for example, an 8-MHz 8088 versus an 8-MHz 8086. The only difference between the 8088 and the 8086 is that the 8088 has an 8-bit data path, the 8086 a 16-bit data path. Now, both the 8088 and the 8086 have 16-bit registers, so a programmer would issue the same command to load 16 bits into either one; the command MOV AX,0200 will move the 16-bit value 200 hex into a 16-bit register called AX. That will take twice as long on the 8088 as on the 8086 because the 8086 can do it in one operation, while the 8088 takes two. Note what's going on—although they're both 8-MHz computers, the 8088 machine computes more slowly for some operations.

Now, you can see that the 8086 is a faster, more powerful chip than the 8088. But did you know that the 8088 was released *later* than the 8086? It's true; here's why.

When the 8086 was first released (1977), it was one of the first microprocessors with a 16-bit data path. Almost every popular microprocessor–based computer available at the time was based on a CPU with an 8-bit data path. ("Almost" because the LSI-11 microprocessor had a 16-bit data path, and a few Heathkit computers used the LSI-11.) As the CPUs all expected eight bits whenever they *read* data, and provided eight bits when they *wrote* data, the motherboards of computers in those days contained enough circuitry to transport eight bits around.

Now, the 8086 was a neat-looking chip, as its 16 bits seemed just the stuff to build a powerful microcomputer around. But consider the *bad* side of a 16-bit CPU: it requires a 16-bit motherboard. An 8086's motherboard must contain enough circuitry to transport *16* bits around, and so could be *twice* as expensive as an eight bit motherboard of some type. That put the 8086 at an economic disadvantage. (It may seem like a trivial matter now, but in the late 70's, hardware was more expensive, and an 8086-based motherboard was significantly more expensive than an 8-bit motherboard.)

So Intel said to themselves, "How can we offer the power of the 8086 and still keep motherboard prices down?" And so they built the 8088, a year after the 8086's release. Inside, the 8088 is identical to the 8086. The only difference is in the size of its "front door"—the path that the 8088 uses to transport data into and out of the chip. As it is only eight bits wide, motherboard designers could easily adapt existing designs to the new chip. As a result, the 8088 enjoyed a moderate amount of success in 1979–1981. Of course, when IBM released the PC in 1981 based on the 8088, "moderate" eventually changed to "amazing."

History repeated itself in 1988 with the 80386SX. The original 80386 was introduced in 1985—Intel's "next generation" chip with a 32-bit data path. The 386 did fairly well fairly quickly, but not quickly enough for Intel. The 286 sold well also, but the 286 had a problem as far as Intel was concerned: Intel didn't *own* the 286. By that, I mean that while Intel invented the 286, it had also licensed several vendors to make the 286, and so many 286es being sold were lining the pockets of Advanced Micro Devices, Fairchild, Siemens, and a number of other chip builders. Intel wanted *all* of the profit from the 386, however, so they refused to license the 386 to any other company.

The 286 was not only a cheap chip, it was also a 16-bit chip. That meant that 286 PCs could be built around 16-bit motherboards. 32-bit motherboards were going to be just plain expensive. Therefore, 286-based PCs would be *tons* cheaper than 386 PCs, and so more 286es would sell than 386es; Intel didn't like that. So they embarked on a campaign of chip infanticide. They ran a huge advertising campaign advising people to stay away from the 286, and to buy 386-based PCs. They also answered the manufacturer's concerns about the costs of building a 32-bit motherboard by offering the 80386SX.

The 80386SX was an 80386 with one difference: its "front door" was 16 bits, not 32 bits. Vendors liked that because they could take their old 16-bit 80286 motherboards, modify their design a bit, *et voilà*! They could offer "386 technology." After a year, it became clear that the original 80386 needed a name, so it became known as the "80386DX."

Is the 80486SX a 16-bit chip, then? Absolutely not. Read on...

Memory Address Space

This talk of megabytes always confuses some people, so let me digress for a minute. A *megabyte* is a unit of storage size, just about the amount of space needed to store a million characters. We use it to talk about the size of *primary memory* or RAM, the kind of memory that goes in expansion boards and that Lotus can run out of if you've got a large spreadsheet; and *secondary memory*, which is on disk drives. When most people say *memory* they're talking about primary memory, meaning chips or RAM. Folks usually just say *disk* when that's what they mean, rather than secondary memory.

Disk memory is also not volatile, which means when you shut it off, it retains its data. Remove power from a memory chip (which happens whenever you turn the machine off), and it forgets whatever it contained; that is *volatile* memory. That's why you have to save your work to disk before shutting off the machine.

But the fact that both disks and memory get measured in megabytes confuses people. I'll say, "I work with a 386 with four megabytes of memory," and they'll think, "What good is *that?* Even *I've* got 20 megabytes on my XT." *I* was talking about primary memory—four megs of RAM. I didn't say anything at all about how much hard disk space I have. *They* were thinking of hard disk space and didn't tell me how much memory their XT has. (Probably 640K, a little over one-half of a megabyte.) End of digression.

You can't just keep adding memory to your PC indefinitely. A particular chip can only *address* a certain size of memory. For the oldest chips, this amount was 65,536 bytes—a 64K memory. The original PC's CPU can address 1024K, or one megabyte (1 MB). Other, newer chips can address even more. The 80386 and 80486 can address gigabytes (billions of bytes).

Details on CPU Chips

In some cases, you'll have to remove and replace these chips in order to upgrade or fix a problem. Here is some more background about them. As we've seen, several CPU chips are used in the PC market. They're all based on a line of chips from Intel called the *iapx86* family. Table 3.3 summarizes their characteristics.

TABLE 3.3: CPU Specifications and Applications

MAKER	MODEL	MAX SPEED (MHZ)	WORD SIZE (BITS)	DATA PATH	MEMORY (MB)	EXAMPLES OF COMPUTERS UTILIZING CHIP
Intel	8088	8	16	8	1	IBM PC, XT, Portable
Intel	8086	8	16	16	1	PS/2 Model 30, Compaq Deskpro
Intel	80C86	8	16	16	1	Toshiba 1100+
Intel	80186	16	16	16	1	3Com 3Server3, Tandy 2000
NEC	V20	10	16	8	1	Kaypro 2000

TABLE 3.3: CPU Specifications and Applications (continued)

MAKER	MODEL	MAX SPEED (MHZ)	WORD SIZE (BITS)	DATA PATH	MEMORY (MB)	EXAMPLES OF COMPUTERS UTILIZING CHIP
NEC	V30	10	16	16	1	NEC Multispeed, Kaypro PC
Intel	80286	20	16	16	16	IBM AT, PS/2 Model 50, 60
Intel	80386DX	40	32	32	4096	Compaq Deskpro 386, PS/2 Model 70, 80
Intel	80386SX	25	32	16	16	Compaq 386S
Intel	80486DX	50	32	32	4096	PS/2 Model 95
Intel	80486SX	25	32	32	4096	ALR 486SX
Intel	80486DX2	66	32	32	4096	Compaq 66M
Cyrix	80486SLC	33	33	32	16	ZEOS SLC
Cyrix	80486DLC	33	33	32	4096	ZEOS DLC
IBM	80386SLC	20	32	16	16	PS/2 Model 57SLC
Intel	Pentium	66	32/64	64	4096	various

Some of these chips are more powerful than others. Some can actually allow you to improve the throughput of your existing PC. For instance, if you have a PC or PC clone, you can replace your 8088 chip with a V20 chip and see about a 5 to 20 percent increase in performance. The upgrade cost is only about $20.

The 8088

The 8088 is older and less powerful than the 80286 and is used in most XT-class machines. It comes in what is called a *40-pin DIP package*, which means a rectangular plastic case with two rows of 20 pins. *DIP* stands for Dual In-line Package (see Figure 3.5). Older 8088s are called 8088-1, as they can only run at low speeds (5 MHz or slower). *Turbo PC/XT* clones may run at 6.66, 7.16, or 8.0 MHz. To do this, they use the 8088-2, which is rated at up to 8 MHz. The 8088 is the equivalent of about 29,000 transistors.

The 80286

The 80286 is a newer chip, designed by Intel in 1981. Its package is a square of plastic called a *PGA,* or Pin Grid Array package (see Figure 3.3). It also comes in a cheaper package called a *PLCC,* or Plastic Leadless Chip Carrier. The PGA package has an inner and an outer square of solid pins; the PLCC arranges thin tinfoil-like legs around its perimeter. The 286 packs a lot more power into a small package than the 8088 does: The 80286 is the equivalent of about 130,000 transistors in about the same volume as the 8088's 29,000 transistors. Because of this, the 80286 runs hotter and may require extra cooling provisions such as *heat sinks,* small metal caps, or metal cooling fins that fit on top of a chip and enable the chip to better dissipate the heat it generates.

FIGURE 3.5

Chip package types

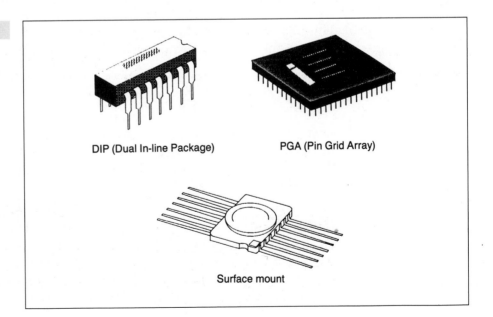

DIP (Dual In-line Package)   PGA (Pin Grid Array)

Surface mount

The 80386DX and 80386SX

The 80386 or, as it's officially called by Intel, the 80386DX is a powerful member of the iapx86 family. Introduced in 1985, the 80386 comes in a PGA package and is the equivalent of about 250,000 transistors. It incorporates a wealth of programming features, including the ability to multitask DOS programs with the help of a "hypervisor" program like DesqView/386 or VM/386. Its 32-bit data path speeds data access, although to date few expansion boards except memory boards and a few LAN and disk controller boards use this full 32-bit capability.

The 386SX is identical to the 386DX except that it has a 16-bit data path to allow it to be more easily incorporated into AT-type hardware designs (recall that the AT's 286 has a 16-bit data path also).

The 80486DX and 80486SX

The newest member of the iapx86 family, the 80486, is sort of an upgraded 386. It combines a tuned-up 386 with two chips that speed up a 386 system: the 385 cache controller and the 387 numeric coprocessor. The microcode is larger and faster—there are the equivalent of 1.25 million transistors in this chip—so a 25-MHz 386 with a 385 and a 387 will execute only half as many instructions per second as a 25-MHz 486.

Better yet, the 486 chip is actually cheaper than a 386, 385, and 387 together, so theoretically 486 computers could be cheaper than 386 machines. Time will tell.

In an effort to stave off 386 compatibles' makers, Intel introduced a new chip in 1991—the 80486SX. It has a full 32-bit data path, memory controller, and 8K cache, like the 80486DX, but lacks the numeric coprocessor.

Actually, it doesn't *lack* it. The coprocessor is there; Intel just disabled it before shipping. (As far as I know, there's no way for a user to re-enable it.) The 486SX is only supplied in a 20-MHz speed. It is intended to offer an alternative to 20- and 25-MHz 386DX systems. The 486SX is attractive because it's a reasonably priced and fairly efficient 20-MHz CPU; it would be even more attractive if they hadn't disabled the coprocessor. Think about it: It cost extra money to disable the coprocessor. If they hadn't, vendors would be able to offer full-blown 486DX machines at the respectable speed of 20 MHz for under $1000. Too bad, I say.

Worse yet, Intel sells a 487SX. This chip, supposedly the coprocessor that matches the 486SX, is actually a complete 486DX in a strange package: Not only is it a math coprocessor, it's a complete processor. When you install it, the 487SX actually shuts down the 486SX and does all of the work itself. Bizarre, eh? That's marketing for you, I guess.

The 80486DX2, the Overdrive Chip, and Clock Doubling

The 80487SX, as it turns out, was a mere harbinger of the wide variety in CPUs that was to follow. To recap, the 80487SX is *not* a floating-point coprocessor. It is a fully functional 80486DX, but packaged a bit differently—the pins on the bottom of the chip are arranged differently from the way they're arranged on the 80486DX, so you can't just pop an 80486DX in the 80487SX socket.

Furthermore, unlike the floating-point coprocessors of yore (the 8087, 187, 287, and 387 families), the 80487SX does not work with the erstwhile main processor—it *takes over altogether*, effectively disconnecting the 80486SX.

Intel took things a step further with a chip called the Overdrive chip. The Overdrive chip does a neat trick—it runs at two clock speeds simultaneously. Placed in a 25-MHz 486SX motherboard, it fits in the 487SX socket, taking over from the 486SX. When it transfers data to or from the bus, the memory, or any other items outside of itself, it does those operations at 25 MHz. But *internal* operations—arithmetic operations, decision making, logical operations, and the like—are done at *twice* the clock rate— 50 MHz internally! The net effect is that the Overdrive chip does everything at least as quickly as a 25-MHz 80486DX, and many operations *twice* as fast! The net effect is that the Overdrive chip will speed up your PC by about one-third to one-half.

Is it worth it? An Overdrive chip costs around $500, not a small amount, but then not a budget-buster either.

Recall that chips built for the 487SX socket are full-fledged CPUs with pin arrangements different from the CPUs that go into sockets designed for the main processors like the 486DX or 486SX. There is then, also, a version of the Overdrive chip that goes in a main processor socket. It's called the 80486DX2, known popularly as a "clock doubler" chip.

The 80486DX2, like the Overdrive chip, runs outwardly at "X" MHz, but works internally at "2X" MHz. Thus, a 66-MHz 80486DX2 works in a motherboard designed for a 33-MHz chip, but runs internally at 66 MHz. The value is, again, that a PC vendor need only take one of its already-existing 33-MHz 80486DX models, replace the 33-MHz 80486DX processor with a 66-MHz 80486DX processor, and they've instantly got a "66-MHz 486."

There's a small "gotcha" about this. Notice the speed designation. If a CPU runs at 33 MHz when it is working with every component in the system but itself, but works internally at 66 MHz, is it really legitimate to say that its speed is 66 MHz? Personally, I'd say not. So, when you see a computer based on the DX*2* chip, don't be amazed by the seemingly transwarp speeds. The actual throughput you'll get from a DX2 computer advertised at "X" MHz is going to be about two-thirds that speed when compared to a DX computer of the same clock speed.

Clock Triplers: 486DX4 and Blue Lightning

Once, clock doublers were the fastest thing around. In late 1993, however, that changed.

Intel once made all the 386 and 486 chips. But they had an agreement with IBM from way back that gave IBM the right to manufacture honest-to-God 386 and 486 chips, using the Intel masks.

So IBM decided to use that agreement.

First, IBM created a chip called the 486SLC. A 486SLC was a 486 SX (no numeric coprocessor, recall) with just *1K* of cache (rather than the normal 8K) and a 16-bit data path. The resulting chip was somewhere between a 386SX and a 486SX in performance. IBM then used it to replace 386SX processors in its PS/2 line, resulting in faster computers using 16-bit hardware. It was a nice idea, but it was a bit silly, as 32-bit hardware is pretty cheap to manufacture these days. If they'd built the 486SLC in 1988, then that would have created a small revolution; but introducing it in 1991 created only minor interest among the IBM-buying faithful.

More recently, however, IBM has taken the idea of a clock doubler and gone it one better. They have taken a 25 MHz 486DX and created a clock *tripler* called "Blue Lightning." Like the clock doubler, a tripler chip can run in a slower motherboard, only running faster inside the CPU.

An existing 486DX-25 MHz system could become partially 75 MHz in speed by just the simple expedient of changing CPUs. IBM also plans 33 MHz chips tripled to 99 MHz.

Not to be outdone, Intel has also announced a 486DX4-99. This chip will communicate with its motherboard at 33 MHz, but will do internal calculations at 99 MHz. That would allow people to take a 33 MHz 486 and upgrade it to 99 MHz by just changing the CPU chip. Intel has also announced a 50-MHz Pentium chip that will run internally at 100 MHz. At this writing, none of those Intel chips are available yet.

The Pentium

In March of 1993, Intel introduced the Pentium processor. In some ways, it's just a souped-up 486. In other ways, it's much more. There's a lot to like about the Pentium. Here's a whirlwind tour of Pentium features.

Greater Raw Speed The Pentium comes in 60-MHz and 66-MHz flavors. If offering two speeds that are so close together seems odd, it is—usually. The Pentium is so difficult a chip to make, however, that the percentage of manufactured chips that can operate at the goal rate of 66 MHz—the *yield,* in chip talk—is much lower than it is for, say, the 386 or 486 chips. Lowering the bar of acceptability to 60 MHz allows Intel to sell the chips that *almost* made it. That means that the 60-MHz Pentiums failed the 66-MHz test and passed the 60-MHz test, whereas the 66-MHz Pentiums passed both tests. Personally, I'd look closely at a return and service policy before buying a PC based on a 60-MHz Pentium.

Why is the Pentium so difficult to make? For one thing, it's much bigger than the 486. The 486 contains 1.2 million transistors; the Pentium contains 3.1 million—over two and half times as many. (That's not the biggest jump we've seen, however. For example, the 386 was only a quarter million transistors.) The Pentium is also a hot chip in not only a figurative but a literal sense. The Pentium overview document from Intel says that it should be expected to run at up to 85 degrees centigrade—that's 185 degrees Fahrenheit, prompting the inevitable observation that it'll not only crunch your numbers, it'll cook your dinner. Look for makers of Pentium-based computers to tout their unique cooling facilities; I guess the 686 (the Sexium?) will need a refrigeration unit. As a laptop user, I look forward to a Pentium notebook that will serve double-duty as both a fast computer and a portable hot plate for us road-warrior types. (Just kidding.)

Seriously, though, think twice about buying this first generation of Pentiums (or is Pentia?); heat spells death for electronic components. Better to buy Pentium computers based on the Pentium II, which runs much cooler. The Pentium II was announced in late November 1993; it's also known as the "P54C," Intel's internal development name for that chip.

The Pentium's greater raw speed refers to the fact that the 66 MHz clock rate is a pure clock rate, unlike the 486DX2-66 chip, which runs 66 MHz internally but interacts with the outside world at only 33 MHz. A 486DX2-66 is a relatively simple chip to design a PC around, as the fact that it communicates at 33 MHz externally means that all a designer need do is to mate a DX2-66 CPU chip with a run-of-the-mill 33-MHz motherboard, and *voilà!* instant "66-MHz computer." With a Pentium-66, on the other hand, both internal and external communication is at 66 MHz, requiring a motherboard that runs at 66 MHz. While it may seem that building a 66-MHz motherboard should be a small incremental change from the currently-available 33-MHz and 50-MHz motherboards, it's not—the task gets harder as the speed gets greater. 66-MHz is around the frequency of US television channel 4, so a Pentium-equipped PC has a serious potential noise problem; run one without the proper shielding (i.e., with the cover off or with an inadequate cover), and you're, well, "on the air." Currently, anyone can design a motherboard with a few chips and a processor. That won't be true with Pentium-based systems. Don't be surprised if the the early 66-MHz Pentium-based PCs vary in actual usable speed by a factor of 50 percent.

The Pentium is also faster than earlier Intel processors because Intel has "hardwired" certain functions that used to be performed in software. Reworking processor parts from software to hardware always ups the transistor count, but repays in improved performance.

Smarter Cache Since the 20-MHz 80386DX's introduction, PC designers have been faced with a difficult choice—what kind of memory to use in their machines. The majority of PC RAM is called "dynamic" RAM (DRAM): It's relatively cheap, but it's not available in the kind of speeds needed to keep up with 20+-MHz systems—you can't get dynamic RAMs in 40, 25, 20, or 15 nanosecond access times, the times required by those systems. As you'll learn in Chapter 8, there is a different kind of RAMs called Static RAMs (SRAMs) that are available in those higher speeds, but they're considerably more expensive than DRAMs. How do manufacturers build high speed machines, and still find RAM that won't drive the price of the PCs out of sight? With a combination of a lot of DRAM and a little SRAM. The DRAM serves as main memory, and most systems have megabytes of it. But many motherboards have between 64K and 512K of SRAM called cache RAM. When the CPU needs the next item of data from the system RAM, it looks first in the fast SRAM cache to see if it is there. If the data is in the SRAM cache, then the CPU gets it from the SRAM with no delay. If, on the other hand, the required data is not in the SRAM, then the CPU must go to DRAM for the data, which slows the system down considerably. The whole idea of a cache is that some smart hardware called a cache controller (it's built into the 486, and it's an optional chip on the 386) must essentially look into the future, guess what data the CPU will soon need, and go get that data before the CPU asks for it, so the data will already be in the cache.

While many 386 motherboards incorporated some kind of cache memory and cache controller, the 486 actually built cache and cache controlling into the CPU itself: The 486 contains 8K of cache, and most 486 systems have additional cache on the motherboard ("external" cache). The Pentium's cache system is better than the 486's in four ways. First, the Pentium has twice as much cache, with two 8K caches—one for data, one for program code. Second, the cache's method of organizing its cached data is more efficient, employing a "write-back" algorithm. The opposite of a write-back algorithm, a "write-through" algorithm, forces data written to the SRAM cache memory to be immediately written to the slower DRAM memory. That means that memory *reads* can come out of the cache quickly, but memory *writes* must always occur at the slower DRAM time. Reasoning that not every piece of information written to memory stays in memory very long, the Pentium's cache algorithm puts off writing data from SRAM to DRAM for as long as possible, unlike the 486, which uses a write-through cache. Third, the cache controller wastes time in searching to see if an item is in the cache—the Pentium reduces that time by dividing the cache into smaller caches, each of which can be searched more quickly; that technique is called a *two-way set associative cache*.

To explain the fourth way in which the Pentium's cache is better than the the 486's, I've got to first make an important point about what a cache must do. Recall that a cache must guess what data and program code the CPU will need soon, and then go get that data before the CPU asks for it. But guessing what the CPU will need isn't a straightforward task, particularly when there are decisions to be made. For example, suppose the cache sees that the CPU is currently executing some instructions that mean "compare value A with value B. If A is greater than B, then set the value MAXIMUM to A; otherwise, set the value MAXIMUM to B." That simple statement boils down to a bunch of instructions, instructions in memory that had better be in the cache if the Pentium is going to be able to continue running without delays. But since the cache controller can't know whether the CPU will take the "A was greater than B" or "B was greater than A" fork in the road, then it doesn't know which result's code to go grab and put in the cache. For years, *mainframe* cache controllers have used a technique called *branch prediction* to guess which way the CPU will go, and now a PC chip—the Pentium—has a cache controller built into it with branch prediction capabilities. So that's four ways that the Pentium makes better use of your memory than the 486 did.

Two Processors in a Single Chip ("Superscalar") There are essentially two CPUs in this chip. The first one is a simple 386-like CPU: It does integer operations, not floating-point operations. The second is like the 486—a 386 with floating-point capabilities built right into it. That means that the Pentium is essentially a parallel-processing CPU, with the ability to do two things at once. Those two CPUs-within-a-CPU are called the U and V *pipeline*s, and the fact that the Pentium has more than one pipeline makes it a *"superscalar"* CPU. (Why not "parallel processing" or "multiprocessing" or "dual processing," I don't know—"superscalar" is the buzzword.)

The neat part of this dual pipelining is that the Pentium uses both pipelines *automatically*. It takes a simple non–Pentium-aware program, reads it, and divides it up into two pipelines. Now, that's not always possible, as some programs contain internal dependencies, but the Pentium does the best that it can.

For example, consider these three commands:

```
A=3
B=2
C=A+B
```

The first two commands—**A=3** and **B=2**—are not dependent. You can manipulate A and manipulate B, and there's no interaction. Once they're done, then you're set to do **C=A+B**. As a result, **A=3** could go over the U pipeline while **B=2** went over the V pipeline, and then **C=A+B** could run on the U pipeline once **A=3** was done. But now consider this sequence:

```
A=1
A=A+2
```

The second command can't be executed until the first command is done. Therefore, in this case, the Pentium would be forced to put the first command, **A=1**, into one of the pipelines, and then wait for it to finish before being able to execute **A=A+2**.

You'll see programs advertised as being "designed for the Pentium". What that means is that the instructions have been arranged so that the Pentium can keep both pipelines stuffed and busy. So-called "Pentium programs" will run fine on a 486 or, usually, a 386, except that they'll run more slowly, as those processors only have one pipeline.

Fault Tolerant The Pentium is designed to be linked with another Pentium on a motherboard designed for fault tolerance. The second Pentium constantly monitors the first; if the main Pentium malfunctions, the other one jumps right in and takes up without skipping a beat.

How Much Faster Is a Pentium? Is a Pentium a good buy? Certainly the dual pipelines are quite impressive, as are the enhanced cache and the like. But is the Pentium that much faster? The answer is that it depends on what you're doing.

When the 386DX appeared, it was clearly faster than the 286. Put a 16-MHz 386 next to a 12-MHz 286 (the fastest 286 at the time), and the 386 would run rings around the 286. You didn't need benchmark programs—the newer chip just *felt* faster.

Working with a Pentium's not like that. I don't think that I could tell the difference between a Pentium and a 486DX2-66 just by running Windows on them. So the vendors of Pentium computers are trotting out benchmark tests that prove "conclusively" that the Pentium is two and half times faster than a 486DX2-66.

Ahem.

The Pentium can be much faster than the 486, but *only* if *1)* the benchmark program can fit entirely in the 16K cache that's included in a Pentium and *2)* the program is easily separated into two pipelines. Real-world programs usually fail on one or both of those requirements. In practice, the large programs that I've tested on a Pentium run about 20 to 30 percent faster than a 486DX2-66. So should you shell out lots of extra bucks for a Pentium? Only if you've got software optimized for a Pentium. Additionally, my recommendation is not to buy a Pentium until they've solved the heating problem. I can't see how a chip that runs at temperatures near the boiling point of water can run reliably.

The "Pentium SX"—the P24T

There are a number of 486-based computers that claim to be "Pentium ready." Now, if you think about that, it seems impossible, or at least improbable. After all, as the Pentium has two 32-bit pipelines, then it must be supplied with a 64-bit data path. But a 486 motherboard would only be built with a *32-bit* data path, as that's all that a 486 needs. So how could a 64-bit chip use a 32-bit motherboard?

The answer is that it *doesn't*. The so-called "Pentium ready" motherboards aren't ready for the Pentium, they're ready for yet another upcoming chip. That chip is a Pentium chip that's been designed with just a 32-bit data path, a chip called the P24T. It is 64-bit inside the chip—that is, it still contains two pipelines—but the "front door" is just 32 bits. In a sense, you could consider it to be a "Pentium SX."

Now, the main differences between a 66-MHz Pentium and a 66-MHz 486, *vis-a-vis* speed, are the larger amount of cache RAM (16K on the Pentium, 8K on the 486), the two pipelines, and the hard-coded instruction set. But the biggest speed increase comes from the two pipelines, and the pipelines are no good unless they're both getting constantly fed. But that's impossible with just a 32-bit motherboard. So the bottom line is that the P24T will run faster than a 486, but not much faster.

Main Memory

Memory used to be easy to understand. Computers (pre-PC) all had something like 1K, 4K, 16K, 32K, 48K, or 64K. Then the PC came along with bigger numbers—up to 640K of memory! Larger numbers, but no more confusing.

Now there's *extended, expanded, LIM,* and *conventional* memory, to say nothing of ROM. Why so many kinds of memory? Mainly because of unfortunate planning: Nobody ever thought the PC would need more than 640K of memory. Here's a look at how memory works.

The PC, like all computers, must have *main memory*. Main memory is high-speed memory that the CPU can read from or write to. "High speed" here means less than a microsecond to read or write. The other name for such memory is *RAM* or Random Access Memory, a particular kind of chip on circuit boards. (Again, don't confuse it with disk memory, which is sometimes called *secondary memory,* because disk drives also store data but at rates that are hundreds of thousands of times slower than main memory. Hard disks take longer than a millisecond to respond to requests.)

Memory is easy to pick out on a circuit board. It's packaged either as a *bank* of eight or nine small chips, or it's a mini-circuit board with several square chips mounted on it called a *SIMM* for Single Inline Memory Module (depicted in Figure 3.6). Memory is always organized into banks, either eight or nine discrete chips, or a SIMM. Most motherboards have room for four banks of memory. Some of the newer machines have no memory on the motherboard at all but instead have a large circuit board with room for megs and megs of memory. As each SIMM is the equivalent of nine chips, SIMMs make replacing bad memory easier but repair options less flexible—changing one chip is a lot cheaper than changing nine.

CHAPTER 3

FIGURE 3.6

SIMM (Single Inline Memory Module)

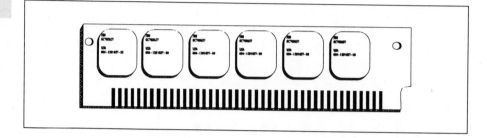

The familiar first 640K of a PC's memory is called *conventional memory*. It's supplemented by reserved areas containing *ROM*, Read Only Memory. The 286 and later machines can address memory beyond that called *extended memory*. Also, a small but important number of applications can use special memory called *expanded memory* or, as it's also known, *LIM memory*. Let's look at each of these in turn.

Conventional Memory

PCs can use 640K of main memory when running DOS and DOS programs. This first 640K is called *conventional memory* and is located on the motherboard and/or expansion boards. *K* refers to 1024, so for example, 64K equals 64×1024=65,536 *bytes* of data. Each byte can hold the equivalent of about one character. A picture called a *memory map* is a common way of depicting memory usage, so let's use it to show what uses the conventional 640K. I'll build one as we go through the various kinds of memory.

Figure 3.7 shows a map of how my system uses memory when I'm working with Lotus 1-2-3 Release 2.1. The map shows decimal memory addresses and hex addresses. Read it from the bottom up. Lower on the page is a lower address.

The bottom 1K is an area reserved by a piece of software called the BIOS that I'll explain soon. DOS (this is PC DOS 3.3) then takes up the next 53K.

An additional 15K are taken up with *TSR*s (Terminate and Stay Resident programs). You probably use these every day in your work. The program to use your IRMA board, if you've got one—you know, the one that connects you to the mainframe when you hit both Shift keys—is one example.

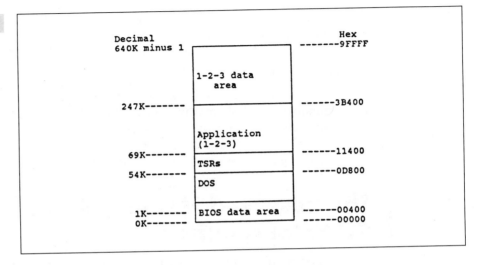

FIGURE 3.7

Example memory map for conventional 640K

Borland's SideKick is another. I use utilities named RELOCATE and DOS 5.0's MODE to speed up my screen and keyboard response time, and DOS 5.0's DOSKEY remembers the last 20 commands I've typed so if I make a mistake I can recall a previous command, edit it, and resubmit it to the PC. These programs are examples of TSRs: They load and essentially "attach" themselves to DOS, extending the system's abilities and, unfortunately, its size.

The next 178K is taken by the 123.EXE program itself. The remainder is then available for 1-2-3 worksheets. The top address is *640K minus 1* rather than *640K* because we started counting at *zero*, not one.

Memory can be physically located either on the motherboard, an expansion board, or, more likely, on both. The original PCs had an old system board called the PC-1. The PC-1 motherboard could only accommodate four banks of 16K memory chips, so only 64K memory could be put on it. In 1983, IBM changed the PC motherboard so, among other things, four rows of 64K memory could be put on it, for a total of 256K. The third recent motherboard was introduced in 1986, allowing two banks of 256K chips (512K total) and two banks of 64K chips (128K total) for a grand motherboard total of 640K. Virtually all clones available since 1985 have allowed 640K on the motherboard. The most recent IBM XT-type motherboard is on the IBM Model 30, a faster new XT-type machine.

Many 286- and 386-based clones allow up to 4 MB right on the motherboard. Again, only the first 640K is conventional memory, the kind easily usable by DOS. The remainder is configured as either extended or expanded memory, covered in the following pages.

Nowadays, most new PCs can accommodate between 16 and 64 MB of memory on their motherboard. Other PCs use a special slot on their motherboard that works with a special memory board. Together, they can boost maximum memory capacity on a PC. The IBM term for main memory on the system board, by the way, is *planar memory.*

The Reserved Memory Area: ROMs and Buffers

The careful reader will have noticed that the original PC's CPU, the 8088, can address one megabyte (1024K), yet PCs only use 640K. Why?

In addition to the BIOS data area and the space taken up by DOS, the PC needs to steal from the CPU's memory address space for the following:

- Video memory
- Small amounts of memory called *buffers* or *frames* used by some expansion boards
- Special memory containing system software called *ROMs* (Read Only Memory)

Back in 1981, IBM reserved the area from 640K to 1024K in the PC's memory address space for these purposes. Here are some details on the three uses for the addresses.

Video Memory

Video memory is memory used by video boards to keep track of what's to be displayed on the screen. When a program puts a character or draws a circle on the screen, it's actually making changes to this video memory. IBM set aside 128K for video memory, but most video boards don't actually need or use that much memory space. Table 3.4 shows the common video boards and their memory capacities.

TABLE 3.4: Typical Video Memory Requirements

BOARD	MEMORY ADDRESS SPACE USED	TOTAL MEMORY ON BOARD (K)	ROM ON BOARD
Monochrome Display Adapter (MDA)	B0000–B1000 (4K)	4	None in memory address space
Color Graphics Adapter (CGA)	B8000–BC000 (16K)	16	None in memory address space
Enhanced Graphics Adapter (EGA)	A0000–BFFFF (128K) (B0000–B1000 can be disabled)	256	C0000–C3FFF (16K)
Video Graphics Array (VGA)	A0000–BFFFF (128K) (B0000–B1000 can be disabled)	256	C0000–C5FFF (24K)
Super VGA	A0000–BFFFF (128K)	512–1024K	C0000–C7FFF (32K)

As you'll see in the table, *Memory Address Space Used* differs from *Total Memory on Board* for the EGA and VGA because these video modes use a technique called *paging* that allows them to put lots of memory on the video board. Lots of memory means better video without taking up a lot of the CPU's total 1024K memory address space. (I'll explain *ROM on Board* in the next section.)

Note that the EGA and VGA can be convinced to disable memory usage from B0000 to B1000, the addresses the MDA uses. That's so your system can run two monitors. Why run two video boards and monitors? Some debugging systems let you test-run your program with output going to the

CGA, EGA, or VGA monitor while displaying debugging information on the MDA.

ROM (Read Only Memory)

Another kind of memory exists that cannot be altered but only read, so it's called Read Only Memory or ROM. This is memory someone (usually the computer manufacturer) loads just once with a special device such as a PROM blaster, an EPROM programmer, or the like. You can read information from ROMs, but you can't write new information. (Well, you *can* write the information, but the ROM will ignore you. Think of ROM as a chip that can give advice but not take it.)

Why have a memory chip you can only store information in once? Well, unlike normal RAM, ROM has the virtue of not losing its memory when you turn the machine off—techy types would say it's *nonvolatile*. You use ROM to store software that won't change. In essence, you can say that ROM contains the software that tells the system how to use a circuit board.

ROMs are found on expansion boards like EMS, LAN, or EGA cards. It's also found on the system board. The ROM on the system board contains a piece of software called *BIOS*, the Basic Input/Output System. DOS doesn't communicate directly with your hardware but issues commands through BIOS. That's why the BIOS is so important: It determines in large measure how compatible your PC-compatible is.

As you'd expect, IBM's BIOS is the standard of compatibility. Back in the early 1980s, the first cloners developed BIOSes that conformed in varying degrees to the IBM standard, so the question "Does it run Lotus 1-2-3 and Microsoft Flight Simulator?" was the acid test of compatibility. Nowadays, two companies, Phoenix Software and Award Software, derive large incomes from their main business of writing compatible BIOSes for clone makers. This has simplified the business of cloning considerably.

I've said that ROM contains software. As you know, software changes from time to time. Occasionally a problem can be fixed by "upgrading the ROM"—getting the latest version of the ROM-based software from the manufacturer. For example, you may end up upgrading the ROMs on your motherboard to make your system BIOS more current—perhaps to support a new type of floppy drive. I've had to change hard disk–controller ROMs to make them work with some newer versions of DOS.

For this reason, you've got to know exactly what ROMs are in your computer or the computers you're responsible for maintaining. In a maintenance notebook, keep track of the serial numbers or dates on the labels pasted on the backs of the ROMs in your PCs. Whenever you install a board, note any ROM identifying marks. It will save you from having to pop the top to find out about ROM when you call for service.

ROMs can usually be identified because they're generally larger chips—24- or 28-pin DIP chips. They're socketed (so they can be easily changed), and often have a paper label pasted on them with a version number or some identifier printed on it. (IBM BIOS ROMs don't carry paper labels on most PCs, XTs, and ATs, but do on later machines.) ROMs are memories, albeit inflexible ones, and so require a place in the memory addresses in the reserved area from 640K to 1024K.

Buffers and Frames

Some boards need a little memory space reserved for them. A Local Area Network (LAN) board, for example, might require 8–16K of storage space used to buffer LAN transmissions. A LIM board (described a little later) needs 16–64K of "page frame" memory space to buffer transfers into and out of LIM memory. Those memory pieces must fit somewhere in the reserved area from 640K to 1024K in the PC memory address space.

Before we leave this section, let's add reserved areas to our memory map (see Figure 3.8).

Extended Memory

Not content with the 8088/8086, Intel began in 1978 to develop processor chips with power rivaling that of minicomputers and mainframes. One thing early micros lacked that more powerful computers had was larger memory address spaces. So from the 80286's introduction in 1981 onward, Intel chips could talk to or *address* megabytes and megabytes. An 80286 can actually address 16 megabytes. An 80386 or 80486 can address four gigabytes of RAM. The term for normal RAM above the 1-MB level is *extended memory*.

FIGURE 3.8

Memory map of the first 1024K

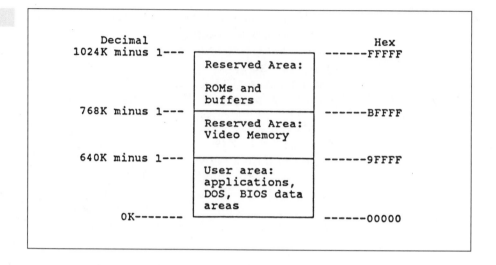

But there's a catch. In order to use this extra memory, the 286 and later chips must shift to a new processor mode called *protected mode*. Protected mode has lots of virtues, but one big flaw: When a chip is in protected mode, it's incompatible with an older 8088 or 8086. Here's why.

Most early CPUs used in microcomputers were more glorified calculator chips than computers—the 4004, 8008, 8080, 8085, 8086, 8088, 80188, and 80186. Intel intended for the 80286 to have some powers that were mainframelike; in particular, it would be able to talk to more memory and to protect that memory.

Mainframes run multiple programs at the same time, which is called *multitasking*. Basically, the memory space of the computer gets parceled out to the applications ("Okay, text editor, you get 120K, and database, you get 105K, and spreadsheet, you get 150K—no, you may *not* have more!"), and everyone's expected to stay in their places. But what about the odd program that accidentally strays from its area? If the text editor stretches a bit, it overwrites the database's area—what to do?

That's why mainframes have memory protection. The CPU has hardware built into it that keeps track of what application gets to use what memory. If an application tries to reach out of its space, the protection hardware senses this and stops the application, probably by ending the program and informing the user. The 286 and later chips have this memory protection.

These chips can also address memory beyond 1024K, but only while in protected mode. Again, the 8088, 8086, and earlier chips cannot under any circumstances address memory beyond 1024K, and so cannot ever have extended memory.

Basically, programs that run while in protected mode don't try to do *any-thing* with memory without first requesting memory blocks from the operating system; then they stay in their places.

And that's the problem.

This whole notion of first asking the operating system's permission before using memory is totally unknown in the DOS world. Programs pretty much assume they're the only program in the system, so they just take whatever they want without asking for it. So for the 286 to have memory protection, it would not only have to be a *different* chip, it would have to be an *incompatible* chip—incompatible with DOS and DOS programs, in particular.

Now, designing and releasing a new chip that was totally incompatible with any previous Intel offerings would be suicidal. So Intel gave the 286 and subsequent chips split personalities: When they boot up, they act just like an 8088, except faster. They can talk to 1024K, and no more. (This is the 8088 emulation mode or, as the documentation calls it, the *real mode*. Why is it called real mode? I don't know—maybe it was real hard to program.) With a few instructions, it can shift over to protected mode and talk to lots of memory beyond 1024K. But, again, once the 286 or later chip is in protected mode, it can't run programs designed for real mode— DOS and DOS programs, that is; it can only run programs designed for protected mode.

You might be wondering, why don't they just write an operating system that uses this protected mode? They have—that's the whole idea of OS/2. So memory beyond 1024K on a 286 or later machine is mainly unusable to DOS. I say "mainly" because there are a few programs that, thanks to some snazzy programming, can make use of the memory beyond 1024K. Probably the best-known of this class of programs is Lotus 1-2-3 Release 3.0; earlier versions can't use extended memory. This need for extended memory explains why 8088-based machines cannot run 1-2-3 version 3.0.

Additionally, Windows 3.0, when in Standard or 386 Enhanced modes, is a protected-mode operating system. Ever see the message "Unrecoverable application error" or "This application has violated system integrity"? That means that a Windows program has attempted to overstep its memory bounds, but the built-in memory protection has thwarted it.

As XT-type machines are based on 8088/8086 chips, they cannot have extended memory. ATs and 386-based machines can. When you see your computer count up to 1024K, 2048K, 4096K, or the like during the power-on self-test, you've got some extended memory.

Most common is a 286 with 1024K of memory. This is divided into two sections: The first 640K is addressed from 0 to 640K and is thus conventional memory. The remaining 384K gets moved above the 1024K mark, getting addresses from 1024K to 1408K. As it's addressed above 1024K, this 384K is extended memory. (Why break it up? Why not just address the memory as 0 to 1024K? Recall that the reserved area from 640K to 1024K must not have user memory in it.) Here's how it would look on our memory map (see Figure 3.9).

FIGURE 3.9

Memory map of the first 1024K and 384K of extended memory

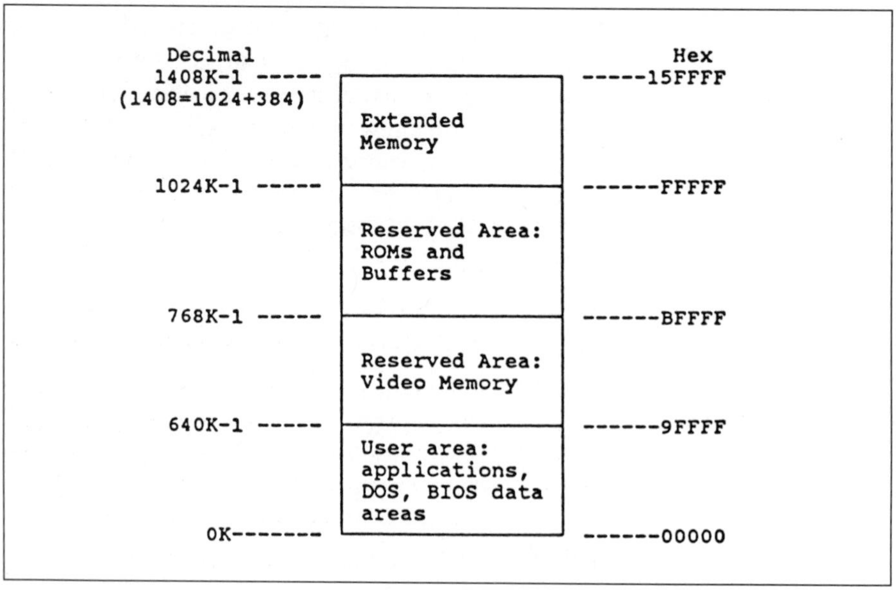

```
        Decimal                                      Hex
     1408K-1 -----         ┌──────────────┐     -----15FFFF
     (1408=1024+384)       │ Extended     │
                           │ Memory       │
                           │              │
     1024K-1 -----         ├──────────────┤     ------FFFFF
                           │ Reserved Area:│
                           │ ROMs and     │
                           │ Buffers      │
     768K-1 -----          ├──────────────┤     ------BFFFF
                           │ Reserved Area:│
                           │ Video Memory │
     640K-1 -----          ├──────────────┤     ------9FFFF
                           │ User area:   │
                           │ applications,│
                           │ DOS, BIOS data│
                           │ areas        │
     0K-------             └──────────────┘     ------00000
```

EMS, LIM, Paged, Expanded Memory

Most PC users eventually come to feel that 640K of memory, the most DOS will allow, is insufficient for most needs. But, as we've seen, extended memory is mainly useless under DOS. So what can be done?

Spreadsheets are a very popular application for the PC, but most spreadsheets on the market have the flaw that all of their data must be in main memory. Thus, a data file of a megabyte or two is impossible for a spreadsheet under DOS.

Lotus, Intel, and Microsoft (LIM) got together and developed a standard for a product that bypasses the DOS limitations through *memory paging*. Up to 32 megabytes of paged (it's also called expanded) memory can be installed in a PC. It's sometimes known as the *Expanded Memory Standard (EMS)*.

Basically, the LIM memory isn't viewed by the system as memory. All the PC knows is that there are 16K-sized pages of storage available. LIM can support up to 2,000 of these pages, hence the 32 MB maximum size. LIM boards allocate 64K of memory, enough space for four pages, somewhere in the reserved area between 640K and 1024K, so a program can manipulate up to four pages at a time.

LIM is manipulated, then, by pulling in a page from LIM memory to the memory in the reserved area, reading and/or modifying the page frame, and possibly writing the page frame back to the LIM memory. This memory is called a *page frame,* and moving data to and from LIM and page frames is called *paging*.

We can now finish our memory map by adding expanded memory off to the side of the normal memory column, as in Figure 3.10.

Perhaps you're wondering if all this paging takes time. It does, so LIM memory is slower than conventional memory. LIM gets around DOS's 640K limitation, but at a cost of speed. Even if you're willing to accept the speed cost, LIM isn't a panacea: Remember that only software written specially for the paged memory can use this memory. There are only a few applications that do this; Lotus is the best known. Two common examples of this kind of memory board are the Intel AboveBoard and the AST RamPage cards.

FIGURE 3.10

Memory areas

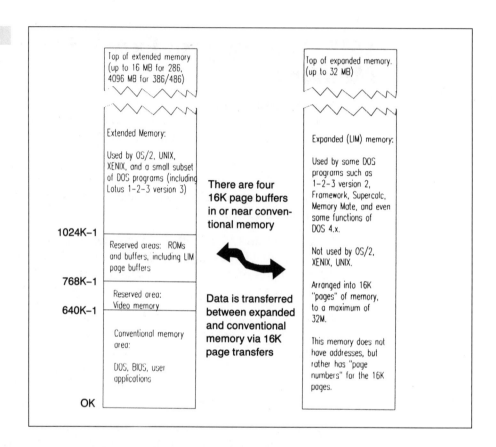

Making Extended Memory Look Like Expanded

I know this has been confusing, but it's about to get worse, so buckle up. So far I've made the extended versus expanded barrier sound like an unbridgeable one, but it's not.

- Many 286 memory boards are reversible for extended or expanded memory. These are good buys, as you might need expanded today and want to be able to use extended later. Some machines, like Zenith's LP286, allow you to configure memory beyond 640K as any combination of extended and expanded.

- The 386 computers have the ability to make extended memory act like expanded memory. This conversion requires a program to emulate LIM memory, so (of course) such a program is called a *limulator.* Good examples are 386 to the Max from Qualitas and QEMM386 from Quarterdeck. Many 386 vendors offer such a program free, as Compaq does with its CEMM program. Their addresses can be found in Appendix A. DOS 5.0 also includes the program EMM 386 to perform limulation.

- In general, limulators for 286s aren't a good idea, as full LIM 4.0 powers can't be emulated and the 286 isn't built to limulate. But All Computing in Toronto offers a solution: the ChargeCard 286. Priced at $400, the ChargeCard gives your 286 the power to limulate, as well as adding an extra 90-odd K to DOS memory.

That ends our tour around memory. Let's review:

- Conventional memory:

    Available to all PCs

    Limited to 640K

- Extended memory:

    Only possible with ATs or 386-based machines

    Impossible with XTs or PCs

    Useful with programs that can use it, such as Lotus 1-2-3 version 3.X.

    Used by OS/2, XENIX

    Used by Lotus 1-2-3 Release 3.0

- Expanded memory:

    Also called LIM (Lotus-Intel-Microsoft) memory

    Can be used with PCs, XTs, ATs—any PC machine

    Useful under DOS *with programs that can use it,* such as Lotus Releases 2.1 and 2.2

    Generally can't be used by OS/2

The only problem remaining is how to keep them distinct in your mind. I always remember extended versus expanded by pronouncing the latter *exPanded*, so I can remember that it's *Paged*.

Buses: PC, AT, ISA, Micro Channel, EISA, Local Bus, PCI, PCMCIA, and More

What is a bus? The CPU must talk to memory, expansion boards, co-processor, keyboard, and the like. It communicates with other devices on the motherboard via metal traces (the shiny lines on the circuit board) in the printed circuit. But how can expansion boards be connected to the CPU, the memory, and so on?

Some computers, like the earlier Macintosh line, didn't allow easy expansion. To expand a 128K or 512K Mac, the circuit boards had to be partially disassembled or modified in ways not intended by the original developers. Installing a hard disk actually involved disassembling the computer, soldering connections onto the Mac motherboard, and reassembling the machine. Making modifications difficult puts the user at the mercy of the modifier, as virtually all such modifications are done at the expense of the manufacturer's warranty and service agreement, if any. You don't have to do such brain surgery on a PC, thankfully. PCs have expansion slots that allow easy upgrades. (Today's Macs also have expansion slots, thankfully.)

Another disadvantage of the old Macintosh approach is that average people couldn't do the modifications themselves. This would be like your having to cut a hole in the wall of your house to find a main power line every time you wanted to use an appliance. Without standard interface connectors, you'd have to find the power line and then splice the appliance into it to get power for the appliance.

This scenario, as we know, is silly, since we have standard outlet plugs. Any manufacturer who wants to sell a device requiring electrical power needs only to ensure that the device takes standard US current and then to add a two-prong plug. "Upgrading" my house (adding the new appliance) is a simple matter: just plug and play. Many computers adopt a similar approach. Such computers have published a connector standard: Any vendor desiring to offer an expansion board for a particular computer need only follow the connector specifications, and the board will work in that computer. From the time of the earliest computers, such a connector has existed. First called the *omnibus connector*, as it gave access to virtually all important circuits in the computer, it quickly became shortened to *bus*, and so it has remained.

So a bus is a communication standard, an agreement about how to build boards that can work in a standard PC. For various reasons, however, there aren't one but *four* different such standards in the PC world, and a few oddballs in addition.

The First PC Bus

The first microcomputer, the Altair, had a bus that was a standard in the industry for years and is still used in some machines; it was called the S-100 or Altair bus. The Apple II used a different bus. The IBM PC introduced yet another bus with 62 lines (the now-familiar bus inside most PC compatibles).

The 62 lines mentioned above are offered to the outside world through a standard connector. These connectors are called expansion slots, as expansion boards must plug into these slots. There are five on the PC and eight on the XT and AT.

The most common are the simple 62-line slots found on the original IBM PC and XT. Because those machines were based on the 8088, and the 8088 has an 8-bit data path, eight of the 62 wires are data lines. That means this bus is eight bits wide, so data transfers can only occur in 8-bit chunks on this bus. Expansion slots on a computer with this bus are called *8-bit slots*.

The AT (ISA) Bus

When developing the AT, IBM saw it had to upgrade the bus (see Figure 3.11 for a comparison of XT and AT bus slots). One reason was because the 80286 is a 16-bit chip, as you recall. They certainly could have designed the AT with an 8-bit bus, but it would be a terrible shame to make a 286 chip transfer data eight bits at a time over the bus rather than utilize its full 16-bit data path. So it would be nice to have a 16-bit bus. On the other hand, there was backward compatibility with the PC and XT to think of. So IBM came up with a fairly good solution: They kept the old 62-line slot connectors and added another connector in line with the older 62-line connector to provide the extra eight bits and some other features as well. Slots with both connectors are called, as you'd expect, *16-bit slots*. Most AT and 386-type machines have at least two of the older 8-bit slots for purposes of backward compatibility.

As the 16-bit slots are just a superset of the 8-bit bus, 8-bit boards work just fine in 16-bit slots. If you have an AT-type machine, you might have noticed that it has not only 16-bit slots but also the older 8-bit connectors (see Figure 3.12). If the 16-bit slots can use 8-bit boards, why have any

FIGURE 3.11

XT versus AT bus slots

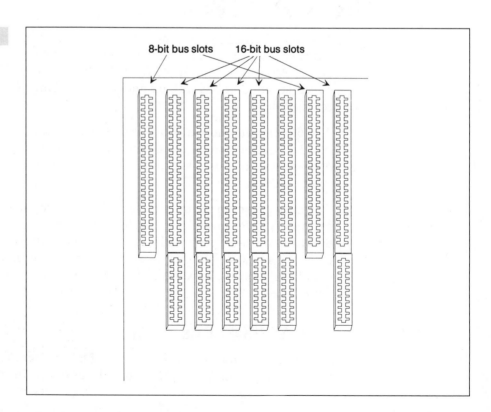

8-bit bus slots   16-bit bus slots

8-bit slots on an AT-type machine at all? The answer isn't an electrical reason but a physical one. Some older 8-bit boards have a "skirt" (see Figure 3.13) that extends down and back on the circuit board, making it physically impossible to plug it into a 16-bit connector (see Figure 3.14).

FIGURE 3.12

PC board with 8-bit connector

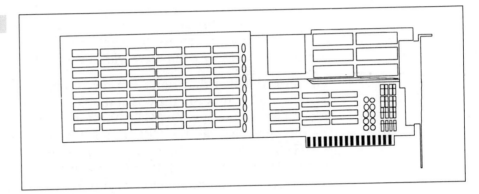

FIGURE 3.13

8-bit board with skirt

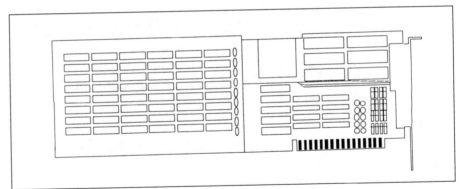

FIGURE 3.14

PC board with 16-bit connector

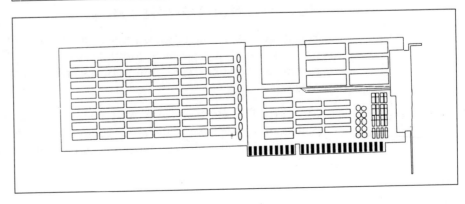

Lately the trade press has taken to calling the AT bus the *ISA* or Industry Standard Architecture bus.

Just How Fast Is That Bus?

The AT bus is tough to get to run at high speeds. It's noisy and tends to be pretty unworkable above 10 MHz. Many circuit boards won't even work properly when forced to operate above 8 MHz. So how do companies offer 33-MHz computers with the old AT bus?

The answer is that they don't run the bus at the full CPU rate. Up to 8 MHz, most clones run the bus at the same rate as the CPU—a 6-MHz computer runs the bus at 6 MHz. Above 12 MHz, Compaq started offering machines that ran the CPU at one rate—12 MHz—and the bus at 8 MHz. Everybody copied the idea, so there are a lot of machines running at 12 MHz and above with buses creeping along at a mere 8 MHz. This is good because you can put a regular old LAN board into your 33-MHz Zenith and use it as a server without having to spend $20,000 for a mythical 33-MHz LAN board. This does, however, have its drawbacks.

The big drawback is that some boards, such as memory boards, should run at CPU speed. If you have a 16-MHz 386 clone (with an 8-MHz bus), buy an extended memory board, and pop it into one of the computer's 16-bit slots. You'll have extended your memory, but all memory accesses on that board *will be at 8 MHz, not 16 MHz.*

That all changes with the *local bus*—but you'll read about that in a few pages.

Beware the 10-MHz Bus!

You might have noticed that I talked about machines with CPU speeds up to 8 MHz having buses running at the same rate as the CPU, and machines over 12-MHz running buses at 8 MHz, skipping over the 10-MHz machines.

Most 10-MHz machines with AT-type buses seem to be designed with the philosophy, "Well, we really *ought* to go to the extra trouble and expense to run the bus at a different speed (8 MHz), but 10 is close enough, isn't it?" So most 10-MHz machines run the bus at 10 MHz. That means 10-MHz computers actually have the fastest buses in the PC/ISA world!

Most boards run fine at 10 MHz, but some will give you some trouble, in particular IBM's 8-bit Token Ring board and many video boards. Recall that video boards need memory. As very few video board makers get praised for the speed of the memory chips they choose for their video boards, most video board memory is selected assuming that the board will be plugged into a slot running no faster than 8 MHz.

The result is that most of the time the board runs fine. But sometimes you get a video failure on bootup. The answer is to buy a video board with fast memory on-board. Headlands Technology (Video 7) and Paradise make video boards that seem to handle 10-MHz buses just fine.

The bottom line: Be careful with what you put into 10-MHz slots. If a board seems to fail, lower the speed (there's usually a turbo switch) and then reboot. If the problem goes away, it may have been caused by the 10-MHz bus slots. The answer probably is to replace the board with a faster one.

Buddy, Can You Spare 32 Bits?

When Compaq introduced the first 80386-based desktop, it wanted to exploit the 32-bit power of the 386 chip. They included a new 32-bit slot, mainly for use with memory. Some 386 clones have adopted this, but it's not a very significant part of the market. It seems that each vendor has developed its own 32-bit "standard." Intel has one it's been pushing, AT&T has another, Micronics a fourth, and so on. This is not really a standard; but expect to see a strange 32-bit slot of some kind on a 386 motherboard for a memory board.

Not too many vendors are pushing their proprietary slots very hard any more, as they're all looking ahead to the new EISA standard (see a couple of sections ahead).

Why Improve the Bus?

Since 1987, IBM and other vendors have offered two alternatives to ISA—the Micro Channel (MCA) and EISA buses, as you'll see in a bit. Before we look at these buses, however, it's reasonable to ask, Why improve the bus at all?

While there are many minor improvements offered by these new buses, four stand out:

- They offer 32-bit widths.
- They support *bus mastering*.
- They are "quieter" in that signals are less susceptible to noise.
- They offer the convenience of setting up add-in boards through software.

The ISA bus, as you recall, only comes in 8-bit and 16-bit formats. But 386DX and 486 (both SX and DX) chips have a 32-bit data path, so PCs built around those chips are hobbled by the ISA bus: They can never realize their full speed potential. Both MCA and EISA offer 32-bit versions.

The bus, as you've seen, is the "data highway" around the PC: the path for information transfer inside the system. But this highway is controlled entirely by the CPU. That's fine for the PCs built currently, as nobody minds the CPU being in charge—there are no other CPUs in the system.

But as PCs get faster and more complicated (and as CPUs get cheaper), we'll see CPUs dedicated to particular tasks: a CPU on the hard disk system, another on the video board, and so on. The overall system may become more efficient if these peripheral CPUs can communicate directly with each other, without having to use the main CPU as an intermediary. That's hard (although not impossible) to accomplish with an ISA machine. But MCA and EISA support the idea of bus mastering.

In a few words, bus mastering means that the peripheral CPUs could request permission to take over the bus for a short period of time. The main CPU would then grant permission for them to take over the bus, and it would drop temporarily "out of the loop," enabling swift communications between, say, the hard drive and the floppy drive.

It should be noted that while bus mastering is possible with MCA and EISA, the vast majority of EISA- and MCA-compatible boards do not exploit this feature currently. Furthermore, using bus mastering devices often puts you in a position of incompatibility when running Windows or OS/2.

As buses tranfer more and more data in a given time, they are more prone to noise. The ISA bus is fairly noise-prone because it relies on edge-triggered interrupts. "Edge-triggered" means that whenever the voltage level on a data line on the bus exceeds some threshold value, the devices on the bus interpret that as data. The alternative is "level-triggered," which requires that the transmitting achieve and hold the higher voltage level in order for data to be recognized by the devices on the bus. Edge triggering can lead to "transients"—brief power surges that can confuse the devices on the bus into thinking that data is on the bus when it's not. Level triggering lowers the noise level, and MCA and EISA employ it.

As you'll see in Chapter 6, installing new circuit boards can be a real headache: You set some jumpers and flip some switches on the board, install it, and see if it works. If it doesn't, you've got to extract the board, try other switch and jumper settings, and reinsert and retest it. That gets to be a pain.

So MCA and EISA support the idea of software configuration: There are no switches or jumpers on add-in MCA or EISA circuit boards. Just pop one of these boards into a system and run a piece of software. The software allows you to experiment with different board settings without having to remove the board between each experiment. Sometimes, the software can even do all the hard work automatically.

Here are some more details on the two new buses.

The PS/2 Bus: Micro Channel Architecture (MCA)

IBM changed the rules again on April 2, 1987, when they announced the PS/2 line. In order to facilitate faster data transfer within the computer and to lower noise levels, the PS/2 Models 50 to 80 (*not* the 25 or 30) have a new bus called the *Micro Channel Architecture (MCA)* bus. It's completely incompatible with the old bus. Expansion boards made for the PC, XT, or AT won't operate in the PS/2 line. Be sure when you buy expansion boards that you know what kind of machine they're destined for, and buy ISA or MCA as appropriate. Figure 3.15 shows both an ISA and an MCA board.

MCA is neat because it's cleaner, as I said before, so it should be able to transfer data at higher speeds than the current ISA machines. It also includes something called *Programmable Option Select*, or *POS*, that allows circuit boards to be a lot smarter about how they interact with the computer. For one thing, DIP switch and configuration problems lessen considerably. We'll talk more about POS in the section on configuration of new boards.

FIGURE 3.15

ISA board and MCA board

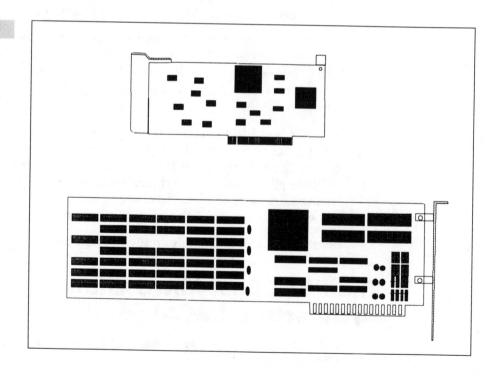

EISA (Extended Industry Standard Architecture)

MCA is a pain because IBM has got it locked up six ways to Sunday, patentwise.

Companies can't clone the MCA without paying a Draconian *five percent of their gross* to IBM as fealty (oops, that's supposed to be "royalties") for use of MCA. Five percent of gross is probably more than most companies are making as *profits*. For the five percent, you don't even get the plans for MCA. First, clone makers are supposed to spend hundreds of thousands of dollars figuring out how to clone MCA—IBM offers no help—and then they get to pay Big Blue the five percent.

So Compaq talked eight other compatible makers (the usual guys— Tandy, AST, Zenith, AT&T, and some others) into forming a joint venture to respond to MCA—they're called the Gang of Nine. Now released, EISA has MCA's good features without sacrificing compatibility with the old AT (ISA) bus, and presumably it has turned out to cost less than five percent of profits.

At this writing (end of 1992), EISA is moderately successful. The premium you'll pay for EISA is about $300 on a clone-type 486 machine—not exactly an "EISA" amount to part with, but not exorbitant either. Much of EISA's potential market, however, is being taken by local bus (the next bus I'll discuss). EISA seems to fit well in the LAN server market.

EISA has a full 32-bit data path, POS-like features, and speeds to about 20 MHz. That means memory probably will still require its own proprietary slot for faster machines; MCA has the same problem.

In the XT and AT days, you just expanded memory by buying a memory expansion card, put memory chips on it, and put the card into one of the PC's expansion slots. But by the time that PCs got to 12 MHz, that easy answer disappeared. No matter how fast your PC is—20, 25, 33 MHz— *the expansion slots still only run at 8 MHz.*

Why do the slots run so slowly? Because most expansion boards can't operate above 8 or 10 MHz. So whenever the system is accessing an expansion board, it slows down to 8 MHz. If that *sounds* unbelievable, consider that supporting boards at only 8 MHz isn't that bad in general: most boards in expansion slots communicate with things that are fairly slow anyway, like floppy drives, printer ports, modems, and the like.

What *really* hurts, then, is having to put a *memory* card in an expansion slot. Memory runs best when it runs at the full speed of the CPU, so it's a crime to make a 25- or 33-MHz machine slow down to 8 MHz when accessing memory. (By the way, a few motherboards give you the option to experiment with a faster bus: for example, I've got a 20-MHz 386 system that lets me set my bus speed to 6, 8, or 10 MHz. If all of your expansion boards are a bit faster than the average bear, you can get away with running the bus at the practically-illegal rate of 10 MHz, and speed up video and disk access in the process.)

VESA Local Bus

Manufacturers have found two ways to avoid slowing down the machine. First, some manufacturers design a special high-speed slot for the motherboard that will only accommodate a particular card—typically, a memory board. This bus slot is called a "local" bus slot. Now, the only people who make boards compatible with that slot will be the people who made the motherboard in the first place, so if you buy a motherboard of this type, make sure you get the memory board at the same time that you buy the motherboard, or you won't be able to put any memory on the system.

That's worth repeating: although people talk as if local bus were a new standard, it's not—at least, not *usually*. An industry group is promulgating and promoting a local bus standard called VESA after the group's name—Video Electronic Standards Association.

Local bus slots currently support three kinds of boards: memory boards, video boards, and disk controllers.

Most local bus machines today do not use a standard local bus, but rather a home-grown proprietary bus slot. That means, again, that if you buy a computer with a bus slot for local bus video from *one* company, you can't then just go out somewhere else and get a local bus video board from some other computer place—you've got to get a local bus video board (or memory board or disk controller board) from the same company that you got the computer that includes the local bus. Unless, of course, you've got a *VESA* local bus computer.

The VESA folks developed a local bus standard because nowadays not all local bus slots are intended for video, as they once were; instead, PC designers are using the local bus slots for high-speed video. Local bus video computers are available these days for only a little more that equivalent computers *without* local bus video.

I said a few paragraphs back that there're *two* answers to the "how do I put fast devices on a slow bus" problem. The first answer was local bus; the second is to put sockets for memory right on the motherboard, obviating the need to deal with the expansion slots. (Some PCs also include VGA integrated on the motherboard; that may be fast local bus video, but it may *not* be—many integrated VGAs are fairly slow.) If you buy one of *these* motherboards, ensure that there's enough room for 16+ MB of RAM; be warned, however, that many of the boards on the market still only have room for 8 MB, so pick carefully.

Some motherboards combine the above two methods: they have room for about 8 MB on the motherboard itself, and also have a high-speed memory slot for a board that will hold another 8 MB. If you get a motherboard like this—one that uses a combination of space on the motherboard and space on a special local bus memory board—you won't need the memory board until you're ready to exceed 8 MB total system memory, *but buy the board immediately anyway*. Why? Because the board may not be available when you need it, in a year or two. These boards generally run $100–$200.

Final thought on local bus video: if you buy local bus video, make sure the video is based on a big-name video chip set, or you'll find yourself without drivers for the video when future versions of the popular Graphical User Interfaces (GUIs), such as OS/2 and Windows, appear. I've seen many based on the Tseng Labs ET4000 chipset, for example; the S3 video chip is another good alternate possibility. Stay with either ET4000, S3, or the Trident TVGA chipsets. See the video chapter for more information on setting up a video system that won't slow down modern software.

PCI: Intel's High-Performance Local Bus

VESA Local Bus (VLB) is an important step in the evolution of computers, but it's not enough. VLB is really just a 32-bit, high-speed extension of the older, dumb ISA architecture. VLB actually hurts the PC world in a way. When I say that, I mean that VLB offers improved speed, but no better ways of *using* that speed: It just perpetuates the old PC approach of doing everything in a fast, brute-force manner. "Brute-force" here refers to the fact that the VLB does not offer most of the attractive features of the Micro Channel and EISA buses; it does not offer software setup of boards or bus mastering. VLB systems are still saddled with jumper-setting installations, and the CPU must babysit every single data transfer over the VLB bus. Forcing the CPU to manage each transfer keeps the CPU squarely in the middle of the system, making it a bottleneck to system performance. Making computers faster, then, requires the near-impossible technology enhancement of creating cheap, reliable processors that run in the hundreds of megahertz. A bus that supported bus mastering, in contrast, could support a system composed of dozens of medium-speed processors—one on the disk controller, one on the video board, one on the serial port, and so on. The benefit? A community of 33-MHz CPUs would be one heck of a lot faster than a fiercely centralized system dependent on a fragile, super-fast 60–100 MHz CPU driving a bunch of dumb, slow peripherals—the kind of systems that are manufactured today.

Intel was aware of this, and was worried. In many ways, having to support the old 1981 8088 ways of the PC was (and is) baggage that's hurting the PC world. Whatever hurts the PC world hurts Intel sales, so Intel designed an even newer, faster bus slot called PCI, Peripheral Component Interconnect. (Obviously, Intel believes in clinging to at least *one* PC tradition—dumb acronyms.)

Wider Data Path   PCI distinguishes itself first because it is a 64-bit bus. PCI supports a data path appropriate for the newer Pentium-based computers, which require 64 bits at each clock cycle. PCI also supports a 32-bit data path, however, making it appropriate for use in high-performance 486 systems.

Higher Speed VLB can only run at up to 33 MHz. PCI can run at up to 66 MHz in the current specification, and Intel believes that it will become faster in the next version. The net throughput of a PCI bus can be as large as 132 MBps.

Backward Compatibility While ISA or EISA boards cannot fit in PCI slots, the chipset that supports PCI also supports ISA and EISA. That means that it's easy to build a PC with PCI, ISA, and EISA slots all on the same motherboard.

Bus Mastering Like EISA and Micro Channel—and *unlike* VLB—PCI supports bus master adapter boards, paving the way for the "community of processors" that I referred to earlier.

Software Setup PCI supports the "plug and play" standard developed in 1992 by hardware vendors. There will be, in general, no jumpers or DIP switches on PCI boards. To set up a PCI board, you just run the PCI Configuration Program. Reconfiguring a system can be done without popping the top on the computer, a great convenience to users and support people. And finding out "what interrupt is that sound card on, anyway?" is as simple as running the configuration program and simply asking it to list out information about all of the boards in the system and what resources that they use. (By the way, if you don't know what an "interrupt" is, don't worry; it's explained in Chapter 6.)

PCMCIA: The Portable Bus

The early 90s have seen big changes in the bus world. EISA has become affordable; VLB has become very common; and PCI is on the way. But they could *all* be superceded by a bus that's been around for years, getting very little attention, but that's finally come into its own.

Laptop computers are an absolute must for traveling professionals; I have personally owned *twelve* of them in the past 10 years. Laptops are great because they're almost 100-percent software compatible with their bigger cousins, the desktop machines. But there's one thing that laptops have always been difficult about supporting: add-in circuit boards.

Over the years, it's been customary to add two kinds of hardware to laptops: an internal modem, and more memory. But, as laptops never had standard expansion slots, laptop owners would have to go to the laptop vendors and buy their proprietary memory—often an expensive proposition. But cost wasn't the worst part of this lack of a standard bus; in fact, cost was less important than the fact that lack of a standard bus led to the lack of a *market* for add-in boards for laptops.

Japanese vendors of memory products tried to address this problem in the late 80's by founding the Personal Computer Memory Card Industry Association, or, in its hard-to-remember acronym, PCMCIA. (The head of the group recently said, "If we had known how important the acronym would be, we would have picked another name.") PCMCIA agreed on a kind of slot for a memory card that was about the dimensions of a credit card, but a mite thicker.

Type 1, Type 2, and Type 3 PCMCIA Slots   The PCMCIA standard proved extremely popular, so popular in fact that hardware vendors said to PCMCIA, "Why not also support modems or hard disks?" So the memory card interface became a "PCMCIA Type 1 slot." A Type 1 (or "release 1," in some references) slot is 3.3 millimeters thick, with a 68-pin connector. Again, most Type 1 cards are memory cards, either normal RAM or "flash" memory cards loaded with a piece of software (for example, Lotus 1-2-3 and Word Perfect are available on these cards.)

The need for internal modems drove the Type 2 slots. While developing Type 2, an important software standard called Card Services and Socket Services was developed—more on that later. Type 2 cards can be designed to act as an object placed directly into the PC's memory address space. Why is this different from Type 1 cards? If you bought a software-on-a-card Type 1 card, like the WordPerfect example that I just gave, then the PC would have to copy the data from the Type 1 card into the PC's memory before it could run the software on the card. That took time *and* used up some of the PC's memory. With Type 2, that's not necessary, making startup faster and increasing the amount of free memory available. Type 2 cards are 5 millimeters thick, allowing more space for more complex circuitry. Type 1 cards will work in Type 2 slots.

Most recently, PCMCIA has defined a Type 3 specification, one flexible enough to support removable hard disks. The main difference of Type 3 is that it's a lot thicker—Type 3 cards can be 10.5 millimeters thick. When purchasing Type 3 cards, be sure that what you're buying meets the standard—there are so-called "Type 3" hard disks that are 13 millimeters thick.

Socket and Card Services PCMCIA supports the ability to remove and install a PCMCIA card *on the fly*. All other buses require that you power down the computer before installing or removing a card, but PCMCIA supports "hot swap." The computer supports this capability with two levels of software support.

> **Socket services** is the PCMCIA name for the BIOS-like software that handles the low-level hardware calls to the card. They are loaded like a device driver. While cards can be swapped without powering down, changes in cards *do* require a reboot. (It is rumored that PCMCIA version 3.0—2.01 is the most recent version—will allow changes without reboots.)

> **Card services** is a higher-layer set of routines that manage how the PCMCIA memory areas map into the CPU's memory area. They also provide a high-level interface supporting simple commands that are common to almost all PCMCIA cards, commands like erase, copy, read, and write data.

PCMCIA Features Let's compare PCMCIA to the other buses that we've discussed, feature for feature.

> **Memory address space:** PCMCIA supports a 64-MB addressing ability. (This is because the bus uses 26 bits for addressing, and two to the 26th power is around 64 million.) This will be adequate for current machines, but will look sparse in a few years, as more demanding operating systems like OS/2 and NT become more popular.

> **Bus mastering:** PCMCIA does not support bus mastering or DMA.

> **Plug and play setup:** PCMCIA allows—*requires*—that hardware setups be done with software. Because of the physical size of a PCMCIA card, you'll never see jumpers or DIP switches.

> **Number of PCMCIA slots possible in a single system:** Most of the other buses support no more than 16 slots. PCMCIA can theoretically support *4,080* PCMCIA slots on a PC.

Data path: The data path for PCMCIA is only 16 bits, a real shame but one that will probably be fixed in the next version of the standard.

Speed: Like other modern bus standards, PCMCIA is limited to a 33 MHz clock rate.

The smaller size of PCMCIA cards, coupled with their low power usage, makes the new bus quite attractive not only for laptops, but also for the so-called "green" PCs, desktop computers designed to use as little power as is possible. For that reason, PCMCIA could become an important *desktop* standard as well as a laptop standard. No matter what happens, one thing is sure: if you're buying a laptop computer these days that will be your one and only computer, make sure that it's got one or, preferably, two PCMCIA slots.

System Clock

The system clock mentioned before is the "metronome" for the computer system. It's implemented on the PC on a chip called the 8284A. The 8284A is located near the 8088 on the system board. The AT-class machines don't have an 8284; they'll either have an 82284 or a clock circuit embedded in their motherboard chip set.

The clock chip is easy to find, if your machine has such a chip (some manufacturers, like Compaq, blend the chip in with some others, so there's no discrete chip). Just find the crystal—it's a small, flat, rounded silver box—and the CPU. The clock is often between the two of them.

You'll need to find the clock chip to install a reset switch in a PC later in the book. Unfortunately, however, most modern computers do not have a separate clock chip, and so you can't install a reset switch.

Many modern motherboards include a set of pins that support a CPU-reset function, however.

Numeric or Math Coprocessor

Next to the 8088 on a PC or near the 80286 on an AT is an empty socket. From 1981 to 1983, IBM wouldn't say officially for what the socket on the PC was intended. But then they announced what everyone already knew: It was for the Intel 8087, a special purpose microprocessor. The 8087 is a microprocessor that's only good for one class of tasks: floating-point numeric operations. If you do a lot of floating-point calculations (calculations with numbers that have decimal points), *and if the software that you use is written to take advantage of an 8087,* such a chip is a good investment. The classic program people think of is Lotus, but most spreadsheets, CAD/CAM, or engineering applications can benefit. An 8087 costs under $100 at this writing, a 287 runs from about $100, and a 387 from about $300 to $900, depending on speed. The 486 actually includes floating-point instruction support right on the chip, so there's no such thing as a 487 save for the companion to the 486SX. The 487SX costs around $700.

Some programs insist on a coprocessor. The latest versions of AutoCAD, for example, refuse to run on a machine without a coprocessor. I can't stress enough how important a coprocessor is for some applications. I used to use a CAD program called Generic CADD—a nice cheap CAD package that would use a coprocessor, if present. I did a bunch of work on a turbo XT (9.54 MHz) with an 8087 coprocessor, then moved to a 386 *without* a coprocessor. The 386 was actually slower when it came to screen redraws. (Now my 386 has a coprocessor, and it runs blindingly fast.) Transcendental operations (sines, cosines, logarithms, and the like) can be 20 times faster on a coprocessor than on the CPU.

You need to know two things about coprocessors: which go with what processor, and what speed to buy.

Matching Processors and Coprocessors

Intel markets six coprocessor chips, presented in Table 3.5.

TABLE 3.5: Coprocessor Chip Information

CHIP	MAXIMUM SPEED (MHZ)	PACKAGE TYPE	TYPICAL CPU
8087	10	DIP	8088/8086
80287	12	DIP	80286
80387DX	33	PGA	80386DX
80387SX	25	PLCC	80386SX
80486DX	33	PGA	80486DX
80487SX	25	PGA	80486SX

In general, the 8088 and 8086 go with the 8087, the 80286 goes with the 80287, and the 80386 goes with the 80387. There are, however, occasional exceptions. Early in the 386 game, several companies released motherboards based on the 386 with a 287 coprocessor. The reason is simple: The 387 wasn't out yet. (In some senses, the decision to use the existing and known 287 was a good one. Intel tried to beat everyone to the punch with their first 386/387 motherboard. Unfortunately, the board was released before Intel finished the 387. Subsequent changes to the 387 made the Intel motherboard's 387 socket useless.) Generally, hybrid 386/287 motherboards run the 287 at 6 to 10 MHz. A 386 running by itself at 16 MHz can often outperform an 8-MHz 287! Therefore, when working on old 386DX machines, don't be surprised if you come across a motherboard with a *287* socket.

Matching Coprocessor Speed to CPU Speed

The coprocessor is an independent CPU, and as such can be run at any speed within the chip's limits. The decision of how fast a coprocessor *actually* runs is made by the board designer. How do you know how fast a coprocessor you need? There are two simple rules:

- For anything but an AT or AT clone, coprocessor speed should be equal to or greater than processor speed.

- For an AT or AT clone, coprocessor speed should be equal to or greater than *two-thirds* of processor speed.

AT designs with slower coprocessors are unfortunate, as a coprocessor running at two-thirds processor speed is often worse than no coprocessor at all. Why do designers do it? The answer is that IBM started it with the AT. Slower coprocessors are cheaper. Designers, wanting to be compatible, aped the IBM decision.

Note that not all 286 machines have this problem—IBM runs the Model 50/60 coprocessors at the full 10 MHz of the processor. As the circuitry in most 286 AT-type systems only drives the coprocessor at $2/3$ CPU speed, there's no point in buying a coprocessor that runs at full CPU speed—it would cost more money, and would still only be run at $2/3$ CPU speed.

The other exception is in the 487SX socket, which can accommodate a clock-doubling overdrive chip.

Power Supply

U.S. line current is 120 volts Alternating Current (AC). PCs, like most digital devices, are set up to use Direct Current (DC) at 5 and 12 volts. The conversion process is done by a *power supply.* The power supply is the silver or black box to the right rear side of the PC.

Power supplies are rated by the amount of power they can handle: 63.5-watt power supplies are used on original IBM PCs, 130-watt power supplies on IBM XTs and clones, and 200-watt power supplies on ATs and clones.

Your power supply determines in part how long your computer components last. A good power supply costs less than $200. Chapter 9 discusses selecting, replacing, and installing a power supply. The power supply can't always cope with environmental conditions, so the chapter also discusses add-on products: surge supressors, spike isolators, and uninterruptible power supplies.

The power supply is easy to find in the system: It's the silver or black box in the back of the chassis that has a label on it that in five languages says, "If you open me, I'll kill you." Figure 3.16 depicts a power supply.

Keyboard

The PC is useless without an input device, and the keyboard is the input device used by most of us. The keyboard is subject to a number of hazards, however, and needs maintenance—and sometimes replacement. The PC's keyboard actually contains a microprocessor of its own called the Intel 8041, 8042, or 8048. Taking apart a keyboard isn't hard; reassembling one is. Attacking both of those problems, and discussing alternative and replacement models, is the subject of Chapter 19, *Keyboards*.

FIGURE 3.16

Power supply

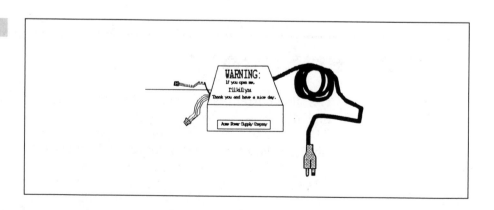

The Notion of a Controller

From here on in this chapter, you'll see add-in boards of various kinds. Most are *controllers* of some kind. All peripheral devices, whether internal or external, need something to communicate between them and the computer. Sometimes these are called *controllers, interfaces, ports,* or *adapters.*

For example, a hard disk needs a hard-disk controller. Basically, a controller is a translator between the CPU and a peripheral device such as a hard disk, floppy disk, keyboard, or video monitor. Controllers mainly perform the following functions:

- They isolate the hardware from the software.
- They match speeds between devices that operate at different speeds.
- They convert data from one format to another.

Isolating the Hardware from the Software

UltraStar's 22CA bus master hard-disk controller is as different from IBM's original XT-type controller as a Corvette is from a Chevette, yet 99 percent of the software written to work with the latter works just fine (or better) with the former.

The underlying hardware is much better and a lot different, so you'd imagine there would be big compatibility problems; but the hardware has been housebroken to respond to CPU requests in the same manner (although faster) as the old Xebec-designed IBM controller. The same is true of video controllers designed by ATI or Paradise: they respond to the same software as IBM's original CGA, EGA, or VGA, but are cheaper and generally work faster. Using controllers with well defined interfaces makes building compatible hardware possible.

You can understand the value of well defined interfaces and modularity by looking at an automobile. Perhaps (if you're my age) you learned to drive in an old '60s car or, if you're my Dad's age, in a car from the '40s.

Both of us now drive cars designed and built in the '80s. The old 1967 Country Squire station wagon was a car radically different from the Honda I now drive. The Hudson my dad drove in the '40s is an even more radical difference from his current Toyota truck. But despite our education on different cars, we're both as well prepared to drive an '80s car as someone who's only driven '80s cars, because the *interfaces* are the same. Because I interact directly not with the car but with the dashboard gauges and controls, I don't need to know the innards. If somebody stole into my backyard tomorrow and replaced my internal combustion engine under the hood with an engine that runs on air, I wouldn't know the difference.

Handling Speed Matching

Most peripherals are considerably slower than the CPU in transferring data. Even the hard disk, for example, is thousands of times slower than the CPU.

Most microcomputers (like the PC) have been designed to control everything in their systems, but that's not necessary. A company named Cogent Data Systems makes a hard disk controller for AT-class machines with memory and a microprocessor right on it: The main CPU just makes a request of the hard disk controller, and then (with the right software) goes off to handle something else while waiting for the controller to do the job. Eventually, the controller informs the CPU that it's finished with the data request, and that the controller has already transferred the data into the CPU's memory.

Truthfully, the "speed-matching" benefits of controllers haven't been really exploited in the PC world, as intra-PC "distributed computing" doesn't really exist—yet.

Converting Data from the CPU's Format

Controllers convert data from the CPU's format (±5 volts, digital, and so on) to whatever format the peripheral uses (for example, something called *Modified Frequency Modulation* for older hard disks).

The CPU speaks its own electrical language to other chips on the motherboard. But it's a language without too much power—a CPU wouldn't be able to "shout" loudly enough to be heard any appreciable distance on a LAN. Devices like video monitors need signals massaged into forms they can utilize. Again, controllers serve this function.

A typical system will have a keyboard controller, a video controller, controllers for the floppy and hard disks, and interface controllers for parallel and serial ports.

A Common Misconception

Many think a controller must be on a board all its own. Not at all. The keyboard controller is generally not a board, but just one chip on the motherboard. The hard and floppy disk controllers are usually on separate boards in XT-type machines, but on the same board on most AT-class machines. As we've seen, many of the newer machines put the video, hard disk, floppy disk, parallel, and serial controllers *all* on a single board—the motherboard.

Let's take a quick look next at the common controllers in the system.

Display and Display Adapters

The PC, like most computers, uses video Cathode Ray Tube (CRT) technology to display information for user reception. To allow the computer to communicate with a display monitor, a display adapter must be inserted into one of the PC's expansion slots. Several display adapters are available:

- The IBM Monochrome Display Adapter (MDA) and compatibles. These offered really out-of-this-world (for 1981) text on a microcomputer screen—sadly, however, no graphics.

- The Hercules Monochrome Graphics Adapter and compatibles. One company took the MDA and added graphics. Most programs don't support the Hercules graphics (which is a shame, as they're pretty good for the price), but some of the biggies like 1-2-3 do.

- The IBM Color/Graphics Adapter (CGA) and compatibles. Introduced with the MDA for use with games, the CGA offered lousy text and lousy graphics.

- The IBM Enhanced Graphics Adapter (EGA) and compatibles. It was really annoying that people with Commodore 64s had better games than PC owners. A lot of that was due to the lousy graphics. To allow better games on the PC (no, that's not really true), IBM introduced the EGA in 1984. It was very expensive at first—over $1,100 for the board and monitor—but now an EGA system with a monochrome monitor that shows you colors as shades of gray can be assembled for under $300. The EGA offers good text and good graphics. An EGA board is shown in Figure 3.17.

- The IBM Professional Graphics Adapter and compatibles. The PGA was a $3,000+ package IBM offered as a more powerful alternative to the EGA in 1984. It never caught on.

FIGURE 3.17

EGA board

- The IBM Video Graphics Array. Sporting PGA-quality graphics, the VGA made its appearance in 1987 with the PS/2s. The graphic and text quality are better than EGA, but not so much that one is tempted to throw away a $400 EGA monitor and $150 EGA board to embrace VGA. Not so much a revolution as just simple evolution. A nice board, nonetheless, and preferred over EGA if you're upgrading from CGA or MDA.

- The IBM Multi Color Graphics Array. This is a cut-down version of VGA for the Models 25 and 30.

- The IBM 8514/A Very High Resolution Graphics Adapter. This does some nifty stuff, including allowing you to see two 80×25 screens right on one monitor. The screens are in Squint-O-Vision, but it's awfully nice for debugging or desktop publishing. At the moment, however, it's a bit rich for most of our tastes—$3,000 for the monitor and board.

- The XGA (Extended Graphics Array) is a lot like the 8514, but faster and more compatible with earlier computers. It also supports up to eight adapters in a single computer.

- Non-IBM High Resolution Graphics Adapters.

Each adapter may service one or more types of displays. The major families of displays are the following:

- Monochrome TTL monitors

- Composite Video monitors

- RGB monitors

- High-resolution RGB monitors

- Multiscan monitors

I have no intention of telling you how to open up and attempt to service one of these monitors—it's dangerous and not particularly cost effective. However, some simple maintenance and troubleshooting techniques can be done with the monitor cover in place. I'll discuss them in Chapter 20 on displays and display adapters.

Floppy and Hard Disk Controller and Disk Drives

The floppy disk drive is an essential peripheral. Since it's a peripheral, it requires an interface card. This card is called a *floppy disk controller board*. These will, in general, not give you many problems. They do fail, however, so you need to know how to recognize and address this.

The much more fertile ground for failure lies in the floppy disks and floppy disk drives themselves. Floppy drives can require speed adjustment, head alignment, and head cleaning. Speed adjustment and head cleaning can be done simply and cheaply. Alignment can require some specialized equipment and isn't always cost effective, but I'll discuss it later.

Beyond adjustment is the problem of compatibility among drive types. There are two kinds of $5\frac{1}{4}$-inch floppies, two kinds of $3\frac{1}{2}$-inch floppies, and Zenith makes a laptop that uses two-inch floppies. Nowadays, I don't even consider outfitting a machine without a $3\frac{1}{2}$-inch drive. The floppy chapter talks about floppy installation and includes a section on installing $3\frac{1}{2}$-inch drives in older XT-and AT-type machines (it's fairly simple).

Hard disks are a godsend if you've been using floppies, because they store more data and are faster, but they bring their own host of problems. Hard disk (IBM calls them *fixed disk*) controllers can develop problems, or they may contain the key to better hard disk performance. There are a lot of options in hard disk controllers these days, and we'll examine them. Figure 3.18 shows a hard-disk controller.

Some hard disk failures, like precipitous drops in speed or loss of data, can be addressed at either the controller or the drive level. Problems like head crashes can be avoided with some simple techniques explained in the chapter on hard disks. Even the ultimate disaster—a reformatted hard disk—can be reversed in some cases.

We tend not to think of certain boards, like parallel ports or video boards, as AT-specific or XT-specific. However, hard disk controllers on the XT are radically different from hard disk controllers on the AT. In general, they're not interchangeable.

FIGURE 3.18

Hard disk controller

Printer Interfaces

Despite the "Electronic Age" and the "Paperless Office," we still don't believe something is true until we see it on paper. Would you *really* believe you had gotten that promotion until you received the letter? You don't use E-mail for that kind of stuff. Printers and plotters produce this *hard copy* output for us.

As should be familiar by now, such devices require an interface, generally a *Centronics parallel port* or an *RS232C serial port*. In the case of the parallel port, the interface usually poses few or no problems. Serial ports can be troublesome sometimes, but inexpensive diagnostic tools described later in this chapter can quickly isolate problems.

Printer ports have been given names that DOS can use to refer to them. DOS calls the first printer port on a PC *LPT1*, or *Line PrinTer 1*. Also, DOS supports LPT2 and LPT3.

The actual printer is the greater source of failures. Printers employ a large number of moving parts. Some dot-matrix and laser printers are very reliable, while some daisywheel printers can offer no end of problems. Chapter 17 examines printer maintenance.

Worse yet, as printers get more powerful, their software gets more complex. It's a shame that so many people fail to exploit the full power of their computers simply because WordPerfect or Word isn't programmed to do the exploiting. Chapter 16 introduces you to the world of escape codes and Hewlett-Packard's LaserJet Printer Control Language (PCL) to let you unlock the power of your PC printer.

Modems and Communication Ports

The other common printer interface is the serial port. It's more commonly used, however, for *modems*—modulator/demodulators. Modems allow computers to communicate remotely with other computers via phone lines. Virtually all modems use serial ports, also known as a *comm port,* an *RS232* or *RS232C,* or the new official name that no one seems to know or use, the *EIA 232D port.*

The DOS names for the communications ports are COM1 and COM2. DOS 3.3 and later versions will also allow COM3 and COM4, but they're limited in their usefulness (more on that in Chapter 18).

RS232 is a source of many cable problems. Either the wrong cable is configured, or environmental problems (electronic noise) cause communication errors. Figure 3.19 depicts an IBM RS-232 adapter. Data communications troubleshooting is an entire book in itself—several books, in fact—but we cover the essentials in Chapter 18.

System Clock/Calendar

The system clock/calendar keeps the date and time even when the unit is turned off. The AT-type machines are designed to include the clock right on the motherboard. XT types don't have it, so they must get by with the help of add-on boards. The vast majority of the time, the only problem from the clock will be with 1) the battery or 2) the software to use it.

The battery causes problems, of course, when it runs down and no longer keeps time. Replacement is no problem, save for some clock/calendar boards that solder the battery on the board. You have to wonder if the people who designed those boards want to be able to charge you $120 three years later to replace the battery.

FIGURE 3.19

IBM RS-232 adapter

The other clock problem is how to change the time and date, and how to get the time and date from the clock/calendar board into DOS's time and date. Again, on AT-type machines it's a piece of cake—DOS directly supports it. But XT-type machines need a separate program, like SET-CLOCK, ASTCLOCK, or PWRUPCLK, to name a few I've seen. The only trouble is that the programs tend to get lost. If you're a technical support person, you should become packrat-like when you see disks with programs to support various boards. Nobody else will know where these disks are, so it's up to you.

By the way, don't confuse this with the clock that raps out the beat that the PC dances to—the one I mentioned a few pages back based on the 8284 or 82284 chip. They're different circuits. The CPU clock doesn't run when the power is off to the PC. The clock/calendar, on the other hand, has a battery to allow it to run even when the system is off.

SCSI Interface

More and more computers come with a Small Computer Systems Interface (SCSI) host adapter board. (Many people call them "SCSI controllers," but that's not actually a correct characterization, as you'll learn in Chapter 11.) You'd use a SCSI host adapter to connect your PC to some kinds of hard disks, most optical drives, scanners, or some tape drives.

Less Common Boards

That's about it for the commonly-found boards. You might also see the following boards:

- Mouse interface boards. Some mice interface via the serial port, but others use their own special interface card. Such a mouse is called a *bus mouse,* as opposed to a *serial mouse,* which is attached with the serial port.

- Local Area Network (LAN) boards. If your company has a Token Ring or Ethernet network, there's got to be a physical connection to the network. That's supplied by a LAN interface card. The most common ones you'll see are:

    Ethernet or its variation, StarLAN

    Token Ring

    ARCnet

- 3270 emulation cards. Despite improvements in IBM's *SNA* (Systems Network Architecture) in the past few years, it's probably easiest to get your PC to talk to the mainframe by making it look like a dumb 3270 terminal, the familiar IBM "green screens" you see in offices around the world. *Dumb* in terminal parlance means it lacks stand-alone processing power. DCA (the IRMA guys), Attachmate, and others make a nice business filling this need. Plug one in your system and your PC can hook up to the same old coaxial cable that's been serving IBM mainframe users for years.

- Tape controllers. If you want to install a tape drive for backup to your system, you'll need a controller of some kind. Many tape drives can use the floppy controller, but it's not recommended—such tapes are painfully slow, and remember that you bought the tape to quickly back up the hard disk. Some tapes are internal, some external. I'd recommend external, because then you can buy a tape controller board for all of your machines, buy only a few of the expensive tape drives themselves, and let the users share the occasional use of a tape drive. (That's *occasional* only when compared to the frequency of use for the hard disk. Backups should be near daily if you generate work of any importance at all. Yes, I know it's a pain, but can you really afford to lose a whole day's work?)

- Scanner interface cards. Graphical and character scanners are becoming more and more popular, and with good reason—desktop publishing really shines with graphics. Today's audience demands lots of visuals. Scanners offer a way to add pictures to text in a computer-readable form. *Character scanners* allow easier entry of text in computer-readable form.

Some Identification Hints

The above descriptions look good on paper, but how can you actually disassemble a computer and hope to identify the parts? Here are a few hints.

Once you've opened the computer, look around and orient yourself. A few things should leap out at you:

- The power supply is, as we've said, marked prominently with a "Do not open" label.

- The hard disk, if one exists, is likely to be a sealed box with air vents on the top and a circuit board on the bottom.

- The floppies should be self-evident.

The circuitry can be identified with some simple rules:

- RAM Memory is usually easy to spot—it's nine small chips in a row or column, often socketed. It may alternatively be in SIMM form.

- ROM Memory is usually a large chip or pair of chips in sockets, often with a label on the top indicating the software version number.

- Note where boards are attached. The board that's attached with a ribbon cable to the floppy drives is probably the floppy controller. Ditto for the hard disk.

- Although the best way to find the hard disk controller is just to follow the ribbon cable from the hard disk back to a circuit board—that board is probably the controller—another method is to observe the extremely unusual nature of the hard disk–interface connectors. You see, many hard disks use a single 34-pin connector and two 20-pin connectors right on the circuit board. These connectors mate directly to the ribbon cables mentioned before. They're quite hard to miss; in fact, the hard disk controller is the board you can find in the dark, because it looks (and feels) like a pin cushion extends out from it (see Figure 3.20). Some hard disks, on the other hand, do not employ the three-connector interface; instead, they use a single 40-pin connection.

FIGURE 3.20

Hard disk "pin cushion"

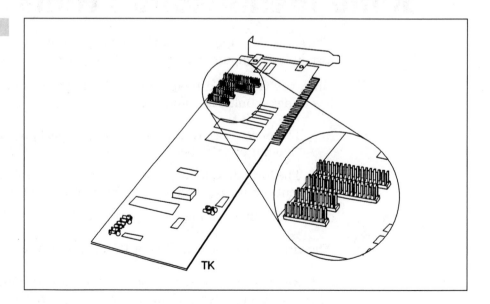

TK

- Note what kind of connectors you find on the back of a circuit board. A common connector type is the D shell, so called because it looks like a capital D. It may have 9, 15, 25, or 37 pins or sockets in it, so it could be referred to as a *male DB9* (nine pins in a D shell), *female DB25* (25 sockets in a D shell), and so on. Table 3.6 is a good reference to the connectors you'll most likely see on expansion card backs. Figure 3.21 identifies some common adapter boards.

- Finally, there's the *process of elimination:* you know there's a hard disk–controller board here somewhere, and you've identified everything but one board—good chance that's it. (This is, of course, a last-ditch method.)

TABLE 3.6: Common Connectors and Probable Uses

CONNECTOR TYPE	COMMON USE
Male DB9	Serial Port
Male DB25	Serial Port (or, sometimes, a SCSI port)
Female DB9	Video, either RGB or EGA color, or Monochrome TTL
Female DB15	Game/Joystick Port
Female DB25	Parallel Printer Port
Female DB37	External Floppy Port (IBM XT floppy controller usually)
Female D shell, 3 rows, 15 sockets	VGA
BNC "push and turn"	3270 coax or LAN
Genderless connectors	IBM Token Ring
RJ11, RJ13, RJ45	Internal Modem, ARCNet, or Ethernet
Female DB9, one RCA jack	Color Graphics Adapter
Female DB9, two RCA jacks	Enhanced Graphics Adapter
50-wire Centronics connector	SCSI port

FIGURE 3.21

Rear view of common adapter boards and probable identification

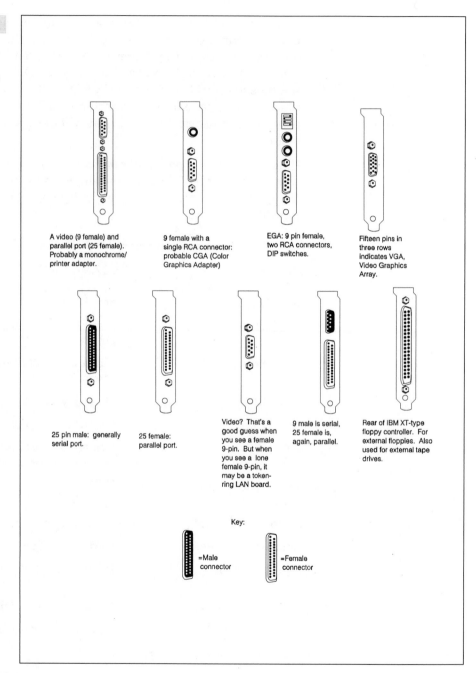

A video (9 female) and parallel port (25 female). Probably a monochrome/printer adapter.

9 female with a single RCA connector: probable CGA (Color Graphics Adapter)

EGA: 9 pin female, two RCA connectors, DIP switches.

Fifteen pins in three rows indicates VGA, Video Graphics Array.

25 pin male: generally serial port.

25 female: parallel port.

Video? That's a good guess when you see a female 9-pin. But when you see a lone female 9-pin, it may be a token-ring LAN board.

9 male is serial, 25 female is, again, parallel.

Rear of IBM XT-type floppy controller. For external floppies. Also used for external tape drives.

Key:

=Male connector

=Female connector

Model Identification Revisited: Specifics of Particular Machines

Now that you've heard of clock/calendars, ROMs, and such, we're ready to finish the PC differentiation that we started earlier. Although the IBM XT and PC are very similar machines, they have a few differences that are apparent under the hood.

IBM PCs and XTs differ by:

- The number of slots: the PC has five, the XT has eight.

- The number of DIP switches: the PC has two banks of eight switches, the XT one bank of eight switches.

- The number of ROM chips: five for the PC, two for the XT. (Generally only one for XT clones. Strictly speaking, there aren't too many PC clones.) The PC has room for a sixth chip, but it's an empty socket.

- The first bank of memory: As I've mentioned, the IBM XT and PC have four *banks* (nine-chip groups) of memory chips. The first bank (*bank zero*) is the most important, as it is the memory where DOS loads itself. This first bank of memory is soldered onto the PC's motherboard, and socketed on the XT's motherboard. This might seem a subtle point, but it's not. If the first bank of memory is bad on the system board, the motherboard can't run DOS—you see, DOS isn't smart enough to load itself somewhere else if that first bank is bad. Result: Bad memory in bank zero means a dead motherboard (in fact, a bad bank zero is the cause of over half of all "dead" motherboards).

I've already said the *big* differences between the XT machines and AT machines are in the bus and the processor. Other differences between XT-type and AT-type machines are:

- Clock/calendar: AT-type machines have a built-in clock/calendar. XT machines generally need a separate board.

- Configuration: AT-type machines have only a few or no switches. XT machines generally have eight or more DIP switches for configuration.

- ROMs: The AT has two ROMs, and room for two more. XT clones usually only have one ROM on their motherboards.

- Motherboard size: People often ask me, "Can I upgrade my XT-type machine by replacing the motherboard with an AT-type motherboard?" In general, AT-type motherboards are physically larger than XT motherboards and can't fit in XT boxes. (There are, however, a group of AT-type motherboards called "baby" AT motherboards. They do fit in XT boxes and are discussed later.)

- Maximum memory: XTs generally can't accommodate more than 640K of user memory. AT-type machines can have just under 16 MB of memory. 386-based machines could theoretically have 4096 MB of memory.

Remember that "AT-type machine" refers to machines as recent as 66-MHz 486 PCs. "AT-type" probably describes 70 percent of the PCs in the world today.

After considering the XT-type and AT-type machines, we have the PS/2s and PS/2-like computers. These machines generally have a smaller *footprint,* or amount of space they take up on the desktop. They put on the motherboard functions like the video, hard disk controller, floppy disk controller, serial ports, and parallel ports that are on separate circuit boards on older machines. This is both a blessing and a curse, as we'll see later. Besides the actual PS/2s, machines like the Zenith LP286 fall into this category.

PS/2 and PS/2-like machines may have the following:

- Bus: Micro Channel bus slots.

- Memory: Older machines use a bank of nine small chips to comprise a bank of memory. PS/2-like machines tend to use the small "miniboards" of memory chips called SIMMs (Single Inline Memory Modules) mentioned before.

- Smaller drives: Many of the PS/2-like machines only have space in their chassis for a $3\frac{1}{2}$-inch drive. If you want a $5\frac{1}{4}$-inch drive, you've got to install an external $5\frac{1}{4}$-inch drive.

- Unusual drive interfaces: Earlier machines use an industry standard drive interface called ST-506/412. (Don't worry, you'll hear more about it later in Chapter 12.) That's nice because you can buy any drive you like and put it into most PC-compatible machines. PS/2-like machines (Compaqs; the Zenith LP286; and the PS/2 Models 50, 50Z, and 70) seem to be going in the direction of strange disk proprietary interfaces. What that means in English is that you've pretty much got to buy PS/2 drives from IBM, and Zenith LP286 drives from Zenith.

By now, you've disassembled your PC and poked around its insides, identifying its vital organs. Let's rest the screwdrivers a minute and take a look at how to make your PC live a bit longer with the next chapter's section on preventive maitenance.

Avoiding Service: Preventive Maintenance

THE most effective way to cut down your repair bills is by good preventive maintenance. Some of this involves common sense. But there are many misconceptions in the PC community about what does and does not make good maintenance sense.

A number of factors endanger your PC's health:

- Heat
- Dust
- Magnetism
- Stray electromagnetism
- Water and corrosive agents

Heat and Thermal Shock

Every electronic device carries within it the seeds of its own destruction. More than half of the power given to chips is wasted as heat, and heat destroys chips.

One of an electronic designer's main concerns is to see that an electronic device can dissipate heat as quickly as it can generate it. If not, heat slowly builds up until the device fails.

You can help your PC's heat problem by doing the following:

- Install an adequate fan.
- Ensure that you're using the proper size of power supply.

- Run it in a safe temperature range.
- Keep the insides dust-free.

The second point—ensuring that your power supply is sized correctly—is taken up in Chapter 9. The others are discussed below.

Removing Heat with a Fan

Some computers, like the Atari 520 or the Commodore 64, don't require a fan, as enough heat dissipates from the main circuit board all by itself. But the PC will surely fail without a fan.

When designing a fan, engineers must trade off quiet operation for cooling power. The fans in the power supplies of most XT-type machines don't seem to do a very good job in either category—they're noisy, and the temperature inside the case of an operating PC or XT can be 30 degrees Fahrenheit warmer than the room outside. ATs are generally cooler, with case temperatures around 15 degrees warmer inside than outside—the phrase is "15 degrees over ambient."

The fan is needed to transport away the heat being generated by the circuit boards, drives, and power supply. Lots of memory and large disk drives are contributing heat factors, as are internal modems (they seem to run fairly hot). One Deskpro 386–like computer I work with was 25 degrees warmer inside the case than outside. If I remove everything but the minimum memory, video, and disk controllers, there's only a ten-degree difference.

You can buy a better fan for your PC in one of two ways. Either get a new power supply containing a better fan or buy an extra "helper" fan. One company, PC Power and Cooling Systems, specializes in improved power supplies for PCs. They sell a Turbo-Cool 200 for PCs, XTs, and smaller ATs, and a Turbo-Cool 300 for full-size ATs and AT-like 386s. They're no noisier than the standard power supplies, yet have been measured to lower temperatures by as much as 35 to 40 degrees in some machines. Obviously, my 386 wouldn't be cooled by 35 degrees, since it's only 25 degrees over ambient; the best a fan can do is to lower the temperature inside the machine to the surrounding temperature. However, installing a PC Cooling Systems fan cooled my machine from 25 degrees over ambient to only 4 degrees over ambient.

PC Cooling Systems also makes add-in "helper" fans for PCs. These are very thin fans that fit inside the case between the case and the chassis. They cost $59 for PCs and XTs, and $75 for ATs. See Appendix A for PC Cooling Systems' address.

Safe Temperature Ranges for PCs

Electronic components have a temperature range within which they're built to work. IBM suggests that the PC, for instance, is built to work in the range between 60 and 85 degrees. This is because although the circuit boards can run as hot as 125 degrees, a typical machine might be as much as 40 degrees hotter *inside* the case than outside it. 125–40=85 degrees, the suggested maximum temperature.

Obviously, if you've got a good fan, the acceptable range of room temperatures expands considerably. If you have a really good fan, the temperature inside the machine will be the same as that outside. You don't want the inside of the PC to get any higher than 110 degrees—hard disks fail at that point, although, again, circuit boards can function in higher temperatures than that. (So my floppy-only laptop can function in the Gobi Desert, although I've not had the chance or inclination to try it yet.)

Since the temperature inside the PC is ambient plus some constant, there are two ways to cool the inside of the PC: lower the constant with a good fan or lower the ambient temperature. Keep the room cooler and the PC will be cooler.

Heat speeds up corrosion. Corrosion is a chemical process, and chemical processes roughly *double* in speed when the temperature of the process is raised by 10 degrees Centigrade (about 18 degrees Fahrenheit). Chips slowly deteriorate, the hotter the faster.

How do you measure temperature and temperature changes in your PC? Simple—get a digital temperature probe. You can buy one from either Radio Shack or Edmund Scientific; see Appendix A for details.

The easy way to use the probe is to tape it over the exit vents by the fan's power supply. An indoor/outdoor switch lets you quickly view the PC's inside temperature and ambient temperature.

Duty Cycles

I said before that a device should get rid of heat as quickly as it creates it. Not every device is that good, however. Devices are said to have a *duty cycle*, a number expressed as a percentage that is the proportion of the time a device can work without burning up.

For example, a powerful motor might have a 50 percent duty cycle. This means it should be active only 50 percent of the time. A starter motor on a car, for example, must produce a tremendous amount of power. Powerful motors are expensive to produce, so instead, cars use a motor that can produce a lot of power for a very short time. If you crank the engine on your car for several minutes at a stretch, you will likely damage or destroy the starter motor.

Floppy disk–drive motors are similar: Run a floppy motor continuously and you would likely burn up the motor. Hard disk motors, on the other hand, run continuously and must be designed with a 100-percent duty cycle. Disk-stepper motors for PC hard disks aren't designed to run continuously. Thus, it's okay to leave your hard disk turned on 24 hours a day, but probably not acceptable to make it read or write data constantly.

Thermal Shock

Because a PC is warmer inside than outside, changes in room temperature can become multiplied inside a PC. This leads to a problem called *thermal shock*. Thermal shock comes from subjecting components to rapid and large changes in temperature. It can disable your computer by causing expansion/contraction damage.

The most common scenario for thermal shock occurs when the PC is turned on Monday morning after a winter's weekend. Most commercial buildings turn the temperature down to 55 degrees over the weekend. Your office may contain some of that residual chill early Monday morning. Inside the PC, though, it still might be 55 degrees. Then you turn the machine on. Within 30 minutes, the PC has warmed up to 120 degrees. This rapid, 65-degree rise in temperature over a half hour brings on thermal shock.

This is one argument for leaving the PC on 24 hours a day, 7 days a week. (You'll soon see some more reasons to do this.) The temperature inside the PC will be better modulated. By the way, you can't leave portable PCs on all the time, but be extra careful with portables to avoid thermal shock. If your laptop has been sitting in the trunk on a cold February day, be sure to give it some time to warm up before trying to use it. Also, let it warm up in a *dry* place, or water vapor will condense on the cold platters. Water on the platters is a sure-fire way to reduce your drive's life.

Sunbeams

Another heat effect is caused by sunbeams. Direct sunlight isn't a good thing for electronic equipment. A warm sunbeam feels nice for a few minutes, but sit in one for an hour and you'll understand why PCs don't like them. Direct sunlight is also, of course, terrible for floppy disks. Find a shadowy area or use drapes.

Dust

Dust is everywhere. It consists of tiny sand particles, fossil skeletons of minuscule creatures that lived millions of years ago, dead skin, paper particles, and tiny crustaceans called dust mites that live off the other pieces. Dust is responsible for several evils.

First, dust sticks to the circuit boards inside your computer. As it builds up, the entire board can become coated with a fine, insulating sheath. That would be good if the dust was insulating your house, but thermal insulation is definitely a bad thing for computers.

You want to keep your PC as cool as possible. One way to keep it cool is to make it easy for heat to radiate from inside the computer. You should remove dust from inside the computer and from circuit boards periodically. A good period between cleaning is a year in a house and six months in an office. A simpler approach is to use the "while I'm at it" algorithm—when you need to disassemble the machine for some other reason, clean the inside while you're at it.

A can of compressed air can assist you. Just as effective for the case and bracket assemblies is a dust-free cloth wetted with a little water and ammonia (just a few drops). Don't use the cloth on circuit boards; get a can of compressed air and blow the dust off.

This should be obvious, but when you blow dust off boards, be aware of where it's going: If you can have the vacuum cleaner nearby, or take the board to another area, you'll have better luck. *Please* don't hold the board over the PC's chassis and blow off the dust with compressed air—all it does is move, not *re*move, the dust.

The second dust evil is that it can clog spaces, such as:

- The air intake area to your power supply or hard disk
- The space between the floppy disk drive head and the disk

To combat the floppy drive problem, some manufacturers offer a floppy dust cover that you put in place when the machine is off. The sad part of this is that you really need the cover when the machine is on. The reason is that CRT displays have an unintended, unpleasant, unavoidable (the three *U*s) side effect: They attract dust. Turn your screen on, and all the dust in the area drops everything and heads straight for the display. Some of the particles get sidetracked and end up in the floppy drives.

Some vendors say the way to cut down on dust in floppy drives is to close the drive doors. This is wrong for two reasons: First, the door isn't dust-tight. Second, double-sided drives should be stored with the doors open. This is because the heads don't touch each other and so cannot damage each other when the drive doors are open. Obviously this is a moot point for half-height drives, which don't allow you to close the doors unless a floppy is in the drive.

A place that creates and collects paper dust is, of course, the printer. You should periodically vacuum or blow out printers, away from the computer (remember, dust goes somewhere when blown away).

Another fertile source of dust is ash particles. Most of us don't burn things indoors unless we're smokers. If you smoke, don't do it near the computer. A study by the U.S. government's Occupational Safety and Health Administration (OSHA) estimated that smoke at a computer workstation cuts the computer's life by 40 percent. That's a loss of $1,200 on a $3,000 workstation.

Magnetism

Magnets, both the permanent and electromagnetic type, can cause permanent loss of data on hard or floppy disks. The most common magnetism found in the office environment is produced by electric motors and electromagnets. A commonly overlooked electromagnet is the one in phones that ring or chirp (rather than beep). The phone forces the clapper against the bell by powering an electromagnet. If you absentmindedly put such a phone on top of a stack of floppy disks and the phone rings, you'll have unrecoverable data errors on at least the top one. Your stereo speakers can do the same thing to floppies.

Don't think you have magnets around? How about these?

- Magnets to put notes on a file cabinet
- Paper clip holders with magnets
- Word-processing copy stands with magnetic clips
- Magnetic screw extractors

Another source of magnetism is, believe it or not, a CRT. I've seen disk drives refuse to function because they were situated inches from a CRT.

X-ray machines in airports similarly produce some magnetism, although there's some controversy here. Some folks say, "Don't run floppies through the X-ray machine—walk them through." Others say the X-ray device is okay but the metal detector zaps floppies. Some people claim to have been burned at both. Personally, I walk through an average of three to four metal detectors per week carrying 3½-inch floppy disks and have never (knock on wood) had a problem.

Airport metal detectors should be sufficiently gentle for floppies. Magnetism is measured in a unit called *gauss*—a power of 25 gauss is required to affect a 360K floppy, more for denser floppies. Metal detectors *in the U.S.* (notice the stress) emit no more than 1 gauss. I'm not sure about Canada and Europe, but I notice that the fillings in my teeth seem to set off the metal detectors in the Ottawa airport.

What about preventive maintenance? For starters, get a beeping phone to minimize the chance of erasing data inadvertently. Another large source of magnetism is the motor in the printer; generally, it isn't shielded and, in case you're wondering, the motors on the *drives* don't produce very much magnetism. Mainly, go on an antimagnet crusade. Magnets near magnetic media are disasters waiting to happen.

A sad story: A large government agency's data center bought a hand-held magnetic bulk floppy eraser. (I'm not sure why—they weren't a Secret-level shop, and thus did not have the need.) The PC expert in the shop tried erasing a few junk floppies, turned it off, and then forgot about it. The next day he remembered that he had left it on top of a plastic floppy file drawer. This meant that the eraser, even though turned off, was about an inch from the top of the floppies. He spent the next day checking each of the floppies one by one, to see if they had been erased by being near the eraser. Most had been. The data center got rid of the bulk eraser. I'm not sure what they did with the PC expert.

Stray Electromagnetism

Stray electromagnetism can cause problems for your PC. Here, I'm just referring to any electromagnetism you don't want. It comes in several varieties:

- Radiated Electromagnetic Interference (EMI)
- Power noise
- Electrostatic Discharge (ESD)—static electricity

Electromagnetic Interference

EMI is caused when electromagnetism is radiated or conducted somewhere you don't want it to be. I discuss two common types—crosstalk and RFI—in the next two sections.

Crosstalk

When two wires are physically close to each other, they can transmit interference between themselves. This doesn't mean short circuits—the insulation may be completely intact. The problem is that the interfering wire contains electronic pulses, which produce magnetic fields as a side effect. The wire receiving interference is touched or crossed by the magnetic fields. Magnetic fields crossing or touching a wire produce electronic pulses as a side effect. (Nature is, unfortunately, amazingly symmetrical at times like this.) The electronic pulses created in the second wire are faint copies of the pulses—that is, the *signal*—from the first wire. This interferes with the signal we're trying to send on the second wire.

Crosstalk isn't really a problem when applied to power lines, although I've heard of cases where the alternating current in power lines creates a hum on a communications line through crosstalk. The larger worry is when bundles of wires, such as data cables, are stored in close quarters.

There are five solutions to crosstalk:

- Move the wires farther apart (not always feasible).
- Use twisted pairs; varying the number of twists reduces crosstalk.
- Use shielded cable. The shield reduces crosstalk—don't even think of running ribbon cables for distances over six feet.
- Use fiber optic cable—it's photonic, not electromagnetic, so there's no crosstalk.
- Don't run cables over the fluorescent lights. The lights are noise emitters.

Radio Frequency Interference

Radio Frequency Interference (RFI) is high frequency (10+ KHz) radiation. It's a bad thing. Sources are:

- High speed digital circuits, like the ones in your computer
- Nearby radio sources
- Cordless telephones and keyboards

- Power-line intercoms

- Motors

Worse yet, your PC could be a *source* of RFI. If this happens, the FCC police come to your place of business and take your PC away. (Well, not really, but they will fine you. More on this later.)

RFI is bad because it can interfere with high-speed digital circuits. Your computer is composed of digital circuits. RFI can seem sinister, because it seems to come and go mysteriously. Like all noise, it's an unwanted signal. (How would you go about receiving a *wanted* radio frequency signal? Simple—construct an antenna. Suppose you want to receive a signal of a given frequency? You would design an antenna of a particular length. Basically, the best length is one-quarter of the wavelength, so a 30-meter wavelength is best picked up by a 7.5-meter antenna. It's not important to know that. To learn more about antennas, pick up an amateur radio book.)

Now suppose there's some kind of RFI floating around. You're safe as long as you can't receive it. But what if your computer is connected to its printer with a cable that, through bad luck, happens to be the correct length to receive that RFI? The result: printer gremlins. Fortunately, the solution is simple: Shorten the cable.

Electric motors are common RFI-producing culprits. I recently saw a workstation in Washington where the operator had put an electric fan on top (to cool the operator, not the workstation). When the fan was on, it warped the top of the CRT's image slightly. Electric can openers, hair dryers, electric razors, electric pencil sharpeners, and printers all are candidates. Sometimes it's hard to determine whether the device is messing up the PC simply by feeding back noise onto the power line (you can correct this by putting the devices on separate power lines), or whether it's troubling the PC with RFI.

Your PC also *emits* RFI, which can impair the functioning of other PCs, televisions, and various sensitive pieces of equipment. By law, a desktop computer cannot be sold unless it meets Class B specifications. The FCC requires that a device three meters from a PC must receive no more than a specific amount of RFI (see Table 4.1).

AVOIDING SERVICE: PREVENTIVE MAINTENANCE

TABLE 4.1: Permissible RF Output (FCC Class B Specification)

FREQUENCY	MAXIMUM FIELD STRENGTH (MICROVOLTS/METER)
30–88 MHz	100
89–216 MHz	150
217–1000 MHz	200

RFI became an issue with personal computers when the PC came out, because IBM had shielded its PC line from electromagnetism, and then sought to use the government to shield the IBM PC from the competition. By pushing the FCC to get tough on PCs, IBM got a bit of a jump on the market. Unfortunately for IBM, getting Class B certification isn't that hard, and most clones qualify these days. Clone makers now say their machines are *FCC Class B Certified.* This has caused the reverse of IBM's original intent, as the FCC certification seems to be a mark of legitimacy. In reality, FCC certification doesn't necessarily indicate good design, quality components, or compatibility.

Protecting your PC from the devices around it, and the devices from your PC, are done in the same way. If the PC doesn't leak RFI, it's less likely to pick up any stray RFI in the area. Any holes in the case provide entry and exit points. Use the brackets that come with the machine to plug any unused expansion slots. Ensure that the case fits together snugly and correctly. If the case includes cutouts for interface connectors, find plates to cover the cutouts or simply use metal tape.

You can use a simple AM radio to monitor RFI field strength. A portable Walkman-type radio is ideal, as it has light headphones and a small enough enclosure to allow fairly local signal-strength monitoring. A cheap model is best, since you don't need sophisticated noise filtering. Tune in an area of the dial as far as possible from a strong station (lower frequencies seem to work best), and you'll hear the various devices produce noises. The system I'm currently using has an XT motherboard, a composite monitor, an external hard disk, and a two-drive external Bernoulli box. The quietest part of the system is the PC; the hard disk screams and buzzes, the Bernoulli makes low-frequency eggbeater-like sounds, and the monitor produces a fairly pure and relatively loud tone.

The PC sounds different, depending on what it's doing. When I type, I hear a machine gun–like sound. When I ask for a text search, the fairly regular search makes a *dee-dee-dee* sound.

Power Noise

Your wall socket is a source for lots of problems. These basically fall into a few categories:

- Overvoltage
- Undervoltage
- Transients—spikes and surges

Also, there's one power problem *you* cause:

- Power-up power surges

Let's consider the last first, then the others.

Power-Up Power Surges

I'd like to discuss one power-related item here: user-induced power surges. *What* user-induced power surges? you ask. Simple: Every time you turn on an electrical device you get a power surge through it. *Some of the greatest stresses electrical devices receive is when they are turned on or off.* When do light bulbs burn out? Think about it—generally, it's when you first turn them on or off. One study showed that when a device is first turned on, it draws up to four to six times its normal power for less than a second. (This is according to *Computer Electric Power Requirements* by Mark Waller, published in 1987 by Howard Sams.) It's called *inrush current* in the literature of electricity. For that brief time, your PC might be pulling 600 to 900 watts—not a prescription for long PC life.

What's the answer? Leave your PCs on 24 hours a day, 7 days a week. We've done it at my company for years. Either turn the monitor off, turn the screen intensity down, or use one of those annoying automatic screen blankers or screen savers so an image doesn't burn into the monitor. Turn the printer off, too. Leaving the machines on also modulates temperature and reduces a phenomenon called *chip creep*, which I'll discuss in the next chapter.

What? You're still not convinced? Yes, it seems nonintuitive—most people react that way—but it really does make sense. First of all, consider the things you keep on all the time now:

- Digital clocks, which incorporate some of the same digital technology as microcomputers.

- Calculators—I've seen accountants with calculators that are on all the time.

- Mainframes, minis, and your phone PBX, which never go off.

- Televisions—part of the TV is powered up all the time so it can warm up instantly, unlike older sets.

- Thermostats—the temperature-regulating device in your home or business is a circuit that works all the time.

In addition to the things already mentioned, consider the hard disk. Many 10- and 20-MB hard disks were built to use low-power motors so they could work with the underpowered PC power supply.

You know from real life that it's a lot harder to start something moving than it is to keep it moving. (Did you ever push a car?) The cost, then, of these low-power motors is that sometimes they can't get started in the morning. At my company there's a 10-MB disk that requires a "jump-start" when it has been off overnight: If the thing doesn't want to work, you just remove it from the system, take off the hard disk's circuit board to expose the motor, and give the motor a spin. After a couple of spins, it can be reassembled, and it will start up fine. (Yes, we should throw it away, but we're cheap and stubborn.)

Here's the point: As long as we don't turn the system off, the hard drive works quite well, at least as well as old 10-meg hard drives work. This applies to hard disks in general—in fact, to anything with a motor. Yes, the motor's life is shortened when continuously on, but even then the expected life of the motor is beyond the reasonable life of a hard disk.

There's another reason you should keep the power on, as far as the hard disk is concerned. The initial power surge runs through *everything*, including the hard disk head. Let's suppose you don't park your hard disk head (more on that in the chapters on hard disks), so the head just ends up wherever it was when you turned the machine off. Now the surge goes through the head. It ends up blasting the data that happens to be sitting under the head with a "BLEAHHH!"—the surge blurs the data under the head.

Finally, consider what happens when you don't turn the machine off at all: The head never crashes onto the platter, as happens when the machine is shut off normally.

A final word of caution. Leaving the machine on all the time is only a good idea if:

- Your machine is cooled adequately. If your machine is 100 degrees inside when the room is 70 degrees, it'll overheat when the room goes to 90 degrees on summer weekends when your building management turns off the cooling system. Make sure your machine has a fan that can handle higher temperatures.

- You have adequate surge protection. Actually, you shouldn't run the machine at all unless you have adequate surge protection.

- You have fairly reliable power. If you lose power three times a week, there's no point in leaving the machines on all the time—the power company is turning them off and on for you. Even worse, the power just after a power outage is noise-filled.

Transient

This is any brief change in power that doesn't repeat itself. It might be an undervoltage or an overvoltage. *Sags* (momentary undervoltage) and *surges* (momentary overvoltage) are transients. Being brief, the transient can be of a high enough frequency that it slips right past the protective capacitors and whatever in your power supply and punches holes in your chips. (No, they're not holes you can *see*, at least not without some very good equipment.)

Transients have a cumulative effect: The first 100 might do nothing. Eventually, however, enough chickens come home to roost that your machine decides, one day, to go on vacation. Permanently. We'll talk about protection against these things in Chapter 9.

Overvoltage

You're said to have an *overvoltage condition* when you get more than the rated voltage for a period greater than 2.5 seconds. Such a voltage measurement is done as a moving average over several seconds.

Chronic overvoltage is just as bad for your system as transient overvoltage: The chips can fail as a result of it.

Undervoltage

Summer in much of the country means air conditioners are running full blast, and the power company is working feverishly to meet the power demands they bring. Sometimes it can't meet the full needs, however, and so announces a reduction in voltage called a *brownout*.

Brownouts are bad for large motors, such as you'd find in a compressor for refrigeration. They make your TV screen look shrunken. And they confuse power supplies. A power supply tries to provide continuous power to the PC. Power equals voltage times current. If the voltage drops and you want constant power, what do you do? Simple—draw more current. But drawing more current through a given conductor heats up the conductor. The power supply and the chips get hot, and might overheat.

Surge protectors can't help you here. *Power conditioners* can—they use transformers to compensate for the sagging voltage. We'll discuss them in greater detail in Chapter 9.

Electrostatic Discharge

ESD, or, as you probably know it, static electricity, is annoyingly familiar to anyone who has lived through a winter indoors. The air is very dry (winter and forced hot-air ducts bring relative humidity around 20 percent in my house, for example), and it's an excellent insulator. You build up a static charge and *keep it*. On the other hand, in the summer, when relative humidities might be close to 100 percent (I live in a suburb of Washington, D.C., a city built over a swamp), you build up static charges also, but they leak away quickly because of the humidity of the air. Skin resistance has a lot to do with dissipating charges. The resistance of your skin might be as little as 1,000 ohms when wet and 500,000 ohms when dry (according to *Flying Circus of Physics* by Jearl Walker, published in 1977 by John Wiley).

You know how static electricity builds up. Static can damage chips if it creates a charge of 1,000 volts or more. If a static discharge is sufficient for the average person to notice it, it's 3,000 volts.

Scuffing across a shag rug in February can build up 50,000 volts. This is an electron "debt" that must be paid. The next metal item touched (because metal gives up electrons easily) pays the debt with an electric shock.

If it's 50,000 volts, why don't you get electrocuted when you touch the metal? Fortunately, the amperage—and the power—is tiny. (Power equals voltage times current.) Different materials generate more or less static. Many people think certain materials are static-prone, while others are not. As it turns out, materials have a *triboelectric value*. Two materials rubbed together will generate static in direct proportion to how far apart their triboelectric values are.

Some common materials are listed below in order of their triboelectric values. (The source of this information is Robert Brenner's *IBM PC Troubleshooting and Repair Guide,* published by Howard Sams in 1985.)

Air

Human skin

Asbestos

Rabbit fur

Glass

Human hair

Nylon

Wool

Fur

Lead

Silk

Aluminum

Paper

Cotton

Steel

Wood

Hard rubber

Nickel and copper

Brass and silver

Gold and platinum

Acetate and rayon

Polyester

Polyurethane Polyvinyl chloride

Silicon

Teflon

Once an item is charged, the voltage potential between it and another object is proportional to the distance between it and the other item on the preceding list. For instance, suppose you charged a glass rod with a cotton cloth. The glass would attract items below it on the list, like paper, and would attract even more forcefully things below paper.

Why does static damage PC components? The chips that largely make up circuit boards are devices that can be damaged by high voltage, even at low current.

The two most common families of chips are CMOS (Complementary Metal Oxide Semiconductor) and TTL (Transistor–Transistor Logic). TTLs are an older family that is faster switching. Potentially faster chips (memories, CPUs, and such) could be designed with TTL.

But TTL has a fatal flaw: It draws a lot of juice. TTL chips need much more electricity than CMOS chips, so they create more heat. So, while fast TTLs could be constructed, designing CPUs that way is difficult because densely-packed TTLs produce so much heat that they destroy themselves. (The 8088 is TTL inside, but the 80386 is CMOS.) One common family of TTL chips has ID numbers starting with 74, as in 7400, 7446, 74LS128, and the like.

CPUs and memories are generally CMOS chips. CMOS has a lower theoretical maximum speed, but it runs on a lot less power. Sadly, that also means it's more subject to static electricity problems. TTL chips can withstand considerably more static than CMOS chips. CMOS chips can be destroyed by as little as 250 volts. Even if static doesn't destroy a chip, it could shorten its life. Static is, then, something to be avoided if possible.

Another effect occurs when the static is discharged. When the fat blue spark jumps from your finger to the doorknob, a small *ElectroMagnetic Pulse* (EMP) is created. This is the thing you've heard about that could cause a single nuclear explosion to destroy every computer in the country, except a lot smaller. It isn't too good for chips, either.

I discharge my static buildup on something metal other than the computer's case. A metal desk or table leg is good. (A number of articles and books say, "Touch the case of the power supply." You *can* do this, but I prefer to use a table leg. The reason is simple: If I'm going to create an EMP, I want it as far from the chips in the PC as possible. The way these effects work, if you double the distance from the discharge to the PC, you divide its effects by *four*. By the way, touching the case of the power supply only makes sense if it's plugged in.)

For your computer, however, you might want something a trifle more automatic. The options are:

- Raise the humidity with an evaporative humidifier—ultrasonic ones create dust.

- Raise the humidity with plants, or perhaps an aquarium.

- Install static-free carpet.

- Put antistatic "touch me" mats under the PCs.

- Make your own antistatic spray (see below).

From the comfort point of view, I recommend the first option strongly. You don't feel dried-out, and the static problem disappears. Raise humidity to just 50 percent and the problem will go away.

You can make inexpensive, homemade antistatic spray. Just get a spray pump bottle and put about an inch of fabric softener in it. Fill it the rest of the way with water, shake it up, and you've got a spray for your carpets to reduce static. Just spritz it on the rug; the rug will smell nice, and everyone will know you've been busy. (I can hear you ask: "How long will this last?" The answer is: "You'll know.")

In a similar vein, a person from a temporary services agency once told me that they tell their word-processing operators to put a Bounce sheet under the keyboard to reduce static.

Technicians who must work with semiconductors all the time use a *ground strap* to minimize ESD. The idea with a ground strap is that you never create a spark (and therefore EMP) because you've always got a nice ground connection that's draining off your charges. A good ground strap is an elastic wristband with a metal plate built into it to provide good electrical connection, attached to a wire with an alligator clip. You put the clip on something grounded—the power supply case is the most common place—and fasten the strap around your wrist. Since you're connected to a ground, you continuously drain off your charges. A resistor in the ground strap slows down the discharge process a bit (from a microsecond to a few milliseconds), so you don't end up with one of the dangerous sparks we've discussed before. If you do a lot of board work in a dry place, ground straps are essential.

When you *must* handle electronic components, use these precautions:

- Remember my advice from Chapter 3 about the power supply? If you don't have an antistatic strap, just leave the power supply plugged in and touch the power supply's case before touching any component.

- Reduce the amount of static you transfer to a chip with a ground strap, or remember the high-tech equivalent of knocking on wood— touch unpainted metal periodically. One member of my staff has suggested only handling chips while naked on a wooden floor. This is an effective measure, provided your work environment is compatible with it.

- Don't handle components in areas having high static potential. For example, avoid carpets (unless they're antistatic) or low humidity environments. Don't wear an acrylic sweater when changing chips. Get leather-soled shoes. If your work environment allows it, you can really avoid static by removing your shoes and socks.

- Don't handle chips any more than necessary. If you don't touch them, you won't hurt them.

- Use antistatic protective tubes and bags to transport and store chips.

- If possible, pick up components by their bodies. Don't touch the pins any more than necessary.

Avoiding Water and Liquids

Water is an easier hazard to detect and avoid. You don't need any sophisticated detection devices. Shielding is unnecessary; you just keep the computer away from water.

Water and liquids are introduced into a computer system in one of several ways:

- Operator spills
- Leaks
- Flooding

Spills generally threaten the keyboard. One remedy recommended by every article and book I've ever read on maintenance is to forbid liquids near the computer. In most shops, this is unrealistic. Some people use clear flexible plastic covers on the keyboard, similar to ones Burger King uses on their cash registers. They're normal cash registers, but they have a plastic skin over them that allows the user to spill "special sauce" all over the cash register without harming it. With the plastic covers, they can just hose down the register. With a plastic cover, you could just hose down the keyboard. (Just kidding.) With one of these keyboard "skins," you can practise safe typing.

One such product, SafeSkin, is offered by Merritt Computer Products. (See Appendix A for more information.) They offer versions for the various odd keyboards in the PC world. On the other hand, should someone spill a Coke on a keyboard without one of these covers, all isn't lost so long as you act quickly! Disconnect the keyboard and flush it out at a nearby sink. Let it dry *thoroughly,* and it'll be good as new.

A similar disaster, flooding, sometimes occurs. Don't assume that flooded components are destroyed components. Disassemble the computer, clean the boards, and clean the contacts and edge connectors. You can buy connector cleaner fluids, or some people use a hard white artist's eraser. Don't use pencil erasers: A Texas Instruments study showed they contain acids that do more harm than good to connectors. Blow out crevices with compressed air. (If you *do* disassemble, clean, dry, and reassemble your computer, and find that it works, write the manufacturer a letter. They might put your face in an advertisement!)

Avoid floods by thinking ahead. Don't store any electrical devices directly on the floor where they'll be damaged when the floor is cleaned. Generally, flooding indoors is less than six inches deep. Be aware of flooding from improper roofing. When installing PCs, don't put one under the suspicious stain on the ceiling ("Oh, that—it was fixed two years ago. No problem now.")

Corrosion

Liquids (and gases) can accelerate corrosion of PCs and PC components. Corrosive agents include:

- Salt in sweat

- Water

- Airborne sulfuric acid, salt spray, carbonic acid

Your fear here isn't that the PC will rust away. The largest problem corrosion causes is oxidation of circuit contacts. When a device's connector becomes oxidized, it doesn't conduct as well, and so the device doesn't function, or worse, malfunctions sporadically. Salt in sweat can do this, so be careful when handling circuit boards; don't touch edge connectors unless you have to. This is why some firms advertise that they use gold edge connectors: Gold is resistant to corrosion.

You don't believe you have detectable traces of finger oils? Try this simple experiment. Pour a glass of soda or beer into a very clean glass—preferably a plastic cup that has never been used before. There will be a noticeable "head" on the drink. (Diet soda seems particularly fizzy.) Now put your finger into the center of the head, just for a second. The head will rapidly dissolve, as the oils damage the surface tension required to support the head.

Carbonated liquids have carbonic acid, and coffee and tea contain tannic acids. The sugar in soda is eaten by bacteria that leave behind conductive excrement—like hiring some germs to put new traces on your circuit board. Generally, try to be very careful with drinks around computers.

Don't forget cleaning fluids. Be careful with that window cleaner you're using to keep the display clean. If your AT is on a pedestal on the floor, and the floor is mopped each day, some of the mopping liquid gets into the AT. Cleaning fluids are *very* corrosive.

Summary: Making the Environment "PC Friendly"

Let's sum up what we've seen in this chapter. Protect your PC by doing the following:

- Check power considerations (see Chapter 9):

    No heating elements (Mr. Coffee, portable heaters) in the same outlet as a PC.

> No large electric motors (refrigerators, air conditioners) on the same line as the PC.
>
> Some kind of power noise protection.

- Check temperature ranges:

  Maximum 110 F. (43 C.)

  Minimum 65 F. (18 C.) This can be considerably lower as long as the computer remains *on* all the time.

- Control heavy dust. You can buy (from PC Power and Cooling) power supplies with a filtered fan that sucks in air through the *back,* rather than the usual approach of pulling it in through the front.

- Make sure there isn't a vibration source like an impact printer on the same table as the hard disk.

- Make sure you're familiar with, or (if you're a support person) teach your users about:

  Parking hard disks

  Leaving the machines on all the time

  Keeping cables screwed in and out of the way

  Basic don't-do-this things in DOS, like formatting the hard disk

- Protect against static electricity.

A Sample Preventive Maintenance Program

While this chapter has discussed some Preventive Maintenance (PM) concerns, I've mainly talked about environmental problems PCs face. The fact is, if you're a PC support person, you're probably too overworked to do actual preventive maintenance.

PM implies that you take a machine off a person's desk at regular intervals, perhaps as often as every six months, and move it to your "shop" to give it a good going-over so you can anticipate problems.

If you actually have a support staff to do this, here's the PM procedure I use. If you have only one machine, it's particularly important. These steps should take about two hours.

Some of these things won't make sense yet, as they're discussed in later chapters. Don't worry about that. It will become clear once you've seen the rest of the book. I just wanted to collect the advice all in one place.

1. Pick up the PC at its worksite. Yes, this takes more time than if you have it delivered to your workplace, but you'll learn a lot. Examine:

   - Are the connectors screwed in?
   - Have screws disappeared from the back of the machine?
   - What else is plugged into the PC's outlet? No Mr. Coffees?
   - Is the PC on a rickety table?
   - Is the PC near a window? Is the PC ever exposed to direct sunlight during the day?

2. Ask if the machine is doing anything strange.

3. Ensure that the hard disk (if any) is backed up.

4. Park the hard disk and take the machine back to your shop.

5. Run the machine's diagnostics (see the next chapter).

6. Examine AUTOEXEC.BAT and CONFIG.SYS for any obvious problems—lack of a BUFFERS command, for example.

7. Repark the head.

8. Disassemble the PC.

9. Clean the edge connectors with a connector cleaner and a lint-free cloth or a hard white artist's eraser.

10. Push the chips back into their sockets (discussed in the next chapter).

11. Use canned air to remove dust from circuit boards—don't forget the circuit board under the hard disk.

12. Reassemble the PC. Ensure that all of the cables are securely in place.

13. Rerun the diagnostics.

14. Ensure that all screws are present. If they're not, add screws.

15. Low-level format the hard disk with a nondestructive reformatter program like SpinRite (Gibson Research), Disk Technician, or the like. (We'll discuss this in greater detail in the hard disk chapters.)

CHAPTER

5

Troubleshooting Problems: What to Do When Something Goes Wrong

OKAY, suppose you dust out your PC fortnightly. You clean and adjust your disk drives semiannually. You have a robot that shoots anyone carrying food or drink who comes within 50 feet of your PC. But, one day, WordPerfect refuses to print your purple prose. How do you proceed?

General Troubleshooting Rules

These rules have kept me out of trouble for a long time. I know they'll be of use to you.

THE RULES OF TROUBLESHOOTING ALMOST ANYTHING

Don't Panic

You Will Win

Write Everything Down

Do the Easy Stuff First

Reboot and Try Again

Remove Memory-Resident Programs

Draw a Picture

Separate the Problem into Components and Test Components

Never Guess

Trust No One: Documentation Sometimes Lies

Observe like Sherlock Holmes

Wish for Luck

The answer to the question above—"How do you proceed?"— is the topic of this chapter. I want very much to instill in you a philosophy of troubleshooting, a philosophy built after much trial and even more error.

You've got to have confidence in yourself as a troubleshooter. Look, this stuff isn't that hard. My technical training is as a Ph.D. economist, I've got ten thumbs, and people pay *me* to fix machines—you can do it too. There's not that much to these machines. When it comes right down to it, the only thing you really can't replace for (at most) a hundred dollars or so is your data, and you can protect that with frequent backups.

If you don't go in there *knowing* you're going to win, you're going to get beaten—these machines can *smell* fear. A former girlfriend, a black belt in tae kwon do, tells me that an important tenet of that discipline is to "have an indomitable spirit." Sounds good to me—practice some tech kwon do, and don't forget that indomitable spirit.

Your computer is affected by fluctuations in the power supply of a duration as brief as four milliseconds. That means if your power disappeared for only $1/200$ of a second, you wouldn't see the lights flicker, the microwave would still work, and the TV wouldn't skip a beat—but several bytes of your computer's memory would get randomized (not a lot of the memory, or you'd see a memory error message of some kind). The result is that a program that has always worked pretty well all of a sudden stops dead. You'll never find out why it locked up that one time in a thousand. Maybe all the people in the building were running their photocopiers at the same time. Maybe radiation from a solar storm assaulted your memory chips. It doesn't matter. The quick answer to this problem is just to start over.

Now, don't get too trigger-happy with the reboot if you're in the middle of an application. Try everything you can to make the machine respond and let you get back to DOS. If you reboot in the middle of an application, the application may have left files open, and any such files will be lost if you reboot before the application has closed them. (Such half-finished files lead to a phenomenon you might have seen called *lost clusters*; more on that in the hard disk chapters.)

Memory-resident, or *TSR*, programs can interfere with system functions. It might just be that your drive E won't format because you've got your LAN software loaded. Don't ask me why—just try it. Remove all those pop-ups by rebooting without them, and see if the problem goes away.

Software troubleshooting is just like hardware troubleshooting: Divide and conquer. Each piece of software you're running is a piece of the system, and you want to minimize the number of pieces you have to deal with. TSRs are the easiest part to remove.

I am, by nature, a lazy person. That's why I got interested in computers: They were machines that could free me from some drudgery. The *inexperienced* and lazy troubleshooter tries to save time by not making notes, by acting before thinking, and *swapping* when he or she ought to be *stopping* to consider the next move.

What I've eventually figured out is that well-planned laziness is a virtue. An *experienced* lazy person looks ahead and says, "Oh, heck, what if I can't fix this thing? I don't want to create any more trouble for myself than necessary." So the lazy person keeps diagrams and writes down every action, to prevent tearing out hair while trying to put the thing back together.

The experienced lazy person does the easy stuff first. If it's a video, not a software, problem, there are four things that can be swapped: the motherboard, the video board, the cable, or the monitor. What gets swapped first? The easy thing does—the cable. I know a nonlazy troubleshooting type who was called one day about a WordPerfect problem:

"Mike [not his real name]," the caller said, "WordPerfect isn't printing with the new laser printer!"

Now, the experienced lazy person listens and says, "Gosh, how can I fix this without leaving my chair?" Personally, I'd zero in on the word *new* before laser printer. My next question would be something like, "What kind of printer did you have before the new laser printer?" (It probably was a daisy wheel.) "Have you ever seen WordPerfect print on this laser printer before?" (Probably not.) "Have you reinstalled WordPerfect for the laser printer?" (A confused "What?" is the most likely answer.)

Mike, on the other hand, attacked the problem by first swapping the motherboard on the PC that was attached to the laser printer. Yeah, yeah, we could observe that Mike is, umm, shall we say, "a couple sandwiches short of a picnic" when it comes to troubleshooting. But I see people do less extreme, but just as unnecessary, things all the time. Heck, I still do a lot of dumb things myself, like playing Macho Man with a screwdriver. But I hope to get better at remembering to be lazy when troubleshooting.

When you open up a machine, you expose the machine to a certain risk that you'll do something dumb to it. PC troubleshooting differs from, say, automotive troubleshooting in that the thing that's most commonly broken is the user. If you separate out the "broken user" stuff, like forgetting to turn it on and so forth, software is the next most common problem. Honest-to-God hardware problems are actually quite uncommon compared to user and software problems, which leads me to the seven specific troubleshooting steps.

Troubleshooting Steps

The lazy person makes the troubleshooting job tractable by breaking down problems into steps. Don't panic; be methodical, or you'll thrash about helplessly and get frustrated. Once you're frustrated, you're lost, and you start creating new problems.

Following is the method I use. It looks a lot like methods suggested by other people, but it's not the only method. You certainly don't have to use my method, but find one you like and stick to it. It's the "this will only take five minutes" repairs that get me in trouble. (It's like when someone giving you directions says, "You can't miss it." You *know* you're in trouble then.) I'll assume for this discussion that you're interacting with someone else (the person with the PC problem), but you could just as easily interview yourself.

Before opening up the computer, do the following:

1. Check the nut behind the keyboard, even if the "nut" is *you*. (I find it's often *me,* in my problems.)

2. Check that everything is plugged in: power, monitor, phone lines, printer, modem, and so on.

3. Check the software.

4. Ask, "What am I doing differently?"

5. Check external signs, and make notes of them.

6. Run whatever diagnostics you like—a commercial product like CheckIt or QAPlus, or (if supplied by the manufacturer), the specific diagnostics for your computer.

Only then, if you still haven't solved the problem,

7. Disassemble the machine, push the socketed chips back into their sockets, clean the connectors, and put the machine back together.

Check for Operator Error

Operator error is responsible for 93.3 percent of PC failures. (That's a made-up statistic, but it got your attention and probably isn't far from the truth.)

There are lots of things an operator can do wrong. For example, when I used to teach hands-on dBASE III+ classes, I'd regularly see students looking bewildered at the screen, saying, "It didn't work." I'd ask, "Did you type in exactly what I told you to?" "Yes," they would reply. I'd look at the screen. Indeed, they did type in exactly what I told them to *this time*. Several commands back, however, they miskeyed something and ignored the resulting error message. These are intelligent people, they were just under some stress (having to pay attention to me *and* the computer), and they missed a detail. It's easy to do.

By the way, this section, and in fact most of this chapter, is written as if you are fixing somebody *else's* machine. However, the same information applies if you're fixing your own. No matter how much of an expert you are, you'll mess up sometimes: I get painfully reminded of this all the time. One particularly embarrassing incident occurred in Jacksonville the first time I taught my "Advanced PC Troubleshooting" class. One person in the class wanted to show me his graphics tablet, a device used to simplify drawing pictures on a computer. He brought it into class and plugged it into the computer. It didn't work. As it was plugged into an RS-232 port, I spent 30 minutes testing the RS-232 port. The port checked out okay. I scratched my head, trying to figure out what was the matter. Then a student said, "Doesn't the tablet have to be plugged into power?" and held up the power plug for the tablet. Arrggh.

So when I say something like "some dopey user did so and so," I mean "some dopey user did so and so—and beat *me* to doing it."

The language of computers confuses people. You've heard the stories about users doing goofy things: They're true. I've seen them. I once watched a user follow the dBASE III 1.0 installation instructions to "Insert System Disk 1 in drive A and close the door." After inserting the disk in the drive, the user then got up (looking a little puzzled, I'll admit) and closed the door to the office. If I hadn't actually been there to see it, I probably wouldn't have believed it.

When teaching those same dBASE classes, now and then I'd get this problem. A student was staring at the keyboard in puzzlement.

"What's wrong?" I asked.

"I'm looking for a key," he replied.

"Which one—I'll point it out," I offered.

"The 'any' key," he said, still puzzled. I looked at the screen. dBASE was prompting, "Press any key to continue..." I had just finished my "pay attention to what the computer is doing" lecture, so this poor soul was trying his hardest to follow my directions. (Nowadays, there's an answer for the "any key" searchers. Egghead Discount Software sells an "any key" kit. It's a keytop sticker that says *ANY KEY.* You install it on, well, any key.)

Even worse, sometimes users will (horrors!) prevaricate slightly. "I didn't do anything. It just stopped working." Please note: I'm not one of those techy types whose motto is, "Assume the user is lying," but sometimes it happens. More often, it's not that they lie; they just don't know what's important.

People sometimes feel defensive calling a support person. You want to collect as much information as possible. If you make them feel defensive, they'll remember incorrectly or withhold information. Here's a trick telemarketers are told: *Smile* when you're on the phone with someone. It works. (As Sam Kinnison says, "It creates the illusion that you care.")

Being a support person can be wearing. There's a great tendency to feel that "these people must get up early in the morning to think up dumb things to ask," but you can't let it get you down. Remember, these folks can't be too dumb; after all, the same company that hired them hired you, too.

Another source of operator error is inexperience. The PC isn't the simplest thing in the world to master. The author of a book titled *Computer Wimp: 100 Things I Wish I'd Known Before I Bought My First Personal Computer* observes in that book that learning to use a computer system can be the most difficult learning endeavor a person can undertake in his or her post-school life. (Things like raising kids are undoubtedly tougher, but they're different kinds of learning experiences.) It doesn't take a genius to recognize that most PC hardware and software manuals aren't the easiest things to comprehend.

Is Everything Plugged In?

I know this sounds stupid, but we've all done it. A friend bought a Hayes Smartmodem 2400 and couldn't get it to work. It accepted commands all right but couldn't dial out. The phone line was tested with a regular phone and it worked fine. He was quite puzzled until he realized that he'd plugged the phone line into the *out* jack in the modem (intended for connection to a phone line that would be shared between the modem and a phone), rather than the *in* jack.

Another time, I ran the IBM diagnostic disk on my PC and kept getting *bad address mark* errors on my disk drives. I was all set to spend a lot of money for new drives until I realized that the scratch diskette I was using wasn't formatted. (The drives were fine.)

When you ask the user, "Is it plugged in?" be diplomatic. (Don't you hate when tech support people ask *you* that question?) But be firm.

- Is the PC plugged into some kind of multi-outlet strip?
- Is the strip on? Did the user kick off the power switch?
- Can the user actually see that the power strip is plugged into the wall?
- Is the outlet on the wall switched on?

I know of a large communications company that kept sending technicians to try to determine why a LAN server kept dying at odd hours of the night. They would set up the software at the user site, leave it running, and then eventually get called back to the site because, after a day or two, all kinds of files had been trashed. The techs would always ask, "Has this been turned off in the middle of an operation?" The users would shake their heads "no" solemnly and with annoyance—this tech guy wasn't going to weasel out of fixing the company's buggy software *that* easily, they thought. Finally this large company sent their Supertech—the guy who'd seen it all. He looked over the server and listened to the users' story.

Now, this guy *knew* from the symptoms that the server was getting shut down improperly. So he looked for easy ways to turn the machine off accidentally. Noticing two light switches on the wall and only one fluorescent ceiling panel, he flipped both switches. You guessed it—the server was plugged into a switched outlet. The security staff, in making the rounds each night, was shutting off the lights.

- Are the peripherals plugged in? Are they plugged *into the computer*?

Not only is everything plugged in, but is everything in *tight*? Multiple-pin connectors slowly bend under gravity unless the mounting screws are tightened. As someone stretches his or her legs under the desk, a loose power cord can be moved enough to disconnect it, or to disconnect and reconnect it. Connectors on the floor take a lot of abuse.

Check the Software

Software problems arrive in several guises:

- Operator error
- Keyboard/screen/disk/timer conflicts with memory-resident software
- Software that doesn't clean up after itself
- Software that requires hardware that isn't connected or activated
- Buggy software

Memory Resident (TSR) Problems

Memory-resident software, like SideKick, Metro, Prokey, Superkey, and others, are great. You don't have to exit dBASE or WordPerfect to do a simple calculation, make a note, or enter an appointment in an electronic calendar. Just press a particular key combination and SideKick pops up. You do your work, then press Escape, and SideKick goes back to sleep. And those are just a few uses.

At least, that's the way it's supposed to work. Often it doesn't, however. Sometimes you press the key combination and the PC goes to sleep.

TSR programs are programs that load themselves into the system and then go to sleep and return control of the system to the user, *without removing themselves from memory*. They remain dormant until an outside condition of some kind wakes them up. They can be activated either by the timer that's built into the system or by some kind of device access (disk access, a keystroke, or certain characters being printed or displayed on screen).

Common kinds of TSR programs are the following:

- Screen blankers. Called by the timer and lack of keystrokes, these programs shut down the video when the machine is waiting for the user.

- Popups like SideKick add some useful features like a phone book or calculator to the system, making it available at any time. They're awakened by special keystrokes.

- Disk cache programs (covered later) silently monitor disk activity and try to anticipate the file the user will want next. They then preload the data from that file so the disk seems blindingly fast. They're invoked by disk activity.

- 3270 emulation and LAN programs. These must handle communications in the background. If they get busy, or try to get busy when the system is in the middle of something else, they can bring things to a grinding halt.

- Viruses are memory-resident programs that sit inside the system, sometimes awakening with each disk access or timer tick, waiting for the right moment to do whatever their job might be. (Most likely that job is something destructive, although some viruses have been benign, just displaying messages of some political import.)

The problem arises because the software is awakened by some event like a keystroke or the timer. What happens if *two* different TSRs coexist in the system, and both try to monitor the keyboard, or the timer, or the disks? Often they can confuse each other, causing the system to either crash or misbehave. (For example, the disk cache program I used three years ago "misbehaved." Now and then it would lead the disk to tell me it had saved a file, when in actuality it had done nothing of the kind. Needless to say, I dumped that program pretty quickly.)

When odd things occur with software, memory-resident applications are the first suspect. Reboot without the memory residents and try the operation again. (That's how I narrowed the problem down to the cache program.) If the problem goes away, try to reproduce the software failure and contact the manufacturer. Sometimes you can rearrange the "hot" keys in memory-resident applications. Other times, rearranging the order in which you load memory residents solves the problem. When you find a workaround, make a note of it so you and your successors can save time later.

These conflicts are a major reason for OS/2, the new PC operating system. OS/2 creates multiple *virtual* PCs, each running a separate program. A program like SideKick, then, thinks it has its own machine and doesn't conflict with WordPerfect's ability to get to the keyboard. This presumes that SideKick is written to play by the rules that OS/2 lays down. Virtually no one played by the PC-DOS rules. How well OS/2 rules will be followed, only time will tell.

Poorly Terminated Software Most software is careful to restore your PC to its original state when it ends. Some, on the other hand, aren't so careful. Most software effects are fairly innocuous, like leaving the background of your display blue and the foreground yellow. The simple DOS command MODE BW80 will fix that. Perhaps you have both a color display and a monochrome display, and the software has left you in the color display: MODE MONO will fix that. Occasionally, software will disable Ctrl-Alt-Del (older versions of Flight Simulator are good examples) or set the disk drives to nonstandard parameters. The only option then might be the big red switch or a soft reboot.

Other programs can leave a peripheral in a strange state. DisplayWrite 4, for example, doesn't reset the printer before terminating, so the printer could still be printing Times Roman when you try to print a DIR.

Hardware-Related Software Faults For a while, you occasionally saw people writing in to computer magazines about a mysterious bug in the original Compaq Portable. For no reason at all, it would sometimes freeze up, and nothing would save it. Eventually, the computer world figured out that the problem was sloppy fingers on the part of the operator.

The Compaq, like all PC compatibles and clones, has a PrtSc (Print Screen) key. Pressing Shift and PrtSc sends an image of the screen to the printer. If a printer isn't present, a PC does several retries and finally decides there's no printer attached. This is called *timing out*. The PC doesn't wait very long—just a few seconds. The Compaq, on the other hand, waits quite a long time. Thus, when the stray finger pressed Shift-PrtSc, the computer would wait and wait and wait for a printer to be attached. Actually, had the user waited long enough, the computer would have come back.

A number of mysteries can be linked to software that doesn't recover well from disabled or nonexistent hardware:

- Trying to print to a nonexistent printer

- Trying to print to an Epson printer when a C. Itoh printer is attached

- Trying to print to a printer that is off line

- Trying to display graphics data on a non-graphic monochrome monitor

- Running a program that assumes (generally for copy protection) that the PC is 4.77 MHz speed, or that the floppy drive has 41 tracks

- Running a program that needs more memory than the PC contains

But here's my favorite hardware-induced software error. The PS/2s insist on being properly configured before they'll do any work for you. If they're configured wrong—if they boot up and find they have more or less memory than they expected, or more or fewer disk drives, or the like—they print a "162" error (see the table of codes later in this chapter) on the screen and wait patiently for an F1 to continue.

If you have an external floppy disk drive on a PS/2, it has its own power supply and power switch. If you forget to turn on the external floppy before booting up the PS/2, you'll get a scary-looking 162 error. Just turn the floppy drive on and reboot. Do *not* rerun the configuration program found on the Reference Diskette: Assuming the floppy is still off, it will sense there isn't an external floppy anymore and stop looking for it. Then when you do turn the external floppy on, the PS/2 won't talk to it. Argggh. (By the way, there are a number of PS/2 motherboards floating around that just plain won't hold a configuration for very long—that's another problem altogether.)

Faulty Software   Sometimes the problem is buggy software. Even the most popular programs can misbehave when faced with a full disk, insufficient memory, or some other situation the designer didn't anticipate or test.

Try to make the bug reproducible. If it's a suspected bug in a compiler product, trim off as much of the other code as possible while retaining the bug. Ideally, a program no longer than ten lines of code should demonstrate the problem. Then report it to the manufacturer and other users in your company.

What Am I Doing Differently?

When I worked in a large programming shop, junior people would often come to me for diagnostic advice on their code.

"This code worked before, but it doesn't now." "What did you change?" I'd ask. "Nothing," they usually replied. "Then why did you run it again?" I wondered.

There *has* to be something different. Otherwise, why are you running the software? Was some code changed? New data? A new machine? It's the first place to look. Did you add a memory board? Some early PC programs (Infocom games and early WordStar, in particular) would refuse to run if more than 512K memory was in the PC. "Illegal Operation," the Infocom games would complain, and then reboot the PC. WordStar would say you didn't have *enough* memory! You'd think that adding memory couldn't cause problems, particularly if you had already checked the memory and found it error-free. In the case of the Infocom games, "Illegal Operation" isn't much of a hint about what's wrong. I barked up a lot of trees until I went back and examined the single change to the system: a memory upgrade.

If you have a problem like that, you've got to convince your system that it has less memory than it actually does. Probably the easiest way to do that is to load a VDISK of some size. VDISK.SYS is a program that comes with DOS. It fools your system into thinking some of your memory is in fact a very fast floppy disk. In the process, however, it steals that memory from DOS programs. Create a 256K VDISK on your 640K machine, and you end up with only 640K–256K=384K space for programs. You install it in your CONFIG.SYS with the command

```
device=vdisk.sys nnn
```

where *nnn* is the size of the VDISK. So, in my WordStar situation, I just ran a VDISK of 128K to bring the system memory down to 512K and then ran WordStar—no problem. By the way, both WordStar and Infocom have resolved these problems.

Hardware upgrades can conflict. Suppose, for example, you install an Intel AboveBoard paged memory board and a 3Com LAN board in the same PC. (This example isn't based on actual experienced problems—I picked the boards arbitrarily for this example.) Suppose the AboveBoard uses the same memory window as the LAN board. Most of the time, the AboveBoard is inactive: It's only called into action when you're working on a spreadsheet too large to fit into 640K. The LAN board, on the other hand, is used periodically to store and retrieve data, and to receive electronic mail. The user boots up all right, sees that the LAN works fine, and then starts working on Lotus. As long as the spreadsheet is small, there's no problem. Then the spreadsheet gets larger, and the spreadsheet program begins using the AboveBoard memory. Still no problem. *Then* disaster strikes: Someone sends an electronic mail message. The LAN and the AboveBoard are active at the same time, and either the system freezes up, the LAN goes south, the spreadsheet is minced, or some combination of the above problems occurs.

Software upgrades can bring problems. Perhaps an application running under DOS 2.1 has just barely enough memory space to run: The extra 20-odd kilobytes required by DOS 3.2 makes it unable to work. A macro that required three minutes to run under version 2 of some spreadsheet might take two hours or not run at all under version 3.

One final story in this section. I was working with an early copy of OS/2 on a 386 clone. I hadn't booted OS/2 in several days, and I needed to get into OS/2 to run a program. I tried to boot, but I got a very scary-looking error message. I'd try again—no luck. I spent four hours (very late at night) swapping memory chips. No luck. Then I remembered I had enabled the video card's autoswitch capability the day before to run a DOS program. That couldn't be the problem, could it? But just in case…I flipped the switch back and tried again. Five minutes later, OS/2 was running my program, and I was kicking myself.

Check External Signs

If the computer has indicator lights, what do they indicate? Are all of the lights glowing on the modem? Does the printer indicate "ready"? Is the hard disk squealing or grinding? Does the monitor image look bent? Your drives and other peripherals produce hums, whirs, and clicks. After a while, these noises become familiar, and any variation in them signals a problem. Pay attention to these signs.

The first step in successful troubleshooting is in isolating the problem component. Note what lights are on and off, the positions of switches, and so on.

Run Diagnostic Programs

The IBM PC and AT come with diagnostic programs that can help pinpoint the problem (assuming, of course, that the computer is well enough to run them in the first place). Other computers do not come with such programs, but you can get various public domain diagnostic programs. See Appendix A for more information.

Truthfully, the programs aren't so valuable for locating errors. They mainly make you feel confident that there's nothing wrong with the PC. After all, what must be running in order to run these programs? Well, the system board must be running, the video must be working so you can see the screen, the keyboard must be active to accept commands, and the floppy must be able to load the program. So merely loading the diagnostic program (or any other program, for that matter) tells you some things about the system. When I talk to vendors, I question the value (in a nice way, of course) of their software.

"Some of what you say is true, of course," admitted one author. "But to boot DOS requires over 64K of memory. Our program is self-booting and its first section loads in less than 16K of memory. That means that, in a case where you had a memory error between the first 16K and the first 64K, DOS would lock up when you tried to boot, but our diagnostic could run. Besides, the big value of a program like this is that a technician can go to a strange machine and get an overview checkup of the machine fairly quickly." So there you have the other side of the issue.

Running the IBM Diagnostic Programs

The IBM diagnostic disk is a bootable disk; put it in drive A and then reboot the system. It uses a simpler version of COMMAND.COM, so don't put it directly on your hard disk. This text won't dwell on running the diagnostic disk, as it's pretty simple—all menu driven. The IBM manual lacks some information on interpreting error codes, however, so a table of diagnostic error codes is presented in the section called "IBM Diagnostic Error Codes," later in this chapter.

For PS/2 50, 55, 60, 70, 75, 80, and 90 owners, there is hidden on the Reference Diskette a set of Advanced Diagnostics. If you buy the Advanced Diagnostics from IBM, you only get a (generally unnecessary) manual for $500. It turns out that the Advanced Diagnostics are already on the Reference Disk! The programs are activated from the Reference Diskette's Main menu with the Ctrl-A key combination. Just boot from the Reference Diskette, wait for the Main menu to appear, and press Ctrl-A (*A* for *Advanced*).

The Power-On Self Test (POST)

One short diagnostic routine runs on the PC every time the PC is powered up. It does a memory test and checks to see that the basic important hardware exists. It's called the *POST*—Power-On Self Test, or, in the BIOS listing, *POD* (Power-On Diagnostics). The documentation given with the PC (at least, the documentation given with my PC) doesn't explain the error codes. Hopefully, you'll never see them. If you do, however, you'll want to know what they mean. They're shown in the section called "IBM Diagnostic Error Codes," later in this chapter.

The following description is taken from my reading of the assembly language listing for the PC-1 BIOS. It varies slightly for the AT and later PCs.

PROCESSOR

1. POST tests the 8088 registers and flags. If it fails, the system just halts.

ROM

2. POST computes and checks a checksum for the ROM. If it fails, the system just halts.

DMA

3. POST checks the DMA (Direct Memory Access) controller, the 8237. If it fails, the system just halts.

IRQ's

4. POST tests the 8259 interrupt controller. If it fails, the system does a long beep and a short beep, then halts.

TIMER

5. POST tests the 8253 timer: Is it running at the right speed? If it's not, the system does a long beep and a short beep. The code actually jumps to the same point as for the error message for the 8259, above. This is unfortunate, as it would have been nice if IBM could have added eight more bytes of code so the 8253 could have a different error message from the 8259.

6. POST performs a checksum test on the BASIC ROM. If the ROM fails, there's a long and a short beep, and then a halt. Again, this is a bit shortsighted. We can live without BASIC, so locking up the computer seems extreme.

VIDEO

7. POST tests the video. If the 6845 video controller isn't present (which either means no video card or a defective 6845), there is one long and two short beeps. *& screen message showing video card type.*

EXPANSION CARDS

8. POST asks installed adapters if they must initialize themselves. Common examples are hard disk controllers, EGA, and LAN adapters. If the boards respond *yes,* POST lets them initialize. When they finish, POST returns to BIOS startup.

9. POST tests the CRT interface lines. If horizontal and vertical sweep don't appear, there are two long beeps and a short one. If everything is okay, the cursor on the PC will blink.

RAM

10. POST tests the memory and all system RAM.

KEYBOARD

11. POST tests the keyboard. Stuck keys are detected here. Any keyboard problems are indicated by a 301 code on the screen followed by a short beep. The system is not halted.

12. POST tests the cassette interface. If there are problems, it shows code 131 and sounds a short beep. It doesn't halt the system.

FLOPPY

13. POST tests the diskette adapter and drive A; and attempts to reset the drive and activate the drive motor. If problems appear, it shows code 601 and sounds a short beep. Goes to Cassette BASIC.

14. POST determines how many printers, serial ports, game ports, and so on are attached. It issues a short beep, loads the boot record, and transfers control to it.

from boot disc

ROM-Based Diagnostics

Some firms (Supersoft and Windsor Technology, in particular) offer a diagnostic tool that works even when the system won't boot. Such a tool is called a *ROM-based diagnostic.* Generally, you remove the BIOS ROM and replace it with a "miniboard" containing a ROM and some support electronics. This miniboard allows the diagnostic to boot the system and do chip-specific tests; it costs about $300. Separate ROMs are required for AT- and PC-class machines.

Award Software (the folks who write the AWARD BIOS that some clones use) makes a plug-in diagnostic board called the POST Card. Another company, Ultra-X, makes a similar product called RACER (Real-time AT/XT Computer Equipment Repair); see Appendix A for particulars. These tools are nice to have, but I'd caution anyone thinking of buying one: They're only of value if you intend to use the information they give.

You have to be willing and able to remove and replace components on the system board, and here we're talking about soldering.

On the other hand, if such a tool is free, it might be handy. Zenith owners needn't hunt around for a diagnostic disk: Zenith diagnostics are built into the machine. Ctrl-Alt-Ins gets them going.

IBM Diagnostic Error Codes

If you've got a true-Blue IBM computer emitting scary-looking error codes, don't buy the expensive IBM manual that lists what they mean. Tables 5.1 and 5.2 tell you what the IBM audio and video diagnostic codes mean. There are POST diagnostic codes in Table 5.2 also.

TABLE 5.1: POST Audio Messages

SIGNAL	PROBABLE CAUSE
No beep, nothing happens	Power supply bad or not plugged in
Continuous beep	Power supply bad
Repeating short beep	Power supply bad
1 long beep, 1 short beep	System board
1 long, 2 short beeps	Failure or lack of display adapter/cable
1 short beep, blank screen	Failure or lack of display adapter/cable
1 short beep, no boot	Floppy drive adapter failure

TABLE 5.2: IBM Hardware Diagnostics/POST Messages

CODE	DESCRIPTION
01x	Undetermined problem errors
02x	Power supply errors
1xx	System board errors
101	Interrupt failure
102	Timer failure
103	Timer interrupt failure

TABLE 5.2: IBM Hardware Diagnostics/POST Messages

CODE	DESCRIPTION
104	Protected mode failure
105	Last 804 command not accepted
106	Converting logic test
107	Hot NMI test
108	Timer bus test
109	Direct Memory Access test error
121	Unexpected hardware interrupts occurred
131	Cassette wrap test failed
161	AT battery failure
162	AT setup info incorrect (rerun SETUP)
163	Time and date not set (run SETUP)
164	Memory size error (run SETUP)
165	PS/2 does not know how to configure board
199	User-indicated configuration not correct
2xx	Main memory (RAM) errors
201	Memory test failed
202	Memory address error*
203	Memory address error*
3xx	Keyboard errors
301	Keyboard error. If followed by a number, the number is the scan code of the key in question.
302	User-indicated error from keyboard test or AT keylock locked
303	Keyboard or system unit error
304	CMOS doesn't match system

TABLE 5.2: IBM Hardware Diagnostics/POST Messages (continued)

CODE	DESCRIPTION
4xx	Monochrome monitor errors
401	Adapter memory, horizontal sync frequency test, or video test failure
408	User-indicated display attributes failure
416	User-indicated character set failure
424	User-indicated 80×25 mode failure
432	Parallel port test failed
5xx	Color monitor errors
501	Color adapter memory, horizontal sync frequency test, or video test failure
508	User-indicated display attributes failure
516	User-indicated character set failure
524	User-indicated 80×25 mode failure
532	User-indicated 40×25 mode failure
540	User-indicated 320×200 mode failure
548	User-indicated 640×200 mode failure
6xx	Diskette drive/controller failures
601	Adapter or drive failed POST
602	Diskette test failed: boot record not valid
606	Diskette verify function failed
607	Write-protected diskette
608	Bad command diskette status returned
610	Diskette initialization failed
611	Timeout
612	Bad NEC chip on diskette controller
613	Adapter failed DMA test

TROUBLESHOOTING PROBLEMS

TABLE 5.2: IBM Hardware Diagnostics/POST Messages (continued)

CODE	DESCRIPTION
621	Bad seek
622	Bad CRC found
623	Record not found
624	Bad address mark
625	Bad NEC seek
626	Diskette data compare error
7xx	8087 or 80287 math coprocessor errors
9xx	Printer adapter errors
1101	Asynchronous (RS232) adapter failure (COM1)
1201	Asynchronous (RS232) adapter failure (COM2)
13xx	Game port failure
1301	Adapter test failed
1302	Joystick test failed
14xx	Printer errors
1401	Printer test failed
1402	Dot-matrix printer test failed
15xx	SDLC adapter (mainframe connection) failures
1510	Failure of 8255 port B
1511	Failure of 8255 port A
1512	Failure of 8255 port C
1513	8253 timer 1 did not reach terminal count
1514	8253 timer 1 stuck on
1515	8253 timer 0 did not reach terminal count
1516	8253 timer 0 stuck on
1517	8253 timer 2 did not reach terminal count
1518	8253 timer 2 stuck on

TABLE 5.2: IBM Hardware Diagnostics/POST Messages (continued)

CODE	DESCRIPTION
1519	8273 port B error
1520	8273 port A error
1521	8273 command/read timeout
1522	Interrupt level 4 failure
1523	Ring Indicate stuck on
1524	Receive clock stuck on
1525	Transmit clock stuck on
1526	Test Indicate stuck on
1527	Ring Indicate not on
1528	Receive clock not on
1529	Transmit clock not on
1531	Data Set Ready not on
1530	Test Indicate not on
1532	Carrier Detect not on
1533	Clear To Send not on
1534	Data Set Read stuck on
1536	Clear to Send stuck on
1537	Level 3 interrupt failure
1538	Receive interrupt results error
1539	Wrap data miscompare
1540	DMA channel 1 error
1541	Error in 8273 error check or status reporting
1547	Stray interrupt level 4
1548	Stray interrupt level 3
1549	Interrupt presentation sequence timeout
16xx	Terminal emulation errors (32xx, 5520, 525x)

TROUBLESHOOTING PROBLEMS

TABLE 5.2: IBM Hardware Diagnostics/POST Messages (continued)

CODE	DESCRIPTION
17xx	Hard disk/disk controller errors
1701	POST error
1702	Adapter failure
1703	Drive failure
1704	Drive or adapter failure: cannot be determined
1780	Drive 0 failure (drive C)
1781	Drive 1 failure (drive D)
1782	Adapter failure
1790	Drive 0 failure (couldn't read the LAST cylinder—probable misspecified drive)
1791	Drive 1 failure
18xx	Expansion chassis failures
1801	POST error code
1810	Extender card failure
1811	Extender card failure
1816	Extender card failure
1820	Receiver card failure
1821	Receiver card failure
1812	Address or wait state failure
1813	Address or wait state failure
1819	Wait Request switch set incorrectly
19xx	3270 PC communications controller failures
20xx	BSC adapter (mainframe connection) failures
2010	Failure of 8255 port B
2011	Failure of 8255 port A
2012	Failure of 8255 port C

TABLE 5.2: IBM Hardware Diagnostics/POST Messages (continued)

CODE	DESCRIPTION
2013	8253 timer 1 did not reach terminal count
2014	8253 timer 1 stuck on
2015	8253 timer 0 did not reach terminal count
2016	8253 timer 0 stuck on
2017	8253 timer 2 did not reach terminal count
2018	8253 timer 2 stuck on
2019	8273 port B error
2020	8273 port A error
2021	8273 command/read timeout
2022	Interrupt level 4 failure
2023	Ring Indicate stuck on
2024	Receive clock stuck on
2025	Transmit clock stuck on
2026	Test Indicate stuck on
2027	Ring Indicate not on
2028	Receive clock not on
2029	Transmit clock not on
2031	Data Set Ready not on
2030	Test Indicate not on
2032	Carrier Detect not on
2033	Clear to Send not on
2034	Data Set Read stuck on
2036	Clear to Send stuck on
2037	Level 3 interrupt failure
2038	Receive interrupt results error
2039	Wrap data miscompare

TABLE 5.2: IBM Hardware Diagnostics/POST Messages (continued)

CODE	DESCRIPTION
2040	DMA channel 1 error
2041	Error in 8273 error check or status reporting
2047	Stray interrupt level 4
2048	Stray interrupt level 3
2049	Interrupt presentation sequence timeout
21xx	Alternate BSC (Binary Synchronous Communications) adapter failures
2110–49	Same as above, but with 21 prefix rather than 20
2201	PC wiring cluster adapter failure
2401	EGA failure
2901	Color dot matrix failures
3301	Compact printer failures

NOTE: *See Chapter 8 for how to decode these error messages

Third-Party Diagnostic Software In addition to the Post and the diagnostic software offered by PC hardware vendors, there is also an entire portion of the software business whose major occupation is in writing and marketing diagnostic software. The main functions of these programs are the following:

- **Inventory**. These programs display an inventory of what they can detect in your system. That can be useful not as inventory of itself; its greater value is in inventorying what the system can *see*. If you know darn well that you installed that mouse interface, but it doesn't show up on the system inventory, then you've got a problem. Before looking too hard for the answer, however, ask yourself first: Is the driver for the mouse loaded? Diagnostic programs, like DOS and applications programs, usually can't detect an unusual piece of hardware unless the driver for that program is loaded.

- **Burn-in**. When you first get a computer, it's common to "burn it in." This means to run it continuously for at least three days, running some kind of diagnostic software over and over again. Simple diagnostics are no good for this kind of thing for two reasons.

  First, most simple diagnostics insist on informing you of any errors, then *requiring* you to press a key to acknowledge that you've seen the error message. Higher-quality diagnostic programs allow you to run the diagnostic in a "logging" mode whereby any error messages are saved to a logging file, and do not require confirmation of an error.

  Second, good diagnostics let you run the diagnostic in a "continuous" mode, whereby it runs over and over and over until you tell it to stop. Burn-in is not an unimportant step, so don't ignore it! Of the last ten computers I've installed, two didn't fail until after four days of constant testing. If I'd not done a burn-in on it, I probably would have ended up with mysterious error appearing at a no doubt inopportune time (Mr. Murphy and his law seem to have taken up residence in my office).

- **Interrupt/DMA/input/output address summary**. As you'll learn in the next chapter, the hardest thing about installing a new circuit board is adjusting some things called the "input/output port address," the "DMA channel," the "IRQ level," and the "ROM address." (Don't sweat about what they are—it's all explained in the next chapter.) The reason that you adjust these things is to make sure that they don't conflict with the port/DMA/IRQ/ROM of any other boards. For example, if you're putting a board in a system, and that board must use either interrupt number 5 or interrupt number 7, but there's already a board in your system that uses interrupt number 7, then you can't let the new board use interrupt number 7. But the question arises, how do you find out what interrupts are currently in use on your system? Diagnostic programs *try* to report these things. I say "try" because they unfortunately can't be trusted in this task, not due to inadequacies on the part of their programmers but because of a simple fact: There's no way to reliably detect ports, DMAs, IRQs, or ROM addresses. (How *do* you find out this information? The only reliable way is to consult the documentation on the boards that are already in your system—more on this, again, in the next chapter.)

- **Diagnostics**. A diagnostic program should provide you with a way to give your hardware a "workout." It will test your computer's memory thoroughly, test every possible data pattern on your hard disk, run your serial port at its maximum speed—in short, a good diagnostic program should be a sort of cybernetic boot camp for your computer.

- **Setup**. Some of these programs do things more associated with setup responsibilities than diagnostic ones. For example, most of these programs will low-level format a hard disk, an important step in setting up an older type of hard disk. Others may have a built-in system setup program that sets up the CMOS chip in a computer.

If you read those bullets carefully, you no doubt noticed a lot of *should*s, as in "a good diagnostic program should..." All the equivocation had a purpose, believe me: Most diagnostic programs are junk. Look carefully before you spend the ton of money that you can easily spend on a diagnostic package.

The science fiction author Theodore Sturgeon is said to have been approached by a literary critic who said, "Ted, you write such good stuff; why do you waste your time writing science fiction?" Sturgeon asked, "What's wrong with science fiction?" The critic answered, "Ninety percent of science fiction is crap." [Well, he didn't say "crap," but this book is rated for general audiences.] Sturgeon is reported to have replied archly, "Ninety percent of *everything* is crap." I'm afraid that this truism, dubbed "Sturgeon's Law" by generations of science-fiction fans, applies well to the diagnostics world. Let me then not waste ink beating up on the chaff; let's look at the wheat.

- **Checkit**, from Touchstone Software. Checkit is a nice, inexpensive (compared to most diagnostic programs) package that is largely inexpensive because it leaves out some of the hardware that you need to do a system checkout. That's not meant to be a negative assessment; I like Checkit and use it quite a bit. But Checkit does not include a few diagnostic tools, namely (1) a loopback plug for the parallel port, (2) a loopback plug for the serial port, or (3) a digital diagnostic test disk for the floppy drive. My guess as to *why*

they didn't include those things is that they can be found elsewhere, and Touchstone wanted to offer an inexpensive package—
adding the extra doodads can double the price. There're two
things that I really like about Checkit: It's got a good set of
motherboard checkout routines (DMA, timer, IRQ, and the
rest) as well as one of the better memory testers.

- **QAPlus** is another good package in the same market niche as
  Checkit. No loopbacks or other doodads, just a good system inventory and memory tester.

- **PC-Technician** is an industrial-strength package from Windsor
  Technologies.

    I first looked at PC-Technician back in 1988, and I must
  truthfully say that I didn't think much of it then. But it's quickly
  matured into a nice general inventory/setup/deep-diagnostic
  routine. It's a bit pricier than the previous two—$395 when last I
  checked—but it's a complete package. There're the test disks, the
  loopbacks, a nice manual, and a carrying case with enough space
  for your tools. (Just make sure you don't put any magnetic screwdrivers next to the disks in the case!) Windsor also sells a program
  that will put your PC printer through its paces, as well as one with
  a plug-in BIOS POST code checker like the ones discussed elsewhere in this section. The features that I like best about PC-Technician are the memory test—again, a good one in the same league
  as QAPlus's and Checkit's—as well as the serial and parallel tests.

- **DisplayMate**, from Sonera Technologies, only checks one thing—
  your display. But it does an extremely thorough job, testing aspects of your monitor that you probably didn't even realize were
  testable—"pincushioning," for example. The accompanying manual is a tutorial on monitor problems and solutions. It won't test
  your memory or your printer, but it deserves a place on your
  diagnostic shelf.

- **SpinRite** from Gibson Research ($99) will be discussed in the
  disk chapters, but I mention it here because it's a disk diagnostic
  that you should keep in your toolkit; it's one of the most comprehensive disk testers around. Better yet, unlike most diagnostic

programs, it can do more than *detect* trouble—it can often head trouble off.

- **MicroScope** from Micro 2000 has received a fair amount of press for one reason, and it's not even a diagnostic reason. Unlike every other hard disk low-level formatter I've ever seen (I'll explain low-level formatting in the hard disk chapters), MicroScope can low-level format a class of hard disks called Intelligent Drive Electronics (IDE) drives. That's something of a feat—one that I take my hat off to Micro 2000 for—but the program has very little worth as a diagnostic program. I mention it in this section, however, as it *is* sold as a diagnostic program. It is a bit expensive ($395) for one function, but if you find yourself having to wipe data irretrievably from IDE drivers, perhaps for reasons of security, then this deserves a look.

One word of advice when running a diagnostic: Although I told you to load all drivers before running the diagnostic, *don't* run your memory manager; it just confuses a memory test. As I've suggested, you can spend a *lot* of money on these programs, so it's a good idea to take advantage of the option that many computer dealers today provide whereby you can buy software and return it within a few weeks.

Under the Hood: Troubleshooting Step 7

Assuming you've performed steps 1 to 6, you might actually have a circuit board problem. Many circuit board problems can be handled simply and without any fancy equipment. Step 7 is just to:

- Take the PC apart
- Clean any connectors with an artist's eraser or connector cleaner
- Push all socketed chips back into their sockets
- Reassemble the PC

As we saw in Chapter 4 on preventive maintenance, edge connectors get dirty and make circuit boards fail. Sometimes "dead" boards will do a Lazarus if you clean their edge connectors.

If you examine most circuit boards, you'll see that most chips are soldered right onto the board. Soldering is a great technique for mass-producing electronic components. The downside is that when you must fix soldered components, you must first de-solder the components. This isn't much fun, and most people don't have soldering skills.

Not all chips are soldered to boards, however. Some are put in *sockets*. A typical board might have thirty soldered chips and four socketed ones. Chips are socketed either because they've been voted "most likely to fail"; or because the designer wanted to put off a decision until the last minute; or because the chip will likely have to be replaced periodically, because it contains software that changes over time—remember ROMs? So socketing chips makes our jobs as troubleshooters easier.

On the other hand, heating and cooling of systems make these socketed chips "creep" out of their sockets, producing the *chip creep* mentioned in the last chapter. That's why you should push socketed chips back into their sockets when inspecting a board for whatever reason. One particularly persnickety tech support person I know actually takes the socketed chips out of their sockets, cleans their chip legs with connector cleaner, and *then* puts the chips back in the sockets.

This should be obvious, but let me point it out anyway. Don't push *soldered* chips. The best that it can do is nothing. The worst it can do is to damage a board, and maybe a chip. When you push socketed chips back into a board, be sure you're supporting the back of the board. If you just put a board on a table and push down on the chips, you might end up bending and damaging the board.

I know advice like "take it apart, clean the connectors, push the chips back in the sockets, and reassemble" doesn't sound very dazzling, but, darn it, *it works!* Buying a board to replace a defective one is a pretty rare event for me as a troubleshooter, and I don't do much soldering. Besides, if you're working on someone else's machine, it impresses the people whose machines you're fixing; basically, all they see you do is touch the boards. Eventually, you'll get a reputation as a person who can just lay hands upon the board and make it whole!

Documenting Trouble Calls

If you're a professional troubleshooter (and even if you're not), one of the biggest favors you can do for yourself is to keep a log of trouble calls, problems, and solutions for the following reasons:

- It provides a record of your contribution to the organization.

- It can be used to justify requests for equipment or personnel.

- It allows you to track trends so you can anticipate future problems, either with particular individuals ("Mr. *X* calls us whenever he can't figure out how to turn the printer on") or situations ("We can expect a call on files called *Y* from everyone with WordPerfect").

- Documented problems and solutions can serve as an excellent training tool for new troubleshooters.

If you're *not* a professional troubleshooter, keep a log of computer fixes anyway. That way, when you solve something *once,* you have the information to solve it quickly *again.*

Whether you use a computerized database or just paper sheets, you should have a method for documenting trouble calls. Here are a few things that should be on each trouble report:

- Trouble report ID#

- Preliminary information:

  Who reported the trouble?

  When was the trouble reported?

  How was it reported (electronic mail, phone, walk-in)?

  Is it related to a previous trouble call? What was the trouble report ID#?

  Where was the trouble reported?

  What was the specific complaint?

  Is this repeatable? Will your client be able to duplicate the problem before a technician's eyes?

When did this first appear?

What was done differently between the time before and after the problem appeared (if anything)?

Does it occur periodically? When?

- On-site information:

    Comments on PC environment: power, temperature, others

    Technician's observation of trouble

    Actions taken onsite

- If the PC was taken to the shop:

    The date it was brought in

    The actions taken

    The result of these actions

    Was the PC returned to the client? On what date?

- Summary information/keywords:

    Hardware, software, and/or user problem?

    If software, what package or packages?

    If hardware, what device or devices?

CHAPTER

6

Installing New Circuit Boards (without Creating New Problems)

CIRCUIT boards and chips are fairly reliable, so long as you keep them above water and don't subject them to the old 1,000-volt torture test. Most boards you handle won't be defective. Much more often you'll be upgrading existing machines, like replacing a video board with a faster, more powerful one or adding a LAN board to a machine that isn't yet on your company's network.

Installing a new circuit board involves:

- Configuration. Make sure the board and the rest of the system communicate.

- Installation. Put it in the system and make sure the cables are all on correctly.

- Testing. Weed out the boards that either don't work or soon will stop working.

Installation looks scary the first time you see it, but it's really a snap once you wend your way through the terminology. Are you the kind of person who always flips past the part of the manual that talks about DMA, IRQ, ROM addresses, and the like? Stick around. The concepts are easy (and essential). It's only the names that are off-putting.

Configuring New Circuit Boards

Most circuit boards are fully functional when you take them out of the box. But most circuit boards seem not to work when you install them in a PC. Why? The main reason is that the new board may *conflict* with existing boards or, more specifically, some resource on the board.

Configuration consists of:

- Resolving device conflicts
- Providing software support (BIOS and/or device drivers)

Configuration involves setting jumpers or DIP switches to select exactly the services the expansion board will provide. Here are some examples of configuration:

- Tell an expansion board how much memory is on the board
- Tell a serial port whether it's COM1: or COM2:
- Tell a printer port whether it's LPT1, LPT2, or LPT3
- Select DMA channels on a board (more on this later)
- Select IRQ lines on a board (ditto)
- Select the I/O address on a board (ditto)

In many cases, the board is preconfigured at the factory to the correct settings, but not always. It's hard for the manufacturer to know what the proper settings should be for four factors: I/O addresses, DMA channels, IRQ lines, and ROM addresses.

Examples: Real-Life Configuration Conflicts

Getting down to brass tacks, here are a few examples of installation woes.

1. You install an internal modem in a PC with a floppy disk controller, color graphics board, and multifunction board. The modem refuses to work. A little testing shows that the serial port, which *used* to work, now doesn't work either. What do you do?

2. You install a multifunction board in a computer with a floppy disk controller and a generic monochrome graphics card. The printer won't work. What do you do?

3. You install a Lotus/Intel/Microsoft expanded memory board in an XT, and you notice the next time you boot up that the clock/calendar has been reset to January 1, 1980. What do you do?

Each of these problems is caused by *resource conflicts*. Here's what caused these conflicts.

In the first case, both the serial port on the multifunction board and the modem sought to be recognized by the computer as COM1, communications port number 1. The basic PC-compatible system can support two serial ports, named COM1 and COM2.

(You may be thinking, "Wait a minute—can't you support *four* COM ports under DOS 3.3 and later?" This is a common misconception, so let me take a minute and clarify that in most cases you're still stuck with two COM ports. First, the question of whether or not *DOS* supports your COM port is fairly irrelevant, as most software that uses the COM port—communications software, mouse drivers, and the like—bypasses DOS altogether, making DOS's opinion in the matter fairly unimportant. Second, and more important, COM ports require an "interrupt" or "IRQ" line, something that I'm about to explain. IRQ lines are important here because there are only two allocated to serial ports—originally one for COM1, and another for COM2. To use COM3, you must *steal* COM1's serial port. To use COM4, you must steal COM2's serial port. Most uses of the serial ports require the interrupt, so the practical upshot is that you can *either* have COM1 or COM3, and you can either have COM2 or COM4.)

A circuit board can call itself COM1 or COM2. But in this case, *two* circuit boards claimed to be COM1. As a result, neither would work. The answer is to convince one of the boards to be the other communications address, COM2.

Before we go on to the next case, I hear you asking, "*How* do I convince one of the boards to be COM2?" The answer is the basis of configuration: You move a DIP switch, a jumper, or (on PS/2 machines) run a program to reassign the board's function from COM1 to COM2. (I'll have more to say about this in a minute, but I didn't want to leave you hanging.)

Figure 6.1 shows examples of a jumper and a DIP switch. Figure 6.2 provides a detailed look at jumpers. Figure 6.3 shows DIP switches on an expansion board.

On some boards, you have something that looks like a striped chip called a *jumper pack* (see Figure 6.4). It's basically several wires in a chip package. You break some wires and leave others unbroken so as to enable or disable board functions. For example, IBM uses one on their RS-232 boards to select whether the board is COM1 or COM2 (see Figure 6.5). There are eight bands: four are broken, four left whole. To move from COM1 to COM2 or vice versa, remove the jumper pack, rotate it, and replace it.

FIGURE 6.1

Jumper and DIP example

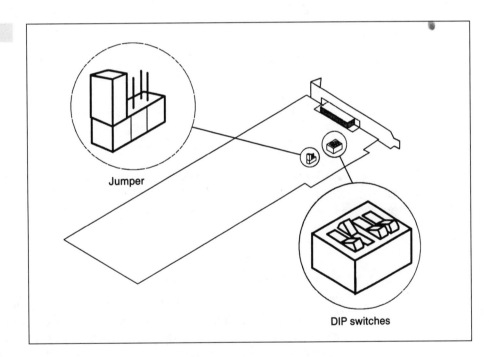

FIGURE 6.2

Jumpers and how they work

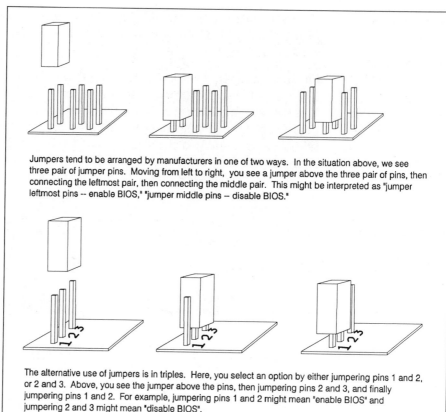

Jumpers tend to be arranged by manufacturers in one of two ways. In the situation above, we see three pair of jumper pins. Moving from left to right, you see a jumper above the three pair of pins, then connecting the leftmost pair, then connecting the middle pair. This might be interpreted as "jumper leftmost pins -- enable BIOS," "jumper middle pins -- disable BIOS."

The alternative use of jumpers is in triples. Here, you select an option by either jumpering pins 1 and 2, or 2 and 3. Above, you see the jumper above the pins, then jumpering pins 2 and 3, and finally jumpering pins 1 and 2. For example, jumpering pins 1 and 2 might mean "enable BIOS" and jumpering 2 and 3 might mean "disable BIOS".

A Clue to Device Conflicts

If you've installed a new board and it doesn't work, don't just pull it out. Test the rest of the system. Does something that worked yesterday not work today? That's your clue that the board is probably not broken, but rather is conflicting with something; and you now know with what it's conflicting, so it's easier to track down exactly what you've got to change to make the thing work.

In the second sample configuration conflict described above, both the multifunction board and the monochrome graphics board had a parallel

FIGURE 6.3

DIP switches on
expansion board

port, both trying to be recognized by the PC as LPT1 (parallel printer port 1). Again, we're faced with a scarce resource. The PC can only recognize three parallel ports: LPT1, LPT2, and LPT3. The answer is to either convince one of the ports to be LPT2 or LPT3, or perhaps to disable it altogether. You might choose to disable it if you had no need for two printer ports.

The third example described above is a bit more "advanced" a topic, but it illustrates the same problem. In this case, the expanded memory board and the clock/calendar tried to talk to the CPU chip via the same input/output address, called an *I/O address*. The answer, as before, is to convince one of the boards to use a different I/O address. (Again, the answer to "how?" is coming.)

Resolving Device Conflicts

The simplest kind of installation problem is a conflict on the easy stuff, like COM1 or LPT1. In most cases, you can't have two video boards, as they'll stomp all over each other's video, ROM, and the like. You usually

FIGURE 6.4

Board detail showing jumper

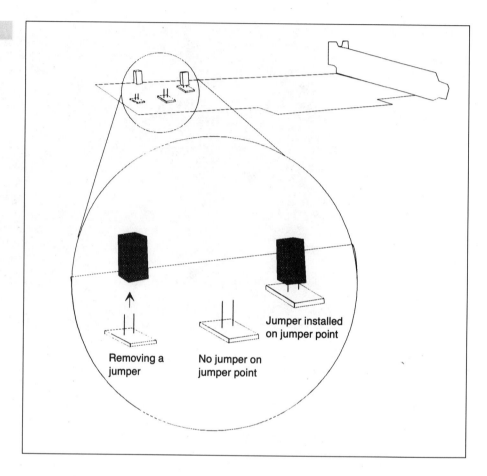

Removing a jumper

No jumper on jumper point

Jumper installed on jumper point

can't get away with two floppy controllers for the same reason. COMs and LPTs can conflict in the same way, except you are allowed multiple COMs and LPTs. You are *not*, however, allowed multiple COM1s.

Again, a COM or LPT conflict arises because two boards have the same COM or LPT name. If two boards both have a COM1 on them, move a jumper or DIP switch to change one of them to COM2, or disable the COM function altogether. How do you know what switch to move? Look at the documentation. People commonly bring me a circuit board and say, "What does this do?," pointing to a jumper. I just shrug my shoulders. There's no way to know without the documentation, so remember to become a documentation packrat.

FIGURE 6.5

IBM RS-232 board
showing jumper pack

FIGURE 6.5

IBM RS-232 board
showing jumper pack

A Word about DIP Switches and POS

Since we're discussing configuration, here are few points about DIP switches. (Figure 6.6 shows two types of DIP switches.)

First, not all DIP switches say ON or OFF. Some say OPEN or CLOSED: If they do, just remember that OPEN is equivalent to OFF and CLOSED is equivalent to ON. Sometimes they say 1, which corresponds to ON, or 0, which corresponds to OFF. Sometimes (grrrr...) they don't say anything at all. In this case, play around with them until you've figured out their ON/OFF positions, and then write them in your notebook.

Second, if you've set the switches correctly but the PC refuses to recognize the settings, be aware that sometimes DIP switches are defective. (It has happened to me.) To test this, remove the system board and test the switches for continuity with an ohmmeter.

FIGURE 6.6

Types of DIP switches

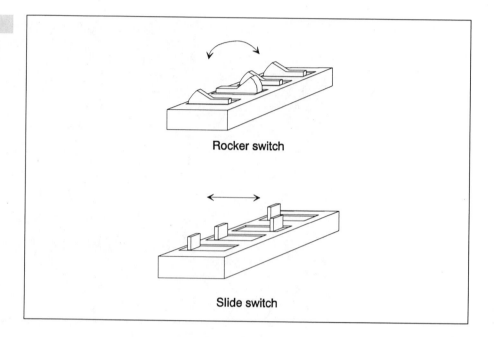

Rocker switch

Slide switch

Finally, remember that sometimes manufacturers mislabel DIP switches or install them upside-down. It *does* happen—rarely, but it happens.

By the way, PS/2 owners will grapple with configuration also, but they'll be spared DIP switches and jumpers. PS/2 expansion boards are intended to do all that with software. Micro Channel machines have a neat feature called *POS* (Programmable Option Select) that allows you to reconfigure a board without removing it or setting switches. I'll discuss this more later.

Can You Have JUST the LPT2 Port?

Here's a real PC configuration brainteaser. I have a PC with *only one* parallel port, which I configured as LPT2. There *is* no LPT1 in this machine. I boot it up. Once the system is running, what LPT port do I have on my system?

Answer: LPT1.

PCs have a strange feature when it comes to parallel ports. On bootup, the BIOS checks the LPTs. If there is no LPT1, it looks for an LPT2 or LPT3. If you've got an LPT2 but no LPT1, it actually converts the LPT2 to an LPT1. This is, of course, a *software* adjustment. I'll repeat: It's flat impossible to have an LPT2 without an LPT1. If you *do* install an LPT2 without LPT1, the LPT2 gets made into an LPT1 on bootup.

This is a nice feature. I just wish the documentation had *told* me about it. You see, it was late one night, and—oh, heck, I don't even want to talk about it. Now *you* know.

Next Step: I/O Addresses, DMA, IRQ, ROM Addresses

If all you do is install internal modems, you probably don't need this section. But there are more possible conflicts in your system—problems you can experience when you install things like LAN boards, scanner interface cards, 3270 boards, mouse interfaces, or basically anything that wasn't offered with the original IBM PC.

These four conflicts are

- I/O addresses—the addresses the circuit board uses to communicate with the CPU.

- DMA channels. They're used to speed up I/O to and from the system's memory, but your system is severely limited in how many boards can be hooked up to use DMA.

- IRQ levels. Hardware must interrupt the CPU to force it to service these in some time-critical fashion.

- ROM addresses. Many boards include some of their low-level control software in ROM. The ROM requires a memory address, which cannot conflict with other ROMs or any RAM in the system.

- RAM buffers. Some add-in cards maintain a little (8–64K) RAM on board to hold data temporarily. That RAM should not conflict with other RAM or ROM in your system.

Here's the scoop on these obscure-sounding resources.

I/O Addresses

How is information actually transferred from a peripheral like a serial port to the microprocessor? You know that CPUs have a range of memory addresses; well, there's also something similar called an *input/output address,* or *I/O address.* Much as the CPU can read and write memory addresses, it can also read and write these I/O addresses.

Each device that must communicate with the 8088 gets assigned an I/O address or, more likely, a range of addresses. This address cannot be used by any other device. I'll steal an old analogy here. Think of I/O addresses as being like post office boxes. Say the keyboard has PO Box 200. When the keyboard has data for the system, it puts the data in box 200. When the CPU wants to read the keyboard, it looks in box 200. *Box 200* is, in a very real sense, a better definition of *keyboard* from the CPU's point of view than is the keyboard itself. Table 6.1 shows the probable addresses for your machines.

TABLE 6.1: Common I/O Address Uses in PCs

HEX ADDRESS RANGE	USER
00–0F	DMA Controller 8237 #1
20–21	Programmable Interrupt Controller 8259A #1
40–43	Timer 8253
60–63	8255 Peripheral Controller (XT only)
60–64	Keyboard Controller (AT only) 8742
70–71	Setup RAM Access Address (AT only)
80–8F	DMA Page Registers
A0–A1	Programmable Interrupt Controller #2 8259 (AT only)
A0–AF	NMI Mask Register (XT only)
C0–DF	8237 DMA Controller #2 (AT only)
F0–FF	Math Coprocessor (AT only)

TABLE 6.1: Common I/O Address Uses in PCs (continued)

HEX ADDRESS RANGE	USER
1F0–1F8	Hard Disk Controller (AT only)
200–20F	Joystick Controller
210–217	Expansion Chassis
238–23B	Bus Mouse
23C–23F	Alt. Bus Mouse
258	Expanded Memory (LIM) Board
278–27F	LPT2
2B0–2DF	EGA
2E0–2E7	GPIB (AT only)
2E8–2EF	COM4 Serial Port
2F8–2FF	COM2 Serial Port
300–30F	Ethernet LAN Board
300–31F	Prototype Card
320–32F	Hard Disk Controller (XT only)
330–337	Bernoulli Box Controller
378–37F	LPT1 Printer Port
380–38F	SDLC Card
3A0–3AF	BSC Card
3B0–3BF	Monochrome Adapter
3BC–3BF	LPT3
3D0–3DF	Color/Graphics Adapter
3E8–3EF	COM3 Serial Port
3F0–3F7	Floppy Disk Controller
3F8–3FF	COM1 Serial Port

Now you can understand I/O address conflicts. Suppose you run a company called ABC Electronics that makes PC upgrade stuff. You come out with a device that IBM doesn't offer for the IBM PC—a clock/calendar, say. You need to assign this clock an address. IBM hasn't assigned an I/O address to the clock/calendar function for the PC (again, see Table 6.1), so you get to pick one. It would be monstrously stupid to create the clock to conflict with the address of a common peripheral like COM1, so you would pick one of the addresses IBM left unassigned—say you pick address 250. You'll sell lots of clocks, and you'll be fat and happy, and so will your users.

Down the street, XYZ Electronics, a competitor, is working on a mouse interface board. IBM hasn't assigned a mouse interface address for the PC, so XYZ just picks an address out of the "unassigned" range. Through an unfortunate coincidence, they pick address 250, and sell *lots* of mice and mouse boards.

One day, a customer puts your board using address 250 into the same machine as the XYZ board, also using address 250. The customer loads software to read the clock, as well as software to interact with the mouse, not realizing what's about to happen. The first time the machine tries to read the clock, it goes to address 250 to read the date. But the mouse (unbeknownst to the computer) has just dumped some data in address 250. The clock program reads the data and tells you that the date is August 2031, or something like that.

What you basically have at this point is a mouse that tells time, which isn't going to work reliably. The answer is to change the I/O address (examples coming up soon!).

This is where the jumpers and DIP switches come in. Realizing that they cannot know what addresses are currently in use on your computer, manufacturers give you a choice of possible addresses. Moving the jumpers or DIP switches allows the choice. Now, you probably won't have a clue which DIP switches do what without the documentation, so be sure to hang on to any switch-setting documentation you have.

Note: When the I/O addresses are changed, the software usually must be notified of these changes. You might not be able to resolve I/O address conflicts, as not all boards even give you the chance to change I/O addresses. It's hard to believe, but some boards are hard-wired to use only one I/O address range. I had a LIM board that conflicted with a clock/calendar, but unfortunately neither board gave me a chance to change the I/O address. One board had to be removed—the conflict couldn't be resolved any other way.

You've seen that the PC only implements 1024 addresses. The bottom 256 (hex locations 000 to 0FF) are only available to components on the system board. Plug-in expansion boards must use the 768 top locations (hex 100 to 3FF). Therefore, if they're designed properly, expansion boards will only allow you to set your I/O addresses somewhere between 100 hex and 3FF hex.

If troubleshooting is your job, it's probably a good idea to keep a roster of PCs and busy I/O addresses. Table 6.1 also tells the common addresses taken up on PCs.

DMA Channels

Transferring data from a device into the computer via the CPU can be very slow, so some devices have the power to write data into the computer memory directly, without CPU intervention. This is called *DMA,* or Direct Memory Access. The PC has a single DMA controller chip, the 8237. It allows up to four DMA channels. One—channel 0—is required for dynamic memory refresh.

There are two kinds of memory: *dynamic* and *static.* "Dynamic memory" sounds better than static, but it isn't. When you tell a static RAM something, it remembers it until you turn off the power or change it. Dynamic RAMs, on the other hand, forget whatever you tell them within four milliseconds. The PC is designed to drop everything and do a RAM refresh every 3.86 milliseconds. This takes five clocks out of every 72, or about seven percent of the PC's time. Of course, if the CPU is doing a lot of INs, OUTs, internal calculations, or the like, you don't notice the slowdown, as the whole idea of DMA is to work in parallel with the CPU.

Wouldn't static RAMs make a slightly faster computer? Yes, but they're more costly; Dell Computing (PCs Limited) used them in their 16-MHz 386 machine. The floppy disk controller usually employs channel 2. The hard disk controller uses channel 1. In general, 3 is unused. On AT-type machines, there's on-board circuitry that refreshes the memory and the hard disk doesn't use DMA, so channels 0 and 1 are available *usually*—I say usually because you'll sometimes see an exception.

AT-type machines (those with 16-bit bus slots) have two DMA controllers, and thus eight DMA channels to the XT's four. Note that not all AT clones have this second DMA controller. *Four DMA channels are just plain not enough,* so don't even think of buying a 286/386/486 without eight DMA channels.

Notice that this implies you have only *one* free DMA channel on your average XT-type machine. AT-types have the 16-bit bus and extra DMA channels, but your circuit board must be a 16-bit board to use the extra DMA channels.

Some well-designed boards recognize that, while DMA makes boards fast, a given system may not have *any* DMA channels available. So these boards offer you the chance to disable DMA and just force all data to go through the CPU. It's not the greatest thing in the world, because it is slower, but at least it makes the board work.

So, in summary, if you have an expansion board that needs a DMA channel, the only one available on the 8-bit boards is generally DMA channel 3. If you're installing a 16-bit board, try whenever possible to use the extra 16-bit–only DMAs, channels 4 through 7, to leave room for the 8-bit boards in your system. If you're out of DMAs, see if the board offers the option to disable DMA. It will be slower, but it will work. Table 6.2 shows common DMA channel uses.

TABLE 6.2: Common DMA Channel Uses in the PC Family

CHANNEL	USE
0	Dynamic RAM refresh (XT—free on AT)
1	Hard disk controller (XT only—free on AT)
2	Floppy controller
3	Unused
4–7	Available on AT & PS/2, but often not exploited

IRQ (Interrupt Request) Levels

To get the CPU's attention, Interrupt Request (IRQ) lines are used. The PC's bus implements lines 2 through 7. They're prioritized, with line 2 more important than line 7. When a line is activated, the processor drops everything and loads a special subroutine written to handle ("service") that particular interrupt.

Peripherals sometimes need to get the CPU's attention in a time-critical fashion. Here's an example: The keyboard controller is pretty dumb. It has no memory to speak of, so every time a keystroke arrives at the controller, it must hand off this keystroke to the CPU (which then puts it in the keyboard buffer) before another keystroke comes in. Essentially, once the keyboard controller gets a keystroke, it wants to say to the CPU, "HEY! STOP EVERYTHING! COME SERVICE ME NOW BEFORE THE USER PRESSES ANOTHER KEY!," so it "rings the bell"—it activates its interrupt line (line number 1, as you can see in Table 6.3). The CPU stops and executes the program that moves the keystroke to the keyboard buffer.

Order of IRQ's on AT

TABLE 6.3: Common IRQ Uses in the PC Family

INTERRUPT LINE	DEVICE	COMMENTS	
0	Timer		
1	Keyboard		
2	Unused	Used in ATs as a gateway to IRQ 8/15, also by "autoswitching" video boards	
3	COM2		*2*
4	COM1		
5	Hard disk	PC and XT only—usually free on ATs	*1*
6	FDC		
7	LPT1		*3*

Modem ? (next to line 3)
Sound Card ? (next to line 5)
Printer? (next to line 7)

TABLE 6.3: Common IRQ Uses in the PC Family (continued)

INTERRUPT LINE	DEVICE	COMMENTS
8	Clock	Interrupts 8–15—only available on 286/386 machines (often not accessible from expansion boards)
9	PC network	
10–12	Unused	
13	Coprocessor	
14	Hard disk	
15	Unused	

If, in the above instance, the CPU was busy doing something else, or if the CPU had chosen to ignore interrupts (some programs can tell the CPU to do that), the keyboard controller might well have waited for quite some time. Then the user might have pressed a key, and the original keystroke could have been lost.

If you're installing a board and it needs an IRQ, look first to interrupt 2 on a PC or 5 on an AT. If those aren't available, try 3; if you don't have a COM2, there's no conflict. Some texts claim that you can steal the IRQ7 from the parallel port. That's true *only if you do not use Windows or OS/2.*

As with DMAs, 16-bit machines have extra interrupts. You can use them only if you're inserting a 16-bit board in a 16-bit slot. Use them if possible, so as to leave room in the lower eight IRQs for other boards. PCs and XTs only have IRQs 0–7, as Table 6.3 shows.

I've mentioned this earlier in the I/0 address discussion, but let me repeat: Some boards don't have jumpers and DIP switches. This means *there's no way to get them to work with conflicting boards.* For example, a client I regularly visited had installed an IBM 5251 (System 36 terminal emulator) board and an old Quadram Quadboard in a PC. The printer port on the Quadboard and the terminal emulator wanted the same resource—which one, I'm not sure. In any case, neither had jumpers. One board was thrown away.

Moral: Find out if the expansion boards you buy have adjustable DMA, IRQ, and I/O addresses.

I hesitate to mention this, but sometimes device conflicts can be solved by doing surgery on the boards. Just lobotomize the chips performing the function you wish to defeat. An example I've seen a couple of times is in serial ports. A client wanted me to set up a multifunction board in a PC with clock, memory, printer, and serial ports. He already had a board installed that provided both serial ports COM1 and COM2. The jumpers on the multifunction board allowed me to set the multifunction board's serial port to either COM1 or COM2, but not to disable it altogether. What to do? A chip called the *8250 UART* (Universal Asynchronous Receiver/Transmitter) is the heart of most serial ports. I found the 8250 on the multifunction board and removed it. The problem was eliminated. *Please don't try this unless you understand what you're doing.*

ROM Addresses and RAM Buffers

Added to I/O addresses, DMA channels, and IRQ lines is a fourth source of conflict: ROM addresses. Some controller cards (like EGA and hard disk controllers) require some ROM on board to hold some low-level code. For example, many hard disk controller cards contain code to do a low-level format of the hard disk; just load DEBUG (a DOS command) and type **G=C800:5**. (Please don't even think of doing this before you read the chapter on hard disks unless you know what you're doing.) The XT controller board's ROM starts at C800:0000. As before, a possibility exists that two different boards may require some on-board software, and if the two boards *both* try to locate their ROM at the same location in the PC's memory address space, neither one will work.

Fortunately, some boards include jumpers to allow you to move the start address of the ROM. Most of the major boards that include ROM (like the EGA, VGA, XT-type hard disk controller, and the like) should *not* have their ROM addresses changed, even if it's possible. Too many pieces of software rely on their standard addresses.

A few boards, like LAN boards, may have a little RAM right on board. A LAN board needs it to buffer incoming or outgoing messages. A LIM memory board needs 64K of RAM for the 16K page buffers, so most LIM boards incorporate some ROM also. Table 6.4 documents some common ROM and RAM requirements for a few boards. Your boards may differ, so consult your documentation.

Conflict between 16-Bit Boards and 8-Bit Boards with ROM

Here's an oddity.

If you have two boards in your system—one 16-bit, one 8-bit—both with ROM, the 16-bit board may cause the 8-bit board to malfunction.

Why? It has to do with a characteristic of the 16-bit ISA bus. It recognizes that it must talk to some boards that are 8-bit, and some that are 16-bit. It doesn't know which are which. So the extended part of the 16-bit slots have three "cheater" lines, lines that are duplicates of three lines on the 8-bit part of the slot. The way the extra lines work is this: Every time a memory access is to occur, the CPU sends out a "warning" message on the three cheater lines, describing roughly where the upcoming memory request will be going.

TABLE 6.4: Common ROM and RAM Buffer Addresses

FUNCTION	ADDRESS RANGE (HEX)	ADDRESS LENGTH
XT hard disk controller	C8000–CBFFF	16K
EGA	C0000–C3FFF	16K
VGA	C0000–C4FFF	20K
LIM boards (may vary)	D0000–DFFFF	64K
Token ring ROM	CC000–CFFFF	16K
Token ring RAM	D8000–D9FFF or DBFFF	8K or 16K
PC network card	CC000–CFFFF	16K

"Roughly" means "within 128K of the desired memory address." If a board has memory that is addressed anywhere in that 128K area, it responds with an "okay, I'm ready" signal. *But* only the 16-bit boards have the cheater lines—so if the upcoming memory access is to or from an 8-bit board, the CPU will receive no response to the warning. In that case, it just conducts 8-bit transfers.

If, on the other hand, the CPU *does* receive a response, it conducts the memory access using 16-bit transfers. To review,

1. The CPU sends out a warning message: "I'm about to do a memory access. It will be somewhere in the following 128K memory area..."

2. This message is only audible to 16-bit boards.

3. If a 16-bit board contains any memory—RAM or ROM—in that 128K address range, it responds, "*I've* got some memory in that range—do the memory access as 16-bit transfers." Any other 16-bit boards that happen to have memory in that range also reply likewise. 8-bit boards, on the other hand, are deaf to the warning, and so would make no response, even if they did have memory in that 128K range.

4. If the CPU hears a 16-bit response, it conducts the memory access 16 bits at a time. Otherwise, it just transfers the data 8 bits at a time.

Where's the problem? What if there are *multiple* boards with memory in a given range? Well, if they're all 16-bit boards, that's no sweat. But what if, within a given 128K memory range, there were 8-bit *and* 16-bit boards? Then every time the CPU wanted to access the 8-bit board, it would send out a warning message that the 8-bit board, logically, would not hear or respond to—*but the 16-bit boards would!* Result: The CPU would send 16-bit data blocks to a board that could only accept 8-bit blocks—an apparent malfunction.

This sounds like a dire scenario, but it really only pops up in one area: the ROM reserve. The addresses from 768K to 896K are, you may recall, where the ROMs are addressed: a 128K-sized memory area, notice. Every ROM access causes the CPU to issue a warning to the entire ROM area. If there are 8-bit boards and 16-bit boards with ROM on them, the 16-bit boards may respond to the CPU's attempts to access the ROMs on the 8-bit boards, with the result that the CPU, again, attempts 16-bit transfers to and from an 8-bit board. So if adding a 16-bit board kills an existing 8-bit board, that may be a reason why.

Resolving Installation Conflicts: An Example I'd like to provide you with as many installation examples as I can. Later, we'll look at the installation documentation for a few boards. But before I go on, I'd like to relate a few brief examples of installation problems and solutions that I encountered while putting a half dozen Ethernet LAN cards into some computers.

The first LAN card I installed was an Ethernet board that used everything we've discussed—an I/O address range, a DMA channel, an IRQ level, and some shared RAM. I left the I/O address at 300 hex, as that wouldn't conflict with the computer that I was installing the board into. The IRQ I chose was IRQ5, avoiding the more commonly–used IRQ2.

I avoid IRQ2 because it *can* be used in some systems, but the fact that it cascades to IRQs 8/15 makes me a bit nervous; in the past, using IRQ2 has caused conflicts with Windows. I set the DMA to channel 1, and put the shared RAM between CC000–CFFFF, as I knew that it would then not conflict with the hard disk controller ROM between C8000 and CBFFF.

When I plugged the board in, however, it refused to function. A little fiddling around made me realize that the DOS memory manager that I was using was placing its memory at the same addresses as the shared memory on my LAN board, which in turn was clobbering the LAN board. I told the memory manager to "exclude" the range of addresses from CC000–CFFFF (consult your memory manager's documentation to see exactly how; for a complete discussion of DOS memory managers, look in Chapter 3 of *Troubleshooting Windows*, also available from SYBEX). The board worked fine after that.

I set the second board identically, and it refused to work. A quick check of my notebook reminded me that a sound board was using IRQ5, causing a conflict. The LAN board only offered IRQs 2 through 7, and I didn't want to use any of them, as I like to avoid 2 if I can, and 3 through 7 were busy, so I needed an alternative approach. A quick look at the sound board showed that it could support any IRQ up to IRQ10, so I reset the sound board to IRQ10, leaving IRQ5 free for the LAN board. Problem solved.

Trouble appeared on the next machine as well. After I inserted the LAN board, not only did the LAN board not work, the video screen showed some odd colors upon bootup. It was a special Windows accelerator board, so I checked its documentation. The accelerator, as it turned out, employed the I/O address range 300–30F, causing a conflict with the Ethernet card. I reset the I/O address on the Ethernet card, and all was well with *that* machine.

The next computer booted up okay, but got strange flickers on the video screen whenever I tried to test the Ethernet card with the test program supplied with the Ethernet board. The Ethernet card was failing its tests, also, so I looked closer, and realized that I'd never opened this particular computer before.

This computer was equipped with a super VGA board. Almost all super VGA boards have an "autoswitching" feature that they'll optionally support, a feature whereby they automatically detect what video mode the currently-running software needs, and then switch to that mode.

This feature should be disabled for two reasons. First, it causes OS/2 and Windows NT to fail, as well as a number of other programs. Second, the autoswitch mode requires that the video board use a combination of interrupts 2 and 9, which is less than desirable because it steals a much-needed interrupt; in some cases, it causes a system to falsely report memory errors.

This super VGA card, as you can imagine by now, had the interrupt enabled, allowing for super VGA. I removed the interrupt jumper from the board—its location varies, so you'll have to consult your board's documentation to find the interrupt jumper before removing it. The Ethernet board ran without a hitch afterward. By the way, if you *are* planning to check your super VGA documentation to find out whether or not the interrupt's enabled, be aware that some manuals just refer to "the interrupt" and some refer to "autoswitching." If you can't find one, look for the other.

By now, as I approached the final machine, I was trying to *anticipate* problems. The LAN board placed in this last machine, like its comrades, refused at first to work. I struggled with this for a while, idly running diagnostic programs on the entire system. As I've explained before, I reasoned that if I could figure out what *didn't* work on this system that worked *yesterday*, that would give me a clue about what the board was conflicting with. (Of course, there *was* the possibility that the board just plain didn't work, but the earlier experiences of the day seemed to render that doubtful.)

Then I noticed that the diagnostic programs failed to notice that the PC had a mouse. Eureka! I recalled at that moment that this particular machine didn't have a serial mouse, unlike most machines in my office—it had a *bus* mouse. A bus mouse requires an interrupt-using circuit board of its own, and I was fairly sure that I'd set the interrupt on the bus mouse interface board to IRQ5. Not wanting to remove the cover from the PC unless necessary, I tried loading the mouse driver, and got the error message "interrupt jumper missing." I opened up the PC, checked the mouse board, and sure enough, it was using IRQ5. With its interrupt changed, I replaced the mouse board, and the last of the LAN boards fired up, ready to go.

I don't want to discourage you with this story. I just want to underscore how important it is to keep documentation of what's installed in your current machines, and to share a war story with you that may give you an idea or two the next time you're having trouble making a new board behave.

PS/2 Configuration Notes

Those of you with the "real" PS/2s (Models 25, 30, and 35 owners excluded) may never have to deal with the pain and suffering described in the preceding sections.

The Personal System line includes the Micro Channel Architecture (MCA) bus, an improvement in some ways over the old PC bus. It includes a feature called POS (Programmable Option Select) that eliminates the need for DIP switches. Like the ISA-based 286s and later machines, PS/2 machines have 8 DMA channels and 16 IRQ lines—plenty for any application.

You may know that the AT uses battery-backed memory (called *CMOS memory*) to retain some configuration information: It recalls things like how much memory the system has, what kind of drives it has, whether or not it has a coprocessor, and the like. It does not, however, assist in installing new expansion boards.

The PS/2s have taken this idea and extended it to expansion boards. In PS/2s, CMOS memory remembers IRQ, DMA, and I/O port information for circuit boards as well. When the machine is powered up, it checks each board against CMOS configuration information. If a new, unknown board is detected, the user will be requested to run a setup program.

There has been a lot of hype in the popular press about how you'll never have to worry about configuration again with the PS/2. It's not really true. You still have to worry about two boards not using the same IRQ lines, but fixing the problem is easier—you run a setup program rather than pull the board out and set DIP switches. The extra DMA and IRQ channels make the configuration job easier, too.

By the way, IBM wasn't the first manufacturer in the PC business to make this possible. Orchid Technologies has been building boards that use software setups since 1986.

Support for the New Board: BIOS Upgrades

If you have one of the earliest PCs, the ones manufactured in 1981 or 1982, you must upgrade your BIOS software in order to use an EGA board, a hard disk, a LAN card, or any other expansion board that has ROM on it. BIOS, you may recall, isn't loaded from disk, but rather is stored in a ROM chip, the one farthest from the empty ROM socket. For details on upgrade products, see Appendix A.

A Configuration Example

To underscore these concepts, let's look at installing two new real-life boards in a 286-based machine:

- A Bernoulli Box controller
- An HP ScanJet interface card

In addition, to make it more interesting, we'll add a mythical LAN board:

- A 16-bit LAN Lightning card

Also, I've included (with their kind permission) excerpts from the two real manufacturers' installation manuals dealing with configuration, as examples of typical manuals. The documentation for these two companies is a bit better than the average manual. An important part of this section is to allow you to see some examples of actual documentation. The manual excerpts follow.

ScanJet Manual Excerpts

Figures 6.7 through 6.10 include excerpts courtesy of Hewlett-Packard.

Resetting the Switches

Remove the plastic cover from the configuration switches. Change the position of the switches to a new setting as described in the following paragraphs. See Figure A-1.

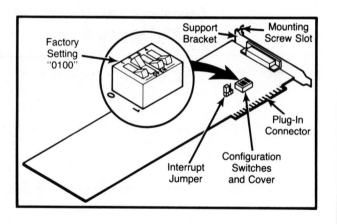

Figure A-1. HP 88290A Interface Card

FIGURE 6.8

ScanJet Installation
Manual Excerpt
(2 of 4)

Background Information

Your computer has two different types of address space: memory space and I/O space. Within the memory space is a section called Expansion ROM memory space. Most computer cards use addresses located in either I/O space or Expansion ROM space, or both. If two cards are configured to use the same address locations, a conflict occurs and your computer system does not operate correctly.

Most cards, including the HP 88290A interface card, have switches which determine the locations in the computer address space that the card will occupy. Addressing problems can be resolved by changing the switches on one of the conflicting cards to choose a new location within the computer address space.

The HP 88290A interface card uses eight bytes of computer I/O space and 16 kilobytes of Expansion ROM memory space. The exact address locations used by the card are determined by the settings of the configuration switches.

Switch 1 on the HP 88290A determines which one of two starting addresses in the computer I/O space is used by the card. Switches 2, 3, and 4 determine which of the eight possible starting addresses is used in the computer Expansion ROM memory space.

Figure A-1 shows where the configuration switches are located on the interface card. Notice that the switch positions 1 and 0 are written upside down to the left of the configuration switch module (when the card is held as illustrated in the drawing). Each configuration switch can be set by pushing one end of it--bottom for position 1 and

FIGURE 6.9

ScanJet Installation
Manual Excerpt
(3 of 4)

top for position 0. The factory setting is illustrated
in Figure A-1.

Selecting I/O Switch Position. Switch 1 is used to
select the I/O address for the card, with position 0
selecting addresses 278H through 27FH and
position 1 selecting addresses 268H through 26FH.
Change Switch 1 from the factory-set position 0 to
position 1 *only if* a parallel printer port is configured
as Port 2 in your computer system.

See Table A-1 to find the situation that applies to
you. Then, select the correct position for Switch 1.
If you decide to change Switch 1 from the factory
setting to position 1, make sure no other card in
your system occupies addresses 268H through
26FH.

Other Parallel Ports		HP 88290A	
Quantity	**Port Assignment**	**Switch 1 Setting**	**Addresses**
None	None	"0"	278H – 27FH
1	Port 1	"0"	
1	Port 2	"1"	268H – 26FH
2	Port 1 & Port 2	"1"	

Table A-1. I/O Table

FIGURE 6.10

ScanJet Installation
Manual Excerpt
(4 of 4)

Selecting ROM Switch Positions. Switches 2, 3, and 4 select the Expansion ROM location for the card. Table A-2 shows all possible settings of these switches with corresponding Expansion ROM locations and their standard uses. The factory-settings for switches 2, 3, and 4 are **1, 0,** and **0,** respectively (addresses C4000-C7FFF).

Expansion ROM Address (Hexadecimal)	Configuration Switch Setting			Common Usage
	2	**3**	**4**	
C0000-C3FFF	0	0	0	EGA Cards
C4000-C7FFF Factory Setting HP 88290A	1	0	0	
C8000-CBFFF	0	1	0	IBM/XT Controller Card
CC000-CFFFF	1	1	0	IBM/PC Network Card
D000-D3FFF	0	0	1	
D4000-D7FFF	1	0	1	
D8000-DBFFF	0	1	1	IBM/PC Cluster Card
DC000-DFFFF	1	1	1	

Table A-2. Commonly Used Addresses

Bernoulli Host Adapter Manual Excerpts

The following excerpts (Figures 6.11 through 6.13) are courtesy of Iomega Corp. By the way, for those who don't know, a *Bernoulli Box II* is a high-density, high-speed floppy disk that offers the same performance as a hard disk. This involves putting a Bernoulli controller (called the PC2/50 by its manufacturer) into the PC.

Lightning LAN "Manual" Highlights

Recall that our LL card is a 16-bit card. For the LL card, let's just say you need to worry about:

- DMA channel. Options are

    1 or 3 (when used in an 8-bit or 16-bit slot)

    5, 6, or 7 (when used in a 16-bit slot only)

- Interrupt level. A wide range of options:

    3, 4, 5, 6, 7 (when used in an 8-bit or 16-bit slot)

    9, 10, 11, 12, 14, or 15 (when used in a 16-bit slot only)

- I/O addresses. It uses 16 consecutive addresses, with the following options (addresses are, of course, in hex):

    300–30F

    310–31F

    320–32F

    330–33F

    340–34F

And that's it. Now let's configure these things.

CHAPTER 4
PC2/50 and PC2B/50
Technical Information

The information contained here is not necessary for the normal operation of the PC2/50 and PC2B/50 host adapter boards with removable cartridge drives. This information is provided for help in configuring the host adapter board for special applications.

Option Switch Settings

The option switches were set at the factory for the most typical configuration used with your computer. However, you can change the switch configurations for special applications. Figure 4-1 shows the purpose and factory setting of each option switch.

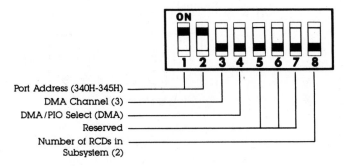

Figure 4-1. Option Switch Factory Settings.

Switches 1 and 2 — Port Addresses. These switches select one of four groups of port addresses to communicate with RCD systems. The switches were preset at the factory for port addresses 340H through 345H. (See Figure 4-2.)

NOTE: If you select a new group of port addresses, make certain no conflicts exist with other hardware accessing the same addresses.

FIGURE 6.12

Bernoulli Host Adapter
Installation Manual
Excerpt (2 of 3)

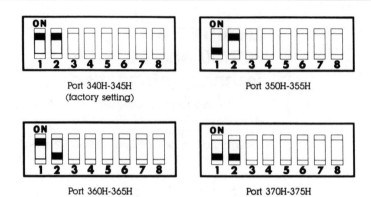

Port 340H-345H
(factory setting)

Port 350H-355H

Port 360H-365H

Port 370H-375H

Figure 4-2.   Port Address Switch Settings

Switch 3 — Direct Memory Access (DMA) channel used to communicate with your computer.   This switch selects DMA channel 1 or DMA channel 3.   Most networking schemes use DMA channel 1 for communication; so if the computer is part of a network, you should use channel 3.   (See Figure 4-3.)

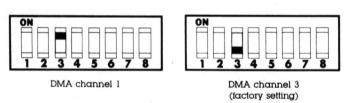

DMA channel 1

DMA channel 3
(factory setting)

Figure 4-3.   DMA Channel Switch Settings

Switch 4 — DMA or Programmed Input/Output (PIO).   Selecting PIO disables DMA communications and decreases transfer rates, but prevents problems with other hardware using DMA.   (See Figure 4-4.)

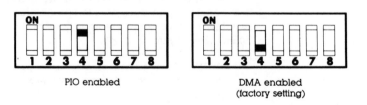

PIO enabled

DMA enabled
(factory setting)

Figure 4-4.   DMA/PIO Switch Settings

FIGURE 6.13

Bernoulli Host Adapter
Installation Manual
Excerpt (3 of 3)

Switches 5, 6, and 7. These switches are reserved. Do not change these settings.

Switch 8 — Number of drives in subsystem. This switch selects the number of 8 inch drives in an RCD external subsystem connected to the host adapter board. The switch is set at the factory for 2 drives. (See Figure 4-5.)

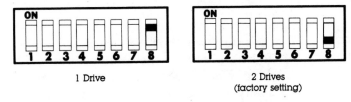

1 Drive   2 Drives
(factory setting)

Figure 4-5. Drive Switch Settings

So now we've seen the documentation (real and, in the case of the Lightning LAN board, imaginary). First, the Bernoulli controller (Iomega PC2/50) documentation tells us there are DIP switches to set the following items:

- I/O addresses
- Whether or not to use DMA
- If used, which DMA channel to choose (options are 1 or 3—it's an 8-bit board, so no DMA 4–7)

The Lightning LAN board is, again, a 16-bit adapter card that attaches your PC to a Local Area Network. It has jumpers to select:

- I/O addresses
- Which DMA channel to use (0 through 7)
- Which interrupt line to use (options are 2 through 15)

The ScanJet manual shows that you have to worry about:

- I/O addresses
- ROM addresses

The Bernoulli controller offers the option to avoid the DMA conflict by opting not to use DMA at all. That's a nice option, but the fact is that you bought these guys for *speed,* and missing out on DMA is *not* the way to get it.

Let's start with the LAN board, as it looks to be the largest pain here. I/O address is easy, as the default (300–30F hex) doesn't conflict with anything. Which DMA channel to use? Well, since it's a 16-bit board, with the ability to use DMAs 4-7, let's just go for DMA 4, so we can leave channel 3 for the Bernoulli. IBM "reserved" interrupt 9 for a LAN board, so we'll go with IRQ 9, again exploiting the 16-bit nature of the board (it'll work faster in 16-bit mode).

Now on to Bernoulli. The manual outlines several I/O port possibilities. The factory switch settings use 340–345 hex, which don't conflict with anything. DMA options are pretty scarce, only 1 (the hard disk, recall) and 3. Thankfully, nothing uses 3—if something did, we'd be forced to forgo DMA—so we set the DMA to 3.

As I've said before, a log of this information makes configuration easier. It's no good knowing that a new board needs IRQ 7 if you don't know whether some currently installed board already uses it.

The scanner board is fairly simple. It needs I/O addresses (options are 278–27F and 268–26F) and a ROM address. Either I/O address is fine, as neither conflicts with anything, although if we set it to 278–27F it will conflict with a second parallel port if we ever install one.

Now the tougher question—where to address the ROMs? Hmmm… I'm not sure what ROMs I currently have in this system. It's an AT-type system, so there is no extra ROM for a hard disk. The only thing in the system with ROM is a VGA, but what is its ROM's address? Checking Table 6.4 (earlier in this chapter) gives us C0000–C4FFF. Figure 6.10 shows that the scanner interface has a factory default of C4000–C7FFF. That would be okay for an EGA, as the EGA's ROM ends at C3FFF, just short of C4000. But note that the VGA's ROM goes all the way up to C6000, which tromps all over the range C4000–C7FFF. What other ranges are available? C0000–C3FFF is also available, but that's of no value either. Next is C8000–CFFFF—perfect! Now it'll work. Notice that it works because this is an *AT*—if it were an XT, the XT hard disk controller's ROM would conflict with addresses C8000–CFFFF.

Board Installation

Once the switches have been set, it's time to insert the new board. The physical process of installing or removing circuit boards is quite straightforward.

1. The power must always be off. You won't hurt yourself; you could damage the circuit board.

2. Before you can use the free slot on the bus, you must remove the metal bracket cover. The bracket cover is fastened to the case with a screw—the same screw that you'll use to secure the board to the system. Remove the screw and the bracket cover. Keep the bracket cover somewhere in case you need it at some time in the future.

3. Remember that the power supply should be plugged in (even though the PC is turned off) so as to provide you with a simple method of discharging static electricity from yourself. Touch the metal case of the power supply to drain away any static charges that you may have on your hands. Then grasp the expansion board that you're about to install. *Do not* touch the board by the gold edge connectors, as you'll remember from Chapter 4.

4. Grasping the board fore and aft, align the board with the empty slot. Apply gentle pressure to insert the board's edge connector into the bus slot. You may find that a slight rocking motion makes it easier to insert the board in the slot.

5. Using the screw that you removed to extract the bracket cover, secure the expansion board to the chassis.

6. If the board that you inserted was a memory board, don't forget to inform the system via the DIP switches or SETUP that system memory has changed.

Which Slot? Unusual Slots in Various Machines

People often think there's some electrical difference between slots, as if the video board must go in slot 2, the floppy controller in slot 7, and so on. In general, that's not true. In most cases, it makes *no difference* which slot boards are inserted in. The only criterion for board placement is ease of cable routing.

In Chapter 3, we looked at the common bus slots. Here are some of the more obscure slots and slot characteristics.

- The "bad slot" on the IBM XT. You generally can't use the slot on the IBM XT motherboard that's closest to the power supply. Its timing lines are a mite different, and most boards won't work in this slot. IBM makes a serial card that can go in there.

- Some accelerator boards recommend that you install them as close to the CPU as possible, short of using the bad XT slot.

- Backplane slots. Backplane systems (most Zeniths, Wyse, Telex, some Kaypros) include slots with extended connectors to accommodate the extra lines required for a split motherboard design. These designs usually divide what would be the motherboard into *two* expansion slots. Because the motherboard contains within it some electronic lines that aren't usually included in the bus, backplane manufacturers add an extra connector to a few slots to accommodate these extra control lines. If you've got one of these backplane computers, the two boards that do motherboard duty *must* go into these slots with the extra connector.

- The 16-bit AT&T Slot. The 8086-based AT&T systems sought to exploit the full 16-bit capabilities of the 8086, and the 6300 systems include an extra connector on several slots—kind of a poor man's 16-bit slot. Sadly, it has no relation to the 16-bit slots found on AT-bus machines, and isn't really of any value. It *can,* however, be used with no trouble as an 8-bit slot.

- As I mentioned in Chapter 3, 386DX and 486 systems are hampered by the lack of a 32-bit slot for memory access. Most other boards really wouldn't benefit from 32-bit access, so the lack of a 32-bit standard isn't a real handicap. But 386 memory needs 32-bit access for full functionality. While waiting for EISA or whatever the bus of tomorrow is, vendors have taken two approaches to providing a 32-bit path for memory: motherboard memory and proprietary 32-bit slots.

Some systems have room for up to 8 MB or more of RAM right on the motherboard. Others, like the Zenith Z-386, have a proprietary slot that can only be used for a memory card. Other compatible vendors do this also: Compaq, Intel, and Micronics are three names that spring to mind. IBM has a proprietary slot as well; the Micro Channel can't transfer data fast enough to support the Model 70's memory.

Power Requirements

Once you've got the new board in, can you feed it?

Sure, you've heard about how PC disk drives draw a lot of power, imperiling your power supply and PC, but what about those expansion boards—any worries there? Surely not, many people say: no moving parts. Actually, memory boards draw a considerable amount of power. According to a datasheet from Mostek, a memory chip manufacturer, a 256K chip draws 0.412 watts maximum. A bank of them (nine) is 3.7 watts. 64K chips draw 0.33 watts, so a bank of nine draws 3.0 watts. A full complement of 640K would require 3.7+3.7+3.0+3.0=13.4 watts at peak—21 percent of a 63.5 watt PC power supply! By comparison, some hard disks' peak power consumption is 10 watts. This gets worse if you have an older PC or XT that only accepts 64K chips. Ten banks of 64K chips would draw 30 watts peak.

It might be difficult to get power requirement figures for some expansion boards, so use the following rough test: Run the PC for a while with the board installed. Then touch the board while the PC is running. A hot board is probably drawing a lot of power. That heat must be removed from the machine; again, use an improved fan in your machine to handle this.

Board Testing

It's in. Now let's figure out if it works.

Burn-In

Most *solid-state components* (that is, electronic things without moving parts) tend to be very reliable if they live past the first few days ("If it works, it'll work forever."). Because of this, initial testing of circuit boards is valuable. Such testing is called *burn-in*.

When a new component like a memory board is installed, it should be tested for a 24- to 72-hour period. Some diagnostic program—generally a simple programming loop of some kind—retests the component over and over again. Some components have warranties of only 90 days, so the burn-in increases the probability that a bad component will be spotted in the warranty period.

Some manufacturers claim to do burn-in for you. You should *still* do it yourself. Why? They burned it in in the factory. Since then it has been subjected to the rigors of shipping.

Where Do You Find Diagnostic Programs?

Chapter 5 mentioned the names of several generic diagnostic programs, like the Supersoft and Windsor products. You could use those to test a board such as a motherboard or a memory board; they're perfectly good for that. But don't do what some folks do. I know of a group who buys a lot of PS/2s. They load up the Reference Diskette that comes with the PS/2, tell the diagnostics to run over and over, and leave the machine. Hours later, they come back and see if there are any errors reported on the screen. If there are no errors, they ship the machine to users. But users complained that a lot of machines had malfunctioning video. It turns out that the VGAs on Model 50s had a higher-than-average failure rate; I myself saw a classroom with 30 Model 50s develop video problems in about 20 percent of the machines. (If you have this problem, it seems most prevalent when the room is above 75-80 degrees. Maybe turning up the air conditioning will help.) The support staff was puzzled. How did this slip by them? Simple. Video diagnostics often require a user to look them over. If your reds are greens and blues are blacks, the monitor doesn't know. The video board doesn't know. You need an operator to audit the video tests.

Here's a cheap memory test. Build a spreadsheet of some kind—1-2-3, Excel, SuperCalc, or whatever—that fills memory. It just consists of a single cell A1 with the value 1, then a cell A2 with the formula A1+1. Then copy that cell until you run out of memory. Set Recalculation to Manual. Write a short macro that loops continuously, recalculating and recalculating again. If you really want a level of elegance, calculate the sum of this large column of numbers, and check it against the actual value: The sum of $1, 2, 3, 4, \ldots N$ is equal to $N(N+1)/2$).

If you've got something like our previous configuration example, where we installed a Bernoulli controller and a ScanJet interface card, you've got to rely on the manufacturers. And in all three cases, they come through. Iomega supplies an RCDDIAG program that tests the controller. LAN boards are generally tested by putting a "loopback" connector of some kind on them to allow them to hear what they broadcast. They send out test messages, and then compare them to what they receive. 3Com ships a program called 3C505 with the Etherlink+ to test it. And HP provides a very thorough ScanJet test program. When you get these programs, *use them*. Remember that just running them once isn't enough; some boards don't fail until they get hot.

Installing Motherboards

The last part of this chapter focuses on a particularly important circuit board—the motherboard. Most add-in boards can generally go right into the computer at the factory default settings, but motherboards almost always require some configuration. Like some people you've probably known, computers won't do any work until you flatter them—"Tell me about myself," they say.

But this process differs between XT-type machines and AT-type machines, and Micro Channel machines vary the technique still further. Here are the details.

System boards must be informed whenever you install (at a minimum) a new drive, more memory, a coprocessor, or different video. For years, circuit boards were configured, as we've seen, with jumpers and DIP switches. But IBM views having to ask users to open machines and flip switches as particularly undesirable. So the AT used a different approach, a more software-oriented one using a memory chip to hold the configuration information, as we'll see.

Configuring the XT and PC System Boards

The original IBM PC has two sets of eight DIP switches for configuration. The first set of DIP switches, labeled SW-1 on the motherboard, describes everything but the memory size:

- Kind of display installed
- How many floppy disk drives are installed
- If a numeric coprocessor is installed

The second set of DIP switches (and two of the switches from the first set) tell how much memory is on a PC motherboard. The IBM XT doesn't have the second set of DIPs, and instead deduces with its POST memory test how much memory the system has. Most XT-type machines follow the XT's lead and have only one set of DIP switches. PCs and other machines with a second set label the second set SW-2. Figure 6.14 shows a detail of DIP switches.

FIGURE 6.14

XT motherboard with
DIP switch detail

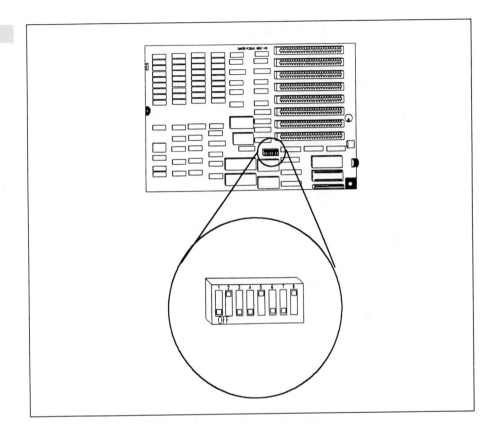

PC System Board DIP Switch Settings

Refer to Tables 6.5 and 6.6 to set the PC's DIP switches. Use a ballpoint pen or small screwdriver to change the switch settings.

Configuring an AT

An IBM AT has one DIP switch to set. The rest of its configuration information is retained in a battery-backed memory. So AT setup involves setting one switch and running a SETUP program. AT-type compatibles usually do *not* have this switch, but instead keep the video type in configuration memory.

CHAPTER 6

INSTALLING NEW CIRCUIT BOARDS

TABLE 6.5: Non-Memory DIP Switch Settings

COPROCESSOR			
Installed	SW-1	#2 OFF	
Not installed	SW-1	#2 ON	
Disk Drives			
No floppies	SW-1	#1 ON	#7 ON	#8 ON
1 drive	SW-1	#1 OFF	#7 ON	#8 ON
2 drives	SW-1	#1 OFF	#7 OFF	#8 ON
3 drives	SW-1	#1 OFF	#7 ON	#8 OFF
4 drives	SW-1	#1 OFF	#7 OFF	#8 OFF
Monitor type			
None	SW-1	#5 ON	#6 ON	
CGA, 40×25 video		SW-1		#5 OFF
CGA, 80×25 video	SW-1	#5 ON	#6 OFF	#6 ON
Monochrome Display	SW-1	#5 OFF	#6 OFF	

NOTE: Always set SW-1 #1 OFF on an XT.

Setting the AT DIP Switch

The one DIP switch on the IBM AT motherboard tells the AT whether it has a monochrome display board or a color display board. The switch isn't labeled. To remember which way it goes, remember CAB: Color Away from Back, meaning the back of the case. You can see the location of the video switch and configuration hardware in Figure 6.15.

TABLE 6.6: Common ROM and RAM Buffer Addresses

MEMORYSIZE	SW-1	SW-1	SW-1	SW-1	SW-1	SW-1	SW-2	SW-2	SW-2	SW-2
(KB)	#3	#4	#1	#2	#3	#4	#5	#6	#7	#8
16	1	1	1	1	1	1	1	0	0	0
32	0	1	1	1	1	1	1	0	0	0
48	1	0	1	1	1	1	1	0	0	0
64	0	0	1	1	1	1	1	0	0	0
96	0	0	0	1	1	1	1	0	0	0
128	0	0	1	0	1	1	1	0	0	0
160	0	0	0	0	1	1	1	0	0	0
192	0	0	1	1	0	1	1	0	0	0
224	0	0	0	1	0	1	1	0	0	0
256	0 '	0	1	0	0	1	1	0	0	0
288	0	0	0	0	0	1	1	0	0	0
320	0	0	1	1	1	0	1	0	0	0
352	0	0	0	1	1	0	1	0	0	0
384	0	0	1	0	1	0	1	0	0	0
416	0	0	0	0	1	0	1	0	0	0
448	0	0	1	1	0	0	1	0	0	0
480	0	0	0	1	0	0	1	0	0	0
512	0	0	1	0	0	0	1	0	0	0
544	0	0	0	0	0	0	1	0	0	0
576	0	0	1	1	1	1	0	0	0	0
608	0	0	0	1	1	1	0	0	0	0
640	0	0	1	0	1	1	0	0	0	0

TABLE 6.6: Common ROM and RAM Buffer Addresses (continued)

MEMORYSIZE	SW-1	SW-1	SW-1	SW-1	SW-1	SW-1	SW-2	SW-2	SW-2	SW-2
IBM XT MEMORY DIP SWITCH SETTINGS										
64	1	1								
128	0	1								
192	1	0								
256+	0	0								

FIGURE 6.15

AT motherboard detail with video switch, battery connection, and CMOS chip

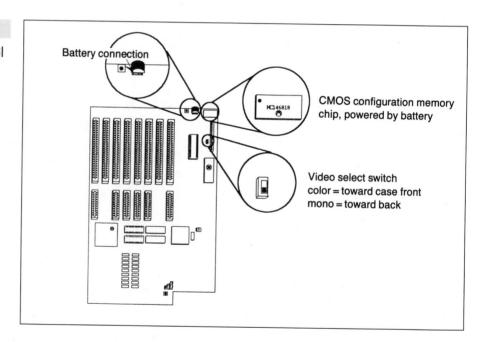

Battery connection

CMOS configuration memory chip, powered by battery

Video select switch
color = toward case front
mono = toward back

Configuration CMOS Memory

There are no DIP switches to set on an AT or AT compatible. Configuring a system board for most 286/386/486 machines should involve no DIP switches, but rather a memory chip that holds 64 bytes of configuration information. Commonly called the *CMOS chip*, it's often a Motorola 146818 24-pin chip. It's volatile, like all semiconductor memory, and so requires a battery to maintain the integrity of its data when the system is turned off.

When the battery runs down, the computer starts acting aphasic (look it up, but it means what you'd expect it to mean). Some systems, like the AT&T 6386, use nonrechargeable lithium batteries that have lives of three to ten years. Others (the Zenith Z-248 comes to mind) use rechargeable nicad batteries.

Newer systems (like the PS/2 Model 30-286) use a memory-and- battery-all-in-one chip from Dallas Semiconductor. It's distinguished by the alarm clock on its face and contains a battery that Dallas Semi claims is good for ten years.

Running the Configuration Programs

Such configuration memory chips must be loaded, and the program to do the loading is generally called SETUP. Conveniently, the SETUP program for Zeniths and for those with recent BIOSes is in ROM, so you're not required to hunt around for a disk—quite nice. The Zeniths activate the program with Ctrl-Alt-Ins. The Award only offers the option when you boot up; if you have an Award BIOS, it'll note that you can press Ctrl-Alt-Esc on startup if you desire. It's extremely annoying to have to paw through your floppies looking for SETUP when you change a battery or add an option, so be sure you know where SETUP is.

When running SETUP, it will ask you things like:

- Date and time
- Floppy drive type (360K, 1.2M, and so on)
- Hard drive type (a number from 1 to 47, generally)
- Amount of conventional memory (it might call it *base* memory)
- Amount of extended memory (it might call it *expansion* memory)
- Primary display type (monochrome, CGA, EGA/VGA)

Most of the questions are easy to answer, except *What hard disk drive type do you have?* That's a bit more intricate, so I'll save discussion of that for Chapter 12.

Replacing the Configuration Battery

As I said above, if your AT-type system insists on being set up every day, you probably need a new battery. New batteries can be bought in the $17–$30 range. See Appendix A for details.

When you replace the battery, you'll notice it's connected to the motherboard with two wires, a red and a white. If you didn't pay attention when you took the old battery off, you might wonder how the new battery is connected. In that case, remember RAP: Red Away from the Power supply.

Setting Up the PS/2 with the Reference Disk

Like the AT, the PS/2s (the *real* PS/2s, the Models 50 to the 80) use some nonvolatile RAM to hold configuration information. But the PS/2s take it a bit further. They have no DIP switches at all and, in fact, can configure their expansion boards in software, also.

PS/2's come with a *Reference Disk* (RD), which contains, among other things, configuration software. The very first thing you should do with a new PS/2 is copy the Reference Disk, as the RD is write-protected and you'll want to write your configuration onto the disk. Figure 6.16 summarizes the PS/2 setup process.

Next, boot the PS/2 from the backup RD. If you haven't configured the machine before, it'll squawk about not being configured and because the date and time hasn't been set. If you've booted from the RD, you'll eventually see a main menu like Figure 6.17.

Now choose 3, Set Configuration. A submenu appears (see Figure 6.18).

If you choose Automatic Configuration, the system will configure itself and reboot. At this point, everything's fine, provided you haven't added any expansion boards. If you have added a board or boards, the system will continue to squawk, because it doesn't know how to configure the expansion boards. By the way, note option 3, Backup Configuration. It does the same thing for your PS/2 that the program SAVECMOS on the utility disk does for your AT-type machine.

FIGURE 6.16

The PS/2 setup process

Setting Up A PS/2 With POS (Programmable Option Select)

First, make a copy of the original IBM Reference Disk. Do your work with the copy.

The backup will be sufficient to configure a basic PS/2 with no expansion boards added.

If you want to add a board, however, the Reference Disk doesn't know anything about it: you must supply some more information to the Reference Disk in order for it to configure the system. Every Micro Channel board comes with an Option Diskette that contains a file or files that must be copied to the backup Reference Disk. (That's why you backed it up -- the original is write protected.) An option on the Ref Disk Main Menu, "Copy Option Diskette" will transfer the configuration files to the backup Ref Disk. *Then* the backup Ref Disk can configure your PS/2.

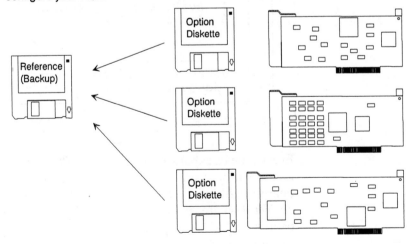

```
┌──────────────────────────────────────────┐
│ Main Menu                                 │
├──────────────────────────────────────────┤
│   1. Learn about the computer             │
│   2. Backup the Reference Diskette        │
│   3. Set configuration                    │
│   4. Set features                         │
│   5. Copy an option diskette              │
│   6. Move the computer                    │
│   7. Test the computer                    │
│                                           │
├──────────────────────────────────────────┤
│ Use ^ or V to select. Press Enter.        │
│ Esc=Quit    F1=Help                       │
└──────────────────────────────────────────┘
```

```
┌──────────────────────────────────────────┐
│ Main Menu                                 │
│  ┌───────────────────────────────────────┤
│  │ Set Configuration                      │
│  ├───────────────────────────────────────┤
│  │   1. View configuration                │
│  │   2. Change configuration              │
│  │   3. Backup configuration              │
│  │   4. Restore configuration             │
│  │   5. Run automatic configuration       │
│ U├───────────────────────────────────────┤
│ E│ Press a number to select.              │
│  │ Esc=Quit    F1=Help                    │
└──┴───────────────────────────────────────┘
```

Every type of expansion board in the PS/2 universe has a unique five-digit identification number called its *Micro Channel ID*. A 2-MB memory board might have ID 10000, an ESDI controller might be 20000, and so on. Vendors are expected to ask IBM for an MCA ID when designing new boards.

Once a new board is in a machine, the system—the RD, in this case—must be informed of just *how* to configure the board. That information is summarized in a 2K file called an *Adapter Definition File,* or ADF. The name of the ADF file for a board with MCA ID *xxxxx* is *xxxxx*.ADF; so in my above example, the file for the ESDI controller would be called 20000.ADF.

When you buy an expansion board for a PS/2, you should get a disk containing, among other things, the ADF file to configure the board. This must be merged onto the RD with choice 5, Copy an option disk. You can see choice 5 on the Main Reference Disk menu, shown in Figure 6.17.

Alternatively, you can just copy the files with the extension .ADF to the root directory.

Once you've merged the option diskette onto the RD, reboot and configure again. Now the RD has the information it needs to configure everything in the computer.

The auto-configuration feature is nice, but sometimes it gets confused as to what kind of hardware you have. At that point, you'll have to edit your configuration directly. When you do, you'll see the two screens of information presented in Figures 6.19 and 6.20 (these are from a Model 50 with a 3270 adapter card in it).

FIGURE 6.19

First sample screen from PS/2 Model 50 Setup Program

```
 ┌──────────────────────────────────────────────────────────────────────┐
 │  Change Configuration                                                  │
 │                                                                        │
 │   Total System Memory                                                  │
 │       Installed Memory ...................... 1024KB (1.0MB)           │
 │       Usable Memory ......................... 1024KB (1.0MB)           │
 │                                                                        │
 │   Built In Features                                                    │
 │       Installed Memory ...................... 1024KB (1.0MB)           │
 │       Diskette Drive A Type ................. [1.44MB 3.5"  ]          │
 │       Diskette Drive B Type ................. [Not Installed      ]    │
 │       Math Coprocessor ...................... Not Installed            │
 │       Serial Port ........................... [SERIAL_1]              │
 │       Parallel Port ......................... [PARALLEL_1]            │
 │                                                                        │
 │   Slot1 - Empty                                                        │
 │                                                                        │
 │   Slot2 - The IBM 3270 Connection                                      │
 │       Resources Used ....................... [Only Choice]            │
 │                                                                        │
 │   Esc=Quit    F5=Previous    F10=Save                                  │
 │   F1=Help     F6=Next                  V    End     PageDown           │
 └──────────────────────────────────────────────────────────────────────┘
```

FIGURE 6.20

Second sample screen from PS/2 Model 50 Setup Program

```
  Change Configuration

  Built In Features
      Installed Memory ...................... 1024KB (1.0MB)
      Diskette Drive A Type ................. [1.44MB 3.5"  ]
      Diskette Drive B Type ................. [Not Installed      ]
      Math Coprocessor ...................... Not Installed
      Serial Port ........................... [SERIAL_2]
      Parallel Port ......................... [PARALLEL_1]

  Slot1 - Empty

  Slot2 - The IBM 3270 Connection
      Resources Used ........................ [Only Choice]

  Slot3 - Empty

  Slot4 - IBM Fixed Disk Adapter
      Type of drive ......................... [ 30]
      Arbitration Level ..................... [Level_3 ]

  Esc=Quit    F5=Previous    F10=Save    ^   Home    PageUp
  F1=Help     F6=Next                    v   End
```

Setting Up EISA Systems

Like Micro Channel, EISA systems have a setup disk that requires information about the boards in your PC; the setup program on the disk can automatically configure your boards. The procedure is almost identical to Micro Channel, with a few differences.

- **The file names are different.** Instead of having the extension "ADF," EISA board definition files have the extension "CFG."

- **You've got to tell it about your ISA boards.** EISA will accommodate ISA boards, but the setup disk can't detect the ISA boards. For the configuration program to work, you've got to hand-enter the information about your ISA boards.

- **Do the setup *first*, then install the boards.** It sounds odd, but I've seen cases where an EISA disk controller goes "dead" if you insert an EISA board that the system does not recognize. As a result, I put the CFG for the new board on my EISA setup disk, then install the board with the setup program *before* actually inserting the board. I get a warning from the setup program that it can't find the board that I'm installing, but that's no problem. Then I shut down the system, install the new EISA board, boot up, and I'm up and running the first time.

EISA systems are getting cheaper and cheaper; think about making your next system an EISA system, and start getting the benefits of EISA speed.

A Possible Future: Plug-and-Play Technology

By now, you've read about interrupts, DMA, and the like. You know that you've got to flip DIP switches or set jumpers to ensure that your boards don't conflict, and if you've installed a SCSI host adapter, a LAN card, and a sound board, then doing all this installation stuff may start looking less like a job and more like a puzzle.

To combat that problem, Microsoft, Intel, and Compaq have proposed a standard called Plug and Play (PAP). The idea behind PAP is that board manufacturers will add circuitry to their add-in boards so that the automatic setup and resource query ("resource" here means IRQ, DMA, I/O address, ROM address, or RAM buffer address) capabilities of EISA and Micro Channel will become available to machines with ISA buses. The PC's operating system could then configure and query boards directly, eliminating the need to pop the top of the PC except when actually removing or inserting a board.

PAP's two features—backward ISA support and software setup/query—sound good, but there's a high price for it. First, while you don't have to replace your bus, you *do* have to replace your system BIOS, your board's device drivers...and your operating system.

Yes, that's right: Plug and play sounds good, but it won't run under DOS. You'll have to run some future version of Windows NT, or perhaps Windows 4.0, to support plug and play. So be very careful when considering computers that offer plug and play; I'd say if you want software control of your hardware's configuration, then you'd do better to buy an EISA or Micro Channel computer.

CHAPTER

7

Repairs with Circuit Boards and Chips

IF the problem isn't software, everything's plugged in, and it isn't something obvious like a burnt-out motor, a broken wire, a gummed-up printer, or an imploded display, then it's probably a circuit board. Step One is to identify the faulty part. I'll talk about diagnostic approaches (they don't cost anything but time) in this chapter. Step Two is repair. There are two levels of repair here: board level and chip level.

The more important, and the more difficult, of these operations is the first, *identification.* How do you know which board is bad? There are several approaches we'll examine here. Next, should you fix or replace the bad board? You'll see the pros and cons. Further along, some repairs can involve chip replacements. Finally, we'll examine diagnosing and repairing memory problems—the chips you'll most likely install and replace.

How Do You Find the Bad Board?

Later, I'll discuss the matter of "replace or repair."

First, let's hunker down to the tough part—figuring out which board is the problem child. Here's the overall roadmap.

1. Make *sure* you've checked steps 1 through 7 in Chapter 5. You *know* by now that a switched outlet (or one with a tripped circuit breaker) isn't the culprit. You're not ripping the machine apart to figure out why it won't boot when the last thing you did was install a new expansion board (and the machine hasn't worked since you put the board in) without first removing the new board to see if

the problem goes away. Again, just be lazy and follow the beaten path. Don't get original. Just make sure you've followed the seven steps.

2. Assuming the machine does boot, use the machine to help diagnose its own problems. Run the diagnostics to see if it's the keyboard, video, and so on. That will give you an indication of what's wrong.

   Suppose the problem is clearly video. What now? Again, be lazy. Before you remove the top and begin to swap, check the easy stuff. First swap the cable, not the monitor or the video board. To be even lazier, is the problem specific to something like a time of day or, more likely, a piece of software? If the video works well enough to boot the system, run DOS commands, and the like, but dies when you're running, say, PageMaker, the problem is likely to be software, not hardware. One of the following is likely:

   • You've installed PageMaker incorrectly (easy to do, as it's a Windows product, and not simple).
   • There's a bug in the PageMaker/Windows code that talks to your video board.
   • Your video card isn't 100-percent compatible with the IBM standard.

In the above situation, I'd take the exact same copy of PageMaker on a floppy disk and move it to an identical system— identical right down to the version of DOS and contents of CONFIG.SYS and AUTOEXEC.BAT. If the problem shows up on the second machine, common sense tells us it's either a software problem with PageMaker, an installation problem, or that the brand of video board both machines have isn't 100-percent compatible. We can't fix the first or third problem (I assume you can't debug machine code or redesign circuit boards), so look more closely at the second. Is the installation right? Call the vendor of the software and hardware—do they know of the compatibility problem and have a fix?

3. Assuming the machine boots, but the above alternatives don't fix the problem, *then* you can start swapping boards to figure out which is the problem. You very rarely get to this point.

4. If the machine doesn't boot at all, consult the next section.

Night of the Living Data: Making a Dead Machine "Undead"

Suppose your machine is completely unresponsive. You can't run the diagnostics, as the machine won't talk at all. Here are two approaches for bringing your machine back from the dead, and a few other possibilities and solutions.

Identifying the Problem Board with Two Machines

First of all, assume there's only one problem. Ideally, you have two machines, one sick and one well. A simple strategy here is to swap boards, one by one. Each time you swap a board, turn on *both machines* and note which machines are currently well. Ideally, you'd like to induce the problem from the originally sick PC to the originally well PC.

By the way, did you check the old "intensity turned down on the monitor" trick? I've turned down the intensity on my monitor, left the machine, come back to the machine after a while (forgetting I had turned down the intensity), and panicked, thinking that (at best) I had a bad monitor.

Ghost in the Machine (Contagious Components)

Be careful here, however. Sometimes you end up with *two* sick machines. Why? I've seen components that, being damaged, damage other components. Suppose you have a dead system, and you've stripped the system to the motherboard and power supply. You try to ascertain what's causing your problems, so you swap motherboards. Still no luck. You try swapping power supplies. *Still* no response. What's happening?

You've got a demon in the power supply: Not only is it not working, it destroys motherboards. Originally it stung motherboard number one; then you fed it another one. I've seen this in two situations: bad power supplies damaging motherboards, and bad keyboard interfaces on motherboards damaging keyboards.

The moral is:

- Swap the power supply before the motherboard.
- Before swapping the keyboard, test the keyboard interface with a voltmeter, as described in Chapter 18.

Identifying the Problem Board with Just One Machine

If all you've got is one machine, here's a nice, minimalist approach. Some people call it the *min/max* technique, short for *minimum/maximum*.

Start with a machine that won't boot up at all and assume there's only one thing wrong with it. We'll break it down to the bare essentials, and then add pieces until the machine refuses to boot. Once the machine refuses to boot, we'll know that the last item that we added is the trouble board.

Start off by removing everything but the following:

- Power supply
- Motherboard
- Speaker

Turn on your computer. You should observe several things. For one thing, the fan on the power supply should start right up. If it doesn't, either the power supply isn't getting power, or the fan's burned out. If the fan is burned out, the problem's easy—you cooked your PC the last time you used it.

There's *one* other reason the fan wouldn't start up. The power supply's pretty smart and can sense short circuits on the motherboard. If it senses such a short, it will shut down and refuse to do anything until the short's resolved. You don't believe me? Try taking a board out while the power's on. If you do it just right, you'll create a short and the machine will shut down. (This isn't a particularly smart idea, actually, and it's not recommended. You might want to just trust me on this one.)

In addition, the power supply should also produce a "click" on the speaker (you've probably never noticed it, but it happens each time you turn on the machine). Another aspect of the intelligent power supply is that, once it feels it's up to the task of getting to work, it sends a signal to the motherboard that resets the system. The result is the "click." Once you hear that, you know the power supply believes itself to be functional.

Assuming the two above things happened, you'll probably get a long beep and two short ones out of the speaker; this is the motherboard's way of saying, *I can't find the video card.* You may hear a different beep combination than one long and a short—different BIOSes respond differently to the "no video" condition.

If the above three things have happened, congratulations—the machine booted. (It didn't do that before, remember?) If it didn't, there are only three possible culprits: the motherboard, the power supply, or the speaker. It's child's play now to figure out which is the offending component: Just swap the speaker, power supply, and/or motherboard. Remember what I said before about swapping the power supply first, in case it's got a demon. Remember that in the PC repair business the cheapest and most effective piece of test equipment is a spare part. At this point, it's a quick swap.

Assuming the machine booted, the next step is to add the video card. Try to boot the machine. Again, if it doesn't boot, try another video card. If it boots, you'll get error messages complaining about the lack of keyboard and drives—errors 301, 601, and 1701 on an IBM machine. (You'll not see the 1701 error on an XT-type machine, as the BIOS error is generated by the hard disk BIOS on the XT controller itself. Because the controller board isn't yet in the machine, the error can't be generated.)

Keep adding boards until the machine fails. As you reassemble the machine, you'll probably see the results shown in Table 7.1. Note that this information isn't gospel—your machine, depending on the manufacturer, will probably do something different from the above. Try it sometime, on a functioning PC, and note the outcome. Do it before you must work with an ailing PC so that you can see what a healthy machine looks like at various stages of reassembly. If you don't know what healthy looks like, you can't recognize diseased.

Now, you may have gotten down to the last board, the machine may have been booting fine, and you inserted that last board, thinking, "Aha! Gotcha. Now to prove it...." But then the machine booted fine. Why? Either 1) it just wanted some attention; 2) it fails when boards are hot, and the disassembly and reassembly cooled it to the point that it works; or 3) you didn't do the greatest job the first time you took it apart, cleaned it, and put it back together.

TABLE 7.1: Steps in Assembling an IBM PC

ADD THIS	EXPECTED OUTCOME
Motherboard, power supply	1 long, 2 short beeps
Video board and display	Blinking cursor, 301, 601, 1 beep
Keyboard	Blinking cursor, 601, 1 beep
Disk controller	Blinking cursor, 601, 1 beep
Floppy A	Blinking cursor, 1 beep, boot
Floppy B	Same—try B
Hard disk controller	Boots from hard disk
Other boards	They should function

What Makes Boards Fail?

If you're reading this, you might already have a dead board. I've said to just replace it, but if you're interested, here's what generally zaps boards.

Most component problems boil down to either environmental trouble, damage due to mishandling, or faulty manufacture. The most common ailments are the following:

- Socketed chips creep out of their sockets because of expansion and contraction; you should rock the chips.

- Bad solder joints can disconnect or cause short circuits; you should resolder.

- Weak components fail under heat.

- PC board traces can be scratched.

- Dirt and dust build up heat.

- Edge connectors or chip pins corrode.

- RFI/EMI noise impairs board operation.

Fix or Replace Boards?

Assuming that you can find the bad board (which we'll discuss presently), do you just replace it, or do you try to fix it? Sure, it's macho to get out the soldering iron and fix an errant board. But, in general, you won't find it cost-effective to repair a circuit board. This is basically because 1) the inexpensive boards are far cheaper to replace than to repair and 2) the more expensive boards require even more expensive equipment to repair them.

Inexpensive boards, like a PC floppy controller, can be bought for $30 to $80. You can see typical board prices in the accompanying Table 7.2, but a cursory glance shows that most boards are indeed cheap. Chips on these boards are primarily soldered, not socketed, and so can only be fixed by someone trained to solder chips without destroying them. Add the hourly cost of this person to the cost of replacement chips, and the amount soon adds up to a total in excess of the cost of $30 a board. More and more boards are four-layer boards, which are tough to solder correctly. *Four-layer* means the board not only has printed circuit traces on the top and

TABLE 7.2: Typical PC Board Prices

PRODUCT	APPROXIMATE COST
486DX2-66 EISA/VLB System Board	$700
386 System Board (40 MHz)	$125
Floppy Disk Controller Board	$29
IDE Hard Disk Controller Board	$12–$50
Hard/Floppy Controller (AT)	$39
Display Controller Boards:	
Monochrome Display Adapter (MDA) with parallel port	$12
Video Graphics Array (VGA)	$80
Memory Expansion Board (XT)	$50
Memory Expansion Board (AT)	$140
Parallel/serial port	$10
Real Time Clock/Calendar	$49
Multifunction Board (clock, printer, serial, memory)	$18
Power Supply	$60
More "Exotic" Boards:	
3278 Emulator Board	$600
Local Area Network (LAN) Board	$99–$500
Expanded (Paged) Memory Board	$99

bottom, but two layers in the middle! Even if the board is a simple two-layer, don't forget that time is wasted inserting the board and powering up the computer after each chip replacement.

More expensive boards (those in the $1,000+ range) could be financially, rewarding to fix, but two factors hinder such repairs. First, more and more boards are being designed as *Surface Mount Design* (SMD) boards. These require expensive tools to solder and desolder, and normal soldering skills don't directly translate to SMD. Even more ominous for the do-it-yourselfer is the greater and greater use of *ASICs* (Application Specific Integrated Circuits). ASICs are used by companies to reduce the chip count on a board; what were once 20 chips are reduced to one chip. They introduce problems for a troubleshooter because they're *proprietary*—you can't buy replacements. You might be the best engineer in the world, but you can't fix bad ASICs. If you can't fix 'em and you can't buy 'em, you've got no choice but to replace the entire circuit board.

There are exceptions to the above, of course. Some manufacturers are farsighted enough to take the chips that are most likely to fail and socket them. That doesn't help the proprietary chip problem, but it addresses the "it's a pain to solder" problem.

Maintenance Considerations for the PS/2 Family

As I've said previously, the PS/2s have workaholic motherboards: the video, disk, parallel, serial, mouse, and keyboard controllers all exist on proprietary chips (ASICs), mounted using surface-mount technology to the motherboard. Auggh! Worst-case scenario for troubleshooting!

Now, it's not *all* bad news. There are fewer boards to worry about, and you have to fuss with fewer DIP switches. Reducing chip count should produce a more reliable machine overall. But it limits what you can troubleshoot. IBM markets upgrades for older PS/2s at a reasonable price—around $1000 for a 486DX2-66 motherboard—but they're still expensive and can't be repaired. Again, it doesn't matter how good or bad an engineer you are, fixing a faulty PS/2 motherboard is just plain impossible.

A PS/2, then, is a risky proposition. It's not likely to fail, but if it does, it will cost lots of money.

By the way, while I'm discussing the PS/2s, you should be aware of a few known problems.

- The early (1987) 60 and 80 ESDI hard disk controllers have a problem that will, over time, cause loss of data. If you have one, contact IBM to see if you have one of the bad ones. Don't wait to see if a problem arises; get the serial number off the board and call IBM.

- An uncertain number of motherboards (some say as many as 40 percent) will not take a configuration. They may stay configured for a while, but turn the machine off overnight and it will forget the configuration. You can replace the battery, and the problem will reappear in a few weeks or months. Engineers tell me the problem is that the design of these motherboards drains batteries too quickly, and a motherboard swap for a more recent model is necessary to solve the problem. Be sure you actually have a problem: Recall from the previous chapter that you've got to merge .ADF files onto your PS/2 Reference Disk in order to enable the RD to configure third-party add-in boards. If the PS/2 is complaining about newly added third-party boards, your problem isn't with the motherboard but with your configuration job. On the other hand, if it was configured fine yesterday and now complains of not being configured when no changes have been made, you could have a problem motherboard. Another favorite cause for a false 162 configuration error is forgetting to turn on the external floppy disk. In any case, if you have a truly troublesome motherboard, remember that the PS/2s have a one-year warranty, and *get on it before the warranty expires*! Those motherboards are expensive if you're beyond your warranty.

- The PS/2s and DOS 3.3/3.2 don't get along very well. IBM has released a patch program called DASDDRVR.SYS that you should get a copy of (IBM offers it free of charge). DASDDRVR.SYS fixes many, but not all, DOS-PS/2 problems. DOS 4.0 and later require DASDDRVR.SYS.

The most striking example of the PS/2's trouble with DOS 3.3 and 3.2 arises when formatting floppy disks. Suppose you format a floppy successfully, and DOS asks if you'd like to format another. You say *yes* and try to format a second floppy, but FORMAT tells you the diskette is bad. No matter how many diskettes you try, it says each is bad. You must reboot to format any more diskettes unless, again, you have DASDDRVR.SYS on your hard disk and it has been activated by putting DEVICE=DASDDRVR.SYS in your CONFIG.SYS file.

Finding, Identifying, and Replacing Bad Chips

As long as we're trying to replace chips, let's see how to find the silly things in the first place; and what do those numbers atop the chip mean? A chip can be described by its function, its identification number, and its manufacturer.

Function: A chip can be something as simple as just four NAND gates, each with two inputs (called a quad two-input NAND chip), or as complicated as a microprocessor. Physical size is some indication of a chip's complexity, but it isn't tremendously important. Memory chips are fairly small, but they're complex.

Identification Number: When a manufacturer designs a new chip, it's given an identification number. For example, an 8088 is a particular microprocessor chip, and a 7400 is a quad two-input NAND chip. Generally, chip designs are patented, so another manufacturer must be licensed before it can offer a chip it did not design. Intel designed the 8088, but Advanced Micro Devices (AMD) probably makes more of them than Intel does, now. I don't know who developed the first 256K×1 dynamic RAM chip, but virtually everyone in the chip business makes them now.

Prefixes and suffixes can be added to a chip's ID number. The suffixes refer to the package it's in (usually *DIP,* for Dual Inline Pin, which is indicated by the suffix AN) or the temperature range (S is military specification, N is normal). Thus, 7400AN refers to a 7400 chip in a DIP package.

A two-letter prefix refers to the manufacturer. Some manufacturer codes are: HD for Hitachi, WD for Western Digital, DM for National Semiconductor, R for Rockwell. Another code might be present, like B8544. This means (ignore the B) the chip was made in the 44th week of 1985. Some vendors, like Intel, don't put a date code on their chips. Instead, they put a serial number on the chip. A motherboard in front of me has a chip with serial number L5450275. If you have a 80286- or 80386-based computer, it's probably a good idea to examine and write down your serial number. Periodically, bugs will pop up and certain serial numbers will be recalled. Understand that there's no single 8088 chip; it has gone through several revisions.

Other suffixes refer to performance, as in the 8088-1 and 8088-2 microprocessors. The -2 runs up to 8 MHz, but the -1 only runs reliably up to 5 MHz. In the case of memory chips, there are more specific speed codes, as we'll see in the upcoming memory chapter.

Okay, you *insist* on trying to fix some boards? Sometimes, you *can* be a real hero and actually fix a circuit board. Most maintenance shops do very little board repair, instead returning the boards to the manufacturer or, more often, just disposing of them. Board repair can be time consuming and therefore expensive, not a great idea when most boards are under $100–$200. You'll spend a minimum of an hour and a maximum of forever fixing a board.

This isn't to say it should never be attempted. The most prominent chip level installations/troubleshootings are for:

- Memory chips
- Replacement microprocessors
- Coprocessors
- ROMs (Read-Only Memories)

If you're going to handle chips, please first take a look at the section on chip handling in Chapter 8. In general, finding bad chips is done in one of the following ways:

- Manufacturer notification
- Software identification of chip malfunction
- Temperature testing
- Digital probe and pulse testing

- Use of specialized (and expensive) signature analyzers
- Exhaustive chip replacement

Chip "Recall"

The most common method is the first, *manufacturer notification*. That is, the manufacturer will send you a replacement chip and a notice that "some boards built in 1986 malfunction due to a faulty 65X88 chip. Enclosed find a replacement 65X88...." This is like a car recall.

Software Chip Testing

Software identification is possible when the chip isn't so vital to the system that the system can't run without it. For instance, if the 8088 or 80286 microprocessor goes on vacation, there's no way to run a diagnostic program. Many memory problems can be tested with software, however, as well as some problems with some major chips, like the 8284 clock chip and the 8237 DMA controller. ROMs often contain a checksum that can be used to verify that the contents of the ROM haven't been damaged. You usually get the program that checks the checksum with the board that has the ROM in question. For example, most PC system diagnostics know where the checksum for the BIOS ROM is, and they check that as part of their routine.

Temperature Chip Testing

Some faulty chips can be traced through their temperature. A properly functioning chip should be slightly warm to the touch— warmer, at least, than after a night of deactivation. A completely cool chip, particularly a large one (large chips tend to run warmer) is probably dead. Similarly, a very hot chip of the finger-burning variety is probably dead or dying.

A worse situation is when the device works *sometimes* but fails after a while (generally just before you're going to save your work). Heat can make a marginal component stop working, and the marginal component might not seem unduly warm. In this situation, how do you locate the bad component? By controlled application of heat and cold.

First, start up the device—PC, modem, whatever—with the cover off. Then use a hair dryer to blow warm, *not hot,* air onto the circuit board (100 degrees will do nicely). The intermittent chip will fail eventually. Now get a can of component coolant (Radio Shack part number 64-2321, for example) and direct the cold blast directly onto the suspect chip. If there's no suspect chip, start with the big ones. Now try to restart the device. If it starts, there's a good chance that the cooled chip is the bad one. If it doesn't restart, try another chip. Keep notes.

The quickest way to find the bad chip with the hot/cold method is through a *binary search.* Start off by cooling only *half* of the circuit board. If the problem goes away, the bad chip is on the cooled half. Warm up the cooled half until the failure occurs, and then cool half of the half that you cooled before. Keep doing this—heat the board, then cool half of the previously cooled area—until you zero in on the bad chip. Finally, there's the brute force method. Get a digital probe and pulser and test each chip, one by one. This method's sure-fire, but slow.

Soldering and Desoldering

If you're going to change chips, a few words about soldering are in order.

It isn't hard, but it *does* take some practice. *If you have never soldered before, the place to learn isn't your PC!* Get some practice elsewhere, or just decide not to bother with soldering tasks. If you *do* want to learn, Heathkit has an excellent "Soldering Self-Instruction" kit. It's $20 and comes with a simple printed circuit project. The kit has a fair amount of information, and I like it quite a lot.

The trick with soldering is to heat up *both* components to the desired temperature, and then apply the solder. You want just enough heat to melt the solder, but not so much as to destroy whatever it is that you're soldering.

Soldering irons come in various powers or wattages. For PC work, you want a low power-iron, like a pencil iron under 50 watts.

Here are a few tips to remember when soldering:

- Use a pencil iron under 50 watts.
- Use a 60/40 solder that is $1/32$ inch in width, with a rosin (*not* acid) core.

- Don't apply the tip more than ten seconds—this should be more than sufficient.

- For desoldering, *do not* use solder suckers or vacuum bulbs unless they have grounded tips. They can build up static charges. Use wire braid instead.

- Remove the board first. Don't try to solder things on or off boards that are installed in the PC.

- When replacing chips or transistors, socket them first (see the next section).

- Buy a solder *jig* (sometimes called a *third hand*) so you have enough hands to hold the board, the soldering iron, the chip, and the desoldering tool. Edmund Scientific (see Appendix A) sells one for $25.95 called the "Extra Hands Work Station."

    (By the way, my friend Scott, a coworker, claims true techies scoff at solder jigs. To the true techies, I apologize. *I've* used the things, and I like them.)

- If replacing a diode, transistor, or capacitor, draw a picture of how the original is installed. Memory (the human kind) gets faulty when faced with the normal frustration of soldering. It doesn't matter which way you insert a resistor.

- When desoldering a chip from a circuit board, don't desolder each pin in order. This builds up too much heat in one area. Jump around. Use a heat sink. Alternatively, use a solder tip designed for DIP packages.

- As mentioned before, many system boards are now four-layer boards. They're *very* tough to work on competently with the usual inexpensive equipment.

Chip Sockets and Chip Insertion and Removal

Chips need not be soldered directly to the motherboard. Chip *sockets* (like light bulb sockets) are available. As long as you're removing and replacing a chip, think about installing a socket for the replacement. Most chips are soldered directly onto the printed circuit board.

The advantages of socketed chips are that they're easy to remove and replace, and it's a lot easier to damage a chip by soldering it in place than by inserting it into a socket. On the other hand, a soldered chip saves money—no socket must be bought. Also, it can't creep out of the socket.

As mentioned before, a socketed chip's problem may be only that it has crept far enough out of the socket to impair electrical connection. Recall that an early step in troubleshooting is to push all socketed chips gently back into their sockets.

Whether you're installing a socketed or directly-mounted chip, you must be sure to install it with the correct side up. Chip pins are numbered counterclockwise, with the farthest pin on the left-hand side labeled 1, then counting down on the left side and finally up the right side (see Figure 7.1). A chip, then, can fit into a socket in one of two ways. Install a chip backwards, and you generally destroy the chip. So pay attention when installing.

The top of the chip generally has a notch (see Figure 7.2) to orient you when installing. To make things even easier, most circuit boards are designed so all the chips face the same way. This is essential: Insert a chip with the notch facing the wrong way, and you may damage the chip. Just make sure you place the new chip so that its notch is facing in the same direction as the chips already on the board.

FIGURE 7.1

Chip numbering

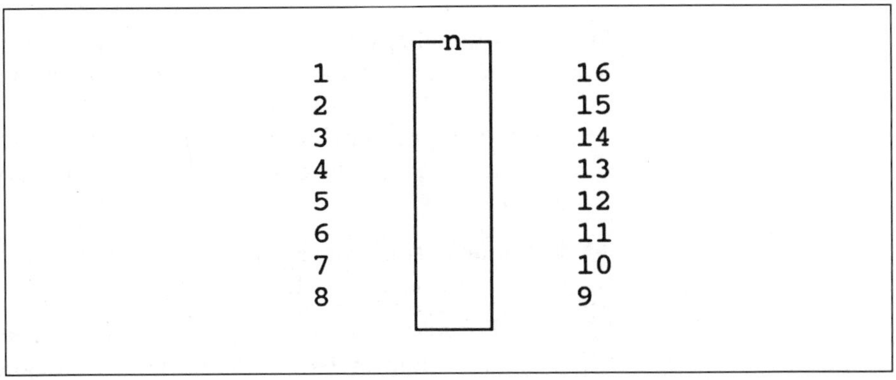

1		n	16
2			15
3			14
4			13
5			12
6			11
7			10
8			9

FIGURE 7.2

Chip notches

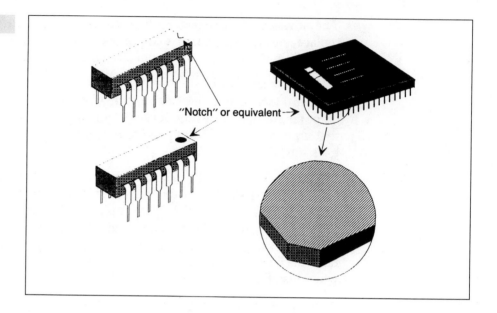

Other Problems and Solutions

The remaining chapters in the book cover peripherals in depth, but here are some ideas and pointers to other sections in the book.

- Hard disk problems. If you seem to have a hard disk problem, look at the extensive coverage of drive recovery in Chapters 13 and 14.

- Keyboard problems. Keyboard problems are covered in Chapter 18, but here are a few possibilities:

  The system board may be at fault. Test keyboard test points (see Chapter 18). Is the keyboard plugged in?

  Is it an AT keyboard on a PC? Vice versa?

  Are you leaning on the Spacebar accidentally?

Is this a turbo AT? Some ATs are so fast that they get confused during a reboot (Ctrl-Alt-Del) unless you take your fingers off the keyboard *very* quickly.

- Many beeps when booting, no video. If you get one long beep and two short beeps, and the drive A light goes on, but there's no display, the problem is most likely the display board. Type *dir b:* and press ↵. If the drive B light comes on, the system is responding—you just can't see it. Swap the display board. Take a look at Chapter 19.

- Drive A light stays on. You try to access drive A, and the floppy light comes on and stays on. Are you loading a program from floppy? The problem could be insufficient memory to run your application. Try your backup diskette, too. Also, check Chapter 14.

- PARITY CHECK error (memory error). See Chapter 8.

CHAPTER

8

Semiconductor Memory

SAID in the last chapter that you generally won't handle troubleshooting down to the chip level. However, there are exceptions, and memory is one of them. So let's talk about the chips you will replace.

No discussion of circuit board and chip problems would be complete without some talk of memory chips. Memory, or RAM, chips are the chips you're most likely to mess with. Generally, you'll handle *Dynamic RAM* (DRAM) chips, but some computers use *Static RAM* (SRAM).

This chapter acquaints you with memory characteristics and organization, how to read the numbers on the top of a chip, how to read memory error messages, what kinds of things can lead to false memory errors, and some tips on handling and installing memory chips.

Reading Memory Chips: Size, Access Time, and Wait States

Chips come (as of this writing) in the following sizes:

16K bits (unusual)

64K bits

64K nybbles (groups of 4 bits)

128K bits

256K bits

256K nybbles

256K SIMMs

1024K bits

1024K SIMMs

4096K SIMMs

16,384K SIMMs

In general, dynamic RAMs used in PCs and ATs are 64K×1 bit or 256K×1 bit. This means that each chip stores 64K bits or 256K bits. Thus, to store 256K bytes, eight 256K-bit chips are needed—8 bits equals 1 byte. That's why each 64K or 256K group is a row of eight chips. (Actually, nine chips are used. The extra chip is for error checking with parity.) A 256K chip is the same physical size as a 64K chip.

On the PS/2s and other high-end machines, manufacturers are using more and more SIMMs (Single Inline Memory Modules). These look like mini-circuit boards containing a number of tiny chips. SIMMs are an entire bank of memory on a miniboard. You can't change a single chip; you must replace an entire bank. SIMMs come in sizes of 256K, 1 MB, 4 MB, and 16MB.

Another important criterion is *access time*, which is part of a chip's cycle time. *Cycle time* is how quickly the chip can respond to a request: If the CPU says, "Get me the value in location 31,824," what's the longest that the memory chip will require to respond? Access time, like cycle time, is measured in *nanoseconds* (ns), or billionths of a second. Typical access times in nanoseconds are:

250 (slowest)

200

150

120

100

85

80

70

65

53 (fastest)

Chips are classified by their access, not cycle, time; see the forthcoming section on wait states. The slowest memory you'll ever see on the PC is 250 ns. Access times of 100 ns and faster are being used in speedier 286/386 AT compatibles.

How do you know what memory speed your PC needs? Either look at the documentation that came with it, or look at the memory it *currently* uses, or see the list of memory speeds in the next section.

Finding Memory Chips: Memory Organization

You've already seen in Chapter 2 that memory is organized into banks, groups of nine chips. That was a bit of a generalization. Here are the details about how memory is laid out on your motherboard.

8088 Memory Organization

You may recall from Chapter 2's discussion of CPUs that the 8088 has an 8-bit data path. That means that every time the 8088 wants to do a memory access, it needs eight bits of data. Now let's look at the memory chips themselves.

Most memory chips are *bit-oriented* chips. A "64K chip" is really a chip with 64K *bits* capacity. Furthermore, that memory chip has a one-bit data path: It can only supply one bit of data at any given point in time. As the 8088 needs eight bits at any given point in time, but each memory chip can only supply one bit, it should be clear that an 8088-based system that uses bit-oriented chips will require a minimum of eight chips for each bank of memory.

The ninth chip is the "parity" chip, used by the system to do a check of the internal integrity of the memory. The parity bit is set when data is first stored in the memory, and then checked when the data is read from the memory. If the parity bit is found to be set incorrectly when the data is read, the system knows that there's been a failure of some kind in the memory system: This leads to the notorious "parity error" that we'll discuss in a few sections. Note that you won't always see parity chips: A few manufacturers decided to save a few bucks and forgo memory checking, sticking with a simple eight-chip memory bank—some of Radio Shack's computers come to mind. So if you see an eight-chip bank, don't be puzzled—you're just looking at a cheaply built machine.

Memory for an 8088-based system can, then, be presented as nine bit-oriented chips. There are also, as mentioned in Chapter 2, SIMMs—small circuit boards that contain memory components on them. Most SIMMs do the work of nine chips, so a bank of memory on an 8088-based system could be supplied by a single SIMM.

The third type of memory organization uses chips like the first approach, but they're different kinds of chips. Where the most common memory chip is bit-oriented, there are also chips that are *nybble-oriented*. A nybble is four bits—half of a byte. A "256K nybble" chip is a memory chip that contains 256K nybbles' worth of data, and that has a four-bit data path.

Since the 8088 needs eight bits of data for memory accesses, an 8088 bank could be constructed of just two nybble chips, with a bit chip thrown in for the parity. The three kinds of memory organization are summarized in Figure 8.1.

80286 and Higher Memory Organization

For more advanced chips, the organization is a bit different. Remember that the newer CPUs have larger data paths— 16 bits for the 286 and 386SX and 32 bits for the 386DX and both kinds of 486.

A 286 or 386SX would require a minimum of 16 bit-oriented chips for a single memory bank, or 18 chips in total with parity; when parity chips are added, one parity chip is added for each group of eight bits. This bank would be 18 bit-oriented chips, two standard SIMMs, or four nybble and two bit-oriented chips. There are even a few vendors—Compaq, IBM, and Toshiba are examples—who have designed their own "16-bit SIMMs," single SIMMs that comprise an entire bank for 286 or 386SX machines.

FIGURE 8.1

Common memory layouts

The most common memory organization in computers designed from 1981 through 1988 uses banks of nine single bit memory chips that together provide the nine bits required for an error-checked bank of memory. A few computers use only eight chips, as they forgo error checking. As the chips are of the DIP variety, this kind of memory organization is sometimes called "DIP memory."

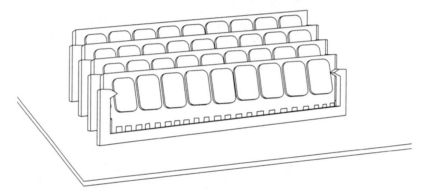

A system's memory may be organized with SIMMs. Some SIMMs take the place of nine single-bit chips. Some manufacturers reduce the space needed for SIMMs even further by building *16 bit SIMMS,* SIMMs that take the place of 18 chips. (One example is the PS/2 Model 70.)

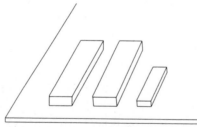

Some banks are composed of only three chips: two larger "nybble" chips that provide four bits apiece, and one more normal-sized single bit chip providing one bit. 4+4+1=9, the number of bits in an error-checked bank.

A 386DX or 486, with its 32-bit data path, would then require 32 bit-oriented chips for data and four more for parity, leading to a 36-chip bank. Four SIMMs would be required for a full bank, or (I've never seen this, but it could happen) nine nybble chips.

Memory Chip Markings

The official names of memory chips reveal two things: their capacity (16K, 64K, 256K, 1024K) and their access time. Chip names take the form 41xx-yy, where *xx* represents the size and *yy* represents the access time in tens of nanoseconds. Here are some examples:

4164-25	64K, access time=250 ns
41256-10	256K, access time=100 ns
4164-15	64K, access time=150 ns

See Figure 8.2 for an example of a 64K, 150-ns chip. Recall that the number may be hidden in a longer ID code, like SN4164-20N. Some manufacturers don't use 64 for 64K or 256 for 256K, but some nearby number, like 65 or 257. (Perhaps they're suggesting that their chips are just a *bit* better than the competition's?) The 41 may be replaced by some other two-digit code, most likely 66, 37, or 42.

Memory Sizes and Data Widths

Memory chips come in varying sizes (and, as you'll see later, speeds). Memory chips have a capacity, and a *data path*—the size of the "front door" of the chip. Once, a group or "bank" of memory consisted of nine small chips called "bit" chips. Now it may be configured as three chips or a small miniature circuit board called a SIMM—Single Inline Memory Module. (There are also SIPPs, which are SIMMs with unusual connectors, but they're few and far between.)

Computer chips are largely responsible for transporting and storing data. CPUs and memory chips each have a data path, the "front door" of the chip. Data paths for memory chips are either one bit (as in the case of the 16K bit, 64K bit, 256K bit, and 1024K bit chips), one nybble—four bits—as in the case of the 64K nybble, the 256K nybble, and 1024K nybble. SIMMs are built up out of either nybbles and/or bits, and usually have a cumulative data path of eight or nine bits.

Data path is more than just a techie side-issue—it's vital to arranging banks of memory. For instance, consider a 64K nybble chip and a 256K bit chip. Notice that the 64K nybble chips have 64K groups of 4 bits (nybbles), for an internal capacity total of 256K bits. A 256K bit chip also has an internal capacity total of 256K bits, but it's arranged differently: the 64K nybble chip can deliver four bits at a time, whereas the 256K bit chip can deliver 256K separate bits only one at a time. A one-megabyte SIMM can provide 1024K of bytes—8-bit groups.

So, to summarize, you'll see the following chip paths/packages and sizes:

- Single bit data path—the most common memory chip. Comes in 16K, 64K, 256K, 1024K.

- Nybble—less common. Comes in 64K, 256K, 1024K.

- SIMMs—the fastest growing sector of the market. Most new machines use SIMMs. SIMMs come in 256K, 1024K, and 4096K sizes.

Memory Organization

PC processors have appeared in three main families: the 8088 family, the 80286, and the 80386 families. Like memory chips, CPU chips also have data paths. Here are the data paths for some common CPU chips:

CPU chips have different-sized data paths, and the data path is essentially the "front door" of the chip. The 8088 has an 8-bit data path, and so can read or write eight bits at a time, the 80286 and 80386SX have a 16-bit data path, enabling them to transfer twice as much data in or out in one operation, and all of the 386 family except the SX have 32 bit data paths. That data path will affect how memory banks are arranged.

Memory Banks on 8088 Computers

Figure 8.3 shows a block diagram of the 8088. The eight lines below it represent the eight data bits that it needs every time it reads or writes data.

A 256K memory chip usually means 256K bits. Adding it to the previous diagram, you see something like Figure 8.4.

The chip you see in Figure 8.4 contains 256K bits of memory, and it has a one-bit data path. As you can see, it would do your PC no good if you added a single memory chip: it would provide data to one of the 8088's data lines, leaving the other seven dangling.

FIGURE 8.3

The 8088 chip

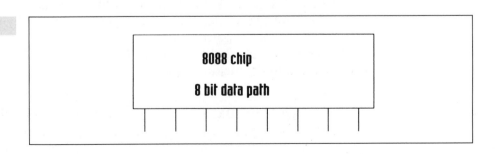

FIGURE 8.4

The 8088 chip with a 256K memory chip

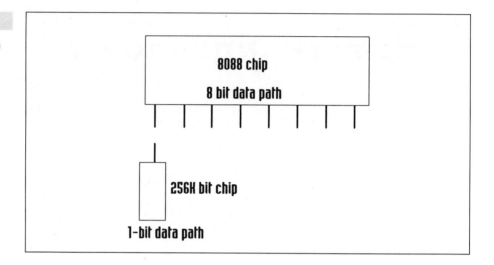

It seems logical, then, that eight 256K bit chips would nicely meet the memory needs of the 8088: one chip for each data line. That would provide a total of 256K bytes of data. Of course, you wouldn't stop there—most XTs have 640K of memory. But we're just talking about a single bank of memory in this case. And a few PCs do indeed use eight-chip memory banks (see Figure 8.5).

But most use a ninth chip called a "parity" chip—I've labeled it with a "P" in Figure 8.6. It and another chip called a "comparator" are used to check the integrity of the data in memory.

When eight bits of data are written to RAM, the comparator generates the ninth parity bit based on the contents of the other eight. Then, when the data is read back, the comparator uses the parity chip to check to see if the eight bits of data have been damaged either by a hardware error in the memory, a power surge, or the like. If it detects an error, it generates something called a *nonmaskable interrupt*, or *NMI*, calling the CPU's attention to the memory problem.

What the CPU does with that data depends on the kind of computer you've got, but IBM computers respond by putting the words "Parity Check" on the screen, and then locking up the computer. You've got to turn the PC off and on again to get it to respond to you.

FIGURE 8.5

FIGURE 8.5

Eight-chip memory
banks

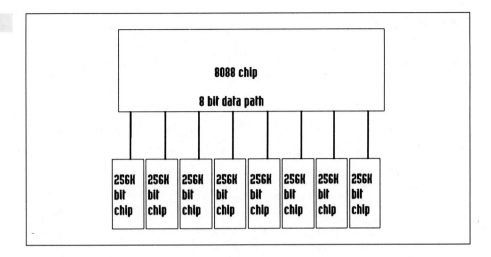

FIGURE 8.6

Eight-chip memory
banks with a parity
chip

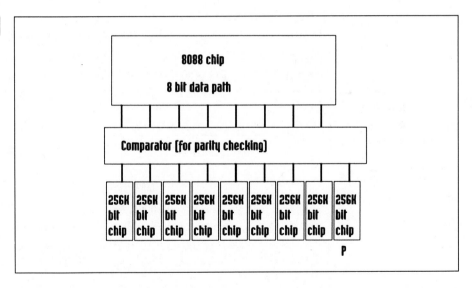

Now you've seen why so many memory banks consist of nine chips. Most
XT memory banks require nine chips: there would be no value to adding
just two or three of these bit oriented memory chips. But you'll see
another kind of bank, one consisting of two larger-than-normal RAM
chips and one small memory chip. Those larger chips are *nybble* chips, as
shown in Figure 8.7.

FIGURE 8.7

A nybble chip

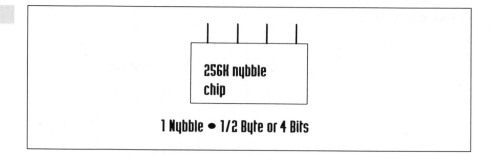

Again, a nybble is one half of a byte—four bits. I hear you chuckling out there, but I assure you, I'm not joking—nybble is the word for it. A 256K nybble chip stores 256K four-bit groups: four times as much as a 256K bit chip.

Using nybble chips, a three-chip bank can be constructed: two larger nybble chips and one smaller bit chip, as shown in Figure 8.8.

The third kind of bank you'd see is a SIMM—a Single Inline Memory Module. The SIMM is a small circuit board that has memory chips mounted right on it, as in Figure 8.9.

FIGURE 8.8

A three-chip bank with two nybble chips and one smaller chip

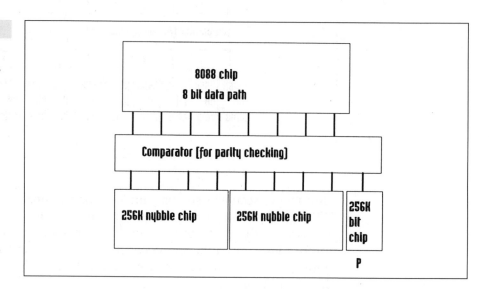

FIGURE 8.9

A SIMM

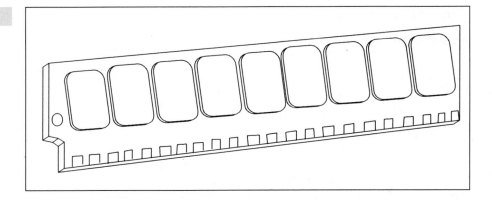

You needn't remove these chips, and you can't, in fact, at least not without a soldering iron. Its small edge connector plugs into a special socket on the motherboard or a properly-equipped memory expansion board. It generally does the job of nine chips, so one SIMM would equal one bank of memory on our 8088 computer. So, summarizing what we've seen so far, there are three basic ways to organize memory on a simple 8088. First, there's the simple nine-chip bank composed of chips with a data path of one bit apiece. Take a gander at Figure 8.10.

Alternatively, two nybbles and a bit will do the job (see Figure 8.11).

Or, as is the case with most recent PCs, a single SIMM may do the job. More likely, however, a PC's motherboard has room for several SIMMs, as you see in Figure 8.12.

FIGURE 8.10

A simple nine-chip bank

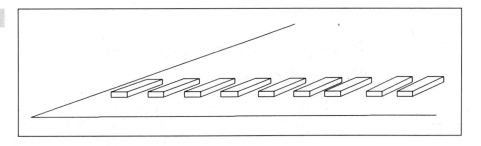

FIGURE 8.11

Two nybbles and a bit

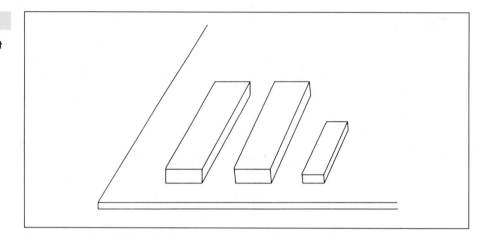

FIGURE 8.12

Motherboards on recent PCs have room for several SIMMs.

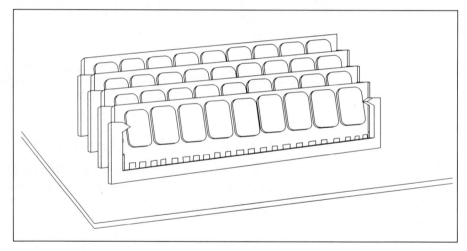

Memory Banks on 16-Bit Computers

What you've learned so far explains how 8088 memory banks work. But recall that the 286 and 386SX computers don't have an 8-bit data path—they've got a 16-bit data path. So eight or nine chips wouldn't do the job for them. As the 286's "front door" or data path is sixteen bits wide, we'd need sixteen 256K bit chips to create a bank for the 286—and that's if our

286 computer was designed to work without parity. With parity, we need a parity bit for each 8-bit group, requiring two extra bits on the bank, for a total of 18 chips.

So the minimum number of memory bit chips you've got to add to a 286 system is eighteen. With nybble chips, we'd need four nybbles and two bits—hmmm, this is starting to sound like a dog-food commercial. As ordinary SIMMs provide 9 bits, you'd need two SIMMs to provide a full bank for 286 systems. Some vendors, like IBM and Toshiba, have designed their own special proprietary 16-bit SIMMs. That's why the IBM PS/2 model 55SX, which uses a 386SX, only requires one SIMM to make a bank—it's a special 16-bit SIMM.

On a typical 386SX computer, you'll see room for four SIMMs. Again, two SIMMs is one bank, as far as the 386SX is concerned, so this motherboard has room for two banks of memory.

How would you configure that memory? Here are the rules:

1. On computers that use banks that require multiple SIMMs (such as 286 and later CPUs), all SIMMs in a bank must be the same size and speed.

2. You may be able to put any size SIMM that you like in a bank, but not always. It's fairly common to see SX machines that won't take 4-MB SIMMs. Other motherboards restrict you from putting in a second bank that is smaller than the first bank—for example, if you'd used 1-MB SIMMs in bank 0, you couldn't put 256K SIMMs in bank 1.

Assuming that our hypothetical computer could take four SIMMs, how many possible memory configurations do we have? The table following summarizes all of the possibilities.

BANK 0	BANK 1	TOTAL (MB)
256	0	0.5
1024	0	2
4096	0	8
256	256	1

BANK 0	BANK 1	TOTAL (MB)
256	1024	2.5
256	4096	8.5
1024	256	2.5
1024	1024	4
1024	4096	10
4096	256	8.5
4096	1024	10
4096	4096	16

Notice that there are some particularly inefficient layouts. Ever notice how many 386SX computers ship with 1 MB of RAM? But look at how it's arranged—the only way to do it is by filling up all of the SIMM sockets with 256K SIMMs. As an exercise, you might want to map out all of the possibilities with an SX motherboard that supports eight SIMM sockets, as some do.

Finally, what about 386DX and other CPUs with 32-bit data paths?

The 386DX and all of the 486 chips all have a 32-bit data path. 32 bits for data plus four bits for parity means a 386 that uses bit chips requires 36 chips per memory bank—that's a lot of chip stuffing! While I've never seen a 386 with nybble memory, only nine nybble chips would be needed to create a 32-bit memory bank, and four normal 9-bit SIMMs would be required. Again, vendors using 16 bit SIMMs would only need two SIMMs to make a complete 386 memory bank.

Room for eight SIMMs is quite common for 386DX and 486 motherboards, so let's take a look at the possibilities there. There's room for eight SIMMs—how many banks is that? Just two, because the 32-bit data path of the CPUs we're discussing here demands four SIMMs per bank. The combinations look like this:

BANK 0	BANK 1	TOTAL (MB)
256	0	1
1024	0	4

BANK 0	BANK 1	TOTAL (MB)
4096	0	16
256	256	2
256	1024	5
256	4096	17
1024	256	5
1024	1024	8
1024	4096	20
4096	256	17
4096	1024	20
4096	4096	32

Again, there're some "clunker" combinations, perhaps the worst of which is the 2-MB arrangement—all of the SIMM sockets filled with 256K chips! Notice also that you've got a bit of a tough choice in the area of 8 MB. You really need 8 MB to make Windows or OS/2 work well, and you will want 16 MB eventually. But notice that to get 8 MB you'll fill your motherboard with 1-MB SIMMs, SIMMs that you'll have to throw away when you upgrade to 16-MB—an upgrade that will require four 4-MB SIMMs.

Most modern PC CPUs can accommodate quite a lot of memory. Unfortunately, many motherboards aren't designed well, and so can't use very much memory. So, when buying a PC, you should look closely at how much memory you can put on the motherboard. It's surprising how little memory motherboards from some big names can accommodate. Look for the ability to put at least 16 MB on the motherboard, even if you're not going to use it immediately: believe me, you'll get there eventually.

Now, of course, there's an exception to that rule. Some vendors, like Compaq, have built quite a number of fast PCs that are equipped with one special high-speed slot designed specifically for memory. If you have a memory board with an unusual connector, more than likely you have a high-speed slot.

This is an important thing to know if you're buying one of these computers. It's not unusual to see a computer today that has room on the motherboard for just 8 MB of memory. That computer will probably expand to 16 MB with the addition of the special board that goes into that high-speed slot: The extra 8 MB goes on that board. That special board is only available from the PC's vendor: The special Compaq board won't work in the same slot as the special Everex board, which won't work in the same slot as the special AST board, and so on.

Many people see that their computer will take 8 MB on the motherboard, and say, "No point in buying the expansion board for the second 8 MB yet—I'll wait until I need more than 8 MB total, and buy the memory expansion board then." The trouble is, once you need the special board, the PC maker will have gone on to more advanced computers, and won't sell your special expansion board any more, so you'll be stuck. The board generally costs only around $100, so buy it when you buy the PC.

Summarizing, you may see any of the following codes atop a 64K, 200-ns memory chip:

    4164-20

    3764-20

    6665A20 4264-20

You may also see a 4464, 41464, 414256, or 44256 chip. This is, as you'd surmise, a 64K or 256K chip respectively, but it's unusual in that it's a chip not with 64K bits, but with 64K *nybbles* (4-bit groups). That means a bank of 64K need not be nine 64K single-bit 4164s, but rather (as is seen on some motherboards) two 64K-nybble 4464s and a 4164 to total nine bits. IBM used 4464s on the motherboard of the XT286: two 256K SIMMs (for a total of 512K), and four 4464s and two 4164s to add the 128K needed to bring system memory to a grand total of 640K. The key seems to be that if the *last* digit before the size is a *4*, it's a nybble chip.

Finally, when identifying memory remember also that manufacturers can do anything they like—there are no Memory Label Police—so you could come up against a 128K chip that simply says Z1250L. You wouldn't find anything out about this chip short of getting a copy of the manufacturer's spec sheets on it.

Beware of Eight-Bit SIMMs!

Now that you understand how memory chips relate to the memory addressing abilities of your processor chips, let me explain how some companies *cheat* at designing your memory subsystem.

Recall that in 8088-based systems, the CPU chip only needs eight bits of data delivered to its front door ("data path"), but that most PCs use nine—eight for data, one for parity. Parity tests memory integrity every single time that you read data from memory, a good idea when you consider how important the things in your computer's RAM are.

Similarly, SIMMs are usually built around a number of memory chips, a number that's usually a multiple of nine. For example, four-megabyte SIMMs are often called *4M × 9 SIMMs*, referring to the fact that the SIMM contains nine groups of four million bits. Simply providing four megabytes could be accomplished with 4M × 8, but the extra bit is the watchdog for your RAM.

Memory prices fluctuate. Changes in the political climate (threats of tariffs and trade sanctions), industry shortages, or just wild speculation can make memory prices jump up 100 percent in a week, and then plummet the next. The spot market for RAM is as volatile as the spot market for crude oil. That makes life difficult for PC vendors, who try to offer lower and lower prices. RAM can be a major cost component of a PC; for example, at this instant, 16 MB of RAM costs around $600 on the street, but a 16-MB 486 PC will cost around $2500. That means that *one quarter* of the PC's cost is RAM! (I'm sure that those two prices will be obsolete by the time that you read this, but the ratios tend to stay pretty constant, so the point that I'm making remains unchanged.) If, then, memory prices go up 40 percent in a week, then it gets pretty tough to offer those same low prices that are advertised in the latest *PC Magazine*. After all, the ad was prepared a month or two ago, and who could know what memory prices would do?

Some vendors have begun to hedge their bets by silently re-designing their motherboards to use not the *4M × 9* SIMMs, but instead *4M × 8* SIMMS! As they've got fewer memory components, the eight-bit SIMMs are a bit cheaper … but you lose the parity protection. So, when you're buying PCs these days, add a question to your information-gathering checklist: "Do your PCs use eight-bit SIMMs or nine-bit SIMMs?" (If the sales person doesn't know what you're talking about, then just go buy somewhere else.)

Background: Wait States

Although they really don't have anything to do with troubleshooting, it's common for people at this point to ask, "What's a wait state?" Here's the answer.

On 286/386 machines, memory must be able to respond to a CPU request in two clock ticks. *Clock ticks* are just the reciprocal of the clock rate: 8 MHz means 8 million clock ticks per second, so each clock tick is 1/8,000,000 second. Punch 1 divided by 8 million into your calculator, and you'll get 0.000000125, which is 0.125 microseconds, or 125 nanoseconds. You can do this for all the popular 286/386 clock rates (see below).

CLOCK SPEED (MHz)	DURATION (ns)
16	167
18	125
10	100
12	183
16	163
20	150
25	140
33	130

The memory must be able to respond to a memory request in two of these clock ticks, so, for example, the memory for a 10-MHz computer must be able to respond in 2×100 ns=200 ns. Most people think the access time is the only time required by the memory when fetching data, but there's another part. The chips have a *charging time* that may equal or exceed the access time. (Typical charging times for a Mostek 64K and 256K DRAMs are shown in Table 8.1.) So access time is important, but the total cycle time is more important:

```
Memory Cycle Time=Memory Access Time+Memory Charging Time
```

TABLE 8.1: Memory Timing Statistics for 64K and 256K DRAMS

ACCESS TIME (NS)	PLUS CHARGING TIME	EQUALS CYCLE TIME
200	170	370
150	120	270
120	90	210
100	75	175
80	65	145

For example, suppose we're going to design a computer using a 10-MHz clock and 256K, 120-ns chips, as cited above. We've got to keep an entire memory cycle below $2 \times 100 = 200$ ns. The cycle time equals the access time plus the charge time, and we know that the access time is 120 ns. Charge time for the 120 ns 256K chips is 90 ns, so total cycle time for the chips is $120 + 90 = 210$ ns—the memories are just 10 ns too slow.

What to do? Obviously, we could install faster memories (for more money), or slow down the processor. There's a third alternative—add wait states. A wait state is just an extra clock tick added to each memory access. Thus, instead of requiring that each memory cycle be done in just two clock ticks (200 ns, in our case), we relax the constraint, requiring that a cycle be finished in just *three* clock ticks. Three clock ticks is 300 ns— plenty of time for our memory to complete its 210 ns cycle.

Sounds great, eh? Not really. Consider that a 10-MHz computer is supposed to get a memory access done in two cycles. With a wait state, it takes *three* cycles (300 ns). What computer would normally require 300 ns to complete a memory access in two clock ticks (no wait states)? One with a $300 \div 2 = 150$ ns clock tick. That would be a 6.7-MHz computer, which is considerably slower than a 10 MHz computer. Thus, adding a wait state really means slowing the computer down by *50 percent* whenever memory accesses occur.

Put together memory cycle times and clock durations, and you can compute Table 8.2.

TABLE 8.2: Memory Requirements for 286/386 Computers

CLOCK SPEED (MHZ)	DURATION (NS)	CYCLE TIME FOR 0 WAIT STATE (2 CLOCKS)	CYCLE TIME FOR 1 WAIT STATE (3 CLOCKS)	MINIMUM MEMORY SPEED FOR 0-WAIT STATE	MINIMUM MEMORY SPEED FOR 1-WAIT STATE
16	167	334	501	150	200
18	125	250	375	120	200
10	100	200	300	100	150
12	183	166	249	80	120
16	163	126	189	60	100
20	150	100	150	53	80
25	140	180	120	N/A	53
33	130	160	190	N/A	N/A

Caches: Why There's No Such Thing as a "Zero Wait State" 386

A topic that gets raised more and more is the question, "What is a memory cache?" Put simply, a *memory cache* is a way to get around the fact that CPUs nowadays are faster than the memory available for a reasonable price. (There's something called a *disk* cache, but that's for later in the book.)

As you've seen, memories come in different speeds. From 1981 to 1986, memory chips pretty much got faster at about the same rate as processors: An 8-MHz computer could generally be outfitted with memory of like speed without breaking the bank.

Then 16 MHz came around.

At 16 MHz, the usual dynamic memory chips just couldn't keep up. Nobody makes a dynamic memory chip with a 126-ns total cycle time.

Manufacturers would either be forced to insert wait states, (a sleazy way, as we've seen, of making a slow machine sound fast), or they'd have to look elsewhere for faster memories.

As it turns out, there *are* faster memories, but they're *static* RAMs, and they're expensive—ten or more times the cost of dynamic RAMs of comparable size. One company did indeed go to all-static memory, but they soon discontinued the product, cost no doubt having something to do with it.

As has happened before, a leaf was taken from the mainframe's book, and *cache memory* was included in most 16-MHz and faster computers. Cache memory is a small amount (generally no more than 64K) of the expensive static RAM, which is fast enough so the CPU can address it at no–wait-state speed. There's also a larger amount, perhaps megabytes, of the relatively slower 80-or-so–ns dynamic memory. The last piece of hardware is a *cache controller* to manage the whole mess.

A cache controller tries to speed up the much larger RAM using an assumption about computer use. The idea is that computer programs tend to stay within one area of code for a while, then move to another area and stay there for a while, and so on. The same phenomenon occurs with data. The cache controller gets an idea of what part of memory to work with and guesses that the CPU will soon need the data that follows in that part of memory. Then it goes to that area in the slow dynamic memory and grabs a piece of it—not the whole 64K, more commonly 4K or thereabouts—and transfers it into the cache. Now, if the cache has guessed right, the next data the CPU needs won't be in the slow memory: It'll be in the cache. The cache is fast enough to accept reads and writes at zero–wait-state speed.

That's *if* the cache has guessed right. If not, the CPU must go all the way out to the slow dynamic memory and endure *two wait states*. (Auggh!) That means the cache had better be good, or you'll have a two-wait-state machine. In practice, caches are right 80 to 99 percent of the time, so you should end up with a machine that's zero-wait state 80 to 99 percent of the time and two-wait state the other 1–20 percent of the time.

Most 386 machines use the Intel 80385 cache controller to handle cache management. The 486 actually includes the 385 right in it with a small amount of static RAM. It's only a *small* cache, at 8K. When buying 486-based systems, buy at least 256K of supplemental *external* cache.

Reading Memory Error Messages

So much for the theory. Now let's look at diagnosing memory error messages. There are three ways to find memory problems: 1) run a rigorous memory test periodically; 2) get a memory error message when the PC does the POST; or 3) get a PARITY CHECK error while in the middle of an application. Let's see how to read the cryptic POST messages for memory problems.

PARITY CHECK 1 means the problem is on the motherboard. PARITY CHECK 2 is on an expansion board.

The POST runs a memory test each time you power up the PC. How does the test know how much memory the system has? You tell it by setting DIP switches on the PC system board, or by running the SETUP program on the AT. Most XT-type computers (the IBM PC excepted) deduce the amount of memory in a POST memory test.

The IBM PC and AT-type machines depend on the setup information, and they're distressed when a memory test finds a different amount of memory than the setup information lead them to expect. So, if you've just installed new memory on an IBM PC or an AT-type computer, and you get a PARITY CHECK message, the first thing to check is whether you reset the system board switches correctly (for a PC) or ran the SETUP program and updated the memory size correctly (for an AT-type system). If you installed 512K on a PC and told the system that 640K exists, you'll get a parity error every time. This is, again, not true for XT-type machines. They really don't pay attention to the DIP switches to determine how much memory they have. For example, if an XT-type computer does the power-up test and finds a problem in the 384K block of memory, it won't issue an error; it will just assume that only 320K memory exists. An IBM PC or most AT-type machines would issue an error message saying in effect, "You lied to me about memory."

Recall that the POST memory error message is a code 201. A POST 201 error will be accompanied by a four-digit code such as

    1020 201

followed quickly by the familiar PARITY CHECK 1 or PARITY CHECK 2 error. On an XT, the same message would look as follows:

    10000 20 201

An AT error message might look like

    10000 0020 201

All three messages allow you to narrow down the memory error to a single chip. All three messages can be decoded to point to first the bad bank of memory, and then the bad chip within that bank. Figure 8.13 shows the part of an XT motherboard that stores the memory.

Decoding IBM PC and XT Error Messages

First, simplify the XT error message to look like a PC error message. In general, you can convert an XT message to a PC message by ignoring the last three digits in the 10000. Thus, a **20000 04** for the XT is the same as 2004 for the PC. The four digits will help you locate the bad chip. So first collapse the XT message to a PC message.

Next, understand that the two leftmost digits point to the bad bank, and the two rightmost digits identify the bad chip in that bank.

Suppose you have an error message such as 3008 201 (30000 08 201 on an XT). The first two digits identify the bank with the bad chip, the last two digits identify the bad chip within the bank. The 201 just tells you that you have a memory error, and that's no surprise. So the problem is in the bank referred to by 30, (not bank 30, there isn't one) and the bad chip is the one with ID 08 in that bank (no, it's not the eighth chip). Figure 8.14 shows how to read a memory error message.

In order to use these error messages, you must first identify which kind of motherboard you have. There are three types for PC- and XT-class computers:

- Original PC (1981–1982)
- PC-2 and original XT (1983–1987)
- 640K XT motherboard (1986–1987)

FIGURE 8.14

How to read a memory error message

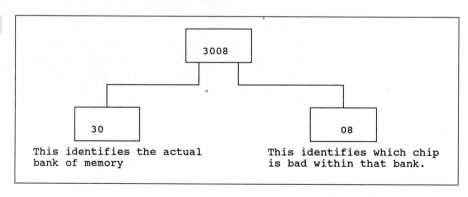

The following pages show an outline of an IBM PC or XT motherboard. On the left is the 201 message: 30xx 201 refers to any 201 message that starts with 30. The *xx* refers to the chip ID, which is written in the chip position on the board.

Original 1981 PC–Early 1983 Motherboard

The marking on the motherboard reads 16-64K CPU. This motherboard contained four 16K banks for a total of 64K on the motherboard (see Figure 8.15). The following examples show you how to locate a chip that is causing an error message:

0C01 201 is on the bottom row, first chip on the extreme left. There's a plus sign (+) in the chip in the diagram in Figure 8.15.

0440 201 is on the second row (counting from the top), second chip over from extreme right. There's an asterisk (*) in the chip in the diagram.

PC-2 (1983–1987) and XT (1983–1987) Motherboard

The marking on the motherboard reads 64-256K CPU. This motherboard contained four 64K banks for a total of 256K on the motherboard. (See Figure 8.16.) The following examples show you how to find a chip causing an error message:

3008 201 on the PC, or **30000 08 201** on the XT, indicates the last row, middle chip, as designated by an asterisk (*) in Figure 8.16.

2080 201 on the PC, or **20000 80 201** on the XT, indicates the third row, rightmost chip, as designated by a plus sign (+) in the diagram.

FIGURE 8.15

16K–64K
motherboard memory
arrangement

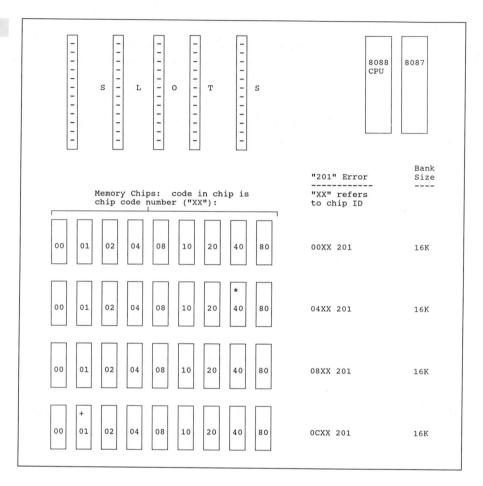

640K XT Motherboard: (1986–1987)

The marking on the motherboard reads 256K-640K CPU. This mother-board contained two 256K banks and two 64K banks for a motherboard total of 640K. (See Figure 8.17.) The following examples show you how to find a chip causing an error message:

> Again, looking at **300000 08 201**, it's now in the first row. Note that codes 00000 08 201, 100000 08 201, and 20000 08 201 would all designate the same chip, indicated with an ★ in Figure 8.17.

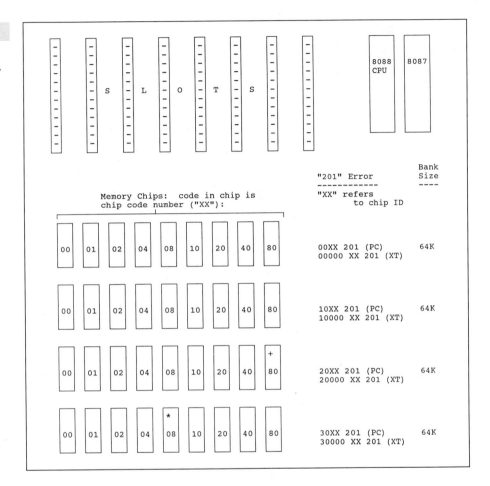

FIGURE 8.16

64K–256K
motherboard memory
arrangement

Error **80000 10 201** is in the third row, one of the 64K rows, the first chip to the right of the middle chip as designated by a plus sign (**+**).

Special Case: "40FF 201" Error

One special case is an error message of the form 40FF 201 followed by a *Parity Check 2* message on a 256K PC. Examine the preceding motherboard memory decoding guides and you'll see that 40*xx* errors aren't on the motherboard—30*xx* is where errors stop on the 256K motherboard. That means 40FF refers to the first bank on an expansion board for this

FIGURE 8.17

640K XT motherboard
memory arrangement

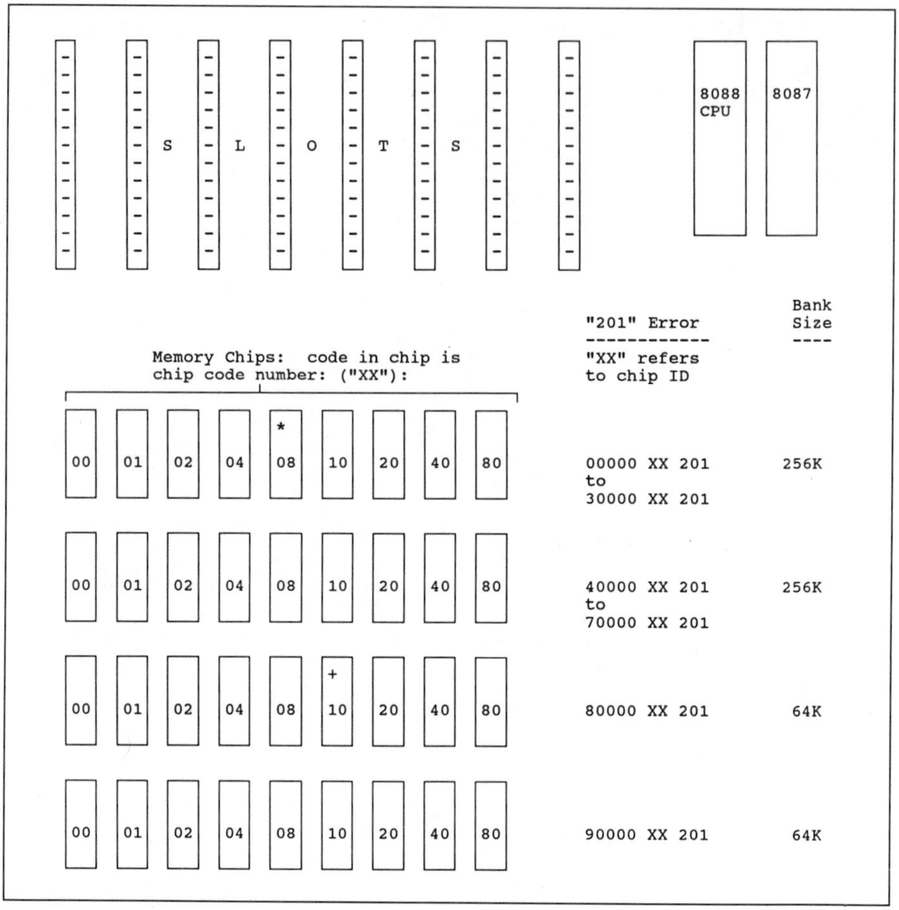

Memory Chips: code in chip is chip code number: ("XX"):	"201" Error "XX" refers to chip ID	Bank Size

00	01	02	04	08*	10	20	40	80	00000 XX 201 to 30000 XX 201	256K
00	01	02	04	08	10	20	40	80	40000 XX 201 to 70000 XX 201	256K
00	01	02	04	08	10+	20	40	80	80000 XX 201	64K
00	01	02	04	08	10	20	40	80	90000 XX 201	64K

machine. The chip ID, however, is FF, so the FF indicates that all nine chips in the bank are failing! (Add up the codes for the chips, and they come to FF hex.) This error occurs when the memory expansion board cannot be accessed at all. You'll see this message when the dip switches indicate that there's more than 256K installed but there's no expansion board, or when the memory board is defective.

An Example PC Error Message

Assume you've got the 256K PC motherboard. You turn the computer on and get a cup of coffee while it goes through the memory test. When you return, you see PARITY CHECK 1 on the screen. To diagnose the problem, you need to see the 201 error. The only way to get it back is to turn the machine off, count to 5, and then turn it back on. *Keep your eyes open!* The 201 message will only last for a second. You would see, for example, 3008 201 and then the PARITY CHECK 1 message.

First, 30 indicates that it's in bank 3, the one nearest the front of the computer. Code 08 indicates it's chip 5, the one in the middle of the row. Simply replace the middle chip in the forwardmost row and you'll be up and running again.

Understanding Error Messages in 8088 Clones

We've already seen that memory is organized into banks of nine chips. Virtually no non-IBM computers offer chip-specific diagnostic information; rather, they just tell you which bank is in error. You'll see a message like

```
Error at 3000:12A0
```

The number of interest is the leftmost one, 3. Think of memory addresses as being organized into 64K groups. If 0 is the first, 1 is the second, and so on, then 3 refers to the fourth 64K group, and that's the bank to replace. So if you've got a motherboard with four banks of 64K on it, you would replace the fourth 64K bank to resolve the above error.

But the memory might not be organized in physical 64K banks. The AT&T 6300, for example, commonly uses physical 64K banks for the first two logical banks, then two physical 256K banks for the latter eight 64K banks. (Just to make things confusing, it also has the option to do the reverse. It can alternatively put 256K chips in the first two banks and 64Ks in the following banks.) When there are 256K physical banks, just consider one physical 256K bank as standing in for four 64K banks:

PHYSICAL BANK	ERROR ADDRESS
First (64K)	0XXX:XXXX
Second (64K)	1XXX:XXXX
Third (256K)	2XXX:XXXX 3XXX:XXXX, 4XXX:XXXX, 5XXX:XXXX
Fourth (256K)	6XXX:XXXX, 7XXX:XXXX, 8XXX:XXXX, 9XXX:XXXX

A typical motherboard's memory arrangement might look then like Figure 8.18.

Again, now you've got to replace the whole bank. Generally non-IBM computers give only enough information to identify the bad bank, not the bad chips. If you had a lot of time, you could change them chip by chip to find the bad one. At chip prices these days, it might not be worth it.

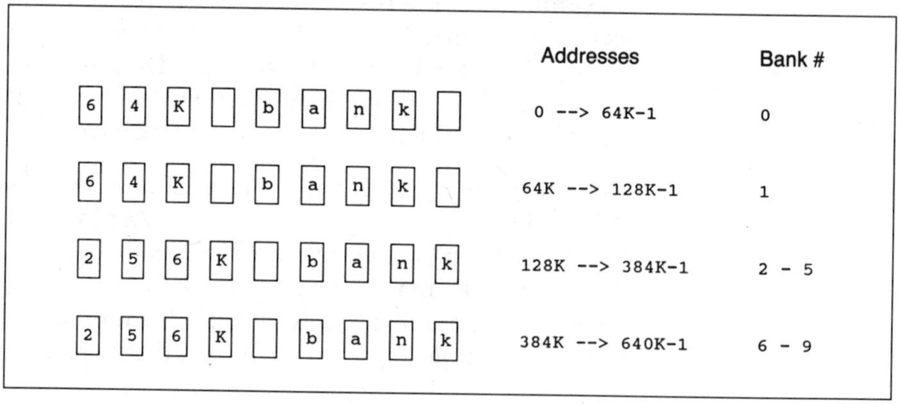

FIGURE 8.18

Hypothetical 8088 motherboard memory arrangement

	Addresses	Bank #
6 4 K [ ] b a n k [ ]	0 --> 64K-1	0
6 4 K [ ] b a n k [ ]	64K --> 128K-1	1
2 5 6 K [ ] b a n k	128K --> 384K-1	2 - 5
2 5 6 K [ ] b a n k	384K --> 640K-1	6 - 9

Understanding Error Messages in 8086–Pentium Compatibles

Before I explain the IBM AT's error messages, I want to discuss AT-type clones so that the AT's memory diagnostics, which are pretty Byzantine, will make some sense.

The notion of 64K banks is simple enough with the 8088-based machines. That's largely because the 8088 has an 8-bit data bus. That's where the nine chips come from: eight for data, and one for error checking. Recall that the 8086 and 80286 are 16-bit chips. It turns out to be a lot faster to access memory 16 bits at a time by alternating nine-chip groups when reading the memory. If the machine in the previous section was a 286 machine, its memory organization might look like Figure 8.19.

FIGURE 8.19

Hypothetical 80286 motherboard memory arrangement

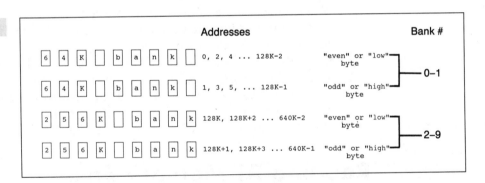

Notice why each "bank" is 18 chips. You couldn't just add 9 chips to the motherboard. If you did, *you'd only get the even-numbered locations!* (You'd need pretty fancy software to run on such a machine, eh?)

Be very sure you understand this: The top two rows together act like a single 128K bank, not two 64K banks. Any error messages referring to the first 128K could point to a problem in either one of the top two rows. Similarly, the bottom two rows act like a single 512K bank.

In fact, we can state a general rule: *The size of a physical bank is the same as the data path to that group of memory.* The 80286 CPU in the AT has a

16-bit data path, so memory on the motherboard is in 16-bit banks. The 8086 CPU used in the Compaq Deskpro also has a 16-bit data path and, once again, chips are in 16-bit banks. For 80386-based machines, we need 32-bit groups, if we use the 32-bit bus, and there must be 36 chips in a bank. If you put an AT memory card into the 16-bit bus of a 386 machine, then you'll be dealing with 16-bit banks on that card.

The idea that the physical bank is the same as the data path is important when you add memory to a PC. For the 386, you must add either 36 chips or four SIMMs. Since chips and SIMMs come in two sizes, 256K and 1 M, you can add memory in groups of $4 \times 256K = 1$ MB or 4×1 MB = 4 MB. Be careful when you choose a 386 machine if you need lots of memory now! Several popular machines are using static column SIMMs that vary greatly in price depending on size. A 256K static SIMM costs about $200, so it will cost me $800 to add a megabyte. But if I need to use 1-MB SIMMs, I'll have to pay $2,000 each for a cost of $8,000 for 4 MB. Ouch!

You should use the same rules as before to identify which bank is the bad one, but now do you have to change *18 chips?* Nope. Look at Figure 8.19 again—you can tell which of the 9-chip groups is the bad one because one group has the even addresses (the *low* ones) and the other has the odd (*high*) addresses. Go back to the memory error address (recall that it looks something like 1234:5678). Look at the *rightmost* digit now. If it's 0, 2, 4, 6, 8, A (no, that's not a misprint—this is hexadecimal), C, or E, change the low 9 chips. Otherwise, change the high 9 chips.

Reading AT Memory Error Messages

Like all 286 clones, the AT is a 16-bit machine and so organizes memory into 18-chip banks, not 9-chip banks.

There were two models of the AT motherboard:

- The earlier motherboard with 36 128K chips
- The model 339 with just 18 256K chips

Remember that 286s use 18-chip banks, so from the AT's point of view the old motherboard has only two 256K banks on it, and the 339 has only one 512K bank. See Figure 8.20 for a close-up view of AT memory banks.

IBM error messages are designed as if memory still only came 64K to a chip. *This means that one* physical *bank of 256K chips is treated as four* logical *banks of 64K chips. If that's not clear, let me restate it: A given 256K chip, if it fails, could display one of* four *error messages—one for each of its four logical 64K areas.*

Recall that the PC error messages were in two parts identifying the 64K bank and the chip in the bank. Both models of the IBM AT contained a total of 512K on the motherboard. The first version used four rows of 128K chips with nine chips in a row. Two rows formed a physical bank totalling 256K, which is equivalent to four logical banks of 64K. Thus, the two rows in the first physical bank contain errors with the logical bank numbers 0, 1, 2, or 3.

FIGURE 8.20

AT motherboard with memory bank detail

The second version of the AT contained two rows of 256K chips totaling 512K in bank 0. Errors in logical banks 0 through 7 all occur in the one bank of memory.

If two rows are now one logical bank, how do I find the bad chip? Four digits are used with the AT to indicate the chip error, with the first two digits indicating a chip in the high byte (bits 8 through 15) and the second two digits indicating an error in the low byte (bits 0 through 7). For example, you might get the error message 30000 0008 201, with the middle four digits indicating the bad chip. Either the first or last two digits will be zero; the error is in the byte with the nonzero digit. Here, you would look to the chip indicated by 08 in the low byte, namely, bit 3. What if a parity chip is bad? Then the chip error is 0000, and you have to swap a parity chip to isolate a problem.

On clones and memory expansion boards, you might see the bits labeled (as IBM does) or simply indicating the high and low byte. As you might expect, boards with no label whatsoever are quite common. In this case, you have to build your own error message map. A useful tool for this situation is simply a 256K chip with a bent address pin (pins 5 to 7 and 9 to 13), which will help you map out an unlabeled board by giving you a complete error message. Just put the chip with the bent pin in a bank of otherwise good memory. It will cause an error message. Create errors for each bank and write them down; you'll have full documentation for the board. Remember, you can use the 256K chip in place of a 64K chip as well.

AT Motherboard Type 1

The marking on the motherboard reads 256/512K. It contains two physical 16-bit banks consisting of 18 128K chips, for a total of 256K in each physical bank and a total of 512K on the motherboard (see Figure 8.21).

FIGURE 8.21

Original AT
motherboard memory
organization

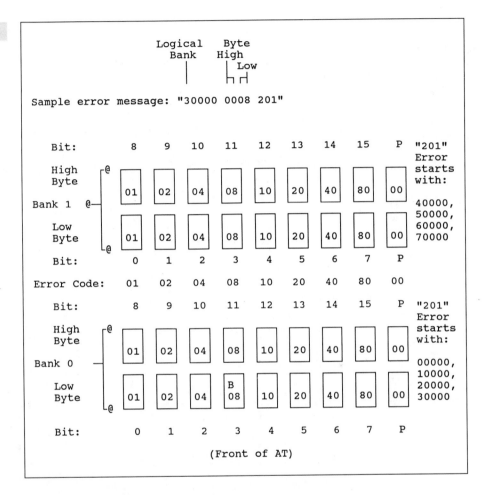

AT Motherboard Type 2 (Model 339)

The marking on the motherboard reads 256/512K. It contains one physical 16-bit bank consisting of 18 256K chips, for a total of 512K in the bank and on the motherboard. (See Figure 8.22.)

FIGURE 8.22

AT Model 339 motherboard memory organization

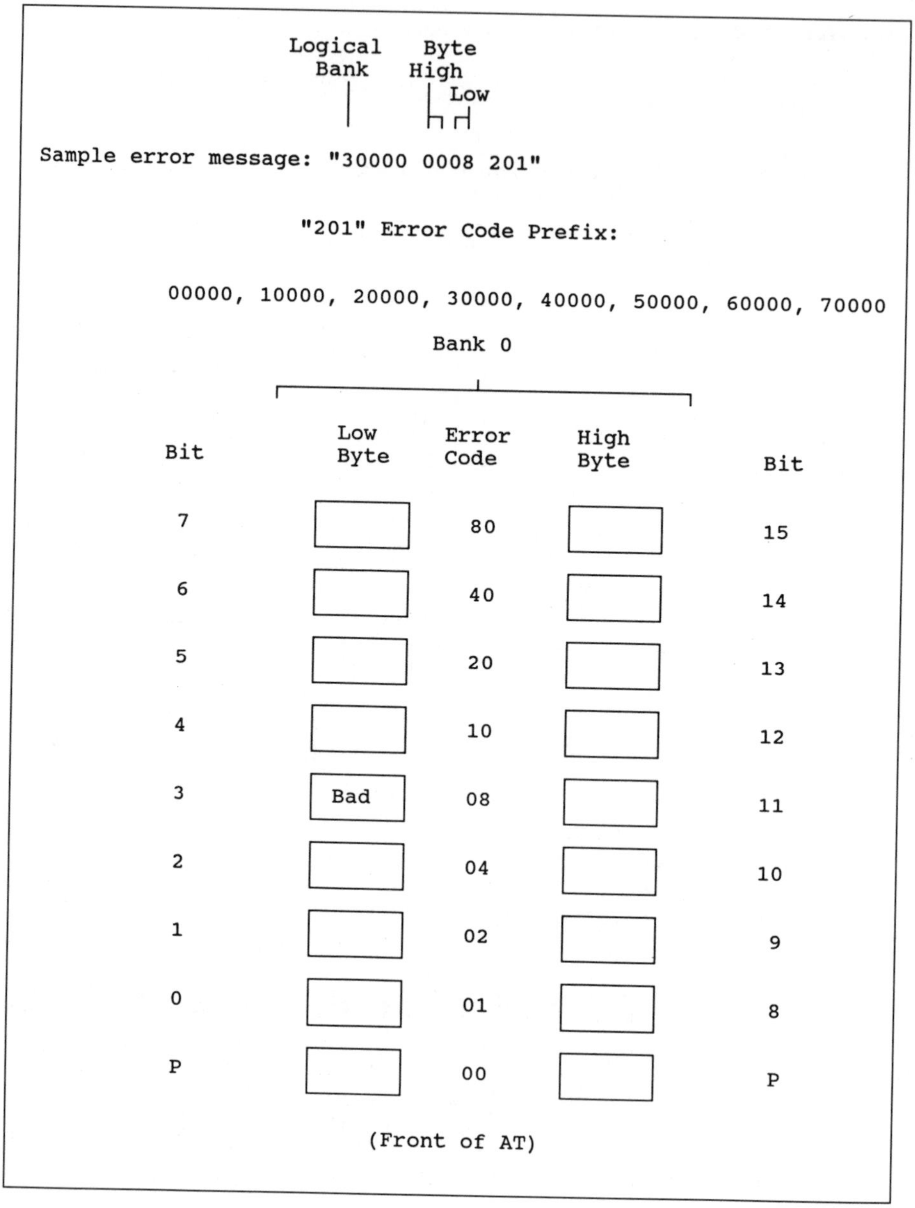

Logical Bank   Byte High Low

Sample error message: "30000 0008 201"

"201" Error Code Prefix:

00000, 10000, 20000, 30000, 40000, 50000, 60000, 70000

Bank 0

Bit	Low Byte	Error Code	High Byte	Bit
7		80		15
6		40		14
5		20		13
4		10		12
3	Bad	08		11
2		04		10
1		02		9
0		01		8
P		00		P

(Front of AT)

Other Causes of Memory Errors

If a chip seems okay but causes errors, consider the following rules:

- Never mix chip speeds in the same row. Don't install a row with some 200-ns chips and some 150-ns chips, even if 200 is the speed required. Remember that if your computer requires 200-ns chips, then a speed of 200 or faster (like 150, 120, 100, or 75 ns) will work fine. You can have one row of 75s, a row of 120s, a row of 150s, and a row of 200s for all it matters—*just don't mix chip speeds in the same row!* (Actually, if your computer only requires 200-ns chips, there's no point in spending the extra money for faster, more expensive chips.)

- Whenever possible, avoid mixing *manufacturers* in the same row. I cannot explain this, but I've seen cases like the following. I've had two rows of chips—one entirely Mitsubishi, another entirely Toshiba—that worked fine. Then I mixed the rows. Errors occurred. I restored the rows, and the problem disappeared.

- Remember to check chip seating: Has the chip crept out of its socket? Are all the legs in their socket holes, or is one bent under the chip, barely touching the contact?

- Is there enough power? Insufficient power can cause parity errors. This one can be a real pain, since it waits for some large disk access to trigger the parity error, like when you try to save your data to disk. You see this problem with underpowered clones and Lotus. Your 1-2-3 spreadsheet might work fine until you want to save the file, and then you get a parity check. The problem is that you're running the power supply to the poor thing's limits, and then you want to fire up the hard disk. There's not enough power; the memory gets shortchanged, and bang! a memory error happens.

- Noisy power can cause memory errors. A surge, such as a static electricity zap, can randomize memory contents, looking like a memory failure to the system.

- Improperly shielded sources of RF noise can alter memory, causing parity errors.

Tips on Installing Memory Chips

A lot of manuals include some really scary instructions for installing memory chips. I've probably installed a gigabyte or so myself (1-MB chips have made it easier to get to the 1-GB level), so here's what works for me.

First, as always, be aware of static electricity. Your acrylic sweater and the soles of your shoes are powerful producers of static. If I'm worried about the static level of an area, and I'm not prepared with a ground strap, *I take my shoes and socks off.* I know it sounds a little bizarre, but I kill very few chips that way, probably fewer than half a dozen in all the time I've been installing memory.

Second, the memory chips go into sockets in a circuit board. As before, don't insert memory into boards while the power is on. Orient the chip so its notch is facing the same way as the notches on other chips on the board. The legs of a new chip will be spread a bit too much to fit into the socket. Just insert one row of pins into their holes, and then coax the other row into *their* holes. At this point, you've got some tension, since the legs on both sides are eager to just spring out of the socket. Double-check that the legs are all positioned to slide into their holes, and then push the chip into the socket firmly with your thumb.

If you make a mistake or must remove old chips, use a small "tweaker" screwdriver. With it, gently pry up one end of the chip, and work the screwdriver completely under the chip. It will come up easily. Make sure you put the screwdriver under the chip, not the socket. The socket won't come up easily, and if it does, you'll have damaged the motherboard.

DO NOT use one of the "chip remover" tongs that seem to get included in every PC toolkit these days. They work okay if you've had practice with them, but they scare me because they make it a lot easier to damage a chip while taking it out. Stick with a small screwdriver, and remember that *patience* is the keyword here. Look at what you're doing, and take your time if you're new to the process.

CHAPTER

9

Power Supplies and
Power Protection

THE PC doesn't come with batteries included (unless it's a laptop). You plug it into the wall socket and it works. The PC itself doesn't directly use wall current, as this is 120-volt alternating current. Like most digital devices, it needs fairly low-power direct current at 5 and 12 volts.

By the way, a word to European readers: Everything I say here applies to you *except* for references to the power mains. Your mains aren't 120 volts but more like 230, and the power frequency is 50 cycles per second, not 60. DO NOT try any of the tests here that refer to the actual alternating current unless you already know about working with the mains safely.

Enter the power supply. The power supply doesn't *supply* power—it *converts* it from AC to DC, so it's a *switching* power supply. A switching design means it can handle quite a range of power problems without trouble. The alternative, a *linear* power supply, isn't quite so robust, and it's found on virtually all PC peripherals. Power supply troubles can be mysterious and annoying. Just as bad are similar-looking troubles with the supplied power itself. This chapter looks at both.

The line current isn't squeaky clean, and that can damage PCs. Safeware, a computer insurance firm, reports that 1986 saw $250 million in insurable PC damage, *$35 million of which came from PCs damaged by surges.*

Cautions about Opening the Power Supply

The power supply is the black or silver box in the back of the PC with the large yellow label telling you in five languages not to open the box up, warning you that it's dangerous. Despite the fact that I can only understand a few of the multilingual messages, I'm inclined to take them at their word.

The reason for the danger is mainly a large (1000 microfarad) capacitor in the power supply. The capacitor is utilized to smooth out some power glitches, which is a good thing, in general. But the capacitor retains power like a battery. Thus, even when the power supply is unplugged, it can still do you some harm. Power supplies cost under $100; just replace them if they're faulty. I recommend replacing and not repairing floppy drives just because it's a pain to repair them, but I recommend not repairing power supplies because they can hurt you. (I still recall a shock from a high school power-supply project.)

Power Supply Connections

On one side of the power supply is the on/off switch for the computer. Sprouting out of the other side are the power connectors. You'll recall P8 and P9 from the discussion of PC disassembly. The other connectors— two or four of them—are for floppy, tape, or hard drives.

The motherboard receives power through the power strip in the upper-right corner of the board. (This is for most motherboards, assuming that you're looking at the board so that the memory chips are closest to you, and the expansion connectors, the CPU, and the keyboard connector are farthest from you.) The connector is actually two six-pin connectors lined up one atop the other. They're generally labeled P8 and P9. P8 has only five wires and connects above P9, which has six wires (see Figure 9.1).

The power supply lines (the yellow, blue, and red wires) can be tested against a ground (any of the black wires). If you're actually testing a power supply, all of the black wires should be tested. Table 9.1 lists the specifications for these lines.

FIGURE 9.1

System board detail
with power connectors

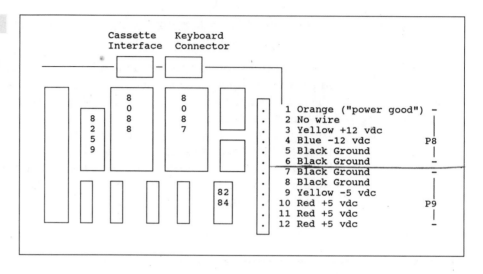

TABLE 9.1: Specifications for PC Power Supply Output

WIRE COLOR	RATED VOLTAGE (VOLTS)	ACCEPTABLE RANGE (VOLTS)	CURRENT RANGE (AMPS)
Yellow	+12	+8.5–+12.6	0.0–2.00
Blue	–12	–8.5– –12.6	0.0–0.25
Red	+5	+2.4– +5.2	2.3–7.00
Yellow	–5	–4.5– –5.4	0.0–0.30

You can then do a resistance test of the motherboard. The tests are conducted on the power supply pins. Table 9.2 contains the *minimum* resistance for each connection. If the measured values are less than this, the motherboard is definitely faulty.

If you've never used a multimeter before, you'll notice that it has a dial on its face with markings like "DC volts," "AC volts," "Amps," "R X 1," "R X 10," and so on. The "R X" markings indicate the ohmmeter part of the multimeter. Set the dial to "R X 1." The meter will have two test probes, one red and one black. On the table, you'll see two *test points*—places to touch

TABLE 9.2: System Board Resistances

COMMON LEAD (BLACK PROBE)	VOM LEAD (RED PROBE)	MINIMUM RESISTANCE (Ohms)
8	10	0.8
8	11	0.8
8	12	0.8
5	3	6.0
6	4	48.0 7
	9	17.0

the probe to. Place the red on one, and the black on the other; it doesn't matter which. Then read the resistance off the meter and compare it to the correct value. If it's out of the proper range, the circuit board—the motherboard, in this case—is faulty and must be replaced.

As we've seen, P8 connects to the motherboard toward the back, with P9 in front of it. As to P10 and P11, the drive power connectors, *it doesn't matter which connector goes to which drive*—they're interchangeable. You can use either connector for floppies, hard drives, or whatever.

IBM ATs have a third connector, P12. It can't be used on most hard disks because it doesn't supply enough power, so use it for a floppy. Clone power supplies generally have four full-power connections. They can be used for anything from hard disks to floppies. Also, they don't need to be used; just because you have four drive power connectors doesn't mean you must have four drives (I get asked that now and then).

Maintenance

Good news here: There's no maintenance required on the power supply. The fan and the power switch are the only moving parts. If you suddenly notice that the PC is very quiet but still operating, then your fan might have died. If that happens, save everything and *shut down immediately!* The computer's heat can quickly damage or destroy the computer if the fan isn't present to dissipate it.

Don't block the vents the PC uses for cooling, and use compressed air to blow the dust out of the fan now and then. Please remove the power supply first so that the dust doesn't immediately settle on the computer.

Upgrading the Power Supply

IBM PCs and some clones have wimpy 63.5-watt power supplies. This is insufficient for many applications. Memory boards, hard disks, 3278 emulators, and other plug-in enhancements can raise the total power requirements over the 63.5-watt supply's capability. But even if you're only using 50 watts, you should think about upgrading. The standard sizes of power supplies for various computers are included in Table 9.3.

TABLE 9.3: PC Power Supply Capacities

COMPUTER TYPE	POWER SUPPLY SIZE (WATTS)
PC	63.5
XT	130.0
AT	192.0
Model 50	94.0
Model 50Z	94.0
Model 60	225.0
Model 70	105.0
Model 80	225.0

A 63.5-watt power supply works harder to supply 50 watts than a 135-watt power supply. Both a Volkswagen Beetle and a Porsche 944 can travel at 65 miles per hour, but it seems like real work in the Beetle. A power supply running near its limit won't be as reliable as one with a little comfort space, so be sure you've got at least 20 percent excess capacity.

Don't confuse *watts capacity* with *watts used*. Sure, a 150-watt bulb uses more power than a 60-watt bulb. A 130-watt power supply is a power supply that can convert *up to 130 watts*. Notice the *up to;* putting a 130-watt power supply on a system that only requires 50 watts will only cause the power supply to convert 50 watts. A lot of folks misunderstand that. Even an IBM engineer in 1983 warned me that putting an XT's 130-watt power supply on an IBM PC would "burn up the motherboard." That was wrong, but I didn't know any better.

You've got worries with the desktop PS/2s, also. The Models 50 and 50Z have fairly inadequate power supplies. Their maximum power output is 92 watts, but the Model 50 requires 73 watts *with no expansion boards*. This hasn't been a problem so far, but wait until people start putting extra memory, internal modems, and the like into the systems.

So pushing a power supply too far isn't a good idea. How do you know how much power your machine is using? One simple device is the Power Meter from PARA Systems (see Appendix A for their address).

When buying upgrade power supplies, consider the fan. Recall that the power supply's fan is responsible for heat dissipation in the PC, as we saw in Chapter 4. Another benefit from an upgraded power supply is the availability of additional floppy connectors. The IBM XT and IBM PC power supplies only offer two connections for drives, the IBM AT only three. Many third-party supplies have four connections. You could then have two half-height drives, a hard disk (half-height), and a tape drive, as well as the power to drive them.

The XT and PC use the same case type for the power supply. PC and XT replacement power supplies are about 135–150 watts. The AT power supply case is a bit larger, and replacements are in the 190–200-watt range. You probably wouldn't replace your AT power supply for reasons of power except in unusual circumstances. You might, however, replace it because the fan is too noisy or to improve cooling.

Speaking of replacement power supplies, look back to the discussion of power supply lines earlier in this chapter. You may have noticed the first line on P8, called *Power Good*. This is a digital signal enabled by the power supply once it views itself as warmed up and ready. A flaky Power Good leads the computer to issue either a long beep, short beeps, or generally unusual noises. Some inexpensive replacement power supplies cause computers to emit a loud or long beep, then settle down to good service. I've experienced this myself, and can only account for the beeps by saying that sometimes the power supply doesn't wait quite long enough to first enable Power Good. A little initial up and down activity on the line would induce the clock to issue a RESET command to the PC.

Troubleshooting the Power Supply

You turn the computer on and nothing happens at all. It's plugged in, so it's not that—what do you do next?

The Power Supply Troubleshooting Trail

First, check the outlet. The outlet should be providing between 104 and 130 volts of AC current. Just set the VOM to read AC voltage and put one lead in each hole of the outlet.

Second, check the cables. The cables should be in place on the system board.

Third, is power getting to the power supply? The fan gets it first, so if it isn't turning, the power supply isn't getting power. When some power supplies are first turned on, the speaker emits a low click.

Fourth, test the power supply with another power supply.

Replacing a Power Supply

If you suspect that the power supply isn't working, replace it. It's simple.

1. On the back of the PC, you'll see four screws bolting the power supply to the chassis. Remove these.

2. Disconnect the system board (P8 and P9) and the drives. Draw a picture and make notes of what connects to what. Note wire colors. P8 goes toward the back, P9 toward the front.

3. Slide the power supply forward just a bit—it's hooked to the chassis from below. It will now lift out.

4. Install the new power supply by reversing the procedure.

5. To be extra careful, strip the PC down to the minimum circuit boards. Then power up and do whatever diagnostics you use.

Protecting the PC from the AC

You can control a lot of things in your environment, but you have little control over one aspect of the PC environment: the power delivered by the electric company. For various reasons, it doesn't come out clean and regular like it's supposed to. Worse yet, you can't even always blame the power company; sometimes it's your or your building management's fault.

Do You Have Power Problems?

Power or wiring problems can show up in these ways:

- The computer mysteriously "freezing up"
- Random memory errors

- Lost data on the hard disk
- Damaged chips on a circuit board
- Data transmission noise and peripheral errors

Recently, I was at a hotel doing a presentation that involved a demonstration PC. The PC did the strangest things:

- Once, it stopped the memory test at 128K and froze.
- Another time, it gave a memory error message around 400K.
- The hard disk wouldn't boot about 30 percent of the time, despite a fresh format.
- It stopped talking to the keyboard a few times, requiring the power switch to be flipped.

What was wrong? The old "hotel power" problem. When the coffee machine was on, the machine did strange things. Additionally, the PC shared an outlet with two 600-watt overheads in continuous use and a slide projector. I moved it to another outlet, and the problems disappeared.

Having said that, what can you do about power problems? The four steps to power protection are:

- Check that your outlets are wired correctly.
- Find out what else is on the power line.
- Provide a common ground for all devices.
- Protect against noise: surges, spikes, and under- and overvoltage.

Following are the facts to "empower" you to solve your line problems.

Check Outlet Wiring

AC outlets have three wires: a large prong, a small prong, and a center cylinder. The cylinder is the safety ground, the first (smaller) prong is the *hot* or *phase* line (the "official" term is *phase*, but anyone who has ever accidentally touched it calls it *hot*), and the second (larger) prong is called the *return, common,* or *neutral* line. The wires in the wall are supposed to be wired so that green is ground, white is return, and whatever's left (usually black) is phase.

It's not unheard of for the hot and the return to be reversed. This actually isn't a problem so long as everything is wired backwards. But if you plug, say, the PC into a correctly wired outlet, and a printer into a wrongly wired outlet, and if one of the devices connects the ground and the common—again, not an unusual occurrence—*and* there's a break in the neutral, then you'll get 120 volts across the cable from the printer to the PC. Lots of destruction will follow. Worse yet, miswired outlets can hurt you; if you're touching both the PC and the printer, you're the electrical path.

You can buy circuit wiring testers from most hardware stores. I got mine at Sears for $6.

Check What Else Is on the Line

Ensure that there isn't any equipment that draws a lot of power on the same line as the PC. That includes:

- Large motors, such as those in air conditioners, refrigerators, or power tools
- Heating coils, such as those in small space heaters or coffee makers—even "personal" coffee makers
- Copiers and their cousins, laser printers

Anything that draws a lot of current can draw down the amount of voltage being delivered to a PC on the same breaker or fuse. Worse yet, heating coil devices like coffee makers inadvertently create something called a *tank circuit* that can inject high-frequency spikes into the power line: This is noise that can slip through your power supply and go straight to the chips on the circuit boards.

One simple solution is just to get a separate power circuit to the box. Another is to get an isolation transformer such as we find in a power conditioner. An RF shield between the primary and secondary coils of the transformer removes the high-frequency noise.

Lasers draw 15 amps all by themselves. That means that, like it or not, you've got to put in a 20-amp breaker and circuit for each laser printer/PC combination. PCs without lasers don't draw much power, and so don't require a separate breaker.

Ensure Common Ground among Devices

Electrical ground is intended, among other things, to provide an electrical *reference point*, a benchmark value like *sea level*. A computer communicates 1s or 0s to a modem, for instance, by varying voltage relative to ground: Greater than +3 volts means 0, less than −3 volts means 1. A voltage near 0 means nothing is being transmitted.

The problem arises when the two communicating devices don't agree on the value of *ground*. If, in the above example, the modem's ground were a 7-volt potential below the computer's ground, the modem and the computer would each think the other was sending data when neither actually was.

Generally, it's not that bad. But if the computer's ground is 3 volts different from the modem's, the occasional bit will be lost or garbled.

The answer? Simple—just ensure that all devices plugged into your PC share the same ground. A simple six-outlet power strip will do this. But there's one flaw in this approach: What about a Local Area Network? Basically, a LAN is one big ground problem. Some people have suggested grounding the shield of the network cables every hundred feet or so. The only true solution is to use fiber-optic LANs, but they're still a wee bit expensive.

Please note: Ensuring that all equipment has a common ground has nothing to do with having a "good" ground. A proper ground is mainly for safety, not data protection. (If someone insists that you must have a good ground for proper data transfer, ask him or her how airplanes and spaceships manage it, hmmm?) We'll look at proper grounding soon.

Protect against Power Noise

We've already discussed undervoltage, overvoltage, spikes, and surges in Chapter 4 on preventive maintenance. Remember:

- *Undervoltage* is undesirable because the power supply reacts to too *little* voltage by drawing too *much* current. This heats up and can destroy components.

- *Overvoltage* can damage a chip because too much voltage destroys the circuits inside the chip.

When some outside force causes your power line to deliver more voltage than it's supposed to, this is called an *overvoltage condition.* Such conditions are, in general, dangerous to the computer.

The physics of it is this: The heart of the computer resides in its chips. The chips are specially designed crystals. Crystals are highly structured molecules; many of them would be happier in a less structured environment. Applying electronic and heat energy to the crystals allows this breakdown in organization to occur. One spike might not do it, but even small spike damage is cumulative.

Damage is proportional to energy. Energy is Voltage × Current × Time.

Brief overvoltages under a millisecond in length are called *spikes.* Spikes are temporary overvoltages that may be of high enough frequency to introduce RFI-like problems. Longer overvoltages (milliseconds to seconds) are called *surges.*

You (or your boss) could be skeptical about the actual level of power problems. This may all be, you suspect, a tempest in a teapot. If you don't think you have power problems, spend $130 on a simple device that can monitor the quality of your power. Called the AC Monitor, it's from Tasco Ltd; you can find more information on it in Appendix A.

Solutions to Power Problems

Solutions to power problems fall into three categories:

- Isolation
- Shielding
- Proper grounding

Isolation means isolating the noise (surge, spike, and so on) from the computer and draining it off harmlessly. This is done with filters, transformers, gas discharge tubes, and *MOVs* (Metal Oxide Varistors). An MOV is an important part of a surge protector. When a surge comes in, an MOV shunts it off to ground. Unfortunately, the MOV is a kamikaze component, since it "throws itself onto the grenade." Each MOV is only good for one big surge, or a bunch of little surges. (No, there's no easy way to test to see whether an MOV is still working or not, at least not without a $2,000 tester.) Power conditioners and surge protectors provide isolation in varying quality.

Shields minimize high-frequency noise. Shielding is in the filter capacitors in surge protectors, the RF shields between the primary and secondary coils in a power conditioner, the metal case of the computer, and the shielded cable.

Grounding is viewed by some people as a magic answer to noise problems. Just run a wire from the device in question to a metal stake pounded into the ground (called a *ground stake*), and all of your ground problems go away (kind of like an electronic Roto-Rooter, "And away go troubles down the drain...").

Nahhh.

First, having a proper ground *is* important. It makes electronic equipment safer (it keeps you out of the circuit), but, as we've seen, a *common* ground is important to minimize communication errors between devices. So the main reason for a proper earth ground is safety.

The idea behind a ground stake is to provide a nice electrical path to earth ground. It *doesn't* eliminate noise, however: Two ground stakes a few yards apart will pass current and noise between themselves. Ground stakes are less effective when there's a drought. I once heard of a ground stake that provided a better connection to ground than others on a particular site because it was, er, "watered" by local fauna. (No, I'm not sure I believe it, but ground *is* magic, and magical stories accompany it.)

A final thought on grounding: Some companies are extra careful to ground their computer rooms, thinking this will somehow protect their data. They're not so careful about the other areas in the building, however, so you've got a computer room with a cleaner ground than the rest of the building. Step back for a moment and ask: What effect would differential grounding have on lightning protection? If lightning strikes a building, it takes the easiest path to ground. If the easiest path to ground is through your computers, so be it. Basically, if you ground your computer room well, but not the rest of the building, it's like putting a big EAT AT JOE'S sign on the computer room, as far as lightning is concerned.

Devices to Remedy Electronic Problems

Okay, now we've seen the problems and some solutions. Now let's look at what's available on the market to solve the problems.

If you're looking here for a recommendation, please understand that I don't have good news. Electric power in the '90s in most of the western world is getting worse and worse because of aging equipment and the lack of new capacity pitted against an ever-growing energy demand.

The PC really needs cleaner power than the stuff you feed your refrigerator, coffee maker, or desk lamp. The only absolutely reliable way to get clean power is to rectify the power, put it in a battery, and then use the DC power in the battery to reconstruct the AC power. A device that does this is a sine wave UPS (Uninterruptible Power Supply); a good one will cost about $800 minimum. So choose the best compromise. Some of the people I work with use surge protectors, some use SPS's (Standby Power Supplies), and others use power conditioners. Me? I'm building the ultimate electromagnetic shield—a Faraday cage—for my office (just as soon as I get some time and money...).

Surge Suppressors and Spike Isolators

Many of us have purchased *surge protectors,* or as they're also known, *spike isolators* (see Figure 9.2).

The idea with suppression devices is that once they detect a large surge coming, they redirect it out to the electric ground, kind of like opening the flood gates. The most common redirection device is the Metal Oxide Varistor, or MOV. It's an impassable barrier between the supply voltage and protective ground until the voltage reaches a certain level. *Gas discharge tubes* and *pellet arrestors* are slower but beefier devices. *Coaxial arrestors* fit somewhere in the middle.

The best suppressors use several lines of defense: MOVs, coaxial arrestors, and gas discharge tubes, for example. Of course, an overzealous surge suppressor can redirect too much power for too long, creating a worse surge of its own.

Another important question is, *what* voltage level triggers the surge suppressor? They're not going to get going at 120.00001 volts; some will pass 1000 volts before calling in the Marines. By then, your PC is toast.

PC magazine did tests of surge suppression devices in its May 27, 1986, issue. They created spikes and measured how much of the spike was allowed through. Some suppressors emitted smoke and flames when subjected to a real surge. Others died quietly, not informing the owner that they no longer protected the PC (they still pass electricity, so there's no way to know). The most impressive performance was turned in by PTI Industries' Datashield 85, a six-outlet suppressor that let no more than

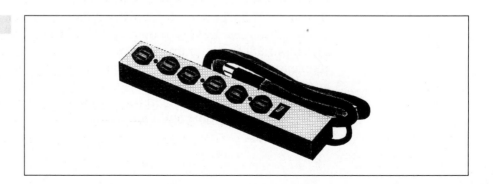

290 volts through (see Appendix A for more information). Some of the more commonly known ones, like Curtis Manufacturing's Diamond six-outlet suppressor, passed 1,440 volts.

The Bad News about Surge Protectors

I can't, in good conscience, recommend surge protectors to you.

As mentioned previously, the best suppressors use several lines of defense: MOVs, coaxial arrestors, and gas discharge tubes, for example. But the heart of surge protectors are MOVs. As we've said before, MOVs are one-time-only devices. One surge, and they're history. Worse yet, they can't be tested.

Yes, some surge protectors come with a little light that goes out when the surge protector doesn't protect any more. But those little lights can't be trusted, either. The light is in series with a fuse, and the fuse is in series with the return from the MOV—it's called a *bleeder fuse*. Given a large enough surge, the fuse will blow (along with the MOV, recall) and the light will go out. So in the case of a single large surge, the light *is* effective. But an MOV can also be destroyed by a number of smaller surges. In that case, the fuse would be unaffected, and the light would stay on.

Summarizing, there's no way to know whether or not your surge protector is still protecting. If you have a light on your surge protector, and it goes out, you definitely have a dead surge protector. But if the light's on, that's no guarantee of surge protector effectiveness.

Power Conditioners

Between a surge protector and a backup power supply is another device, also moderate in price, called a *power conditioner*. A power conditioner does all the things a surge protector does, filtering and isolating line noise, and more. Rather than rely on MOVs and such, the power conditioner uses the inductance of its transformer to filter out line noise. An isolation transformer is a far superior device for removing noise than a capacitor or an MOV. Additionally, most power conditioners will boost up undervoltage so your machine can continue to work through brownouts.

Recall that the surge protector's MOVs fail with no sign, so there's no good way to know if your surge protector is doing any good. Power conditioners don't have that problem; when a transformer fails, you know it—the power conditioner just plain doesn't provide any power.

Which power conditioner is right for you? The one I use is Tripplite's LC1800. I've seen it in mail-order ads for as little as $190.

Backup Power Supplies

In addition to protection from short power irregularities, you might need backup power. I've lived in a number of places in the northeastern U.S. where summer lightning storms will kill the power for just a second—enough to erase your memory and make the digital clocks blink. Total loss of power can only be remedied with battery-based systems. Such systems are in the range of $350 to $1200 and up.

There are two types, *Standby Power Supplies* (SPS) and *Uninterruptible Power Supplies* (UPS). Figure 9.3 shows how these work. SPS's charge the batteries while watching the current level. If the power drops, they activate themselves and supply power until their batteries run down. A fast power switch must occur here, and it's important to find out what the switching time is. Four milliseconds or under is fine. Fourteen milliseconds, in my experience, isn't fast enough.

A UPS constantly runs power from the line current to a battery, then from the battery to the PC. This is superior to an SPS because there's no switching time involved. Also, this means that any surges affect the battery-charging mechanism, not the computer. A UPS, then, is a surge suppressor also.

A UPS or SPS must convert DC current from a battery to AC for the PC. AC is supposed to look like a sine wave. Cheaper UPS and SPS models produce square waves (see Figure 9.4). Square waves are bad because they include high-frequency harmonics that can appear as EMI or RFI to the computer. Also, some peripherals (printers in particular) can't handle square-wave AC. So, when examining a UPS, ask whether it uses square wave or sine wave. Some produce a pseudo-sine wave. It has the stairstep look of a square wave, but not as many harmonic problems.

FIGURE 9.3

How UPS's and SPS's work

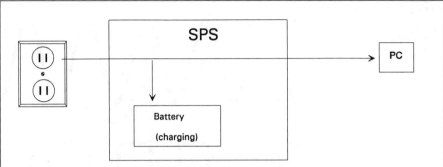

When power is normal, an SPS passes current through to the PC, spikes and all, while siphoning off a bit of the power in order to keep the battery charged.

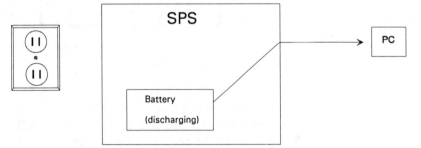

When the power is interrupted, the SPS supplies power to the PC from the battery for as long as the battery lasts. The SPS must also sense the power-down condition and get the battery on-line quickly enough that the PC can continue to work uninterrupted.

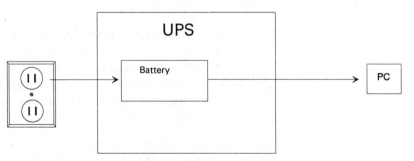

A UPS sends power from the socket right into the battery, then takes the power out of the battery and gives to the PC. Benefits: constant surge protection and zero switching time.

FIGURE 9.4

UPS AC waveforms

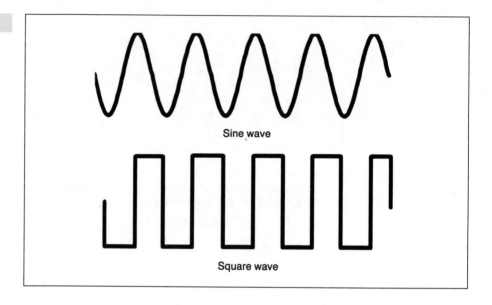

Sine wave

Square wave

Ordinarily, the purpose of a UPS is to allow you enough time to save whatever you're doing and shut down gracefully. If you're in an area where the power might regularly disappear for hours, you should look for the ability to attach external batteries to the UPS so you can run the PC for longer periods.

Remember that a sine-wave UPS is the only way to really eliminate most power problems. The reason *everyone* doesn't have one is cost.

A decent compromise can be found in a fast ($\leq$4 ms) square-wave SPS. I know I said square waves are bad for your peripherals, but consider: How often will the SPS actually be doing anything? Not very often—remember that it only supplies power when the line voltage drops out, not a common occurrence. The brief minute or two each month of square-wave power that your peripherals end up getting won't kill them. And you'll save a pile over a UPS.

On the other hand, remember that a UPS is always on line, and so must produce sine-wave output. But UPS's have the benefit that they provide surge protection by breaking down and reassembling the power; SPS's *do not* provide this protection. You must still worry about surge protection when you buy an SPS, but not if you buy a UPS. So make the choice that your budget allows.

Something to look for in backup power supplies—either UPSs or SPSs—is a serial port.

Serial port? Yes, a serial port. Windows NT and OS/2 can monitor a signal from a serial-port–equipped UPS/SPS. When power fails, the backup power supply informs the operating system, and the operating system does a graceful shutdown in the battery time remaining.

Summarizing, here are buying pointers for backup power supplies:

- If it's an SPS, it must switch in less than or equal to four ms.
- If it's an SPS, square-wave output is acceptable.
- If it's a UPS, it *must* have sine-wave output.
- Get a serial port on the backup power supply.

And notice that battery-powered laptops have the best power supply—a built in UPS.

The Grandaddy of Power Problems: Lightning

When Thor's hammer falls near your site, you won't need any special equipment to note its occurrence. Curled-up, blackened circuit boards are pretty easy to spot.

I travel around North America and Europe teaching troubleshooting classes. You know what *everyone* tells me? No matter where they are, the natives tell me they're in the "lightning capital of the world." Take a look at Figure 9.5 to find out where you rate (if you live in the U.S.).

Here are some points to understand about how lightning affects you:

- Lightning affects your system even if it doesn't strike your building.
- It's *good* to leave a machine plugged in—the lightning has an easy path to ground.

FIGURE 9.5

Mean annual number
of days with
thunderstorms

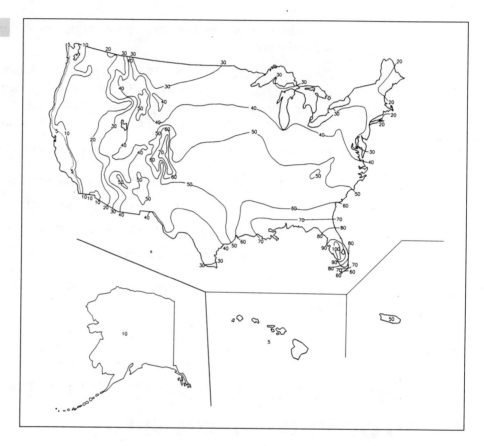

- As mentioned earlier, taking special care to ground the part of the building that the big computers are in just makes those computers more vulnerable. A better-grounded path is the one lightning will take.

- Lightning arrestors can reduce the likelihood of lightning damage.

- Newer hi-tech lightning rods are being used in some sites. They look like an umbrella built of barbed wire standing about 30 feet tall.

- A cheap lightning protection is overhand knots in the power cord. Believe it or not, some researchers discovered this one. It makes the lightning surge work against itself and burn out the power cord, *not* the PC. And it works—Washington had the biggest thunderstorm it had seen in years in the summer of 1989, and my stuff with knots in the cords rode it out without a hitch. My TV didn't have knots in the cord, and I had to buy a new TV.

- Optical isolators will protect you from lightning. They break the electrical connection and transfer data optically.

Hard Disk Drive Overview and Terminology

HARD disks have become an absolute necessity. Some programs require them, and most are enhanced by them. But they're a common source of failure, and so require some maintenance attention.

As hard disks are sealed, you can't directly fix some hardware disk problems. Other hardware, however, is directly accessible and can be replaced, and there are many programs to help you monitor your disk's health, tune up its speed, and recover from disaster.

Disk Structure: Hardware and Software

First, some terminology. Disk technology has gone through a lot of changes in just a few decades. There are a lot of options for disks today, and a wide variety in price. *Sectors, seek time, clusters,* and the like—what do they mean? I will briefly explain them here.

Geometry: Cylinders, Heads, Platters, Tracks, and Sectors

Let's begin with the factors that determine how large your drive is; the items that comprise your disk's "geometry."

Disks are divided into areas called *sectors,* each of which holds 512 bytes of information. Sectors are grouped together into *tracks* on a disk *surface.* A disk has at least two surfaces.

Let's start off by discussing floppy disk structure, as it incorporates the same basic elements as a hard disk in a simpler form.

A floppy stores 360K in the following way:

- The floppy disk itself is like a hard disk's metal *platters.*
- A floppy disk has two sides, or *surfaces,* and thus the drive has two *heads.*
- Each side contains data.
- Each side is divided into 40 concentric *tracks.*
- Each track is divided, like the pieces of a pie, into eight or nine wedges called *sectors.*
- Each sector stores $1/2$ K (512 bytes) of information.

Hard disks are organized first by their metal platters stacked atop one another. Each side, or surface, of each platter is divided into concentric tracks. Typically, the single "platter" that is a floppy is divided into 40 or 80 tracks; but hard disks start at 305 tracks and go up from there. The platter is commonly 5¼" in diameter like a floppy, so, obviously, the tracks are squeezed closer together on a hard disk than on a floppy. In fact, floppies put only 40 or 80 tracks in the same space that a hard disk can put over a thousand tracks, so you can see why hard disks are more fragile than floppies. Figure 10.1 illustrates the layout of tracks on a floppy disk.

FIGURE 10.1

Forty tracks on a floppy

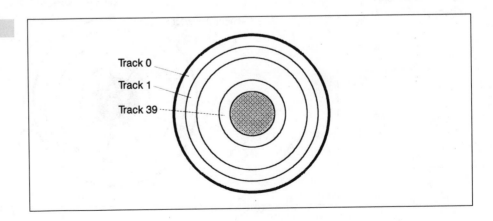

Each surface is then figuratively divided radially, like a pie. Floppies typically divide tracks into 8 to 18 sectors apiece. Figure 10.2 illustrates this division. Hard disks divide each track into 17, 26, 33, or 34 sectors. Drives with 26 or more sectors are called *RLL* (Run Length Limited). Seventeen-sector disks are called *MFM* (Modified Frequency Modulation). (More on those later.) Most drives nowadays use RLL. In fact, most use a version of RLL that puts *more* than 26 sectors on a track, called *Advanced* or *Enhanced RLL* (ARLL or ERLL).

Both hard and floppy disk devices store 512 bytes on a sector—$^1/_2$ K of data, as 1K = 1024 bytes. (See Figure 10.3.)

To summarize, a 360K floppy is composed of:

$$
\begin{array}{rll}
& 2 & \text{Sides or surfaces or heads} \\
\times & 40 & \text{Tracks per side} \\
\times & 9 & \text{Sectors per track} \\
\times & ^1/_2\text{K} & \text{Bytes per sector} \\
\hline
= & 360\text{K} & \text{Bytes/Disk total}
\end{array}
$$

FIGURE 10.2

Tracks and sectors on a floppy

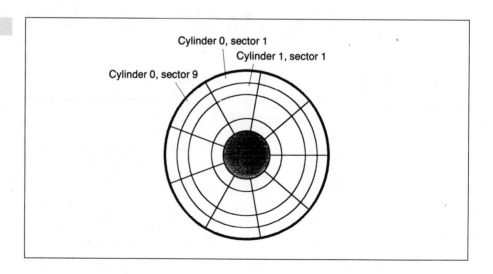

FIGURE 10.3

Each sector contains
512 bytes of data

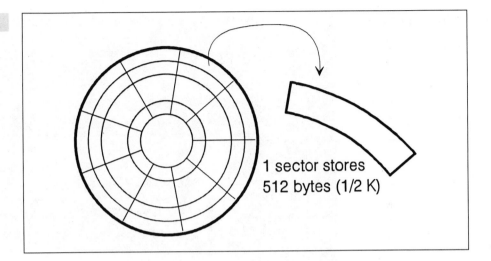

1 sector stores
512 bytes (1/2 K)

Hard disks work in a similar manner, but pack a lot more data space. Figure 10.4 shows a hard disk with its cover removed. The original 10 MB XT hard disk has the following specs:

- There are four surfaces
- There are 305 tracks on each surface
- There are 17 sectors to a track
- There are $\frac{1}{2}$ K on each sector

A hard disk, then, is comprised of $4 \times 305 \times 17 \times \frac{1}{2}$ K=10,370K bytes.

As you examine other disks, you will find that 512 bytes per sector is pretty constant. The number of tracks, the number of surfaces, and the number of sectors all vary. Remember that some manufacturers call them "heads" rather than "surfaces." Since there is one head per surface, in practice, they mean the same thing. The XT 10-MB hard disk has four heads.

You may be wondering about the different sizes of sectors. The sectors nearer the center of the disk are, indeed, smaller than those out on the disk's rim, yet they store the same amount of data. Doesn't it seem smarter then to put more sectors on the outside tracks, where there's more

FIGURE 10.4

Hard disk with cover removed

space? Doing so, however, turns out to complicate drive electronics considerably. Nevertheless, a few of the really high-capacity drives do employ unequal numbers of sectors per track: This technique is called *ZBR* (Zone Bit Recording) and is used on many of today's drives that are larger than 200 MB.

All of a disk's heads—whether the two heads of a floppy, or the 16 found on some large drives—are attached to a bracket called an *actuator arm*, shown in closeup in Figure 10.5. That means that when head 0 (as usual in the computer business, we count 0 to 3, not 1 to 4) is positioned over track 142 on surface 0 by the head actuator, head 3 is also positioned over track 142 on surface 3. Disk heads cannot be independently positioned.

The process of reading a sector involves two steps. First, move the read/write head over the desired track. Then wait for the disk to rotate so that the desired sector is under the head, then read. In general, moving the head takes the most time. This means that we can most quickly read a file whose sectors are all on the same track, and *whose tracks lie above one another*—one head move reads a pile of data.

FIGURE 10.5

Closeup of hard disk
actuator arm and
heads

Thus, if you need track 271, surface 0 for the first 17 sectors of your data on some file, then it is convenient to have track 271, surface 1, 2, and 3 for the rest of that file. Then these data (512 bytes/sector × 17 sectors/track × 4 tracks=a maximum of 34,816 bytes) can be read without moving the read/write head. The collection of a given track number on all surfaces is called a *cylinder*. Our example XT 10-MB hard disk's 200th cylinder is the collection of side 0/track 200, side 1/track 200, side 2/track 200, and side 3/track 200. Most manufacturers do not report the number of tracks; instead they report the number of cylinders. As with surfaces and heads, there's a one-to-one correspondence between tracks-per-surface and cylinders, so the terms can be used interchangeably.

Let's apply this, and calculate the size of a hard disk. One of my XTs uses a Rodime disk drive. It has 639 cylinders and six heads. What is its capacity? Assume that, as with most of the PC drives today, it has 512 bytes per sector and 17 sectors per track.

The capacity can be expressed as 512 bytes/sector × 17 sectors/track × 639 tracks per surface × 6 surfaces=33,371,136 bytes. Recall that a megabyte is not a million bytes, but 1,048,576 bytes, and you will see that this is a 31.8-MB drive.

Getting Information on Your Disk: CORETEST

CORE International is a company that sells some of the fastest disks around. It's no good being number 1 (or close to it) if no one knows it. So they wrote a benchmark program and put in the public domain. It's called (appropriately) CORETEST.EXE. See Appendix A if you want to get this program.

To run it, just type **CORETEST**. Take a look at a sample run, depicted in Figure 10.6. Here's how to interpret it.

For our purposes, CORETEST offers five interesting numbers:

- Cylinders
- Heads
- Sectors
- Average seek time
- Data transfer rate

FIGURE 10.6

Sample CORETEST screen

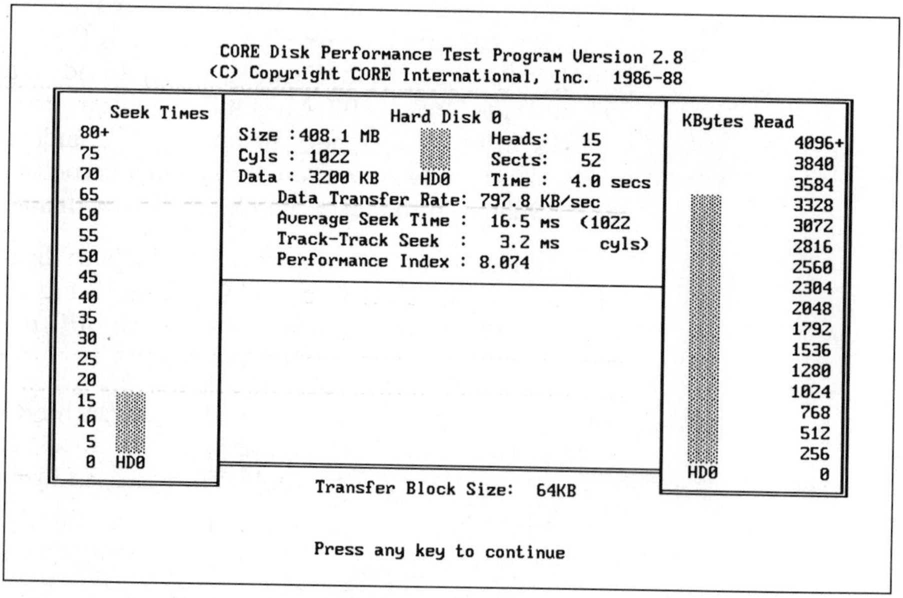

```
                CORE Disk Performance Test Program Version 2.8
                  (C) Copyright CORE International, Inc.  1986-88

    Seek Times                    Hard Disk 0                    KBytes Read
    80+         Size :408.1 MB           Heads:   15                  4096+
    75          Cyls : 1022              Sects:   52                  3840
    70          Data : 3200 KB    HD0    Time :  4.0 secs             3584
    65             Data Transfer Rate: 797.8 KB/sec                   3328
    60             Average Seek Time :  16.5 ms   (1022               3072
    55             Track-Track Seek  :   3.2 ms       cyls)           2816
    50             Performance Index : 8.074                          2560
    45                                                                2304
    40                                                                2048
    35                                                                1792
    30                                                                1536
    25                                                                1280
    20                                                                1024
    15                                                                 768
    10                                                                 512
     5                                                                 256
     0  HD0                                                       HD0    0

                       Transfer Block Size:   64KB

                         Press any key to continue
```

CORETEST is a quick-and-dirty way to find out how your existing hard disk is currently set up. You cannot use it to, say, plug in a mystery disk and find out its sectors, tracks, and/or heads. I know you're wondering what *seek time* and *data transfer rate* are, but I'm going to explain them in an upcoming section about disk performance measurement, so hang on until then.

Software Structure of a Disk

DOS doesn't concern itself with tracks, cylinders, and the like. It organizes data on a sector-by-sector basis. As far as DOS is concerned:

- Disks are divided into *absolute* sectors.

- Absolute sectors map into *DOS* sectors.

- The DOS sectors are grouped into *clusters,* a space allocation unit I'll discuss soon.

- A *directory* entry refers to the first cluster number in the file, which is our initial pointer into something called the *File Allocation Table* (FAT). The FAT keeps track of where files are located.

- The FAT also contains information that DOS uses to locate the remaining clusters. There's a FAT entry for each cluster.

- A FAT entry can be 1) a number pointing to another cluster, 2) a 0 indicating an unused cluster, 3) a *bad sector* marking, or 4) an End Of File (EOF) indicator.

Absolute Sectors and DOS Sectors

Identifying an area on a disk by its cylinder, head, and sector is what DOS folks call indentifying it by its absolute sector cylinder x head y sector z. DOS doesn't directly use absolute sector locations. Instead, it refers to sectors with a single number called the *DOS sector number.* As DOS traverses a disk, it orders sectors by starting at cylinder 0 head 1 sector 1: This is *DOS sector number 0.* (Note that cylinder 0 head *0* doesn't have a DOS sector number designation; it's out of bounds, so far as DOS is concerned.) The remaining sectors on the track are DOS sectors 1 through 16. DOS then moves through the next head, number 2. The 17 sectors on cylinder 0, head 2 are the next 17 DOS sectors. DOS keeps moving up the heads until the cylinder is exhausted, and then it moves to the zero head of cylinder 1. It continues in this fashion, moving further and further inward toward the center of the disk.

Why use DOS sector numbers? I don't know, really. It's probably because every four or eight sectors are grouped into a *cluster,* and it's easier to divide up a nice one-dimensional number like a DOS sector than it would be to have to constantly figure out that cluster 200 is on cylinder 40, head 2, sectors 15–17 and cylinder 40, head 3, sector 1. (I just made those numbers up, so don't try to figure out from where I got them.) Supposing you had the XT 10-MB hard disk described earlier, Table 10.1 relates the two sector notations.

Clusters

Finally, DOS sectors are grouped into *clusters.* A cluster is the minimum space allocated by DOS when DOS gives space to a file. For example, if you create a file that is one byte long, you take up not just a byte on the disk, but instead the minimum allocation, a cluster. Cluster size varies with the disk type, as you can see from Table 10.2. A single-sided floppy

TABLE 10.1: Some Absolute and DOS Sectors for a Four-Head Disk

CYLINDER	HEAD	SECTOR	EQUIVALENT DOS SECTOR
0	0	1	N/A (outside DOS sectors)
0	0	17	N/A
0	1	1	0
0	1	17	16
0	2	1	17
0	2	17	33
0	3	1	34
0	3	17	50
1	0	1	51

TABLE 10.2: Cluster Sizes

DISK TYPE	CLUSTER SIZE (BYTES)	SECTORS/CLUSTER
Single-sided floppy	512	1
Double-sided floppy	1024	2
3½-inch floppy	1024	2
1.2-MB floppy	512	2
0–15-MB disk or disk partition	4096	8
16–128-MB disk or disk partition	2048	4
128–256-MB partition	4096	8
256–512-MB partition	8192	16 ✳
512-MB–1-GB partition	16,384	32

uses clusters that are just one sector long, but a 10-MB hard disk uses clusters that are eight sectors long, or 4096 bytes (4K). That means a one-byte file on a single-sided floppy would take up 512 bytes on the disk, as would a 500-byte file. A one-byte file would take up 4096 bytes on a 10-MB disk drive.

Think of the following analogy. Suppose you're the guy running the Trump Shuttle. The Trump Shuttle promises a seat on a jet going from Washington, D.C. to New York every hour, without a reservation. Let's say the DC-9 jets they use can accommodate 100 people. How many jets must you run this hour? If you've got 1–100 people, run one jet. Just one person, the 101st person, forces you to go to a second jet. There are no "half" jets.

Depending on what kind of storage medium DOS uses, different size "jets" are used. First the floppies appeared, then the 10-MB disk drive, then the 1.2-MB floppies and the 16+-MB drives. If you're feeling brave,

DOS 4.*x* even supports drives up to 512-MB in size—it uses a 16-bit FAT (65,536 entries) and clusters of up to 8192, and will support up to a 512-MB drive.

You've seen that cylinders and heads are counted starting at 0, and sectors starting at one, so it won't be *too* strange when I tell you that clusters start at number 2. By the way, clusters only start in the data area, after the FAT and directory.

Table 10.3 relates cylinders, heads, sectors, DOS sectors, and clusters for our 10-MB XT disk. In this case, the important factor is that the disk has 17 sectors/track.

TABLE 10.3: Partial 10-MB Disk Geography

CYLINDER	HEAD	SECTOR	EQUIVALENT DOS SECTOR	CLUSTER NUMBER	DESCRIPTION
0	0	1	N/A (outside DOS sectors)	N/A	Partition Record
0	0	17	N/A	N/A	Unused 0
0	1	1	0	N/A	DOS boot record
0	1	1	1	N/A	FAT sector 1
0	1	17	16	N/A	FAT sector 16
0	2	1	17	N/A	Root directory sector 1
0	2	17	33	N/A	Root directory sector 17
0	3	1	34	N/A	Root directory sector 18
0	3	15	48	N/A	Last root directory sector
0	3	16	49	2	First data sector
0	3	17	50	2	Second data sector
1	0	1	51	2	Third data sector
1	0	2	52	2	Fourth data sector
1	0	6	56	2	Eighth data sector
1	0	7	57	3	Ninth data sector

The FAT and the Directory

As mentioned previously, the directory and the FAT are a team in locating files. The directory tells you names of your files, and the FAT tells you where the file is located. They're all located near each other on your disk, as you can see in Figure 10.7.

FIGURE 10.7

DOS data areas

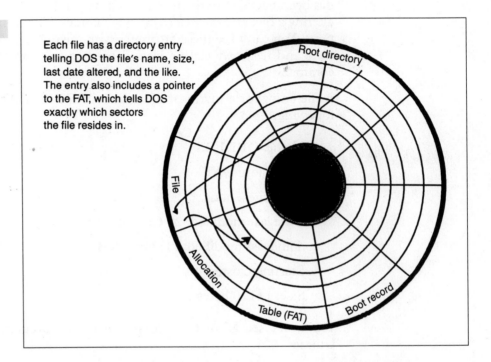

Each file has a directory entry telling DOS the file's name, size, last date altered, and the like. The entry also includes a pointer to the FAT, which tells DOS exactly which sectors the file resides in.

Root directory

File

Allocation

Table (FAT)

Boot record

A directory entry contains 32 bytes of information about a file:

- The file name (eight bytes)
- The file extension (three bytes)
- Its attributes (one byte)
- Ten bytes, unused, kept for future DOS functions
- The date (two bytes) and time (two bytes) of last update

- The starting cluster number (telling DOS where a file begins) and the FAT (where the rest of the file is found)
- Four bytes containing the file size in bytes

Each bit of the attribute byte refers to a particular attribute. The most interesting bits are: the *archive* bit, which refers to whether or not a file has been backed up; the *read-only* bit, which keeps DOS from erasing or altering a file; and the *hidden* bit, which hides a file from most DOS functions. You can't see these attributes with the normal DIR command. *Archive* and *read-only* can be viewed or changed with the DOS ATTRIB command.

A file entry for a mythical file called ORDERS.DAT might tell us the following:

Name: ORDERS

Extension: DAT

Attributes: none

Date last modified: 28 October 1989

Time last modified: 11:23:44 AM

Starting cluster: 40

Size: 11120 bytes

You won't see all of this unless you have a program like the Norton Utilities.

You don't have enough information yet to know exactly where this file is on disk. You *do* know that it starts in cluster 40. You can even deduce how many clusters the file occupies. How? Simple. Say it's a 30-MB drive. Since it's larger than 15 MB, you know the clusters are 2K, 2048 bytes apiece. Since the file is 11,120 bytes long, that would imply it takes up $11120 \div 2048 = 5.42$ clusters. But, recall, DOS won't give a file a partial sector; 5.42 clusters is no good, so DOS rounds up to six clusters.

But which six clusters? The FAT answers that question. The FAT is a table of numbers representing which clusters belong to what files. There are two kinds of FATs:

- Twelve-bit FATs with enough entries for 4096 clusters maximum, used on floppies and hard drives up to 15MB. A hard disk with a 12-bit FAT has clusters 4K in size.

- Sixteen-bit FATs with enough entries for 65,636 clusters maximum, used on drives larger than 15 MB. (Sixteen-bit FATs are only available under DOS 3.*x* and later.) Clusters are 2K on drives with 16-bit FATs up to 128MB disks.

Each cluster on the disk has a corresponding FAT entry. Given an entry for cluster *x,* the entry must be one of the following:

- A zero (0), indicating the cluster is unallocated

- An EOF, indicating it's the last cluster in a file

- A BAD, indicating the cluster contains a bad sector or sectors and shouldn't be used

- A non-zero cluster number that is a pointer to the *next* cluster in the file of which *x* is a part

Figure 10.8 adds to the ORDERS.DAT directory example an excerpt from the FAT table with the entries relevant to ORDERS.DAT.

Reading this FAT excerpt, you see that cluster 39 is the end of some file—you don't know which one. You start looking for ORDERS.DAT in cluster 40 because the directory entry tells you to: Entry 40 contains 41, meaning that 41 follows 40 as the next cluster in ORDERS.DAT. Entry 41 contains 42, meaning that 42 is the next cluster in ORDERS.DAT. Entry 42 contains 44, telling us to skip 43, which was skipped because it's a cluster with unusable areas in it—a *bad cluster.* Entry 44 tells us to skip up to cluster 102 for the next cluster, and 102 points us to 103, which is the end of the file. You skipped over 45, which is the end of some file; again, you don't know which file.

FIGURE 10.8

Directory and FAT
example

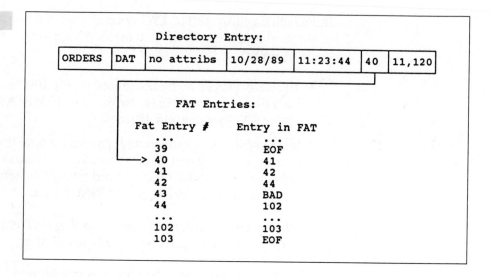

Note that each cluster's FAT entry in a file links to the next cluster's FAT entry in that file. This is called a *one-way linked list;* one-way because you can only follow it in one direction. (If this is unclear, look only at entry 103, the EOF for ORDERS.DAT. Looking only at that information, what would tell you that 102 was the previous entry? Nothing. On the other hand, the FAT *will* tell you to go from 102 to 103.)

Disk Performance

Some disk/controller combinations are faster than others. You measure drive speed by looking at 1) how long it takes to find a particular piece of data, and 2) once there, how quickly it can be read off the disk. The first measurement is called the *access time* and the second is called the *data transfer rate.*

Access Times, Seek Times, and Latency Periods

The hard disk drive is somewhat like a phonograph. The platter itself is like the record, and the read/write head is like the phonograph stylus. To play a selection on a phonograph, you do two things:

1. Position the stylus arm to the beginning of the song.

2. Wait for the music on the track to come around.

Step 1 takes a lot longer than step 2. Almost instantaneously after positioning the stylus, the music is found.

Disk reads and writes work the same way. The head must first be positioned over the track, and then it waits for the desired sector to come up.

The formula to remember is this:

ACCESS TIME = SEEK TIME + ROTATIONAL LATENCY PERIOD

In other words, the amount of time required to find a sector equals the time it takes to move to the sector's cylinder plus the time it takes to wait for the sector to rotate around.

The two components are called *seek time* and *latency period*. Seek time is the time required for the head to position over a track. Latency period is how long it takes for the desired sector to move under the head.

Disk Seek Time

Of the seek time and the latency period, the seek time is usually the longer wait. It varies according to how many tracks must be traversed. A seek from one track to the next is usually quick, 5 to 16 milliseconds, but most seeks aren't so convenient. A common measure of an average seek is the time required to travel one third of the way across the disk. This is the one used in most benchmark programs. You might wonder, Why not halfway across the disk, rather than one third? The reason is that most accesses are short seeks—just a few tracks.

The list below shows some typical average seek times for a range of hard disks.

DRIVE DESCRIPTION	SEEK TIME (MS)
Toshiba 3100 10 MB	175
XT original 10 MB	94
PS/2 Model 50 original 20 MB	80
Seagate ST225 (20 MB)	75
Rodime 33MB in XT	57
AT original 20-MB	30
Priam HD 60-MB	22
Maxtor 140-MB in AT	19
Typical IDE drive	14
Fujitsu 504 MB IDE	9

Seek times are "built in" to a drive. There's no way for you to improve upon it, short of getting a new drive.

Seek times vary in part because there are two approaches to seeking: *band steppers* and *voice coils.* A band stepper is never quite sure over what track it's positioned, because it has no guidance mechanism. It does, however, have a *track zero indicator,* so it knows when it's at track zero. To find a track, it just seeks out track zero and then steps, track by track, to wherever it's going. A voice coil, on the other hand, is much faster because it devotes an entire surface to head position information. I've got a Seagate ST4096, for example, with nine surfaces. (In actuality, it's got ten, but the tenth is used for head positioning information.)

Rotational Latency Period

Once a head is positioned over a track, the job's not done: Now the head has to wait for the desired sector to rotate under the head. How *much* time is a matter of luck. If you're lucky, it's already there; if you're really unlucky, you just missed the sector and will have to wait an entire revolution. This waiting time, whether large or small, is called the *rotational latency period.* A common number cited is *average latency period.* This makes the simple assumption that, on an average, the disk must make a half-revolution to get to your sector. Since the disk rotates at 3600 rpm, one half revolution then takes $1/7200$ of a minute = $60/7200$ second = 8.33 ms (milliseconds). This contributes to the amount of time the system must wait for service.

The sum of the average seek time and the latency period is called the *access time,* and is oft quoted in product advertisements.

Data Transfer Rates and Interleave Factors

Once a disk has found the desired data, how fast can it transfer it to the PC? This is called the *data transfer rate.* It's the last significant number in the CORETEST output. It all makes sense if you keep the following assumption in mind: Remember there are only 512 bytes in a sector. That means whenever an application requests, say, sector 1 of track 100 of side 2, it'll probably need sector 2 of that track and side next. In fact, most of the times you need one sector from a track, you'll end up needing them all. So what's the best arrangement of sectors to allow them to be read at maximum speed?

By the way, if you have an IDE drive—which most modern PCs have— then this discussion is irrelevant. All IDEs are arranged for maximum data-transfer rate, and even if they *weren't,* you couldn't do anything about it anyway. This discussion *is* important, however, if you've got to maintain older PCs.

When a disk, whether hard or floppy, is low-level formatted (more on this process later), milestones are laid down on each track called *sector IDs.* These IDs separate one sector from another and are discussed in some more detail in the section on low-level or physical formatting. What I really was asking in the last paragraph, then, is this: The IDs can be laid out in any order, so in what order should the sectors be arranged? The answer to this question is the optimal *interleave factor.*

On floppies, the nine sectors are laid out like numbers on the face of a clock (Figure 10.9). That's because reading all of the sectors on a floppy in one pass doesn't tax the controller, speed-wise. They have nine sectors on a track, and the disk only rotates five times per second. At maximum, the biggest burden a floppy could put on its controller would be to throw it $^1/_2$ K bytes per sector times 9 sectors per rotation times 5 rotations per second, or 22.5K bytes per second. Heck, the serial port on most PCs can run at almost that rate; consecutive sectors on a floppy are no big deal.

Hard disks usually don't work that way. The problem is that hard disks rotate a lot faster than floppies. Hard disks spin at 60 rotations per second, and floppies rotate at 5 revolutions per second. In addition, hard disks pack more sectors on a track, as you'll recall. To see the problem, suppose you had a hard disk with the sectors in numerical order (called a *1:1 interleave*), as pictured in Figure 10.10.

As the hard disk rotates 60 times per second, the maximum this disk could throw at the controller per second would be $^1/_2$ K bytes per sector times 17 sectors per rotation times 60 rotations per second=510K bytes per second! Most hard disk controllers (and some computers) can't handle half a megabyte per second.

FIGURE 10.9

Simple floppy interleave order

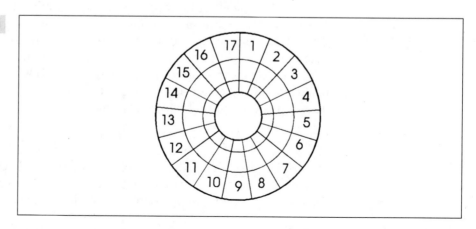

FIGURE 10.10

1:1 interleaved hard disk

So let's look in detail at what happens when two sectors are read in succession on a 1:1 interleaved disk:

1. DOS and BIOS request the hard disk controller to read a sector.

2. The controller instructs the disk head to move to the track and read the sector.

3. The head reads the data and transmits it to the controller.

4. As hard disks are fragile devices, the controller always includes *extra* data when it writes information to the disk. This information, when read back, enables the controller to detect whether or not errors have arisen in the data. This extra information is called the *ECC* (Error Correcting Code). It involves a mathematical function and takes a little while to compute. (The microprocessors on hard disk controllers aren't the fastest things in the world. I mean, you don't find too many 386s on disk controllers.) Meanwhile, the disk continues to spin.

5. Once the controller has checked the data, it passes it to BIOS and DOS, which are also paranoid about hard disk data loss. BIOS and DOS have their own small amount of overhead—proportionately less than the controller's, but relevant nonetheless. Meanwhile, the disk continues to spin.

6. Now that everyone is happy with the data, DOS wants the next sector. But since the controller, DOS, and BIOS were taking so long with the last sector's data, the disk continued spinning. If you had put sector 2 right after sector 1, you would *always miss the subsequent sector.* That implies that you would have to wait a whole rotation to get the next sector. This process would *always* occur. Figures 10.11 illustrates this problem.

Thus, on a disk with the sectors laid out clock-fashion in numerical order, you'd always end up getting only one sector read per rotation. As the disk rotates 60 times per second, it's only read 60 sectors per second. Each sector holds, as you'll recall, $1/2$ K; so the maximum data transfer rate from this disk would be 30K bytes per second, a rather poor transfer rate. (A 1.2-MB floppy could outperform this disk, since it transfers data at 45K per second!)

FIGURE 10.11

How interleaving
affects disk speed

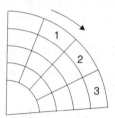

Step 1: An instruction to read sector 1 on a given track is executed. The head has been positioned over the right track, and now the data is read as the disk turns under the head.

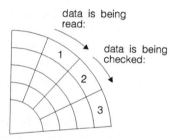

Step 2: The data has been passed from the disk head to the controller. The controller checks that the data was not corrupted while on disk by using a mathematical computation called the Error Correcting Code (ECC) test. Meanwhile, the disk keeps turning.

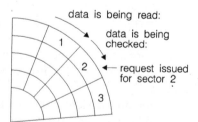

Step 3: After the controller pronounces the data OK, DOS and BIOS must be consulted again. Finally, they are ready to request sector 2—but sector 2 has just passed by. We are in a perfect location, however, for sector 3; why not put sector 2 where sector 3 is now?

But suppose you staggered the sectors, to give the controller time to get ready for the next sector. IBM did that on the XT, as pictured in Figure 10.12.

This is called a *1:6 interleave*. Start at 1 and then count clockwise six sectors. You're now at 2. Count six more. You're now at 3, and so on. This gives the XT time to do computations and still catch the next sector. Inspection will show that the XT can read *three* sectors on the first rotation, or about 180 sectors per second. That means we can get three times the data transferred per second from an XT by changing from a noninterleaved disk layout to a 1:6.

As controllers get faster, they can compute error correcting codes faster. The AT controller is fast enough that you can move your disk's sectors closer together than the XT controller allowed. IBM interleaved the AT disk at 1:3, as illustrated in Figure 10.13.

This is a *1:3 interleave factor*. Six sectors can be read on a single rotation—twice the XT's throughput, or 360 sectors per rotation. Remember why we can't make the IBM XT a 1:3 disk—the sectors would be too close, and we'd always miss the next sector. The net effect would be, again, getting only one sector per rotation.

FIGURE 10.12

1:6 disk interleave

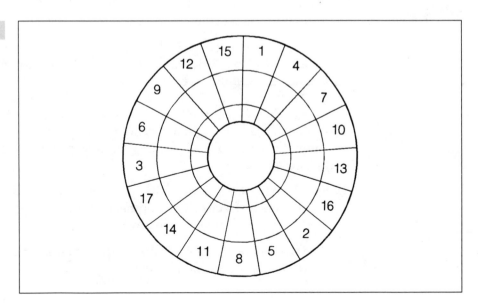

FIGURE 10.13

1:3 disk interleave

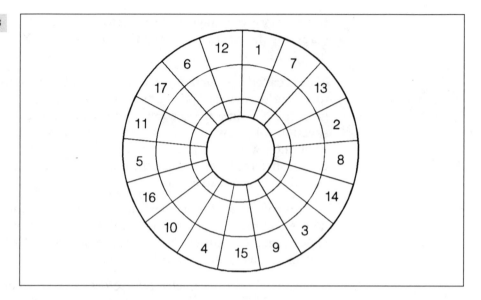

This might seem like a somewhat academic discussion, but you'd be surprised how many computers are interleaved incorrectly. For example, IBM formatted XT drives at 1:6 even though 1:5 is the best interleave, and they formatted AT drives at 1:3 even though 1:2 is the best interleave for that machine. How important is this? Take a look at Table 10.4.

You can see that on an IBM XT, reformatting from IBM's default 1:6 interleave to a 1:5 interleave would improve disk throughput by 20 percent. Changing the interleave on an IBM AT from 1:3 to 1:2 would increase disk throughput by 50 percent. Other companies are guilty of the same thing. The AT&T 6386, for example, is formatted at 1:3, although it should be 1:2. The right interleave factor means that your controller, your computer, and your disk are right in step, pulling data off the disk as quickly as possible.

So it's up to you to ensure that your machine disk is formatted to its optimal interleave factor. The optimal interleave factor is determined, again, by the kind of controller you have.

One way to breathe new life into a tired old machine is to replace the disk controller with one that allows a smaller interleave. You can speed up an

TABLE 10.4: Theoretical Disk Data Transfer Rates

DRIVE TYPE	MAX DATA TRANSFER (K BYTES/SECOND)	SECTORS READ/ ROTATION
360K floppy, XT	22.5	
360K floppy, AT	27	
1.2-MB floppy, AT	45	
Hard disk 1:6 (17 sectors/track)	85	2.8
1:5	102	3.4
1:4	128	4.3
1:3	170	5.7
1:2	255	8.5
1:1	510	17.0

XT-type machine with either the XT-type controllers from Data Technology Corporation (DTC5150CX) or Western Digital (WD1002-WX1 or XT-GEN), dropping the interleave factor on your XT to 1:3. Adaptec even makes an XT-type controller that'll handle 1:2 on an XT. You can replace the standard-issue Western Digital WD1003 1:2 interleave controller on AT-type machines with Western Digital's WD1006 or Data Technology's DTC7280, both of which actually support 1:1 interleave factors.

Recall that the interleave factor is set when you low-level format a hard disk. Recently, some software writers have started offering *interleave fixer programs*. These both measure your disk's optimal interleave, and then allow you to reset your disk's interleave factor without backing up, reformatting, and reloading. Their approach is really a simple one: just read a track, store it in memory, reformat the track to the proper interleave factor, and rewrite the original information.

There are several such programs on the market; Steve Gibson's SpinRite is probably the best known. I use and recommend HOPTIMUM from Kolod Research. HOPTIMUM is packaged in the hTEST/hFORMAT program set, a set of utilities that I feel everyone must have if they're to do major data surgery on a hard disk. Appendix A describes some interleave fixers. Some sample HOPTIMUM output is shown in Figure 10.14.

Cautions about Using Interleave Fixers

HOPTIMUM and company are nice to have around (and the rest of the hTEST/hFORMAT collection is indispensable as well), but here are a couple of cautions.

FIGURE 10.14

Sample HOPTIMUM program output

```
C:\MACE>hoptimum
HOPTIMUM - Hard disk interleave OPTIMIZER Program          Version 1.0.3
  Copyright (C) 1986 Kolod Research, Inc.
                Box 68 * Glenview, Il. 60025 * 708-291-1586
Licensed Program Materials
Drive - C - will be formatted and tested as:
            read/write heads:    6
                  cylinders:  639
                    sectors:   17
Formatting parameters will be:
            beginning surface:    0 (surfaces start internally at 0)
              ending surface:    5
          beginning cylinder:  628 (cylinders start internally at 0)
            ending cylinder:  638
          sector interleaves    1 through    7
                machine type: PC/XT (or compatible)
Do you wish to change
any of the above formatting parameters ? (Y/N): n
        ... more output ....
Summary is as follows...
    Interleave              Total access time        Total clock ticks
                            (rounded to nearest sec.)  (normally 18.2 / sec)
    ----------              -------------------------  --------------------
            1                      20                       364
            2                      20                       365
            3                       4                        65
            4                       5                        86
            5                       6                       106
            6                       7                       126
            7                       8                       146
Program has terminated normally
```

First, it's perfectly fine to test your XT-type controller's optimal interleave with an interleave adjuster program, but don't actually allow the program to do a *nondestructive reformat*. The problem is that the nondestructive format consists of a lot of separate *format track* commands, rather than the more normal destructive format's single *format multiple tracks* commands. At the beginning of each format command, the controller *recalibrates* by moving back to track 0. In the case of a format multiple tracks command, one recalibration is required for the entire destructive format. But, again, the nondestructive formats work by reading a track, formatting the track, restoring the track, and then repeating the process on the next track until the disk is done. XT controllers insist on recalibrating, then, for *each track!* That's a lot of head movement; in fact, it's not unusual to see HOPTIMUM or SpinRite require eight or more hours to run on an XT-type machine. That's a real torture test of what is probably a low-end drive anyway. It would be nice if it worked, but it really isn't a good idea. Instead, do it the hard way: Back up, reformat, and restore.

Second, it's likely that, if CORETEST reports that you have more than 17 sectors on a track (likely values are 25, 26, 33, or 34), these low-level format or interleave adjustment programs won't work *and will destroy all data on your hard disk.* So back up your data before you use them for the first time. (Don't say I didn't warn you.) CORETEST, on the other hand, is nondestructive; I've seen a couple of controllers it won't run on, but it never destroys data.

Finally, be aware that Western Digital XT-type controllers write important information on the first sector of the disk. This information often doesn't get rewritten on reformat, rendering the drive useless. Avoid this if possible by telling the reformatter not to touch cylinder zero. HOPTIMUM lets you do this; SpinRite does not.

1:1 Hard Disk Controllers

Controllers waste a lot of time checking data and rereading data they've read just recently. Full-track and caching controllers seek to eliminate that waste and speed up disk access.

Some controllers, like the Western Digital WD1006 for ATs, and the hard disk controllers shipped with the PS/2 Models 50 through 80, take another approach to interleaving. They assume (reasonably) that most of the time when you want *one* sector on a track, you'll end up wanting *most* sectors on a track. Think about it: Why look at a track as 17 sectors, each requiring separate read operations, when another approach is to read the whole track in one operation? In this case, you don't really have to worry about plucking out a single sector and checking it before you go on to the next. This is called *full-track buffering*. In this approach, you read the whole track, then do the error checking on the entire track.

For instance, if you have an AT-type 286 or 386 clone, you almost certainly use the Western Digital WD1003 hard disk controller. For under $110 (when last I checked), you could buy the WD1006, a 100-percent compatible replacement that reads entire tracks at a time. Reading an entire track in one shot means the disk can support a 1:1 interleave, allowing a 510K/second data transfer rate from your hard disk—quite nice indeed, and highly recommended.

If you use such a controller, DOS, of course, knows nothing of this and continues to request only single sectors. The net effect is that the first sector requested of each track takes a little longer to retrieve than normal. Subsequent sectors are instantaneous, requiring no disk work at all.

Will this approach always work better than sector-by-sector reads? Not if for some reason the program only wanted one or two sectors per track. This is, however, unlikely.

Caching controllers are another story. The idea here is to put a microprocessor and some memory on the controller, and allow the controller to cache requests for data. The problem is that it often confuses DOS or an application, and may render you unable to run OS/2 or UNIX. This is a nice option, but only if you're certain it will cause you no regret.

Encoding Schemes: FM, MFM, RLL...

As time goes on, everyone finds that hard disk space is like All Good Things in Life: There just isn't enough of it. The same microcomputer market that grinned from ear to ear just six years ago when IBM offered the voluminous 10-MB disk (most manufacturers were only offering 5MB at the time) is now saying, "Just *how* do I get a third 300-MB drive on my Novell server?" Then there's the second question, "And can I get those 300-MB disks to read data *faster?*"

Well, mass storage manufacturers are eager to meet those needs, so they're constantly working to put more space on a hard disk and to figure out how to pull it off the disk faster. This section tells you how they're doing it.

The method to increase storage space that most quickly comes to mind is to add platters to a hard disk, or perhaps to squeeze more cylinders onto the disk. But there are limits to that, both space and cost constraints. To go further, manufacturers have looked to putting more sectors on a track.

To an extent, all one needs to do to put more sectors on a track is just to write some software: Most disks could accommodate an extra few sectors without too much trouble, so all the 17-sector disks out there could become 20-sector disks, and become $3/17$ larger. But manufacturers are looking for a quantum leap to allow them to build drives that reach to near-gigabyte levels. They do this by changing the *encoding scheme*. *MFM* (Modified Frequency Modulation) is the encoding scheme that has been used for years on disks. In 1988, a newer one, *RLL* (Run Length Limited), put 50 percent more data on a given disk (although, as you'd expect, at a cost of reliability). Here are some more details.

Basically, data is stored on a magnetic medium by encoding what are called *flux reversals* onto the magnetic medium. A reversal means either negative to positive or positive to negative. The reversal shows up as a "pulse" when reading the data, so I'll refer to reversals as *pulses.* Disks use pulses and the lack of pulses to represent data on a disk drive.

The easiest approach, it seems, would be to encode something like

```
0=no pulse
1=pulse
```

But there's a practical obstacle to this simple method. You see, if there's a long string of zeros, then there would be a long period of no pulses. Too much silence and the controller gets lost. Pulses not only send data, they keep the controller's internal clock in synch with the data on the disk.

Think of it this way: If you set your watch to the same time as some time service, both your watch and the time service's clock will match each other for a while. But as a few months go by, you'll find that your watch is getting a little ahead or behind the time service, so you'll reset your watch periodically.

Data comes off the disk in a time-dependent fashion, so the timing that was used to *write* the data must match the timing that's used when *reading* the data. It sounds simple to do, but it's not. The clock circuit on the hard disk controller is less precise than, for instance, the clock circuit on your digital watch. It may run a bit slower or faster from day to day and second to second. Pulses help resynchronize the data and the controller. (There's more to it, but that's as technical as I want to get, since I assume you're not going to design hard disk controllers for a living.)

So if we used the simple *pulse=1, no pulse=0* approach, and got a long string of 0s, the resulting silence could cause the controller to get out of synch with the data. Therefore, we need an encoding scheme that ensures that we never go too long without a pulse.

One way to handle the synchronization problem is to include clocking bits with the data. A simple approach called *Frequency Modulation,* or *FM,* encodes a 1 as two pulses, and a 0 as a pulse followed by no pulse:

    1 0 0 0 1 1

becomes

    PPPNPNPNPPPP

(P=pulse, N=no pulse).

This seems fairly effective, eh? Yes, but it's wasteful—I only told you half the story before. To see why it's wasteful, you need one more piece of the puzzle: You can fit more *pulses* and *no pulses* on a disk if the number of *pulses* is relatively small. (Yes, that conflicts with our desire to ensure that we never go too long without a pulse.) The scheme pictured above, as you can see, includes a lot of pulses. It does eliminate the "long run of 0s" problem, however. The minimum length run of 0s is 0; that is, sometimes two pulses occur next to each other. The maximum length is 1, so you never have more than one 0 in a run. We can say that this is a (0,1) run length limited scheme. FM is an old encoding scheme that's not used much any more.

So our criteria for a good encoding scheme are:

- It should minimize the number of pulses necessary to store a given piece of data so that the maximum amount of data can fit on the disk, *but*
- It should be careful not to allow too long a run of "no pulses" to occur, as the clock on the disk controller board can lose track if it doesn't recalibrate with a pulse now and then.

FM led to *MFM,* or Modified FM. MFM is a bit more daring, creating minimum zero runs of one 0 and maximum runs of 3, for a (1,3) run length limited scheme. IBM uses this for floppy and most hard disk encoding.

MFM is encoded so:

- 1 is always no pulse, then a pulse (NP)
- 0 as in 00 is coded pulse, then no pulse (PN)
- 0 as in 10 is coded as two no pulse's (NN)

So 101100 looks like

```
1 0 1 1 0 0
NPNNNPNPNNPN=4 pulses
```

Compare this with FM:

```
PPPNPPPPPNPN=9 pulses
```

Recently, a new kind of controller has arrived called *2,7 Run Length Limited,* or, as it's usually referred to, *2,7 RLL* (or just *RLL*). It pushes the density of data on a hard disk 50 percent further. RLL first appeared on mainframes in the early '80s, and it will be an important technology in the PC field in the years to come.

RLL uses a more complex encoding scheme, which is compared to that of MFM in Table 10.5.

TABLE 10.5: Encoding Patterns Compared to MFM

PATTERN TO ENCODE	RLL ENCODING (N=NO PULSE, P=PULSE)	# PULSES	MFM ENCODING	# PULSES
00	PNNN	1	PNPN	2
01	NPNN	1	PNNP	2
100	NNPNNN	1	NPNNPN	2
101	PNPNN	2	NPNNNP	2
1100	NNNNPNNN	1	NPNPNNPN	3
1101	NNPNNPNN	2	NPNPNNNP	3
111	NNNPNN	1	NPNPNP	3

So 101100 encodes as 101 100 or

    PNNPNNNNPNNN=3 pulses

One common RLL configuration combines the Seagate ST238R (a 21 MB drive, actually the ST225 with a different label) and an RLL controller to yield a 30-MB system. Always use RLL-rated drives with RLL controllers.

A final benefit from RLL is that, since the data is stored in a denser fashion, it's transferred off the disk faster. When RLL works, it makes your disk *faster* and *bigger*.

Drive Interfaces: ST506, ESDI, SCSI, IDE

How does the controller talk to the drive? They must agree on a "language" to speak between themselves, called an interface. The definition of the interface is partly hardware, partly software. For example, when you use the telephone, you are using a standard interface: The hardware is the phone and all the phone company equipment, and the software is the phone etiquette like the fact that when you call someone, they talk first, not you.

If you wanted a hard disk on a microcomputer in the late '70s, you'd buy a controller and a drive from the same company, so you wouldn't worry about the interface, and that's good, as both the controller and the drive would speak some strange language cooked up by the hard disk and controller manufacturer. Nowadays, however, you're likely to want to buy a controller from one vendor, like Western Digital or Data Technology Corporation, and a drive from another vendor, like Seagate, Maxtor, or Mitsubishi. That implies that they both must support some common standard interface.

ST506

Originally, the now-defunct Shugart Technologies used something they called the *ST 506/412* interface, or as it's more commonly called, *ST506*. This interface is installed on both the controller side and the disk side: you need an ST506 controller to talk to an ST506 drive. The cabling is standardized by this interface, also: a 20-wire cable for data and a 34-wire cable for control signals.

Most drives are ST506. An ST506 interface is 5 million pulses per second, which can translate to about 7.5 million bits per second if using 2,7 RLL encoding (only about 5 Mbps for MFM). But it's also a simple interface: Raw bits are transmitted from the drive to the controller, timing bits as well as data bits. The ST506 controller then must separate the timing from data bits (this is called "data separation"), slowing down the whole process. Any loss or damage of the timing bits can invalidate the data bits under this scheme. That's why most hard-disk cables are fairly short, to address this problem: Shorter cables mean lower error rates.

The ST506 interface is not only noise-prone, it's fairly dumb. Under ST506, the controller can't tell the drive to move the head to a particular cylinder. Instead, it can only issue the commands "move up one cylinder" or "move down one cylinder." Moving from cylinder 100 to cylinder 200, then, requires 100 separate commands.

ESDI

In the early '80s, a group of drive vendors got together with the goal of developing a drive interface standard that could succeed ST506. They wanted it to keep as much of 506's aspects as was possible—the same cabling, for example—but to remove as many flaws as was possible. The new standard was called the Enhanced Small Device Interface, or ESDI.

ESDI improved upon ST506 in these ways:

- where ST506 can only support up to 16-head disks, ESDI can support up to 256 heads, making way for much larger disks.

- ESDI can support a much higher data transfer rate than ST506. ESDI allows for 24 million bits per second data-transfer rates.

- An ESDI drive can send to its corresponding controller information about its disk layout. Where ST506 drive/controller combinations require some extensive configuration to ensure that the controller knows how many heads, cylinders, and sectors are on its disk, an ESDI controller just gets the information directly from the drive.

- ESDI does the data separation right on the disk, allowing for longer cables and more noise-free communication between the drive and controller.

ESDI was intended to be the interface for real "muscle" drives. It never really got popular, however, and it's fading away like ST506, to be replaced by SCSI and IDE.

SCSI

About the same time as ESDI was being developed, the small computer world ("small computer" here refers to PCs, Macs, UNIX workstations, and small minicomputers) realized that there were an ever-growing number of peripherals that an ever-growing number of vendors were trying to interface to an ever-growing number of types of computers.

One way to solve this problem would be to agree on a kind of computer bus that would be used by all types of small computers. That would be very tough to implement, however, over a wide variety of CPUs. So, these vendors developed something akin to a hard disk interface that could support not just hard disks, but also things like:

- CD-ROM drives
- WORM (Write Once, Read Many times) optical disks
- WARM (Write And Read Many times) optical disks
- Optical scanners
- 21+-MB "super" floppies
- Bernoulli Box–cartridge storage devices

That led to a PC interface called SCSI (pronounced—honest!—"scuzzy"), Small Computer Systems Interface. Macintoshes use SCSI as a drive interface. SCSI has become the drive interface for "power" systems, like disk servers.

Eventually SCSI will support over 100 megabits per second, but for now it's in the ESDI range of speed. SCSI hard disks actually put the disk controller on the drive; the board in the computer really doesn't have much to do, and is strictly speaking not a controller but a "host adapter." If you have Iomega Bernoulli Boxes, you may have wondered why Iomega calls the adapter card a "host adapter," rather than a "controller," the SCSI interface is the reason. Another SCSI plus: the simplicity of the host adapter (remember, it doesn't have much to do, as the controller is on the drive) means that a single host adapter can support up to eight devices. All the SCSI host adapter does is to connect all the SCSI devices to the PC bus.

SCSI is an intelligent "system-level" interface. That means it responds to more complex commands than the "read this sector" commands that ST506 and ESDI use.

SCSI is hampered when working with DOS in the following way. SCSI identifies sectors with a "linear" notation. Rather than asking a SCSI controller for "head 0, cylinder 0, sector 1," a program just asks for "sector 1 on the drive." All sectors are numbered consecutively. Programs need only worry about the sector number, be it 1 or 1,000. No worrying about drive geometry.

DOS, in fact, *also* thinks like this: it organizes sectors internally with a linear notation, rather than the "three-dimensional" head/cylinder/sector approach. It actually must convert from linear to 3-D notation when making a disk request, as BIOS expects disk requests in 3-D format. And there's the problem. As SCSI adapters must look BIOS-compatible, they must accept the 3-D notation and convert it back to linear notation before trying to read a sector.

Consider, then, the plight of a SCSI drive under DOS: DOS converts linear sector addresses to 3-D sector addresses, then the SCSI adapter takes the 3-D addresses and converts them back to linear for its own use! (Actually, there is yet another linear-to-3-D conversion on the SCSI drive, slowing things down even further.)

This is meant to be just a brief introduction to SCSI. We'll talk more about it in Chapter 11.

Which Is Better, SCSI or ESDI?

A logical question. Answering it requires understanding a simple idea: SCSI and ESDI are different interfaces, designed to serve different ends.

- ESDI is basically a souped-up version of ST506. It was designed to allow drive makers to build big, fast drives for single-user systems. The drive management is basically done by the CPU, which, again, is not a problem for single-user systems.

  But what about a server that must manage six or seven ESDI drives, and multiple requests from different workstations for data on those drives? That's a lot of work for the CPU, and would benefit from distributed intelligence.

- SCSI provides that distributed intelligence. The SCSI host adapter is a CPU all in itself. All the PC's CPU would have to do in the six-drive scenario is to just issue six data requests rapid-fire to the SCSI host adapter, then sit back and wait for the data to come in. (Actually, it wouldn't sit back and wait. A good multitasking system would do something else while waiting for the responses to come in.)

Here's a more down-to-earth example of how SCSI differs from ESDI. Suppose you were remodeling your house. If the remodeling just means replacing the sink in the downstairs bathroom, you'd just hire a plumber and manage her directly. You wouldn't need a general contractor—in fact hiring a general contractor to oversee one person would be expensive and time-consuming. Even though you're not a professional plumbing overseer, you can see whether a simple job is getting done or not. This is the ESDI situation.

But if remodeling involves a lot of work, you need painters, plumbers, carpenters, and electricians. You could just go out and hire them directly and manage them, as before, but it would be a nightmare. You'd save lots of time and maybe money by getting a general contractor, who would find and manage the workers separately. The "interface" that you see is the general contractor, who doesn't do any of the work himself—in fact, he may end up hiring the same plumber that you would have, had you done the management all by yourself. That's the SCSI scenario. SCSI is a higher level of management.

ESDI would be superior in a single-user system where speed is of the essence.

SCSI would be superior if :

- you have an operating system that can exploit its multitasking power

- you are controlling a diverse range of devices, and do not want to have to lose one bus slot for your drive controller, another for your tape, yet another for your CD-ROM, etc.

    (Reality check time: As SCSI hasn't settled down as a standard, there's no real guarantee that any SCSI device can be controlled by any given SCSI host adapter. We're talking mid 1990s before it's a reliable standard.)

- your PC has a smart bus. You've read earlier in Chapter 3's discussion of buses that that the Micro Channel and EISA buses offer a "bus-mastering" capability, and that this is a Good Thing. It refers to the fact that the standard AT bus is controlled by the CPU. Even if you've got a smart board (like a SCSI host adapter) plugged into the bus, it can't initiate transfers across the bus without the permission of the CPU. Bus mastering is a Good Thing because it allows the bus to be more easily shared among "smart" boards boards with autonomous CPUs on them. That implies that a well-designed SCSI adapter in a bus master system (and the right software) could do some nifty things that an ESDI adapter could not in the same environment. Again, SCSI shines in a multiprocessor environment.

By the way, I should point out that both SCSI and ESDI universally use RLL for data encoding, allowing great data sizes (I'm saving this data on a 621-MB ESDI drive that is physically no larger than the 10-MB drive I installed in an XT in 1983). When people refer to an "RLL drive," they really mean an ST506 drive that is rated to handle RLL encoding. Strictly speaking, all ESDIs and SCSIs are "ESDI/RLL" and "SCSI/RLL"—one could design an ESDI or SCSI using MFM, but there would be no point.

IDE

Well, if the vendor committees that developed ESDI and SCSI had their way, we'd be all using those standards. But one vendor's view of how to save a buck and squeeze a bit more performance out of some existing hardware changed the business, and created an "ad-hoc" standard that changed the whole industry.

In 1986, Compaq wanted to speed up ST506 drives, as well as reduce manufacturing cost and increase reliability. So they approached Western Digital. WD and Compaq realized that, as you've read earlier, one of the big weak links in the ST506 system was the cable connecting the hard disk to the controller. The longer the cable, the lower the maximum data transfer rate and the higher the noise level. So, they reasoned, with a shorter cable, we can get better performance out of cheaper drives. That led to a new drive/controller interface approach called IDE—Integrated Drive Electronics.

Perhaps the shortest controller/drive cable in the world is found on an IDE drive. This packs 26 to 35 sectors on a track using basically ST506 technology with a twist: Rather than the usual separate drive and controller, IDE puts the controller right onto the drive in a quest to eliminate data loss between the drive and the controller. As the data transfer between controller and drive is, then, pretty reliable, manufacturers are emboldened to put 30 or more sectors per track.

In earlier ST506 systems, the controller took the data from the drive, converted it to a format that the PC bus could understand, and then (as the controller was plugged right into one of the bus' expansion slots) handed the data to the bus. What about IDE? Is the drive/controller combination plugged into the bus? Generally not, only because it's physically awkward to have a cable from the back of the drive end up in a bus slot connector. IDEs connect to the bus in one of three ways.

- The IDE drive/controller indeed connects to a bus slot, if it is a *hardcard*. I'll explain more about hardcards in a few pages.

- Most IDEs nowadays connect to the bus with with a simple *pass-through* or *paddle* board. Under this scheme (Compaq does it, for example), a 40-wire cable runs from the IDE drive/controller to an *IDE adapter card,* really nothing more than a board plugged into an expansion slot that just hands the data to the bus. Remember, the data comes off the IDE drive already formatted for the PC bus. IDE drives like this are easily spotted by the 40-wire cable connection, rather than the more familiar ST506 dual-cable approach.

- More and more motherboards include an IDE connector right on the motherboard.

Sounds good? It is, basically, with one twist: You can't maintain it with software. You're not supposed to low-level format it, and in fact I've seen a low-level format damage an old Compaq IDE drive. Norton will work for some data recovery, but the real low-level products like Disk Technician can't help you at all. Once upon a time, I would have said that there's something a bit too disposable about these drives for my taste: They're basically reliable, but you're helpless if they do develop a problem.

But I've got to bow to the times and recognize a simple fact: ST506 and ESDI are dead. Virtually any drive you buy today under 300 MB is an IDE drive. Drives in the 300–600-MB range are either IDE or SCSI, and anything bigger than 600 MB is almost certainly SCSI … as of today.

IDEs keep getting bigger. And getting better, as well: I find myself at this moment working at a desk that has three computers on it. One's got a 660-MB ESDI drive, the second has a 340-MB IDE drive, and the third has a 540-MB IDE drive. The IDEs have been as reliable as the ESDI. Some of that is due to the fact that all three drives are from Maxtor, a maker of top-quality stuff.

Write Precompensation and Reduced Write Current

Here are two intimidating-sounding terms that you ordinarily wouldn't even hear of, except for when you had to low-level format a drive. Everybody's curious about what they mean, however, so here they are.

Write precompensation corrects a problem that occurs when the hard disk uses the higher numbered cylinders, the ones closer to the center of the platter. There's less space there to store data, yet recall that the same amount of data gets stored on each track. That means the linear density of, say, cylinder 500 is considerably higher than that of cylinder 0. Recall that data is stored on the hard disk by magnetizing the disk to create pulses that the head detects as the platter whizzes by underneath it. These magnetic areas are like small magnets, with *north poles* and *south poles*. Remember north and south poles from science class? Put two souths or norths together, and they repel. Put a north and a south together, and they attract.

Sometimes the data on a disk works out so that the magnetic areas for two adjacent bits end up with their north poles facing each other (souths would do the same thing). The bits actually move *away* from each other, and the data on the disk actually changes because of magnetic repulsion.

Write precompensation "precompensates" for this by writing the data closer together than it should be, so when the magnetic areas repel each other, they end up exactly where the controller wanted them in the first place; see Figure 10.15. The *write precompensation value* is the cylinder at which to start the write precomp. If a drive has 600 cylinders and the write precomp cylinder is 600, that means the drive doesn't require write precomp. The manufacturer determines when designing the drive at which cylinder to start write precompensation.

FIGURE 10.15

What write
precompensation does

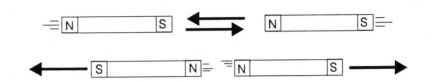

Data is stored on disk by magnetizing areas of the disk platter with north and south poles.

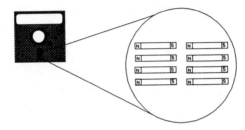

Data is represented by magnetism at any one spot and also by the lack of magnetism in some spots. The spaces between the magnets are also important.

This   becomes this;

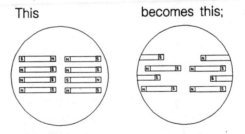

The inner cylinders of most hard disks are sufficiently small so the data ends up being crammed pretty close together. Attraction and repulsion take effect immediately, affecting the spaces between the magnets (and therefore the stored data).

Reduced write current cylinder refers to a similar problem. Think of writing data on a magnetic medium as being like writing on paper with ink. The "ink" here is the electric current used to create the magnetic field. The more ink, the "larger" the letters. Large letters are easier to read later, and a little smear or smudge (some kind of data corruption) won't make the data unreadable. So disk-drive designers prefer to turn up the juice as far as possible to make the data as safe as possible.

But if you write too big, the letters run over each other. That happens on those troublesome inner cylinders as well. Too much electric current makes magnetic domains that are physically too large, and they overrun each other. The drive turns down the current starting from the reduced write current cylinder to the center of the drive.

Again, you'll see these numbers when formatting a drive. Some disk controllers insist on knowing when to start precompensating or turning down the write power.

Hardware: The Controller and the Drive

The hard disk subsystem consists of the sealed drive itself and a controller board, which plugs into a slot in the PC expansion bus. Controllers are available that act as both floppy and hard disk controller, saving you a slot. Some firms have developed *hardcards*, which mount a narrow drive on a short controller board to yield a plug-in hard disk and controller all in one. We'll consider the two components separately.

The Controller

The controller is a printed circuit board that generally contains some *VLSI* (Very Large Scale Integration) chips on it and, commonly, a simple microprocessor. More than 10,000 transistors on a chip makes it VLSI. More than a thousand transistors per chip is *LSI* (Large Scale Integration);

more than one hundred is *MSI* (you guessed it, Medium Scale Integration); and more than ten is *SSI,* the meaning of which is left as an exercise to the reader. The controller acts as the go-between for the hard disk and the system board. Controllers are identified by the factors discussed below.

XT-type or AT-type

Unlike most expansion boards, the hard disk controllers in the XT and the AT are designed differently and are largely incompatible (see Figures 10.16 and 10.17). Some controllers talk with the computer via DMA (XT types) and others use an odd IRQ approach (AT types).

FIGURE 10.16

IBM XT hard disk controller

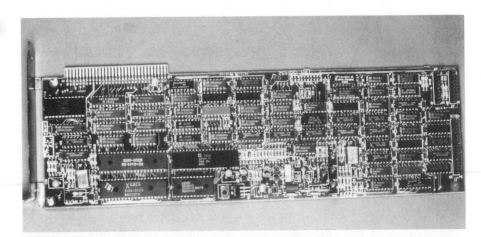

FIGURE 10.17

IBM AT hard disk controller

In the IRQ approach, the controller first fills a 512-byte buffer on the controller board itself. Then a hardware interrupt type 14 is issued, and the 80286 CPU reads the data from the buffer and stores it in memory. It uses interrupts—IRQs—to transfer data more quickly than DMA. This sounds contradictory, as the whole idea behind DMA is to be able to transfer data into memory without the CPU forcing you to slow down. The reason the interrupt-driven approach works is the design of the interface between the controller's buffer and the 80286. Most controller designs spoon out data in 8-bit bytes. The AT controller hands data to the CPU in 16-bit chunks. A second reason for the success is two 80286 commands that the earlier chips don't have, which allow fast block transfers from an I/O port. The raw transfer rate for these transfers can be as fast as 16 million bits per second.

What Interleave the Controller Can Handle

Controller manufacturers are turning out faster and faster controllers—1:1 controllers are becoming a common sight in AT- type machines, and 1:3 is now the most common in XT-type machines.

The Controller's Encoding Scheme (MFM, RLL, ARLL)

There's no such thing as an RLL drive—the controller determines the encoding scheme. But there is the fact that some drives are of higher quality than others, and to squeeze 26 sectors on a track, we can't usually get away with a run-of-the-mill drive.

The Controller's Interface (ST506, ESDI, SCSI, IDE)

There *is* such a thing as an ST506 or ESDI drive. Ensure when you buy a drive that it uses the same interface as your controller.

Cabling on the Controller's Interface

You'll see a few types of cables in the PC hard disk world:

- Normal two-cable

- Single 40-pin IDE (Integrated Drive Electronics), like Compaq and Zenith (for LP286), and SCSI connector

- Very oddball edge connector types, like the PS/2 desktop models (25, 30, 50, 50Z, 70)

I'll talk more about this in the drive installation chapter, but for now let me just say that *most* microcomputer drives use a fairly standard set of hard disk cables, a 34-wire and a 20-wire cable. Those cables are used for both ST506 and ESDI drives. And that's great; it means you can buy a drive from Dastardly Dan's Double Discount House of Clones, and then buy a drive from someone else, and they'll work together. And it means you can get a new 80-MB drive and put it in your vintage 1985 XT.

Usually.

Some vendors have apparently decided that all this compatibility wasn't doing a thing for their profit margin, so they've retained the ST506 (or ESDI) signals but rearranged the cable! The underlying electronics are exactly the same, but the cable's different. That means you must buy a drive with the same unusual cable connections as the controller.

Who does this? Compaq was the first I can remember. The Deskpros were the first to use a strange cable (one 40-wire cable, not the usual 34-wire or 20-wire) to connect to a drive that was ST506 electronically, but which used the strange one-cable connector. That was the first IDE drive.

Because the demand for drives that have the strange one-cable connector is much lower than the demand for the usual drives, fewer vendors offer them, and those who do charge about a $600 premium over the equivalent two-cable drive. Your choices were either to dump your already-bought Compaq drive and controller and replace them with a normal two-cable drive and controller, or to pay through the nose for a second Compaq-ready drive. Zenith did the same thing with their small footprint LP286. Ditto IBM's PS/2s, all of them. Nowadays, *everyone* uses this IDE approach.

The Winchester Sealed Drive

Most microcomputer hard disks are *sealed* units: The heads and platter are in a sealed, air-filtered compartment. It isn't always like that for hard disks.

On some mainframe disk drives, the disk is in a separate *disk pack* that mounts atop the drive motor and control circuitry. The drive motor and circuitry contain the heads. The disk packs, which look like Tupperware cake carriers, just contain disk platters. They're not sealed, since they must be "mounted" atop the drive motor and control circuitry. It's convenient to be able to have a whole shelf of disk packs, each storing megabytes and megabytes of data. But they're less reliable because dust can more easily get on the platters; the heads can pick up the dust and scratch it across the platters, sometimes damaging them irreparably. IBM changed this years ago with the *fixed drive,* a drive sealed in an air-filtered compartment that couldn't be mounted or dismounted. That's why IBM calls the hard disk the fixed disk drive. (And all this time, I thought *fixed* meant it wasn't broken...)

How did it get to be called a *Winchester* drive? I've heard two stories. The first one: The model number was the 3030 drive. The model number reminded technicians of the Winchester .3030 rifle, and the drive became known as a Winchester drive. The name has stuck through model numbers. The second one: The drive was invented at the Hursley Research Center in Winchester, England. Either way, the name stuck—any sealed drive is called a Winchester drive (see Figure 10.18).

Until recently, Winchesters for microcomputers have been based on $5\frac{1}{4}$-inch platters. It's interesting that, whether the drive is 5 MB or 180 MB, it's contained in the same size housing. You can't look at a drive and detect its capacity by its physical size.

We're seeing the appearance of more and more $3\frac{1}{2}$-inch hard disks. They're nice in that they have lower power requirements, and oddly enough, they often seem *more* reliable than their older $5\frac{1}{4}$-inch cousins.

FIGURE 10.18

10MB Winchester-
type hard disk

Hardcards

A *hardcard* is just a printed circuit board with the controller and drive mounted on the same board. To work this minor miracle, vendors mate the most advanced—and physically compact—technologies.

A hardcard's design goal seems to be, *Minimize drive power consumption and space taken up in the computer.* I can't disagree more. Larger power supplies are cheap and easy to install, and I'm certainly not willing to give up reliability just to save some space. Remember that *normal* hard disks are probably the least reliable things in your system. You cannot afford to give up even more reliability in the disk department.

All I'll say here is *be very careful when buying hardcards.* Are you only buying the drive because it's low-powered? Remember my comments on that in the previous section on $3\frac{1}{2}$-inch drives.

On the other hand, Plus Technology makes the original Hardcard, and they still make the best. They've matched an RLL controller with a high-quality drive to produce a good quality product, given (again) the design goals.

The reliability of hardcards is questionable. I'll echo Paul Mace's advice at this point: "If you've got a hardcard, fine. Just be sure to back it up regularly." Thankfully, they've just about disappeared.

CHAPTER

11

Understanding and Installing SCSI Devices

OVER the years, a number of mass-storage interfaces have come and gone. The first crop of hard disks in the PC world used an interface called ST412/506, which was inexpensive but limited in capabilities. So the computer industry set to work building a next generation of interfaces, leading to the development of the Enhanced Small Device Interface, or ESDI. ESDI is a fast and flexible interface, but it's an interface only for hard disks; as it turns out, that's something of a liability.

Introducing SCSI

Prior to the mid 80s, every type of storage device had its own kind of controller. If you wanted to add a scanner, a hard disk, a tape backup device, and a CD-ROM to your computer, you'd have to install one board into the system that would act as the interface for the scanner, another for the hard disk, one for the tape, and one for the CD-ROM. That meant not only four controllers, it also meant having to *configure* four separate boards (see Figure 11.1).

The computer industry responded to this with the following idea: Build PC peripherals that have controllers built right in, so those peripheral/controller combinations are configured correctly, right out of the factory. The only interface problem that would remain would be interfacing the controller/peripheral pair to the bus of the target system—the PC, in this case, but it would be just as easy to interface (in theory) to a Macintosh, a UNIX workstation, or a minicomputer. A new interface arose called the Small Computer Systems Interface, or SCSI (see Figure 11.2).

Standard
peripheral-to-PC
interface layers

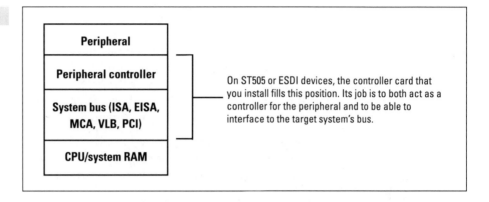

Peripheral-to-PC
interface with SCSI

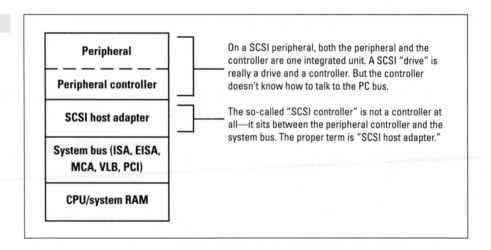

The benefit of putting a controller on each device in the SCSI world is that you know that the controller and drive are a matched set. In particular:

- The cables between the controller and the drive, which are a troublesome source of noise, can be extremely short, leading to much lower noise levels.

- The controller and drive (or peripheral) can be more closely matched. That means that built-in diagnostics can be included on the SCSI device, and also that there's no need to support the full range of some kind of interface standard like ST506 or ESDI. An

ESDI function that's irrelevant for a particular drive/controller combination can be discarded under SCSI. That wouldn't be possible under ESDI because you buy the ESDI drive from a different vendor than the vendor that you buy the ESDI controller from; as a result, the ESDI controller designer must build in every ESDI function, whether it'll be used or not. SCSI devices can concentrate solely on doing what they're intended to do, and nothing else.

- It saves having to configure the controller for the peripheral. Anyone who's spent hours trying to convince a "standard" drive to communicate with a "standard" controller knows what I mean here.

SCSI peripherals can be focused to do a particular task, but they lack the ability to talk to any real-world bus. SCSI devices don't know what a Macintosh, a PC, or a Sun computer is. That's where the SCSI board that you install in your system comes in. The SCSI "controller," then, is not a controller at all; it's just a kind of "universal translator" that allows any drive/peripheral combination to communicate with a particular computer's bus. So the SCSI *host adapter* (its true name) is the "glue" that cements your SCSI devices and your computer.

In this chapter, you'll learn more about what SCSI does, how to physically install SCSI devices, and how to set up software to support SCSI devices. Once you know that, you will be better equipped to attack problems with SCSI.

And that's essential information, because believe me—there's SCSI in every PC's future.

Defining a SCSI Configuration

Making SCSI work involves these items and issues. This is just an overview; we'll examine all of these issues in detail.

Item: SCSI host adapter

Issues:

- The host adapter must be compatible with the system's bus.

- There are different versions of SCSI: SCSI, SCSI-2, and SCSI-3. The host adapter must be able to support the same level of SCSI as the peripherals.
- Bus mastering and 32-bit interface SCSI host adapters are preferable.
- The host adapter must be assigned a SCSI ID between 0 and 7.
- The host needs a SCSI driver that follows the same SCSI standard as the SCSI drivers on the peripherals. There are three standards here: ASPI, CAM, and LADDR. These are *not* related to SCSI, SCSI-2, and SCSI-3; this is a different dimension in SCSI compatibility.

Item: SCSI-compatible peripheral

Issues:

- Each peripheral needs a SCSI driver that is compatible with the SCSI standard on the host's SCSI driver.
- All SCSI devices follow SCSI, SCSI-2, or SCSI-3; it may be important to know which level the device follows when installing it.
- Each peripheral must be assigned a unique SCSI ID from 0 to 7.
- Devices can be mounted internally or externally.
- Some devices have optional built-in termination (see below); others may have termination that's not optional (this is very bad, but more common than you'd like), and still others do not include termination of any kind.
- Devices should be able to be daisy chained, so they *should have two SCSI connectors if they are external.*

Item: SCSI cabling

Issues:

- There are several kinds of SCSI cables, and even variations within categories like SCSI, SCSI-2, and SCSI-3.
- You can't run cables more than a few feet, or the SCSI signal degrades and the peripheral doesn't work.

Item: SCSI termination

Issues:

- Each SCSI system needs two terminators, one on each extreme end of the chain of devices.
- SCSI and SCSI-2 use different types of terminators. (One is the T-100, the other is the T-1000...) They are generally incompatible; see later sections of this chapter for more details.
- Some devices have built-in terminators, others require separate termination devices. SCSI-II usually *requires* built-in termination.
- The host adapter probably supports termination of some kind. This should be considered when terminating the system.

Item: SCSI drivers

Issues:

- The SCSI system will need a driver for each SCSI device, as well as a driver for the host adapter.
- SCSI hard disks may *not* require drivers; instead, they may have an on-board BIOS that serves in that function.

SCSI Physical Installation

Actually putting SCSI adapters and peripherals into your system is pretty much the same no matter whether you're using devices that are SCSI or SCSI-2, or if you're using the ASPI, CAM, or LADDR standards (I know I haven't explained these yet; hang on for a minute and I'll get to them, I promise). So let's look at physical installation first.

Installation Overview

Basically, putting a SCSI device into the PC involves these steps:

1. Choose a SCSI host adapter, if you don't already have one.
2. Put a SCSI host adapter into the PC.

3. Assign a SCSI ID to the peripheral. This is usually done with a jumper or a DIP switch.

4. Enable or disable SCSI parity on the peripheral.

5. If the peripheral is an internal peripheral, mount it inside the PC.

6. Cable the peripheral to the SCSI host adapter.

7. Terminate both ends of the SCSI system.

That's the physical end of a SCSI setup; software installation follows, but for the moment let's focus on the physical setup.

Choosing a SCSI Host Adapter

Many computers—more and more—have SCSI support right on their motherboard; others come with SCSI adapters in a slot as standard equipment. If this is true for you, then skip to the next section. But otherwise, just a few thoughts about choosing host adapters.

-   There are host adapters for 8-bit ISA, 16-bit ISA, 16-bit Micro Channel, 32-bit Micro Channel, and 32-bit EISA. The wider your interface, the better your maximum data transfer rate.

-   Many SCSI host adapters use bus mastering to improve their performance. Bus mastering is very similar to Direct Memory Access (DMA) in that it allows the host adapter to transfer data straight into memory without having to involve the CPU. But DMA only allows high speed transfer from peripheral to memory or from memory to peripheral... not from peripheral to peripheral. Bus mastering makes peripheral-to-peripheral transfers possible without CPU intervention, often leading to higher-speed data access. Anyone who's heard of bus mastering has probably heard that the MCA and EISA buses support it. While it's not generally known, bus mastering is possible with ISA bus machines. Adaptec makes an AHA1542C controller that's almost jumper-free and that will do bus mastering on an ISA bus machine, providing some admirable data-transfer rates.

    By the way, there's another benefit to bus mastering: it means that your host adapter doesn't need to use one of your precious DMA channels.

- Some SCSI devices come with optional cache RAM. While it sounds like it'll make your system really scream, what it mainly does is to make the *benchmarks* look good. A system that provides no hurdles between the bits on the platter and the CPU's RAM will provide pretty good data-transfer rates that are *real* data-transfer rates, not bogus ones. For example, with my SCSI drive, I get a data-transfer rate of about 1.5 MB/second—so fast that the CORETEST benchmark accuses me of cheating and using a cache program. Bus mastering should reduce or remove the need for cache RAM on the controller.

- Look for an adapter that supports SCSI-2, and potentially one that supports Fast SCSI, Wide SCSI, and Fast-Wide SCSI (I'll explain those towards the end of the chapter).

- Make sure that your adapter has drivers that support either the ASPI or CAM standard, with ASPI preferred. (See *SCSI Software Installation* later in this chapter for more information.)

Choosing the wrong host adapter isn't the end of the world, but it *can* mean more installation and troubleshooting headaches.

And if you're in a tight spot and need to interface a SCSI device with a computer that doesn't have slots, look into the MiniSCSI Plus from Trantor Systems. It's around $200, and will convert your parallel port into a SCSI-1 adapter. The provided software is ASPI compatible, as well. There're even OS/2 2.0 SCSI drivers included.

The Trantor *does* suffer from one serious problem. It needs actual power applied to the end of the SCSI chain, power called *termination power*. SCSI-1 devices don't provide termination power, but SCSI-2 devices do. As a result, the Trantor will only work with about half of the SCSI devices. Try it before you buy it. (More information about termination later in this chapter.)

Installing the SCSI Host Adapter

Putting a SCSI host adapter into the PC is pretty much the same as installing any board. SCSI adapters are a bit more of a pain than the average board to install because they typically require DMA channels, IRQ levels, I/O addresses, *and* a ROM address.

It's usually possible to connect SCSI devices to a host adapter both *internally and externally*. In Figure 11.3, you see that there is a 50-pin header connector on the SCSI host adapter for internal connections, and an external connector, a Centronics 50-pin female connector used to attach to external devices.

FIGURE 11.3

Adaptec 1542B SCSI
host adapter

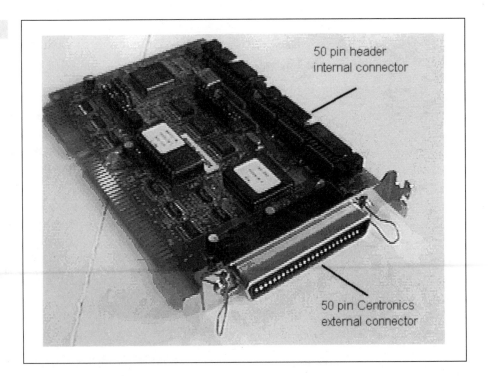

50 pin header
internal connector

50 pin Centronics
external connector

More recent SCSI adapters will use a miniature 50 socket "D" shell connector.

Assign a SCSI ID to the Peripheral

Now consider the SCSI peripheral that you're going to install.

A basic SCSI configuration assigns an identification number called a "SCSI ID" to each device on the SCSI system. The values for this ID range from 0 to 7, and the host adapter typically is set to 7. You typically *can* change the host ID from 7, but *don't*—you'll expose yourself unnecessarily to software incompatibilities.

Choosing SCSI IDs   Before installing a peripheral in your system, you should assign it a SCSI ID. You typically set a SCSI ID with a DIP switch, a jumper, a thumbwheel, or the like. There are just a few rules for setting SCSI IDs:

- Each device on the SCSI chain must have its own ID.

- Do not use ID 0 or ID 1 for anything but hard disks.

- If you plan to boot from a SCSI hard disk, make it ID 0.

- Check your system documentation to see if it expects a device at a particular ID. For example, my advice to put a hard disk on ID 0 or 1 is really DOS, OS/2, and NT-based advice. Other operating systems (SCO UNIX, for example) may not care about which ID you use for a boot drive. At the same time, SCO *must* see any CD-ROMs at ID 5.

- Regardless of what I recommend, or what your documentation says, the only way to solve some SCSI problems is to just try out different ID combinations until something works. I've never fixed anything by fiddling around with the adapter's ID, but I've fixed things by messing with *other* IDs.

- IBM PS/2 machines with SCSI drives use ID 6 for bootable hard disks.

If some of what I've included here sounds vague, then forgive me; you can see here a perfect example of the fact that SCSI is still something of an evolving standard.

Target IDs and LUNs   I've thus far been talking about "SCSI IDs." But installing my Adaptec SCSI hardware—Adaptec is the SCSI market leader, and a manufacturer whose products I can recommend—I see a message upon bootup that says

```
Host Adapter #0 - SCSI ID 6 - LUN 0: NEC CD-ROM DRIVE:
   841 1.0
```

And a later message says

```
Host Adapter #0, Target SCSI ID=6: NEC CD-ROM DRIVE:8411.0
```

First of all, "Target SCSI ID" is the same thing as "SCSI ID." So when you see "Target," just ignore it.

"LUN" is short for "Logical Unit Number." It refers to the fact that a SCSI device can have "sub"-devices. For example, consider the Iomega 44+44 Bernoulli backup device. It's a metal case containing two 44-MB cartridge drives, and is SCSI compatible. If I connect an Iomega 44+44 cartridge device up to one of my SCSI systems, then I'll see a new SCSI ID, which refers to the 44+44 system. The two drives will be distinguished not by different SCSI IDs but by different *logical unit numbers* under the same SCSI ID.

This is actually fairly unusual in the SCSI world, and as a result will probably give your system heartburn—that is, your drivers may not be able to address the second 44-MB drive. But now you'll know what "LUN" refers to. Again, the vast majority of devices only include one LUN.

In theory, each SCSI device can have up to eight LUNs. To make things even worse, each LUN can have a *sub-sub-device* name called an *LSUN*, or *Logical Sub-Unit Number*, which can range from 0 to 255.

Notice also the "NEC CD-ROM..." information. That's an actual example of the information that the CD-ROM gives to the host adapter about what it—the peripheral—is.

Enable/Disable SCSI Parity

The SCSI bus can detect and use parity signals to detect errors in transmission over the SCSI cabling. Errors can and do occur, particularly as the cable gets longer from end to end.

To use SCSI parity, *all* devices must support it. If only one device does not support SCSI parity, then you must disable it for all devices on the chain.

Some operating systems, like Windows NT, will not work *at all* with a SCSI CD-ROM unless it supports SCSI parity. That implies that you should plan to support SCSI parity from the very beginning; buy only devices that support SCSI parity (and SCSI-II, by the way.)

SCSI Daisy Chaining

Many of you will only end up putting one or two SCSI devices on a PC, but SCSI can easily support seven peripherals off a single SCSI host adapter, or it can support hundreds of devices with a lot of rocket science. (The "hundreds of devices" works if you put eight SCSI adapters in a system, which are each connected in turn to eight SCSI adapters—that's possible; remember LUNs? The second level SCSI adapters can be externally connected to other SCSI adapters, leaving the possibility of *lots* of devices. In the real world, it's impossible to find PC software that supports such a thing, so forget it.)

Multiple devices are attached to a single SCSI host adapter via daisy chaining. There are several kinds of cables in the SCSI world.

SCSI-1 and SCSI-2 Cables   External SCSI devices tend to have two 50-pin female Centronics connectors, as you see in the view of the back of a SCSI device shown in Figure 11.4.

A 50-pin male connector, such as you'd see on a SCSI cable, looks like Figure 11.5.

FIGURE 11.4

The rear of a SCSI device, showing two SCSI connectors (for daisy-chaining)

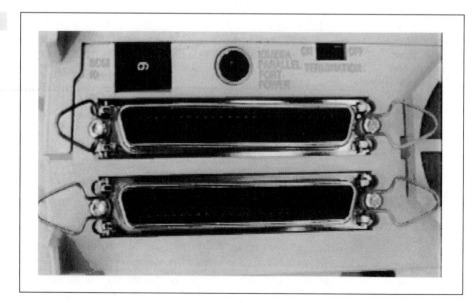

50-conductor
Centronics connector

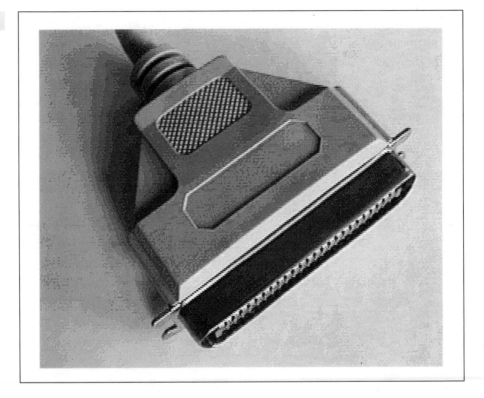

Some external SCSI cables have a Centronics connector of the type you see in Figure 11.6 on both ends of the cable. Such a cable is called a "SCSI-1" or "SCSI" cable. Use them to either connect between SCSI-1 host adapters and SCSI devices or when daisy-chaining from SCSI device to SCSI device.

Other SCSI cables have a male DB-25 connector on one side, and a Centronics 50-conductor connector on the other side (see Figure 11.7). Those are called "Macintosh SCSI" or "SCSI-1" cables.

Newer SCSI adapters often do not employ a Centronics connector for external devices, but rather use a miniature 50-socket D shell connector. You can see the male version of that connector—the version that you'd see on a cable—in Figure 11.8.

FIGURE 11.6

SCSI peripheral cable

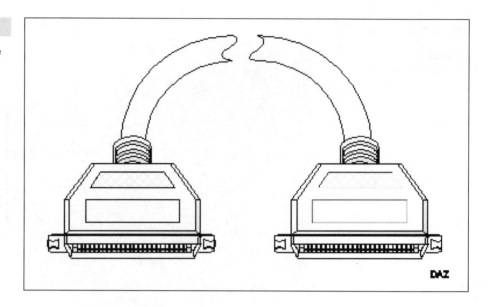

FIGURE 11.7

SCSI-1 cable

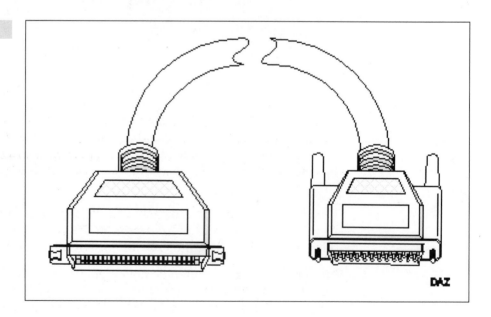

FIGURE 11.8

Miniature 50-socket D
shell connector

The cable incorporates two buttons on either side that you must squeeze together in order to connect or disconnect the cable to or from the adapter. You will occasionally see this connector instead of the Centronics on peripherals, and more commonly on the backs of SCSI adapters—Adaptec since 1993 has put them on the backs of their 1742 adapters in lieu of the more common Centronics 50. As a result, a common cable has a mini DB50 on one side and a Centronics 50 conductor connection on the other side. Such a cable—Centronics 50-conductor connection on one side, miniature D 50 pin connector on the other—is called a *SCSI-2 cable* (see Figure 11.9).

The names *SCSI-1 cable* and *SCSI-2 cable* are misleading. Even if you've got a SCSI-2 adapter, you'll probably only use a *SCSI-2 cable* to connect from the adapter to the first external SCSI device.

FIGURE 11.9

SCSI-2 cable

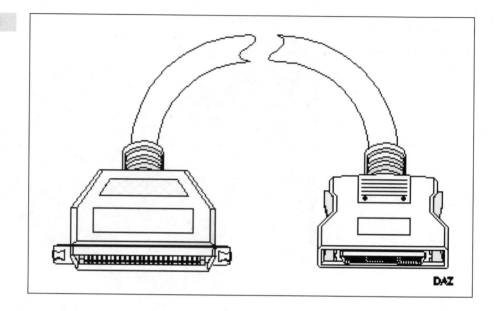

Through Thick and Thin: Not All Cables Are Equal While we're discussing cables, let me relate a short war story that taught me an important lesson about cables.

I installed a CD-ROM onto a server so that I could install Windows NT Advanced Server on my LAN. The CD-ROM was an external drive that used the 50-conductor Centronics connector, so I walked over to my cable pile and pulled out a standard SCSI cable with 50-conductor Centronics connectors on both ends. I plugged the CD-ROM into the SCSI adapter's interface port on the back of my PC, and the problems started. My existing tape drive and hard disk drive—both internal—started acting up.

After an hour or two of playing around with the system, I found that if I downgraded the SCSI system from SCSI-II to SCSI-I (I did this by reconfiguring my SCSI host adapter, an Adaptec AHA1542C), the problems went away. I had vague forebodings about losing SCSI-II compatibility—SCSI parity doesn't work under SCSI-I, recall—but everything seemed to work, so I figured that I'd live with it.

Then came time to install NT Advanced Server. And the README file said, "The SCSI and CD-ROM support built into Windows NT 3.1 requires that CD-ROMs provide SCSI parity to function properly." Great, I thought, and started fussing with the SCSI devices to get the CD-ROM to support SCSI parity. I mean, there was a jumper specifically included on the CD-ROM to control whether or not SCSI parity would be used, so why wouldn't it support SCSI parity?

Just on the off-chance that I had a bad cable, I went back over to the cable pile to see what else I had. I found another dual 50 Centronics cable identical to the cable that I was using, and another dual 50 Centronics cable that was about twice as thick as the first two. I tried swapping the original thin cable for the other thin cable—no difference. But when I used the thicker cable, everything started working! I got full SCSI-II support, as well as SCSI parity functionality.

A few calls around to cable places brought the information that, yes, there were two kinds of dual 50 Centronics cables. The thin ones work fine for SCSI-I but not for SCSI-II. The thick ones are good for both. Look for cables from Amphenol, Quintec, and Icontec, and your cables will work fine under SCSI-II; Amphenol is at (607) 786-4370.

Internal SCSI Cabling External devices, as you've read, tend to have two SCSI connections on them so that they can support the SCSI daisy chain. Internal devices, in contrast, only use a single 50-pin header connector. Internal SCSI cables are just ribbon cables with 50-pin IDC connectors, as you see in Figure 11.10.

As the connectors are sitting in the middle of the cable, one connector does the job for daisy-chaining.

"Macintosh" SCSI Cabling As the Mac includes SCSI connections right on the motherboard, and SCSI support right in the Mac kernel, there are many SCSI devices that originated in the Mac world. As a result, you may see a final kind of SCSI connector—a 25-pin female connector, just like the parallel port that you find on the PC. There is a so-called "Mac SCSI cable" that consists of a 25-pin male connector on one side and a 50 conductor Centronics male on the other side.

FIGURE 11.10

50-conductor SCSI
ribbon cable

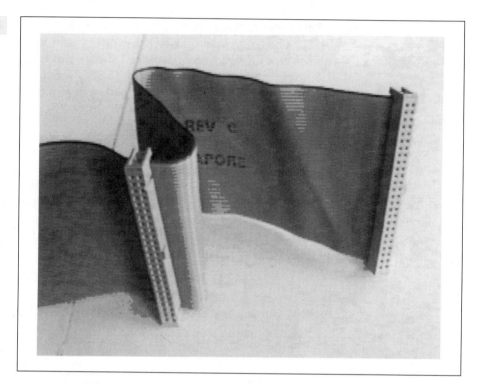

WARNING

Some people call the "Mac SCSI cable" a "SCSI-1"
cable; as a result, it's a good idea to double-check
when ordering cables.

Terminating the SCSI Chain

Before popping the top back on your PC, there's one more thing that
needs doing: You must terminate the SCSI chain.

Now, for some reason, whenever we discuss this in class, people seem to
take on an Austrian accent, but termination just means providing a voltage and resistance on either end of a cable, so that the entire bus has a particular set of electrical characteristics. Without this resistance, the SCSI

cables cannot transport data around without significant error rates. (It *will* work sometimes, despite what some people claim; but it won't work reliably.)

NOTE

SCSI-1 termination was a simple resistor. SCSI-2 termination requires a small amount of power applied *by* the SCSI device. (600 milliamps at 4–5.25 volts, to be precise.) Some devices do provide termination resistance, but not termination power, making them potential troublemakers in a SCSI-2 setting.

Internal and External Terminators You've seen that some SCSI devices are installed internally in the PC, and connect to the host adapter with a ribbon cable, and that other devices are installed externally, and connect to the host adapter with a SCSI-1 or SCSI-2 cable. There are also internal and external terminators, as well as SCSI devices that have terminators built right in. In sum, the kind of terminators that you'll see are:

- an external SCSI terminator
- an internal Single Inline Pin Package (SIPP) terminator on the host adapter and/or a hard disk
- a device with built-in termination that's enabled or disabled with a DIP switch or a jumper
- a device with built-in termination that *cannot* be disabled

External terminators look like a Centronics connector sitting all alone, as you see in Figure 11.11. They clip onto one of the Centronics connectors on the back of the last external device on your SCSI daisy chain.

SIPP-type terminators often show up on the host adapter itself, as it needs termination and SIPPs don't take up too much space. You can see a SIPP in Figure 11.12.

There are typically three of these SIPPs on a host adapter. You'll also find SIPPs on many internal SCSI hard disks. You just remove them (*gently*, as you may need to reinstall them one day) by working them out

FIGURE 11.11

Centronics-type
SCSI-1 terminator

FIGURE 11.12

SIPP-type SCSI
terminator

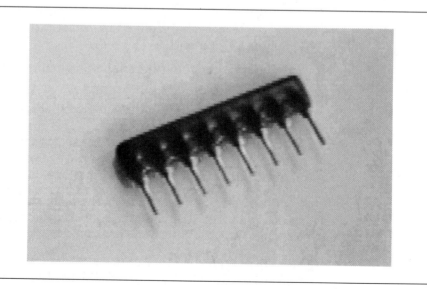

with needlenose pliers. Once you've done that, put them in an envelope, seal it and label it "SCSI Terminators," and put it somewhere.

If you look back to the picture of the back of the external SCSI device, you may notice a switch labeled *termination*. It can be flipped on or off, so if this SCSI device is the last on the chain, then all I need do is to flip it ON; else, I flip it OFF.

Active and Passive Compatibility You've already read that SCSI-I uses "passive" termination, and SCSI-II uses something different, called "active" termination. What's the difference? Are they compatible?

First, the differences. *Passive* termination was used in SCSI-I. It employs two resistors on either end of the SCSI bus. A 220-ohm resistor is tied to the termination voltage—one of the SCSI lines—and a 330-ohm resistor is tied to ground. *Active* termination is a more reliable approach that just uses a single 110-ohm resistor to the termination line.

Second, what about compatibility? While you may experience different results, most SCSI-II setups that I've ever worked with *require* active termination. If you use one of the old plug-type terminators, like the one in the "terminator" picture in Figure 11.8, then SCSI-II will often not work. Active termination requires electrical power, so there's no simple plug that will provide active termination on a SCSI-II chain. You've pretty much got to have a device that supports active termination on either end of a SCSI-II chain, or you're quite likely to experience problems.

Sample SCSI Setup: One Internal Drive When I say "Put terminators on the end of the chain," it's worthwhile taking a minute and making sure that you know what I mean. Let's look at a few sample SCSI applications; take a look at Figure 11.13.

In this setup, you've just got a SCSI hard disk. There must be terminators on each side, but there are only two sides, so it's simple to figure out where the terminators go. Both terminators are probably SIPP-type terminators. The host is ID 7, the hard disk is ID 0; this means that you're intending to boot from the hard disk.

Sample SCSI Setup: Two Internal Devices Now let's make it a bit more complex. Take a look at Figure 11.14.

FIGURE 11.13

One-device (internal)
SCSI application

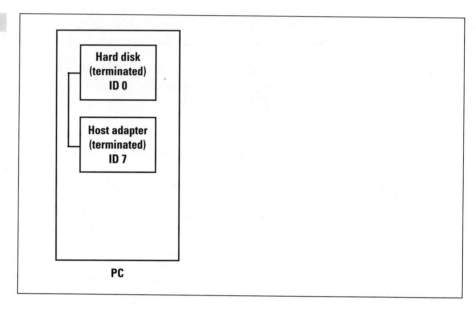

FIGURE 11.14

Two-device (internal)
SCSI application

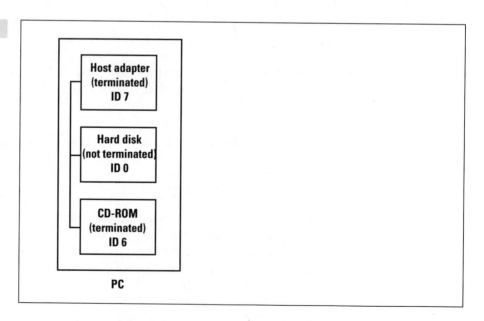

Now we've added an internal CD-ROM. It's got to have a different ID, so ID 6 is good; remember, I want to avoid ID 1 for anything other than a hard disk. The hard disk terminators must be removed, as the hard disk is in the middle of the chain, and the CD-ROM is terminated.

Sample SCSI Setup: One External Device Now let's do the same things, but now with external devices (see Figure 11.15).

FIGURE 11.15

One-device (external) SCSI application

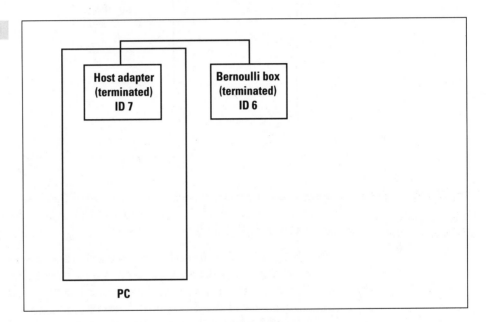

Now there's just one external device, a cartridge storage device that we won't try to boot from. I've set the Bernoulli Box to ID 6, and terminated it, as it is the extreme end of the chain.

Sample SCSI Setup: Two External Devices Continuing, I'll now add a second external device (see Figure 11.16).

This time, I'll make the CD-ROM ID 5, as ID 6 is taken. The Bernoulli shouldn't be terminated, as it is now in the middle of the chain, and the CD-ROM is terminated.

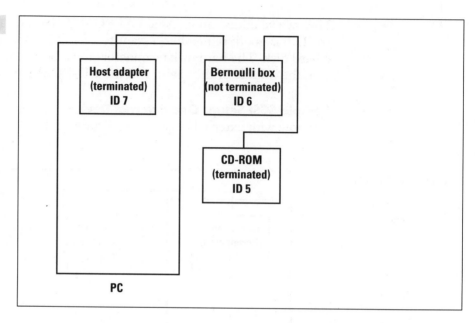

FIGURE 11.16

Two-device (external) SCSI application

Sample SCSI Setup: Internal and External Devices   For the grand finale, let's put two external devices and two internal devices on this system. Take a look at Figure 11.17.

The thing to notice about *this* scenario is that the termination has been removed from the host adapter, as it is now (for the first time) in the middle of the chain. The external devices are attached to the external connector on the back of the SCSI host adapter (the Centronics or miniature D connector), and the internal devices are hooked to the internal 50 pin header connector. Every device has a unique SCSI ID, and there's termination on the ends of the chain.

N O T E   The sum total of your SCSI cables should not exceed 18 feet. In general, the shorter your cables, the better.

FIGURE 11.17

SCSI application with internal and external devices

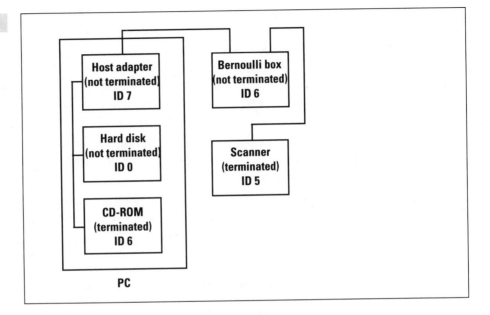

Installation Troubleshooting Notes

Now that I've drilled into your head the idea that you should only have terminators on either side of the chain, let me offer an exception.

Sometimes a SCSI setup doesn't work. You check and recheck the SCSI IDs, but there are no duplicated IDs. You've terminated properly, but things still don't work. What do you do?

It sounds odd, but you can sometimes get things to work by adding back terminators. For example, the Bernoulli switches can be flipped back in place even if the Bernoulli isn't at the end of the cable. The SIPPs can be replaced on the host adapter even if it's in the middle of a chain. Like so much of PC troubleshooting, sometimes fiddling around leads to the answers.

Other things to try:

- Most SCSI host adapters display a sign-on message listing the recognized devices on the SCSI bus. Use that information as your first diagnostic. If the device is seen on the bus, but you can't get it to do tricks, then the problem is probably a driver problem rather than a hardware installation problem.

- If you encounter "phantom disks," disks that you can see but cannot read or write, then you've probably put two devices on the same SCSI ID.

- Sometimes the ID setting device is defective. I've seen a tape drive that could be set for ID 4 but would show up as ID 6.

- Sometimes cables are defective, or *combinations* of cables don't get along. Try this:

  1. Install just the host adapter and its driver. Boot the system and make sure that the host adapter is working—no DMA/IRQ/IO address conflicts.
  2. Turn the PC off, add the first SCSI device and *power it up before you reboot the PC.* SCSI devices often must be active before the host adapter can recognize them. (Be sure also that everything is terminated correctly.)
  3. Once you've got that device in place, power down the PC and add the next SCSI device. Test it as you just tested the first SCSI device.

I find it most convenient to install the internal devices first, *then* the external devices. I usually remove the SIPP terminators from the host adapter, and just place an external SCSI terminator on the connector on the back of my host adapter if it's a Centronics type connector; otherwise, I get a SCSI cable, attach it to the back of the host adapter, and then terminate that.

SCSI Software Installation

Much of the SCSI installation process is like a normal hard disk's installation process: low level format, partition, and high level format. Doing those things isn't much different from doing them on non-SCSI hard disks, save that you may have to use a special program for the formatting and/or partitioning; check your SCSI software documentation for an example.

The tough part about SCSI software installation, however, is the drivers. There seem to be a *million* of them, and none of them appear to be on speaking terms with one another—and what do they do, anyway?

Until a few years ago, SCSI drivers were proprietary. You were crazy to buy a SCSI hard disk and host adapter unless you got them from the same vendor, a vendor that supplied drivers for the two of them. But since 1991, several "universal driver" standards have appeared. Figure 11.18 shows how they work.

Rather than trying to create a hard disk driver, a CD-ROM driver, a scanner driver, and a tape driver that are all compatible with the operating system, a universal driver system defines an intermediate standard and supports that with a driver specific to the host adapter. The SCSI device drivers then need only be written to work with the intermediate standard defined by the host adapter's driver.

The three main competing universal standards are:

- ASPI (Advanced SCSI Programming Interface)
- CAM (Common Access Method)
- LADDR (Layered Device Driver Architecture)

FIGURE 11.18

How SCSI driver software fits together

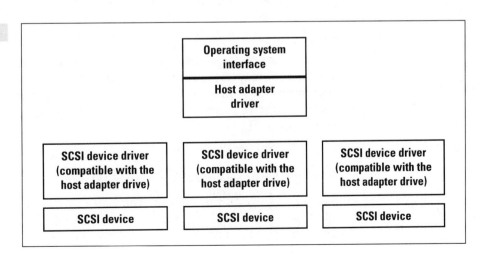

Additionally, no discussion of drivers could fail to include:

- The INT 13 BIOS interface found on many SCSI host adapters

The idea here is that you buy a host adapter from *anyone* and get a driver for that adapter that supports one of these standards—for example's sake, let's use ASPI, as it's the most popular. Then you buy a SCSI tape drive that's advertised as being "ASPI compatible." That means they include with it a driver that controls the tape drive via ASPI communication with the host adapter. Since the driver on your host adapter board speaks ASPI and your tape drive's driver speaks ASPI, everything will work out fine. And if you decide to replace your current SCSI host adapter board with one that's faster or better in some way, then all you need is an ASPI driver for that board—you needn't even change the device driver for the tape drive. (I should stress that this is the *idea*; of course, ASPI compatibility is not a black-and-white thing in the real world.)

Installing SCSI Software

Nowadays, there are two packages that make installing SCSI a snap. CorelSCSI (from Corel Systems) and EZ-SCSI 2.0 (from Adaptec) are both reasonably priced (under $100) and nearly complete sets of SCSI drivers for ASPI. You just load 'n' go to get these systems up and running. Here's a section from a CONFIG.SYS built with EZ-SCSI:

```
DEVICE=C:\ADAPTEC\ASPI4DOS.SYS /D
DEVICE=C:\ADAPTEC\ASPIDISK.SYS /D
DEVICE=C:\ADAPTEC\ASPICD.SYS /D:MSCD001
```

Taken in order, these three device drivers 1) load the base ASPI support for the host adapter; 2) provide an ASPI-to-hard-disk interface for a SCSI hard disk; and 3) provide an ASPI-to-CD-ROM interface for a SCSI CD-ROM. If the first driver didn't load, then the second and third drivers could not load.

With CorelSCSI, the CONFIG.SYS lines look like:

```
DEVICE=C:\ADAPTEC\ASPI4DOS.SYS /D
DEVICE=C:\COREL\UNI_ASP.SYS /C:4 /ID:2 /VOL:1 /DOS4
    /SS:512 /@4:-51
DEVICE=C:\COREL\CUNI_ASP.SYS /ID:6 /N:1 /D:MSCD001
```

(Note that the second and third lines of this example represent one line of the CONFIG.SYS)

Notice that the first line is the same; that's because Adaptec wrote the ASPI driver for its board, the Adaptec AHA1542, which I used for these tests. Notice also the greater number of parameters on the invocation lines. UNI_ASP.SYS is the driver for the hard disk, and CUNI_ASP.SYS is the driver for the CD-ROM.

The **/ID:** parameter specifies which SCSI ID the device uses. The Adaptec drivers figure it out automatically. Personally, I like the Corel approach better, as it allows me to *force* the drivers to do something when I'm troubleshooting. For those who just want to plug it in and make it go, however, the Adaptec approach may be more appealing.

/C: allocates cache buffers. **/SS:** sets the sector size in bytes. **/VOL:** is the number of logical drives that will appear on the hard disk. @4:-51 is, according to Corel, "a reference marker for the software's internal operations, and should never be altered or deleted." **/DOS4** allows logical drives larger than 32 MB. **/D:**, which you will have noticed also in the Adaptec setup, assigns a name to the CD-ROM; that name is required to help MSCDEX, which loads later, to find that CD-ROM.

EZ-SCSI comes with drivers for CD-ROMs, removable cartridge hard disks (like Bernoulli Boxes), and fixed hard disks. EZ-SCSI does not include drivers for scanners, WORM (optical Write Once, Read Many times) drives, WARM (optical Write And Read Many times) drives, and tape drives. If you get a device that supports ASPI *later*, then you can easily add it to a configuration that started out from EZ-SCSI.

CorelSCSI includes drivers for hard disks, CD-ROMs, removable cartridge hard disks, WORM drives, WARM drives, and tape drives. There are no scanner drivers yet, but there soon will be.

Despite the wider variety of drivers that come with Corel's product, I'd recommend Adaptec's EZ-SCSI, as I found installing it to be trouble-free. In contrast, putting a Bernoulli Box on my system involved a lot of fuss and 45 minutes on the phone with Corel. The Corel software tends to be rather terse in its error messages. When it works, it works great. When it doesn't, well, you can always call Corel, right? That recommendation may change with new versions.

About the SCSI Standards

The fact that there are three "universal" standards points out the truth that SCSI is still a standard in flux. Here's an overview of the three standards.

ASPI (Advanced SCSI Programming Interface) ASPI was invented by Adaptec, and the first time I read anything about ASPI, the "A" stood for Adaptec. But ASPI has been adopted by other hardware manufacturers, and, as you've read, it's the home of two very fine suites of SCSI drivers. I'd recommend that you stay within the ASPI standard, as it's easiest to find drivers that are ASPI compatible.

Let me underscore that there is no such thing as an "ASPI-compatible SCSI hard disk;" the compatibility question relates to the drivers, not the hardware. If someone wanted—and she were technical enough—then she could write an ASPI, a CAM, and a LADDR driver for a given SCSI device.

ASPI support for DOS is provided by Adaptec for their boards and Ultra-Stor for their boards. (UltraStor calls their drivers "USPI" drivers, but they are ASPI.) Another personal recommendation: don't buy UltraStor stuff. They have a tendency to not write drivers for any board of theirs that's two years old or older. For example, I've got an UltraStor 22CA controller, a quite expensive controller that I picked up in 1991. They don't have drivers for OS/2 2.1, LAN Manager 2.2, or Windows NT in any version. Adaptec, in contrast, has proven quite prompt and responsible in the past few years; there's even Adaptec drivers right in the box for OS/2 2.1 and Windows NT.

If your concern is for your Novell server, then don't worry too much; it seems that writing Novell drivers comes second only to writing DOS drivers in importance.

CAM (Common Access Method) Another strong contender in the SCSI world is a company called Future Domain. Future Domain has a decent-sized share of the SCSI host adapter market because they make an inexpensive eight-bit host adapter that's spread far and wide.

It hasn't spread far and wide because it's a top quality adapter. Instead, the Future Domain adapter is so popular because it's cheap. You see, if a company wants to sell a "complete CD-ROM package" for a SCSI-based

CD-ROM, then they must include a SCSI host adapter. Now, SCSI host adapters aren't cheap, in general. Future Domain's model 840 controller nicely fills the market niche for eight-bit, non–bus-mastering SCSI controllers. I'm not a big fan of the board mainly because of the painfully slow speed that results from using an eight-bit board, but on the other hand it's inexpensive, and so could be a nice "experimenter" board to have around.

Unfortunately, however, you can't get ASPI drivers (that I know of) for this board. Instead, there is an alternative standard proposed largely by NCR and Future Domain called the Common Access Method, or CAM. It's a very good standard, perhaps better in some ways than ASPI. But it's not as well served.

If you *do* wish to go with CAM, then you'll find a universal driver set from Future Domain called PowerSCSI!; it should soon even contain a CAM-to-ASPI converter, which may eliminate altogether the ASPI versus CAM question. OS/2 2.1 and SCO Unix both include CAM support in the shipped installation disks. Even better, PowerSCSI! should be free with a Future Domain controller. In contrast, EZ-SCSI costs $75 from Adaptec.

Layered Device Driver Architecture (LADDR) LADDR is a proposed Microsoft standard that Microsoft developed for OS/2 1.x. It never really caught on, although there's LADDR support shipped with the OS/2 1.x used as the basis of Microsoft's LAN Manager. Even that will probably disappear as Microsoft gets the NT Advanced Server into more and more markets.

SCSI without Drivers: On-Board BIOS Support

After all this talk of mixing and matching drivers, you may be getting a bit queasy. But if all you're going to install is a hard disk or two, then you may never have to trouble with drivers.

Why SCSI Adapters Have BIOSes Using SCSI hard disks, if you think about it, can lead to a sort of chicken-and-egg problem. The SCSI device isn't accessible until the SCSI device drivers are loaded, and device drivers are generally loaded from the hard disk. But how can you load SCSI drivers from a SCSI hard disk? I suppose one answer would be to boot from a floppy and then don't reboot, but it's a somewhat cumbersome answer.

The answer to the question of, "How does my PC boot from a SCSI hard disk?" is that most SCSI adapters have an on-board BIOS that contains enough software to run the hard disk, even if there are no SCSI drivers loaded.

Size Limits on BIOSes   That's a real life-saver, allowing us to use SCSI hard disks without having to worry about drivers. But this BIOS can only support hard disks with the following characteristics:

- They must each be under 504 MB in size, and
- they must be configured as SCSI IDs 0 and 1.

The 504-MB limit is a little flexible, but here's where it comes from. The SCSI BIOS can't stray too far from the basic PC BIOS's handling of hard disks. In general, the BIOS can't handle a hard disk with more than 63 sectors, 1023 cylinders, and 16 heads. Given a normal 512-byte sector, that means that the largest hard disk addressable under normal DOS conditions is $63 \times 1023 \times 16 \times \frac{1}{2}$ K in size, or 515,592K, which is 504 MB. Now, *some* SCSI controllers use the fact that the sector size is not strictly set in stone to up the sector size to 1024 bytes, raising the maximum size to 1 GB; I recommend against it, as disks with sector sizes other than 512 bytes may confuse your operating system or applications.

When to Disable a BIOS   Many SCSI installations that I have done are not intended to support a hard disk. For example, installing a CD-ROM in an already-running system means that I've already got a functional IDE drive in the system, so there's no point in replacing it with a SCSI drive.

In that case, I don't need the BIOS, so I disable it. You do that either with a piece of setup software or with some kind of physical setting, like a jumper or DIP switch. That's a real benefit, as it creates more space in my Upper Memory Area for larger Upper Memory Blocks. So disable your BIOS if you are not booting from a SCSI hard disk.

Bus Mastering Alerts

Many SCSI host adapters use a kind of "super DMA" called "bus mastering". Again, it's a terrific feature, but be aware that it confuses Windows and SmartDrive unless you load SmartDrive with the "double buffer" option, or bypass loading SmartDrive into upper memory.

Now and the Future: SCSI-1, SCSI-2, and the Rest

I have referred to the different SCSI generations throughout this chapter. At this point, the different generations make little difference, as much modern software can't make the full use of the modern SCSI generations. But some can, and that makes it worthwhile knowing and purchasing more advanced SCSI. Here's a rundown on the different SCSI generations.

SCSI-1: The Beginning of a Good Idea

In 1981, Shugart Associates—the company that eventually became Seagate—developed a parallel block-oriented transfer protocol called the Shugart Associates System Interface, or SASI.

SASI became the Small Computer Systems Interface, or SCSI in 1984, when the ANSI's X3T9 committee formalized the specification.

SCSI is an eight-bit parallel interface between a SCSI host adapter and a SCSI device. ("Eight-bit" here has nothing to do—or very little to do—with your bus interface.) The standard calls for a maximum data transfer rate of 5 MBps. It incorporated a command set that could be only partially implemented by a vendor, but the vendor could still claim that their device was "SCSI compatible."

SCSI-1 left so much undefined that it was nearly inevitable that the actual SCSI-1 implementations on the market would be incompatible.

SCSI-2 Improves on a Good Thing

SCSI-1 was a bit vague in some of its direction in things like exactly how the command language should be implemented, leading to the beginning in 1986 of work on the SCSI-2 standard. The final proposal isn't done, but most devices nowadays support SCSI-2 verbs. Strictly speaking, however, SCSI-2 devices nowadays are "draft SCSI-2 devices".

SCSI-2 incorporates *scripting*, where a series of transfers can be "batched" across the bus. For example, a hard disk could be backed up to an optical drive—with no processor intervention.

SCSI-2, as you've already read, also forces the termination circuits to get a bit more complex. Instead of simple resistors, SCSI-2 termination must include voltage regulation circuits that keep the bus voltage between 4 and 5 $\frac{1}{4}$ volts. That means a less noisy bus, but it also spells trouble for an SCSI-2 configuration with an old SCSI-1 device at either extreme. Additionally, parity is required by the SCSI-2 standard, but the prevalence of SCSI-1 devices (many of which don't support parity) will probably render this "requirement" moot for a while.

Fast and Wide SCSI

As originally defined, SCSI is an eight-bit parallel interface between a SCSI device and a SCSI controller. Several variations have been defined in SCSI-2.

Fast SCSI doubles the data transfer rate over the existing data path. If SCSI-1 eight-bit transfers are 5 MBps, then, Fast SCSI eight-bit transfers are 10 MBps. Fast SCSI can only occur with particular cables and circuitry on the SCSI interface called differential cables.

Wide SCSI uses an extra cable to increase the data path to 16 or 32 bits. Using non-differential cables and interface, Wide SCSI can increase data transfer rate to 20 MBps.

Fast-Wide SCSI uses a greater data transfer rate over a wider (differential) cable to support a data transfer rate of up to 40 MBps.

SCSI-3

A standard now under construction, SCSI-3 will expand SCSI's capabilities in these ways:

- It will support up to 32 devices, rather than the current 8 (7 not including the host adapter).

- The command set has been expanded for DATs and file servers.

- The electrical standard will support longer cable lengths and fiber optic cabling.

- "Serial" SCSI, a *six-wire* version of SCSI that's designed to be "plug 'n' play". Can't wait...

Even though SCSI is an emerging standard, I wouldn't wait before buying. SCSI support is widespread enough nowadays that the time to start implementing SCSI on your high-end workstations and servers is *now*.

CD-ROMs on Your SCSI System

One of the major reasons to buy a SCSI host adapter is to install a CD-ROM; most CD-ROMs interface via SCSI. Here's a bit of background on CD-ROMs.

Optical Disks and Disk Drives

Optical disk drives are available in different sizes. The sizes you will probably use are 3.5" and 5.25". There are also 8" and 12" optical disk drives for specialized image storage markets. The larger disks have a much greater storage capacity than the standard-sized ones, so imaging applications that need to store gigabytes of data on a single disk use the larger optical disks.

Optical disks come in a variety of different types: CD-ROM, WORM, Rewritable—Phase Change or Magneto Optical (MO)—and mixed media (part is CD-ROM, part is rewritable). Each type has specific uses peculiar to itself. Of these different types of optical disks, only the CD-ROM does not come in a cartridge (a protective case that looks just like a 3.5" diskette, having a hard plastic shell and a shutter that covers a slot in the shell. The shutter is pulled back when the cartridge is inserted into the optical disk drive so the drive can read the disk). Since they don't come with cartridges, computer CD-ROMs are often kept in caddies to protect them from damage.

A 5.25" optical disk has a 654-MB capacity, using a standard International Standards Organization (ISO) format. A 3.5" optical disk has 128-MB

ISO format, though a 256-MB capacity is in the works. A CD-ROM normally contains 680 MB (74 minutes of music), although 580-MB (63 minutes of music) disks are available.

How Optical Disks Work

The optical disk drive reads the CD-ROM disks just like a home-CD player reads CDs. With a laser, the drive (or player) reads pits that have been stamped into the disk's surface with a master mold. Optical disk drives that write data work a little differently, having a laser inside that heats the surface of the disk. This heating either creates a pit (in the case of WORM disks), changes the plastic so it doesn't reflect anymore (in the case of Rewritable, Phase Change disks), or makes it non-magnetic (in the case of Rewritable, Magneto Optical disks). It's possible to create your own CD-ROMS, but the equipment to do that is expensive—currently over $7,000.

Though the coating on WORM disks can only be written onto once (hence the name), a rewritable drive uses media with a surface coating that can be reheated to restore or change the "pit." A regular optical drive changes the reflecting quality of the coating. A MO (magneto optical) drive changes the magnetic property of the coating.

Some of the rewritable drives are dual media drives, able to play either a disk with a rewritable coating or a disk with a WORM coating. With these drives, you can permanently archive payroll records (for example) on WORM disk, yet still be able to store frequently changed files on a rewritable disk, without needing two drives for the two capabilities. (Frequently changed files quickly fill up a WORM disk, since a new file must be written every time the file is saved.)

Although the software for WORM drives (or a WORM cartridge in a dual media drive) prevents data from being written over the same area twice, it is possible to use special software to directly control the disk drive and write over an existing area, sabotaging the existing data. This destroys any information present.

CD-ROMs on the Market Today

When buying or installing a CD-ROM, here are the things to consider:

- Proprietary or SCSI interface? You can find CD-ROMs (the cheaper ones) that come with their own non-SCSI interface. I strongly recommend against buying them because

  - you will not be able to get drivers for anything but DOS and Windows 3.1. If the company isn't around when Windows 4 arrives, you'll be out of luck. Staying within ASPI or CAM ensures that you'll have drivers in the future.
  - the drives tend to be lower performance drives.

- Data transfer rate can vary wildly from one drive to another.

- Seek (access) times also vary a lot from one system to another.

- Your drive should support a *multisession* CD, a CD with more than one database. Look for CDs that are "Photo CD ready," even though you'll probably never do Photo CD.

- SCSI-2 compatibility is a good idea nowadays.

They're a bit expensive, but I like the NEC CDR74 (external) and CDR84 (internal) CD-ROMs quite a bit. They're fast and trouble-free. Toshiba also makes good CD-ROMs.

Working with MSCDEX

In the process of installing your CD-ROM, you'll have to put a driver in your CONFIG.SYS that makes the system able to support the actual machinery of the CD-ROM, and then you'll install in AUTOEXEC.BAT a program that tells DOS how to handle a thing that has the speed of a floppy, the capacity of a hard disk, and that you can't write to. I can't give you any general rules about what the device drivers will look like, as they vary from drive to drive, but here's an example dissected a bit.

A Sample Drive Installation Here's the line for the Adaptec ASPI CD-ROM driver; you've seen this line already.

```
DEVICE=C:\ADAPTEC\ASPICD.SYS /D:MSCD001
```

The thing that I want you to notice is the **/D:MSCD001**. It basically *names* the drive; it's called the *driver signature*. You could alternatively call it ASPD001 or something like that. That driver signature on the device driver invocation must match the driver signature on the MSCDEX invocation, which looks like this:

```
C:\DOS\MSCdex /D:MSCD001 /S
```

Even the Corel driver, which looked like this:

```
DEVICE=C:\UTILS\CORELDRV\CUNI_ASP.SYS /ID:6 /N:1
     /D:MSCD001
```

still incorporated a driver signature. (Again, note that this has to be *one* line in the CONFIG.SYS.) If you had two CD-ROMs, then you'd have two device drivers in CONFIG.SYS, both with different driver signatures—for example, MSCD000 and MSCD001. Then the MSCDEX invocation would look like this:

```
C:\DOS\MSCdex /D:MSCD001 /D:MSCD000 /S
```

Here, I've instructed DOS to give the *first* drive letter available to MSCD001, and the *second* available letter to MSCD000.

Other interesting parameters on MSCDEX are:

- **/S** is required to allow MSCDEX to share this drive over a peer-to-peer network; some CD-ROM software will not, however, run over a network.

- **/E** allows MSCDEX use of expanded memory for its buffers.

- **/V** is "verbose," giving details of memory usage at boot time. Older MSCDEXes are verbose by default, requiring a **/Q** ("quiet") to suppress their bootup information.

- **/L:*letter*** forces DOS to give the CD-ROM a particular drive letter.

- **/M:*number*** specifies the number of sector buffers.

MS-DOS 6.2, by the way, improved DOS support of CD-ROMs with SmartDrive 5.0. Previous SmartDrives would not cache CD-ROMs.

SCSI Removable Drives

The last thing we'll consider briefly in the SCSI world are removable cartridge storage devices. There are two popular brands of removable hard disks, Syquest by Syquest Technology and Bernoulli by Iomega. The Syquest disk drive has been available to original equipment manufacturers (OEMs) and through distributors from the beginning in 1987. Consequently, many companies that supply or manufacture mass storage peripherals, such as hard disks and tape drives, include Syquest drives in their product line. Bernoulli drives, on the other hand, are only available from Iomega. In fact, when Iomega recently introduced a portable Bernoulli drive, they designed it so that only their parallel port SCSI adapter would work with the drive.

Syquest

Syquest has been the standard removable drive for Macintosh users since 1987. A Syquest drive uses a single hard disk platter in a removable plastic shell. Syquest started out with 44-meg cartridges, but now has 88-meg cartridges, requiring an 88-meg Syquest drive. The 88-meg drive will read, but not write to, the 44-meg cartridges. (The 88-meg cartridge has twice as many tracks on the disk.) To get around this problem, some suppliers of mass storage peripherals offer an external drive containing a 44-meg and an 88-meg Syquest drive. If you plan to send large desktop-publishing data files to a service bureau to have them make negatives and proofs, you will probably have to have a Syquest drive. You should check with the service bureau to see if they prefer 44-meg or 88-meg cartridges.

Syquest has been working to shrink their Syquest cartridges as computers and hard disk drives get smaller. For several years, they have shown prototypes of removable cartridge drives with 3.5" or even 2.5" cartridges. Both sizes of cartridges have a 40-meg capacity.

Bernoulli

Iomega makes the Bernoulli drive, which uses a flexible disk in a removable plastic shell. When the disk is spinning, it becomes rigid and creates a pillow of air on which the data read/write head floats. This is known as the Bernoulli effect, after its discoverer.

The Bernoulli drive has also increased its capacity over time. When first developed, Bernoulli drives used large 8" sized cartridges that stored only 20 meg. Later, the cartridge capacity was increased to 40 megabytes, and then 90. Next, the drive was redesigned so it was the same size as a half height 5.25" floppy drive that used 45-megabyte cartridges. The 5.25" form factor allowed the drive to also be added to a PC as an internal drive. Today, the standard cartridge capacity of the Bernoulli box is 150 meg, and, like the Syquest, it will only read, not write to, the old 40- and 90- meg cartridges.

Other Brands?

It's probably a good idea to stick with the popular brands (Bernoulli and Syquest) when buying removable disk drives. There are many orphan removable drives and cartridges out there, but if you get one and the company goes out of business, you're stuck. After buying an off-brand, you may find out that you can no longer get disks for the drive and that you have to buy a second drive as a spare to ensure that you can get your data off when you need it (after the first drive fails from old age or component failure).

CHAPTER

12

Hard Disk Drive
Installation

OKAY, you went out and bought a new 16,000-MB, 1-ms–access disk, and you want to put it in your Belchfire 8800 clone. What do you do? You've got to handle first the hardware end of the installation, then the software end.

Non-IDE Hard Disk Hardware Installation

Most older drive interface specifications have much in common. IDEs are a bit different, however, and so require special treatment.

To get the hardware installation on an ST506, SCSI, or ESDI drive done, you've got to:

1. Find the *drive select jumper* and set it properly to tell the system if the drive is the first drive in the system or the second.

2. Find the *terminator chip* and remove it if it's on the second drive in the system. (If you're only installing one drive, you needn't worry about this.)

3. Cable the drive properly and install it in the chassis.

4. Inform the controller with what kind of drive it will be dealing.

Drive Select Jumpers on the Drive

As I've hinted, drive controllers can usually service more than one drive; two is the most common. (The desktop PS/2s are an exception, as they only allow one drive.) You don't buy a "drive 1 or drive 2" from a manufacturer—any drive can act as drive 1 or drive 2 in a system. How, then, does the controller know which is which?

On the drive's circuit board, near the data connections, you may find a number of places to put a jumper. The places are generally labeled *DS0, DS1, DS2,* and *DS3.* There should be a jumper on one, *and only one,* of these positions. Alternatively, there may be only a *jumper pack,* a chip-shaped piece of black plastic with metal bands across it. You might recall that I mentioned them in the chapter on installing new circuit boards. You'll notice that most of the bands are broken, but at least one is intact; it's serving as the drive select jumper. I've even seen a few drives with DIP switches to select their drive address. Figure 12.1 provides an example.

Finding these things could take some study, and even when you've found them they're often not labeled. My experience is that you'll see at least four jumper positions, one for each drive address. Only one is jumpered. If it's one on the end, I assume that's location DS0. If it's one in from the end, I assume that's DS1. This works most of the time. So, assuming that *O* means a jumper point that's open (no jumper) and that *J* means a jumpered jumper point, you might see this arrangement:

OOOJ or JOOO means DS0

OOJO or OJOO means DS1

Don't take that information to the bank; it's just a guideline. If you ask, the vendor will often send documentation on the location of the drive select jumpers and terminators.

FIGURE 12.1

Hard disk drive select
jumper and terminator

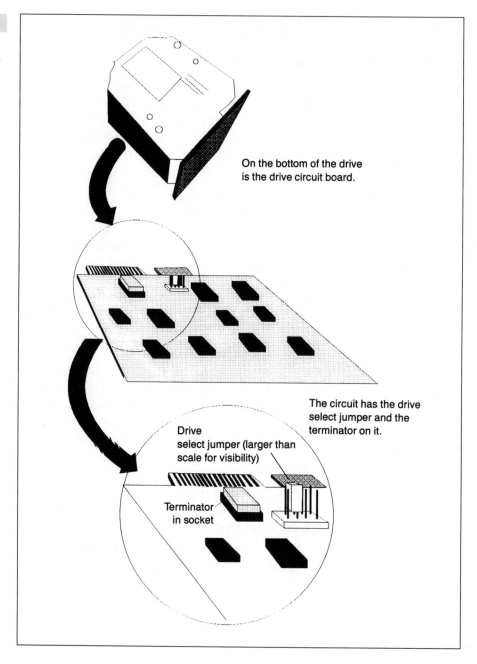

On the bottom of the drive
is the drive circuit board.

The circuit has the drive
select jumper and the
terminator on it.

Drive
select jumper (larger than
scale for visibility)

Terminator
in socket

The Terminator "Chip"

Once you've found the drive select jumper, look around on the circuit board. Near it may be a chip-like object in a socket—the socket is the giveaway here. It's called the *terminator,* and you only need worry about it if you're installing a second hard drive. Putting more than one drive on a single cable requires some special considerations. How do we have multiple devices talking on a single line without having them interfere with each other and blow up the poor chips that are listening to them? The same problem exists on the motherboard, which, you might recall, must talk to a variable number of expansion boards. The generic answer is a *bus.*

There are different kinds of buses, but the drives (floppy and hard) use a design called an *open collector bus.* In order for the bus to work, it must have a resistor called a *pullup resistor* at the physical end of the bus. This resistor "terminates" the bus, so it's called a *terminator.* It's not in a typical resistor package, however. It's in a chip-like package, so it often gets called the *terminator chip,* even though it isn't technically a chip. This bus circuit is designed to work best with a particular resistance value.

So one drive—the one on the physical end of the cable— must have a terminator chip. Drives come with standard terminators, so you'll need to find it on the drive attached to the middle connector and remove it. If you leave both terminators on the drives, you'll have two of these resistors in parallel, which looks to the controller like a single resistor with *half* the resistance of either of the terminators. Less resistance means more current runs through the chips, which can cook the chips on the controller. Leave both terminators off, and the bus is "open"—it has near-infinite resistance. That makes signals "float" and introduces noise into the bus. So, either way, pay attention to your terminators; you want just *one* between the two drives, and that one must be on the drive that's on the physical end of the cable.

Hard Drive Cabling

A controller board is commonly connected to a drive with two ribbon cables. The larger cable has 34 lines, the smaller one 20. Many controllers have one 34-pin connector and two 20s. The second 20-pin connector is for connecting a second drive.

In about half of the cases, there's a twist in lines 25–29 in the middle of the 34-pin cable. In the rest of the cases, there's no twist. There could be one or two 34-pin connectors on the cable. So check to see if your cable has a twist.

With the no-twist cable, just set the first drive to DS0 and the second to DS1. The twist, however, throws the controller a curve: The drive connected to the twist gets its DS0/DS1 reversed. Set the jumper for DS0 on the drive connected to the twist, and it behaves like DS1. Set the jumper for DS1, and it behaves like DS0. That means you set *both* drives to either DS1 or DS0. Set both to DS0, and the drive with the twist becomes the second drive. Set both to DS1, and the drive with the twist becomes the *first* drive. I hope that's clear. If it isn't, look at Figure 12.2. It covers all four twist/no-twist cases.

Telling the Controller What Kind of Drive You Have

Controllers and disks aren't manufactured together. Controller manufacturers like OMTI, Data Technology Corporation (DTC), and Western Digital build controllers to be generic. For example, when I first received my 33-MB Rodime drive (from a company called PCs Limited, since renamed Dell Computers), it was supplied with a Xebec controller. I formatted the drive and used it for a while, finding it a bit slow. A CORETEST showed an access time of 639 milliseconds that was substandard or, as the tech support person said, "sub-substandard." I got a DTC 5150X controller and connected it, again with standard cables and connectors. It was built to handle a variety of disks. Disk type 4 was 639 cylinders, 6 heads—the Rodime. I selected disk type 4 with a set of jumpers. (On an AT controller, recall, you do it with the SETUP program.) The drive formatted without trouble and yielded a seek time of 57.5 ms.

That's just one example. Every disk/controller combination must be, in essence, "properly introduced." There are three ways, by my reckoning:

- The Western Digital WD1002 XT-type controller keeps the "what kind of drive is this?" information on the partition record of the

FIGURE 12.2

Hard disk
configuration and
cabling

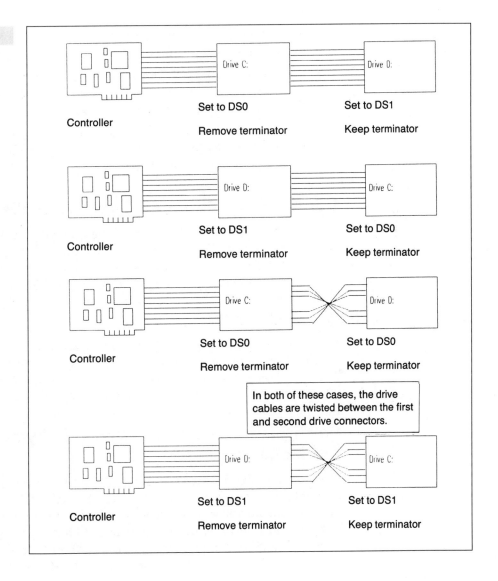

drive. The drive comes with software that allows you to put that information on the partition.

- Most other kinds of XT-type controllers require you to move a jumper, so the controller knows what kind of drive it's using, and some really old ones aren't configurable at all.

- AT-type and PS/2 computers use software, storing a "drive type number" in CMOS configuration memory. You use SETUP to tell the system what kind of drive it has.

Configuring Older XT-Type Controllers

On most XT-type controllers, either the controller will only talk to one kind of drive (IBM XT types) or you must move a jumper to tell the controller what kind of drive you have. Many older controllers, like the IBM XT controllers, will only communicate with a 10-MB or 20-MB drive. That's unfortunate, but a replacement from DTC, Western Digital, or OMTI won't cost much.

There's not much to say about controllers that use jumpers. You just find the drive type that fits your hard disk, move the jumper, and you're off! This *does* assume, by the way, that you have the controller card's documentation. If you don't, you could be out of luck.

Configuring Western Digital XT-Type Controllers

More and more XT clones use a different, more flexible (but also troublesome) controller made by Western Digital. WD has an entire family of XT-type controllers, all with similar (but not identical) characteristics. They're called *autoconfigure* controllers. (There are, by the way, other autoconfigure controllers, such as most ESDI controllers, but the WDs are the most common and so we'll focus on the WD 1002s in this section.)

On these controllers, you have to run a program in the controller's ROM to tell the controller what kind of drive you have. That's nice, because the controller can then accommodate an infinite number of drive types.

On an autoconfigure controller, this infinite flexibility is possible because the controller doesn't mess with jumpers; drive information is encoded onto a sector on the drive. *So be very careful with these drives!* If you run most utilities that can low-level format a drive, such as SpinRite, IAU, or HOPTIMUM, they might destroy this configuration information. The information is stored in the first few bytes of the partition record (also known as the *Master Boot Record,* or MBR). These controllers tend to confuse people, so I've summarized the high points of WD configuration in the next couple of pages.

When you run one of the WD controllers and activate the low-level formatter with DEBUG (a program supplied with DOS), you'll be prompted for the following things:

- Drive number (0 for first drive, 1 for second)
- Interleave factor (probably 3 for the MFM controllers, 4 for the RLL controllers)

Then it may (depending on the BIOS version) ask, *Do you want to dynamically format this drive (y/n)?* Respond **y.** Then it wants to know:

- The number of cylinders
- The number of heads
- The lowest cylinder that uses reduced write current (RWC)
- The lowest cylinder that uses write precompensation (WPC)
- The maximum correctable error burst (legal values 5 or 11)
- The ccb option byte

You can obtain the number of cylinders, number of heads, RWC cylinder, and WPC cylinder from your drive's documentation or by contacting the drive's manufacturer.

Maximum correctable error burst refers to the *Error Correction Code* (ECC) used by the controller to ensure that data read off the hard disk wasn't corrupted in storage. An ECC is much like a checksum, or the parity bit in memory. It goes beyond simple error *detection,* however; it can actually correct a short string of bad bits. Depending on how complex the controller's ECC method is, it can correct from 5 to 11 bad bits in a row. That's what the controller wants to know—how far should it go in writing error-correction stuff on the disk. Go for the security and pick 11 bits.

The *ccb option byte* prompt refers to the *step rate* of your drive. Step rate refers to how quickly multiple seek commands can be sent to a disk head. The numbers vary considerably, and WD has chosen an odd bunch of values, as you can see in Table 12.1.

TABLE 12.1: WD1002 ccb Option Byte Codes

CCB	STEP RATE
0	3 microseconds/step
1	24 microseconds/step
2	24 microseconds/step
3	24 microseconds/step
4	8 microseconds/step
5	24 microseconds/step
6	24 microseconds/step
7	8 microseconds/step

The step numbers can be hard to find, so I just usually go with the majority and use value 5, the default. No, I don't know why there are so many *24 microseconds/step* options.

As mentioned above, these drive characteristics are written to the first half of the sector that contains your MBR. I cannot stress this enough—*back this up!* The only program I know that will do this is XFDISK, another part of the extremely useful hTEST/hFORMAT collection I've mentioned before.

Installation Details on Some WD 1002 Controllers

Nearly every XT compatible you'll come across has one of the WD 1002 controllers in it. Western Digital, in its quest to retain its amazing control of the XT controller market, offers a version of the WD 1002 for every occasion. That means there are quite a number of controllers available in this line, but I'll restrict my discussion to the six most common ones.

To tackle setting up a WD controller, you need to do the following:

1. Make sure you've got an MFM controller for an MFM drive or an RLL controller for an RLL drive.

2. Check the date of the BIOS chip on the controllers that have a separate BIOS chip (some incorporate the BIOS into other chips). The latest BIOS is dated 62-0000094-*xxx*, where *xxx* is three digits that could be anything—they'll vary. If you have a controller with a lower BIOS ID number (such as the 62-000043-010 I have in my hand at the moment), upgrade the BIOS.

3. Set the jumpers, if there are any on the board.

4. Configure and low-level format the drive, as described in the previous section.

Table 12.2 summarizes which controllers have BIOS chips and jumpers and whether they support dynamic configuration, and shows their encoding scheme.

TABLE 12.2: Western Digital WD1002 XT Controller Features

CONTROLLER NAME	ENCODING	BIOS CHIP?	WHICH JUMPERS?	SUPPORTS DYNAMIC CONFIGURATION?
WD 1002A–WX1	MFM	Y	W1–W8, SW1	Y
WD 1002–27X	RLL	N	W1–W9, SW1	Y
WD 1002A–27X	RLL	N	W1–W2	Y
WD 1002S–WX2	MFM	Y	W1–W7, SW1	Y
WD 1002S–WX2A	MFM	Y	W6 only	Y
WD XT–GEN	MFM	N	None	N (except model F300)

In general, you'll see from zero to ten jumper locations on a WD 1002. They're labeled from W1 to W9, and there's often a larger jumper set called SW1 with nine positions. *Not every board has all ten jumpers,* and indeed most don't have more than seven. The jumpers are set as follows (* indicates factory defaults):

W1 and W2   On most WD drives, these are hardwired—and WD ain't tellin' what they do anyway.

W1/W2 RLL Translation (1002-27X Only)   On one RLL controller, the WD 1002A-27X, you have the option to "fool" the system into thinking it has an MFM controller and drive. So long as your drive has 663 or fewer cylinders, the 1002A-27X will translate instructions to read or write 1024-cylinder, 17-sector disks into instructions to read or write 663-cylinder, 26-sector disks. The translation mode is enabled by jumpering *both* W1 and W2. Disable translation by removing both jumpers. My recommendation: Don't do it. It confuses disk utilities, and an otherwise innocuous program could trash your data because of it.

W3 BIOS Enable   1–2 to enable the BIOS.* No jumper; disable BIOS.

W4 I/O Address   1–2 selects address 324 hex; 2–3 selects address 320 hex.* Note: This must agree with Controller Select jumper if W8 is present.

W5 ROM Size   1–2 is hardwired and allows the use of 2732 and 2764 ROMs.* Break 1–2 trace and solder 2–3 to allow use of 2716s.

W6 Reduced Write Enable   1–2 drive can have up to 16 heads, but no RWC. 2–3 drive can have up to 8 heads, *and* RWC enabled.*

W7 Interrupt Select   1–2 hardwired controller uses IRQ5.* Cut 1–2, jumper 2–3, and jumper position 7 on SW1 to enable IRQ2 instead.

W8 Controller Select   1–2 controller is first controller in PC.* 2–3 controller is second controller in PC. Note: Controller Select jumper position must match I/O Address jumper position.

W9 (Unused)   If you have W9, as in a WD 1002-27X, just leave it open—no jumper.

SW1   This is actually a set of jumper positions labeled from 1 to 8. In most cases, don't put jumpers across any of the positions.

That's your quick and dirty guide to configuring WD 1002 controllers. It's not the whole story, but it'll cover 99 percent of the cases. WD provides semiautomated tech support service at (800) 777-4787. If you're outside of the U.S., dial direct (714) 747-2033, extension 34700.

IDE Hard Disk Installation

As I said earlier, IDE installation is a bit different from other hard disks. That's not bad, just different. In general, you'll find that installing IDE drives is easier than installing any other kind of hard disk. The steps to installing a single IDE drive in a system are:

1. Install the IDE adapter. (Remember that IDE puts the disk controller right on the drive itself; there is, therefore, no such thing as an "IDE controller.")

2. Mount the IDE drive in the case.

3. Attach the power connection to the IDE drive.

4. Attach the single 40-wire ribbon cable that connects the drive to the adapter to the adapter and drive connections.

That's all there is to it. IDE connections are definitely easier than the other kinds of hard disk connections. No twists in the cables, no terminators, and you only rarely deal with drive select jumpers.

If all you're doing is installing an IDE drive in with a basic IDE adapter, then you're done—progress to the next section, *Specifying an AT Hard Drive Type*. But stay with me if you've got one of the following items.

• A second IDE drive to install.

- An IDE adapter with ROM on it.
- An IDE adapter with cache on it.

Installing a Second IDE Drive

You saw previously that you must set a drive-select jumper, kind of an address indicator, for each non-IDE hard disk, no matter how many hard disks you've got. With IDEs, however, that's not the case.

The reason why is because the IDE controller is, again, right on the drive itself, and so it does not have to worry about addressing drives; it knows that there's only one drive in its "universe."

But what happens when you install a *second* IDE drive?

Well, two IDE drives means *two controllers in the same system,* which is, as you'd imagine, a prescription for trouble. (If you've forgotten why, look back to Chapter 6 for a reminder about circuit board conflicts.) Modern IDE drives are equipped for this problem, and have a provision to essentially shut off their onboard controllers. Installing two IDE drives in the same system, therefore, boils down to getting one of the controllers on one of the IDE drives to control *both* drives. In IDE terms, we say that one controller is the "master" and one is the "slave," or that we must "slave" one controller to the other in order to make them work together.

When you've only got a single IDE drive, there's no question of master or slave, so you usually needn't do anything with jumpers. But once you add the second drive, you've got to configure both the old drive and the new, annointing one the master and the other the slave.

Careful readers will have noticed that I said "usually" in the last paragraph. That's because *not every IDE drive can be configured for mastering or slaving.* That's true mainly of older IDEs, but it's still something to look out for. I mention it particularly because the most common scenario for installing a second drive is one wherein you've already got a 40-MB IDE drive from a computer that you bought in 1990, but now you've purchased a 210-MB IDE to replace it. As you're going to install the 210, however, you say to yourself, "hey, why not keep the 40 in there? That way, I'll have *250* MB on line!" It's a good plan, but make sure that you can set one drive to "slave" and the other to "master."

Specifying an AT Hard Drive Type

How do you tell a 286/386/486 type machine what kind of hard disk you have? Not with jumpers—the SETUP program does the job here. The information is, as you might recall from our discussion of motherboard configuration, saved into a battery-powered memory chip generally called the CMOS chip.

Supplying hard disk information to the CMOS chip is, sadly, the most troublesome part about running an AT's SETUP program. The program asks, "What type is your hard disk?" If you answer *Seagate ST225*, or the like, it just beeps at you. Unfortunately, the drive type number isn't particularly descriptive. Table 12.3 shows the drive types offered for IBM machines. Your clone may well vary in its drive table, although the first 14 drive types are almost invariably the original IBM drive types.

This drive type information is in your computer's BIOS ROM, not on the hard disk controller. If you don't know what drive types your BIOS supports, consult your computer's documentation. Some clones will tell you what hard disk table they have if you respond with a question mark (?) when their SETUP program asks, *What drive type is your hard disk?*

Now, there might not be a prestored drive type that exactly matches your hard disk, so you could have to find the closest one. Here's how. Suppose you get a machine from Table 12.3, and you want to install a drive with 1024 cylinders, seven heads, and no write precompensation? (You might be wondering, "Where would I get that information about the drive anyway?" Simple—call the manufacturer.) You quickly see there are no exact matches. Now what? Find the best match. There are four steps:

1. Eliminate all drives with write precompensation different from that of your drive. If it's just a few cylinders different, you can get away with it, but the write precomp *is* important. Notice in the drive type table that IBM thought it sufficiently important to include *two* 21-MB drive types in the original 14—types 2 and 6 only vary by their write precompensation values. Since your drive doesn't need write precomp, you eliminate the drive types that *do*, so what remain are types 6, 8–12, 14–16, 18, 26–28, 37, 41–42, and 44–46.

TABLE 12.3: Built-In AT Drive Types

DRIVE NUMBER	NUMBER OF CYLINDERS	HEADS	WRITE PRECOM- PENSATION	CAPACITY	EXAMPLES
1	306	4	128	10.6	Seagate ST412, ST212, ST112
2	615	4	300	21.4	Seagate ST225
3	615	6	300	32.1	Tulin TL240, Rodime RO206
4	940	8	512	65.4	Atasi 3080
5	940	6	512	49.0	
6	615	4	no	21.4	The CMI 20 MB
7	462	8	256	32.1	Quantum Q540
8	733	5	no	31.9	Seagate ST4038
9	900	15	no	117.5	Maxtor XT-1140
10	820	3	no	21.4	Micropolis 1302, Vertex V130
11	855	5	no	37.2	Vertex V150
12	855	7	no	52.0	Vertex V170
13	306	8	128	21.3	Seagate ST425, Rodime RO204
14	733	7	no	44.6	
16	612	4	no	20.3	
17	977	5	300	40.5	
18	977	7	no	56.7	Priam HD60
19	1024	7	512	59.5	

TABLE 12.3: Built-In AT Drive Types (continued)

DRIVE NUMBER	NUMBER OF CYLINDERS	HEADS	WRITE PRECOM-PENSATION	CAPACITY	EXAMPLES
20	733	5	300	30.4	
21	733	7	300	42.5	
22	733	5	300	30.4	
23	306	4	0	10.1	
25	615	4	0	20.4	
26	1024	4	no	34.0	
	1024	5	no	42.5	
28	1024	8	no	68.0	
29	512	8	256	34.0	
30	615	2	615	10.2	
35	1024	9	1024	76.5	Seagate ST4096
36	1024	5	512	42.5	
37	830	10	no	68.8	
38	823	10	256	68.3	
39	615	4	128	20.4	
40	615	8	128	40.8	
41	917	15	no	114.1	
42	1023	15	no	127.3	
43	823	10	512	68.3	
44	820	6	no	40.8	
45	1024	8	no	68.0	
46	925	9	no	69.1	
47	699	7	256	40.6	

NOTE: Your AT might not have all 47 types. IBM added them over time.

2. You can't exaggerate about cylinders. It's all right to use a drive type that doesn't exploit all your drive's cylinders, but if you pick one with *more* cylinders than your drive has, the computer will try to format nonexistent cylinders. Trying to format, say, cylinder 900 on a 700-cylinder machine could destroy the drive. No drive types exist that have more than 1024 cylinders, so you're still looking at the same possibilities as before.

3. Eliminate all drive types with more heads than your drive. You also can't exaggerate about heads. Remove the drive types with more than seven heads, and you are left with types 6, 8, 10–12, 14–16, 18, 26–27, and 44.

4. Now choose the greatest capacity. Any of the remaining drive types are fine to use, but you want the largest amount of drive space possible, so examine the capacities, and you'll come up with type 18. Now, note that the actual drive is a 60-MB drive, and type 18 describes a 56.7MB drive, so we're wasting 3.3MB. But it's as close as this ROM allows.

Expanding Your AT's Drive Types

If you have a drive that won't match any AT drive type within a reasonable number of megabytes, think about buying an add-on ROM to enlarge the AT drive table. Alternatively, there are software answers, such as products called SpeedStor or DiskManager, but I don't recommend using a device driver to communicate with your hard disk. One reason is that it's another piece of software that must be functioning properly in order for your programs to use the hard disk, and thus it can complicate your troubleshooting hassles. Another is that a ROM is usable for any operating system, so you'll have no trouble going to OS/2, Novell, or UNIX systems in the future. One such ROM is sold by OnTrack Systems, and is listed in Appendix A.

Hard Disk Software Installation

There's more to hard disk preparation than FORMAT C:/S. There are three steps to drive preparation:

- Physical (low-level) format
- Partition creation
- DOS (high-level) format

Physical Formatting

Physical, or *low-level,* formatting is a process whereby 17 sectors are "drawn" on each track, using magnetism as the "ink." Each sector is then filled with ASCII 229 (the sigma character). It's at this level that the interleave factor is set. This formatting is generally done by the manufacturer. You cannot low-level format an IDE drive.

The low-level format process not only tests the disk medium itself, but also writes out the *sector IDs* that will be used by DOS to locate data on the disk. The physical format process matches up a drive and a controller. Since every controller and drive has its own quirks, this means a controller might not be able to read a disk formatted by a different controller, even if the new controller is the same model as the old one.

You'll do a physical format for one of four reasons:

1. You've purchased a new controller or drive.

2. You experience a large number of disk problems. Try backing up the hard disk, do a new physical format, create a partition and directory format, then reload your files. They'll come back. Recall that sector IDs are laid down at physical format time. These IDs, like all magnetic images, fade over time. (Ever seen a *Sector Not Found* error from DOS? That's what causes it.) You could have a perfectly good disk with old, faint IDs that ends up looking like

it's bad. A new physical format will make it good as new. As I've said before, it's a good idea to reformat the drive every year or so.

3. You wish to experiment with the interleave factor to increase your data transfer rate from your hard disk. We covered interleave factors in Chapter 10.

4. You suspect a faulty format, as in a case where a disk is accidentally formatted as a 20-MB drive when it's actually a 10-MB drive.

Once I tried to use a rental XT under DOS 3.1. The XT was delivered to me with the disk formatted under 2.1, so I tried to reformat it. The drive ground a lot and finally told me that it had formatted a 20-MB disk and had found 10-MB of bad sectors. It was, of course, a 10-MB disk, which in reality had gotten an odd formatting. I ran a physical format, then created the partition, and did the DOS format; there was no further trouble.

How you physically format is a controller-specific question. If you have:

- Any XT-type MFM controller other than a Western Digital WD1002, WD XT-GEN, or RLL controller: Either use the HDAT program on the utility disk or HFORMAT from the Kolod collection. Alternatively, your dealer may have included a low-level format program with your disk.

- A WD1002, WD XT-GEN, or an RLL (XT or AT) controller: Each requires its own format program. It's sitting in the ROM on the hard disk controller, so you need only use DEBUG to activate it. The built-in program is generally at address C800:5 or C800:6. Adaptec RLL controllers put the program at C800:CCC. *Warning: The procedure I'm about to describe will irrevocably destroy any data on your hard disk drive. Don't do it unless you've backed up the drive in its entirety!* Load DEBUG with the following command:

```
C>debug↵
–G=C800:5
```

(I've discussed formatting the WD controllers in the earlier section on setting up and using WD XT-type controllers.) You'll get some kind of prompt, like *What interleave factor would you like to use?* The prompts will depend on the manufacturer. See the documentation that came with the controller. If you don't have documentation, call the manufacturer's tech support line.

- An MFM AT-type controller: Again, use hDAT or hFORMAT. Alternatively, the IBM AT Advanced Diagnostics disk includes a low-level format program.

- PS/2 Model 25, 30, or 30/286: You've *got* to use hFORMAT. It's the only program I know of that seems to format these drives reliably.

- PS/2 Model 50 to 80: If you have a PS/2, there's a low-level format program on the Reference Disk; boot from the Reference Disk. Once you're at the Main menu, press Ctrl-A and an Advanced menu will pop up. One option is a low-level format of the PS/2 disk.

Make sure you know how to do physical formats. If you're responsible for several or many machines, get the instructions and try it out once. The reason for this is that you want to see all diagnostic procedures on a properly functioning system. Then you'll know how to spot troubles.

Partitioning

In order to accommodate multiple operating systems, DOS allows you to create multiple *partitions* with the program FDISK. Suppose you have a 30-MB drive and want to run both DOS and XENIX. Using FDISK, you can create a (say) 20-MB partition for DOS, and a 10-MB partition for XENIX. Even if you're going to give it all to DOS, you still must run FDISK.

Until recently, using FDISK has been a two-minute operation: You tell it to give DOS the entire disk; then it reboots the system, and you're ready to format. But nowadays, you could find yourself spending a little more time in the partition process.

You see, as of DOS 3.3, FDISK has another value. DOS 3.*x* can't handle a disk larger than 32-MB. Previously, this meant that an 80-MB drive either wasted 48-MB or required a device driver to access the latter 48-MB.

As of DOS 4.0, this problem has disappeared; you can create a single drive of sizes over a gigabyte.

Under FDISK 3.3, you can divide the disk into a drive C with 32-MB, a drive D with 32-MB, and a drive E with 16-MB. Here's how to do so.

The disk gets divided into two partitions, a *primary DOS partition*, and an *extended DOS partition*. The primary DOS partition can't be larger than 32 MB, but the extended can be as large as you like. So Step 1 is to divide the example 80-MB drive into a primary DOS partition of 32 MB, and an extended DOS partition of 48 MB.

Next, the extended DOS partition gets divided up into "logical" drives. You can have as many as you like, each of any size up to 32-MB. If you wanted, you could create drives D, E, F, G, H, I, and so on, each 1-MB in size. (However, you should probably consider professional counseling if you'd really like to create piles of tiny logical drives.) All of this is pictured in Figure 12.3.

FIGURE 12.3

DOS 3.3 partitioning of sample 80MB drive

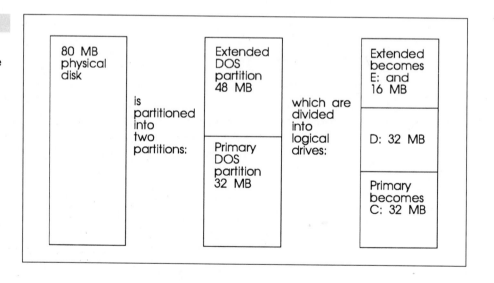

Here are the steps to set up an 80-MB disk under DOS 3.3.

1. **Invoke FDISK (called PART in some older OEM's versions of MS-DOS) and create the primary DOS partition.** You'll see an opening screen with four options:

   1. Create DOS Partition
   2. Change Active Partition
   3. Delete DOS Partition
   4. View Partition Information

   If you have two hard disks, there will be a fifth option to allow you to choose on which disk to work. Right now, select option 1, Create DOS Partition. You'll then see another menu offering:

   1. Create Primary DOS Partition
   2. Create Extended DOS Partition

   First, we will make the primary partition, so select 1 again. FDISK will then offer to automatically create the maximum size DOS partition and make it bootable. Don't take this option, as it immediately reboots the system. Answer **no**. It will then say something like:

   ```
   Enter number of cylinders for partition......[450]?
   ```

   It has already computed the number of cylinders that will allow a 32MB primary DOS partition. Press ↵ and it will display the information on the new partition. Press Esc and you'll return to the FDISK Main menu. By the way, it will beep at you—that's normal.

2. **Create the extended partition and logical drives.** Enter 1 to go to the Create DOS Partition menu again, but this time choose 2, Create Extended DOS Partition. It will, by default, suggest that you devote the rest of the disk to the extended partition. Like the main menu, it will display a message somewhat like this:

   ```
   Enter number of cylinders for partition......[550]?
   ```

   Take its suggestion. It will beep again and remind you that no logical drives have been created. The extended partition must be further divided into logical drives. Press Esc and it will suggest a number of cylinders to allocate to logical drive D (the amount needed to bring it up to 32 MB). Again, take its suggestion. It will then suggest the remainder for drive E. Accept its suggestion. You'll see the information on the new partitions and logical drives on the screen. Press Esc, and you're back to the Main menu.

3. Make the DOS partition bootable. Oops, that's "active." The PC has to know to which partition it should go in order to boot. That partition should be called the bootable partition (in my opinion, anyway), but FDISK calls it the *active partition.* Choose option 2, Change Active Partition. It will ask which partition to make active. The primary DOS partition should be partition number 1, so choose number 1. Then press Esc once to get to the Main menu, and another time to get out of FDISK. The system will reboot, and you're partitioned.

Under FDISK 3.3, you can create as many volumes as you like, all 32 MB or smaller. Perhaps even better, Compaq DOS 3.31 and PC DOS 4.0 and 5.0 allow you to create disks up to 512 MB in size. It's a nice innovation, but be careful: Some hard disk utilities, like older versions of Norton, Mace, or PC Tools, were written before such DOSes existed and might not know how to talk to your disk. Worse, some can actually damage your data when you run them.

Having gone through all that work to create the DOS partition, you might wonder, "What happens if the partition information is destroyed?" This is a real problem; in this situation, the PC will refuse even to recognize that a disk exists. Kolod Research offers some utilities to help. XFDISK, one of the programs that comes with hTEST/hFORMAT, can back up your partition record. You can also back up the partition record with Norton 4.5, Mace 5.0, or PC Tools 6.0 and later.

The latest editions of the popular disk utilities—the Norton Utilities version 6.0, the Mace Utilities version 6.0, and PC Tools 7.0—all support the latest disk formats.

DOS Formatting

Finally, you run the DOS FORMAT program. The FORMAT command creates the DOS boot record, FATs, and root directory—it doesn't touch the MBR or the user data area. The FORMAT program also does not actually overwrite sectors and physically format hard disks. Disks have five areas, some of which we've heard about earlier in this chapter:

- The partition record or Master Boot Record (MBR). This contains the disk partition information to divide the physical drive into logical drives. On autoconfigure controllers, it also contains a few bytes that describe the disk. This resides (under DOS 3.*x*) on cylinder 0, head 0, sector 1. The remaining 16 sectors on the first cylinder/head are unused.

- The DOS boot record. Originally, this only contained a snippet of code used to start booting up the system. In later versions of DOS, other disk ID information was added. Among other things, the DOS boot record contains a pointer to the FAT, so if the boot record is damaged, the FAT will look strange to DOS. The boot record resides on *DOS sector 0*, which is cylinder 0, head 1, sector 1.

- DOS numbers sectors sequentially starting at cylinder 0, head 1, sector 1. Sectors 2 to 17 of that cylinder/head are the next 16 DOS sectors. The next group is the 17 sectors on cylinder 0, head 2. Next is head 3, and so on. To traverse the DOS sectors in order, first increment sectors until you're out of them; next, increment the head numbers until they're exhausted; then increment the cylinder numbers.

- The FAT (File Allocation Table). The FAT is a map of what clusters are associated with what files. DOS keeps two copies of the FAT, the primary and the secondary. There are two kinds of FATs: a 12-bit FAT, with 4096 12-bit entries, requiring 6K total on the disk for each copy; and a 16-bit FAT, with 64K 16-bit entries, requiring 128K for each copy. Under DOS 3.*x*, 4.*x*, and 5.*x*, floppies and 10MB hard disks use the 12-bit FAT, and 20+MB hard disks use the 16-bit FAT. DOS 2.*x* uses the 12-bit FAT for all disk types.

- The root directory. The root directory is the basis of the tree-structured file system. There are 128 entries for a disk with a 12-bit FAT and 512 entries for a disk with a 16-bit FAT. *Entries* means room for directory information for a file. Twelve-bit FAT disks can only have 128 files in their root directories. Try to create a 129th, and you get an *unable to create directory entry* error message. The root directory immediately follows the second copy of the FAT on the disk.

- The data area. Actual user data goes here. It follows the root directory.

- IBMBIO.COM or IO.SYS. If the disk is bootable, the first directory entry, and the first cluster, refer to the first *hidden file*, IBMBIO.COM (for PC-DOS) or IO.SYS (for MS-DOS).

- IBMDOS.COM or MSDOS.SYS. If the disk is bootable, the second directory entry will refer to the second hidden file, IBMDOS.COM (for PC-DOS) or MSDOS.SYS (for MS-DOS).

Since the FORMAT program doesn't destroy or overwrite data in the data area, this implies that *formatted hard disks can be recovered*. DOS 5.0 even includes an "unformat" program. See Chapter 14 on failure recovery for more information.

There are, incidentally, a few exceptions to this rule. Earlier versions of AT&T, Compaq, and Unisys MS-DOS actually torpedo the whole disk. There's no recovery from this.

A Note about Bad Areas

One of DOS's most important jobs is to ensure that unreliable, or "bad," areas on a disk aren't used. The FAT helps DOS avoid these bad areas.

Bad areas have either *hard errors* or *soft errors*. Hard errors are problems in the disk surface itself, so that it cannot record data at all. This is caused by manufacturing defects or later abuse. Soft errors occur when some data has faded on the disk to the point where it cannot be read. The idea is, "If it faded once, it could again, so we'll cordon off the area and not use it again" (kind of like a hazardous waste dump for your system). Programs like Norton Disk Doctor or Mace Remedy detect these things.

Hard errors are designated by the system at low-level format time. Low-level format programs can format an area with a specific code that will upset the DOS FORMAT program when FORMAT does its quick sector scan. When FORMAT can't read the sector, it marks it as bad in the FAT.

Soft errors, on the other hand, can allow FORMAT to read the sector just fine, so a cluster previously marked bad might not be remarked on a subsequent format. Soft errors, you'll recall, don't always show up when tested. The fact that FORMAT hasn't remarked all of the bad areas as bad leads some people to think that they can get rid of bad sectors by just reformatting the drive. All that does is erase DOS's information about where bad areas exist, which is not a great idea. Low-level formatting, on the other hand, might help a failing drive, for reasons I've already mentioned.

CHAPTER

13

Hard Disk Preventive Maintenance

HARD disk preventive maintenance mainly refers to protecting the data and the drive. The drive is fairly fragile, so some careful handling and simple procedures can minimize chances of harm. The disk's data is also important, more so in fact than the drive itself. Backups are the key here, although you probably never even thought of making the kinds of backups we'll discuss here.

Hard Disk Mechanical Protection

Following these tips will help protect your hard-disk hardware:

- Leave the machine on all the time. I think I've beaten this one to death, so I'll say no more on the subject.

- Get good surge protection. Surges go through the whole system, including the drive head. And if the drive head happens to be near the FAT or partition....

- Don't smoke around drives. There's more information on this below.

- Park the head. There's more on this too below.

- Be careful what length screws you use to secure a drive, particularly Seagate ST2*xx* drives. I've mentioned it before, but it's a common mistake, so I'll mention it again. DO NOT use the standard ⅜-inch screws to secure Seagate ST225, ST238, or ST251 drives. They're too long and can actually push in the drive housing. Back off the screw, and the problem is often solved.

- Don't secure Seagate ST2*xx* drives on all four sides. Some of the ST2*xx* drives seem to have their mounting holes drilled out of line with one another. That means that when you tighten four screws to secure the drive, two on each side, you warp the drive and it stops working. Panic ensues. The answer is simple—just loosen one of the screws, and the problem disappears.

- Format a drive in the position and at the temperature it will be used. The small effects of gravity are important. If you're going to use the machine on its side, low-level format the drive on its side. Don't format a drive when it's cold. Don't run test programs on it when it's cold, either.

- Using a disk-caching program can lengthen the life of your drive, as it reduces wear on the drive. See below for more information.

- Attend to squeaky drives. Not only are they annoying, they might be trying to tell you something.

You Can't Fix It, So You Must Protect It

There's not much that can be done in the way of regular maintenance on the sealed Winchester drive. You can't clean the heads, and you can't align them. If the drive itself is fried, about all you can do with it is cut it open and leave it on your bookshelf as a conversation piece.

What kills hard disks?

- Smoke (the filters aren't perfect)
- Vibration

I've mentioned the effects of smoke before. When a smoke particle sits on the disk, the head whips around and crashes right into it. Then it drags it around the platter, leaving scratches in its wake. On a 5¼-inch platter rotating at 3600 rpm, a particle on the outermost track would travel at

56 miles per hour. The outermost track is, by the way, the most important track, as it contains the directory information for the rest of the disk.

Vibration is a problem because of the way in which the head travels above the disk platter on a cushion of air. The distance between the platter and the head (called the *head gap*) is fairly small. Any bouncing around, then, can cause the head to literally crash onto the platter below. This plows a small furrow in the platter and grinds down the head. Do this enough, and you'll lose the data in the furrow and possibly the head.

A similar thing happens whenever you turn off power from the hard disk. Deprived of its cushion of air, it crash-lands onto the platter below. If you always have the head positioned over the same spot when you power down, you'll eventually create a new bad sector there.

Another way you can protect your data is to buy quality drives. How is the magnetic material put on the platters in the first place? The cheaper and less effective approach is to simply *coat* the platters—in effect, to glue rust onto the platters. A better and more expensive approach is to *plate* the magnetic oxide onto the platters. Plated media are superior and more expensive. Best of all are *sputtered* media: a magnetic compound high in cobalt (there are only three magnetic elements—iron, nickel, and cobalt) is vacuum-welded to the platter. It makes a smoother surface, which in turn allows the head to fly closer to the platter, which allows higher bit-density on a disk.

Disk Protection: Parking the Heads I

One of the best ways to reduce the damage from the head hitting the platter is to move the head outside the data area, and then power down. This is possible because the actual number of tracks the disk has is greater than the number you use, by a few. For example, on the 305-cylinder XT hard disk, you can position the head over cylinder 306, then power down. This is called *parking the heads.* Do it when you're going to be away from your machine, at lunchtime or for the evening.

Parking the Heads II: The Deadly SHIPDISK

Most of us have heard of disk parking, and many know that IBM includes a head parking program on the IBM Diagnostics disk called SHIPDISK. The notion is that when you're going to subject the disk to some jarring, such as when you're moving the XT, you should first boot the Diagnostics disk and use SHIPDISK to position the head, then turn the system off.

In general, SHIPDISK works fine *when you use it this way:* Boot off the Diagnostics disk and then run the program. But a lot of people decided to just copy SHIPDISK off the Diagnostics disk onto their hard disk, and run SHIPDISK before powering down for the night. This is a bad move, as SHIPDISK presumes the presence of some software routines that only exist on the special version of DOS included on the Diagnostics disk. Run under regular DOS, SHIPDISK can destroy data.

Here's another SHIPDISK item to watch: If you use XT SHIPDISK on an AT hard disk, the disk is zapped. (In the words of Bill Cosby, "'Zap' means 'dead.'")

Parking the Heads III: Safe Remedies

What, then, should you do? Two possibilities: First, you could leave your PC on all the time, as has been discussed earlier. Second, use a generic park program, a "safe" parking program.

If you work in an environment with a lot of vibration, don't hesitate to park the heads whenever you're not using the PC, even if it's still turned on. In this case, or if you're just plain forgetful, use a program like the shareware program TIMEPARK from Sanford J. Zelkovitz (see Appendix A). TIME-PARK will park the heads on your disk *automatically* every few minutes.

Just put it in your AUTOEXEC.BAT file with this command:

```
TIMEPARK 2
```

This will instruct the program to park the heads on your disk every two minutes.

Disk-Caching Programs

The most demanding mechanical activities for a drive are starting up in the morning and moving the head throughout the day. You can avoid the first stress by leaving your machine on all the time. You can avoid the second with a cache program, as a cache minimizes the number of head movements the disk must do. In the process, it also makes the system work more quickly. Here's how.

A disk cache works on the principle that a sector used on disk tends to be reused soon. It watches each disk "read" operation, and copies the information read into a section of memory set aside for disk caching. Subsequent DOS requests to read anything from disk that the cache already has in memory are intercepted by the cache, which delivers the data to DOS by transferring it from the cache memory. Reading memory is, again, lots faster than reading disks, so the system speeds up considerably.

If bug-free, disk caches are truly neat. They make the disk do less work, and they can use some memory that you haven't been doing anything with anyway. Remember that extended memory that's only good to heat up the room under DOS? There are disk-cache programs that change all that and use the extended memory as cache space. (You don't really want to have to give up some of your 640K, do you?)

There are lots of cache programs out there, but let me recommend the best: Multisoft's Super PC-Kwik version 4.2. (No, they can't spell, but they can sure write code.) You can find Multisoft listed in Appendix A.

Here are some cache tips. You can load a file into the cache by copying it to NUL:. Copying to NUL:, DOS's "bit bucket," doesn't really do anything except force DOS to look at the file. Cache programs watch what DOS is watching, and so a side effect of copying to NUL: is to load a file into a cache. For example, if I had a file called BANANA.WK1 that I wanted in the cache, I'd just type **COPY BANANA.WK1 NUL:**. Caches don't know which sectors are most likely to be read, so they take a while to "learn" which sectors are most profitably cached. And, of course, if you have an application that jumps all over the disk (unlikely, but possible), the cache will actually slow you down.

What if cached data is sitting in memory and the computer is powered down? Won't that lose data? No—any *writes* requested are done directly to disk. It's really disk *reads* that benefit from caching, although a smart cache observes when a sector that the system wants to write doesn't vary from the current disk value.

Squeaky Drives

Many hard disks make high-pitched squeals and squeaks. How to handle this? There are three reasons for squeaky drives.

First, ensure that the disk is fully secured, and either lying flat or on its side. A slightly askew disk will whine. By the way, it's perfectly acceptable to store a hard disk on its side, but you'll get better results if you also format (a low-level format, described later in this chapter) the drive in this position.

Second, check how well supported the drive is. The XT- and PC-type machines ordinarily only support the drive on one side. This makes the drive bend just a little and sets up vibration. The vibration is then picked up by the case, and the whole computer starts squealing. The answer is simple: Damp the vibration between the drive and the case. This can be done by using a small piece of cardboard or folded construction paper as a shim between the drive and the chassis.

The third approach involves something on the drive called the *static wiper*, shown in Figure 13.1. Remove the drive. On its bottom there's generally a circuit board. The board may have a cutout in the middle: if not, remove the board. You'll see a flat piece of spring metal lying on a small bearing. This piece of metal is a static wiper. It drains off static charges from the drive. Over time, the charges and the friction of sitting against the bearing cause the wiper to become pitted. The pitted surface against the rotating bearing is the source of the squeak.

One answer is to remove the circuit board (you can remove the circuit board without unsealing the disk), and use a fine emery cloth to shine the static wiper. An easier answer is to use some GE silicone putty. Just a drop

FIGURE 13.1

View of static wiper
on underside of hard
disk

on top of the wiper (*not between it and the bearing!*) changes the mass of the wiper just enough to damp the squeak. The small blob of silicone will fall off after six months; when it does, just replace it.

At my company, we once tried lubricating the bearing to stop the noise. We used WD-40 (a common silicone-based lubricant) to quiet a drive. It quieted the drive somewhat, and in a few months it quieted it completely: The WD-40 attracted gunk, and the gunk dirtied the whole works so badly that the drive stopped working.

There's actually a fourth reason for squeak, but there's really nothing you can do about it. Sometimes the bearings fail and start to grind against each other. You can tell for sure by using a stethoscope (any long narrow piece of metal will do, actually) and listening to the bearings while the disk is running. If the bearings are grinding, you'll hear it. The answer is to back up the disk, throw it away before it fails, and replace it.

Hard Disk Data Protection

The essence of data protection is to make good backups.

- Back up user data periodically (see below).

- Back up, low-level format again, and reload your data on the drive once or twice per year. Recall that each track is divided with sector IDs recorded by the head at format time. Those IDs can fade and/or the mechanical head-positioning equipment can move, causing a host of problems. Reformat periodically to keep the mechanicals in line with the data, and to refresh the IDs on the disk. A nondestructive low-level format program like Spinrite or HOPTIMUM can greatly simplify this task, as you needn't reload your data after each reformat. Remember that nondestructive low-level formats probably aren't a good idea for a machine with an XT-type controller. It's better just to do it the hard way with such a machine and back up, format, and reload.

- Back up the first track (actually, the first *sector*—head 0, track 0, sector 1). This protects the partition record and possibly the autoconfigure record. Use a program like XFDISK from hTEST/hFORMAT.

- Back up the FAT and root directory automatically with a program like FR (Norton or Image), RXBAK (Mace), or Mirror (PC Tools). *Be sure you have the most recent version of the software!* (An old Mirror once trashed the FAT on our LAN server.) Put the program in your AUTOEXEC.BAT. FAT backup programs make unerasing or unformatting data easier. As we'll discuss in Chapter 14, the major effect of erasing data or formatting disks is seen mostly in the FAT, not the user data areas. So it makes sense to back up the FAT to make things easier for a program like Norton when you're trying to undo some user-created damage.

- Unfragment your files monthly or semimonthly with an unfrag-menter like Norton SpeedDisk, Mace Unfrag, or PC Tools' Compress. These programs basically tidy up your disk so DOS can read the files faster. Most people use them for speed, but truthfully I run them because putting all my files in nice neat consecutive order makes data recovery easier: If a file isn't scattered all over the disk, it's easier to find when the directory and FAT have gone south. See below for more details.

- Run a disk tester program like DiskTest to provide early warning of hard-disk problems. There are a lot of disk problems that DOS doesn't tell us about:

    If DOS detects a read error, it performs several retries without informing the user. If the retries succeed, the user never knows there's a problem.

    In responding to DOS, BIOS might execute retries of its own. DOS knows nothing about this.

    When following BIOS orders to read a sector, the controller can not only detect but actually *correct* a few bad bits in each sector. BIOS knows nothing of this.

    Between all this, it would be nice to have a program around to monitor all the things DOS and the gang aren't telling you. Spinrite and Disk Technician both try to do this while they're doing disk testing. Norton Disk Doctor and Mace Remedy are in this class also. They do sequential disk-read tests, and try to move data from flaky areas on disk to more reliable places.

File Unfragmenters

As mentioned before, files can be *fragmented*. This means that a given file may be divided into sectors 30–40 (one contiguous group) and 101–122 (another contiguous group). Noncontiguous files are bad for two reasons.

First, noncontiguous files take longer to read. The fact that the disk head must go chasing all over the disk to read them slows down disk access. Putting the whole file together makes read operations quicker.

Second, you have a higher probability of recovering an erased file if it isn't fragmented. Keeping disks unfragmented just pushes the odds a little further in your favor.

How do files become fragmented? Well, when DOS needs a sector, it basically grabs the first one available. When the disk is new, only a few sectors have been taken, and the rest of the disk is one large free area. New files are all contiguous. But as files are deleted, they create "holes" in the disk space. As DOS is requested for new sectors, it responds by taking the first sector available. This can easily lead to a new file being spread out over several separate areas. Figure 13.2 shows a fragmented and an unfragmented file.

You can test this with the command **CHKDSK *.***. Here is a sample output from an earlier version of CHKDSK:

```
Volume IC-DISK  created March 17, 1993 9:00a
730112 bytes total disk space
23552 bytes in 3 hidden files
1024 bytes in 1 directories
207872 bytes in 40 user files
497664 bytes available on disk
655360 bytes total memory
363152 bytes free
C:\SETUP10.EXE
Contains 2 noncontiguous blocks.
```

Like most DOS utilities, CHKDSK only operates on a subdirectory at a time. To get fragmentation information about the whole disk, you'd need to run CHKDSK on each subdirectory: CHKDSK C:\DOS to look at the DOS subdirectory, for example. Microsoft attempted to solve this problem with DOS 3.x. DOS 3.x and later reduce the fragmentation problem but don't solve it entirely.

Programs exist that will rearrange the disk so that all files are contiguous and no holes exist. The best known is Disk Optimizer from SoftLogic Solutions. The latest version even allows you to specify the most used files so that they can be moved to the front of the directory, speeding access by a bit. Mace will also do this with its UnFragment option. Norton's Speed Disk program (now part of DOS 6.0 as the DEFRAG command) is another program in this genre.

If you use copy-protected software, like Lotus 1-2-3, talk to the vendor before trying this. Lotus's copy protection scheme will cause 1-2-3 to be destroyed if you optimize a disk with Lotus installed. If you run copy-protected software, uninstall it before optimizing; then reinstall it.

FIGURE 13.2

A fragmented and unfragmented file

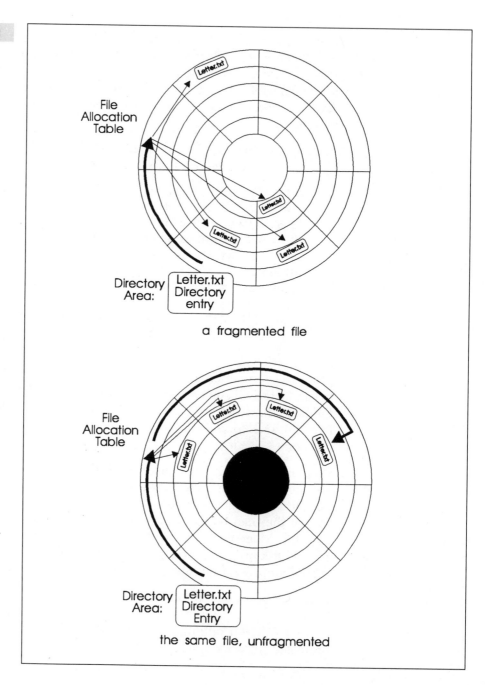

a fragmented file

the same file, unfragmented

Better yet, *remove* the copy protection. Lotus sells a Value Pack that includes two neat utilities and removes the protection from your copy of 1-2-3. Version 2.2 and 3.0 never had copy protection to begin with. I'm *not* advocating piracy, but I *am* advocating protecting your investment.

The Best Insurance: Good Backups

There are two kinds of hard disk users: the ones who have had a disk failure and lost data that wasn't backed up, and the ones who are *going* to. You seek to stay in the latter category as long as possible.

I can't stress this strongly enough: *At the first sign of unusual behavior, back up the entire disk.* Backup approaches fall into three categories:

- SBB—Software-based backup (only uses floppies)
- HBB—Hardware-based backup (tape drives and the like)
- PBB—Prayer-based backup (hope disaster will never happen)

Informal surveys indicate that about 20 percent of corporate users employ special hardware and the other 80 percent claim to use software-based schemes. Many of the 80 percent use a hybrid software/PBB system.

By the way, those of you who are smiling smugly because you use a tape or something to back up, have you ever tried to *restore* that data you've been saving? What's that you say—you trust that the people who sold you the tape drive wouldn't sell you buggy software? Heh, heh...

Software-Based Backup

These programs assist the user in transferring data onto floppies. Their main features are:

- Speed
- Maintaining indexes of backed-up data
- Use of the DOS archive bit
- Splitting large files over several floppies

- File compression
- Error-correcting data formats

Despite its difficulty and bugs, the DOS BACKUP program is probably the most-used software alternative. It isn't particularly fast, and it stores data in a nonstandard format, but it comes free with DOS. It will break up files that are too large to fit on a single floppy onto several floppies, and it manipulates the DOS archive bit. No compression or error correcting is used.

Fifth Generation Systems' Fastback product is well known and widely used. It's much faster than BACKUP and formats disks on the fly. It uses error correction but no compression, and stores data in a nonstandard fashion.

Similar programs are offered by other vendors, but here's another approach. Under DOS 3.2, a new command, XCOPY, appeared.

XCOPY has several features that recommend it for disk backup:

- It's faster than COPY.
- You can tell it to prompt you for file names.
- It operates on the archive bit.
- The resulting files are in DOS format.

The main drawback is that XCOPY isn't smart enough to break up large files over several disks. XCOPY is smart enough only to copy the files that have changed since the last backup, and to search subdirectories (with COPY, you must specify each subdirectory). It will also create subdirectories on the target disk. From the root directory, just issue the command

```
XCOPY C: A: /V/M/E/S
```

/E/S says look at all subdirectories, not just the current one, and create an identical subdirectory structure on the target disk. /M is the important option: It says, *Only copy the files that haven't been backed up and, once copied, mark the files as backed up.* (It uses the file's archive bit.) /V verifies the copy.

XCOPY will then fill up a floppy (it must be formatted first). Insert a new floppy and issue the command again. It won't try to recopy files it has already copied, as their archive bits are cleared. Continue until there's nothing left to copy. Then use BACKUP for the files that are too large to fit on one floppy.

No matter what system you use, inserting and removing floppies is a large pain. If backups are difficult, they won't get done. That's why hardware back-up solutions are superior and worth the money.

Hardware-Based Backup

There are several backup hardware options:

- Tape drives with special controllers
- Tapes based on the floppy controller
- Removable hard disks, like the Bernoulli Box
- LANs
- A second Winchester

Tape drives cost from $450 up. For an office of XTs, a good solution would be to get a portable tape drive that can plug into the back of the floppy disk controller (you wondered what that 37-pin port was good for, eh?). Then one $700 tape drive can be shared among many computers.

Bernoullis are reliable, fast devices that double as an extra hard drive (they are just as fast) and backup device. Because there are two drives, backing up a Bernoulli cartridge is simple. To use a Bernoulli to back up a hard disk, Iomega includes backup software, or you can use the XCOPY approach outlined above.

One writer has suggested that, as hard disk drives have become so inexpensive, it could be cheaper just to install a second hard disk and use it to back up the first.

Hard Disk Failure
Recovery

NOW that you're a hard disk expert and you've started covering your backside (magnetically speaking) with various automatic backup programs, you're beginning to feel virtuous.

But then disaster strikes....

Resurrecting a Dead Drive

What do you do, exactly, when you turn on your computer and the drive doesn't respond? In this section, I'll describe the steps your computer goes through to boot from the hard disk; I'll tell you where failures happen and what to do to try to resolve the problem.

I'll assume that we're talking about a drive that worked yesterday in the very same machine and the very same controller, and that you didn't drop it from the back of a truck or add any new boards between then and now. If you're having installation problems, look back at Chapter 12. (For more detailed information on hard drives, see *The Hard Disk Survival Guide*, also written by myself and published by SYBEX.)

Before we get started, prepare what I call a "toolkit" floppy (on both 5¼-inch and 3½-inch media, of course) to assist in troubleshooting. Remember, you're trying to fix a nonbooting drive, so the floppy should be bootable with whatever device drivers you need to get to your hard disk. It should also contain:

- FDISK
- FORMAT
- HDAT or some other low-level formatter, like Kolod's hFORMAT

- XFDISK from hTEST/hFORMAT
- DEBUG (in case it's needed to activate a low-level formatter)
- A head-parking program, preferably one that you can exit from without rebooting
- Mace Remedy or Norton DiskTest or Disk Doctor
- SETUP, if your computer is an AT or 386
- NU from the Norton Utilities version 4.5 or Disk Editor and UnErase from version 5.0 and on

By the way, that will all take up about 600K, so you'll obviously have to break it up over a couple of 360K disks, but 1.2-MB, 720K, and 1.44-MB disks can handle it with no problem.

The Hard Disk Boot Procedure (Overview)

Here's what the disk does on a normal day to get started:

1. The hardware must function and be configured properly.
2. The partition record is read.
3. The boot record is read.
4. The hidden files are loaded.
5. IBMBIO.COM or IO.SYS executes and reads CONFIG.SYS.
6. IBMDOS.COM or MSDOS.SYS executes.
7. The user shell (COMMAND.COM) loads.
8. The shell loads and executes AUTOEXEC.BAT.

The Hard Disk Boot Procedure (Details and Suggested Fixes)

Now we'll look at the eight steps in detail. On each step, I'll outline:

- What the disk is trying to do: details on the eight steps.
- Recognizing errors at each step: It's not an exact science, but I'll list common symptoms of problems *at each step*.
- Fixing problems at each step: I'll tell you what you can do to fix a problem once you know you have it.

Malfunctioning Hardware

The hardware and cables must be functioning.

Possible Symptoms of Problems The symptoms can include:

- Disk boot failure
- Not even attempting to boot from the hard disk
- The number 1701, 1780, 1781, 1790, or 1791, followed by the message *F1 to continue,* and finally BASIC popping up on your screen

What to Do Let's start from here, before the system even tries to boot. The drive won't talk to you if:

- The drive is too cold, or, less likely, too hot. Is it Monday morning? Did you just bring the drive in from the outside, if the computer is a laptop? Make sure the drive is warmed up to room temperature before you try to use it (this goes double if you're about to format it).

- Its cables have come loose, or have been reconnected incorrectly, or might just be bad. Do you have another set of cables? Give them a try.

- An AT, PS/2, or 386 has lost its SETUP info. If the battery has run down on your 286/386/486 computer, it may have forgotten that it has a hard disk or, worse, it may *misremember* what kind of hard disk it has. Run the SETUP program (or use the program CMOSER.EXE on your utility disk) to check to see that the computer remembers correctly what kind of hard disk it has.

- The drive has been physically damaged. This one is a toughie. Scratches on cylinder 0 (the location of the vital partition record, or Master Boot Record) can be fatal. Some drives fail only because the circuit board on the drive has failed; swap that and the problem could go away.

I've heard of a situation (although I haven't tried it yet) in which a head-stepper motor burned out a Miniscribe drive. Now, the stepper motor is inside the sealed area of most Winchester drives, so replacing it exposes the drive to dust—not a good idea. The repair person did not have the requisite "clean room" (such a room must be cleaner than a hospital operating room!) in which to open the drive, so he used a clear plastic bag. He put his tools in the bag before starting, put the drive and the stepper in the bag, opened it, and swapped steppers without taking the drive from the bag until the operation was over. It allowed him to get the data off the drive. I can think of several reasons why it might not have worked— the plastic bag might have created static that would have damaged the drive, some dust might have been in the bag, and so on—but it worked. Hey, what did he have to lose?

Reading the Partition Record

Assuming that SETUP, the cables, and so on are okay, the drive light will come on very briefly, just a "flash" during a normal boot when the computer is turned on. The controller is reading (at BIOS's insistence) the partition record or Master Boot Record (MBR). The MBR resides on head 0, cylinder 0, sector 1. (The rest of the sectors on that track are unused, by the way.) If this fails, the drive is ignored.

Possible Symptoms of Problems You may see some kind of message indicating that the drive doesn't exist, like *invalid drive specification* when you boot from the floppy and try to read drive C, or a message like *0 drives found* or *0 drives ready.* The PC might act like there's no hard disk there at all. If the hardware is okay but there's no partition record, you won't see any error messages on bootup—it just won't recognize the hard disk at all.

What to Do Find out what's going on with the partition record. Here are some alternatives.

Run FDISK. If it fails altogether, with a message like *There is no drive there,* recheck the hardware items in the previous step.

If FDISK loads okay, select the *display partition status* option. If it says you have a partition, check that the message makes sense: Are they DOS partitions? Do the cylinders range to a silly value, like up to cylinder 900 on a 500-cylinder drive? (You can check this by running FDISK on a machine with an identical drive.) If the partition is okay, move to the next step, checking the DOS boot record.

If you see the message *Non-DOS partition,* don't get trigger-happy with your tools. Since DOS is a pain about talking to disks bigger than 32 MB, a number of vendors have offered various software workarounds to allow large drives to work in a DOS environment. Some common ones are On-Track Disk Manager, SpeedStor, Golden Bow VFeature, and Priam EDISK. You can spot these easily: They have a small DOS partition to allow your system to boot, a large non-DOS partition of their own design, and a device driver to allow the system to use the alien non-DOS partition. I'll have more to say about this later, but for now, don't start repartitioning if you see a small DOS partition up front and a larger non-DOS partition following it.

If FDISK tells you *no partitions defined,* then something trashed the partition record. DO NOT use FDISK to create a new partition record, as FDISK unfortunately also gets a bit gung-ho and zaps the DOS boot record and some of the FAT when asked to create a new partition record. The game plan here is to get an MBR from a working machine, copy it to floppy, and then move the good MBR to the drive. The tools: GETSEC and PUTSEC, two programs that come with hTEST/hFORMAT (the Kolod Utilities, you'll recall). They allow you to grab a particular sector and move it to or from a floppy. Try it. Alternatively, Kolod's XFDISK does FDISK-like duty without the excess data destruction, confining itself exclusively to the MBR.

This might not work, *if the low-level format information has been destroyed.* Sometimes a power surge can cause the disk head to torpedo the sector IDs on a track, effectively deformatting it to a pristine state. Kolod XFDISK and FDISK can't read or write tracks with garbled sector IDs. Try low-level formatting *just* cylinder 0, head 0 with either HDAT on your utility disk or HFORMAT from hTEST/hFORMAT. Then the partition record ought to go on just fine.

If cylinder 0, head 0 has been deformatted on an autoconfigure controller (like the common XT-class WD1002 discussed earlier), you've got extra trouble. Recall that the autoconfigure controllers store a few very important drive identification bytes in an otherwise unused part of the MBR. If they can't find those bytes, they can't talk to the drive at all, just as if your AT-class machine had lost SETUP.

Some of these controllers have a jumper that converts them from *autoconfigure* to *extremely dumb*—that is, they think they're talking to a Seagate 225. Enable the Seagate 225 mode. You don't want to do it forever—just long enough to convince the controller to write out a new cylinder 0, head 0, sector 1. Recall that the autoconfigure information is placed at the start of the MBR, so you'll be fine (as far as the autoconfigure controller is concerned) once you've snatched an MBR off a working machine with a similar controller. Two birds, autoconfigure and the MBR, are killed with the single stone of restoring cylinder 0, track 0, sector 1.

There's a similar story for the RLL controllers that report that there are only 17 sectors on a track. They're lying—there are really 26 sectors on a track, but they don't want to confuse application software. So they translate *on the fly* requests for 17-sector data to requests for 26-sector data. For example, RLL controllers won't report that a Seagate ST238R is what it truly is, a 615-cylinder, 4-head, 26-sector per track disk. Instead, they insist that it's a 910-cylinder, 4-head, 17-sector per track disk. These controllers confuse low-level formatter programs. Again, there's usually a jumper to disable this translation feature. Deactivate the feature, and try just to work on the first cylinder or head.

If you're still having no luck, you might be unable to reformat the first cylinder. This happens sometimes, if the platter is scratched on that position. Now, you're in some trouble, since you can't move the MBR somewhere else; everything else is movable but that.

Here's a powerful trick that might help. *Warning: It may destroy a perfectly good drive.* This requires an already-working, formatted, identical drive, and your bad drive. We'll assume, hope, and pray that the only problem is in the boot section of your disk. The trick here is to get DOS to boot from the disk and recognize it.

You need to connect the good drive, boot from it, and then, with the power still on, park the good drive (using a park program that you can get out of without rebooting) and disconnect it. Then you connect the bad drive and see if DOS can talk to it. If it does, you should back everything up and throw the drive away.

Simple, I hear you cry, but does it work? You bet—I once tried it when all else failed, and I saved the data.

Reading the DOS Boot Record (DBR)

Assuming that the MBR problems are out of the way, the system next tries to load and execute a sector's worth of information called the DOS Boot Record, which I'll call the DBR.

Possible Symptoms of Problems You might see the message *Disk Boot Failure* or *Non System Disk Or Disk Error.* (At this point, some systems even have a bug in their system software that asks you to *Insert a new disk in drive C and press any key to continue.* Nice to know computer designers have a sense of humor.)

What to Do Reconstruct the DBR. It's a similar problem to reconstructing the MBR, with two differences, one minor and one major. The location of the DBR is cylinder 0, head *1*, sector 1. (That's the minor difference.) If the track has lost its sector ID information, however, you can't just zap the track and start over—the FAT uses sectors 2–17 of that track. (That's the major difference.)

If you end up having to reformat the entire cylinder 0/head 1 track, you're basically in the same position as someone who has had their hard disk formatted and is trying to unformat it. So turn to the section on unformatting hard disks later in this chapter.

An excellent first tool to try for reconstructing DBRs is Norton's Disk Doctor version 4.5 or later. Among other things, it rebuilds the DBR if it finds it corrupt.

Loading the Hidden Files

Next, two files that are the heart of the operating system are loaded into memory. The two files might have become corrupt (either from a software or hardware problem), or DOS just might not be able to find them because the FAT has been damaged.

Possible Symptoms of Problems There may be a boot-failure type message, or the system may lock up partway through booting.

What to Do Your best bet is just to reload the hidden files, just to be safe. Ordinarily, you should be able just to boot from a floppy and type SYS C: to retransfer the system files to the hard disk. (SYS, for those who don't sleep with their DOS manuals, is a DOS command that attempts to install the operating system's two hidden files to the hard disk.) If that does the trick, terrific. If not, read on.

Background on Hidden Files

The two "hidden" files are the heart of the PC-DOS or MS-DOS operating system. PC-DOS and Compaq DOS name the files IBMBIO.COM and IBMDOS.COM, even though they're not really .COM files. MS-DOS generally names the files IO.SYS and MSDOS.SYS. DOS 5.0 only requires that the hidden files be somewhere in the root directory, not in a particular cluster or directory entry. However, under DOS 3.x and 4.x, these files *must* be in a particular place in order for the system to find them and boot. SYS requires that several conditions be met, or it will refuse to run, claiming there's *insufficient space on destination disk*.

The three basic rules under DOS 3.*x* and 4.*x* for SYS to work are:

- IBMBIO.COM or IO.SYS must be the *first* file in the root directory of the boot disk.
- IBMBIO.COM or IO.SYS must have its starting cluster as cluster number 2. (By the way, the file need not be contiguous afterward.)
- IBMDOS.COM or MSDOS.SYS must be in the second directory entry in the root directory of the boot disk.

So you try the SYS command, but it fails. What to do? Here's a sure-fire method to bend SYS to your will.

Convincing the SYS Command to Work to Restore Your Hidden Files

Here are some more specifics on SYS's three rules. Again, you must force these conditions to be true on your disk:

- The first two directory entries must be empty—not merely available, as when a file is erased; these entries must be clean as a whistle. (You see, when a file is erased, its directory entry isn't zapped completely. In fact, only the first byte is changed. That's a good thing, as we'll see later, because it helps us recover erased files.)

If there are files currently in the first two entries, copy them elsewhere and erase the files. Remember there are also oddball things that are classified as files: subdirectories and the volume label. Then clean out the first two directory entries by using the Norton Utilities' Disk Editor program. Recall from the disk introduction section that each directory entry has 32 bytes that describe the file's name, size, starting cluster, and the like. *Clean* means there's nothing but binary 0s there. Now, NU will only let you directly punch 0s into the directory in a second editing mode, the hex (hexadecimal) edit mode. Type **NU c:**, and choose **E** for Explore Disk and then **E** for Edit/Display. You'll see the root directory. Press F2 to switch the display to a hex format. Then enter 128 0s—you're filling two 32-byte directory entries with hex 0s.

- Of course, there must be sufficient disk space for the hidden files.

- Cluster 2 must be available for IBMBIO.COM or IO.SYS. If that's currently taken by file *x*, you can free it up by copying file *x* to another file and then erasing file *x*.

Example: Let's force my drive E (a Bernoulli cartridge) to take a SYS. I start off by trying the command SYS E: and am rebuffed. So I take a look with Norton at the E drive. Displaying the root directory as in Figure 14.1, I see the problem.

The first two directory entries are taken. The first entry is the volume label PUBLISHING. (I know that because it has the *Vol* attribute on the right-hand edge of the screen.) That's easy enough to get rid of with the DOS Label command. The second is a subdirectory, WORD. Note that the WORD subdirectory is also using the all-important cluster number 2. WORD can be eliminated easily by creating a subdirectory called WORD2, copying everything over to WORD2, and then just erasing everything in WORD. Finally, enter RD WORD. Now reinvoke Norton (see Figure 14.2). Flip over to the hex display with F2 and you'll see a screen similar to Figure 14.3.

FIGURE 14.1

Norton Utilities display of the root directory of E before SYS fix

```
   Object   Edit   Link   View   Info   Tools   Quit              F1=Help
   Name    .Ext   Size      Date      Time    Cluster Arc R/O Sys Hid Dir Vol
 Sector 83                                                                ↑
   PUBLISHI NG        0    2-22-91    6:35 pm      0    Arc              Vol ▐
   WORD              0    2-22-91    6:35 pm      2                 Dir
   MW                0    2-22-91    6:35 pm      3                 Dir
   σPRINT            0    2-22-91    6:35 pm      4                 Dir
   PE                0    2-22-91    6:35 pm      5                 Dir
   σEPORT          304    2-22-91    6:35 pm      6    Arc
   WIN286            0    2-22-91    6:35 pm      7                 Dir
   DESIGNER          0    2-22-91    6:35 pm      8                 Dir
   CADD              0    2-22-91    6:36 pm      9                 Dir
   WIN386            0    2-22-91    6:36 pm     10                 Dir
   σASRULER DRW    509    2-22-91    6:36 pm     11    Arc
            Unused directory entry
            Unused directory entry
            Unused directory entry
            Unused directory entry
            Unused directory entry
 Sector 84
            Unused directory entry
            Unused directory entry                                       ↓
 ┌─────────────────────────────────────────────────────────────────────────┐
 │ Root Directory                                              Sector 83  ◄ │
 │ G:\                                                    Offset 0, hex 0  ◄ │
 │ Press ALT or F10 to select menus                     │ Disk Editor       │
 └─────────────────────────────────────────────────────────────────────────┘
       Norton Utilities display of the root directory of E: before SYS fix
```

FIGURE 14.2

Norton Utilities
display after erasing
first two entries

```
    Object    Edit    Link    View    Info    Tools    Quit                F1=Help
  Name    .Ext    Size      Date     Time      Cluster Arc R/O Sys Hid Dir Vol
  Sector 83                                                                       ↑
  σUBLISHI NG        0    2-22-91   6:35 PM        0    Arc                    Vol ▓
  σORD               0    2-22-91   6:35 PM        2                     Dir
  MW                 0    2-22-91   6:35 PM        3                     Dir
  σPRINT             0    2-22-91   6:35 PM        4                     Dir
  PE                 0    2-22-91   6:35 PM        5                     Dir
  σEPORT           304    2-22-91   6:35 PM        6    Arc
  WIN286             0    2-22-91   6:35 PM        7                     Dir
  DESIGNER           0    2-22-91   6:35 PM        8                     Dir
  CADD               0    2-22-91   6:36 PM        9                     Dir
  WIN386             0    2-22-91   6:36 PM       10                     Dir
  σASRULER DRW     509    2-22-91   6:36 PM       11    Arc
               Unused directory entry
               Unused directory entry
               Unused directory entry
               Unused directory entry
               Unused directory entry
  Sector 84
               Unused directory entry
               Unused directory entry                                             ↓
  Root Directory                                               Sector 83
  G:\                                                          Offset 0, hex 0
  Press ALT or F10 to select menus                            Disk Editor

            Norton Utilities display after erasing first two entries
```

FIGURE 14.3

Norton hex display
before cleaning
directory entries

```
    Object   Edit    Link    View    Info    Tools    Quit              F1=Help
  Sector 83                                                                       ↑
  00000000:  E5 55 42 4C 49 53 48 49 - 4E 47 20 28 00 00 00 00   σUBLISHING (.... ▓
  00000010:  00 00 00 00 00 00 61 94 - 56 16 00 00 00 00 00 00   ......aöV......
  00000020:  E5 4F 52 44 20 20 20 20 - 20 20 20 10 00 00 00 00   σORD       ►....
  00000030:  00 00 00 00 00 00 6E 94 - 56 16 02 00 00 00 00 00   ......nöV_▓....
  00000040:  4D 57 20 20 20 20 20 20 - 20 20 20 10 00 00 00 00   MW         ►....
  00000050:  00 00 00 00 00 00 70 94 - 56 16 03 00 00 00 00 00   ......pöV_♥....
  00000060:  E5 50 52 49 4E 54 20 20 - 20 20 20 10 00 00 00 00   σPRINT     ►....
  00000070:  00 00 00 00 00 00 73 94 - 56 16 04 00 00 00 00 00   ......söV_♦....
  00000080:  50 45 20 20 20 20 20 20 - 20 20 20 10 00 00 00 00   PE         ►....
  00000090:  00 00 00 00 00 00 74 94 - 56 16 05 00 00 00 00 00   ......töV_♣....
  000000A0:  E5 45 50 4F 52 54 20 20 - 20 20 20 20 00 00 00 00   σEPORT       ....
  000000B0:  00 00 00 00 00 00 79 94 - 56 16 06 00 30 01 00 00   ......yöV_♠.0▯..
  000000C0:  57 49 4E 32 38 36 20 20 - 20 20 20 10 00 00 00 00   WIN286     ►....
  000000D0:  00 00 00 00 00 00 7B 94 - 56 16 07 00 00 00 00 00   ......{öV_•....
  000000E0:  44 45 53 49 47 4E 45 52 - 20 20 20 10 00 00 00 00   DESIGNER   ►....
  000000F0:  00 00 00 00 00 00 7D 94 - 56 16 08 00 00 00 00 00   ......}öV_▯....
  00000100:  43 41 44 44 20 20 20 20 - 20 20 20 10 00 00 00 00   CADD       ►....
  00000110:  00 00 00 00 00 00 81 94 - 56 16 09 00 00 00 00 00   ......üöV_°....
  00000120:  57 49 4E 33 38 36 20 20 - 20 20 20 10 00 00 00 00   WIN386     ►....
  00000130:  00 00 00 00 00 00 83 94 - 56 16 0A 00 00 00 00 00   ......âöV_▓....  ↓
  Root Directory                                               Sector 83
  G:\                                                          Offset 0, hex 0
  Press ALT or F10 to select menus                            Disk Editor

            Norton hex display before cleaning directory entries
```

Notice that we're looking at the same information as before (the root directory); we're just looking at it in a different way. Ensure that the cursor is at the start of the E5 in the upper left-hand corner, then just lean on the 0 key until the first 64 bytes are 0s (each byte is represented by two hex digits, so you must enter 128 zeros). The screen then looks like Figure 14.4. Now flip back to the Directory format with the F4 key, and you'll have good news—the two entries (Figure 14.5) show up as never-used. SYS E: now works like a charm. Again, none of this is necessary under DOS 5.0.

Starting the Boot Process

The drive begins the boot process by loading and executing the first hidden file, which in turn loads and executes CONFIG.SYS commands.

Possible Symptoms of Problems You may encounter CONFIG.SYS error messages or the inability to talk to nonstandard devices like On-Track Disk Manager partitions, Bernoulli Boxes, tape drives, and so on.

FIGURE 14.4

Norton hex display after cleaning directory entries

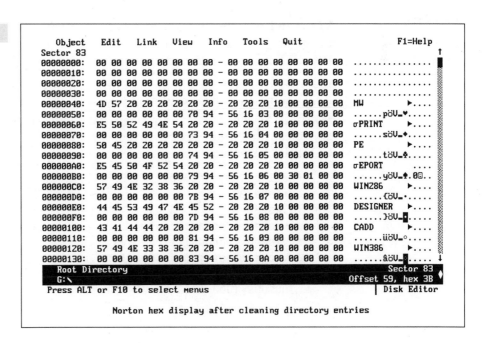

```
       Object   Edit   Link   View   Info   Tools   Quit                F1=Help
       Sector 83                                                               ↑
       00000000:  00 00 00 00 00 00 00 00 - 00 00 00 00 00 00 00 00   ................
       00000010:  00 00 00 00 00 00 00 00 - 00 00 00 00 00 00 00 00   ................
       00000020:  00 00 00 00 00 00 00 00 - 00 00 00 00 00 00 00 00   ................
       00000030:  00 00 00 00 00 00 00 00 - 00 00 00 00 00 00 00 00   ................
       00000040:  4D 57 20 20 20 20 20 20 - 20 20 20 10 00 00 00 00   MW         ►....
       00000050:  00 00 00 00 00 00 70 94 - 56 16 03 00 00 00 00 00   ......pöU_♥....
       00000060:  E5 50 52 49 4E 54 20 20 - 20 20 20 10 00 00 00 00   σPRINT     ►....
       00000070:  00 00 00 00 00 00 73 94 - 56 16 04 00 00 00 00 00   ......söU_♦....
       00000080:  50 45 20 20 20 20 20 20 - 20 20 20 10 00 00 00 00   PE         ►....
       00000090:  00 00 00 00 00 00 74 94 - 56 16 05 00 00 00 00 00   ......töU_♣....
       000000A0:  E5 45 50 4F 52 54 20 20 - 20 20 20 00 00 00 00 00   σEPORT      ....
       000000B0:  00 00 00 00 00 00 79 94 - 56 16 06 00 30 01 00 00   ......yöU_♠.0◙..
       000000C0:  57 49 4E 32 38 36 20 20 - 20 20 20 10 00 00 00 00   WIN286     ►....
       000000D0:  00 00 00 00 00 00 7B 94 - 56 16 07 00 00 00 00 00   ......{öU_•....
       000000E0:  44 45 53 49 47 4E 45 52 - 20 20 20 10 00 00 00 00   DESIGNER   ►....
       000000F0:  00 00 00 00 00 00 7D 94 - 56 16 08 00 00 00 00 00   ......}öU_█.....
       00000100:  43 41 44 44 20 20 20 20 - 20 20 20 10 00 00 00 00   CADD       ►....
       00000110:  00 00 00 00 00 00 81 94 - 56 16 09 00 00 00 00 00   ......üöU_°....
       00000120:  57 49 4E 33 38 36 20 20 - 20 20 20 10 00 00 00 00   WIN386     ►....
       00000130:  00 00 00 00 00 00 83 94 - 56 16 0A 00 00 00 00 00   ......âöU_█.....↓
       Root Directory                                               Sector 83  ◆
       G:\                                                      Offset 59, hex 3B
       Press ALT or F10 to select menus                        │  Disk Editor

                       Norton hex display after cleaning directory entries
```

```
    Object  Edit  Link    View   Info   Tools    Quit                    F1=Help
   Name    .Ext  Size     Date    Time          Cluster Arc R/O Sys Hid Dir Vol
   Sector 83                                                                      ↑
    Unused directory entry                                                        ▓
    Unused directory entry                                                        ▓
   MW               0    2-22-91   6:35 PM       3                       Dir      ▓
   σPRINT           0    2-22-91   6:35 PM       4                       Dir      ▓
   PE               0    2-22-91   6:35 PM       5                       Dir      ▓
   σEPORT         304    2-22-91   6:35 PM       6   Arc                          ▓
   WIN286           0    2-22-91   6:35 PM       7                       Dir      ▓
   DESIGNER         0    2-22-91   6:35 PM       8                       Dir      ▓
   CADD             0    2-22-91   6:36 PM       9                       Dir      ▓
   WIN386           0    2-22-91   6:36 PM      10                       Dir      ▓
   σASRULER DRW   509    2-22-91   6:36 PM      11   Arc                          ▓
              Unused directory entry                                             ▓
              Unused directory entry                                             ▓
              Unused directory entry                                             ▓
              Unused directory entry                                             ▓
              Unused directory entry                                             ▓
   Sector 84                                                                     ▓
                 Unused directory entry                                          ▓
                 Unused directory entry                                          ↓
  ┌─────────────────────────────────────────────────────────────────────────┐
  │ Root Directory                                                  Sector 83 ◆
  │ G:\                                                       Offset 32, hex 20 ◆
  │ Press ALT or F10 to select menus                             │ Disk Editor
  └─────────────────────────────────────────────────────────────────────────┘

        Norton directory display after cleaning directory entries
```

What to Do Basically, this part fails if your CONFIG.SYS has gotten the boot process trashed or if one of the programs called by CONFIG.SYS has gotten trashed.

It's fairly easy to check out the first problem. Just boot from a floppy, then examine the CONFIG.SYS file of the boot drive. If it looks strange, just rewrite it. *Strange* doesn't only mean that it looks hieroglyphic; strange can also mean that your device drivers are missing. Take, for instance, my CONFIG.SYS file:

```
shell=c:\command.com /P /E:512 c:\
buffers=20
files=32
device=d:\dos\ansi.sys
device=d:\bernoulli\rcd.sys
device=d:\dos\driver.sys /d:1
DEVICE=D:\XDOS\386MAX.SYS
  INCLUDE=1000-A000 FRAME=E000
```

The first four lines are pretty basic CONFIG.SYS, but the last four (the last two lines represent one line) look a bit bizarre. Why are they there?

RCD.SYS makes my Bernoulli Boxes work. If my CONFIG.SYS somehow loses the line that says to use RCD.SYS, my Bernoullis are useless.

The next line, loading DRIVER.SYS, makes my 5¼-inch drive work like a real 720K drive. Without it, it reads and writes 720s okay, *but formats 720K disks as only 360K!* This could be a very subtle bug. Imagine: Your 720K disk drive stops formatting properly, but reads and writes okay. Would you think of CONFIG.SYS first?

The last line invokes a program called *386 To The Max,* a program that does a few tricks to squeeze the most out of my 386-based computer. For one thing, it allows me to load my TSR programs out of the 640K DOS workspace. If I forget this device driver, strange things happen later when I try to load programs into the area outside of the 640K.

But my CONFIG.SYS is tame compared to those of some of my clients. Several, for example, use a device driver that I hate called *OnTrack Disk Manager.* The file name of this device driver is DMDRVR.BIN.

OnTrack Disk Manager is a device driver intended to allow DOS 3.*x* users to get around the 32-MB disk–size barrier. Under PC-DOS 3.2 and earlier, you could only use a 32-MB or smaller disk. Put an 80-MB disk on a PC-DOS 3.2 machine and you'd get a 32-MB disk with 48-MB of wasted space.

OnTrack's idea, then, was to write a device driver that would allow DOS to talk to a new kind of device—a disk that could be hundreds of megabytes in size. So you create two partitions on your 80-MB drive: a small (1-MB or so) bootable DOS partition (drive C) that's mainly used to store the boot programs, and a second, non-DOS partition (drive D, 79 MB or whatever's left) that's only accessible once the DMDRVR.BIN has been loaded.

Let me repeat: That second partition is an alien partition. Norton, Mace, PC Tools, and the gang have no idea how to handle this partition unless the device driver has been loaded.

Summarizing, the new potential problems that arise from using a non-DOS partition and a device driver to access your disk are the following:

- If the DEVICE=DMDRVR.BIN statement is lost from the CONFIG.SYS, your users won't be able to figure out why their D drive has disappeared.

- If something goes wrong in the partition, you won't have the panoply of recovery tools available that you'd have in a DOS partition.

- The device driver is another piece of software between your disk and DOS, just one more thing to go wrong on your disk. I'm not saying OnTrack is buggy, but why would anyone want to introduce a new potential source of bugs?

OnTrack isn't the only company that does this. My 60-MB Priam, for example, shipped with a device driver called EDISK.SYS already on it, again to allow me to get around the DOS 32-MB barrier. (I immediately reformatted the drive and got rid of the driver.) A program called SPEEDSTOR was pretty popular for a while in the same genre. Disk Manager is the program you tend to run into more often because Seagate has been giving it away free with their drives. Let me say it again: If you have the choice, avoid device drivers that change the way DOS talks to your hard disk.

Don't get me wrong. OnTrack makes some great stuff; it's just that I hate using device drivers to talk to a hard disk. Hard disks have enough potential problems without creating opportunities for new ones.

What's the alternative to these device drivers? PC-DOS 3.3 or Compaq DOS 3.2. FDISK under DOS 3.3 gets around the 32-MB problem by allowing you to divide the disk into two partitions, a *DOS partition* and an *Extended DOS partition*. The DOS partition can't be larger than 32 MB, but the Extended DOS partition can be any size. You create the DOS partition, and FDISK calls it drive C and makes it bootable. Then you allocate the remainder of the disk to the Extended DOS partition, even if it's larger than 32 MB. FDISK then breaks this Extended DOS partition up into logical drives, which can then be formatted. For example, my 80-MB drive divides into a C drive of 32 MB (the DOS partition), a D drive of

32 MB (part of the Extended DOS partition), and an E drive of 16 MB (the remainder of the Extended DOS partition).

Some of you are out there asking, "Doesn't he know about DOS 5.0, which can format drives up to 512 MB?" Yes, and I highly recommend it. This other advice is for those who, for some reason, have not upgraded.

Another potential device driver problem is the simple one of file corruption. You might have a perfectly bug-free device driver, but if for some reason the file that contains the device driver is corrupted, the system can crash when loading the driver. Try reloading your device drivers from a floppy disk.

Loading the User Shell COMMAND.COM

A corrupted or out-of-date copy of COMMAND.COM can keep the system from booting. One way to avoid users accidentally overwriting COMMAND.COM is to make COMMAND.COM read-only with the DOS ATTRIB command (only in 3.3 and later versions):

```
ATTRIB +R C:\COMMAND COM
```

Possible Symptoms of Problems   The system may crash or, more likely, you may see the message *Bad or Missing Command Interpreter* followed by a system freeze.

What to Do   Boot from a floppy and COMP (a DOS file comparison command) the COMMAND.COM on the floppy to the one on the hard disk. You might find that a user has copied a pile of files to the hard disk, not realizing a COMMAND.COM from an old version of DOS was also copied over the COMMAND.COM on the hard disk's root directory.

A less likely alternative (but one that has happened to me) is that a spontaneous bad sector has arisen in the middle of COMMAND.COM. Just use Norton's DiskTest or DOS's RECOVER COMMAND.COM to locate and lock out the new bad sectors. Then recopy COMMAND.COM from the floppy drive.

Executing AUTOEXEC.BAT

COMMAND.COM executes the commands in AUTOEXEC.BAT. Any bugs in the programs called by AUTOEXEC.BAT will, of course, hang the system.

Possible Symptoms of Problems Symptoms are application-specific. The big question is, did the system do okay *until* AUTOEXEC.BAT started executing?

What to Do Rename AUTOEXEC.BAT to AUTOEXEC.BUG or something like that so it isn't found by COMMAND.COM, and reboot. If the system boots okay, you've got a problem in one of the commands in AUTOEXEC.BAT. It's probably a TSR that's conflicting with another program. As usual, try rearranging the order of the TSRs. Remove one command at a time until the problem goes away, then zero in on the program that caused the crash. Does it run all right by itself? Does it only not run on a particular XYZ Turbo 8800 clone?

The above are the procedures I use to bring a dead drive back to life. It can't solve every problem, but this will resolve 99 percent of your hard disk problems. But if you're *still* stuck....

Data Recovery Services

Still can't get your drive to talk to you? Hey, look, even Dr. Kildare lost a few patients. If you *really* need that data, there's a last hope. It isn't cheap—from $1,000 to $20,000—but you can send it to a service. They disassemble the disk, remove the data, and then send it to you on floppies. OnTrack, the same people who wrote Disk Manager and other utilities, offer the service. They charge $200 to diagnose the problem, and then you negotiate over the recovery cost. It's expensive, yes, but (if you own a company) it's cheaper than going out of business. See Appendix A for their address.

Miscellaneous Drive Problems

Here's a potpourri of "unclassifiable" errors.

Track 0 Bad or Unusable Error

Sometimes a disk won't accept a DOS format, and FORMAT complains that track 0 is bad, rendering the whole disk unusable. If this happens, you probably cannot save your data.

To save the disk, try one of the following remedies.

- Try a low-level format. That solves many of these problems.

- Prepare a diskette with the system on it, and ensure that the CONFIG.SYS file on the diskette contains this line:

```
FILES=99
```

If there's another line with FILES= and some number, delete it. Then reboot and try DOS FORMAT again. DOS is now a lot less picky about what it will and won't format. I don't know why this "trapdoor" is there, but it is. It only exists in DOS 3.1, 3.2, and 3.3, as far as I know. Once the drive is formatted, you can return to the old FILES= value.

Damaged Boot Record

To boot from a floppy disk, early versions of DOS put some computer code onto the first sector of the disk. The ROM in the PC knew just enough on powerup to load that sector and execute the code found within. This sector was called the *boot record*. This sector is, you'll recall, 512 bytes long, like all sectors.

IBM uses the boot record (previously only for bootstrap code) to contain DOS version and disk-type information. The twenty-first byte is important, as it's the *Media Descriptor*. Table 14.1 lists these descriptors. Another boot record item is *number of sectors on disk*. Two bytes are allocated for this. The biggest number you can represent with two bytes is $2^{16}-1$ or 65,535. As sector sizes are 512 bytes, this leads to the current maximum volume size under PC DOS 3.X of 65,535 sectors $\times$ 512 bytes/sector= 32,767K, or 32 MB.

TABLE 14.1: FAT Media Descriptor Byte Values

CODE	DESCRIPTION
FF	8-sector DS floppy (320K)
FE	8-sector SS floppy (160K)
FD	9-sector DS floppy (360K)
FC	9-sector SS floppy (180K)
F9	1.2-MB floppy and 3½-inch floppies
F8	Hard disk

If your boot record is damaged, you'll be completely unable to read the disk, even if you don't need to boot from it. You can reconstruct and repair a boot sector with the help of a special utility like Mace. The Restore Boot Sector command in Mace will either use a backup boot sector (which you must allow Mace to create before the problem exists) or copy a boot sector from an identical disk.

Norton Disk Doctor can rebuild a boot record, but sometimes NDD gets a little rambunctious and fixes a little *more* of the disk than you intended. You can, however, construct a boot record in DEBUG and write over the damaged boot record. Here's one simple way:

1. Read a good boot sector from a similar drive into memory with DEBUG.

2. Then, write the boot sector in the memory to the troubled disk.

How to Fix a Damaged Floppy Boot Record

Fixing a damaged floppy boot record is simplicity itself. Find a formatted disk so you can steal a good boot sector from it.

1. Insert the good disk of the same size, density, and so on as the disk with the bad boot record in drive A.

2. Load DEBUG. It's on the DOS Supplemental Programs diskette, and should be in your DOS subdirectory.

3. Instruct DEBUG to load the boot record off the good disk: Type **L0001**.

4. Remove the good disk from drive A and insert the disk with the bad boot record.

5. Tell DEBUG to overwrite the bad boot record with the good one: Type **W0001**.

6. Quit DEBUG.

Warning: Don't mix boot sectors! Don't try to patch a boot sector on a hard disk with one from a floppy. It won't work.

Tip for PC DOS 3.2

A final point on the boot record: The fourth through the eleventh bytes contain a string with the manufacturer ID (called the *OEM name and version*), like *IBM 3.2* on a PC-DOS 3.2 formatted diskette. This was fairly irrelevant until PC-DOS 3.2. As of 3.2, however, the boot record information became absolutely essential. One of the things in the boot record is the location of the FAT. If you have a disk written under a version of DOS that doesn't bother with the location of the FAT, DOS 3.2 could become confused and try to read a FAT where one doesn't exist. You'll get a *sector not found error* type of message. This only occurs under PC-DOS 3.2 and later as far as I know. This can be remedied fairly easily. Just format a blank floppy under DOS 3.2, and then do the above procedure. Use DEBUG to copy the 3.2 boot record off the blank disk to the other disk.

This problem doesn't always occur, but if it does, try this. Better yet, try it on a *copy* of the disk.

Damaged FAT and CHKDSK Errors

The next area is the FAT, the File Allocation Table. As you've seen, it causes its own share of problems. You've seen that it's a linked list of clusters, one FAT entry for each cluster. There are two kinds of FATs: 12-bit and 16-bit. A 12-bit FAT can keep track of $2^{12}-1$, or 4095 clusters. It's used for floppy disks and 10-MB hard disks. A 16-bit FAT can keep track of $2^{16}-1$, or 65,535 clusters.

Most disk formats keep a second copy of the FAT. I guess it was originally included for fault tolerance or redundancy, but versions of DOS before 3.2 don't use it. If your FAT is damaged, you can copy the secondary FAT back to the primary position with DEBUG, or Mace will do it more simply. Unerasing programs manipulate the FAT.

The FAT causes all of those cryptic CHKDSK woes. You see, CHKDSK doesn't check the disk, it checks the FAT.

Recall how space allocation is managed under DOS with the directory and FAT. A normal file could, for example, have a first cluster of 100; the FAT entry for 100 could be 101, 101 could point to 102, and 102 could contain EOF. That would mean that the file resides in 100, 101, and 102. Potential problems in FAT chains, then, are

- A chain ending with a 0 (invalid cluster, file truncated)
- A chain ending with a bad sector (invalid cluster)
- A chain being extended inadvertently (allocation error)
- A chain without a beginning directory link (lost clusters)
- A chain that cannot match its directory size information; it is either much too small or much too large (allocation error)
- Two or more intersecting chains (cross-linked clusters)
- Damaged subdirectory file (invalid subdirectory)

Another consideration is file size. When a file is created, the creating program tells DOS how big the file is, or rather it gives DOS some clues. Text editors commonly suffix their files with a Ctrl-Z. DOS sees this and then computes file size, which goes in the directory. Even though DOS retains file size in the directory, recall that it actually must allocate space in terms of clusters. Taking hard disks as an example, a cluster on a 20-MB hard disk is 2048 bytes long. If I create a file of a single byte, it still takes up 2048 bytes.

It's important that I stress here: *CHKDSK errors usually don't point to hardware errors.* They either indicate bad software or operators. Let's examine a few of the most popular messages briefly.

Lost Clusters

Sometimes CHKDSK reports *lost clusters*. This basically means loss of the pointer from the directory to the FAT. This pointer is often the *last thing written when the file is created.* This means a program that died in the middle of manipulating the FAT could have created some FAT chains but not yet written the pointer from the directory to the FAT. Another cause of this is operators who realize they've made a mistake, and so turn off the machine in the hopes of saving themselves. If they do this while a file is being written, there will definitely be lost clusters. The problem is often caused by mixing DOS 3.*x* and 2.*x*, or application program bugs such as those found in dBASE and MultiMate.

Remedy: Do a DIR, and print it out. Run CHKDSK/F. New pointers will be created and the lost chains will be given variations of the filename FILE*nnnn*.CHK, where *nnnn* is a four-digit number. Data *might* be recoverable; dBASE or 1-2-3 files may not be recoverable.

Cross-Linked Clusters

Another CHKDSK complaint is *cross-linked clusters.* It refers to multiple pointers into the same cluster. It means that more than one file thinks it owns a disk area: Cluster 14, for example, reportedly might be owned by more than one file.

Remedy: Copy all affected files, then erase the affected files. The copied files will have as much data as can be recovered. In all probability, some data has been lost.

Invalid Subdirectory

A subdirectory's information is contained in a file. If this file is damaged, DOS doesn't know how to get to the files in the subdirectory. CHKDSK reports an *invalid subdirectory* error. *Don't execute CHKDSK/F until you first print out the directory listing of the subdirectory!* The reason: CHKDSK just eliminates the subdirectory information—it isn't too smart about recovering subdirectory information.

Now CHKDSK sees a whole lot of FAT chains without directory entries, as their directory is gone. It then converts these to FILE*nnnn*.CHK files. Your problem is to match up the .CHK files with the former subdirectory contents. Your hints are the order and size of the files. The sizes might not match exactly, as CHKDSK just reports the entire cluster size. The directory, with more specific file size information, is gone, so the best CHKDSK can do is just to add up the number of bytes in the clusters and report that as the file size.

For example, imagine you have these files in an invalid subdirectory:

ORDERS.TXT	2010 bytes
NAMES.DBF	3000 bytes

Let's say this is a hard disk, with 2048 byte sectors. After CHKDSK mauls the subdirectory, you find you have two new .CHK files:

FILE0000.CHK	2048 bytes
FILE0001.CHK	4096 bytes

Notice that the file sizes have been rounded up to the nearest 2048-byte multiple. To finish the recovery job, first rename the files. Second, use Norton Utilities to revise the directory file size. *This is important,* as Lotus will refuse to read a file that has been completely recovered but has the wrong directory file size.

Recovering from and Avoiding Sector Not Found

Found during any DOS operation, fading or loss of a sector ID causes a *Sector Not Found* error.

Remedy: Keep it from happening by doing low-level formats regularly. (But remember that you can't low-level format IDE drives.) As you've seen, programs exist that will do this *without disturbing the data.* If it occurs anyway, see the next section.

Recovering Data Lost Because of Disk Media Failure

As you know if you've ever formatted a floppy disk, not all sectors are created equal. Sectors that started out reliable can suddenly go south for the winter, taking important data with them. There are some things that can be done in this case, however. You're not helpless.

The initial formatting process tests for bad sectors and ensures that DOS doesn't try to use them. The FAT is where DOS keeps track of bad sectors. If the initial FORMAT locates bad sectors, it will inform the FAT. The FAT entry for the cluster where that sector resides would then indicate that this is a "don't-use" cluster.

What about newly created bad sectors, like ones that appear when the disk "crash lands" on your surface too many times? These spontaneous bad sectors must be reported to the FAT.

There are two parts to this problem. The first one is that the sector probably contained data you need; you'd like to recover this data. The second is that the sector must be reported to the FAT.

First, recovering the file: You can use a utility to do this, but I prefer to do it by hand, as some of it's just luck. First, COPY the file. In the process, you'll probably get a message like one of the following:

```
Sector not found reading drive X
Data error reading drive X
General failure reading drive X
```

That's followed by the question *Abort, Retry, Fail?*

The data is probably not *dead,* but rather the magnetic field is weakened. (As Monty Python would say, "It's not dead—it's just *resting.*") Retry it to see if the problem can be resolved. Retry several times. When it's obvious that you're not getting anywhere, use Fail. Here's what Fail does: The sector is probably not completely garbaged. Only one byte out of the 512 may be damaged. Fail tells it to copy it, warts and all. In some cases, this may mean an innocuous error. In other cases, it may mean that the data is irretrievably lost.

Now you've recovered as much of the data as possible. If it has errors and you want to sew the data back together, and you're stout of heart and long of patience, you can load up DEBUG and try patching the data. For example, one bad byte in the wrong place can render a dBASE or Lotus file useless. You can get a book that describes file formats for the big programs, and use it to try to repair data. The name of the book is *File Formats for Popular PC Software,* written by Jeff Walden, published by John Wiley. I stress that this book doesn't tell you how to fix files, but just tells you what undamaged ones look like. It's no simple task to rebuild files, but it can be done sometimes with patience and time.

Now update the FAT. There are several programs that do this. The DOS program RECOVER is one. RECOVER doesn't do the above-mentioned retries and fails; it just assembles whatever doesn't give it trouble, collects it into a file with a name like FILE0001.REC, and marks the bad sectors on the FAT. The .REC file is of no use to you; just erase it (it's in the root directory, by the way).

Another approach is to use the Norton Utilities' Disk Doctor program or the Mace Utilities' Remedy program. These are better programs, as they'll scan an entire disk for you, but they don't do the retry/fail work—you've still got to do that yourself. Mace has a command, DIAGNOSE, that will alert you to bad sector without trying to update the FAT and kill the sectors. Norton will do the same with Disk Doctor. Disk Doctor can also be invoked for a single file with bad sectors.

This bears repeating: As soon as your hard disk starts showing spontaneous new bad sectors, back up the whole disk *now* and run a reformatter program.

Backing Up and Restoring Your MBR

The Master Boot Record (MBR) never changes for most systems, but it's an item of maximum importance. Without it, the system cannot boot. The best protection is a backup. Here are three ways to do it.

NOTE In the examples below, I'll use underscores (_) to indicate spaces in the commands you type in.

DOS 5.0 The easiest method, if you've got DOS 5.0, is to use the MIRROR.COM program. Back up your MBR with these steps.

1. Type MIRROR /PARTN and press ↵.

2. Mirror will prompt you for a drive to save the partition table to. The default is A:, which is fine, so put a floppy in drive A: and press ↵. The floppy should be bootable, and should contain the UNFORMAT.COM program. You'll get a "successful" response if all went well, and your screen will look like Figure 14.6.

FIGURE 14.6

Saving an MBR with MIRROR

```
C:\>mirror /partn

Disk Partition Table saver.

The partition information from your hard drive(s) has been read.

Next, the file PARTNSAV.FIL will be written to a floppy disk.  Please
insert a formatted diskette and type the name of the diskette drive.
What drive? A

Successful.

C:\>
```

Restoring the partition record is simple as well:

1. I'll assume that you're restoring the partition record because of some hard disk disaster, so boot from the bootable floppy containing UNFORMAT and your MBR backup file.

2. Type **UNFORMAT /PARTN** and press ↵.

3. You'll be asked where the MBR backup file, which is called PARTNSAV.FIL, is, with the default of A:. Press ↵ to accept A: as the source drive for PARTNSAV.FIL.

4. You'll then get a chance to review the partition information just to be sure that you're not restoring a nonsensical partition to this disk. Your screen will look something like Figure 14.7.

FIGURE 14.7

Restoring an MBR with UNFORMAT

```
A:\>unformat /partn
Hard Disk Partition Table restoration.

Insert the disk containing the file PARTNSAV.FIL
and type the letter of that disk drive.
What drive? A

Partition information was saved by MIRROR 6M,  6-07-93  5:02pm

Old partition information for fixed disk # 1 (DL=80h):

                 Total_size         Start_partition   End_partition
        Type    Bytes    Sectors    Cyl Head Sector   Cyl Head Sector     Rel#
       ------   -----    -------    --- ---- ------   --- ---- ------    ----
HUGE   Boot     489M    1001889      0   1    1      993  15    63        63

Options:  Q  =  Quit, take no action.
          1  =  Restore the partitions for fixed disk 1.

Which option? Q
```

5. Press **1** to restore to the boot drive's MBR, then press ↵.

6. You'll be asked to confirm that you want to do this. Press **Y**, and ↵.

7. You'll then get a prompt that says *Insert a DOS boot disk in drive A and press ENTER to reboot...*, but that's probably not necessary. Assuming that the only problem on your hard disk was the loss of the MBR, you should be able to pop the floppy out and press ↵, and your system will boot.

DEBUG Even if you don't have MIRROR around, it's possible to back up and restore an MBR. Do this from a *bootable* floppy that contains DEBUG.EXE (MS-DOS users) or DEBUG.COM (PC-DOS users). Remember, I've used underscores to represent spaces.

1. Type **DEBUG_MBR.DAT**. (The case doesn't matter, but I'm showing it in caps for clarity's sake.) You should see a File Not Found message—don't let it concern you.

2. Type **A**. This tells DEBUG that you want to assemble something.

3. Type **MOV_DX, 9000**. This command tells DEBUG to move the value of segment 9000 to register DX. Since you can't write anything to a register, you have to move this information to a extra segment.

4. Type **MOV_ES,DX**. This command moves any information in register DX to the extra segment (called ES).

5. Type **XOR_BX,BX**. BX is the offset; **XOR** is a programming trick to set it to zero.

6. Type **MOV_ CX, 0001**. This command stores the value of track 00 and sector 1 in register CX.

7. Type **MOV_DX, 0080**. Here, you're storing the information at head 0 of drive 80 (your A: drive is drive 00, your B: drive is drive 01, your C: drive is drive 80 and your D: drive is drive 81—these are all physical drives, not logical drives) into register DX.

8. Type **MOV_ AX, 0201**. This command tells DEBUG to read 1 sector.

9. Type **INT_13**. This is the BIOS disk call.

10. Type **INT_20**. This tells the BIOS, "I'm done!", signaling that it won't get any more commands and can leave memory.

11. Press **E** to stop entering commands.

12. Type **G** to run the program. When it's done, you should see a message that says, *Program terminated normally*.

13. Type **R_CX**. This command asks DEBUG to show you the value of register CX, and lets you edit it.

14. Type **200**. This is the size of the file that DEBUG will write.

15. Type **W_9000:00**.

16. Type **Q** to exit DEBUG.

You have just created a file called MBR.DAT. You can see a sample screen of this operation in Figure 14.8.

FIGURE 14.8

Using DEBUG to save an MBR

```
A:\>debug mbr.dat
File not found
-a
25A4:0100 mov dx,9000
25A4:0103 mov es,dx
25A4:0105 xor bx,bx
25A4:0107 mov cx,0001
25A4:010A mov dx,0080
25A4:010D mov ax,0201
25A4:0110 int 13
25A4:0112 int 20
25A4:0114
-g

Program terminated normally
-r cx
CX 0000
:200
-w 9000:0
Writing 00200 bytes
-q

A:\>
```

The process of restoring your MBR with DEBUG is similar to that of saving it. To restore your MBR, first start from a bootable floppy that contains both DEBUG (.EXE or .COM) and the correct MBR.DAT—do *not* try restoring an MBR.DAT from one machine onto another machine unless the two machines are identical! Once you're set, change to the A: drive and do the following:

1. Type **DEBUG_MBR.DAT.** This time, if you get a *"File not found"* message, *stop and exit DEBUG (type Q) immediately!* If you continued at this point, you could blast your MBR. (Seeing that message means that you didn't save it properly.)

2. Type **L_9000:0** to direct DEBUG to load the information to 9000:0, where we'll tell the program to look for it.

3. Assuming that all went well, now type **A** to let DEBUG know you want to assemble a file.

4. Type **MOV_DX, 9000.**

5. Type **MOV_ES,DX.**

6. Type **XOR_BX,BX.**

7. Type **MOV_ CX,0001.**

8. Type **MOV_DX, 0080.**

9. Type **MOV_AX,0301.** This command tells DEBUG that you want to *write* 1 sector.

10. Type **INT_13.**

11. Type **INT_20.**

12. Press E to stop entering commands.

13. Type **G** to run the program. When it's done, you should see a message that says *Program terminated normally.*

14. Press Q to exit DEBUG. Your screen will look like Figure 14.9.

Norton DISKEDIT If you like the capabilities of the Norton DISKEDIT program, then here's a short tutorial on using DE to read and write MBRs. It's also a quick lesson on copying parts of a disk to a file with DE.

1. Start off by loading DE by typing DISKEDIT or DE, depending on how you've got it set up. You may prefer to do this from a bootable floppy in case something goes wrong.

2. Change DISKEDIT from read-only to read-write so that you can do this exercise. Choose Tools, and Configuration from the DISKEDIT menu. You'll see a screen like Figure 14.10.

FIGURE 14.9

Restoring an MBR with DEBUG

```
A:\>debug mbr.dat
-l 9000:0
-a
25A4:0100 mov dx,9000
25A4:0103 mov es,dx
25A4:0105 xor bx,bx
25A4:0107 mov cx,0001
25A4:010A mov dx,0080
25A4:010D mov ax,0301
25A4:0110 int 13
25A4:0112 int 20
25A4:0114
-g

Program terminated normally
-q

A:\>
```

FIGURE 14.10

Enabling read/write
capability on
DISKEDIT

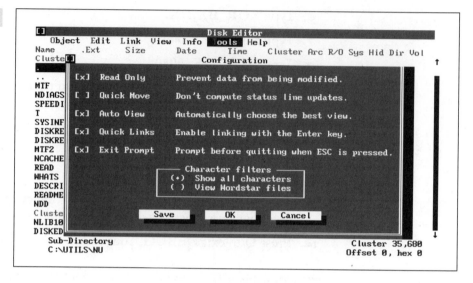

3. The cursor is probably situated right on the "Read Only" box, so press the spacebar to remove the check and enable the read-write capability of DE. Then press ↵, and then ↵ again to clear the confirmation message box.

4. Tell DE that you want to see the MBR by choosing Object (Alt-O), then Partition Table (T). You'll see a screen like Figure 14.11.

5. The object that you selected is one sector—512 bytes—in length. You can tell DE to write it to a file by pulling down the Tools (Alt-T) menu, then selecting Write Object To (W). You'll see a screen like Figure 14.12.

6. You could specify that the information should go to a file, but that's the default value anyway. Just press ↵. You'll then be prompted for a file name. Enter **A:MBRBAK.BIN**, the filename we'll use here. You'll get an "are you sure?" message; press ↵ to clear it.

7. Press Escape and ↵ to exit DE.

FIGURE 14.11

Examining a partition
table with DISKEDIT

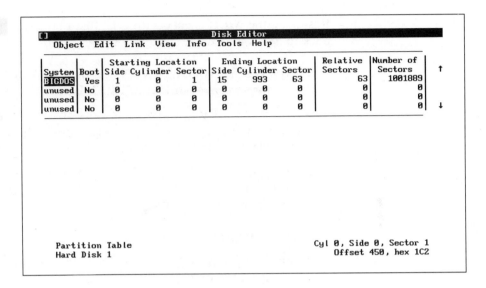

FIGURE 14.12

Writing a partition
table with DISKEDIT

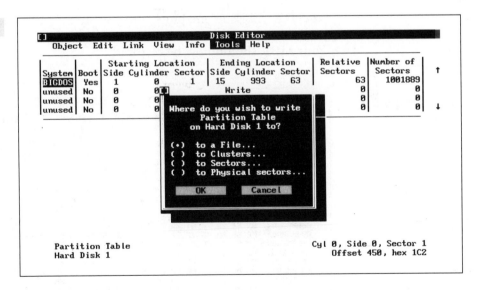

Restoring the MBR is easy with DE. Just make sure that you've got the backup MBR in drive A:, and follow these steps.

1. Type **DE A:MBRBAK.BIN** and press ↵. You'll see some garbage on your screen, as in Figure 14.13.

2. This is the MBR. Now write it to its physical location, which is cylinder 0, head 0, sector 1, by pulling down the Tools menu (Alt-T) and selecting Write Object To.

3. This time, you will not save the information to a file; you'll save it to "Physical sectors", so press **P** and ↵. You'll then see a screen like Figure 14.14.

4. Select Hard Disk 1 and press ↵.

5. You'll be prompted for the particular head, sector, and cylinder to write the data to, but it's already set to the correct value, so press ↵.

6. DE will issue one of its "are you sure?" messages; press ↵.

Your MBR should now be restored.

FIGURE 14.13

Reloading an MBR into DISKEDIT

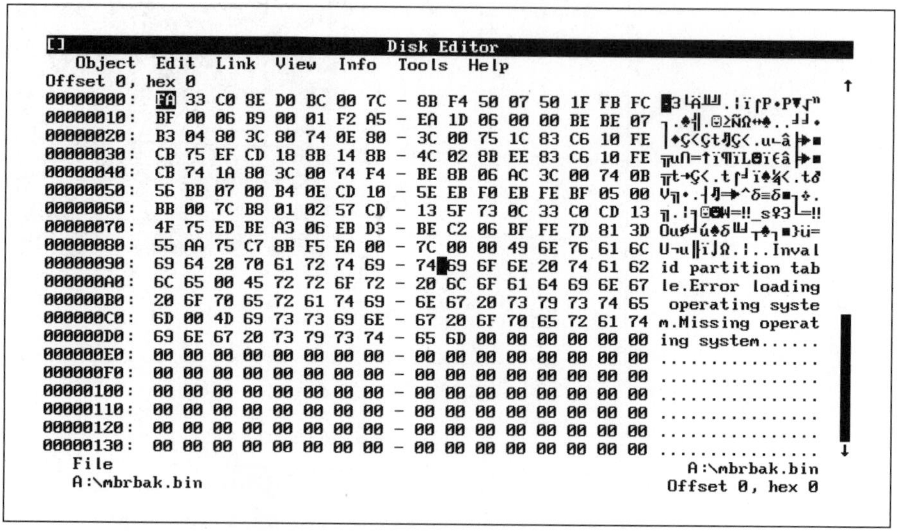

FIGURE 14.14

Restoring an MBR with
DISKEDIT

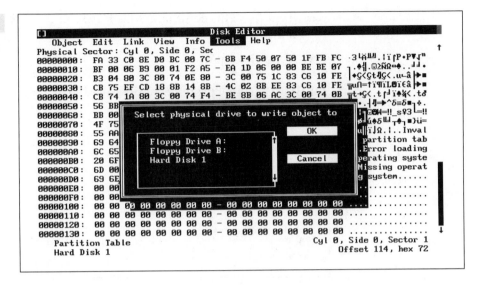

Backing Up and Restoring Your DBR with DEBUG

You can use DEBUG to back up your system's DOS Boot Record (DBR),
or you can grab a DBR off an identical machine and put it on another
machine with a damaged DBR.

Start off with a bootable floppy that contains DEBUG, as you did with
the MBR backup/restore. Note that underscores represent spaces.

1. Change your default drive to the A: drive, which should contain a
    bootable floppy that has DEBUG on it.

2. From the command prompt, type **DEBUG DBR.BIN** and press
    ↵. You'll see a "File not found" message; that's okay.

3. Next, type **L_100_2_0_1**. This command tells DEBUG to load the
    first sector of drive 2 to address 100, and that it is loading only
    one sector.

4. Type **R_CX**. This command tells DEBUG to display the CX
    register and allows you to edit it.

5. Type **200**. Here, you're telling DEBUG that the file you want to
    write is 200 bytes long.

6. Type **W**. This command tells DEBUG to write a file. You will see a message that says *Now writing 00200 bytes*.

7. Type **Q** to quit.

DEBUG has now produced a file called DBR.BIN. Your screen will look like Figure 14.15.

FIGURE 14.15

Saving a DBR with DEBUG

```
A:\>debug dbr.bin
File not found
-L 100 2 0 1
-r cx
CX 0000
:200
-w
Writing 00200 bytes
-q

A:\>
```

To restore the DBR:

1. Work from the A: drive, as with the MBR restore. Type **DEBUG DBR.BIN**.

2. Type **W_100_2_0_1**. This time, you're telling DEBUG to *write* the first (zeroth) sector, and only one sector, drive 2.

3. Type **Q** to quit.

Recovering Accidentally Erased Files

Sometimes, carelessness and haste bring a painful cost: accidental erasure of files. There are lots of ways to do this, and I need not dwell on them. Let's see how to recover from the problem.

First, how can unerasure be done? Recall that a disk has clusters for data, a FAT, and a directory. The directory points to the FAT, which then maintains a list of clusters connected to the file.

Erasure is done not by blanking out clusters, but instead by changing the first letter of the name of the file, as the name is kept in the directory. DOS doesn't go to the trouble of erasing the clusters, so they just sit there, available for use the next time a new file is created (or an old file is expanded). *As long as you unerase before a new file is created, the file can be saved.*

The process could be done by hand with a lot of patience and DEBUG, but fortunately there are products to do this. The best known one is, of course, the Norton Utilities. The original product included UnErase, and versions since 3.1 have included Quick UnErase (QU). The Mace Utilities include a similar program called UnDelete.

Simple unerasures can be done with QU or UnDelete fairly easily. I prefer Mace's UnDelete, as Mace will unerase nondestructively to another disk. If a number of files have been erased or new files have been created, the unerase programs can be fooled. With a program like Mace, you can try the process a few times under different assumptions. With Norton, you cannot do this. DOS 5.0 includes an unerasing program called UNDELETE.

Recovering Accidentally Formatted Hard Disks

This is a more painful problem. It's more likely under DOS 2.0, 2.1, and 3.0 than in 3.1 or 3.2, but it still happens. As mentioned before, the DOS FORMAT command doesn't actually erase sector data, but only erases and creates the boot record, the FAT, and the root directory.

So the sectors are all there, but how do you sew them back together? (A 32-MB hard disk has 65,536 sectors.) There are two approaches, which I call Class I and Class II unformatters. Class I can recover an entire disk but requires some preparation before the format occurs. Class II, on the other hand, can't recover the entire disk but will work even if you've not prepared the disk prior to the format.

The Class I approach is to keep a compressed copy of the FAT, the directory, and the boot record in a specific physical location. (I've already discussed this in Chapter 13, *Hard Disk Preventive Maintenance.*) As long as you keep it up to date, the disk can be restored. Mace uses this approach when it creates a file called BACKUP.M_U. Norton uses the FR/S command in the Norton Advanced Utilities, creating a file called FRECOVER.DAT in the root directory. In Mace, a program called RXBAK.EXE is run periodically and the information is kept up to date. Then, rather than unformatting, just restore BACKUP.M_U and your data is restored entirely. PC Tools and DOS 5.0 use a program called MIRROR to do a similar thing. Great, but you must do the FAT/directory backup first. Many users put either FR, RXBAK, or MIRROR in their AUTOEXEC.BAT files, so the FAT image is backed up daily.

Of course, if you've modified the FAT since the backup (created new files or made existing files larger), FR and its ilk can't help you out. You can't recover what you haven't backed up.

The alternative Class II approach can only recover information in subdirectories, and even then there are no guarantees. Subdirectory information is maintained in files, and those files are recognizable by their format. Unformatting programs first locate these files, then use the information in them to reassemble data files. The subdirectory files contain a link to the first FAT entry. Since the FAT is a blank FAT, it's only of use to tell us what the first sector was. Unformatters then read sectors until they come to another file. This means that fragmented files cannot be saved in entirety, and garbage sectors may be tacked onto the end of data files. But it's better than nothing, and your chances of success can be improved by running an unfragmenting program now and then (also discussed in Chapter 13). It also means that any files kept in the root directory cannot be restored. The only programs I know of that attempt this more difficult unformatting are Mace Unformat and Norton 4.5's FR.

Keeping Users from Accidentally Formatting Disks

Some support people protect users' hard disks by just removing FORMAT from the disk altogether. I don't recommend this, as users often need to format diskettes. Besides, treating users like children often comes back to bite you. If you're fixing your *own* computer, this obviously does not apply to you.

Under DOS 3.3 and later, a user must enter the hard disk's volume label in order to format the disk. It might not be a bad idea to put volume labels on all users' hard disks. That way, they have to *really* want to format the disk in order to get it to work. Any user who actually types in the volume label, responds *yes* to the message explaining that the data on the disk will be destroyed, and then finally explains that he didn't know he would lose all his data when formatting probably can't be helped.

Another approach is to rename FORMAT to TAMROF and create a batch file. Note the effect: Whenever you type FORMAT, you're forced to format only in the A or B drive. This could be moderately effective, but it leaves the TAMROF.COM program on the user's disk. I don't know about you, but I'm a curious person. If I notice a program I've never seen before, I'll try it out.

We can put the icing on the cake with a DOS 3.*x* trick. Most people don't know this, but you can hide a program under 3.*x* (2.*x* won't do this) and DOS can still run it. So, just use the Norton Utilities or something similar to hide TAMROF.

CHAPTER

15

Floppy Disk Drives

FLOPPY disk drives are responsible for some of an average PC's down-time. They're less troublesome than they were several years ago, not because they're manufactured any better, but because we use them less. Hard disks are the medium of choice for many home users and most corporate users. The floppy's role nowadays is mainly a program distribution medium and an archival device. As most hard disks can't travel, most computers still rely on floppies to get information from the outside world.

A floppy disk system is a fairly ingenious device in some ways. Part turntable, part cassette recorder/player, it unfortunately relies on a fair amount of moving parts. This makes floppies a weak point in your computer's reliability armor. Fortunately, they're inexpensive enough ($100 or less) that a fast, relatively cheap repair can be effected by someone with no troubleshooting ability at all by just replacing the bad drive.

In this chapter, you'll look at the components of a floppy system and learn how to test, replace, and adjust these components.

Pieces of the Picture

The floppy disk subsystem is modular, like the rest of the PC. As before, we'll use this modularity to allow us to "divide and conquer." The subsystem consists of the drive, a controller board, the cable connecting the drive to the controller, and the floppy diskettes themselves.

The Floppy Diskette

I said above that the floppy drive is part turntable, part cassette player. The floppy diskette is, then, the combination album/cassette. It comes with a built-in feature that audio records lack, however. You might recall in your past (or present) audio-buff days getting out the Discwasher and cleaning the record prior to playing it. For some people, a ritual like this is comforting. For them, I must sadly report that no such thing exists with floppies.

Floppies are stored inside their own "Discwasher": a semirigid case lined with fleecy material. The case has a hole cut in it so the disk can be read or written to without having to remove it from the case. In general, there's no need to clean a floppy diskette. Figure 15.1 shows $3\frac{1}{2}$-inch and $5\frac{1}{4}$-inch diskettes.

A reasonable life expectancy for a floppy diskette is said by diskette manufacturers to be about three to four years. There are, of course, better and worse diskettes. Any given manufacturer creates all of its single- and double-sided diskettes in the same location. All diskettes are then tested; the question of single vs. double density and single vs. double sidedness is determined by the results of the tests. Most diskettes these days are at least double density. Some double-density diskettes can format quad density—it's a matter of luck. Similarly, some single-sided diskettes can format double sided.

Are the manufacturers ripping you off when they charge extra for double sides or higher density? It would seem so at first glance. If FORMAT likes a diskette, it should be all right, regardless of whether the manufacturer

FIGURE 15.1

Floppy diskettes

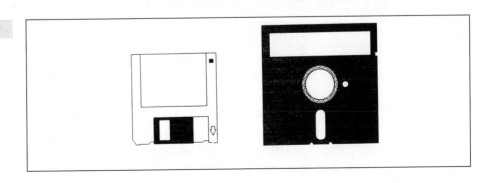

says it's double or single sided, double or quad density, right? Actually, this isn't true. We're not only interested in how well the diskette stores data now, but how well it stores data in the future. FORMAT only tests how well a diskette retains information for a few seconds. That's not a good enough test; put important information on the wrong kind of floppy, and it won't be reliable in the long term.

Take my advice: If the manufacturer says it's single sided, use it single sided. Manufacturers have equipment that can test the signal strength of data written to a diskette as opposed to what's read from the diskette, and thus can distinguish more than just "data is there" or "data isn't there." You only save pennies per diskette like this, and remember that you're using these diskettes to save data that costs you a lot of money to generate. There's also a fundamental physical difference between 360K and 1.2-MB floppies that makes mixing them up not a good idea; the floppies actually have a different coating on them.

In order to hold the floppy so it can be spun, the drive "clamps" onto the edge of the hole in the middle of the floppy. Tandon drives ensured good speed control by clamping rather hard, and so with the advent of the PC (the first major computer to use Tandon drives) we slowly saw the growth of floppy drives with hub rings. (Back in the early '80s, companies sold retrofit hub ring kits: hub rings and glue with an applicator.) Nowadays, virtually all double-density floppies have them. They're actually unnecessary today, as most drives are half-height drives that don't need to exert as much pressure.

The Floppy Drive

The drive itself varies in several ways:

- Half height vs. full height
- Size (8-, 5¼-, 3½-inch)
- Density (double vs. quad)

Half height or full height? Height has no effect on data storage; disks read or written with a full-height drive can be read or written to with a half height. There are even ⅓-height drives (Okidata makes them). Your major concern maintenance-wise is that the half heights are a bit more troublesome to work on, but at $65 for a drive, you won't do much work on them anyway. Occasionally, you'll have trouble putting in two half heights where previously there was one full height. If you're installing two half heights on an IBM PC or XT (the clones have no problem), be sure you have a mounting bracket to allow you to do this.

Most of the PC world uses 5¼-inch 1.2-MB and 3½-inch 1.44-MB drives. More and more machines, like portables, PS/2s, and many "small footprint" computers, lack 5¼-inch drives altogether, so it's worth examining how to put a 3½-inch drive in an existing XT- or AT-type machine. The 3½-inch drives can be outfitted with mounting cases so that they fit where a half-height 5¼-inch would be. The connection is the same, the controller is the same; you'll need to get software support, as I'll discuss later in the chapter. Best of all are the "dual drives" that combine 1.2 MB and 1.44 MB in a single half-height package.

Density varies somewhat. Density is measured in *Tracks Per Inch* (TPI). Regular double-density drives are 48 TPI drives—the 40 tracks fit in ⅚ of an inch. The 1.2-MB floppies used in the AT are quad-density drives with 96 tracks per inch and 80 tracks on a disk. 3½-inch drives are even more finely packed at 135 TPI.

The quality of the drive also determines how many sectors can be placed on the disk. Table 15.1 summarizes these data.

TABLE 15.1: Floppy Disk Formats

DISK TYPE	CAPACITY	TRACKS	SECTORS/ TRACK	BYTES/ SECTOR
360K DSDD	360/320K	40	18 or 9	512
1.2-MB	1.2-MB	80	15	512
3½-inch	720K	80	19	512
Zenith 2-inch	720K	80	19	512
HD 3½-inch	1440K	80	18	512
Super HD 3½-inch	2880K	80	36	512

Many things can go wrong with disk drives. You can learn to fix them (we'll talk about repairs in this chapter), but they're sufficiently cheap that you could reasonably consider them disposable. In any case, if you are responsible for maintaining more than one machine, be sure to have a few on hand for spares. Fixing drives takes time, and you might not have that time when a drive dies.

The Disk Controller Board

As with other devices, the floppy drive needs a controller board. AT-type machines generally put both the floppy-controller and hard disk–controller functions on a single board. On XT-type machines, you can buy combination hard/floppy disk–controllers for about $150. Most computers nowadays put the floppy-controller function right on the motherboard.

A floppy-only controller for the XT-type machines is about $30; this type of board is depicted in Figure 15.2. Again, controllers can be fixed if you have time and are patient (most chips on controllers are *not* socketed), but it can't hurt to have a spare one or two around for quick diagnosis.

FIGURE 15.2

XT-type floppy controller board

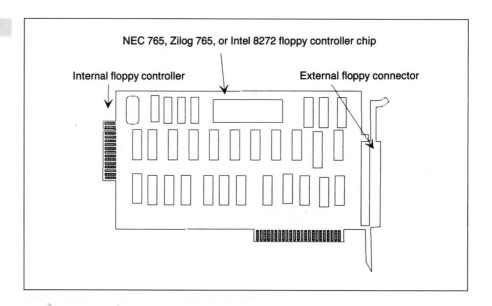

You can swap the controller board in just a few minutes. There are generally no DIP switches to set. You'll see a ribbon cable extending from the edge of the controller card. This ribbon connects to the disk drives; disconnect it from the controller card. The card *should* be keyed so you cannot connect it upside-down, but check at this point. Don't forget the Pin 1 Rule! If there's any ambiguity, draw a picture. Use a magic marker to write **UP**↑ on the connector. Do whatever makes reassembly easy. Then unscrew the mounting screw and remove the disk controller board (you have, of course, turned the power off before doing any of this). Install the spare in the reverse manner and try to reboot. If the problem goes away, fix the controller or throw it away and buy another one. This is an effective diagnostic procedure that literally only takes minutes.

The main chip on a floppy controller board is the big one labeled either NEC 765 or INTEL 8272. It's probably not worth replacing on an XT-type controller, but if you have a "does-it-all" motherboard like an AT&T 6300 or 6386 with the floppy-controller function right on the motherboard, this could save you some money. The controller chip costs about $4, but unfortunately it isn't socketed.

The Cable

The drive is connected to the controller by a 34-wire ribbon cable. The cable is usually "keyed" between lines 4/5 and 6/7 so that it's inserted correctly. Most of the cables have three edge connectors: one for the drive controller, one for drive A, and one for drive B.

The connector from the drive controller to B is a *parallel* cable: pin 1 on the drive controller side is connected to pin 1 on the floppy side, 2 is connected to 2, and so on. The connector to A has a twist in it, however (see Figure 15.3). It's this twist that identifies A from B. The ribbon cable has three connectors, one on one end and two on the other end. The lone end goes on the controller. The one in the middle goes on drive B. The one on the end goes on drive A. If you're likely to forget (as I am), get a magic marker and write **controller**, **B**, and **A** on the appropriate connectors.

It never hurts to have a couple of extra cables around. The cables are about $20–$30 from any mail order house or computer discounter. Keep an extra one around. Swapping the cable is easy. Testing continuity is a pain.

FIGURE 15.3

Floppy cable with twist
for A drive

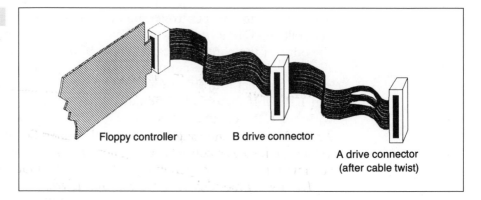

Floppy controller   B drive connector

A drive connector
(after cable twist)

Maintenance

For all of their moving parts, disk drives behave rather well. I still have
the same A drive on my original PC as when I bought it in August 1981.
A few simple procedures will greatly extend the life of your drives and
diskettes.

How Often Should You Clean the Heads?

Like audio cassette drives and videotape recorders, floppies have a magnetic read/write head that collects magnetic oxide. The similarity has lead
some people to conclude that it's a good idea to remove this buildup now
and then. This has lead to floppy head–cleaning kits.

Like all good PC owners, you've probably purchased a floppy-head
cleaner to ward off floppy evil spirits. But then the first question is: How
often should I clean the floppy heads?

The head-cleaner people say to do it weekly. Some people cynically claim
that this is because they want you to use it up and buy some more. Other
people claim that cleaning this often would be disastrous, as the procedure wears away a little of the head each time—you'll always have a clean

head, but it lives a shorter time as a result of the cleaning process. The books are split on the question.

Personally, I clean my heads only when the drive fails. I have some computers I've *never* cleaned the heads on, and they work fine. My recommendation: Clean the heads only when you start experiencing read/write errors.

And *be careful* in choosing a floppy-head cleaner! Some cleaners don't use a cleaning fluid and a cotton cleaning floppy disk but just a *sandpaper* floppy! (I know, it's not sandpaper, just a mildly abrasive cloth, but it might as well be. It's not a good idea to use it on your drives.)

Remember another head-saving tip: On full-height drives, keep the doors open when you're not using the drive. Otherwise, the two heads grate against each other. Some people think it's smart to leave the drive doors closed, as an antidust measure. The doors aren't dustproof by a mile, so it's a silly idea. Leave them open and save your disk heads.

Environmental Factors That Affect Disks and Diskettes

We've all seen the "do not" cartoons on the back of the diskette jackets. They lead you to believe that floppies are very fragile items. As those of us in the real world know, this isn't really true. Yes, you must take care of them, but you needn't get crazy about it. Don't put them on the radiator or leave them on a shelf that gets three hours of direct sunlight every day. Don't store them under the roof leak. Given the choice, store them upright stacked left to right rather than on top of each other.

Remember thermal shock. If your portable computer has been sitting in the back of the car in freezing temperatures overnight, bring it in and let it warm up before using it. Just a little heat expansion/contraction can temporarily realign your drives. More extreme temperatures can damage the diskettes. Vendors claim that diskettes should never be stored below 50 degrees nor above 125 degrees. (The *50 degrees* part may be paranoia: I order software through the mail regularly, and when it's delivered in January, it often sits outside in freezing temperatures for the entire day. I've never had a problem with that. When it sits out in the rain or in the hot sun, or when the postal carrier bends it, that's another story.)

Dust, smoke, and dirt can cause damage to the head and/or to a diskette. As before, don't smoke around the machines. It's nice to work with the windows open on a sunny spring day, but there's a lot of pollen and road dust in the air. To see this, clean your windowsill thoroughly, and then leave the window open for a day. Check it the next day. On a normal spring day when the weather has been dry, you should see a noticeable film after just one day. You sure don't want that on your heads.

A Disk Drive Tester

Part of maintenance is monitoring. Several disk drive–test programs are on the market today. For the price, I like a product called TestDrive from Microsystems Development. The program itself is very inexpensive, but you need an alignment diskette or diskettes to go with it. You'll want three alignment test floppies: one for 360K drives, one for 1.2-MB drives, and a single diskette that serves both 720K and 1.44-MB drives.

MSD even gives away a free version of the program that will only work on 360K floppies. For $25 they'll send you the full-blown version that works on anything. You can order this from MSD; see Appendix A for more information. See the *Floppy Drive Testing* section later in this chapter for details on what drive test programs do and how to understand their output.

Removing, Configuring, and Installing Floppy Drives

You generally won't repair drives; rather, you'll replace them. That means it's most important to be able to take them out and put them back in.

Removing Floppy Drives

Floppy drives are removed in three steps:

1. Remove the screws from the mounting brackets.
2. Remove the power connection.
3. Remove the data connection.

The floppy drive is secured to the computer case with two mounting screws on an XT. These can be a pain to remove, as the two screws on the left side (the A drive) are usually close to expansion boards. To loosen these screws, you sometimes need to remove all of the expansion boards. A useful tool here is an *offset screwdriver*. This is a screwdriver with a bent handle. Get an offset screwdriver, and you won't have to remove all of the expansion boards. As we've seen before, AT-type machines secure the drives in front with metal tabs. Remove the tabs, and the drive slides out like a drawer from a desk.

On the back of the floppy is a connection from the power supply. It has four wires attached to a connector: a yellow, two blacks, and a red. The connector is keyed so you cannot connect it backwards. There are two of these (four on some power supplies), one for each floppy drive. Many power supplies label them P10 and P11, with P10 on the A drive and P11 on the B drive. Actually, it doesn't matter which is connected to which. It's the twist in the drive ribbon cable that decides which is the A drive. The connector may be under the back of the printed circuit board. Disconnect it with a gentle pull, or rock it side to side. You might find it easier to pull the floppy out just a bit so you have room to reach around back and disconnect cables.

A blue or gray edge connector on the data cable connects to the back of the drive. Remove it, being sure as always to diagram it. As before, don't be afraid to get a marker and write right on the cable.

Now the drive will come out fine. As you remove the drive, be careful of parts on the drive that stick up. Don't break them off as you remove the drive.

Installing and Configuring Floppy Drives

Installing a floppy is just the reverse of removing one, except the drive must be configured. To configure a new floppy, you must:

- Terminate the drive properly.
- Set the drive-select jumper.
- Connect the drive using the twisted or nontwisted connector, as appropriate.
- Attach a power connector (P10, P11, and so on).

In Figure 15.4, you see how a floppy controller and drives are cabled and configured.

First, the last drive on the drive cable—A, in the case of the PC—must be terminated. *Termination* just means that a resistance must be present across

FIGURE 15.4

Common floppy cables and configuration

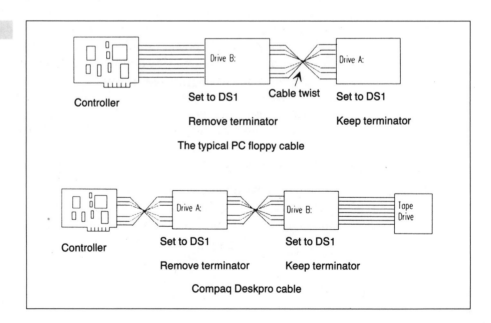

Controller

Drive B: Set to DS1 Remove terminator

Cable twist

Drive A: Set to DS1 Keep terminator

The typical PC floppy cable

Controller

Drive A: Set to DS1 Remove terminator

Drive B: Set to DS1 Keep terminator

Tape Drive

Compaq Deskpro cable

two electronic lines, or the drive controller will think there's nobody home. As with hard disks (see Chapter 12 on hard disk installation), the drives will probably work with both terminators in place; but that shoves twice as much current through the controller, cooking the chips over the long run.

Termination is done with a terminating resistor or *terminator*. It looks like a chip—in fact, it's a resistor in chip's clothing—and is in a socket on a drive's circuit board. To unterminate, just remove the chip. Remember: Drive A must be terminated, regardless of whether or not drive B is present. Note that some half-height drives have the terminators soldered in place. In these cases, there's a jumper labeled *TM*. To remove the terminator, remove the TM jumper.

In many modern floppy drives, there is no terminator at all. So, if you can't find an obvious chip or jumper labeled "TM," don't worry—the termination (and *de*termination) has been handled automatically.

You can see a terminator and a drive-select jumper (discussed below) in Figure 15.5.

Second, the drive must be selected. This means that certain jumpers must be added or removed. On Tandon full-height drives (the most popular ones), there's an area that looks like a socket for a chip. With the jumper installed, it looks like Figure 15.6. Put a jumper across the holes shown above, third from the right. A regular staple works fine and is probably the jumper of choice for 90 percent of the Tandon floppies installed in PCs today. For other drives, look for *DS0* (Drive Select 0) or a marking like that. Some drives show DS0 through DS3, others show DS1 through DS4. *Take the second value:* if the drive jumpers are labeled from DS0, pick DS1; if the drive jumpers are labeled from DS1, pick DS2. Figures 15.7, 15.8, and 15.9 show terminators and drive-select jumpers on three different drive models.

Sometimes you'll see two jumper positions, *RDY* and *CD*. In general, a jumper should be on one or the other, but not both. RDY is used on a PC or XT. CD is used on an AT for *change line* support (see the *Drive Shows Phantom Directories* section later in this chapter for a discussion of change line support).

FLOPPY DISK DRIVES

Remember that the A drive goes on the connector that has a twist between it and the controller board—except for a few strange machines, that is, and Compaq.

Compaq wanted the A drive to be first in line after the controller (look back at Figure 15.4). So they put a twist in between the first connector and the controller. That's fine, but it kind of leaves drive B out in the cold, since it wants *no* twists between it and the controller. What to do?

FIGURE 15.5

Typical floppy with view of drive-select jumper and terminator

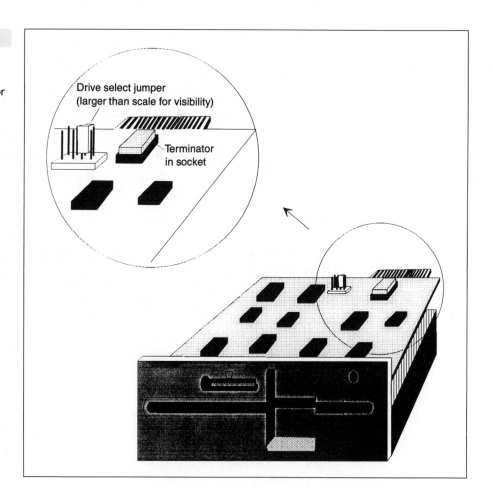

FIGURE 15.6

Tandon drive-select jumper

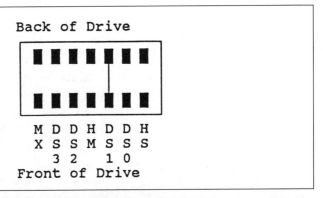

Back of Drive

M D D H D D H
X S S M S S S
  3 2   1 0
Front of Drive

FIGURE 15.7

Terminator and drive-select jumper on Tandon drive

Simple—Compaq just put another twist in the cable *after* the A connection, sort of to "untwist" the twist. That means that when you put a second floppy on a Compaq machine, you must take the terminator off the A drive and leave it on the B drive.

FIGURE 15.8

Terminator and
drive-select jumper on
TEAC drive

FIGURE 15.9

Terminator and
drive-select jumper on
Fujitsu drive

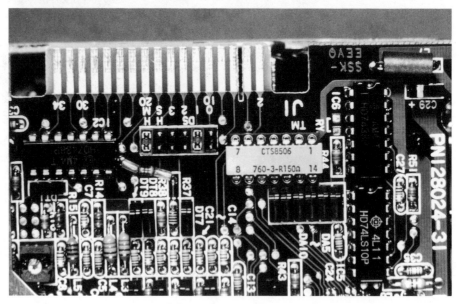

To review floppy drive configuration,

Drive A

- Should be connected to the twist in the floppy cable
- Should retain the terminator chip
- Should be selected as the second drive

Drive B

- Should be connected to the nontwisted cable connector
- Should not have the terminator
- Should also be selected as the second drive

Remember to inform the computer via DIP switches or the SETUP program when drives are added or deleted.

What the Other Jumpers Do

Here's a partial list of the other jumpers you'll see atop a floppy drive board:

- HM: Head/Motor. "Loads" the head when the motor is turned on with the Motor On or Motor Enable command (see the section *More on Drive Select: What Does the Twist Do?* later in this chapter for more information). In a multidrive system, there's just one Motor On signal. That means that all drives would be turned on and their heads could read and write. This isn't supported by IBM's software, however, so don't try to get faster floppy copies this way. IBM wrote all floppy disk software so that only one drive would be on at a time, as the original machine (the PC) had a fairly low-output power supply.

- HS: Head Solenoid. The opposite of HM—you may not select both. (In the PC world, you will, in fact, usually select neither.) It says only to load the head when the drive is selected. In PCs, the heads load as soon as the drive door is closed.

- MX: Multiplex. If activated, the drive is always active. Again, don't take this option in the PC world.

- HI, HO, LHI, LHO, OP: Applies to 1.44-MB drives. Manufacturers include a *media sensor*. This tells the drive when a 720K diskette has been loaded in the drive. An attempt to format it as 1.44 MB will fail because of the media sensor. You can shut off the media sensor with these jumpers. Exactly how you enable or disable it varies with the drive.

Installing 3½-Inch Drives

The 3½-inch, or microfloppy, drives are here to stay. They're a bit slower to seek than the bigger 5¼-inch minifloppies, but they're rugged and store a lot of data. The biggest problem with machines mixing micro- and minifloppies is data transfer. How do you get data from your mini to your micro?

The best answer (and the reason for this section) is to put a microfloppy on the machine you use as your "main" machine, the one on your desk on which you do the most work. Install it as the B drive; then transferring from minifloppy to microfloppy is as easy as **COPY A:*.* B:**. Microfloppy installation is really pretty simple. It's relatively easy to install a 720K drive on an XT- or AT-type machine, or a 1.44-MB on an AT, but an XT-type floppy controller will *not* support a 1.44-MB floppy. Only DOS 3.2 or greater will support 720K floppies.

Installing a microfloppy drive is like installing a floppy drive, but you must ensure that you have software support. You get software support for a 720K floppy with DOS 3.2 in the form of a program called DRIVER.SYS, but it doesn't work very well for 1.44-MB drives. I strongly suggest that you upgrade your BIOS to get BIOS support for these drives if you intend to put a 1.44-MB drive on your AT-type machine.

If you're installing the drive in a system with a SETUP program, such as a 286/386/486 system, check to see if your system supports 720K and/or 1.44-MB drives. Just run your SETUP program and look at the floppy drive options it offers. If your BIOS doesn't support the microfloppies, think about upgrading. BIOS's for IBM ATs that expand the drive table and support 3½-inch floppy drives come from the same place as motherboard upgrades, as discussed in Chapter 6.

Now let's install the microfloppy drive:

1. Remove the B drive, if you have one, from your current system. Keep it as a spare drive.

2. Install the microfloppy in a 5¼-inch mounting kit so that it fits where the old B drive used to be. Most microfloppy vendors sell these "universal" mounting kits. I've used Toshiba's and TEAC's with good results.

3. Install the microfloppy in the computer, just as you would a normal drive. Ensure that the drive-select jumper is in the second position and remove the terminator, if any, from the drive. Again, don't install a 1.44-MB drive on an XT-type machine unless it has a special controller that can support that drive.

4. If you have a computer with BIOS support for the microfloppy, use SETUP to inform it that you've changed the B drive. If it's an older computer that only recognizes either 360K or 1.2-MB floppies, tell it that the microfloppy is a 360K drive or try to get a BIOS upgrade.

5. If you don't have BIOS support, change your CONFIG.SYS file to include the following line:

```
DEVICE=DRIVER.SYS /D:1
```

This instructs DOS to support a 720K floppy. Now, it can't redefine what *B:* means to it, so it creates a new drive letter, such as D:, E:, or whatever. You'll see a brief message something like *driver loaded for drive E:* at boot-time. Use that drive letter when referring to the 3½-inch drive. Again, DRIVER.SYS doesn't work very well for 1.44-MB drives, but if you want to try it, the line should be

```
DEVICE=DRIVER.SYS /D:1 /S:18 /F:2
```

In DRIVER.SYS, you inform the system which physical drive is to be affected with the /D:*d* parameter. If d equals 0, it refers to the first drive, the A drive; d=1 refers to the second drive, the B drive; d=2 would refer to a third, external disk drive. /S:18 says there are 18 sectors per track. /F:2 tells DOS that it's a 1.44-MB disk drive.

Now just use the COPY or XCOPY commands to transfer data between mini- and microfloppies—just refer to the B drive, as in **XCOPY A: B:**. One quirk arises when you format a new disk, however, if you're using DRIVER.SYS. As I said a few paragraphs back, DRIVER.SYS can't redefine what B means, so it creates another drive letter. If you enter FORMAT B:, you'll end up with a 360K microfloppy. You must FORMAT to the new drive letter in order to get a 720K formatted microfloppy.

To put a 1.44-MB drive on an XT-class machine, you need a new controller. A firm called MicroSense sells an alternate controller they call a Compaticard that will do the trick. See Appendix A for further information.

To summarize:

- Check to see if you've got BIOS support.
- 720K disks don't require BIOS support, but it's preferable.
- If the machine is a 286/386/486, consider upgrading the BIOS.
- Unless you have BIOS support, you cannot install the drive as an A drive, so use B if possible.
- If necessary, use DRIVER.SYS (supplied with DOS 3.2 and later). DRIVER.SYS will create a new logical drive. Use that drive's letter for formatting.

More on Drive Select: What Does the Twist Do?

Only read this if you're curious about the twist in the cable, and why DS1 or DS2 is selected.

As I've said, the drive is connected to the controller by a 34-wire ribbon cable. The cable is usually "keyed" between lines 4/5 and 6/7 so it will be inserted correctly. Most of the cables have three edge connectors: one for the drive controller, one for drive A, and one for drive B.

The connector from the drive controller to B is a *parallel* cable—pin 1 on the drive controller is connected to pin 1 on the floppy, 2 is connected to 2, and so on. The connector to A has a twist in it, however. It's this twist that distinguishes A from B. The following table lists the lines on the A side that should be connected to certain lines on the B side.

PIN ON CONTROLLER AND DRIVE B	PIN ON A
10	16
11	15
12	14
13	13
14	12
15	11
16	10

Why the twist? Back in the old days, daisy-chained drives spoke, one at a time, over a shared cable. They knew what address they had by their drive-select jumper. The first drive was DS0, the second DS1, and so on.

IBM decided (perhaps rightly) that actually requiring users to select DS0 for drive A and DS1 for drive B was a bit taxing. Was there an easier way? As it turns out, by putting a twist in lines 10 to 16, *both drives can be DS1,* but the one with the twist looks like DS0 to the controller. The twist, then, makes life easier for the PC installer.

Here are the ugly details. The floppy has an edge connector with 34 lines on it. The controller has an edge connector with 34 lines on it. Just before the connector at the end, the cable is twisted from lines 10 to 16. Thus, there's one connector (the one used by the A drive) with a twist upstream of it, and one with no twists upstream (the B connector). In order for a drive to work, it must receive power on a *drive select* line and a *motor enable* line. The controller only has one generic motor enable line, but separate drive select lines. Twisting the cable, as we'll see, moves around the select and motor enable lines to activate either the B drive or the A drive.

First, consider the situation with a nontwisted cable (this is the normal situation for the B drive). See Table 15.2. Why wouldn't this cable work for drive A? Suppose we had a *straight-through* cable—one that connected 10 on the floppy to 10 on the controller, 12 on the floppy to 12 on the controller, and so on. Well, when the controller began to activate drive A, it would put power both on line 14 to select drive A and on line 10 to turn on A's drive motor. (Why are there *two* Motor Enables on the controller, rather than a shared one between the drives? So that a future, at present nonexistent, version of the PC could run multiple drives simultaneously.)

TABLE 15.2: Interface Functions for Floppy Controller and Drive (No-Twist Cable)

CONTROLLER PIN	FUNCTION	DRIVE PIN	FUNCTION
10	Motor enable for A	10	Select drive 0
12	Select B	12	Select drive 1
14	Select A	14	Select drive 2
16	Motor enable for B	16	Drive motor enable

What would drive A see? Drive A *needs* to see lines 10 (to select the drive) and 16 (to start the drive motor). But recall that the controller has powered up lines 10 and *14*. Powering up lines 10 and 14 would activate *Select 0*—good so far—and *Select 2*. No good.

The B drive, on the other hand, would work okay, as the controller would enable 12 (select B) and 16 (Motor Enable), which would appear to B as Select 1 (correct, as it's jumpered to be drive 1) and Drive Motor On. That's why the nontwisted cable connector works fine for drive B. In Table 15.2, lines 12 and 16 are the ones relevant to operating the B drive.

Now consider what the twist does. When we twist from 10 to 16 *on just the A connector,* the connections work as shown in Table 15.3. Now A is on this twisted connector. As before, the controller powers lines 10 and 14 to enable A's motor and to select the drive. But now 10 on the controller side goes to 16 (Drive Motor On) on the A side, so we're halfway there. Line 14 on the controller side goes to line 12, Select Drive 1. Recall that A, like B, is jumpered to respond as Drive 1. The A drive thinks that it's drive 1 and its motor is enabled, so *voilà!*—the drive responds. Drive B also works because, you'll recall, it was set up fine before we twisted the cable, and the B connector isn't twisted.

TABLE 15.3: Interface Functions for Floppy Controller and Drive (Twisted Cable)

CONTROLLER PIN	FUNCTION	DRIVE PIN	FUNCTION (WHAT DRIVE A SEES)
10	Motor enable A	16	Drive motor on
12	Select B	14	Select drive 2
14	Select A	12	Select drive 1
16	Motor enable B	10	Select drive 0

Floppy Drive Testing

Anyone can run Norton Disk Doctor (version 5.0 and later) on a drive, but perhaps you've never heard of disk-alignment tests, hub centering, azimuth, and hysteresis—impressive, aren't they? Here's how to understand what the tests are telling you (and, of course, be the envy of your floppy-using friends). For this discussion, I'll use Microsystems Development's TestDrive, a test program that I've mentioned previously in this chapter.

A complete floppy check involves tests of:

- **Sensitivity**. How wide a range of space on the disk can a head read from a fixed point?

- **Radial Alignment**. Is the floppy head centered on a track? (See Figure 15.10.)

- **Hysteresis**. Can the floppy find a particular track equally well no matter from which direction it approaches?

- **Hub Centering**. Can the hub clamp hold the floppy well enough to make it turn in a perfect circle, with no wobbling?

- **Azimuth Skew**. Is the head at a tangent to the tracks or skewed a bit?

- **Rotational Speed**. Does the motor drive the floppy at the proper speed?

Since TestDrive is fairly good (and cheap), I'll include sample screens from its tests in the following sections.

Floppy Head Sensitivity

In a perfect world, data is exactly centered on a perfectly thin track on a diskette. But the world hasn't been perfect at *least* since the time the Dodgers left Brooklyn, so you can hardly expect better of floppies. Consider the width of a track. There are three track densities popular at the moment: 48 tracks per inch (TPI) for 360K floppies, 96 TPI for 1.2-MB floppies, and 135 TPI for 720K and 1.44-MB floppies. That works out to track widths of 20.8 milli-inches (mi), 10.8 mi, and 9.4 mi, respectively. Since data doesn't generally reside exactly in the center of a track, a floppy head needs the power to read a range of distance further out and further in from track center. That range is called the *sensitivity*.

FIGURE 15.10

Aligned and misaligned floppy disk heads

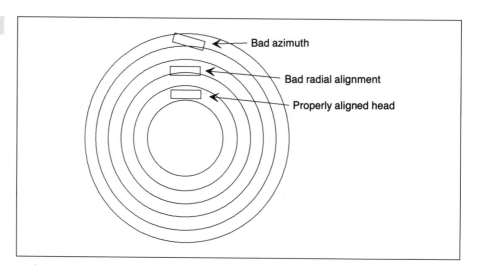

Ideally, a head should be able to sit in the center of a track and be able to read almost all the way to the next track in each direction. (If it could read more than that, it would be confused by information on the adjacent tracks.) Thus, it would be nice if a 360K drive had a sensitivity just under 20.8 mi. We'll settle for about 80 percent of that. In the particular case of 360K floppies, we'll be happy with 16 mi. A 1.2-MB drive can get along with 8 mi sensitivity, and 3½-inch drives are fine with 5 mi. (By the way, Table 15.4 summarizes criteria for 360K, 1.2-MB, and 3½-inch floppies. I'm not just pulling these numbers out of the air.)

Test programs measure sensitivity with a special test disk that has data written at various previously-known distances from the center. They ask the user to put the special test disk (generally known as a *Digital Diagnostic Disk,* or *DDD*) into the drive and run the test program. The program, knowing what to expect, compares what the head could read with what it did read. Then it can report sensitivity.

Take a look at Figure 15.11. Here, the test program is showing results for tests of tracks 0, 6, 32, 40, 67, and 79 (this is a 3½-inch disk being tested). The left-hand side of the page is showing results for the bottom head, 0, and the right-hand side of the page shows results for the top head, 1. The

TABLE 15.4: Typical Critical Values for Floppy Tests

TEST	VALUE SHOULD BE	48 TPI (360K)	96 TPI (1.2-MB)	3½-INCH
Alignment (milli-inches)	≥	±8	±4	±2.5
Hysteresis (milli-inches)	≤	1.5	1.0	1.0
Head Azimuth	Should be readable up to ±39 minutes of arc			
Hub Centering	Must pass tests ≤	8	4	3
Rotational Speed (RPM)	±1%	300	360	300

FIGURE 15.11

Sample alignment test
output

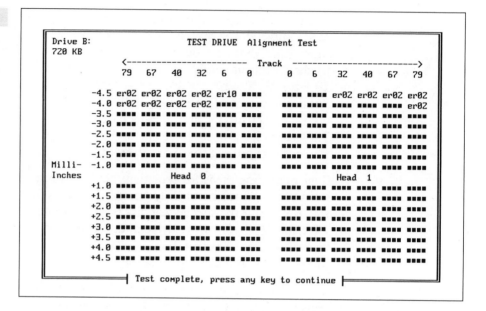

```
Drive B:                    TEST DRIVE  Alignment Test
720 KB
               <---------------------- Track ---------------------->
               79   67   40   32   6    0         0    6   32   40   67   79

       -4.5 er02 er02 er02 er02 er10 ████    ████ ████ er02 er02 er02 er02
       -4.0 er02 er02 er02 er02 ████ ████    ████ ████ ████ ████ ████ er02
       -3.5 ████ ████ ████ ████ ████ ████    ████ ████ ████ ████ ████ ████
       -3.0 ████ ████ ████ ████ ████ ████    ████ ████ ████ ████ ████ ████
       -2.5 ████ ████ ████ ████ ████ ████    ████ ████ ████ ████ ████ ████
       -2.0 ████ ████ ████ ████ ████ ████    ████ ████ ████ ████ ████ ████
       -1.5 ████ ████ ████ ████ ████ ████    ████ ████ ████ ████ ████ ████
Milli- -1.0 ████ ████ ████ ████ ████ ████    ████ ████ ████ ████ ████ ████
Inches                   Head  0                         Head  1
       +1.0 ████ ████ ████ ████ ████ ████    ████ ████ ████ ████ ████ ████
       +1.5 ████ ████ ████ ████ ████ ████    ████ ████ ████ ████ ████ ████
       +2.0 ████ ████ ████ ████ ████ ████    ████ ████ ████ ████ ████ ████
       +2.5 ████ ████ ████ ████ ████ ████    ████ ████ ████ ████ ████ ████
       +3.0 ████ ████ ████ ████ ████ ████    ████ ████ ████ ████ ████ ████
       +3.5 ████ ████ ████ ████ ████ ████    ████ ████ ████ ████ ████ ████
       +4.0 ████ ████ ████ ████ ████ ████    ████ ████ ████ ████ ████ ████
       +4.5 ████ ████ ████ ████ ████ ████    ████ ████ ████ ████ ████ ████

              ┤ Test complete, press any key to continue ├
```

results (in milli-inches) are both positive and negative because the test examines information both toward and away from the drive center. Any cell with four dots is a perfect read; anything starting with *er*, like *er10*, is an unsuccessful read.

Take a look at head 0, track 40. It cannot read –4.5 or –4.0, but –3.5 to +4.5 presents no problem. Since 4.5 to –3.5 is a distance of 8 mi, the sensitivity of this drive is said to be 8 mi, quite adequate for a 3½-inch drive. If a head is insufficiently sensitive, it might only be dirty. Clean the head and try again.

Radial Alignment

Not only must a head be sensitive; it must be placed properly. The ideal head rests over the center of a track. This is its *radial alignment*. Radial alignment is deduced by examining the center of sensitivity. Basically, you should look at the sensitivity criterion, 6 mi in the case of our 3½-inch floppy. (Again, Table 15.4 has these criteria.) That means a properly aligned 3½-inch drive could read ±3 mi. Our drive can indeed cover that entire range, but note that (at least over track 40) it isn't perfectly centered. The pattern isn't symmetrical. If its sensitivity was only 6 mi, it could only read from perhaps +3.5 to −2.5. It would then fall short of being able to read to −3 mi and would therefore be misaligned. So sensitivity and radial alignment go hand in hand. A somewhat misaligned head can be compensated by greater sensitivity.

Older drives have an adjustment screw that can move a head farther from or closer to the center of the drive. Test software like TestDrive generally offer a *continuous alignment test* option so you can try to fix a misaligned head by yourself. It's not easy; you'll need patience and steady hands. Again, you might be able to improve sensitivity by cleaning the head, thereby nullifying an alignment problem.

Hysteresis

The method for positioning a head over a track is imperfect and, in fact, results will generally vary depending on whether the head is moving farther from or closer to the center. Basically, where a head ends up depends on where it's coming from: A head told to go to track 20 from a current location of track 30 will end up in a slightly different position from one that's told to go to track 20 from track 10. That's the thesis of the hysteresis test.

A hysteresis test measures the distance between head position on selected tracks when positioned further out from and closer in towards the center. The difference between the locations in milli-inches is the result. Acceptable values are 1.5 mi for 360K drives, 1.0 for 1.2-MB drives, and 1.0 for 3½-inch drives. You can see a sample output of a hysteresis test in Figure 15.12.

The sample test ran on a 3½-inch drive; 3½-inch drives must show a hysteresis value of 1.0 mi or less. TestDrive ran tests on tracks 32 and 40 for both heads 0 and 1. In all cases, the difference between head position when moving in towards the center of the disk and when moving out towards the edge was 0.25 mi. This figure is well below 1.0, so the drive is working just fine. You can't do much about a drive with bad hysteresis, so replace it.

FIGURE 15.12

Sample hysteresis test output

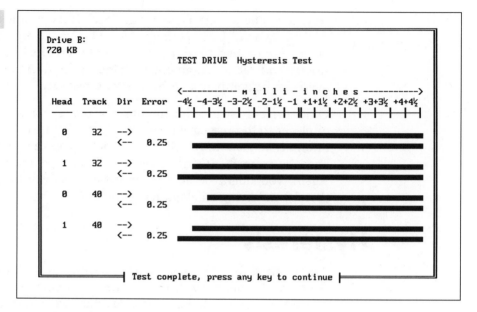

Hub Clamping

The center hub clamp holds the disk in its exact center so it spins in a perfect circle. If it doesn't, that shows up as bad alignment. TestDrive checks this with three test tracks on your DDD that can detect varying amounts of wobble. The smallest value in milli-inches is the loosest test, the largest value is the most stringent one. A sample output is shown in Figure 15.13, again for a 3½-inch drive. There, the disk tests at 2.5, 3.0, and 3.5 mi. Of these, 2.5 is the easiest test; 3.5 is the toughest. We'd be perfectly happy if the disk only passed the 2.5 and 3.0 mi tests, but this disk passes the 3.5 mi test as well. (This is clearly a drive you'd be proud to take home to meet your motherboard.)

A serious hub clamp problem can't be resolved. But sometimes all you have to do to fix the problem is just remove the floppy and reinsert it in the drive.

FIGURE 15.13

Hub centering test
output

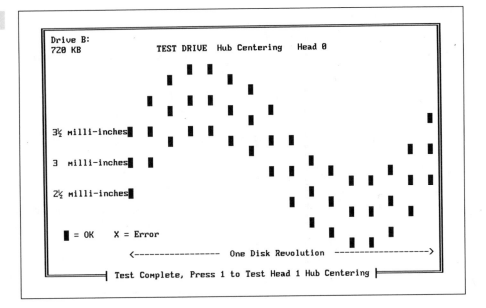

```
Drive B:
720 KB               TEST DRIVE  Hub Centering    Head 0




3½ milli-inches

3  milli-inches

2½ milli-inches


  ∎ = OK    X = Error

                        <---------------- One Disk Revolution ---------------->

  | Test Complete, Press 1 to Test Head 1 Hub Centering |
```

Disk Rotation Speed

Most floppies rotate at 300 rpm, except the 1.2-MB floppy drives, which rotate at 360 rpm. Small variations in this speed (plus or minus one percent) are okay, but greater differences can make the floppy malfunction.

Now, understand that you'll probably never have this problem if you buy half-height drives. They're direct drive rather than belt driven. Some of the newest ones don't even have an adjustment switch; a chip on the drive automatically adjusts the speed, so there's no maintenance.

Speed tester programs exist for 5¼-inch floppies. For example, you might come across Verbatim's Disk Drive Analyzer or Dysan's Readiscope; Test-Drive also tests rotational speed. These programs indicate either graphically or numerically whether the drive is too slow or too fast. You would remove the drive from its bracket and then put it on its side on the top of the power supply, a convenient flat surface where it's easy to get to the speed adjustment screw. Reconnect the cables and run the program, adjust the speed, and run it again. Keep doing this until you get the speed just as you like it. TestDrive's rotational speed test is the "spindle speed test." There's a sample output in Figure 15.14.

FIGURE 15.14

Sample TestDrive
rotational speed test
output

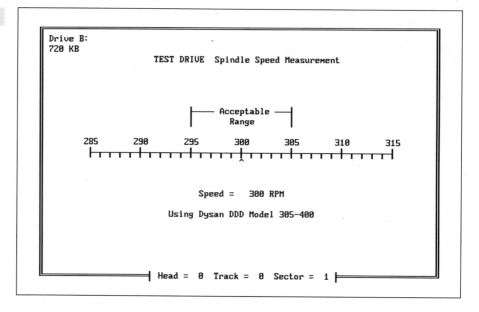

The disk under test again performs stunningly, clocking in at exactly 300 rpm. We'll see how to adjust a drive with a bad drive speed in the "Floppy Troubleshooting and Adjustment" section later in this chapter.

Head Azimuth

The drive head is built along a straight line, but it must read a track that's in a circle. In order to best read the data, the head must sit at a tangent to the circle. If it's not exactly tangent, it's said to have *azimuth skew*. The skew generally isn't much, less than a degree off, so skew is measured in minutes ($\frac{1}{60}$ of a degree, and of course a degree is $\frac{1}{360}$ of circle). As with alignment, a good drive must be able to handle data that's a mite out of spec, so a drive's head azimuth is considered okay as long as it can read from −39 minutes skew to +39 minutes skew. TestDrive can test this with the DDD. Figure 15.15 shows such a test.

The test represents successful reads as four slashes, unsuccessful reads as four *X*s. Reading from left to right, each set of slashes or *X*s represents the range from −42 to −21 minutes of skew, three minutes at a time, and from

FIGURE 15.15

Sample head azimuth
test output

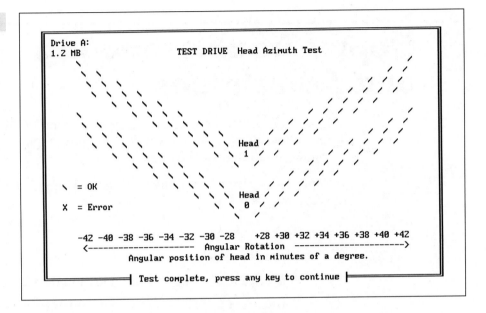

+21 to +42 minutes of skew. Your drive should read with no problem from
−39 to +39 (as does this drive). If it fails the ±42 minute test, it's still okay.

Floppy Drive Test Summary

You test a drive by examining its sensitivity/alignment to ensure that the
drive can write data reliably and read data that has been written by
other drives, even if they're a bit out of alignment themselves. Then you're
concerned with how consistently the drive locates a track when traveling
inward vs. outward on the disk: the hysteresis tests that. If the hub clamp
can't hold the disk properly, it will wobble, so the hub clamping test
checks that.

I've said that the acceptable tolerance—the critical value—for different
drive types (360K, 1.2-MB, 720K, 1.44-MB) varies. You need to know
what those critical values are in order to test each kind of floppy drive.
Those critical values are summarized in Table 15.4.

Floppy Troubleshooting and Adjustment

In a minute, I'll talk about repairing components of the floppy system. But first—how do you know what's wrong? Let's look at some common symptoms and possible causes.

Suppose the drive is malfunctioning, and one of the following things is occurring:

- The drive refuses to read.
- The drive refuses to write.
- The drive reads, but it grinds a lot and displays *Retry?* messages.
- You see a 601 message, and then the computer goes to Cassette BASIC.

Possible causes fall into two categories: software and hardware.

Software Possibilities

The problem could be caused by:

- A bad applications program
- A file destroyed by a software bug or incorrect power-down
- FAT damage
- Directory damage
- Boot record damage
- Accidental file erasure

These software problems are discussed in Chapter 14, *Hard Disk Failure Recovery*. The same software that will help on hard disks will generally work on floppy drives also.

Getting the Floppy Drive Running Again

Given that a floppy drive isn't working and there do not appear to be software problems, what do you do?

At this point, I'd do the following things:

1. Reboot. The disk parameter table could be bad.
2. Check the diskette. Try another floppy.
3. Clean the heads on the disk.
4. Swap the drives. Check that the connections are solid.
5. Try a new A drive.
6. Swap the controller.

You don't want to spend forever figuring out which one of these is the problem. You just want (at this stage) to determine if it's *something* on the drive that is causing the problem. The simplest approach to this is simply to swap the drive. For details, see the previous configuration section. If, after swapping A and B you can now boot from drive A and read and write data, then the former drive A is at fault. Replace or repair it.

Common Repair Points

Supposing you want to fix a drive, what common fixes can you do? Here are a few ideas. Once you have a notion of what part of the floppy subsystem has failed, how do you replace or repair it? This section addresses that as well.

Is It Worth Repairing Floppy Drives?

I want to open this section by saying, as I've done before, that if you only learn how to replace the controller board, cable, and drives, and learn nothing about repairing the components themselves, you're doing fine. Floppy drives are very cheap—about $100—and can be replaced without repair. Even if you want to repair the drives, there are firms that will fix floppy drives for a flat fee of $35–$45. This might be more cost-effective than spending your time trying to repair a drive.

But if you want to fix a floppy-drive problem, here's a potpourri of things that go wrong, and what you can do for them.

The floppy drive itself can malfunction for a variety of reasons:

- The head is dirty.
- The head is misaligned.
- The *index timing light* is dirty. A light-and-sensor combination detects when the index hole on the floppy (the small hole next to the large central hole) lines up with the corresponding hole in the floppy jacket.
- The rotation speed is wrong.
- The drive belt is slipping (in full-height drives only).
- The drive door is broken or cracked.
- On-drive electronics have failed.
- The track zero adjustment is wrong.
- The *servo board* has failed. It's a small circuit board on the back of Tandon drives, and must be replaced if the Tandon drive can't maintain a constant rotational speed.
- The floppy head rails are sticky. Does the head move smoothly with the power off? Try a little lube on the head rails. I use WD-40, but some techs tell me that my drive will live longer if I use a

teflon-based lube like the Tri-Flo that I mentioned in the hard disk chapters.

We will look more closely at some of these problems below.

Mixing 1.2-MB and 360K Floppies

Both 1.2-MB floppy drives (the kind found as drive A on most AT-type machines) and 360K floppy drives (the more common kind) use diskettes that are physically 5¼-inch in size. How much can they be mixed?

- Any diskette created on a 360K drive can be read by a normal 1.2-MB drive.

- Some folks take cheap 360K diskettes and format them as 1.2-MB floppies. You end up with a 1.2-MB floppy with 400K of bad sectors. Is this a good idea? Emphatically, *no.* There is, you see, a fundamentally different kind of surface on a 1.2-MB floppy than on a 360K. It's a much finer grain, which explains why it allows 80 tracks and 15 sectors per track in the same area that only accommodates 40 tracks and 9 sectors on a 360K diskette. The data will go on the disk, but it won't stay there. The surface, by the way, isn't only a finer grain, it also requires more power to record on it. The 1.2-MB drive uses greater electric current than a 360K. That's why it's physically impossible to write information on a 1.2-MB diskette with a 360K drive—the 360K's recording strength is insufficient to get the 1.2 MB's attention. (That also means, by the way, that stray magnetism will affect a 1.2 MB less than a 360K; the magnetism would have to be at a higher strength to erase data.)

- If you create a diskette with a 360K drive and write new information to it on a 1.2-MB drive, the new information is still in 360K format, but it might be unreadable by a 360K drive. Half-height 360K drives seem to have less trouble reading these diskettes than full-height drives.

- If you format a new 360K diskette with a 1.2-MB drive, you'll probably (again) have trouble reading this diskette with a 360K drive. In fact, it's much more likely that you'll have trouble with this than if you simply write new data to a previously formatted diskette. Recall that to format a 360K diskette in a 1.2-MB drive you would use the command FORMAT A:/4.

All of these problems stem from the following: The 1.2-MB drive is an 80-track drive. It writes 80 narrow tracks on a diskette. The 360K drive is a 40-track drive. It writes 40 wide tracks on a diskette. When the 1.2-MB drive is asked to write a 40-track diskette, it writes 40 tracks, all right—40 of its skinny tracks, not 40 fat tracks! That means that if the head trying to read this skinny track is a 360K, it might not happen to be centered in the same place as the original 1.2-MB head was when it wrote the track.

Worse yet, imagine that the 1.2-MB head is *overwriting* old 360K data. The 360K data is written about 16 milli-inches wide. But the 1.2-MB head only writes tracks about 8 mi wide. So the 1.2-MB writes an 8 mi swath through the middle of what used to be a 16-mi image of data. The 360K head then tries to read this and, if it's of normal 360K sensitivity, will see a *very* confusing track indeed! Data written by the 1.2-MB drive, therefore, might not be readable by a 360K drive—the 360K drive isn't built to read skinny tracks.

Why not eliminate the problem by telling the 1.2-MB drive to write pairs of skinny tracks? One company, Microbridge Computers International, has done that. The utility CPYAT2PC tells the 1.2-MB drive to write pairs of skinny tracks. Appendix A has more information on this utility. Another answer is to only format a 360K diskette in a 1.2-MB drive when the diskette has never been formatted before. That implies that to use a 360K floppy on a 1.2-MB drive, just run the floppy past a magnet, so as to create a clean surface for the 1.2-MB drive.

A Turbo Clone Randomly Writes Bad Data to Floppy

I discovered this one when my 386 clone started writing out unreliable data on floppies all of a sudden. I asked, what have I done differently? Simple—I'd upgraded my BIOS. Some clones mimic the Compaq in that they slow the machine down to 8 MHz when doing floppy reads or writes. This is ostensibly done to accommodate the occasional copy-protected program. Turns out this *isn't* always a good thing: I'd use DISKCOPY, then DISKCOMP, and find errors. Then I'd do it again and get errors, but in different places, randomly. I put the old BIOS in, and everything was okay. I'm waiting for the version of the BIOS that doesn't do the floppy switching. If you've got an AWARD BIOS, you can test this: If you can do Ctrl-Alt-– (minus sign) and slow down your computer, then you've probably got the floppy slow-down enabled. This might not be a bad thing for your computer, by the way—it just turned out to be the wrong thing for mine.

Please note that I'm not saying that Compaqs have this problem. Compaqs seem to be able to do speed switching when reading and writing floppies without trouble.

Drive Shows Phantom Directories

The symptom here occurs when you do something, like a DIR command, on a floppy. Then you remove the diskette, put a different diskette in the drive, do a DIR, and you see the *directory of the previous floppy, not the one in the drive now!*

If you see this on a computer, this is a RED ALERT! Don't use the floppy until you get the problem fixed. The reason: Let's say you put a floppy in the drive and do a DIR on it. Then you put a different floppy in the drive, and write some data to the floppy. *The PC writes data to the new floppy using the old floppy's directory!* That means that the newly-written file is probably okay, but everything else on the floppy is trashed.

Where does this problem come from? It's something called the *change-line signal.* Time for a little history.

Back in the old days, when floppies were the major storage medium for microcomputers, software designers wanted to squeeze the most performance from those floppy drives, mainly because they were pretty low-performance. One way to do that was to avoid, wherever possible, rereading information on a floppy. What information gets read the most? The directory and FAT. Way back before DOS even existed, there was an operating system called *CP/M* (Control Program for Microcomputers). To get better speed, some CP/M applications only read the directory when a disk was first inserted in a drive. That meant if you were going to swap a floppy while in WordStar, you had to tell the program or it would trash your floppy. It was a real pain.

The original PC guys remembered the CP/M experience and (I'm guessing) decided they'd sacrifice a little speed for reliability. So the PC and XT (not all XT clones) BIOSes always read the disk directory and FAT before doing anything dangerous—they don't assume that the floppy stays in the same place. And all was well with the world.

But some compatibles makers looking to outdo IBM's performance sold computers with slightly different floppy drives. These floppy drives had something called *change line support*. It was no big revolution; in fact, it had been around since the CP/M days. One of the signals from the drive to the controller was a *change-line signal*—it signaled that the floppy door had been opened since DOS had last looked at the drive. If the change line was activated, DOS would reread the floppy; if not, it wouldn't bother. That meant that writes didn't have to be preceded by directory reads, as in the IBM XT case.

The IBM AT design team, looking to show the competition who was boss, added the *change line* feature to the AT. That means that there's a minor difference between XT floppy drives and AT floppy drives. The XT drives don't really use line 34 on the floppy edge connector, but the AT drives use 34 as the change-line line. To complicate matters, this question of whether or not change line support is really needed is determined by what BIOS your computer has. Some XT clones need it, some don't. Some AT clones need it, others don't. The IBM AT needs it. You really can't go wrong with a floppy with change line support, as a computer that doesn't need it will just ignore it.

If you have a computer that needs change line support, and you install a floppy drive that lacks it, the computer will display the phantom directory (and possibly trash a floppy someday).

Now you know what change line support is, and that some computers need it. Suppose you find yourself with a change line problem—phantom directories. What do you do?

- Check the floppy cable. The aforementioned old XT (a clone) has a scratched cable. I haven't gotten around to replacing it yet, but that's the answer to the problem.

- Check to see if the floppy has change line support. Exactly *how* to activate change line support is tough to know for sure unless you've got the documentation, but look for a DC jumper point. You may alternatively see a RDY line. Move the jumper from RDY to DC.

- Use DRIVER.SYS. This won't solve all woes, but it's a stopgap. The DRIVER.SYS device driver that ships with DOS 3.3 has a */C, change line* option. You use DRIVER.SYS to tell DOS things about a drive. For our purposes, let's just look at the /C option. Assuming that your problem drive is drive B (the second physical drive), and assuming that it's a 360K drive, you'd say

  ```
  DEVICE=DRIVER.SYS /D:1 /C /T:40 /F:0
  ```

  Don't worry about most of the parameters, but the /D:1 says we're describing drive 1, or the B drive. Drive A would, of course, be drive 0. When the system boots, you'll see a message something like *driver installed for drive E.* Use that drive letter henceforth when referring to drive B!

- Another possibility is to fool the controller into thinking there have been lots of change-line signals. One approach to this is simply to construct a cable that disconnects line 34 on the drive side but cross-connects lines 34 and 20 on the controller side. As line 20 is activated with each head step, the controller will believe it's seeing many change-line signals.

- The last approach is just to remember to do a Ctrl-C keystroke when you're in DOS and have changed the floppy. It forces DOS to reread the disk directories. This isn't great, but it's a good emergency measure.

Drive Head Is Dirty

Try cleaning the drive head. Again, it's easy and might solve your problem.

Diskette Is Bad

It's fairly common for diskettes, particularly heavily used diskettes, to develop bad spots. If you always use the same diskette as your work diskette, try another one. If the problem goes away, use a disk tester like Norton's Disk Doctor (version 5.0 and later) or the Mace Utilities DIAGNOSE program on the original disk. Recover what data remains and discard the diskette. (You do keep backups, don't you?)

Cable Is Loose

This sounds silly, but is it plugged in? Expansion or contraction, and vibration can loosen the power and data cables on floppies. Maybe they weren't installed snugly in the beginning.

Cable Is Bad

The cables can get nicked when you install boards, replace drives, or just remove the cover. How bad that is depends on which line gets nicked. A line nick on my XT-compatible laptop that I mentioned before keeps the change line from working. My partner Pete had an AT that just plain wouldn't format the A drive. We always have lots of drives around, so we didn't worry much about it. One day he noticed a nick on the cable. He replaced the cable and the problem went away, never to return. It only takes a two-minute swap with another cable to find out for sure.

Controller Is Bad

Generally, you'll see (on an IBM-BIOS machine) a 601 error on power-up if the controller is malfunctioning. You could run any general diagnostic program to test the controller, but as mentioned earlier, in some cases just swapping the controller is a quicker way.

Power Supply to Floppy Malfunctioning

At the back of the floppy drive where the line from the power supply connects, you'll see four solder points. They'll probably be labeled, left to right, +12V GND GND +5V. These are the power lines the floppy needs to operate. You can test these while the floppy is operating with a multimeter. Put the black probe on GND and the red probe on either +12V or +5V. You should see power in the range 4.8–5.2 for the 5-volt pin, and 11.5–12.6 for the 12-volt pin. If the values are outside of this range, the power supply is faulty.

While we're on the subject, I should mention that some "disk failures" are actually the fault of power spikes. Power protection is a good move here, as always.

Replacing the Drive Door (Full Height)

When the PC first came out, people soon learned that the plastic doors on full-height drives tend to break easily. The spring-loaded doors snap open, sometimes destroying themselves in the process. If the door can't be closed, the drive won't even try to read. Sometimes the door will only crack, leading to the mysterious case where the drive door is closed but DOS says the drive isn't ready.

Replacing the drive door is fairly easy. First, remove the screws that hold the drive to the computer case. Then pull the drive out a bit. The drive is held to the spindle by a metal bar, which is held to the door by two screws right behind the drive-face bezel. The bar is spring loaded, so hold it down with one finger while removing the old door. Then put the new door in, and fasten it to the bar with the two screws.

Saving a Dirty Floppy

Earlier I said that in general there's no need to clean a floppy diskette. That's *in general*.

I *have* seen some occasions when cleaning a floppy is appropriate—after flood damage, or when the odd glob of chocolate Häagen-Dazs ice cream gets onto the floppy. The instances when you clean a floppy are extremely rare.

Here's how to do it: You remove the floppy diskette from its jacket, clean it, and replace it in a clean new jacket. Make sure you can tell which is the top of the floppy when you return the floppy to its jacket. I scratch the floppy near the center, well away from the data area, to mark it; 360K disks don't need this, as they generally have hub rings on top. Cut across the top of the floppy jacket. Carefully remove the floppy and place it on a clean, soft surface—a paper towel will do, but cheesecloth is preferable. The floppy can be wiped clean with a damp soft rag with warm-to-hot soapy water, then *gently* wiped dry with a soft clean cloth, and left to dry on a flat surface. I once saw an article claiming that floppies could be dried by stringing them up through the center hole, but I doubt that this would work well: the floppy could dry in a bent shape.

Wait until the floppy is dry. When I say *dry,* I mean it: Leave it for a day. A damp floppy could flake wet oxide bits onto your drive head and destroy or seriously incapacitate it.

Then remove a blank floppy (this is the "sacrificial" floppy) from its case and throw it away. Use its case for the cleaned floppy. If you make a clean cut with a razor across the top of the disk jacket, the jacket can be reused.

This, by the way, is also useful sometimes when a floppy is mailed and the mailer is bent. If you can't unbend the case by running it along the table edge, take the floppy apart and steal another case.

If you've been successful here, *copy the floppy immediately.* If it's a distribution disk, send away for a replacement just in case. This is only a disaster-recovery procedure, not a maintenance procedure.

The Floppy Drive Electronics

On each floppy drive, of whatever make, there's at least one printed circuit board. As always, these can be defective, but they tend to live fairly long if they survive the first few weeks. Unfortunately, there's no way to "burn in" these boards without burning out the drive-stepper motor.

They aren't difficult to change, but I don't recommend it. I've never seen a floppy drive with a bad PC board. Further, it's very difficult to get replacements. Some floppy drive manufacturers won't sell you replacement doors, boards, and so on unless you're a repair facility licensed by them. Licensing usually requires some franchise money and attendance at their repair seminars. As I said before, for $100 you can replace the bad floppy drive and keep it for parts.

Disk Rotation Speed

As we've seen, most floppies rotate at 300 rpm. The 1.2-MB floppy drives on the AT rotate at 360 rpm. Small variations in this speed (plus or minus one percent) are okay, but greater differences can make the floppy non-functional or dangerous.

Dangerous? Yes. A few years ago, I was asked to install a copy of *dBASE III* version 1.0 on an XT. It was a perfectly legal copy. When I went to install the program, it informed me that it was an illegal copy and refused to load. I tried installing it on other machines. It didn't work. Ashton-Tate first told me I was lying or mistaken, and finally (after threats of violence) sent me another master disk. Thankfully, Ashton-Tate has now commendably removed copy protection from their products. It took a while to reconstruct the problem.

What had happened was this: The floppy on the XT had a drive that was slightly incorrect in speed—not so different as to render it unusable for normal uses, but enough to upset the finicky copy protection system. Worse, the particular system being used at the time (Prolok, by Vault Corporation) would permanently alter a disk that it saw as an illegal copy. Once Prolok thought a disk was bad, it would alter the disk so it would always seem bad. That was why the disk wouldn't run on other XTs. (How did I eventually prove this? I have some friends at a software house who use Prolok. They Prolok-ed some disks, and we tried to load them on the XT. Same problem.) Copy protection is almost a quaint remembrance, but not yet. It pays to be able to test and adjust disk speed.

Big jumps up and down in speed can be due to slippage of the belt that drives the disk. These are only found on the bottoms of full-height drives or Qume half heights. And by the way, many older floppy drives will not work reliably when mounted on their sides.

Testing and Adjusting Disk Speed

Recall that you'll probably never have this problem if you buy half-height drives (hint, hint) because they're direct drive rather than belt driven. Some of the newest ones don't even have a speed-adjustment switch; a chip on the drive automatically adjusts the speed, so there's no maintenance.

There are two basic ways to test disk speed: with a speed tester program and stroboscopically. We discussed using TestDrive earlier; it's an example of a software speed test.

What if you have a floppy with an incorrect rotational speed? Again, if it's a half height, you're basically going to replace its circuit board. You can't really adjust a half height's speed, as the speed is constantly adjusted by electronics on the circuit board atop the drive.

If you've got a full-height Tandon or CDC (also called MPI) drive, its speed can be adjusted by a *variable resistor* on the floppy. It's the tweaker screw with the red epoxy on it. The variable resistor is on a small printed circuit board sitting upright on the back of a Tandon floppy drive. It's a tall (about one inch) blue rectangular component, and there's a small screw atop it. The screw is probably partially covered with epoxy. The CDC drive has the variable resistor on the circuit board on top. A Shugart half height has it on the top circuit board on the right towards the front.

The speed adjustment variable resistor is usually easy to find, as it's often the only one on the floppy. Just break off the epoxy, adjust the variable resister with a screwdriver, and then put a dab of nail polish on it to hold the setting.

The other speed checking approach doesn't involve software. The bottoms of *some* (not all) disk drives have a design that looks like a test pattern. It's two concentric sets of spokes, one inside the other. These are used for a stroboscopic speed test. Here's how it works.

First, remove the drive. Then get the motor running and issue DOS commands. Put the drive under a fluorescent light. The outer spokes will look like they're standing still when the speed is correct. (The inner set frequently is for 50 cycles per second, the frequency of European power mains—and therefore fluorescent lights).

Remember to secure the variable resistor when you finish adjusting it. Either use electrician's epoxy or just regular nail polish. (Nail polish also comes in a variety of colors, unlike boring red-only epoxy.)

CHAPTER

16

Printer Software

PRINTERS have a powerful but complicated command language that allows programmers to tell the printer what to produce on a page. Just as you must know some DOS in order to trouble-shoot your PC, repairing and maintaining printers requires some famil-iarity with printer command languages. Here, I'll discuss writing batch files to test printer features and understanding *your* printer's command language. In the process, I'll focus on the problems of soft fonts and font selection in laser printers.

Why should you learn your printer's programming codes, rather than let-ting the word processor do it? Here are five example batch files I've writ-ten for my laser printers that I find really useful:

- EJECT forces the printer to do a form feed and print whatever in-formation is in its page buffer.

- HP66 tells the HP to print 66-line pages. By default, the HP prints only 60 lines to a page. That confuses some software, which demands that all pages have 66 lines. The software sends 66 lines for what it thinks will be a page, and the HP prints out a full page and then a short page with just 6 lines on it. Argghh! If I run HP66 beforehand, there's no problem.

- RESET saves me the trouble of reaching over, pressing the Off Line button, and then holding down the Continue/Reset key to reset the printer.

- SMALLPRT shifts the printer into lineprinter mode.

- LANDPRT shifts the printer into lineprinter landscape mode, so I can print out really wide text.

I'll use a lot of examples from the HP Series II laser printers, but the general principles apply to all printers.

Most printers have sadly unexploited features. I worked for several years with a Canon A2 laser printer (now remaindered in some catalogs for $1,800, I note). It could not only do the usual underline, boldface, and the like, but it could expand any font horizontally and vertically, shade text, and support an amazing vector graphics language that produced really spectacular output. The problem was that it wasn't supported by most printer utilities. That meant I had to write a few printer drivers.

Many printers are treasure chests of features. This chapter discusses how to use those features.

The First Confusion: ASCII and Control Codes

Computers communicate among themselves and with their peripherals via a numeric code. This code represents characters—numbers, letters, punctuation, and the like. Fortunately, computer vendors have pretty much agreed on the use of a code called *ASCII,* the American Standard Code for Information Interchange. (For a business noted for incompatibility, it's pretty incredible that virtually all vendors support this.)

ASCII, in its most basic form, is just a set of correspondences between numeric codes and the letters they represent. You can see the printable ASCII codes in Table 16.1.

For example, to tell a printer to print *Hello,* a program would send five numeric codes: 72, 101, 108, 108, 111. It's kind of like a cryptogram.

TABLE 16.1: The Printable ASCII Codes

32		42	*	52	4	62	>	72	H	82	R	92	\	102	f	112	p	122	z
33	!	43	+	53	5	63	?	73	I	83	S	93	]	103	g	113	q	123	{
34	''	44	,	54	6	64	@	74	J	84	T	94	^	104	h	114	r	124	|
35	#	45	-	55	7	65	A	75	K	85	U	95	—	105	i	115	s	125	}
36	$	46	.	56	8	66	B	76	L	86	V	96	'	106	j	116	t	126	~
37	%	47	/	57	9	67	C	77	M	87	W	97	a	107	k	117	u	127	DEL
38	&	48	0	58	:	68	D	78	N	88	X	98	b	108	l	118	v		
39	'	49	1	59	;	69	E	79	O	89	Y	99	c	109	m	119	w		
40	(	50	2	60	<	70	F	80	P	90	Z	100	d	110	n	120	x		
41	)	51	3	61	=	71	G	81	Q	91	[	101	e	111	.o	121	y		

Simple Programs to Send ASCII Codes

There are a number of ways to get these codes to the printer. The simplest way:

1. Create a file with the desired printer codes called, let's say, *X*.

2. Then create a batch file that uses the COPY command to send the codes to the printer. Using file *X* as an example, the batch file would look like

```
@echo off
copy x prn
```

Users with a DOS version previous to 3.3 should omit the @ sign from the **echo off** command. The file *X* should be a one-line set of printer codes terminated with a Ctrl-Z, *not* the usual ⏎! For example, suppose you want to create a batch file that just tells the printer to print the word *hello*. Just create a file called, for example, GREET.TXT, with only one line in it:

```
hello Ctrl-Z
```

Then invoke it with a batch file you can call GREET.BAT:

```
echo off
copy greet.txt prn
```

The **echo off**, by the way, tells DOS not to clutter up the screen with a lot of batch messages.

Using DOS's Editor to Enter Batch Files

For my examples, I'll suggest that you enter batch files with the editor supplied free with DOS, EDLIN. Now, wait. Before you turn your nose up, consider: All expert types should know EDLIN. When you're at another person's machine, you can't count on them having your favorite text editor. There's nothing more unprofessional than hearing an expert whine, "Why don't you have a *real* editor...." So here's a handy guide to EDLIN. When you see *n1* or *n2*, that means *Substitute a number here.* The commands you need most are:

n1	Moves EDLIN to the line numbered n1 and allows you to edit that line
n1I	Allows you to type in lines that will be inserted starting at line n1
n1,n2D	Deletes lines n1 through n2
E	Saves the file and exits
Q	Exits without saving

When EDLIN allows you to edit a line, the DOS editing keys come in handy, also. The most useful ones are:

F3	Copies the current line to the end from edit buffer
Ins	Allows you to insert characters
Del	Removes characters from the edit buffer

| $\rightarrow$ | Copies one character from edit buffer; F1 also does this |
| $\leftarrow$ | Backs up one character |

Trust me. One day, you'll thank me.

The Nonprinting ASCII Codes: Control Codes

You may have wondered why the codes started at 32. What about codes 0 to 31? Well, they're there, but they don't tell the printer to print a character; they tell the printer to *do something*. These are called *control codes*.

When a printer gets to the end of a line, it knows to start a new line. How does it know that the line has ended? Simple: The program has not only sent the text to be printed, it also ends each line with two codes you can't see. The first one, called *Carriage Return*, says to send the print head back to the extreme left position. The second, called *Line Feed*, says to scroll the paper down one line. (Otherwise, we'd just overprint the same line again and again. Your document would just be one very black line.) Carriage Return's control code is 13; Line Feed's is 10. Control codes used by printers are listed in Table 16.2.

TABLE 16.2: Selected Control Codes

NAME	ABBREVIATION	DECIMAL CODE	HEX CODE
Tab	HT	19	09
Line Feed	LF	10	0A
Form Feed	FF	12	0C
Carriage Return	CR	13	0D
Escape	ESC	27	1B

Since you now know control code 12 (Line Feed), you can now see how to write EJECT.BAT. Use two files, EJECT.TXT and EJECT.BAT. EJECT.TXT will contain the printer control codes. EJECT.BAT will *copy* that file to the printer: This is the way the codes are transferred to the printer.

Entering ASCII Codes

By the way, how do you enter a code 12? There are keys on the keyboard for A, B, C, and so on, but not too much for the nonprinting codes. You enter them with a PC feature.

1. Hold down the Alt key.

2. With your other hand, type the ASCII code *using the numeric keypad*—it won't work with the numbers on the top key row.

3. Release the Alt key.

The character will pop up on the screen. Try it with 65, the code for capital *A*.

EJECT.TXT is created with EDLIN in the following way:

1. At the DOS prompt, type **edlin eject.txt** and press ↵. EDLIN responds with the words *new file;* its prompt is an asterisk (*).

2. Type **i** and press ↵. This tells EDLIN that you want to enter lines. The screen will display *1:*.*

3. Press Ctrl-L, then Ctrl-Z. This is the code for a form feed.

4. Press Ctrl-Break, then type **e** and press ↵; this tells EDLIN to save the file and exit.

EJECT.BAT then is straightforward:

1. At the DOS prompt, type **edlin eject.bat** and press ↵. EDLIN responds with *new file*.

2. Type **i** and press ↵ to tell EDLIN that you want to enter lines. The screen will display *1:*.*

3. Type **copy eject.txt prn** and press ↵. The screen will display *2: **.

4. Press Ctrl-Z to tell EDLIN that this is the end of the file. Press Ctrl-Break, then type **e** and press ↵ to save the file and exit.

By the way, where the batch file refers to *eject.txt*, it's helpful to include the entire path name, like *c:\pcodes\eject.bat*, so the batch file can be invoked from any subdirectory.

Most of these codes are pretty straightforward. *Form Feed* forces a new page. *Tab* moves the print head to the next tab stop. But what about Escape?

Escape (Esc) is a *prefix*. It's an easy way for printer manufacturers to build a huge library of possible control codes. Esc generally doesn't do anything by itself—it tells the printer the next character is a command, not a character to print. Here's an example.

An Okidata 92 (a kind of dot-matrix printer) receives an Esc and then a *C*. Ordinarily, the Okidata would just print a *C*. But the Esc prefix means the *C* is a command, not a character. The Okidata then looks up what Esc-C means, and sees that it's now supposed to start underlining. It keeps underlining until it sees an Esc followed by a *D*. (How did I know that? I read the manual. Stay tuned.)

Putting Control Codes in Batch Files

Can you write a batch file to induce a printer to print underlined text? Sure, but there *is* one fly in the ointment.

The problem is in entering the Esc character. For DOS, EDLIN, and most text editors, Esc *means* something—it's not just a character to be entered. Some editors can be told, *The next keystroke I enter is just a keystroke—not a command.* It's just so with DOS's editor, EDLIN. I'd like to enter a line something like the following (<Esc> refers to the Esc key):

```
ECHO It's a <Esc>Cwonderful<Esc>D day.>PRN
```

But I don't really want to type *E, s,* and *c*. I want to just enter an Esc character. So there's a special sequence for entering Esc: Type Ctrl-V followed by a [(square bracket). Again, we'll create a text file and a batch file. So, the EDLIN session proceeds in the following way.

To make WONDER.TXT and WONDER.BAT:

1. At the DOS prompt, type **edlin wonder.txt⏎**.

2. At the EDLIN prompt, type **i** and press ⏎ to tell EDLIN that you want to enter lines.

3. At *1:**, type **It's a**, press Ctrl-V, then type **[C wonderful Ctrl-V [D day⏎**. The screen will display *2:**.

4. Press Ctrl-Z.

5. Press Ctrl-Break and type **e** to save and exit.

6. At the DOS prompt, type **edlin wonder.bat**.

7. At *new file*, type **i** to tell EDLIN that you want to enter lines.

8. At *1:**, type **copy wonder.txt prn** and press ⏎.

9. At *2:**, press Ctrl-Z to tell EDLIN that this is the end of the file.

10. Press Ctrl-Break and type **e** to save the file and exit.

Please note that the Ctrl-V trick probably doesn't work on your text editor or word processor. There's probably some other way to enter Esc. Consult your word processor or editor's manual. If you are using EDIT, you can enter an escape as Ctrl-P followed by the Esc key.

Again, control codes other than Esc can be easily generated with the Alt key. It's just Esc that will give you trouble.

Finding Out the Details on Your Printer

How did I know <Esc> C starts underlining on the Okidata, and that <Esc> D stops underlining? I looked it up in the Okidata manual. Since Okidatas aren't the most common printers in the world (as you can see, I buy printers more for their features than their popularity), we'll take the

PRINTER SOFTWARE

rest of the examples in this section from the Hewlett-Packard series of LaserJet laser printers. Figures 16.1–16.4 contain excerpts from the HP manual (from the appendix describing the printer's control codes).

FIGURE 16.1

Excerpt from HP manual (1 of 4)

FUNCTION	PARAMETER	PRINTER COMMAND	DECIMAL VALUE	HEXADECIMAL VALUE
JOB CONTROL COMMANDS				
RESET				
RESET		EcE	027 069	1B 45
NUMBER OF COPIES	# of Copies (1-99)	Ec&l#X	027 038 108 #...# 088	1B 26 6C #...# 58
PAPER INPUT CONTROL				
	Eject Page	Ec&l0H	027 038 108 048 072	1B 26 6C 30 48
	Feed from Tray	Ec&l1H	027 038 108 049 072	1B 26 6C 31 48
	Manual Feed	Ec&l2H	027 038 108 050 072	1B 26 6C 32 48
	Manual Env. Feed	Ec&l3H	027 038 108 051 072	1B 26 6C 33 48
PAGE LENGTH and SIZE				
PAGE SIZE	Executive	Ec&l1A	027 038 108 049 065	1B 26 6C 31 41
	Letter	Ec&l2A	027 038 108 050 065	1B 26 6C 32 41
	Legal	Ec&l3A	027 038 108 051 065	1B 26 6C 33 41
	A4	Ec&l26A	027 038 108 050 054 065	1B 26 6C 32 36 41
	Monarch	Ec&l80A	027 038 108 056 048 065	1B 26 6C 38 30 41
	Commercial 10	Ec&l81A	027 038 108 056 049 065	1B 26 6C 38 31 41
	International DL	Ec&l90A	027 038 108 057 048 065	1B 26 6C 39 30 41
	International C5	Ec&l91A	027 038 108 057 049 065	1B 26 6C 39 31 41
PAGE LENGTH	# of Lines	Ec&l#P	027 038 108 #...# 080	1B 26 6C #...# 50
ORIENTATION	Portrait	Ec&l0O	027 038 108 048 079	1B 26 6C 30 4F
	Landscape	Ec&l1O	027 038 108 049 079	1B 26 6C 31 4F
MARGINS and TEXT LENGTH				
TOP MARGIN	# of Lines	Ec&l#E	027 038 108 #...# 069	1B 26 6C #...# 45
TEXT LENGTH	# of Lines	Ec&l#F	027 038 108 #...# 070	1B 26 6C #...# 46
LEFT MARGIN	Left (col #)	Ec&a#L	027 038 097 #...# 076	1B 26 61 #...# 4C
RIGHT MARGIN	Right (col #)	Ec&a#M	027 038 097 #...# 077	1B 26 61 #...# 4D
CLEAR HORIZONTAL MARGINS		Ec9	027 057	1B 39
PERFORATION SKIP MODE				
PERF SKIP	Disable	Ec&l0L	027 038 108 048 076	1B 26 6C 30 4C
	Enable	Ec&l1L	027 038 108 049 076	1B 26 6C 31 4C
HORIZONTAL COLUMN SPACING				
HORIZONTAL MOTION INDEX	# of 1/20" Increments	Ec&k#H	027 038 107 #...# 072	1B 26 6B #...# 48
VERTICAL LINE SPACING				
VERTICAL MOTION INDEX	# of 1/48" Increments	Ec&l#C	027 038 108 #...# 067	1B 26 6C #...# 43
LINES/INCH	1 line/inch	Ec&l1D	027 038 108 049 068	1B 26 6C 31 44
	2 lines/inch	Ec&l2D	027 038 108 050 068	1B 26 6C 32 44
	3 lines/inch	Ec&l3D	027 038 108 051 068	1B 26 6C 33 44
	4 lines/inch	Ec&l4D	027 038 108 052 068	1B 26 6C 34 44
	6 lines/inch	Ec&l6D	027 038 108 054 068	1B 26 6C 36 44
	8 lines/inch	Ec&l8D	027 038 108 056 068	1B 26 6C 38 44
	12 lines/inch	Ec&l12D	027 038 108 049 050 068	1B 26 6C 31 32 44
	16 lines/inch	Ec&l16D	027 038 108 049 054 068	1B 26 6C 31 36 44
	24 lines/inch	Ec&l24D	027 038 108 050 052 068	1B 26 6C 32 34 44
	48 lines/inch	Ec&l48D	027 038 108 052 056 068	1B 26 6C 34 38 44

FIGURE 16.2

Excerpt from HP
manual (2 of 4)

PUSH/POP POSITION				
PUSH/POP POSITION	Push	Ec&f0S	027 038 102 048 083	1B 26 66 30 53
	Pop	Ec&f1S	027 038 102 049 083	1B 26 66 31 53
FONT SELECTION				
ORIENTATION				
ORIENTATION	Portrait	Ec&/00	027 038 108 048 079	1B 26 6C 30 4F
	Landscape	Ec&/10	027 038 108 049 079	1B 26 6C 31 4F
SYMBOL SET SELECTION				
PRIMARY SYMBOL SET	HP Math7	Ec(0A	027 040 048 065	1B 28 30 41
	HP Line Draw	Ec(0B	027 040 048 066	1B 28 30 42
	ISO 60: Norwegian 1	Ec(0D	027 040 048 068	1B 28 30 44
	ISO 61: Norwegian 2	Ec(1D	027 040 049 068	1B 28 31 44
	HP Roman Extension	Ec(0E	027 040 048 089	1B 28 30 45
	ISO 4: United Kingdom	Ec(1E	027 040 049 069	1B 28 31 45
	ISO 25: French	Ec(0F	027 040 048 070	1B 28 30 46
	ISO 69: French	Ec(1F	027 040 049 070	1B 28 31 46
	HP German	Ec(0G	027 040 048 071	1B 28 30 47
	ISO 21: German	Ec(1G	027 040 049 071	1B 28 31 47
	HP Greek8	Ec(8G	027 040 056 71	1B 28 38 47
	ISO 15: Italian	Ec(0I	027 040 048 073	1B 28 30 49
	ISO 14: JIS ASCII	Ec(0K	027 040 048 075	1B 28 30 4B
	HP Katakana	Ec(1K	027 040 049 075	1B 28 31 4B
	ISO 57: Chinese	Ec(2K	027 040 050 075	1B 28 32 4B
	HP Math7	Ec(0M	027 040 048 077	1B 28 30 4D
	Technical	Ec(1M	027 040 049 077	1B 28 31 4D
	HP Math8	Ec(8M	027 040 056 77	1B 28 38 4D

Examples

Here are some examples of batch files that make your printer perform functions from DOS. I'll only show the text files here. Remember that you must also write an accompanying batch file to copy the text file to the printer.

Compressed Print

Most printers have a way to move to a 15– or 16–character-per-inch (CPI) mode. Having a batch file called SMALLPRT, shown below, to shift the printer into this mode could be quite handy.

```
<Esc>&l00<Esc>(10U<Esc>(sp16.6h8.5vsbT
```

PRINTER SOFTWARE

FIGURE 16.3

Excerpt from HP
manual (3 of 4)

FUNCTION	PARAMETER	PRINTER COMMAND	DECIMAL VALUE	HEXADECIMAL VALUE
	ISO 100: ECMA-94 (Latin 1)	Ec(ØN	027 040 048 78	1B 28 30 4E
	OCR A	Ec(ØO	027 040 048 079	1B 28 30 4F
	OCR B	Ec(1O	027 040 049 079	1B 28 31 4F
	ISO 11: Swedish	Ec(ØS	027 040 048 083	1B 28 30 53
	HP Spanish	Ec(1S	027 040 049 083	1B 28 31 53
	ISO 17: Spanish	Ec(2S	027 040 050 083	1B 28 32 53
	ISO 10: Swedish	Ec(3S	027 040 051 083	1B 28 33 53
	ISO 16: Portuguese	Ec(4S	027 040 052 083	1B 28 34 53
	ISO 84: Portuguese	Ec(5S	027 040 053 083	1B 28 35 53
	ISO 85: Spanish	Ec(6S	027 040 054 083	1B 28 36 53
	ISO 6: ASCII	Ec(ØU	027 040 048 085	1B 28 30 55
	HP Legal	Ec(1U	027 040 049 085	1B 28 31 55
	ISO 2: IRV	Ec(2U	027 040 050 085	1B 28 32 55
	OEM-1	Ec(7U	027 040 055 85	1B 28 37 55
	HP Roman8	Ec(8U	027 040 056 85	1B 28 38 55
	PC-8	Ec(1ØU	027 040 049 048 085	1B 28 31 30 55
	PC-8 (D/N)	Ec(11U	027 040 049 049 085	1B 28 31 31 55
	HP Pi Font	Ec(15U	027 040 049 053 085	1B 28 31 35 55
SPACING				
PRIMARY SPACING	Proportional	Ec(s1P	027 040 115 049 080	1B 28 73 31 50
	Fixed	Ec(sØP	027 040 115 048 080	1B 28 73 30 50
PITCH				
PRIMARY PITCH	# CPI	Ec(s#H	027 040 115 #...# 072	1B 28 73 #...# 48
POINT SIZE				
PRIMARY POINT SIZE	# Pt.	Ec(s#V	027 040 115 #...# 086	1B 28 73 #...# 56
STYLE				
PRIMARY STYLE	Upright	Ec(sØS	027 040 115 048 083	1B 28 73 30 53
	Italic	Ec(s1S	027 040 115 049 083	1B 28 73 31 53
STROKE WEIGHT				
PRIMARY STROKE WEIGHT	Medium (0)	Ec(sØB	027 040 115 048 066	1B 28 73 30 42
	Bold (3)	Ec(s3B	027 040 115 051 066	1B 28 73 33 42
TYPEFACE				
PRIMARY TYPEFACE	Line Printer	Ec(sØT	027 040 115 048 084	1B 28 73 30 54
	Courier	Ec(s3T	027 040 115 051 084	1B 28 73 33 54
	Helv	Ec(s4T	027 040 115 052 084	1B 28 73 34 54
	Tms Rmn	Ec(s5T	027 040 115 053 084	1B 28 73 35 54
	Letter Gothic	Ec(s6T	027 040 115 054 084	1B 28 73 36 54
	Prestige	Ec(s8T	027 040 115 056 084	1B 28 73 38 54
	Presentations	Ec(s11T	027 040 115 049 049 084	1B 28 73 31 31 54
	Optima	Ec(s17T	027 040 115 049 055 084	1B 28 73 31 37 54
	ITC Garamond	Ec(s18T	027 040 115 049 056 084	1B 28 73 31 38 54
	Cooper Black	Ec(s19T	027 040 115 049 057 084	1B 28 73 31 39 54
	Coronet Bold	Ec(s20T	027 040 115 050 048 084	1B 28 73 32 40 54
	Broadway	Ec(s21T	027 040 115 050 049 084	1B 28 73 32 41 54

FIGURE 16.4

Excerpt from HP
manual (4 of 4)

FUNCTION	PARAMETER	PRINTER COMMAND	DECIMAL VALUE	HEXADECIMAL VALUE
	Bauer Bodoni Black Condensed	Ec(s22T	027 040 115 050 050 084	1B 28 73 32 42 54
	Century Schoolbook	Ec(s23T	027 040 115 050 051 084	1B 28 73 32 43 54
	University Roman	Ec(s24T	027 040 115 050 052 084	1B 28 73 32 44 54
FONT PITCH				
PRIMARY & SECONDARY FONT PITCH (Alternate Method)	10.00 Pitch	Ec&kØS	027 038 107 048 083	1B 26 6B 30 53
	16.66 Pitch	Ec&k2S	027 038 107 050 083	1B 26 6B 32 53
DEFAULT FONT	Primary Font	Ec(3@	027 040 051 064	1B 28 33 40
	Secondary Font	Ec)3@	027 041 051 064	1B 29 33 40
UNDERLINE				
UNDERLINE	Enable Fixed	Ec&dØD	027 038 100 048 068	1B 26 64 30 44
	Enable Floating	Ec&d3D	027 038 100 051 068	1B 26 64 33 44
	Disable	Ec&d@	027 038 100 064	1B 26 64 40

Of course, you don't enter the letters *E, s,* and *c*—you enter the Escape code. The initial string *l0O* is *lowercase L, zero,* and *uppercase letter O.* This is the command to select a 16.6 CPI font. For more explanation, see the next section on selecting laser fonts. Here's the LANDPRT.TXT file for landscape lineprinter fonts:

```
<Esc>&l10<Esc>(10U<Esc>(sp16.6h8.5vsbT
```

The only difference between these files is that the initial part starts with llO rather than l0O.

Reset

Sometimes you'd like to restore the printer to its power-on settings. One application in particular that can use this is DisplayWrite. Run Display-Write, and it sets up the printer for its own use and prints your document. The annoying thing is that DisplayWrite doesn't clean up after itself, sometimes leaving your printer in a strange mode of some kind. You can, of course, take the printer offline and reset it, or turn it off and then turn it back on. But a batch file is simpler, and besides, you can add it to the DisplayWrite batch file so the reset is automatic every time you use the program. Here is the RESET.TXT file:

```
<Esc>E
```

Sixty-Six Lines per Page on a LaserJet

One really annoying feature of laser printers is that they don't print 66 lines on a page. Instead, they force a margin of a few lines at the top and bottom, and generally won't print more than 60 lines per page. There are a few programs that just plain assume there are 66 lines on a page, and so using them on a laser is a real pain—each page shows up as 60 lines on one page, 6 lines on the next, and a form feed.

When the LaserJet powers up, it wants a top margin of 0.5 inches and a bottom margin of 0.5 inches for a printing space of 10 inches. You *can* tell it to minimize the top margin (you can't tell it to eliminate it altogether), but can't tell it to get rid of the bottom margin. The laser engine is absolutely bent on only printing within 10.5 inches of 11-inch paper, so you can't do much to change that. But you can subtly change the height of each line so 66 lines fit in the 10.5 inches. Making the lines a bit shorter gives the printer the space to fit 66 lines, but that's not all. Finish by telling the printer that not only *can* it print 66 lines on a page, it *should* print 66 lines to a page.

The whole code string looks like the following:

```
<Esc>E<Esc>&l14c1e7.64c66F
```

Selecting Fonts on an HP LaserJet

If you're working with a desktop-publishing or word-processing program and you want to use the many typefaces available on a laser printer, you generally have a fairly simple task; a couple of keystrokes and you've changed fonts. But suppose you want to convince dBASE (or Lotus) to print a report in something other than the default font?

If you've ever looked at control codes for simpler printers, like an Epson dot matrix printer, you've seen that font selection is a fairly simple matter. But the LaserJet (and its later cousins) have many more fonts available, and so require a more complex font selection approach. Getting a handle on fonts for a LaserJet involves:

- Understanding font terminology (yeah, there's jargon for that too)
- Understanding the font selection codes
- Knowing the printer's limitations in terms of memory and number of fonts

So here goes.

Font Attributes: Courier Isn't a Font

My friend Jane Holcombe, the LaserJet expert, says, "You can always tell LaserJet novices. They call Courier a 'font.'" Courier isn't a font. (Jane *is* a printer snob.) It's a *typeface,* at least in HP terminology. Suppose you've printed a document using Courier typeface—that's all just one font, right? Wrong. You change the font if you use boldface, italics, different sizes, or go to landscape mode, to name just a few possibilities.

Fonts are described by *eight* attributes:

- Orientation (portrait or landscape)
- Symbol Set (don't worry about this for the moment)
- Spacing (fixed vs. proportional)
- Pitch (width of characters)
- Points (height of characters)
- Style (upright vs. italic)
- Stroke Weight (light, normal, boldface)
- Typeface (Courier, Times Roman, and so on)

For example, a typical document may have the following type characteristics:

- Portrait orientation
- IBM-US symbol set
- Proportionally spaced
- 12-point height
- Upright
- Normal weight
- Times typeface

Most of these characteristics are self-explanatory, but here are the details.

Orientation

This just refers to whether the text prints across the width of the page (as does the text that you're reading now), which is called *portrait mode,* or up the length of the page, in *landscape mode.* Landscape mode is mainly used to present wide data, such as a timeline or a spreadsheet. Orientation is selected with the <Esc>&l#O code sequence, where # equals 0 for portrait or 1 for landscape. (Note that it's an ampersand followed by a lowercase *L,* not the numeral 1. The ending character is the letter *O,* not a zero.) The standard paper for portrait mode is aligned 8½ inches wide × 11 inches long; landscape is 11 inches wide, 8½ inches long.

Symbol Set

Recall the discussion of the ASCII codes? Someone, at some point, decided to declare that the ASCII code for *A* is 65, and 65 it has remained. There *are* alternative code sets. The ASCII table earlier in the book did not include all codes, but rather the most-used ones. In actuality, there are 256 different codes that can refer to characters. Some are familiar, such as letters, digits, punctuation, and the like. Others may exist to support foreign-language characters such as the cedilla (ç), or mathematical symbols like the greater than or equal to (≥), or characters used to draw boxes.

There isn't just *one* ASCII code set. Variations are fairly common. Suppose you have an old Ohio Scientific computer. If you print the code 65 on your screen, you'll get the familiar old *A,* just as you would on an IBM compatible. But try printing code 254. On the Ohio Scientific, you'll see a little picture of an army tank. On the PC, you'll see a superscripted 2. Those are different *symbol sets.* Basically, a symbol set relates code *x* with character *y.*

As I've indicated, pretty much all symbol sets have 65 equaling *A,* 48 equaling *0,* and the like. It's the codes from 0 to 31 and above 127 that tend to become strange. A symbol set might vary from the PC symbol set because:

- The symbol set follows some international standard (ISO or ECMA).

- A computer manufacturer decided to be creative. For example, HP's microcomputers are supposed to be PC compatible, but the symbol set they show on their screens is a bit different from the IBM symbol set.

- The symbol set represents nonstandard items. Another example could be a symbol set with mathematical or legal symbols.

- The symbol set represents a non-Roman character set. Greek, Hebrew, Kanji, and Korean could be (and are) available as laser-loadable fonts.

HP has defined a number of symbol sets, but the ones you'll see most commonly are Roman-8 (the symbol set that's built into HP computers) and IBM-US (the symbol set found in most IBM compatibles). Recall that both symbol sets are very similar, in fact identical for the codes from 32 to 127. That means if all you're doing is printing simple English text, it really doesn't matter which of the two symbol sets you use. But the box drawing characters most IBM compatibles have aren't available to you if you use a Roman-8 symbol set. That's why, when your screen looks like

```
Hello
```

the HP printout looks like

```
Öáááááááááááá¢
•   Hello      •
âáááááááááááái
```

By the way, if you have a LaserJet Series II, the answer is to tell the HP to use the IBM-US symbol set. Just take the LJ II offline, and then press and hold down the MENU key for about 8 seconds. (If you don't know where the control is, look at Figure 16.5.) *SYM SET=ROMAN-8* will appear on the LCD panel. Press the + key twice, and *SYM SET=IBM-US* will appear. Press the ENTER/RESET MENU key once. Then press the MENU key until READY appears. Reset the printer, and you're in business from that point on.

Symbol set is selected in software with the sequence <Esc>(###, where ### is the symbol set ID. The IDs for Roman-8 and IBM-US are 8U and 10U, respectively. Check your font documentation for the symbol sets of the fonts you've purchased. You can also find out symbol sets on an LJ II by taking the printer offline and pressing PRINT FONTS/TEST. You get

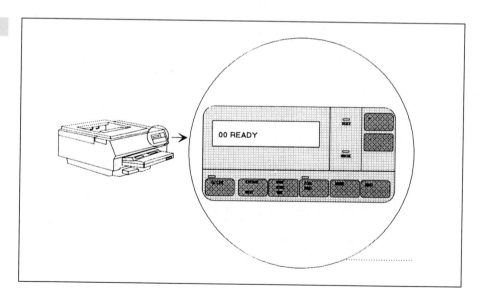

FIGURE 16.5

LaserJet Series II printer with detail showing control panel output something like Figure 16.6. Note that the first Courier font shown has the 10U (IBM-US) symbol set. Note there's also an 8U, the Roman-8, and an 11U, the IBM-Danish/Norwegian symbol set.

Spacing

This either refers to *fixed* spacing as in a typewriter or *proportional* spacing as in this text, where smaller characters take up less space than larger characters. In fixed spacing, all characters take up the same amount of space, which must obviously be the amount required by the largest character in the character set (the capital *M*, for those who are interested). The escape sequence is <Esc>(s#P, where # equals 0 for fixed and 1 for proportional.

Pitch

Pitch is the width of a character. Note that pitch is only used for fixed-spaced fonts—you'd never specify pitch when selecting a proportionally spaced font. Pitch is measured in characters per inch. Courier typefaces are typically 10 or 12 pitch, line printer faces are usually 15 or 16.6 pitch. For the truly brave, you can buy 20+ pitch faces for use in printing superwide spreadsheets. Note that pitch and spacing are reported on the Series II Font Printout under the *pitch* column: If the font is fixed, the pitch is reported. Otherwise, the letters PS under the font indicate that the font is proportionally spaced.

Pitch is selected with the <Esc>(s##.##H sequence, where ##.## is the pitch. To select a 16.6-pitch font, use Esc(s16.6H. The common 10-pitch

FIGURE 16.6

Excerpt from LaserJet Series II Font Printout

```
                 -------- PORTRAIT FONTS --------

FONT                                   POINT SYMBOL
 ID              NAME            PITCH SIZE   SET        PRINT SAMPLE
---- ------------------------- ----- ----- ------ ------------------------

INTERNAL FONTS

I00  COURIER                     10    12     10U ABCDEfghij#$@[\]ˆ`(|)˜123
                                                  íó│┤╢╕╣╗╜┴┼╚╔╦╩╤╨╥╘╫╪█▐απΦ
I01  COURIER                     10    12      8U ABCDEfghij#$@[\]^`(|)~123
                                                  ÀÂ˙ÇÑ¡¿£§êéàèëöÅØåæÄÜßÁÐÒ
I02  COURIER                     10    12     11U ABCDEfghij#$@[\]ˆ`(|)˜123
                                                  íó│┤╢╕╣╗╜┴┼╚╔╦╩╤╨╥╘╫╪█▐απΦ
```

Courier could be selected with <Esc>(s10H. When specifying decimal values, don't use more than two decimal places.

Height

Height is sometimes called the font's *points* because that's the unit used to measure height. A point is $\frac{1}{72}$ inch. Height is reported in the Font Printout as *Point Size*. It's selected with the <Esc>(s##.##V sequence. For example, 12-point type could be selected with the Esc(s12V sequence.

Style

This tells if the font is upright (roman) or if it's italic. The code sequence <Esc>(s#S sets this, where # is 0 for roman, 1 for italic. Note that this doesn't direct the printer to italicize an existing upright font—the printer isn't capable of that. I make that point because people get confused that these commands can't *change* existing fonts, they only *select* fonts that are already in the printer. If no fonts match the criteria, you're out of luck. Beginners often think the LaserJet Series II will make a font with an upright style into a font with an italic style; they don't realize that you must create (or buy) a font that has an italic style. Only then, once it's been downloaded to the printer, can you successfully issue a font select command that includes a request for italic style.

Stroke Weight

Stroke weight specifies whether a font is lightly drawn, normal, or boldface. This is activated with the <Esc>(s#B sequence, where # is an integer from −7 to 7. The setting 0 is normal, and 3 is normal bold.

Typeface

This describes how the typeface is drawn. In Figure 16.7, you can see how four different designers went about creating capital and lowercase *A*s. The different typefaces are supposed to convey different moods and messages. Typefaces are selected with the <Esc>(s#T command, where # refers to typeface number. Typeface numbers are shown in Table 16.3.

FIGURE 16.7

Courier, Times Roman,
Helvetica, and
Lineprinter A

A A A A a a a a

TABLE 16.3: HP Typeface Numbers

VALUE (#)	TYPEFACE
0	LinePrinter
3	Courier
4	Helvetica (Helv)
5	Times Roman (Tms Rmn)
6	Letter Gothic
8	Prestige
11	Presentations
17	Optima
18	Garamond
19	Cooper Black
20	Coronet Bold
21	Broadway
22	Bauer Bodoni Black Condensed
23	Century Schoolbook
24	University Roman
36	Bitstream Charter

Using Font Attributes to Select a Font

Now you understand the eight attributes (seven if you're talking proportional, because—as you may recall—proportional fonts don't need a pitch value). You understand that any given font is a unique combination of these eight attributes. How do you select a particular font?

Selecting Fonts with Complete Information and Using Shortcuts

Let's start with a simple example. This text is mainly in a font that has, as has been already mentioned, the following attributes:

- Portrait orientation
- IBM-US symbol set
- Proportionally spaced
- 12-point height
- Upright
- Normal weight
- Times Roman

Now let's match up commands with attributes:

Portrait Orientation	<Esc>&10O
IBM-US symbol set	<Esc>(10U
Proportionally spaced	<Esc>(s1P
12-point height	<Esc>(s12V
Upright	<Esc>(s0S
Normal weight	<Esc>(s0B
Times typeface	<Esc>(s5T

String them all together, and you get

```
<Esc>&l00<Esc>(10U<Esc>(s1P<Esc>(s12V<Esc>(s0S<Esc>(
s0B<Esc>(s5T
```

(Make sure you enter this as one line.) Now, this will work, but there's no reason to type all that if it's not necessary. That's where LaserJet Shortcut #1 comes in handy. When issuing several escape commands, *all of which begin with the same two-character string*, you can omit the Escape and the two characters on commands after the first. However, you must indicate that the shortened command is part of a series of commands by ending it with a *lowercase* letter rather than the uppercase letter used in the manual. The last command in the string should *retain* the uppercase letter. For example, rather than <Esc>(s0X <Esc>(s0B<Esc>(s5T, use <Esc>(s0x0b5T.

Apply LaserJet Shortcut #1 to the above string, and it becomes

```
<Esc>&l00<Esc>(10U<Esc>(s1p12v0s0b5T
```

You then can apply LaserJet Shortcut #2. When the LaserJet expects a numeric value and you don't supply one, it assumes a value of 0. That'll let us remove the zeros from 0s0b:

```
<Esc>& l00<Esc>(10U<Esc>(s1p12vsb5T
```

And the font is selected. By the way, you can't remove the 0 from the first part of the command, for some reason.

Understanding How Fonts Are Selected in Depth

Suppose you give incorrect information, like requesting an 11-point font when only a 10 or a 12 is available? Suppose you request a font that's Portrait with typeface Courier, when the only fonts available are a Portrait Lineprinter and a Landscape Courier—would you get the Lineprinter or the Courier? The HP uses the following algorithm to match a request to a font.

1. First, look at the Orientation request, if included. If only one font matches the Orientation request, take it *and ignore the rest of the request*. Thus, if you requested a Portrait Courier and all the laser has is Portrait Lineprinter and Landscape Courier, you would get Portrait Lineprinter.

2. If there are *several* fonts that could meet the Orientation criterion (there probably are), look next to the Symbol Set request, if one was included. Is there something that matches both the Orientation and Symbol Set? If there's only one font that matches the two exactly, take it and, again, ignore the rest of the request. Alternatively, if an invalid Symbol Set is requested, the current Symbol Set is taken *as if specified by the user.*

3. If, given the Orientation *and* the Symbol Set, there are several eligible fonts, look next to Spacing. As before, if this narrows things down to just one font, stop examining the font selection command. If proportional spacing is requested, but there are no proportional fonts in the eligible pool, just treat the request as if the user requested fixed spacing.

4. Still have more than one eligible font? Look to Pitch if Spacing is fixed. If you can match the pitch request (a 10-pitch is requested *and* a 10-pitch is in the pool of eligibles), use that to narrow the field of eligible fonts. If there's no match (for example, you requested an 11-pitch but only have 10 and 12 in the eligible pool), take the *next higher* pitch. If none are higher, take the closest lower pitch.

5. If, given Orientation, Symbol Set, Spacing, and Pitch, you still have more than one possible font, choose the font(s) in the pool with the closest Height to the requested Height. As before, stop if this narrows the field to one.

6. Look next to Style. If you can *match* the request to a font or fonts in the pool, do so. If not, just ignore the request. The vast majority of the fonts are 0 (upright) anyway, so it tends not to thin the pack very much.

7. If you're still trying to narrow down font possibilities, use Stroke Weight next. Recall that stroke weight varies from −7 (very light) to 7 (dark bold). If the printer can match the request, it will. If not, it will look for a more extreme weight. For example, if 3 isn't available, it will look first to 4, 5, 6, and 7; if −5 isn't available, it will look first to −6 and −7. Failing that, it will use the closest weight. This doesn't help to narrow things down very well, as most fonts are either 0 (normal) or 3 (bold).

8. Only *now* does the printer look at the Typeface. If there isn't an exact match, the request gets ignored.

9. Finally, if there are *still* more than one possible font that meet all eight criteria, choose first from soft (downloaded) fonts, then cartridge fonts, and finally from built-in fonts. If there are multiple soft fonts that match, pick the one with the lowest font number.

To summarize, font characteristics are ranked in terms of importance. Here, they're arranged in descending order of importance:

1. Orientation

2. Symbol Set

3. Spacing

4. Pitch

5. Points

6. Style

7. Stroke Weight

8. Typeface

A Note on Using the IID and IIP Printers

The Series IID and IIP printers have an extra feature the Series II does not: They can rotate fonts. You needn't worry about whether a font is landscape or portrait. Just specify which you want.

Understand the difference. The Series II uses orientation as a means to narrow down which printer font to use. The IIP and IID use this information as a command about whether or not to rotate an already-selected font. That means that IID and IIP font selection strings look like the II commands with one difference: The orientation string part goes at the end.

That means the previous font selection example would look like the following one on the IID or IIP:

```
<Esc>(10U<Esc>(s1p12vsb5T<Esc> & 100
```

Examples of Font Selection

Suppose your laser printer has the fonts listed in Table 16.4 loaded in it at the moment.

1. You request a Landscape 10U Proportional font, 12-point Courier. What do you get? The printer looks first at Orientation. There's only one Landscape font, so you get the line-printer font with 8.5-point height.

2. You request a Portrait 10U Fixed 10-pitch 12-point Courier font. Which do you get? There's a soft-font Courier and a built-in Courier. Both meet the criteria given: orientation, symbol set, spacing, pitch, and height. It's a tie, and ties go to the soft font.

3. You request a Portrait 10U Proportional 12-point Upright Normal font, as you want the 12-point Times Roman and can't remember the typeface code for Times Roman. Which do you get? Both the Charter and the 12-point Times Roman meet all criteria given. Now it's a tie. Charter happened to be loaded first, and so it got soft font ID S02. The Times Roman got ID S03, so it's ignored in favor of Charter.

TABLE 16.4: Selected Laser Printer Fonts

ORIENT-ATION	SYMBOL SET	SPACING	PITCH	POINTS	STYLE	WEIGHT	FACE	SOURCE
Land.	ON	F	16.6	18.5	Uprt	Normal	Lineptr	B
Port.	10U	F	10	12	Uprt	Normal	Courier	S01
Port.	10U	F	10	12	Uprt	Normal	Courier	B
Port.	10U	PS		12	Uprt	Normal	Charter	S02
Port.	10U	PS		12	Uprt	Normal	Tms Rm	S03
Port.	10U	PS		10	Uprt	Normal	Tms Rm	S04

B—built in fonts. *Sxx*—downloaded soft font #*xx*

4. You look up the Times Roman code, and request Portrait 10U
Proportional 10.8-point Upright Normal Times Roman. What do
you get? Since 10.8 is closer to 10 than to 12, you get the 10-point
Times Roman. Had you asked for 11-point, there would have
been a tie, since 10-point is as far from your request as is 12-point.
The tie would have gone, again, to the soft font with the lower soft
font ID number, and you'd end up with 12-point Times Roman.

Well, those are the basics of tackling control codes on your printer. Take
some time to become comfortable with what your printer can do, and
you'll get more out of what you paid for. Now let's see how to tackle the
hardware....

Printers and Printer Interfaces

PRINTERS can be a real maintenance headache. Because they produce tangible results (pieces of paper), malfunctions with printers can be more upsetting than their wholly-electronic brethren. For example, try telling Lotus that you've got an Okidata printer when you have an Epson, and then print a graph. The printer will start spewing out pages, as if angry for being misrepresented.

Most of my printer problems—the vast majority—are software-related issues. The hardware problems are often cable or printer interface problems. I mainly use dot-matrix and laser printers. Daisywheel printers *are* prone to hardware failure, and I frankly recommend that you don't buy them. Hewlett-Packard even offers a printer (the LaserJet series IIP) that can be found for just a little under $900. At that price, it's cheaper than a daisywheel that's one-fifth its speed, and it has a sheet feeder and peace and quiet thrown in for free.

Components

As always, components usually include a controller (the parallel or serial interface board), a cable, and a printer. The parallel port is simple enough that it's commonly included on other expansion boards.

Remember that the essence of peripheral troubleshooting is *isolate and test.*

Maintenance

A few things can be done to maintain printers of all types. Vacuum out the paper chaff periodically from the inside of the printer. Determine if there's a belt-tightening mechanism for the printer; usually a motor moves the print head via a belt. Find the correct tension values. Keep a replacement belt on hand. In fact, find any small replaceable things and have them around beforehand. (Believe me, they're no picnic to try to find in a hurry.)

With a dry, soft cloth, clean both the paper path and the ribbon path. Most manufacturers suggest cleaning every six months. The ribbon path can build up a film of inky glop that causes the ribbon to jam. To clean this, go to a drugstore and buy a dispenser box of 100 clear plastic gloves. Use them when working on the printer (but not chips and boards—that plastic can build up some *mean* static) so that you don't have to wash your hands for hours to remove the ink. A cleanup tip: Hairspray seems to be good for removing ink from fabric. Cheap hairspray works a lot better than the expensive stuff. Spray it on the fabric, and rinse with cold water. A little soap will pick up the rest.

Most printers don't need to be lubricated in everyday use. In fact, oil can do considerable damage if applied to the wrong places. But if you thoroughly disassemble the printer, you'll probably have to lubricate various points as you reassemble. If you intend to do this, I strongly recommend that you get a maintenance manual from the manufacturer. On dot-matrix and daisywheel printers, you can pretty safely lube the head transport rails: two long metal rods where the print head moves back and forth. As with hard disks, it would be a good idea to use a teflon-type lubricant.

Dot-Matrix Printers

Here are a few things you can do to lengthen your dot-matrix printer's life.

- Be nice to the print head. Dot-matrix printers are, in general, very reliable. But keeping the print head cool is vital. Don't stack up things on or around the printer.

Here's a tip that will extend both the life of your ribbon and that of your head: Put some WD-40 lubricant on a used ink ribbon. Let it soak overnight. It'll produce good output the next day, and you won't damage the print head—in fact, putting the WD-40 in the ink lubes the print heads. Let me stress, however, that this only applies to ink ribbons. If you have a thermal transfer printer, like an IBM Quietwriter or an Okimate 20, this won't work.

You shouldn't re-ink your ink cartridges for the same reason that you shouldn't buy cheap cartridges: There's an acid in cheap inks that corrodes print heads, and a necessary lubricant in the inks of the more expensive cartridges. This isn't to say that kindly Mr. Jones with his discount office supplies store down the street is selling you dangerous cartridges, but it doesn't hurt to find out if the ink is the low-acid, lubricious type.

- Do not turn the print platen rollers when the power is on. The platen roller is turned by a stepper motor. The motor is doing its best to keep the platen right where it is. You frustrate the poor thing if you turn the platen against its will, and so it gets dangerously schizophrenic and commits suicide. Only turn the platen rollers when the power is off. If you're responsible for other users' machines, teach them to follow this rule.

- Don't engage both the friction feed and tractor feeds at the same time. If you enable both the tractor feed and the friction feed, a tug-of-war between the two feeds results. The paper loses.

- Do not be parsimonious with paper. Did you ever have a dot-matrix printer that used fanfold paper that ended up curling around so that the paper exited out the back and ran back in the front? The problem is that when people tear a sheet off the printer, they leave just a partial sheet sticking out of the output end. That gets longer as the output grows, but it doesn't know quite where to go and so sometimes curls back into the box feeding the blank sheets. The answer is to "train" the paper: Shoot out three sheets from the back and start the paper folding up away from the input box. Many times, a piece of cardboard taped between the *in* and *out* reduces the possibility of this happening. Better yet, when you initially feed paper to a printer, feed *several* sheets. Don't be stingy—it's just paper. If this makes you ecologically uncomfortable, don't you recycle all the wasted paper in your office anyway?

Laser Printers

The laser printer is very similar to a copy machine. Having said that, it's amazing that they're as reliable as they are.

The most common laser engines are made by Canon. The HP LaserJets, the AppleWriter, the Canon A1/A2, the QMS Kiss, and others are all built around the Canon engines. These need no maintenance except for a new cartridge every 3,500 copies or so. The cartridges, discounted, cost about $70 and contain all that's needed for routine maintenance:

- Toner
- Print drum
- Main corona wire

So, you're performing a routine maintenance every time you change your cartridge.

Lasers require proper ventilation and a fair amount of power; they draw about a kilowatt of electricity. Other than that, don't pour any Cokes in them and they'll last a long time. Here are a few preventive maintenance tips:

- Lasers need ventilation. They generate a lot of heat. Plan to get rid of that heat somehow.
- Don't use recharged cartridges unless you know that the recharger isn't recharging more than once, and that it's recharging correctly. Should you use recharged cartridges? Here are the pros and cons.

    Pro: They're cheaper. Laser cartridges, especially those using the Canon engine, consist of a number of disparate items that ordinarily wear out: roller brushes, toner, and print drums, for example. These components wear out at different rates, and the recharge services claim that it's a shame to waste a good print drum just because the toner has run out.

    Con: The recharge people are right, up to a point. A print drum can probably stand one extra toner recharge—just one. If you buy recharged stuff, how do you know how many times it's been recharged? Further, some services are better than others. I've seen faultily recharged cartridges that spray toner all over the inside of the printer. It's quite distinctive.

So be careful of the "drill and fill" operators. Ensure that rechargers don't do more than one recharge; they should label their cartridges as "do not recharge" or the like. You should get a refill for the fuser wiper brush, and a cotton swab for your transfer corona (see the diagram in the instructions that come with the refill).

- Never ship a laser with a toner cartridge in place. It can open up and cover the inside of the laser with toner.

- When you change the cartridge, follow the instructions completely. Don't just shake the cartridge, pull out the cellophane, and insert the cartridge. Replace the fuser roller brush and clean the transfer corona.

Troubleshooting Approaches

What should you do when you encounter a printer problem? Here are a few thoughts.

Isolate the Problem

As always, we'll try to isolate the problem: Is it something in the computer or its software? The printer interface? The cable? The printer? Is the printer plugged in, cabled, and *on line?*

I'm assuming that this computer/printer combination has worked before, and that you haven't done anything differently since the last time it worked. The steps I use are:

1. Check if the printer is on line, plugged in, has paper, and is turned on. Does the printer have paper? One of my favorite tricks is to

check that the main paper tray is full, and then accidentally and unwittingly select the empty alternate paper tray.

2. Cycle the power switch on the printer, reboot, and retry. The first thing I'd try would be to cycle the power switch and restart the software. One time I was experimenting with graphics on a daisy-wheel printer, setting the vertical and horizontal motion increment to a very small value and then using periods (.) for graphic points. (I got some impressive results for a daisywheel.) Anyway, I forgot to reset the motion increments. A secretary came by about an hour later, saying, "Mark, were you messing with the printer?" She held out a letter that the printer had typed in a space of about one by two inches.

3. No luck? Do a self test on the printer. Most printers have a built-in self-test mode. Disconnect the printer from the computer and activate the self test (for more info on the HP laser printers, keep reading). Does it work okay? If not, swap the printer until you can examine it further. If it works now, *reconnect it immediately* or you'll embarrass yourself later.

4. If the printer self-tested okay, do a PrintScreen. *Do not* test a printer using WordPerfect or some other application; you don't know that it doesn't have a software problem.

5. Still no luck? Time to swap the cable (it's the easiest part to swap).

6. If necessary, replace the printer interface board and/or printer (not likely).

Cable Troubles

The role of cable lengths in noise and interference has been discussed before in this text, but another problem is overly long cables. Serial and parallel cables aren't supposed to be made up longer than 50 feet, and it's probably not a good idea to make up a parallel cable longer than six feet. If you're using long cables and getting mysterious errors, the cables could be the culprits. The cable won't refuse to work—you'll get odd transient errors.

How to solve this? One solution is offered by Intellicom. Called the Long Link Parallel Interface, it extends parallel cables by up to 7,000 feet.

Remember to use the screws on the connector to secure your cable. I saw a situation wherein an Okidata printer printed consistently incorrect characters. I tried to understand the problem by comparing the ASCII codes of the desired characters to the codes actually printed. I found in each case that bit 6 was *always 1*. It turned out that the wire for line 6 wasn't fully seated. Securing the connector fixed the problem.

I found a similar problem with a broken wire in a cable. Here's an example. Suppose I tried to print *Hello* but got *Iekko*. Compare the codes of the desired and actual characters in Table 17.1. The *e* and *o* aren't affected, but *H* and *l* are. Notice that in all cases the low bit is 1.

TABLE 17.1: An Example Printer Cable Problem

DESIRED CHARACTER	CODE	ACTUAL CHARACTER	CODE
H	01001000	I	01001001
e	01100101	e	01100101
l	01101100	k	01101101
l	01101100	k	01101101
o	01101111	o	01101111

Port Problems

As you know, printers can have either a serial or parallel interface. On the PC, serial and parallel interfaces differ only by male connectors for serial interfaces and female connectors for parallel interfaces.

They're radically different, however. The parallel interface uses different voltages and handshakes than the serial interface. Printers can be bought with either serial or parallel interfaces. Given the choice, take parallel. It's a cleaner and faster interface. As laser printers get faster and, more particularly, support higher resolution, more high-speed interfaces will appear. For example, Apple uses an AppleTalk 230,000 bps interface to an Apple LaserWriter.

If you're using a serial interface, are the communications parameters set correctly? There are four:

- Speed (1200, 2400, 4800, 9600)
- Parity (Even, Odd, or None)
- Number of data bits (7 or 8)
- Number of stop bits (usually 1 or 2)

You'll find the parameters in the technical manual of the printer. Then construct the DOS commands:

```
MODE COM1: speed,parity,data bits,stop bits,P
MODE LPT1:=COM1:
```

In the first case, an example would be

```
MODE COM1:9600,N,8,1,P
MODE LPT1:=COM1:
```

This means *9600 bits per second, no parity, 8 data bits, 1 stop bit.* The *P* means it's a printer.

If you're having port problems, did you install something recently? Could something be conflicting with the printer port? Recall the story of the 5251 emulation board that zapped the printer port in Chapter 4. You'd never imagine it, but the terminal emulation board was killing the port. Is there another printer port? Are they both set for **LPT1:**?

Look at the Software

Following are some points to consider.

Internal Printer Software

Generally, printers must be configured. The most common configuration problem is the AUTO LF, or *automatic line feed.* This says, *Every time you get a carriage return, assume there's a line feed with it.* If your computer sends line feeds anyway, everything comes out double spaced. This is generally adjustable with a DIP switch on the printer.

Another configuration option—a more and more common one—is *printer emulation mode.* Many printers nowadays will emulate a Diablo 630 printer, or an Epson MX80, or an IBM Graphics Printer. If you've got your Hewlett-Packard ThinkJet printer set up for IBM Graphics Printer emulation, don't tell your software you've got a ThinkJet, tell it you've got an IBM. This sounds simple, but you'd be surprised at the number of people who get tripped up on that one.

The final option gives an indication of how international the electronics business is. Many printers speak foreign languages. If you set up your printer for British, you might get the Pounds Sterling sign rather than a dollar sign.

If you have a LaserJet Series II or later, they don't have DIP switches but rather configuration memory. Take a look at the values there. Did the user get adventurous and convert the interface from parallel to serial on the laser printer?

Is the Program Configured for the Printer?

If you just replaced your old Qume daisywheel with an HP LaserJet, the software won't work unless you tell it you have a LaserJet.

Know your printer. If you're the local PC guru, get to know the bizarre escape sequences that put the printer through its paces.

On the DOS disk, there's a program called GRAPHICS.COM. It allows you to use the PrtSc key even when a graphic image is on the screen. (The original PC, without GRAPHICS, will simply ignore graphic data.) Don't install GRAPHICS unless you have an Epson or IBM printer. Otherwise, it won't work. This is because graphic printing commands vary widely among printer types. If you own an HP LaserJet, an Okidata, or some other non-IBM printer, you'll need replacement software. Contact the manufacturer, or learn some assembly language and write such a routine yourself. I've had to do it for two printers, and it's not impossible. It does take some time the first time around, however.

The Mysterious Timeout

Sometimes the computer will sense that the printer is ignoring it: The printer will *time out*. When the computer says, *Abort, Retry, Ignore?,* you say *Retry,* and it works fine. How can you address this problem? Simply add the following DOS command to your AUTOEXEC.BAT:

```
MODE LPT1:,,P
```

This instructs the computer to retry forever. This means, of course, that you must be sure to have a printer connected, or the first attempt to print will lock up the computer.

Beware, however. If you don't have a printer attached and use MODE LPT1:,,P, the computer will wait forever to print. The three-finger salute (soft reboot) or the Big Red Switch are your only alternatives.

Has the Environment Changed?

Everyone talks about it, but...

A printer repairman told me about a day he'd had the previous October. He said that all over town a particular model of printer was failing left and right. He couldn't figure it out. We thought about it. Around the middle of October, we turn on the heat in Washington. That dries out the air and, in turn, the items in the work area. Chips don't mind being dried, but what about capacitors? Could a paper-type capacitor be malfunctioning because it was drying beyond a certain point?

A repair memo came around from the manufacturer a couple of months later. Sure enough, a particular capacitor didn't like it too dry. The answer: Either put a humidifier near the printer, or change the capacitor with a similar, less dryness-sensitive replacement. Moral: Be suspicious when the seasons change.

Power goes in this category, also. If you maintain computers in an office, and see the copier guys rolling in a new Xerox monster copier, ask gently what circuit breaker it'll be on.

Troubleshooting Dot-Matrix Printers

Dot-matrix printers are the cheap, noisy workhorse of the computer printer business. Is it worth trying to fix them? Give it a try; a lot of the tinkering won't take much time and, as the printer generally has a self-test mode, you can do a lot of testing fairly quickly. In this section, you'll see what can be done (by humans, that is) to adjust and fix printer problems. I must caution you, however. I've got to stress an important point:

WARNING

If you're going to be working inside printers, be aware that printers, unlike PCs, don't generally have separate shielded power supplies. When you take the top off of a printer, you generally expose 110-volt AC lines. If the printer is plugged in (accidentally) when you disassemble it and you touch the wrong thing, *you could die*. Period. End of sentence. *Make sure* you unplug the printer before taking the top off of it. I'm not kidding.

Here's a good tip a printer repair tech gave me: Don't open the printer until you have the printer's plug *in your hand*. Don't let someone else do the unplugging. Someone else might inadvertently unplug the wrong thing, leaving the printer plugged in. Yeah, it's paranoid, but just because you're paranoid doesn't mean they're not out to get you.

Here's a look at the things that fail most commonly and what to do about them. The weak points on the printer itself are

- The print head
- The print head data ribbon
- The stepper motor
- The circuit board

The last item, the circuit board, is often the price of the printer itself, so you might not want to bother with circuit boards.

The Print Head and Data Ribbon

The print head contains 9 to 24 stiff wires that are forced with solenoids to strike the ink ribbon and participate in forming characters on the paper. It can't hurt to lubricate the head with a little of the teflon lube mentioned before—just a little!

The print head is sensitive to too much heat. Print for too long a time, and the head just burns up. This isn't as much of a problem for the newer printers as it was for the old Epsons and Okidatas. The models out today have a *thermistor,* which shuts down the printer temporarily if the print head overheats. Generally thermistors are pretty robust, but if one malfunctions, the printer will shut down regularly. If that happens, try changing the thermistor first; it's a lot cheaper than a print head. The exact location varies from printer to printer; consult your printer's shop manual.

Replacement print heads can be quite reasonably priced. Some companies are selling rebuilt Okidata heads for as little as $25.

How do you replace a print head? You have to do two things:

- Release the print head.
- Disconnect the print head from its ribbon cable.

The print head is held down with just two screws or, more often, just a pair of clips. Once it's freed, *be careful*—it's probably still connected to a ribbon cable that lets it communicate with the main circuit board. Removing the print head's cable is usually just a matter of gently pulling it out of a slot at the bottom of the print head. By the way, print heads are *hot,* so be careful when removing one.

Once it's out, take a look at the ribbon. Is it kinked? That can cause problems. I once knew a woman who would *iron* Okidata cables to make them work (first she wrapped them in a cloth). It worked. Clean its edges so it makes a nice contact with the print head.

I should mention also that if you get a continuous black line or white line through characters, it might not be the print head but the connections to the print head.

Replacing print heads on older Epson printers isn't really a reasonable fix, as the print heads and the main circuit board have a suicide pact. When the print head dies, it takes the circuit boards with it when it burns up.

A variation on the typical dot-matrix printer is the *ink jet printer*. Rather than hammering at a ribbon, the ink jet squirts a narrow jet of ink at the paper. This is very quiet, but the jets tend to clog, leaving partial letters on the page. The answer here is simple: Remove the cartridge and push on the ink sack with a long, thin tool, like a straightened-out paper clip. The ink will push out the small holes, unclogging them. With the HP ThinkJet, it's a pretty regular procedure. The Seiko color ink jet has the same problem.

Stepper Motors

The stepper motor drives the platen. As you've seen before, stepper motor failure can be caused by using the friction feed and tractor feed together or by users turning the platen knob by hand when the power is on. When you need one of these stepper motors, the printer companies will sell them to you for big bucks. But remove the stepper and it generally turns out to be a standard stepper that you can get at your local techy electronics supply place.

Stepper problems are sometimes manifested as slipped lines: The printer doesn't do a complete linefeed.

Miscellaneous Problems and Symptoms

Here are some things to look for:

- White bands in the printout. This is a software problem that particularly shows up in graphics printout. There's a software command that controls the distance between lines. Ordinarily, this distance is a bit wider than the height of a character. However, in graphics we wish our lines to just touch, so we can blanket the whole page with dots.

- Vertical lines wobble. The printer is attempting to print a column of vertical bars in order to form a vertical line. Each bar should be the exact same number of inches from the left margin, but the head is moving *bidirectionally*. This means, for example, that if the carriage is eight inches wide and the printer is trying to print a line three inches from the left margin, the print head must alternately move three inches from the left, then five inches from the right. This might sound trivial, but it only needs to be $1/70$ of an inch off, and the wobble will be pronounced.

  The answer is simple: Most printers have a command that tells them to print in one direction only. Set the printer for unidirectional printing, and the registration problem will go away. Also, check the ribbon on the printer. Is it worn out in one spot, near the head? Does the ribbon move? Check the ribbon transport mechanism; it can become jammed.

- Transport motors can fail. Is the ribbon moving? If not, check the ribbon transport motor. Will it turn? Is the connection to the motor intact? What about gears—are they properly aligned?

- Jerky response. This can be due to a bad connection between one of the motors and the drive board, or a bad drive board. Remove connections, clean the connections, and see if the problem goes away. If not, examine the motor—does it turn easily? (Do this test with the power off.) Finally, try replacing the drive board.

- The printer doesn't print the screen accurately. This one is generally a software problem. If box-drawing characters on a screen appear as boldface *P*, *J*, or *M* characters, you've either got a printer that can't print the box-drawing characters or that hasn't been enabled to draw them. (Recall the discussion about this in the previous section about the LaserJet Series II.) As the LJII comes out of the box, it uses something called the Roman-8 character set. Activate the menu on the LJII and choose PC-10. Now it will print screens just fine. For more information, see Chapter 16 on selecting fonts with the LaserJet Series II and later.

Troubleshooting Laser Printers

Some parts of laser printers are very hot and work at quite high voltage. Please observe basic precautions when working inside lasers.

Testing Laser Printers (Including the Secret Service Test)

There are three tests you can perform on the LaserJet Series II:

1. System self test. This is basically what happens when you turn the printer on. You'll see a *05* or *05 SELF TEST* code on the printer status panel. To start this, take the printer off line, and press and hold the PRINT FONTS/TEST key. It tests

   - Program ROM
   - Internal font ROM
   - RAM
   - Printer/Formatter interface
   - All LEDs

2. Engine Test. You can isolate printer engine problems with this test. There's a pen-sized hole on the right side of the printer if you're looking at it from the front. Figure 17.1 shows where to find it. Insert a pen or pencil in this hole and *15 ENGINE TEST* will appear on the status panel. The test output should look like parallel thin lines running from the bottom to the top of the page.

3. The Secret Service Test. You probably already knew about the test button in the side of the laser printer, and of course one of the operator buttons on the front of the laser says TEST. But there's

FIGURE 17.1

Engine test button
location

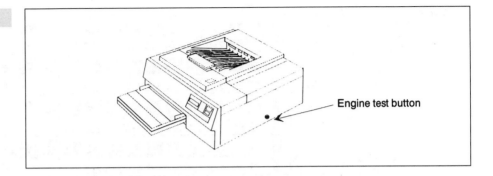

yet another test mode: the *service test mode*. You get to it by turning on the system while holding down ONLINE, CONTINUE, and ENTER simultaneously. The display will power up blank. Now press CONTINUE, and then press ENTER, and the display will show SERVICE MODE. It will do a short 05 TEST. Then press the test button, and a more complex test output will appear, as you can see in Figure 17.2. This printout demonstrates registration and grayscales.

Why is it secret? I don't know. My strong recommendation is to run one of the tests when you first get the printer, and store it someplace. Use it at regular maintenance times as a measure of how the printer is doing as the years go on.

Resolving Laser Printing Problems

The two most common laser printing problems are:

- Cloudy, faded output. The whites aren't white and the blacks aren't black. The probable cause is either low toner or a corona wire that's dirty or damaged.

- Regular horizontal lines or blotches across output. Probable damage to a transport roller or print drum.

The laser works like a copy machine, by applying a large (6 kilovolt) charge to a print drum. The image is "etched" on the drum, then, in

FIGURE 17.2

Close-up of LaserJet
Service Test Output

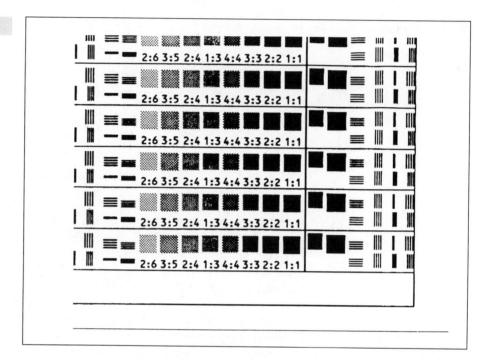

electricity. Toner is attracted to this electric charge, and so an image forms on the drum. Then the paper is fed, charged up to 6 KV in the opposite direction, and pressed against the print drum. This charge is transferred with a *corona wire*, a hair-thin wire. There are two coronas, the main corona (located in the print cartridge) and the transfer corona (located in the printer itself). The toner, being fickle, goes to the opposite charge on the paper, deserting the drum. Now we've got the toner on the paper, but toner is basically just yecchy black dust. How do we keep it from smearing on the paper? The paper runs against a hot *fusing roller* that melts the toner right into the paper. (Laser printers give new meaning to the phrase *hot off the presses.*)

Corona Cleaning

The coronas attract toner, which can eventually get caked all over the wire and render it less useful. If the corona can't adequately charge or discharge the paper or print drum, toner doesn't go where it's supposed to, and so some toner stays in the "white" areas and not enough stays in the "black" areas. So clean your coronas. By the way, that's what the *intensity* dial does on your laser—it controls the amount of voltage put on the corona.

How do you keep the corona clean? The main corona is in the cartridge, so you could just be lazy and replace the cartridge. But don't do that; use the brush right inside the Series II. Open the Series II, and you won't be able to miss the green plastic brush. Note that it has one gray side with a suede-like feel. That's for cleaning the main corona. Now remove the cartridge. Note the slot atop the cartridge. You'll see that the suede end of the brush fits nicely into the slot. Just run it across the slot once, and the corona's clean.

The *transfer corona* is a permanent fixture in the laser, so it *must* be cleaned. Near the brush for the main corona, the transfer corona is a hair-thin wire set in a shallow trough below the paper path. You can't directly get at the transfer corona because there's a web of monofilament criss-crossing above it. The monofilament keeps the paper from accidentally feeding into the trough and getting crunched up and snapping the delicate corona. You can clean it a little bit at a time with a cotton swab, some alcohol, and some patience. Dip the swab into the alcohol, then reach it between the monofilament and wipe the corona. Don't get too forceful, or you can break the corona, and then we're talking tears and sadness. Again, do this each time you change the cartridge or in the event of cloudy output.

Regular Blotches on Output

There are rubber paper transport rollers, metal fusing rollers, and a print drum in the system. Any of them can get bent or scratched or just develop irregularities of some kind. These show up as regular blotches or lines in the output.

There are seven rollers and drums, so diagnosing sounds pretty rough. But HP and Canon helped us out again. All the rollers and drums have different diameters, and, again, two of the problem children are in the cartridge.

Diagnosing: As I've said, rollers and the print drum have different circumferences. Measure the distances between regular blotches to get a clue about which component has failed; then consult Figure 17.3.

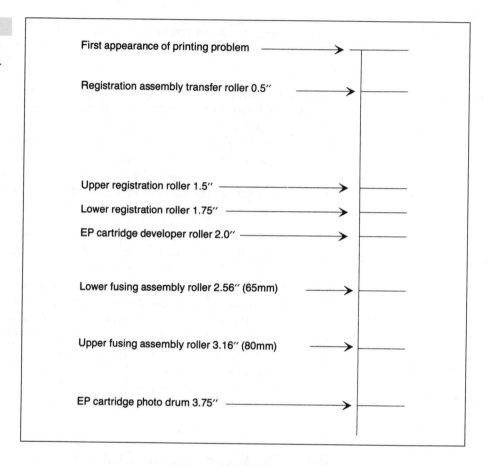

FIGURE 17.3

Actual distances between regular laser blotches and causes

Another reason for smudges in printout can be that the feed rollers or fuser rollers are dirty. Clean these with a damp cloth and then dry. *Do not* try to clean the fuser rollers until the laser has been off for a couple of hours—they run very hot. (Go ahead and try. Believe me, you'll never try it again.)

Another thing that causes blurriness is if the image gets on the paper okay but isn't fused right. Electrical ground to the fuser might be faulty. This causes static buildup on the fuser, which shows up as smudges. Damp paper or paper with an unusual coating can inhibit the fusing or corona processes—try different paper. The controller circuit board could be defective, but I've never seen that.

It seems that everyone knows this, but I'll say it anyway: When a LJII says *toner low,* just remove the cartridge and shake it. The problem will go away for a while.

Images Are Stretched or Squashed

More than likely, this is caused by the drive motor not pulling the paper through at the proper speed. Replacing it isn't fun, but it can be done.

LaserJet Potpourri

Here are some common LaserJet printer problems and solutions.

LaserJet Gives 20 Error

The number 20 means that you asked the LaserJet to do something it doesn't have enough memory to do. One common reason for this is that you bought a LaserJet+ or a LaserJet Series II without a memory expansion. I don't know why they do it, but HP sells both of these printers with only 512K of memory, when they need about 1MB to do full-page graphics. Send a full page and you'll get a 20 error. Just press the CONTINUE key on the printer and you'll get a sheet with half a page of graphics on it, followed by another sheet with the remaining part.

The answer is generally to get more memory. But another possibility is that you've filled the printer's memory with *fonts.* When I set up my printer to do desktop publishing, I end up loading about 650K of fonts into it. Even with the 1.5-MB option I chose when I got my Series II, I get into trouble with some really complicated graphics. The 850K left after loading the fonts is enough for *most* graphics, but complex pages can sometimes trigger a 20 error.

55 Error on Startup

Sometimes you'll get a 55 error when you turn the system on. It's pretty scary, particularly when you get out the shop manual and look it up. There are two main circuit boards in the bottom of the LaserJet Series II: the *DC controller PCA* and the *interface PCA.* (By the way, when you read the HP manuals, they constantly refer to PCAs of various kinds. Look though you may in the manuals, they never define PCA. PCA is *Printed Circuit Assembly*—just another term for a circuit board.)

There are two circuit boards or PCAs—the *DC controller board* handles charging and discharging the coronas, and the *interface board* controls the parallel and serial interfaces. If you smoke your interface with a switchbox, just replace the interface PCA. (In case you've never heard, HP says you can damage your LaserJet interface PCA with a parallel port switchbox. If they catch you at it, they'll void your warranty. I don't know if it really zaps parallel ports. I've used one for some time without trouble, and I've never met anyone who had actually experienced the problem.)

Anyway, when powering up, the two boards do a communications test to ensure that they're talking all right. If there's noise in their communication, the 55 error pops up. The HP shop manual says you must replace the cards if you see this error, but don't sweat it too much. This error can crop up just because of the normal inrush surge you get when you turn the machine on. I have a Series II that was giving me 55 errors about every other day on power-up. I thought I'd have to do some surgery on the printer, but then I happened to move it to another outlet. Bingo! The error never returned. It seems that power noise of any kind on power-up shows up as a 55 error.

Fonts Do Not Appear on Page

Once you become a desktop-publishing maven, you can dazzle others with your documents, replete with fonts galore. But one day you might find that a *really* font-intensive page won't print. What's going on?

You've come up against a printer shortcoming, I'm afraid. HP lasers can only print a page with 16 fonts per page. Remember, Courier isn't a font. *Font* refers to a combination of typeface, size, stroke weight, and so on.

Actually, 16 fonts shouldn't be a great hindrance. The strangest page in this book has no more than 10 fonts on it.

Printer Picks Up Multiple Sheets

Believe it or not, this usually isn't the printer's fault. It's usually the paper. You need dry paper in order to get proper feed. Is the paper sitting in the tray for weeks at a time? Not good. When paper is removed from its ream wrapper, it's supposed to be dry. So how do you keep paper dry afterwards? If it gets used in a day or two, there's no problem. But if it sits in the tray for longer, it could pick up some humidity. Here are two thoughts: First, keep the paper in a large Tupperware lasagna carrier. It'll keep it dry as long as you burp it when you put the paper in the Tupperware. Another approach if the paper is already damp is to dry it out with a microwave oven. Also, make sure you've got the correct side of the paper up (look at the package for the arrow).

Laser Hiccups Periodically When Not in Use

Ever had your laser make a noise kind of like it was going to start printing a page, even when you didn't tell it to do anything? Don't worry. It's normal. There's a roller called the fuser roller that lives longer if it's rotated periodically. The Series II rotates it every 30 minutes or so of inactivity.

CHAPTER

18

Modems and Serial Interfaces

WHEN computers first appeared on the scene, each was an island. Computer-to-computer communication mainly came in the form of moving tapes or card decks from one machine to another. We now jocularly refer to this method as *sneaker-net* or *AdidasLAN*. Today, dozens of communications devices exist, from a simple null modem cable to a 100-Mbps FDDI fiber network adapter.

Communications troubleshooting is a separate book all in itself, so I won't try to cover the entire topic. Instead, I'll look at asynchronous communications in this chapter, and even then the discussion must be brief for reasons of space. A PC troubleshooter dealing with serial communications must understand:

- What an RS-232 is
- How it's supposed to be used
- How it's actually used
- How to test its components

Components

The four parts of an asynchronous communications system are the port, the cable, the modem, and the software. They are described in detail below.

The Asynchronous Port

On the computer end, the computer must be able to speak the language of asynchronous communications. A device to allow this to happen is variously called an asynchronous port, asynchronous adapter, communications port, or RS-232C port. RS-232 and RS-232C are the same thing; in fact, the "official" name now is EIA 232D.

The connector type used is generally the standard 25-pin DB25-type connector (see Figure 18.1), such as you'd find on the back of most modems. Ever since the advent of the AT, some adapters use a 9-pin connector. You won't miss the other 16 pins; asynchronous communication doesn't use them anyway. The signals are the same. You might have a cabling problem, however. We'll discuss cables later.

Most folks don't buy an asynchronous adapter on a board by itself. Instead, it usually appears on a multifunction board like the Quadram Quadboard or the AST SixPakPlus.

The Cable

Communications cables are the bane of a PC expert's existence. The problem is that no manufacturer follows the RS-232 standard exactly. Many manufacturers use a different connector or they rearrange the order of the pins. Neither is a fatal problem, just a pain in the neck.

FIGURE 18.1

A DB25 connector

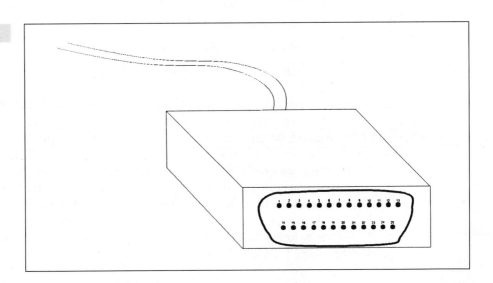

A very good introduction to the art of RS-232 cabling is the book *Computer Connection Mysteries Solved*, written by Gerard Wideman and published by Sams. It's well written, funny, and about $14.

Cables can get broken wires and loose pins, or they can be wired incorrectly. The end of this chapter includes wiring diagrams for common PC cables.

The Modem

The most common use for a serial port is as a modem interface. Modems allow computers to communicate via regular phone lines. They've been around for decades. In the PC world, Hayes Microcomputer Products introduced the Smartmodem (now called the Smartmodem 300) in the early '80s, starting a whole new generation of communications devices. Now 2400 bps is fairly ubiquitous, and various kinds of 9600-bps modems are becoming common. I use the US Robotics Courier HST, a $600 modem that transmits 17,600 bps over regular dial phone lines. (Unfortunately, it talks at 17,600 bps only to *other* Courier HSTs.)

Smart modems are *programmable* modems. What does programmable mean? Well, back in the old days, you had to flip switches to do things like:

- Turn echo on or off
- Adjust speed, parity, data bits, and stop bits
- Turn a monitor speaker on or off

Additionally, you had to dial your calls by hand. However, you can send programmable modem commands via software in the computer. Thus, you can write a program to set some communications parameters, dial a number until it answers, log onto the computer at that number, download a file, and log off, all without the operator having to be present. This is truly useful, but it also means you must learn the modem's rather terse command language in order to get the full benefits of your modem. Or you must trust that the person who wrote your communications software really knew modem programming.

The Communications Software

The best known examples of asynchronous communications software are:

- Crosstalk by Microstuf/DCA
- Smartcom III by Hayes
- PROCOMM, by Datastorm

If you have a programmable smart modem, as most of us do these days, be sure your communications software understands the modem's language. Most smart modems claim to use the same language as the market leader, Hayes, but if you're using a clone modem of some kind, it can't hurt to check with the software vendor. Most software has been checked out on the more popular clones, like the U.S. Robotics modems.

Maintenance

These systems are mainly solid state, and so have no moving parts. Modems tend to run hot, as many are designed around one or two fairly dense chips, so don't pile books atop the modem. Make sure the modem's ventilated. I know the ads all show a phone perched on top of a modem, but I'm not sure it's such a good idea. I know for a fact that it's *not* a good idea to stack up Smart-modems. I've had a fair amount of heat-related modem trouble. Be sure you know where to find the modem's warranty information. Most modems have two-year warranties, so don't throw that information out.

The usual cautions apply: Because they're large connectors with tiny pins, screw in the cables. Don't make the cables longer than they need to be. This increases the noise level in the cable, and if a loop of cable dangles down behind a table, it might get caught in something or be idly kicked. I know of a case where an analyst routinely braced his feet against the cable—just a nervous habit. The cable was even more nervous.

I mentioned power problems in Chapter 9 on power supplies. *The same surge problems can appear on phone lines.* If the line from the phone company switching station to your computer is above ground at any point, think seriously about a *phone line isolator* (sometimes called a *modem isolator*). This sits between the modem and the phone. Another measure of prevention is an RS-232 isolator. It sits between the modem and the PC. I'd rather smoke a modem by itself than a modem and the rest of my system. Such products are offered in the Black Box Catalog (see Appendix A).

You might be wondering why I beat up on surge protectors in the power supply chapter but am suggesting them now. It's mainly cost. Surges really don't occur that often over the phone line, save in the event of lightning. When that unlikely lightning strike occurs, you want something that'll take the brunt of the impulse and hopefully burn out in the process, cutting off the connection between your expensive equipment and the lightning. (I suppose you could also try knots in the phone cord.)

Troubleshooting

Communications troubleshooting can provide you with hours of mind-exercising delight, if you're the kind of person who likes puzzles. Let's see how to decompose the problem and isolate the bad component.

Common Communications Software Problems

By far, the source of the greatest amount of communications trouble is the software. You must ensure that both parties in the communication have agreed on the *communications parameters:*

- Speed
- Parity (can be even, odd, or none)
- Number of data bits (can be 7 or 8)
- Number of stop bits (generally 1, could be 2)
- Local echo on or off

All communications packages have the ability to set these values. Don't worry about what the parameters mean, just be sure they match. Below are some common symptoms that can be software problems.

Cannot Connect

Check the parameters. If you cannot connect, or if you connect and see garbage ({ characters in particular), you've probably got a speed or data bits mismatch.

Cannot See Input

This is when you type but can't see what you're typing. Try a simple command, like whatever command you would use to get a file directory from the distant system. If the command gets a proper response from the other side, even though you can't see what you typed, the problem is that you must set your local echo to ON. *Local echo* tells your PC whether to display the characters you type or not. Sometimes you'll want to disable local echo, as the remote site will echo characters. In that case, you press a key, the key goes out to the remote site, the remote site echoes, and *then* you see the character you typed. Whether or not you need local echo is determined by whether or not the other site provides echoes.

Input Is Double

You type a character, and two appear on the screen. Output from the other computer is normal. Answer: Set your local echo to OFF.

Sometimes, there's no local echo command. In that case, the command has been misnamed (it's a common mistake) to *duplex*. (Duplex is something completely different, an engineering concern in data communications.) Then,

> Half Duplex=Local Echo ON
>
> Full Duplex=Local Echo OFF

Again, it's wrong terminology, but who cares as long as you can get the problem solved?

Is Your Software Set Up to Talk to Your Modem?

You instruct most modems to dial a number by sending the command ATD followed by the phone number. Some modems don't understand the AT command set that most communications software depends on, however. (For a while, IBM sold an internal modem for their luggable PCs that used a strange command set.) Is your software equipped to talk to your modem?

Simple Hardware Problems

Besides software problems, basic hardware incompatibilities can keep your communications from successfully working.

Cannot Dial

You set up to dial the distant computer, but the modem doesn't respond. There are lots of possibilities:

- Is it plugged into the phone jack? It's common to share the modem's phone line with a regular phone and forget to plug the modem back in before using it.

- Is the modem plugged into the computer? Did the cable fall out? (It won't if you screw in the connectors.)

- Is the phone line working? Plug in a phone. Is there a dial tone?

- Is it your phone system? If you have an in-house phone system, like a ROLM or Northern Telecom system, you might have to issue extra commands to dial out of your system (called a PBX). Check with your telecommunications manager.

Line Noise and Quality Problems

Sometimes it isn't hardware or software that's the problem, it's the phone line itself. There are a few areas you can reasonably check:

- Quality of the communications provider
- The in-house wiring
- Whether call waiting is interrupting modem sessions

Controlling Which Long-Distance Carrier You Use

Are you using a sufficiently high-quality carrier? If you're communicating at 2400 bps or faster, you might find that the only choice is (no, I don't own stock) AT&T. I know of only one modem (the US Robotics Courier HST that I've mentioned that I use) that can handle 2400 bps over a non-AT&T line, and even then its success is sporadic. On the other hand, 1200 bps seems to work on *anything*, so I can use Joe Bob's Long-Distance Service and Bowling Alley or whoever's cheaper at the time to save money on a minute-by-minute basis.

How do I do this? Simple. Equal access allowed us to pick our own long-distance service (you remember, back in the early '80s, when the phone system went to pieces?). Most folks think they're stuck with what they've got, but that's not true at all.

You might be using an "off-brand" long-distance service for your combined voice/data switched (dial) needs. You're not quite sure what long-distance service you have? Simple. Dial (700) 555-4141 and you'll get a recorded message telling you. As I said, you'll find that 2400 bps and faster modems don't really do particularly well on a service other than AT&T. (That's not absolute, by the way; some routes are well served by a number of carriers, and this is all based on my own subjective experience dialing into and out of Washington, D.C.) All isn't lost, however.

Rather than dialing long distance in the usual way, 1 (*area code*) (*phone number*), dial instead 10288 1 (*area code*) (*phone number*) to access AT&T, assuming you don't already have AT&T.

Actually, there are codes for many of the big common carriers:

MCI	10222
Allnet	10444
Sprint	10333
ITT	10488

Please note that these codes are subject to change.

This also works for voice only, by the way.

Suspending Call Waiting

Call waiting is a service that allows you to be aware of incoming calls while you are talking on the phone. A "beep" sound announces that someone is trying to get to you. You can tap the switchhook, and you're connected to the second caller.

That's great for busy people, but it's a problem for modems. The modem hears the beep as a suspension of the carrier and it drops the line. That's why the phone companies are in the process of reprogramming their phone switches to allow you to suspend call waiting for the duration of your conversation. How? Simple—just dial *70, then your phone number. The call waiting is suspended for the duration of the conversation. Once you hang up, the service is reestablished. Rotary phones users dial 1170.

Check the In-House Cable Plant

You might find that line noise is being created by the wiring in your building. You could have old wires that don't transmit as well as they once did, or someone may have run the wires near the high-voltage lines in the elevator shaft, or any one of a million things may have gone wrong with the in-house cable plant. Inspect your cable plant periodically. I had phone noise trouble in my building, so I restrung my phone lines and the problem went away. (I actually found that my termination block was made out of four wood screws driven into a rafter in the basement!)

Finally, did you check that the modem and the PC share a common ground? You may recall from Chapter 9 that plugging the PC and a peripheral into different outlets can lead to slight differences in the value of electrical ground, resulting in noisy communications.

The Port

The RS-232 port could be ill. As it's a bidirectional device (that is, it talks as well as listens), you can use a *loopback* to allow it to test itself. This involves putting a connector of some kind on the port to allow it to "hear" what it broadcasts; it can send out test messages and then compare them to what it receives.

Serial ports do become ill. I don't know why. In my case, I presume it has something to do with the plugging and unplugging that I do with my system (I do a large amount of communications consulting, so I try a lot of equipment out on my system). For instance, I've had two Toshiba 1100+ laptop computers, and they both had something wrong with the serial port: Receive Data in the first one, Ring Indicate in the second. Probably 20 percent of the expansion boards I've worked with have had a serial problem; so it's worthwhile knowing how to diagnose such situations.

To test the port, you need to see what is happening on the various control lines. I recommend you get a *breakout box* to assist you in testing the communications port. A simple, cheap, portable in-line breakout box is available from Hall-Comsec (see Appendix A). A breakout box allows you to prototype a serial cable without soldering or pin crimping (the two most common methods of cable assembly). That's nice because you can then figure out what the correct cable configuration is, even if you don't know how to solder or crimp, and then give that cable configuration to someone in your company or a technical service house to make the cable up for you. You see, getting the cable made (soldered) isn't too hard, once you've settled on a design. But making sure the cable is designed right is difficult, so you'll want to do it yourself. A breakout box makes that possible.

Take a look at Figure 18.2. Regular 25-wire RS-232 type cables come in one side and go out the other. All 25 lines are represented on each side with large round metal posts. The breakout box comes with about a dozen wires that terminate in small plugs that mate with the posts. The way the box works is that you first design a cable, then run wires from post to post to make the connections necessary for the cable, and plug in the breakout box (it serves as the cable) to the two devices you want to interface. The cable design either works or it doesn't.

Let's say you're trying to design a cable to allow your laptop to transfer data to your PC. The cables on either end are too short to connect the two devices, so first you'd run a couple of extension cables. Run a regular straight-through cable from the PC to one side of the breakout box, and a regular straight-through cable from the laptop to the other side of the breakout box.

Now you're ready to start prototyping. First, figure to start your cable design with a cable that just connects 2 on the PC side to 3 on the laptop side, 3 on the PC side to 2 on the laptop side, and 7 on the PC side to 7 on the laptop side. (How did I know to try this? Hang on until the next section, when I describe how to design an RS-232 cable.) To set this up, just run one of the wires from 2 on the PC side to 3 on the laptop side, and from 3 on the PC side to 2 on the laptop side. Actually, you don't have to run a wire from 7 to 7, as there are DIP switches for each of the 25 lines, and any time you want a "straight-through" connection all you need to do is close the DIP switch for that particular line. (Make sure the others are all set to "open," or you'll have lots of "wires" in your cable that you didn't intend.)

FIGURE 18.2

A typical breakout box

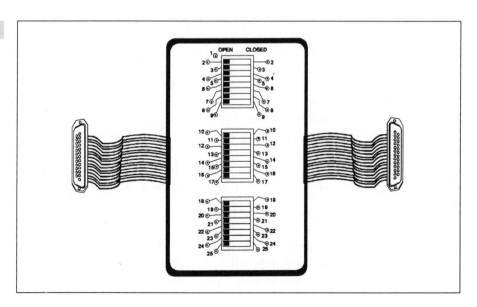

Some breakout boxes have red and possibly green lights to indicate activity levels for various inputs and outputs in the RS-232 connection. Red lights indicate the presence of voltage in excess of +3 volts (interpreted as *0*) and green lights indicate the presence of voltage below −3 volts (interpreted as *1*). The 0 is the signal used to indicate *active* on the control leads. By the way, in RS-232 signaling, values between −3 and +3 are considered neither 0 nor 1.

How to Test a Serial Port Even If You Can't Spell RS-232

We'll use the public domain program PDIAGS.EXE, found on lots of bulletin boards, and a breakout box like the WireTap. Any breakout box will do, as long as it has indicator lights. You could, alternatively, use a voltmeter, but the breakout box is a good investment.

1. Plug the breakout box directly into the serial connector on the back of the computer. Don't use a cable. You'll see activity on just three lines:

    > Line 2=−3 volts (1)   *Green*
    > Line 4=+3 volts (0)   *Red*
    > Line 20=−3 volts (1)   *Green*

2. Activate the diagnostics, PDIAGS. You'll see no change in the lights.

3. Get into the serial port diagnostic menu by pressing **S**.

4. Open the port: **Alt-P** followed by the letter **O** (not zero). Line 20 should reverse to value 0. If it does not, your *Data Terminal Ready* (DTR) line is defective.

5. Attach a jumper on the breakout box from line 20 to line 8. On the computer display, the word below CD should now be *YES*. It was *NO* before. If it does not read *YES*, your *Carrier Detect* line is defective.

6. Now move the jumper so it runs from line 20 to line 6. On the computer display, the word below DSR should now be *YES*. (CD will be *NO* once more.) If it is not, your *Data Set Ready* line is defective.

7. Shut off local echo: **Alt-P** followed by **E.**

8. Move the jumper so it connects lines 2 and 3. Now press **Alt-F.** A "fox" message (*The quick brown fox jumped over the lazy dog 0123456789 times!*) should appear. If it does not, either your *TXD* (Transmit Data) or your *RXD* (Receive Data) lines are defective.

9. Quit by pressing **Alt-Q,** then **Q.**

If there's a problem, how can you fix it? Obviously, swapping the board is an alternative. But I've fixed a few serial ports when the wires connecting the printed circuit board to the connector were broken or when the main chips failed.

RS-232 interfaces (asynchronous ones, that is) are mainly designed around four chips. One is a large, easily identified chip called a *UART*, a Universal Asynchronous Receiver/Transmitter. It's often socketed (yay!), and it's often the problem circuit on asynchronous interfaces. There are three main UARTs:

- 8250, an older, more common model
- 16450, a faster improvement
- 16550, a 16450 with a 16,000,000-byte buffer for greater speed

These chips are upward compatible: You can remove an 8250 and put a 16450 in its place. By the way, that's handy information if you use OS/2. You see, in most applications you can't really see any difference between an 8250 and a 16450. But OS/2 won't recognize a serial port based on an 8250. A new 16450 is approximately $9, so if you're stuck with internal modems or multifunction cards that use 8250s but want to use OS/2, a chip swap could save the day.

The other two chips are driver chips with model numbers 1488 and 1489. There are usually two 1488s and one 1489. When a power surge or lightning has damaged a serial port, it's often one of these two that has died. They're under $1 apiece, but sadly they're usually soldered, not socketed.

Again, there's no dishonor in choosing not to fix bad interface cards, so don't feel pressured to attempt such a fix. If, however, you do want to take a swing at it, try those three chips.

The Cable

If the port checks out okay, maybe the problem is the cable. Detach the breakout box from the computer, and then connect the cable you usually use to the computer. Connect the breakout box to the free end of the cable, and re-run the above tests. If one fails, you have a broken wire.

Remember that with cables, speed trades off for distance. If you have a 100-foot RS-232 cable, you won't be able to run it at 38,400 bps. The exact same equipment and a two-foot cable might be able to run at that speed. The only difference is in the length of the cable.

On the other hand, if you're reading this because the cable has never worked, turn to the section, "Understanding RS-232 and Designing RS-232 Cables," later in this chapter.

The Modem

Some modems have built-in loopback capabilities. (As you'll recall, this means they can send out test messages and then compare them to what they receive.) In that case, you can do simple loopback tests. If not, the best first procedure is just a modem swap. They're small and don't require much work to swap.

Do the front lights tell you anything? Put a breakout box in line between the modem and the computer. You should see the correspondences shown in Table 18.1. When a specific modem light is on, the corresponding breakout box light should be on.

TABLE 18.1: Modem Front Panel Light/RS-232 Line Correspondences

MODEM LIGHT	RED LIGHT ON BREAKOUT BOX
TR	20
MR	6
RD	3
SD	2
CD	8

Are the connections correct? Many modems have two phone jacks: one to connect to the wall and one to pass through to the phone. Connect the "phone" jack to the wall, and you'll dial okay but disconnect as soon as the other side answers!

Do the modems match? Are you calling a 9600-bps modem with a 1200-bps modem? If so, is the 9600 smart enough to drop back to 1200? Is it an error-correcting modem, requiring another error-correcting modem in order to carry on a conversation?

The Phone Line

The phone line has four lines colored red, green, yellow, and black. Only the red and green ones are used. They should offer 48 volts of DC power. If your phone varies greatly from this, call your repair office. Can you try the call on another line? Is it a multiextension phone—could someone be picking up the phone as your modem tries to dial?

Warning: The voltage on a normal phone line is enough to be felt. If you happen to measure the line while the phone is ringing, the voltage shoots up to almost 100 volts. Only do this test if you know what you're doing, please.

The Other Side

Half of the possibility for problems comes from the folks with whom you're trying to communicate. Double-check their parameters with them. Try calling out to another computer, if possible. Have they recently installed a new revision of *their* communication software or a new, "completely compatible" modem?

Going Further

Devices called *analog channel test units* exist that will actually test the phone line between you and the other party. They are, however, quite expensive. An *oscilloscope* can help you measure the frequencies being produced by your modem to see if they're within specification. Again, an individual PC user probably would not want to go this far, as the required investment in test equipment isn't trivial.

Understanding RS-232 and Designing RS-232 Cables

For a "standard," RS-232 sure provides a lot of headaches. Suppose you buy a device from vendor A with an RS-232 port on it and a device from vendor B with an RS-232 port on it, and try to hook them up. When it doesn't work (a common outcome), you start calling people.

Vendor A responds: "Trouble with our unit? Gosh, we don't really ever get bad reports on...wait! What are you trying to connect to? *Vendor B?* That's your trouble. That guy hasn't designed an interface that follows specs since the day he got into business."

So, reasonably, you're annoyed by the temerity of Vendor B and call him. He is jolly.

Vendor B: "Vendor A? Is that old rapscallion [not the actual word used] still lying about me? His problem is that he builds 'em to the standard, all right—the *1964* standard. He's building RS-232A ports. We follow the 1984 conventions, and...".

If you could get these two guys in the same room, you know what they'd say?

"Your problem is the cable; it's the wrong one." You wait expectantly for the solution, but they demur.

"Oh, no, we don't sell cables," they chorus, and then they leave.

You see, you'll probably face about two big RS-232 compatibility problems per year. You'll be a happier person if you can take a swing at fixing them. If a simple country economist like myself can do it, so can you.

So here's the world's shortest course on what RS-232 is and how it works.

Why Is There RS-232?

RS-232 exists basically so that different vendors can offer equipment that can communicate with each other. I can buy a modem built before the PC was even designed and it will work with the PC just fine, as they both use RS-232 to communicate. RS-232 is an example of a *physical interface*—an agreement among vendors about how to make equipment communicate.

For a simpler and more familiar example of a physical interface, think of the plug in your wall socket. It supplies 120 volts, 60 cycles per second (cps) of alternating current. If you plug in something that uses, say, 200 volts, or 50 cycles per second, you'll get very unpleasant results, including possibly burning your house down. So when did you last check to be sure that something used 120-volt, 60-cps current? Probably never. You just figure that if you buy something with a regular power plug, it will use the juice okay—and you're right. There's a standards agency, Underwriter's Laboratory, that concerns itself with power and safety; you won't see a UL sticker on something you could plug into a wall socket and injure yourself with.

So the plug itself seems important. Can you, for instance, use your American microwave oven in London? Nope, they have different power. The first problem you'd run up against is, again, the plug: Your plug won't fit into any wall sockets. Can you just snip off the plug, install a British-type power plug, and use the wall current? No again: It's 220 volts, 50 cps.

Why use different plugs, then? Simple. The plug is a reminder about where the equipment can and cannot be used. The plug tells us something else, too: what devices *supply* power, and what devices *use* power. Female connectors indicate a device (like an extension cord) that supplies power. Male connectors indicate a device that uses power. This way, you don't plug a toaster into a microwave oven and think something will come of the marriage.

Behind the plug lies a lot of information about an interface standard. Know what plug you have, and you don't have to worry about things like the power's number of volts or cps. RS-232 does something similar.

Just as there are two members of the power interface, the user and the supplier, so are there two kinds of RS-232 interfaces. RS-232 was designed basically to allow computing devices called *DTE*s (Data Terminal Equipment) to talk to communications devices called *DCE*s (Data Circuit-terminating Equipment). So there's a DTE-type RS-232 interface and a DCE-type RS-232 interface. RS-232s use DB25 connectors: Male DB25s go on the DTEs, female DB25s go on the DCEs.

DTE-type interfaces are most commonly found on PCs and printers. Devices with DCE-type interfaces include modems, mice, and digitizers. Remember that RS-232 is defined to allow DTE-type interfaces to communicate only with DCE-type interfaces.

How RS-232 Works

RS-232 is a digital interface, intended to communicate no more than 50 feet and at 20,000 bps. (Everybody uses it for greater distances and higher speeds, but 50/20,000 is the standard.) Communication is effected with 25 separate wires, each with its own task. RS-232 is defined for both synchronous and asynchronous communication, so there are a lot of lines in the 25 that we'll never use in asynchronous communications. As mentioned before, lines are either *on* with a voltage level of +3 volts or more, *off* below −3, or *neither* in between. *Flow control* is an important part of RS-232's purpose. Flow control allows a receiving device to say to a sending device, "STOP! My buffers (a small amount of memory in the printer itself) are overflowing—hang on a second and I'll get right back to you," and then allows it to print what's in its buffers and say, "Whew! I'm ready for more now."

There are ten important asynchronous lines in RS-232, as shown in Table 18.2. It's important to understand that each line is controlled by either one side or another. Line 2, for example, is viewed as an input by one side and an output by the other side. If both sides viewed it as an input, then both would be transmitting information that was never received. So each line (except grounds, which are just electrical reference points) is controlled by one side or another. Note, by the way, that there's also a 9-pin version of the RS-232 connector. When I refer to pin numbers, I'm referring to the 25-pin numbers, not the 9-pin.

TABLE 18.2: RS-232C Leads

DESCRIPTION	PIN # (25-PIN)	PIN # (9-PIN)	FROM	ABBREVIATION
Data Leads				
Transmit data	2	3	DTE	TD
Receive data	3	2	DCE	RD
Power-On Indicator Leads				
Data set ready	6	6	DCE	DSR
Data terminal ready	20	4	DTE	DTR
Leads That Announce That an Outside Event Has Taken Place				
Data carrier detect	8	1	DCE	CD
Ring indicator	22	9	DCE	RI
Ready to Send/Receive Handshake Leads				
Request to send	4	7	DTE	RTS
Clear to send	5	8	DCE	CTS
Ground Leads				
Signal ground	7	5		SG
Protective ground	1			FG

Here's the sequence of events for a normal RS-232 session.

1. Both devices are powered up and indicate "power up" status. The DTE powers up line 20 (DTR, Data Terminal Ready). The DCE powers up line 6 (DSR, Data Set Ready). A well-designed RS-232 interface won't communicate further until these two lines are activated. The DTE waits to see a signal on line 6, the DCE a signal on line 20. Lines 6 and 20 are supposed to be *equipment check* signals that only indicate device power status, but they're sometimes used as flow control lines.

2. The modem connects with another modem. Data communication is no good without someone to communicate with, so next (in a modem/terminal situation, the situation envisioned by the RS-232 designers) a distant modem would be dialed. The modems exchange carriers (the high-pitched whine you hear when modems connect), and the modem (DCE) tells the terminal (DTE) about it over line 8, DCD (Data Carrier Detect). If you have a modem with red lights, by the way, you'll see the preceding activity reflected in the lights. Line 6 is attached to the light labeled MR, Modem Ready; line 20 is attached to line 20, Terminal Ready; and line 8 is attached to the light labeled CD, Carrier Detect.

3. The terminal (DTE) asks the modem (DCE) if it's ready. The terminal activates line 4, RTS (Request To Send). The modem, if ready, responds with line 5, CTS (Clear To Send). Now the handshake process is complete. Lines 4 and 5 are flow control lines.

4. Data is exchanged. The terminal (DTE) passes information for the modem (DCE) to transmit along line 2. The modem passes information back to the terminal along line 3.

And that's all there is to the RS-232 interface.

A Note on Reality

The above description is nice and complete, so far as the standard goes. But most RS-232 interfaces aren't complete. Most PC software, for example, only looks at one handshake, such as 8 (Carrier Detect), 6 (Data Set Ready), or 5 (Clear To Send), and ignores the rest. Some software doesn't look at *any* control lines, so DTR, DSR, DCD, RTS, and CTS become irrelevant. That makes cabling easier but ignores the question of flow control.

The Simplest Cable

Let's start our cable discussion with the simplest cable: the straight-through. A straight-through cable connects a wire from line 1 on side 1 to line 1 on side 2, another wire from line 2 on side 1 to line 2 on side 2, another from line 3 on side 1 to line 3 on side 2, and so on. The standard PC-to-modem cable is an example of this cable. RS-232 was designed with this cable in mind.

A Simple Cable Problem

Let's say you have a modem with, it turns out, an unusual property: It never applies power to line 5, CTS. It powers up 6 (DSR) okay, and raises 8 when the carrier is detected, but it doesn't do anything on line 5. The PC side turns out to be "regulation" RS-232, and won't communicate without seeing a signal on line 5. Can a cable help?

Sure. The PC wants to see a signal on line 5, so let's give it one. Just construct a cable that's straight-through except for line 5. Then run a short wire (called a jumper) from line 8 on the PC side to line 5 on the PC side. Now when DCD (8) is raised, CTS (5) will also be raised, so line 5 shows activity, and the PC's interface is happy.

Designing Cables for Serial Printers and PC-to-PC Transfer

Many cables are just a variation on the straight-through cable. Of the rest, most are cables designed to solve something called the "null modem" problem. Recall that RS-232 is designed to connect DCEs to DTEs. Now ask, what kind of cable would connect a printer to a PC? Well, both the printer and the PC have DTE-type interfaces. According to the RS-232 standard, you can't directly connect two DTE interfaces. You're supposed to hook up a modem to the PC (recall that the modem's a DCE), hook up a modem to the printer, and then run the world's shortest phone wire between the modems. Of course, no one does this. A cable that allows us to avoid the two modems is called a *modem eliminator* or *null modem* cable.

What must be different to get two DTEs to talk to each other? First, both are trying to transmit on line 2 and receive on line 3. The answer here is pretty simple—just cross 2 and 3:

```
2-------------3

3-------------2
```

```
8--+
20-|----------6
```

Flow Control

Once you've built your null modem cable, you should test that it handles flow control properly. Flow control is implemented either in hardware or software.

- Software flow control

    XON/XOFF

    ENQ/ACK

- Hardware flow control is done with one of the control lines, usually:

    DSR

    CTS

    DCD

The software approaches send *STOP!* characters back and forth when one side's buffers are overflowing. The hardware approaches just deactivate a line when the receiver needs a rest. Again, here's where your cable design is vitally important. If you neglect to include the particular handshake wire in your cable, there's no way for the computer to know that the printer is overflowing its buffer.

Another handshaking problem shows up when one side is using one method and the other side a different one, as when the PC is looking at CTS and the printer is using XON/XOFF.

You can test your handshake easily. Let's say you're hooking up a serial printer. Have the computer send a bunch of information to the printer to be printed; then do something like pull the paper tray or take the printer off line. See if the computer figures it out: Does it stop sending information to the printer? Then put the paper tray back in, or put it back on line, and see if it picks up where it left off. Another way to force buffer overflows is to set the communications line at a high speed like 19,200 bps on a slow printer; the buffer will fill up fairly quickly.

Common Cables

That's the RS-232 overview. Hopefully you're an RS-232 expert by now. But whether you are or not, here are a few basic cable diagrams. Below, I present cables to connect:

- A PC (25-pin connector) to a modem (see Figure 18.3)
- An AT (9-pin connector) to a modem (see Figure 18.4)
- A PC (25-pin connector) to another PC, a printer, and a PS/2 (see Figure 18.5)
- An AT (9-pin connector) to another AT, a printer, and a PS/2 (see Figure 18.6)
- An AT to a PC, a printer, and a PS/2 (see Figure 18.7)

FIGURE 18.3

Twenty-five-pin DTE to 25-pin DCE cable description

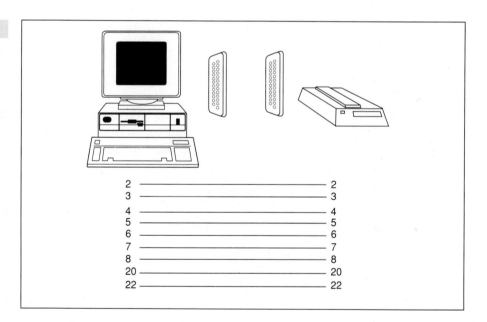

FIGURE 18.4

Nine-pin DTE to
25-pin DCE cable
description

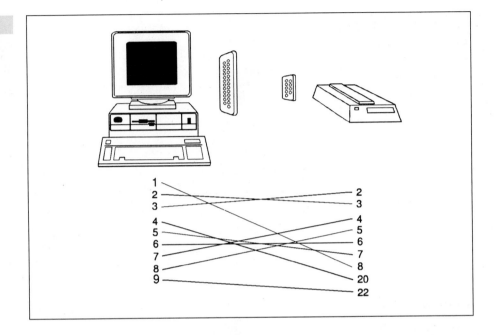

FIGURE 18.5

Twenty-five-pin DTE to
25-pin DTE null
modem cable
description

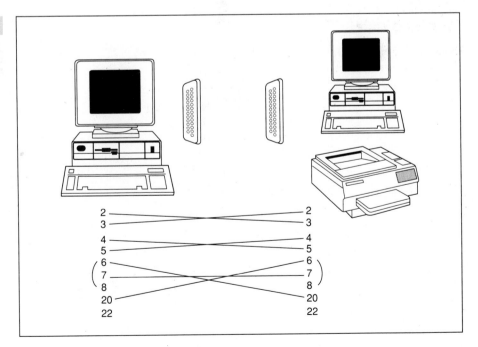

FIGURE 18.6

Twenty-five-pin DTE to 9-pin DTE null modem cable description

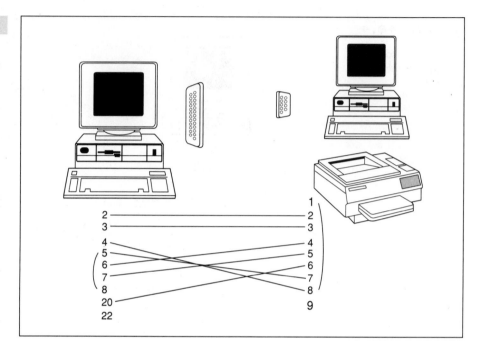

FIGURE 18.7

Nine-pin DTE to 9-pin DTE null modem cable description

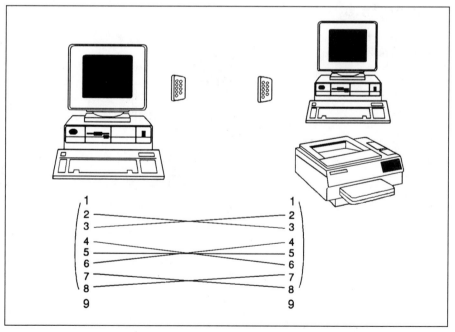

Keyboards

THE design of the PC keyboard has apparently kept IBM fairly busy since the original PC's inception. Every time a new PC is released, a new keyboard follows. They're all the same to troubleshoot, however.

Design and Components

Keyboard systems, as in the case of all peripherals, consist of an interface, a cable, and the keyboard itself. Here's what makes keyboards tick (or click).

Keyboard Interfaces

There are four IBM-type keyboard interfaces, most incompatible with each other. They are:

- The original PC or XT keyboard (generally called the *XT* keyboard)

- The original AT keyboard (generally called the *AT* keyboard)

- The 101-key PS/2 keyboard (generally called the *enhanced* keyboard)

- The 3270 PC keyboard

The XT and AT keyboards are different mainly because the XT keyboard puts the keyboard microprocessor in the keyboard, and the AT keyboard assumes the keyboard microprocessor is on the system board. They're generally incompatible: You can't use an XT keyboard on an AT or vice versa. Clone keyboards generally get around this by putting an XT/AT switch on the keyboard. The enhanced keyboard, on the other hand, will work on any machine without modification.

Switch/Contact Design

You'll find two basic kinds of keyboards:

- Switch-based
- Capacitive

The *switch-based* keyboard uses, as you'd imagine, microswitches for each key on the keyboard. Clones tend to use this switch-type approach. The switches can become dirty. They can be cleaned sometimes, but often it's easier just to replace them. They're soldered, but it's an easy solder, as there are no delicate chips around. Then again, there's the fact (always hovering in the background with keyboards) that they're sufficiently cheap. Perhaps when a problem of this magnitude occurs, you should just throw away the keyboard and buy a new one. I've seen replacement keyboards for as little as $30.

The IBM and AT&T keyboards are *capacitive*. In the bottom of the keyboard is one large capacitive surface. Each keyboard key pushes a spring, which in turn pushes a paddle. The paddle makes an impression on the capacitive module. The capacitive module sends out signals, which are interpreted by the 8048 microprocessor in the keyboard. It sends the key's ID, called a *scan code,* to the PC. The PC then figures out what the key means.

This sounds more complicated (it is), but it involves one large capacitive module rather than a lot of prone-to-failure switches. Unfortunately, it limits you a bit as far as what you can do to repair the keyboard.

Let's see what we can take apart and test.

The System Board Keyboard Interface

First is the interface between the keyboard cable and the system unit. This is a DIN plug, which has five pins (not in consecutive numerical order). Figure 19.1 diagrams the connector on the system unit side.

Voltage between pins 1, 2, 3, or 5 and pin 4 should be in the range of 2–5.5 volts DC. If any of these voltages are wrong, the problem probably lies in the PC, the system board in particular. If they're okay, the problem is probably in the keyboard. Check the keyboard cable next.

FIGURE 19.1

Keyboard interface connector

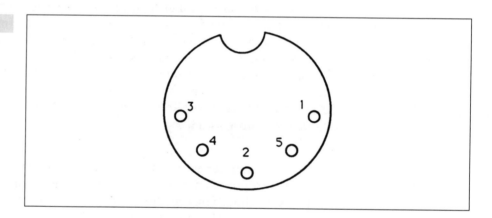

The Keyboard Connector

The keyboard cable runs from a DIN connector, which attaches to the system unit, to a flat-jaw type of connector inside the keyboard housing. The cable has five wires and can be checked for continuity quickly with an ohmmeter. Disconnect the cable inside the keyboard and test each line.

Maintenance

The major item of maintenance for keyboards is *abstinence;* that is, abstinence from spilling things into the keyboard. The SafeSkin was discussed in Chapter 4 on maintenance; this is one protection approach. Another is just to be careful.

Periodically disconnect the keyboard and remove it from the general area of the PC. Pull the keytops off of it (be sure you have a similar keyboard nearby so you can put the keytops back in the right order). Then hold it upside down and blow it clean with compressed air. The keytops aren't that tough to remove; I use one of those chip puller tools that comes with PC toolkits (recall that they're dangerous to use to actually pull *chips*) and find it to be just the tool for the job.

Troubleshooting

As with other items, you might want to view the keyboard as disposable. Replacement keyboards cost about $20 from discount houses. There are some simple things you can do before throwing out a keyboard, however.

Is It Plugged In?

On the back of the IBM PC there are two identical ports, a cassette port and the keyboard port. Plugging the keyboard into the cassette port won't work. You could even destroy the keyboard if cassette instructions are sent to the cassette port. The ports should be labeled, but if they're not, the keyboard port is the one closer to the power supply.

Is It One Key or All Keys?

If only one key is malfunctioning, check that key's spring. Remove the key by grabbing it with your fingers and pulling up. For the tough keys, fashion a hook from a paper clip or, again, use a chip puller. Under the key you'll see a spring. Replace the key cap and see if the problem goes away. If not, try pulling the spring out *just a little*. Then replace the key cap.

Checking the Cable Continuity

Next, test the continuity of the cable. Turn the keyboard upside-down so the cable is coming out of the back of the keyboard, to the right. Remove the two screws. The bottom plate will swing back and up to remove.

You'll now see that the cable splits to a single wire, which is grounded to the bottom plate, and a cable with a flat-jaw connector. Push apart the jaws of the connector to release. You can then test each of the five wires for continuity with your ohmmeter.

Completely Disassembling the Keyboard

This is not recommended for the fainthearted. You have a good chance of making things even worse, so don't do it unless there's no other hope. Warning: It'll take about four hours in total once you've taken the thing apart, put it back together wrong, figured out what you did wrong, taken it apart again, accidentally spilled all the pieces on the floor, and so on, before finally reassembling the keyboard correctly.

Remove the main assembly from the keyboard case. With a vise or C clamps, set up a support for the keyboard assembly on the sides. If you don't support it on the sides, it will fall apart when you remove the back metal plate. (Remember those springs on each paddle?)

Alternatively, you can make your life easier by removing all the key tops. But, again, don't do it unless you have another keyboard around that you can use as a guide to replacing the keytops.

A printed circuit board with capacitive pads on it is held against a metal plate by ten metal tabs (five above, five below) and a hex screw. You must use a pliers to unbend the tabs enough to remove the plate. Position the assembly so that the plate (not the printed circuit board) is on top; then remove the metal plate.

The plate has been holding dozens of plastic paddles against the printed circuit card, one for each key. These are small, flat, easily-broken pieces of plastic shaped like the outline of a castle turret, or the rook piece in chess. You're looking for a broken paddle. Replace any broken paddles and replace the metal plate.

The other reason to attempt this is if you've poured hot coffee into the keyboard. Very carefully remove all of the paddles and clean them, as well as the brackets where they sit. Use alcohol to clean the capacitive PC board. Then reassemble and pray. I've seen this work, but only once.

Replacing the metal plate is a bit difficult. Position it correctly; then use clamps to hold one side together while you bend the tabs on the other side into place. Again, it's very easy to damage paddles at this point. Where do you get replacement paddles? I know of no one who sells them, so get them from the first keyboard that dies: It's good for 83 replacement paddles.

Replacement Keyboards

If you've gotten this far and had no luck, don't despair. Many keyboard problems aren't solvable, and the things aren't that expensive anyway.

Datadesk, Keytronics, and Northgate make good replacement keyboards. Datadesk's keyboards are a bit cheaper, and they have one that's programmable. What this means is that you can move that annoying Esc key somewhere else, set up your keyboard as a Dvorak keyboard, and the like.

Keytronics offers a keyboard with an online bar code reader. Other software allows you to print out bar codes with a dot matrix or laser printer. One firm I know of uses bar codes at the top of their document-tracking forms so secretaries don't have to key (and sometimes miskey) a 12-digit document-tracking ID every time they have to update the document-tracking database.

Another interesting keyboard enhancer product is a touchpad. Keytronics offers the KB5153, which can be AT- or XT-compatible and includes a capacitive touchpad that doubles as a mouse emulator. It's considerably more expensive (about $280), but that, you'll recall, is the price IBM charged for the original simple PC keyboards, and you get a mouse in the process.

CHAPTER

20

Displays and Display Adapters

THE display on a computer is the primary output device. It's the sort of thing people get opinionated about. Personally, I've had the cheapest video combination available for years, simple composite black-and-white monitor and color/graphics adapter, but some folks just gotta have high-resolution displays. What's behind all this, and how much can we fix?

The display system has two components: a display and a display controller.

Displays

The first part of a display system is the monitor. Many options have grown up in the PC world. Some are cheap, some cost thousands of dollars. They all show at least 25 lines of 80-column text.

There are several basic kinds of monitors:

- Composite monochrome (around $75)
- Composite color ($200–$350)
- RGB ($350 or more)
- EGA monitors (about $560 with adapter card)
- Direct drive TTL monochrome ($150)
- Multiscan ($500 or more)

Table 20.1 helps you understand these monitors.

But what if you're going to upgrade your video? VGA, super VGA, and XGA are today's options.

In 1987, VGA was introduced on the PS/2 line. At the time, VGA was about the neatest video around for most PC users. In the half-decade since its inception, however, it has become the minimum ante for new computers. That's largely due to the greater emphasis on graphics: Desktop publishing and Windows applications need graphics, and of course most games require at least EGA graphics to be attractive. The next step up, "super" VGA, has spawned a host of new problems, as there isn't really just *one* super VGA—there're several different major super VGA vendors. And now there's XGA, but mortals like you and me won't be able to afford it for a while, if ever. How do you know what to buy?

In this section, I'll show you how to choose the right VGA board and monitor for your system. I'll define terms and cost ranges, and keep you from spending a lot of money on a dead-end system.

Super VGA Board Basics

VGA has been around for a while. But vendors have been offering *super* VGA for just about as long. Given that super VGA boards are about as inexpensive as VGA boards, it seems to make sense to buy super VGA. Here's what you've got to be concerned about when buying super VGA.

- What resolutions does it support? In those resolutions, how many colors can it display? If you're using a 14" monitor, resolutions above 800 × 600 are useless, so don't worry about them. For 1024 × 768, you'll require a 17" monitor. For resolutions above 640 × 480, your board will have to accommodate more video RAM.

- Can your monitor support those high-resolution modes?

- If the board supports 1024 × 768, does it support it in both interlaced and noninterlaced modes? (Noninterlaced is preferable, assuming that your monitor can display it.)

- Does the board support a 72-Hz "ergonomic" vertical-refresh rate? (This is preferable, but it's only of value if your monitor can support that resolution.)

- Will you be able to get drivers to support the board's super VGA modes?

- Is the board 8 bit or 16 bit? If it's 16 bit, can it be reset to 8 bit for compatibility?

- Did the board's designers include Windows accelerator support? If you're using Windows, that's recommended.

- Is the board interfaced with the system through "local bus?" Again, this is preferable, but it generally requires that you get your motherboard and video board from the same vendor.

In the bulk of this chapter, you'll learn what these features are, and why they're desirable.

How Much Memory Does Your Video Board Need?

Most VGA boards nowadays are super VGA boards, even the cheap clones. You can pick up a no-name VGA board for about $80–$150, and in addition to standard VGA, it'll probably do some kind of 800×600 mode. The more expensive super VGA boards ($200–$300) will support 1024×768, either in interlaced or noninterlaced mode. More resolution means more dots on the screen, which means that the video board needs more memory.

A video board's memory requirements are determined by two things: its resolution and the number of colors that it can display. For instance, the VGA can display a resolution of 320×200 with 256 colors, but when in the higher 640×480 resolution, it can only display 16 colors. That has nothing to do with the constraints of the monitor, or even of the VGA board *except* for the amount of memory on the board. A normal VGA comes with 256K right on the board.

Resolutions like 1024×768 with 256 colors obviously require more memory—that's why you see ads for VGA cards with an option for either

256K, 512K, or 1024K on the board. If all you're doing is regular old VGA, you need only 256K—there's no point in spending the extra money for 512K or 1024K. (I hear you asking, "what resolution *do* I need?" I'm getting there.) Following is the amount of memory that a video board needs for the common resolution/color combinations:

RESOLUTION	COLORS	MEMORY
640 × 480	16	256K
640 × 480	256	512K
800 × 600	16	256K
800 × 600	256	512K
1024x768	2	256K
1024 × 768	16	512K
1024 × 768	256	1024K

Will Your Monitor Support Your Super VGA Modes?

Suppose you buy a no-name VGA card for about $90. Then you leaf through the documentation that came with the board, and notice that it has a super VGA 800 × 600 16 color mode. The problem is, a standard VGA monitor (cost: $200) won't display the 800 × 600 mode. You need a "multisync" monitor (cost: $350) to display 800 × 600. (More on monitors coming up, trust me.) So the "free" super VGA mode will cost you $150 more for a monitor to see the high resolution.

There's generally no problem convincing a monitor to show a wide array of colors, but monitors have definite ranges of resolutions that they can display. Before you plan on using a particular resolution, be sure that your monitor can display it properly.

Vertical-Scan Frequencies: Interlacing and 72 Hz

Your video monitor displays information by projecting a narrow beam of electrons onto a phosphor-covered glass panel—your monitor screen. Wherever the beam hits, the phosphor becomes excited ("excited" here is a relative term), and so the phosphor lights up for brief period of time (see, excitement *is* relative here), then fades out.

Because it fades very quickly—in hundreths of seconds—the electron beam must retrace its path constantly to keep the image on the screen. How often must it travel across the screen? Well, the electron beam in the back of a video monitor must repaint the screen at least 60 times per second, or your eye will probably perceive flicker. (Why "probably?" Hang on for a sentence or two.) And that brings me to a story about the IBM 8514 video system.

Interlacing and the 8514

The 8514 video system is important mainly because it was the first mass-market PC–based video system to support a resolution of 1024×768. But, in order to save money on the monitor, IBM cut a corner on the system. Now, in order to get high resolution images, you need a high-quality (read: expensive) monitor. One way to get higher resolution out of a cheaper screen is to "refresh" it less often. The 8514 does not refresh 60 times per second, but rather 43 times per second.

This isn't the first time we've seen this fewer-than-60-refreshes-per-second approach to high resolution; it's called *interlacing*. What was significant was that *IBM* did it, so the practice of interlacing became acceptable.

But, you see, interlacing is *not* acceptable, at least not from a quality standpoint. The result of interlacing is a flickering screen and eyestrain headaches. That's why you've got to be careful when buying a system with 1024×768 resolution. Check that it's *non*interlaced.

By the way, if you do have an interlaced monitor, there may be a few things that you can do to reduce the effects of flicker, because several factors affect flicker—that's why I said "probably" a few sentences back.

First, you see flicker better with your peripheral vision, because the center of your vision is built around low-resolution color receptors called *cones* on your retina. Surrounding the cones are high-resolution monochromatic receptors called *rods*.

Peripheral vision images fall on the rods. Sailors know this because when searching for a ship on the horizon, they don't look right at the horizon —they look below it, so the horizon falls on the high-resolution rods. In any case, the closer you are to your monitor, the more of its image falls on the cones, which are less flicker-prone.

You can demonstrate this with any monitor. Stand so that your monitor is about 60 to 80 degrees to your left: If the direction you're facing is 12 o'clock, the monitor should be at about 10 o'clock. Hold a piece of paper in front of you and read the text on it. You'll notice that you're seeing the monitor out of the corner of your eye, and that it's flashing. This also suggests that you should buy a small monitor, as a large image will end up falling more on your rods; but 1024×768 on a 12" screen is, well, suboptimal.

Glare screens will also reduce flicker, as will lighting: brighter environmental lighting reduces flicker by closing your pupils and restricting the light to the rods. Another anti-flicker tactic is to keep your room bright. When the ambient light is bright, your pupils contract, which has the side-effect of reducing the amount of light that gets to the peripheral rods. You'll also find that certain color combinations exaggerate the flicker— black and white is one problem combination—so play around with the Windows colors and you'll make the screen more readable.

72-Hz Video

Since I've brought up the subject of video with low refresh rates, it's worthwhile looking at the opposite end of the spectrum—video systems that refresh at more than 60 screens per second. More widespread use of larger monitors means that more people notice flicker on normal 60-Hz VGA. Furthermore, people nowadays use their computers all day, so anyone who has even the slightest sensitivity to flicker will get some eyestrain. As a result, vendors nowadays are offering VGA and super VGA boards that put out a higher vertical-refresh rate. I feel 72 Hz is well worth investing in—my eyes rest much more easily on a 72-Hz screen than a 60-Hz screen. So, when buying your next video board, look for 72-Hz vertical refresh.

There are, of course, a few caveats. First, you need a monitor that can handle a 72-Hz vertical refresh; a basic cheap $200 VGA monitor can't handle a 72-Hz signal. Before you buy a video board, find out what kind of monitor you currently have and ask the video board's vendor if your current monitor can use all of the video board's features. If not, either don't buy the board, or plan to buy a new monitor with your new board. (Don't you just love it when some computer expert tells you to go spend some money? Kidding aside, believe me, better video is worth it.)

The second caution is actually kind of funny or sad, depending on how you look at it. Every single computer I've set up in the past two years that has a video system that will handle both 60- and 72-Hz video came out of the box configured for 60 Hz. Now, reconfiguring the video for 72 Hz usually isn't any harder than just running a short program that comes with the video board, so it's not like I unlocked some hidden feature of the video board. It's just plain inexplicable why a computer company would sell a superior video product as part of its PC, but wouldn't take the two minutes to use those features.

So, if you've got a recently-purchased computer, take a close look at the video documentation that came with it. I've been able to bring more than a few surprised smiles to the faces of owners of PCs recently by running the video setup programs that were sitting right on their hard disks.

Super VGA Requires Drivers

Having super VGA capability is nice, but your super VGA only acts like a super VGA when you've got drivers to *support* super VGA. That means having a super VGA driver for Lotus 1-2-3 version 2.4, one for 1-2-3 version 3.4, another for WordPerfect, one for Windows, one for OS/2, and so on.

Your application software may not support the super VGA modes of your super VGA board, and you have no guarantee that the video board vendor will be around in the next few years to supply you with drivers for the software. In a few years, your super VGA board mode could be a white elephant. You can build-in resistance to obsolesence by buying super VGAs based on a popular super VGA chipset. Perhaps the most widely-used super VGA chipset is the Tseng Laboratories ET4000. You'll find it on Orchid and Diamond VGA boards as well as on many "no-name" video boards.

The second problem arises when you try to *do* anything with the super VGA mode. You need a "driver" program for each of your applications to exploit super VGA—a driver for 1-2-3, one for WordPerfect, and so on. How do you know that the VGA vendor will be around to continue to support his board? On the other hand, this won't be a problem if you buy your boards from a "big name" vendor like Paradise, Orchid, Headlands Technology, Sigma, or ATI—they'll probably all be around for years to come.

Another way to ensure support is to ensure that your VGA supports the "VESA" video standard. A group of VGA vendors called the Video Electronics Standards Association, or VESA, has developed a set of standards for 640 × 480 256 color mode, 800 × 600 with either 16 or 256 colors, and 1024 × 768 with either 16 or 256 colors. Many super VGA boards support this standard, and many pieces of software support the mode.

16- and 8-Bit Video Boards

Video boards were originally designed to cater to the lowest common denominator, PC-wise—the XT-type machines. As XTs aren't too fast, there wasn't any point in designing video boards to be fast. So older VGAs and VGA clones are fairly slow in putting text and graphics up on the screen.

One way to speed up video is to double up on the data-transfer rate by buying a 16-bit video board. Older video boards transfer data at eight bits, as that was the maximum rate that XTs could handle. But any AT-type 286, 386SX, or 386 system can accommodate a 16-bit video board with no problem. So buy 16-bit video boards, rather than 8-bit boards.

Actually, you'll find that most of the VGA boards available today in 1993 are 16-bit boards. But there are still a few 8-bit boards out there, so take a minute to be sure that it's a 16-bit board.

There *is* another feature that you'll see on a few boards: *VRAM, Video RAM*. It's a special kind of memory chip that is not only high speed, it is *dual ported*: The video circuitry can read the memory at the very same time that the program is writing to it. That means snappier screens. It's a nice feature, but it's gawdawful expensive at the moment. Pass it up unless you need the very best.

One small consideration when buying 16-bit VGA boards: Make sure you can slow them down to 8 bits. A look back to Chapter 6 will remind you that if you have several adapters on your system with ROMs, then you must be alert to a potential hardware conflict. If some of the ROMs are 8-bit and some are 16-bit, then any attempt by the CPU to read an 8-bit ROM may fail. Thus, if you have an 8-bit adapter with a ROM on it, it may not work once you install a VGA with a 16-bit ROM. The answer in that case would be to reconfigure the VGA to offer only an 8-bit ROM.

Windows Accelerator Features

The rise in popularity of Graphical User Interface (GUI)–based systems has placed heavy demands on today's video technology. Those demands are answered by a video system called an accelerator, discussed later in this chapter. Accelerator capabilities are offered as an option on many video boards these days. If you're a user of Windows or OS/2, think seriously about getting a graphical accelerator board.

Ride the Local Bus

In Chapter 3, you learned that local bus can greatly speed up interaction with a peripheral. The peripheral that most greatly needs high speed access to the CPU is the video board, so perhaps the best use of local bus is in video. That's probably why the local bus standard was developed by a *video* standards group—VESA.

Local bus is a good idea that's getting cheaper and cheaper. If possible, get local bus video. See the later writeup in the "speeding up video" section for more information.

You can see that buying a video board has gotten to be a complex undertaking. Armed with this information, you'll be able to buy smarter... and when you see the faster, higher quality images that result, you'll be glad you did!

Video Memory Aperture

Some high-performance video accelerators get their speed by mapping their video memory right into the computer's memory address space. This video is called the video aperture, *and* you've got to understand it to solve some configuration problems.

In Chapter 3, I discussed briefly how video memory works. In graphics mode, an EGA, VGA, or newer video board only uses the addresses between 640K and 704K for video memory. But think for a moment, and you'll see that this seems not to make sense. 640K to 704K is just 64K, and even a simple VGA board has 256K of RAM on it. Super VGAs can have one or two *megabytes* of RAM on them. How does all that RAM fit into a 64K address space?

Simple: a little bit at a time.

The VGA uses its 256K of RAM within a 64K constraint by taking the 256K and chopping it up into *four 64K-sized areas*. Most of the video memory is invisible to the CPU at any instant in time. To update the VGA, a VGA-aware program first asks the VGA to make the first 64K area visible to the CPU. The 64K is defined to describe the red part of the image. Once the red 64K is made visible to the CPU—"paged in" is the correct term—then the VGA-aware program can modify the red part of the VGA image. The red 64K—the "red page"—is then paged out, and the next 64K—the green page—is paged in, and modified. The same is done for the third page (the blue page) and the fourth page (the intensity page).

Stop and consider what had to happen just to update a single VGA screen: Move in the red page, modify it, and move it out; then move in the green page, modify it, and then move it out; move in the blue page, modify it, and then move it out; and finally move in the intensity page, modify it, and then move it out. That's a lot of work. The reason why so much work must be done is because of the severe memory-address constraints of DOS-based programs, which in general must live in the bottom 1024K of PC memory.

Now think about what happens with a super-VGA board with 2 MB of RAM. If the super-VGA board is built like most super-VGA boards, then the 64K page approach is still used. 2 MB is, however, *32* different 64K pages. That means that a super-VGA video driver for a 2 MB video board must page in and out 32 different pages in order to update the video screen just once. Now it should be obvious why high-resolution super-VGA screens can be so terribly slow.

Some super-VGA boards take a totally different approach. They reason that they are being used not by DOS-based programs, but instead by OS/2 or Windows programs. Both OS/2 and Windows can easily rise above the 1024K address range, so some super VGA boards place the whole 2 MB of RAM right into the PC's address space, just like the RAM that the system uses to run programs. The value of this approach is that now the video RAM can be updated in a straightforward, *fast* way, without having to wait around for 64K-sized blocks to be paged around. The range of addresses used for this 2-MB block of memory is called the video aperture.

Mapping video memory right into extended memory is a good thing, in general, as it significantly speeds up video operations. But there's one catch. As you've learned in several places in this book, you can't have two things located at the same address. If the video RAM is directly mapped into the PC's extended memory address space, then you've got to be careful that it doesn't end up in the same address as some of the PC's installed extended memory. For example, if your PC has 8 MB of memory, then be sure to put the video aperture above 8 MB so that it will not conflict with your system memory.

Video aperture is usually an *option*; you can usually choose to just use the standard 64K-at-address-640K page approach. While disabling video aperture and using the small-page approach will slow you down, it might be the only way to get a system to work. IBM's accelerator board, the Extended Graphics Array (XGA), will optionally allow you to set its 2 MB of video RAM to a video aperture—but that aperture must be somewhere in the bottom 16 MB of memory addresses. That's a shame, as many Windows or OS/2 "power users" will have at least 16 MB of system RAM. As the video aperture must appear in the bottom 16 MB of addresses, but those addresses are already filled with RAM, then the XGA user would have to disable video aperture. That's not a problem for every high-performance board user, however. For example, the ATI mach32 system can use any address in the first four gigabytes—so until you fill out your 486 with 4 GB of RAM, the ATI can still offer video aperture... and I somehow suspect that before any of us puts 4 GB on a computer, there will be some quite large changes in video.

The bottom line is that you should 1) look for video aperture as an option for high performance video systems, 2) make sure that the video aperture can appear anywhere in the 386/486/Pentium address range of 0–4 GB, and 3) when experiencing video troubles, check to see if the manufacturer has already enabled the video aperture, and has perhaps accidentally addressed it on top of some system RAM. (I've seen that happen with an XGA system sold with 16 MB of RAM and the XGA RAM addressed at the 8-MB level. The system kept crashing Windows and OS/2 until the video aperture was disabled.)

Buying Monitors

Now that you've got a board, what monitor goes with it? Monitors aren't as complex as video boards, but there're a few terms to work with.

Monitor Mumbo Jumbo: Horizontal-Scan Frequency

As I explained earlier, a monitor works by directing a beam of electrons against the inside of its screen. Phosphors on the inside of the screen become "excited," and glow. Making phosphors glow or not glow defines images on the screen.

From a computer's point of view, a video display is just an array of pixels. *Resolution* is the number of dots that can be put on the screen. The electron beam sweeps across the tube, painting lines of dots. CGA used 200 lines top to bottom, EGA 350, and VGA 480. As it uses higher resolutions, super VGA does even more.

Consider the number of horizontal lines that a monitor must draw per second. In a basic VGA, each screen has 480 lines, and there are 60 screens per second. 480 times 60 is 28,800 lines per second. That is called the *horizontal-scan frequency*, as it is the number of times that the beam sweeps horizontally per second. It too is measured in hertz, or kilohertz (kHz)—thousands of hertz.

Actually, a VGA has a somewhat higher horizontal-scan rate than 28,800 Hz (28.8 kHz), as the monitor has extra lines that you can't see (they're called "overscan"). How *many* extra lines a monitor has varies from video mode to video mode. A CGA has a horizontal-scan frequency of 15,750

Hz, or 15.8 kHz. EGA uses 21.8 kHz, and VGA 31.5 kHz. So the horizontal scan frequency your monitor needs to serve your board is determined in part by two important factors: the number of horizontal lines on the screen, and the screen's refresh rate.

Dot Pitch

Monitor ads tout "0.28 mm dot pitch." What are they talking about?

We've seen that more resolution means more dots (pixels) on the screen. The widths of the dots that the monitor can display is the monitor's *dot pitch*, and it's measured in millimeters (mm). The smaller the dots, the higher the horizontal resolution that a monitor can show in a crisp and readable manner. A larger monitor can have a larger dot pitch without sacrificing resolution, as its screen is larger.

In reality, you'll see four dot pitches for VGA monitors: 0.34, 0.31, 0.28, and 0.26 mm. Avoid 0.34 on 12" VGA monitors, but you may find it quite acceptable on 14" monitors—go take a look at one before you buy it. 0.34 on a 14 inch, or 0.31 on a 12 inch is fine for VGA only, but buy 0.28 if you plan to use a super VGA in 800 × 600 resolution, and 0.26 for a super VGA using 1024 by 768 resolution.

Multi-Frequency Monitors

The last monitor feature is *multisyncing*, the ability to handle multiple resolutions automatically. Recall that the horizontal frequency that you need to display an image is determined by the refresh rate (the vertical frequency) and the horizontal resolution.

Until 1986, monitors were fixed-frequency in both the horizontal and vertical directions. When you bought a CGA monitor, it could only do one set of frequencies: 15.75 kHz horizontal, 60 Hz vertical. The EGA monitor had to be able to do double duty, as it could be attached to either CGA or EGA boards, and so had two sets of frequencies: 15.75 kHz/60 Hz for CGA boards, and 21.8 kHz/60 Hz for EGA boards. The VGA knows of three sets of frequencies: one for CGA modes, one for EGA modes, and 31.5 kHz/60 Hz for its native standard VGA mode. So a "vanilla VGA" monitor is a fixed-frequency monitor that only supports CGA, EGA, and VGA—no super VGA modes.

In 1986, NEC changed that with its Multisync monitor. The Multisync could detect and synchronize with any horizontal frequency from 15 kHz to 31.5 kHz, and any vertical frequency from 50 to 70 Hz. That meant that a single monitor could work on any kind of video board out at the time. More important, when IBM introduced the VGA in April 1987, the Multisync was ready—it could handle VGA's 31.5 kHz horizontal frequency with no problem.

Now most video vendors offer their own Multisync-like monitors: They're generically called *variable frequency monitors* (VFMs). NEC doesn't sell the original Multisync any more, but they have Multisync models from the 3FGX (31.5–38 kHz horizontal, 50–80 Hz vertical) to the 6FGX (30–66 kHz horizontal, 50–90 Hz vertical).

The competition's not asleep, however. The most reasonably-priced high resolution VFM is from Sony. The Sony Multiscan HG CPD-1304 (just call it the "Sony 1304," and people will know what you're talking about) is a *great* deal—0.26 mm dot pitch, 28–50 kHz horizontal, 50–87 vertical (usually priced reasonably). It'll display sharp noninterlaced 1024 × 768 screens, as well as 800 × 600 in rock-solid 72-Hz refresh rate. For high-end 14" super VGA, it can't be beat.

Speeding Up Video

High-resolution images are nice, but having all those extra pixels on the screen means that the processor must manage them all. A higher resolution generally means slower screens. You see, the video boards that we use in the PC world are almost all "dumb"—the CPU must do all the work. For instance, if a program wants to put a picture of a circle on the screen, it must compute the location of every dot on the screen, and activate the corresponding pixel, one by one.

More advanced systems use an "object oriented" approach, whereby the CPU just issues a command to the (intelligent) video board: "video board, draw a circle. Place it *here*, and color it blue." That way, specialized hardware (called a "graphics coprocessor") can be developed to speed up the graphical process. The CPU could describe an entire screen with a few commands, and go back to computing while the graphical hardware handled the tough work. Such boards are still very expensive—$1000 and up. But they'd get cheaper if a lot of them were sold. I wish VESA had labored to develop a standard on graphics coprocessors, rather than agreeing on how to burden the CPU further with more pixels to shove around.

Assuming that video is a major bottleneck for PC performance—and Windows performance in particular—what can be done about improving video performance? There're several approaches:

- Get faster video drivers, and make the most of your existing video.

- Get a video board with a coprocessor or an accelerator chip on-board.

- Get a local-bus video board that will exploit the full speed available from your computer.

One Answer: Faster Drivers

In a minute, I'll talk about one answer to the problem, an old answer—spend more money for faster hardware. But it's worth mentioning that there's another way. The Microsoft drivers that come with Windows are, like most Microsoft stuff, good but not great, and could use some improvement.

The drivers got some of that improvement with the upgrade from Windows 3.0 to 3.1—you'll notice that the 3.1 VGA drivers are noticeably faster than the 3.0 drivers were. But are they as good as they could be? A company by the name of Panacea (okay, so they've got an ego problem) makes replacement video drivers for super VGA boards. Called Win-Speed, these software drivers are essentially the software version of a Windows accelerator. Panacea's address is in Appendix A.

My tests of WinSpeed on an Orchid ProDesigner IIs showed speed increases of essentially zero for bitblt alignments, wide line drawing, windows scrolling and erasing, but increases of about 50 percent speed for non-wide line and arc drawing, speed doubling of fills and text drawing, and an amazing ten-time increase in speed of ROPs (Raster OPerations). WinSpeed costs $79. However, understand that WinSpeed only supports super VGA boards in 256-color modes. So, for most of us, WinSpeed is only of value on those occasions where we're doing image processing. There's no point in using the slower 256-color Windows drivers when running most Windows business applications. Compare the Panacea drivers to the 256-color 8514/a drivers that ship with Windows, and you'll see about a 30-percent speed improvement with the WinSpeed drivers.

Video Coprocessors and Accelerators

More and more applications will use 256 colors in the future, however, and more and more applications will use the higher resolutions. What's the answer? Video coprocessors.

You may already know of the sockets for math coprocessors, sockets found on the motherboard of nearly every PC compatible on the market. A math coprocessor is a special-purpose CPU, one designed only to do floating-point math, but to do it much more quickly than a general purpose CPU like your 80386. In fact, the coprocessor for the 80386—a chip called the 80387—can compute sines, cosines, and logarithms twenty times faster than the 80386.

Video coprocessors are just another kind of special-purpose CPU. As you'd expect, they're designed to shove pixels around quickly. Your math coprocessor is just a single chip, but video coprocessors are generally entire circuit boards. Related to a coprocessor is a less-expensive alternative called an accelerator. The difference is that a coprocessor is a full-fledged microprocessor, one programmable to do just about any task that the main CPU can do. An accelerator, on the other hand, is not a general-purpose CPU, but rather just a special-purpose chip that knows how to do a particular Windows task quickly. Accelerators typically include VGA circuitry on-board; coprocessors typically complement a VGA, requiring that you have both a VGA board and a coprocessor in your system.

Most accelerators are good at something called *bit blitting*. As you probably know, a term commonly used by GUI users for pictures is *bitmaps*. Windows wallpaper are bitmaps, screen captures are bitmaps, any picture created with Paintbrush is a bitmap. Much of what slows Windows down is placing bitmaps on the screen, either transferring them from memory to screen, or in moving them from one part of the screen to another part of the screen.

Moving a bitmap is technically referred to as a *bitmap block transfer*, which gets abbreviated to *bitblt*. A number of inexpensive Windows accelerators are just VGA boards with a bitblitter chip onboard. The large number of bitblt operations that Windows does makes this combination of VGA and hardware bitblt support very cost-effective.

The net effect of either a coprocessor or an accelerator is to offload much of the Windows video overhead from the CPU, so there's not much difference between the two from the point of view of most users. Using either is the same: you get the new board, you insert it in the system, and you load the drivers that support the board. From here on in, I'll treat them as essentially the same kind of device.

A video coprocessor board generally consists of a few basic parts: the video CPU special high-speed "video" RAM (VRAM) on-board programs in a Read Only Memory (ROM) a feature connector to your VGA. Most video coprocessors cannot stand alone in your system; they act as a "helper" to your VGA board. If you've ever noticed the edge connector on the top of your VGA board and wondered what it's there for, now you know: It's called the VGA feature connector and it is intended to be connected with a ribbon cable to a video coprocessor board, when you install such a board. The CPU is generally either a Texas Instruments TI34010 or TI34020 CPU. One company, Array Technologies Inc. (ATI) has designed their own proprietary coprocessor, yielding what is arguably the fastest Windows-compatible video board in the world.

As you've seen, video boards need memory. Most use simple RAM, Random Access Memory. The RAM on the video board is accessed by two systems—the PC's CPU and the video circuitry, whether the video circuitry is a simple no-processor VGA or a coprocessor-based system. That means that generally the PC's main CPU writes screen images to the RAM, and the video circuitry reads the RAM so as to display it on the screen.

There's a minor snag with using RAM for that function, however. RAM is *single-ported*, meaning that you can either read it or write it. The CPU cannot place data in RAM while the video circuitry reads that data and displays it on screen. Each must take turns, slowing down the video subsystem.

Dual-ported RAM, which we looked at in the *16- and 8-Bit Video Boards* section earlier in this chapter, is RAM that can be simultaneously written and read. As its most obvious application is in video circuitry, it has gained the moniker *VRAM*, Video RAM. VRAM is required on most coprocessor boards for its speed and it is, as you'd expect, expensive. The biggest change in how your system works with a coprocessor under Windows is how it manipulates the screen. With a "dumb" VGA, the CPU had to handle the screen pixel by pixel.

If a program needed to, say, draw a circle, the system would have to do the following things: Compute the locations of every dot on the circle; check that the video hardware is ready to be modified or change each pixel so that the circle appears on the screen. With a coprocessor, it just says, "coprocessor board, draw a circle at such-and-such location, such-and-such size, and such-and-such color," and the coprocessor board handles it—and quickly! The on-board CPU on some coprocessor boards run at 60 MHz or faster.

Local Bus Video

Fast drivers and bitblitters are two ways to shift Windows into overdrive. But the third, and potentially most effective, is a very simple idea—local buses. Recall that a page or two back I mentioned that any board in a PC runs at a mere 8 MHz. Spend all the money that you like for a 100-MHz 586, but anything in a slot runs at 8 MHz. Whenever Windows manipulates the video board, your 100-MHz "screamer" whispers at 8 MHz.

More and more vendors are bypassing the standard bus, and producing a proprietary bus slot that runs at the full speed of the computer. A quick peek at a Computer Shopper in Fall 1992 shows over a dozen companies offering very inexpensive computers that feature local bus video.

How important is local bus? Well, a standard ISA bus slot can only transfer data 16 bits at a time, at 8 MHz. A local bus slot on a 33-MHz PC would use the full 32-bit data path of the 386DX or 486 chips, and at 33 MHz would run four times faster. Twice the ability to transfer with each clock tick and four times more clock ticks per second adds up to a theoretical improvement of eight times faster! With these capabilites, imagine how much faster a regular dumb VGA running in a local bus slot could be. Ah, you've noticed that I said "could be." Having tested three vendors of local bus video, I've found performance improvements as pathetic as twenty percent, and as good(?) as eighty percent. Please be wary before you buy a local bus system; ask the vendors for some benchmarks demonstrating the speed of the local bus video before you plunk down your hard-earned cash for a red herring.

Maintenance

There's not much to say here. Treat the display board like another PC board. Ensure that the connectors are secured, as the little pins can bend over time. Be very sure not to plug RGB into monochrome and vice versa, even if they *do* use the same connector. Clean the display when it gets too dust-filmed.

Troubleshooting

Some of the dumbest monitor problems are the easiest to solve. Check the following:

- Is it turned on?
- Is the brightness or contrast turned down?
- Is everything plugged in? Is it plugged into the right place?
- If you're using a multiple-display board, are the DIP switches and jumpers set for a monochrome display or RGB? If you set it for RGB and plugged in mono, throw away the mono monitor.
- Has someone cleverly convinced DOS to display black letters on a black background? Reboot.
- Did you hear a long beep and two short ones, indicating a bad video card?

- If you're using a multispeed computer, is it in turbo mode? The display memory might not be fast enough in the higher-speed mode. Drop back to the lower speed. If the problem goes away, you'll probably have to replace the memory on the display board. (Remember the 10-MHz bus problem. A few computers have very fast buses—we discussed this in Chapter 3—that can cause some boards to malfunction.)

- There are non-video reasons for a display "malfunction," such as that the power supply has killed the computer. If the display is dead, do you hear the power supply fan? Try typing DIR. If the computer is okay but the display is bad, you'll see the drive light come on. Use a sound-emitting program to see if the computer is functioning.

- Are the motherboard DIP switches set correctly for your display adapter?

The quickest test is a monitor swap. *Do not do this* if you're working with a multidisplay (one that supports both RGB and mono-TTL monitors) and are unsure about jumper settings. There's no sense in torpedoing *two* monitors today.

If that does nothing, swap the display cards and then the cable. If the display card is the problem, do the usual easy stuff: Check the seating of the socketed chips. Clean the edge connector and the video connectors. Try again.

Still no luck? If you're courageous, you can attack the display board. Many simple monochrome or color/graphics-type display boards are based on a Motorola 6845 chip, a character generator ROM, and memory. If the memory is faulty, you'll only lose some of the display. If the ROM is bad, you'll get funny-looking characters on screen. If the 6845 is bad, just about anything could happen.

Don't try to service the monitor. As I've said before, you can hurt yourself doing that because large capacitors in the monitor can store electricity for a long time after the monitor has been unplugged.

Buying New Systems and Upgrading Existing Systems

IF you're the kind of person who fixes your own or someone else's PC—and if you aren't, why are you reading this book?— then you're likely to be the kind of person who's often looking to the *next* PC, the latest-and-greatest machine. Perhaps your palms itch when you see that someone else owns a Pentium-based PC, when all that you can afford is a 386SX. You eye 1-GB hard drives the way some teenage boys eye Corvettes.

Or maybe you're *not* that way. Maybe computers are just a tool for you, a platform upon which to get some work done. But you've found that your current platform just isn't strong enough to support today's software: Windows, OS/2, and NT require 8 MB of RAM and a clock rate of over 20 MHz on a 386 platform in order to be useful. And you need to know how to either upgrade your existing machines, or buy a *new* one that won't offer as much trouble when it's time to upgrade again in a year or two.

It's a good time to upgrade; with prices these days, everybody can own some of the fastest PCs on the planet. Buyers with tons of money don't have much advantage over the rest of us at present. (Unless, of course, you've *got* to have a Pentium-based notebook with the active matrix screen and 500-MB 1.75-inch drive.) And cheap 486es come *just* in time for those of us who are Windows users, as I've suggested: Windows is the best excuse that I know of for buying a 486.

But *which* one to buy? Well, I'm not going to tell you *that:* There are zillions of honest vendors out there that deserve your money. I'd just like to give you some advice on how to make sure that your vendor is one of the good ones.

I tell my clients that when they're going to buy a PC, they should consider four things: compatibility, serviceability, upgradability (I know, it's not a word), and price/performance.

Because I'm concerned about those things, I recommend that people avoid many of the big names in the PC business and buy a *generic* computer rather than a *proprietary* computer.

Parts of a Generic PC

Now, I've discussed this before, but before I go any further, let me remind you about what I mean when I say "generic" and "proprietary." *Generic* refers to machines designed like the IBM XT, even if the machine is built around a 486. Generic machines are PCs consisting of a few separate industry-standard parts. Those parts include:

- A standard **case**: If you buy a computer with an unusually-shaped case, as you'd see in the "slimline" PCs or the micro towers, then you'll find that all of the boards inside the computer may be unusually-shaped as well. That means that you'll not be able to locate replacement parts easily, should you need them. It also means that you can't put an industry-standard (generic) power supply in your system. That's undesirable because there are some very nice power supply alternatives these days, such as super-quiet fans or power supplies with built-in battery backup.

- A **motherboard**: The circuit board inside the case that contains the PC's CPU chip, its memory, and its expansion slots. On that motherboard should be *eight* expansion slots, rather than the three that you find on some computers these days, so that you can add expansion boards to your PC now and in the future. Three slots just isn't enough.

- A **hard disk/floppy disk controller**: A board that acts as an interface—an "ambassador," essentially—between the motherboard and your hard and floppy disks. The disks are, of course, the essential storage devices that you keep your data on. A PC also contains the hard disk and floppy disk drive or drives.

- A **video adapter** board that allows your PC to display images on a video monitor. It will probably be a so-called "super" VGA board. VGA is Video Graphics Array, a common video standard.

I'll recommend VGA accelerators a bit later.

- An **I/O board** containing two serial ports and a parallel port. You'll use serial ports for your mouse and modem—the device that lets your PC communicate with other computers over the phone—and the parallel port will let you attach your PC to a printer.

Problems with Proprietary PCs

So how is a generic PC different from a proprietary PC? Well, you find all of the same functions in a proprietary PC, but you find all of them on a single circuit board, a kind of "workaholic" motherboard. The big problem with proprietary computers is that you can't upgrade them easily, nor can you fix them for a reasonable price.

Proprietary computer motherboards are typically shaped differently from each other, and from generic motherboards, making it impossible for you to replace an old or damaged proprietary motherboard with anything but another motherboard of the exact same make and model. As motherboards of that particular make and model are only available from that particular vendor (by definition, since the motherboard is proprietary), it may be expensive or impossible to get a replacement. Likewise, it's almost certainly impossible to get an upgrade.

For more specific problems with proprietary designs, let's return to my four criteria.

Compatibility is at stake because if the vendor did anything wrong—for example, if they chose a mildly incompatible video chip, as AT&T did for some of their systems—there's nothing you can do but either throw away the computer, or hope that the designer was farsighted enough to allow you to disable the built-in video function so you can go out and spend more money on a separate video board.

Upgradability is a concern because the one-board design is "all or nothing." It's not shaped like other one-board designs—for example, Compaq's one-board design looks nothing like IBM's one-board design—so you can't replace the board with a better third-party offering. Everyone with a PS/2 Model 50 is pretty much *stuck* with a PS/2 Model 50, short of buying a new computer. This is underscored by the heroic efforts of a few vendors to offer an upgrade path for computers like the 50: We've seen Rube Goldberg schemes like 386SX "daughtercards" that replace the CPU of the computer but that then render the computer largely incapable of running Windows or DOS 5.0, or at the other end of the spectrum that make the 50 a 20-MHz 386 computer—and at only twice of the price of buying a new 25-MHz 386!

Serviceability is a problem for reasons touched on above. A generic design like a Gateway 2000 is a safe buy in many ways, not the least of which is that even if Gateway goes bankrupt tomorrow, their entire machine is composed of generic parts that can be bought at *thousands* of clone houses around the country. And this isn't brain surgery: You've seen in this book that you can break down and rebuild a PC in about 30 minutes, leaving it better than when you found it.

And what about **price/performance**? First, notice that I put this last. That's because compared to what computers used to cost, *any* PC is a bargain, even if you pay list price for an IBM-made. As for the proprietary computers: In theory, a single-board design can be faster and cheaper for many reasons. You don't see that in actual fact because single-board designs tend to be embraced by the big-name companies that need to pay for four-page color spreads in *Byte* and *PC Magazine*. I believe that by the mid '90s we'll see an informal standard among third-tier vendors for single-board designs. Once that happens, single-boards will fall into two categories: the mix-'n'-match group typified by the third-tier group, and the proprietary single-boards sold by the big names.

You don't need to buy a big name to get big performance, reliability, or flexibility. Look in your local paper's business section for the names of companies near you that sell generic PCs. It can't hurt if your company offers service through a national service company like Wang or TRW. Then choose that firebreathing 50-MHz 486DX that you've always wanted and put it to work for you—and smile, knowing that you've bought the security of easy upgrades and independence from any single vendor.

Choosing a Market Niche

Where will you buy your PC from? People in some companies are allowed to buy only from IBM or Compaq; others put machines together from parts. Computer dealers basically fall into three niches.

- **First tier**: IBM and Compaq. The *definitions* of compatibility. Price/performance tends to be fairly low, innovation minimal or gimmicky. Despite reputations for reliability, both companies throw us curves regularly (e.g., try running Laplink in turbo mode on a PS/2 Model 70). Machines *require* service contracts because they are *not* repairable: Everything is on a single proprietary board, and that board's usually only available from the vendor. And have you ever called Compaq with a tech support question? On the other hand, as I just observed, PCs of *any* stripe are so much cheaper than mainframes that by comparison you're not doing terribly even if you pay 1987 list price for a Model 80. And, despite the proprietary nature of the machines, even the lowliest repair shop has a tech who's been certified by Compaq and/or IBM, making *finding* service easier.

- **Second tier**: AST, ALR, Dell, Gateway 2000, Zenith, AT&T, Unisys, and Wyse. These companies tended towards the "modular generic" architectures for years, but are all migrating toward the "proprietary single-board" architecture. (Of the ones named, Gateway is the only one still offering modular designs.) Pros: better price/performance than first tier. Upgrade hardware (e.g. larger drives, better video) will be more available than may be the case with some of the PS/2 machines, although this won't be true with the "small footprint" machines, which tend not to be expandable at all. Con: Being saddled with proprietary architecture may require that you discard machines from a second-tier company altogether when they're obsolete; for example, Zenith Z-248s became popular when the government bought so many of them, but they're falling into disuse because you can't run UNIX, Windows, or OS/2 on a slow 286. Worse yet, their unusual power supply makes it impossible to just go out and buy an upgrade system board. Zenith offers a "386 upgrade kit" for the 248, but it's far too expensive.

- **Third tier**: also known as "box shovers" or "Three Guys and a Goat PCs." This group gets a scary reputation that's not really deserved. Yes, some of them are sleazy, deceptive, and unreliable, but then those are adjectives that have been aptly applied to some of the *big* names in the business, too. On the positive side, these companies are always aware that every sale is a significant portion of their total business, and they'll do just about anything to get a multi-machine contract with a large company or government client. You usually needn't worry about shoddy parts, as they're putting together pieces made by fairly big U.S., Taiwanese, Korean, and Japanese vendors. If you look at the sum total of all third-tier vendors, you'll see that between them they only use about three or four suppliers for any given part (drives, motherboards, controllers, etc.). That means that if you really look at the companies that are *supplying* those parts—Micronics, DTK, AMI, Chips & Technologies—you'll see that they're pretty large and reliable companies. The absolute best part about these machines is that they're the simplest to upgrade and maintain. They also have the best price/performance in the group, and compatibility is usually as good at the second-tier machines.

Choosing PC Parts

In the process of choosing a PC, I look at what it's made of in order to decide if it's the kind of machine that I'm looking for. Let's look at the important parts of a PC and summarize what you should consider when buying a PC. All of these items are discussed elsewhere in the book; this is just a summary. Consult the Index to find out where to read more about any given topic.

- **CPU**: If you're buying today, buy 25-MHz 386DX or faster computers. The extreme price attractiveness of the 386SX is dissolving, and the extra power of the 386DX can be put to good use in a Windows-oriented world. Once the "boutique" nature of the Intel DX2 and OverDrive socket fades and generic motherboards with the OverDrive socket appear in great variety—they're already starting to appear—then they'll be a good buy.

- Additionally, there is a lot of evidence that CPUs running at 50 MHz and greater require some kind of special cooling hardware for the CPU itself. That includes heat sinks, fans mounted on the CPU, or the small refrigeration units (no, I'm not kidding—they're about the size of a matchbox) that fit on top of CPU chips.

- **What about modular "upgradable" PCs?** The idea *sounds* good, but the upgrades are proprietary and can be quite expensive. Generic PCs are the original "upgradable" PCs.

- **Bus**: The trade rags beat this one a lot. In a few words, there are three types of expansion slots in the PC world: the original one, called ISA (Industry Standard Architecture), an IBM offering called MCA (Micro Channel Architecture), and a Compaq-inspired improvement of ISA called EISA (Extended ISA). ISA is going to fade away in the next year or so; you will find many fewer new 386DX or 486 computers with an ISA bus this time next year. MCA isn't a bad bus, it's just too tied to a single vendor *and* won't work with your old ISA expansion cards. EISA is a good bet because it works with the old ISA boards, as well as providing an expansion path to the future. But you won't go far wrong with ISA, as boards that use the full power of EISA are only starting to appear, and slowly at that. **Local bus** is a good idea for your video boards and even now for disk controllers.

- **RAM**: Like it or not, the world is going GUI (Graphical User Interfaces). Name a single major product being developed for DOS—there aren't any. All new development is in Windows, OS/2, or UNIX. Don't get me wrong—DOS will never die. But just as the once-mighty CP/M ("CP *who?*" See what I mean?)

slowly surrendered the stage to the more powerful DOS, so will DOS applications migrate more and more to the GUIs. So you need RAM, and lots of it. At about $35/megabyte, RAM's cheap. I recommend that you buy computers with 8 MB of RAM but be sure there's an easy expansion path to 16 MB.

- If you're buying 33 MHz or higher, get a motherboard with *processor cache* of at least 256K. The option used to be very expensive, but now it's quite reasonable.

- **ROM BIOS**: an important part of compatibility. Buy from one of the big three: Phoenix, Award, or AMI. That way, it's easy to get upgrades. Nice BIOS features:

  - User-definable drive types
  - Bus speeds that can be set in the setup
  - Fast A20 gate speeds up windows
  - Processor cache enable/disable

- **Motherboard/System Board**: the board that contains the above items. If you're buying from a first- or second-tier company, you'll end up with their board. From a third-tier place, look for motherboards from Micronics, DTK, Mylex, Chips & Technologies, and AMI. Avoid "Opti" motherboards.

- **Disks**: You're probably going to end up buying IDE-type drives, mainly because they're so amazingly cheap, fast, and reliable. Just back the silly thing up *regularly,* because there's only a limited array of repair options open to you. Best buy these days is probably a Maxtor 340 MB, a Maxtor 500 MB, or the Fujitsu 500 MB, all IDEs. Costs are around $1/MB. Do not buy ST-506 or ESDI drives. Consider buying a disk controller with cache RAM right on it, but be sure that you can *disable* that cache if need be.

- In the floppy arena, I've seen too many problems with Mitsubishi drives to recommend them; TEACs seem the most trouble-free. I highly recommend the TEAC "double" drive, a drive that fits into a single half-height bay that contains the electronics to work with both 5¼ and 3½ diskettes.

- **Video board**: If you're going to buy regular plain VGA, go ahead and buy the cheapest clone you can find; they all work the same. But if you're buying super VGA, buy from a big name such as ATI, Orchid, Headlands Technology/Video 7, or Sigma Designs. Paradise/Western Digital seems to be fading from the business. Buy from a big name so they'll be around when you need driver software for WordPerfect version 27. If you're doing Windows, consider an accelerator board like the Orchid Fahrenheit 1280 or the blazingly-fast Graphics Ultra from Array Technologies, Inc. The right accelerator can speed up your Windows screens by a factor of up to ten. Look also for local bus video, another way to jazz up screens. You can even find PCs nowadays that offer accelerators that use local bus—very fast Windows machines indeed!

- **Video monitor**: Buy a monitor based on the resolution you'll use it at. If you're doing regular old VGA (with a resolution of 640 dots across the screen by 480 dots down the screen), buy a 12-inch fixed-frequency VGA monitor; it'll cost around $220. For the super VGA 800 × 600 resolution, get a 14-inch multisyncing monitor that can handle that resolution. For 1024 × 768, buy a monitor that's at least 17 inches diagonal. And *do not* buy interlaced 1024 × 768: sure it's cheaper, but the lawsuits from your employees going blind will be expensive. Buy noninterlaced. And only worry about it at 1024 × 768: Nobody I know of tries to interlace 640 × 480 or 800 × 600.

- **Mice**: Although I hate to put more money in Microsoft's pocket, the Microsoft mouse seems the best of all the mice I've worked with. But $100 for a mouse? Arggh!

- **Printers**: Well, they cost a little more, but it's hard to go wrong with HP laser printers. The series 4 produces beautiful output. If you need a high-speed dot-matrix printer, Okidata seems to make the most rugged ones—you know, the ones that can print all 15 parts to your 15-part forms.

- **Serial ports**: Look for serial ports based on the 16550 UART chip. It's built for multitasking.

CHAPTER

22

Multimedia

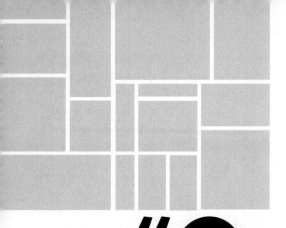

"**O**KAY**, everyone, quiet on the set; make sure all the fans are adjusted to a quieter speed. Somebody check the makeup on that PC—I'm getting a shine off its monitor. And tell that Compaq to turn the damn speaker keyclicks off. Kris, check the PROMPT command on the prompter. Good. Let's do this in one take, people, all right? Now, lights... camera... *action!*" Multimedia is show biz on the PC. If you've got the storage space, the speed, and the equipment, then you can essentially make movies on your machine.

It's not all fun and games, either. Right now, I'm experimenting with building Windows-based movies that depict the process of disassembling a PC. Perhaps a future edition of this book will include a CD-ROM containing an hour of "PC movies" that show what this book talks about in a whole new format. (The project's not anywhere near done, however, so *puhleeze* don't harass SYBEX or me for the thing.)

Making PC movies is an expensive process, and takes a good long time. But at the other end of the money spectrum, multimedia includes something as simple as adding sound to existing programs, announcing over the speaker "Mail call!" when new electronic mail has arrived, or allowing you to pick up a microphone and add a note with some voice emphasis to an E-mail message. Adding sound doesn't *have* to cost a bundle, so it's something we all can experiment with and use.

The hardest part about multimedia seems to be buying compatible equipment and getting it to talk to each other. This chapter looks at understanding what hardware and software you need, installing it, and making it work.

What Is Multimedia?

Multimedia means mixing sound, images, graphics and other information in a digital form on a single compact disk. A compact disk is 12 cm (just under 5") in diameter and can store up to 650 megabytes of data. Unlike disks, which use concentric tracks of data, CD-ROM data are written in a single spiral that starts out at the outer edge of the disk and extends round and round the disk, finally ending near the disk's center. That spiral is nearly *3 miles* long, which helps to explain how it can fit so much data on such a small space.

The term "multimedia computer" is ambiguous, meaning many things to many people. In particular, PC manufacturer's marketing departments have been, well, *creative* with the term. Multimedia seems to have picked up the "games" tag, but that's not fair. Multimedia can be used for games, for training, or for serious business applications. The stress that has been placed on multimedia's game-playing abilities is misleading, and not very helpful if you're trying to sell the purchase of multimedia computers to your company's senior officers. You don't want them thinking of the employees spending all their time playing games.

Explaining everything in the world about multimedia would fill books, so I've got to lower my sights a bit in order to get all of this into just one chapter. For this chapter, I will focus on computers that meet the MPC (multimedia PC) standard. I will also mention some of the accessory boards that enhance the capabilities of these PCs.

What Is the MPC Standard?

The MPC (Multimedia PC) standard is a CD-ROM and hardware standard that Microsoft announced in 1991 in conjunction with a number of major hardware manufacturers. The Multimedia PC Marketing Council was established to administer the program and license the MPC logo and trademark. The MPC standard consists of the following:

- CPU (Central Processor Unit): 80386SX or better.
- Memory: 2 MB of RAM.

- Floppy disk drive: $3^1/_2$" high density.
- Hard disk: 30 MB.
- CD-ROM drive with the following characteristics:

  - servicing it should require no more than 40 percent of the CPU's power.
  - average access time of 1 second or less.
  - data transfer rate of 150 kilobytes/second or better.

- Video display: VGA display adapter with a color VGA monitor.
- Keyboard: 101-key IBM-style keyboard.
- Mouse: two-button bus mouse.
- Data ports: one serial port, one parallel port.
- Music port: MIDI port.
- Game port: joystick port.
- Sound card: sound card compatible with Sound Blaster.
- System Software:

  - Microsoft Windows 3.0 or later.
  - Microsoft Multimedia extensions for DOS.

Microsoft is a driving force on the MPC Council, so it is not very likely that Microsoft will radically change the ground rules and make MPC obsolete. The biggest change happened in early '92 when the MPC council switched the base PC from an 80286 to an 80386 CPU. The only worry now is that Microsoft might change the MPC specifications just to trip up IBM and OS/2.

Although Windows is specified as the Graphical User Interface (GUI) or system software, MPC software can also be run on PCs using the OS/2 operating system, generally by running Windows under OS/2. There also are OS/2-based multimedia packages such as Studio I by Joni Carter. (Studio I is explained in more detail shortly.)

A Sampling of Multimedia Uses

Most people think of multimedia as a way of creating pretty pictures and sounds, but in fact there are many practical applications in its use, including training, education, legal and business applications. There's even a way to make voice annotations to text. Let's take a look at each of these in more detail, with examples of each application. (You can use these examples when selling the idea of multimedia to your boss.)

Training

Multimedia excellence as a medium for training is demonstrated by Studio 1, a program designed by Joni Carter, a famous sports artist who uses multimedia extensively. Studio 1 is the multimedia equivalent of The Miracle Piano Teaching System. The artist walks you through each lesson, then has you do it. Studio 1 will be bundled with all IBM ultimedia PS/2 computers. ("Ultimedia" is IBM's name for their multimedia standard, an alternative to MPC.) The training effectiveness of Studio 1 defines a new standard for business training multimedia on a PC; of course, its major downside is that it runs only under OS/2.

Teaching and Education

A CD-ROM is an excellent way to present materials for learning and review. Front Page News (10/90–9/91) takes advantage of CD-ROM's ability to store a large amount of material in a small space, including the full text of over 200,000 news articles from more than 10 U.S. and international wire services.

Another good learning tool is the Anatomist. This is a complete anatomy textbook, in which you can click on an item and hear its name pronounced. You can look at the reference notes provided and add your own custom notes. Anatomist is currently available only for the Mac, but I hope that it will be available for the PC soon. Most of the on-line dictionaries available on CD-ROM offer an option to pronounce a word, in addition to the usual definitions and synonyms/antonyms.

Legal

In the courtroom, a notebook computer and CD-ROM drive are quickly becoming as essential as a well-prepared case. The case law for many states is now available on CD-ROM as fully searchable text files, so a lawyer can immediately search for a previous ruling or precedent without leaving the courtroom. In other words, the laborious process of poring over mountains of old cases has been supplanted by the pressing of a few keys and the blink of a disk access light. Lawyers don't even have to lug around an external CD-ROM drive for their notebooks, as several different brands of notebook computers are now available with a built-in CD-ROM drive by Scenario.

Business

What do you do when you need access to large amounts of information, but have only limited storage available? A business can get disks with the white and yellow pages listings for different regions of the United States or even the entire country. At only half a dollar for each directory assistance call, these calls can pay for themselves quickly; more important, these directory databases are more up-to-date than the printed phone directories, whose data stales at an appalling rate. A number of businesses with switchboards have even turned directory assistance into a profit center.

In business, the best decision is the well-informed decision, and CD-ROM makes the process of becoming well-informed much easier than it used to be. A small business with international dealings can do a sanity check on the advice from their foreign advisors. The official European Community legal database is available on CD-ROM.

CDs' huge storage capabilities make them the chosen mode of distribution when dealing with large amounts of information. Any business that uses desktop-mapping software for sales analysis quickly finds that the size of the base map files requires getting them on CD-ROM. U.S. Census data and other marketing data are also so voluminous that a CD-ROM is the only realistic way to distribute the data.

Voice Annotation

A multimedia PC makes it possible to do electronic and voice mark-up of a document. I can attach a voice file to a spreadsheet or program that contains the documentation behind the document. How many times have you wished you knew what the author of a document was really thinking? For many of us, it's easier to get a point across verbally than with the written word... but, of course, that's "for many of us." For other people, voice annotation finally gives them the opportunity they've always sought—the opportunity to chatter on at great length for posterity. So voice annotation's got to be done right, or the person listening to the voice annotation will quickly decide to skip the voice document.

Artisoft has been offering their Sounding Board for several years. The Sounding Board allows the user to record, play and store speech in their PC. The speech files can be transmitted over Artisoft's LANtastic LAN to other Sounding Board users. This might be one way of distributing memos in a paperless office without stripping the expression from the words, as electronic mail messages tend to.

Rational Data Systems offers VoiceOver, which adds voice annotation to WordPerfect word processor documents. Now you can attach voice comments to WordPerfect documents. Rational and WordPerfect are working closely together to add VoiceOver to other WordPerfect applications.

More and more banking institutions are moving to a "workflow- processing" model of paper shuffling, and multimedia is at the heart of it. Here's how it works.

Apply for a mortgage, and you're in for a Kafkaesque experience. You end up filling out fifteen forms, many of which want exactly the same information as the *other* fourteen forms. Then you drop the forms off at the bank, and the bank ships them around to the five or six people who must review and approve the loan. If you call the bank looking for information about the status of your loan, you're likely to be told that "Mr. Jones is currently working on your loan, but Mr. Jones is out at the moment." Your forms may even be lost.

With workflow processing, your forms are scanned onto an optical disk, and then burned. The only copy of your forms exists as little burned pits on an optical disk. The data file that contains these optical images then gets shoved into the workflow processor, which knows how the forms must go: first to Ms. A, then to Mr. B, Mr. C, and finally Ms. D.

The forms are shuffled over the LAN to the electronic "in-box" of Ms A, who pulls them up on her screen and looks them over. If all is well, she clicks a button, and the forms move electronically to Mr B. If *not*, however, she can circle the troublesome spot with her mouse, pick up a microphone attached to her monitor, and vocally note what's missing or awry with the form. Then, if you should call in looking for information about what's holding up your loan, the telephone operator at the bank can just pull up the document on his screen, and ask the workflow processor to "search for notations." The workflow processor then highlights for the operator exactly what stumbling blocks exist before your loan can be approved. No chasing around for Ms. A, no losing forms, and those benefits accrue largely to the optical storage device, the LAN, the workflow-processor software, and the audio input/output capabilities of the workstation. Two of those factors are multimedia features.

How to Buy or Make an MPC System

Now that you have an idea of what multimedia is good for, you'll need the setup to try it out. After looking over the list of *all* the stuff that you could buy in order to be fully multimedia-ready, you might conclude that multimedia was designed to get the electronics industry out of its depression. It's true, the amount of equipment required, or that would be nice to have, is impressive. But you don't need all of it in order to get started. You can start small, and build as you go.

Look at your present computer system carefully and consider your needs before upgrading with an MPC kit. First, if your computer is less than a 386SX, it won't meet the MPC standard. Second, if the computer is your primary work-at-home computer, you might not be able to get it out of the kids' hands once it has been upgraded to an MPC PC.

As usual when adding capabilities to your computer, you need to make sure that your PC has enough available slots. Many kits require a slot for the sound card and a slot for the MIDI card or SCSI disk controller card. If the multimedia kit has an internal CD-ROM drive, you need to make sure that you can place the controller card close enough for the cables to reach the CD-ROM drive. You also need to have an available disk drive bay that is accessible from the front of the case and the power supply in the PC.

If you are buying a CD-ROM drive, multimedia upgrade kit, or multimedia PC, you should buy one that has the MPC logo. The MPC logo ensures that the components or system are compatible with the MPC standard. (The MPC standard is listed above.) If you also have a Macintosh, you should look for QuickTime compatibility on the CD-ROM.

Although the MPC standard specifically mentions only a 386SX or better computer, it's best to get the fastest computer possible. A video accelerator board will also help to display the images faster.

Here is a list of things to watch out for in the MPC standard. These can trip you up when upgrading an old system. Also watch out for these bare minimum features of the MPC standard that don't meet real world needs.

- A small case PC may not have enough future expansion room.

- Many of the "pizza box" PCs have only two or three expansion slots. If you add an MPC kit, you may only have a single half length slot available for future expansion.

- The CPU—there is no minimum speed mentioned, but most manufacturers ship at least a 20-MHz 386SX. In truth, you'd be best off with a computer at least 25 MHz in speed, and with a 386DX or better processor. A 486 may actually be a better chip if you can afford it.

- The memory—to be realistic, get at least 8 megs of RAM, as you'll be working with Windows, and Windows needs 8 MB to be useful.

- A 3½" high density drive—this will trip up many people who add an MPC kit. If your PC does not have one, *add it*.

- The hard disk—120 megabytes is the smallest realistic size, and 200 megabytes would be better. Believe me, you'll use it.

- The video:

    - Although VGA is the minimum resolution (480×640 lines), a higher resolution, such as Super VGA (800×600 lines) is better. But remember that more resolution means more CPU overhead. As you read a bit earlier, a video accelerator is a very good idea.

    - You might want a larger monitor than the 14" monitor many systems have. Unfortunately, as of early 1993, monitors larger than 15" are much more expensive than the smaller ones.

- CD-ROM—More on this later.

- Speakers—Not part of the MPC standard, but you have to get the music and other sounds out somehow.

    - Speakers have magnets, and magnetic fields affect monitors. I have seen this proven at software demos at the Grand Hyatt in New York City (above Grand Central station). Every time the electrically-powered trains came in, the displays of the monitors on the third floor would be affected. A number of speakers specifically designed for multimedia PCs have specially shielded speakers. If yours does not, then be sure to put the speakers a few inches away from the case of the PC.

    - You might want to consider a pair of headphones so that you will not have to worry about disturbing others.

Choosing a CD-ROM Drive

Although it seems that choosing a CD-ROM drive would be easy, it is not. In fact, many earlier CD-ROM drives will need to be replaced because they do not have the capability of supporting many of the new features. If you see a CD-ROM for sale in the classified section of the paper, it is probably because that person is upgrading and the old CD cannot support the new multimedia standards. When buying CDs, remember that the access time must be under 1000 milliseconds and the data transfer rate must be above 150 KBps.

Disk Carrier Options (Caddy or Caddyless) Some CD-ROM drives are caddyless, meaning that they don't use a caddy, a carrier, for the CD-ROM. These caddyless systems have a drawer that slides out into which you place the CD-ROM, then push the drawer shut to prepare the disk for use.

The caddy, a plastic cartridge with a shutter, makes the CD-ROM disk look like an optical disk. Just as with a $3\frac{1}{2}$" disk drive, the shutter is moved aside when the caddy is inserted. This enables the disk drive to read the CD-ROM inside the caddy. Caddies are good since they protect the CD-ROM from damage while being handled.

CD-ROMs are fragile. Despite what the advertising suggests, you can't use them as frisbees and still get usable information off them. The CD-ROM is handled just once to load the caddy; after that, the CD-ROM is protected. The drawback of a caddy is that they are an additional cost and you will probably end up buying one for each of your CD-ROM disks.

Which Interface?

CD-ROM drives are available both with proprietary and SCSI interfaces. Buy only the SCSI interface, as it allows you to move your drive to another system in the future. The SCSI interface also provides for expansion room if you want to add a scanner, hard disk or optical disk in the future.

Now, when you scan the ads for CD-ROMs, you may not *like* that advice. You'll see some systems offered for about $200, with some CD-ROMs thrown in for free. It might seem like a good deal to buy one of these drives, but don't do it! First of all, you're buying a drive with a proprietary interface, which means that you'll need for its manufacturer to provide not only updates of drivers for the CD-ROM, you'll also be dependent on that vendor for interface drivers. The chances of getting these drives to work under OS/2 or Windows NT are slim. Buy cheap now, and regret it later. On the other hand, you may want to spend the $200 on a cheap drive now, and use it as an educational device, something that you'll use to learn about CD-ROMs. Just be sure that you've got somebody to sell the drive to when you dump it in nine months for something faster.

If you are placing the CD-ROM drive into a business or library, you should make sure that you can daisy-chain additional drives off the first drive. The first drive is the controller for the other drives. This enables you to have up to eight CD-ROM drives while using only one connection to the PC's SCSI controller.

Internal, External or Portable?

This is determined by either your PC or how you plan to use your CD-ROM. External CD-ROMs don't take up space in a PC drive slot, and they don't require power from the PC. They do cost more, however, because they have their own case and power supply. NEC has a portable CD-ROM drive with its own battery pack. If you really need a CD-ROM drive that's built into a notebook computer, Scenario has modified notebooks to have a built-in CD-ROM drive.

CD-ROM Speed

The fastest CD-ROM drives have an average access time of 280 msec. Some slower drives have an access time of as long as 1500 msec. When a manufacturer makes a less expensive CD-ROM drive, the drive is often much slower than a more expensive drive. If you are planning to buy a CD-ROM drive on sale, you should look carefully at the access time.

Manufacturers are also trying to speed up CD-ROMs by increasing the data transfer rate. The transfer rate in the MPC standard is 150 kilobytes/second. Some CD-ROM drives, advertised as Double Speed drives, have increased this to 300 kilobytes/second. Some drives have even increased the transfer rate to 600 kilobytes/second.

It's clear that CDs are much slower than disks. Why is that? CDs are slower than disks for a few reasons, having to do with the CDs' original design and the discrepancy between their data amount and available cache space.

First of all, CDs were originally designed to play music, playing sequential tracks for a long time, rather than to seek small amounts of data distributed at random. I've seen a CD-ROM that took 15 hours to retrieve a single field for all 50 states from a Census CD-ROM.

Second, the disk speed is varied. CDs are recorded using CLV (Constant Linear Velocity). In this recording system, the speed of the disk varies from over 1,000 rpm at the center to 400 rpm at the edge. Hard disks use CAV (Constant Angular Velocity). CLV varies the speed of the disk so that the read head always covers the same distance. CAV has the disk spinning at a constant RPM so the read head always covers the same angle. It might help to envision a pie. A pie cut with CAV, the method used to record a hard disk, would have wedge-shaped cuts, like a traditional pie. A pie cut with CLV, the way that CDs are recorded, would have rectangles cut in the pies, so that the outside edge of the pie had more rectangles.

Finally, the discrepancy between the huge amounts of data that need to be read from a CD and the much smaller size of the CD's cache can slow things down. A CD-ROM drive will often need to read a large amount (megabytes) of data. This amount of data overwhelms the CD's cache, which is often only 64 kilobytes in size. (The cache is a large buffer and storage area for data which allows the data to be moved from the cache to the computer quickly.) To get around this problem, you might want to buy several megabytes of memory and use it with a caching program. Some people even copy an often-accessed CD-ROM to a 720-MB hard disk. This makes the CD-ROM data available at hard-disk speeds.

Double, Triple, or Quadruple Spin?

As you just read in the previous section, CD-ROMs can be quite slow in accessing data. A slow CD-ROM can be slower than a floppy, a nightmarish thought: reading 680 MB at floppy speed! NEC has developed a faster approach to reading CD-ROM disks, one mainly involving turning the disk faster.

Quick review from the hard disk section: There are two indicators of disk-drive performance. The first is *access time,* which asks the question "how long does it take to find the data on the disk platters?" It's measured in milliseconds; the best values for modern hard disks is around 9 ms, worst for modern hard disks is around 30 ms. The second performance measure is *data-transfer rate,* which asks the question "now that I've found the data, how quickly can I zap it off the disk and onto the PC's bus?" That's measured in KBps. Hard disk data-transfer rates range from about 500 KBps to about 5000 KBps.

With either a hard disk or a CD-ROM drive, the faster the disk spins underneath the read head, the faster the data comes out of the drive. Normal CD-ROMs can only spin CD-ROM disks fast enough to produce data at about 150 KBps. At that rate, it would take about an hour and a half to read an entire CD-ROM disk, assuming that the disk were the maximum size of 680 MB! In 1991, NEC started selling a "double-spin" disk that upped the data transfer rate to 300. 1993 saw the introduction of triple-spin or "30×" drives that offered a data transfer rate of 450 KBps, and "4×" drives that transfer data at 600 KBps. All of the NEC (and competitive) drives are stuck with pretty lousy access rates—access times of 200 ms are about the best that you'll see on the CD-ROM market.

It seems that speed is directly proportional to price. Single-spin CD-ROMs cost around $220, double spins $450, triple spins around $700, and 4× drives are near $1000. Do you need 3× or 4×? To retrieve simple data, no. But if you're intending to use your CD-ROM for multimedia uses, then it is very hard for a 150 KBps drive to shovel enough data out onto the PC bus to support an animated video presentation. 4× is about the minimum to support full-screen (640 × 480), 16 frame per second animation.

CD Red Book, CD Yellow Book

As you read about multimedia and CD-ROMs, you will hear references to a number of different books, such as Red Book and Yellow Book. These book colors refer to standards, with the different names corresponding to different CD types. It's important to pay attention to these different types of CDs, as you have to make sure that the CD-ROM disk drive supports the CD- ROM disk you are planning to play. Below is a more in-depth overview of the different books. You can also order the books themselves from the standards organizations. (See Appendix A for the addresses.)

Here, adapted from "Compact Disk Technology" by James R. Fricks, is an explanation of the alphabet soup you will read about and hear mentioned.

- Red Book—CD-Digital Audio (CD-DA) for music.
- Yellow Book—CD-ROM.
- Mode-1 is computer data.
- Mode-2 is compressed audio data and video/picture data.
- CD-ROM/XA—XA is eXtended Architecture, an extension to Yellow Book that defines a new type of track.

- CD-ROM Mode 2, XA Format, is used for computer data, compressed audio data, and video/picture data.

  The CD-ROM / XA track may mix, or interleave, sectors of Mode 2 data and Mode 2 audio. (Other CD formats require the track to be pure data or pure audio.) This requires additional hardware to separate these interleaved tracks when playing the disk. This hardware separates the audio sectors so they can be decompressed and played through the audio output, then the data sectors are passed to the computer. Some vendors offer an XA interface board that will allow an existing CD-ROM drive to play CD-ROM / XA disks.

- Green Book—Compact Disk Interactive (CD-I). These are played on a stand-alone CD-I player attached to a TV or monitor.

- Orange Book—Recordable Compact Disk Standard

- Part I—CD-MO (Magneto Optical). This has a premastered ("mastered" is CD-ese for "recorded") read-only area (optional), and a re-writable area for recording data. You can read more about these 3½" optical disks in the *SCSI* section of Chapter 11.

- Part II—CD-WO (Write Once). This type of CD, called a CD-WO or "hybrid disk", has a prerecorded read-only area and a recordable area. In the prerecorded area, information is written with Red, Yellow, or Green Book specifications at manufacturing time. (With this information, the CD-WO can be played on any CD-Player.) The recordable area allows additional recordings to be made in one or multiple sessions. This is the format that Kodak's Photo CD uses. As of late 1992, only the first session on the disk is readable by CD players.

- CD-Bridge Disk—The CD-Bridge Disk defines how to add additional information in a CD-ROM / XA track so the track can be played on a CD-I player. The resulting hybrid disk can be played on either a CD-I player connected to a TV set or on a CD- ROM / XA player connected to a computer. Kodak's Photo-CD is also an example of a CD-Bridge Disk. The Photo-CD Disk is designed to be playable in CD-I players, Kodak's Photo CD players, and in computers using CD-ROM/XA drives.

Choosing Multimedia Sound Boards

You've got to put up with some backtalk from your PC if you want to do multimedia. Specifically, you need a sound card that supports FM generation, and potentially MIDI. (FM here doesn't mean that it's got a radio; it refers to the way that sounds get generated by the board.) FM files in the Windows world—and MPC is based largely on Windows—have the extension WAV.

You can spend a ton of money on sound cards—that's probably a big reason why they're relatively unusual in the PC world—but now there are a number of low-end soundcards on the market today. In 1992, Microsoft introduced a sound card designed for low end sound applications, such as voice annotation. Compaq included the same sound chip (Business Audio) on the motherboard of some of their PCs. Artisoft has had their Sounding Board sound card for several years.

Attractive as these low end sound cards are, however, a true MPC- compliant sound card is most appropriate. The true standard in the MPC sound arena is the Sound Blaster Pro, from Creative Laboratories.

The Microsoft PC Speaker Driver

At the extreme "cheap" end of the cost spectrum is the Microsoft PC Speaker Driver, a sound driver that lets you use the speaker in your PC as an FM playback device. The hardware cost is zero, and the software cost is negligible: Microsoft will send it to you if you request it, or you can download it from CompuServe on the MSL forum. The file's name is SPEAK.EXE. When you download the file to your hard disk, put it in a directory all by itself, and type SPEAK. It will decompress to several files, one of which is the documentation that explains how to install the driver.

Should you use the Speaker Driver, and forget getting a sound board? In general, I'd say no. All it's good for is playing back WAV files, and even then voices are nearly unintelligible. It is totally useless on a notebook computer, as most notebooks have extremely basic speakers. Even on a desktop PC, although you'll find that simple tunes play back all right, all I'd use it for is to attach a chime to an error message or the like. But no matter how you cut it, it ain't multimedia.

Sound Card Features

When buying a sound card, consider the following options:

- Can it handle 16-bit sound? Early sound cards stored and represented sound data as 8-bit packets of information. Newer cards support both 8-bit and 16-bit sound. The difference? 8-bit data represents sound as one of 256 possible levels; 16-bit represents sound as one of 65,536 different levels. The Sound Blaster Pro and the Media Vision ThunderBoard are examples of audio boards that support 16-bit sound.

   Do you need 16-bit sound? Well, for simple voice annotation, no. But many multimedia presentations involve some music, and music playback is significantly enhanced by 16-bit sound, provided that it was recorded at 16 bits to begin with. If you want to capture music at CD quality, you will need to buy a 16-bit card, as an 8-bitcard does not have enough resolution to accurately capture sounds at faster sampling rates. Of course, the downside of more information is that it takes more storage space.

- How does it interface to the PC? Most boards will, of course, plug into a normal PC slot. But is it an 8-bit or 16-bit slot? Note that there is no connection between the number of bits in the sound sampling (the topic of the previous paragraph) and the number of bits in the PC interface (the topic of this paragraph). But a 16-bit interface means better speed. Furthermore, many of us live with notebook PCs, which lack slots. Both Media Vision and Creative Labs offer battery-powered devices about the size of a deck of cards that plug into a parallel port, bringing MPC sound to a notebook PC.

- Where will you get drivers? The nice thing about buying something that's Sound Blaster compatible is that there'll be drivers around for it; think of the Sound Blaster as the Hewlett-Packard LaserJet of sound cards.

- Does it support MIDI, or FM, or both? MIDI, as you'll read a bit later, is a standard for playing music on a PC. But MIDI adapters cannot play voice annotation-type files; they are stored in a Frequency Modulation (FM) format that usually uses the extension "WAV" in the Windows world. The Sound Blaster Pro supports both. But it's surprising which boards do not support FM; for example, an old standard in the PC sound business is the AdLib sound board. The AdLib board will only play MIDI files, however; you can't set it up to play back FM files. In contrast, some PC hardware can play back FM files but not MIDIs; one example is the PC speaker driver.

- Does it support sound input as well as output? Not all boards let you record; some only play back.

Once you get the sound board into your system, you can immediately get it doing something. Microsoft sells a package called SoundBits that lets you attach sounds to different Windows events. For instance, when I start up Windows, I get a recording of HAL from the movie 2010 saying, "I am completely operational, and all my circuits are functioning perfectly."

Getting the Sound Out

You can use either regular speakers or sexy-looking speakers designed for multimedia computers. If you are in an office, you might want to consider a pair of headphones so that you will not have to worry about disturbing others.

If you plan to use regular speakers, you should place them several feet away from the computer and monitor. You don't want the magnets in the speakers to accidentally scramble the data on an important floppy. You will need to move the speaker cable from the sound card to the CD-ROM drive when you play CDs.

Most sound cards only have a mono output. If high-quality stereo sound is important to you, get a 16-bit sound card and a separate MIDI card. A good audio store can help you if you want to tie your multimedia PC into your home entertainment center.

Getting the Sound In

Recording is a topic in itself. Entire books have been written on the subject, and there is a professional society for recording engineers. For our purposes here, the key points are resolution and sampling frequency. If you are just recording voice, 11 kHz (kilohertz) at 8 bits is adequate. For CD quality you will need 44.1 kHz at 16 bits (and a big hard disk).

An audio store or Radio Shack store is a good source for microphones, cables and help. Take a look at your sound card before you buy anything. Some sound cards have separate connectors for the right and left audio channels, some have a single stereo connector, and others are mono sound only.

Sound Blaster Suggestions

I've installed about a dozen or so Sound Blasters and Sound Blaster Pros in systems. In the process, I've discovered a few things that you may find useful.

- Once you've installed a Sound Blaster, be sure that there's a speaker attached to it. One of my employees moved a PC and neglected to move the speaker, thinking it unnecessary. By the time I discovered it, a week later, the Blaster's speaker-driver circuit had burned itself out, and the board was scrap.

- When you buy a sound board, whether it's a Blaster or some other board, you'll also end up buying speakers. The speakers have amplification capabilities, requiring either batteries that run down continually, or that you fiddle around with one of those power adapters that look like a power plug on steroids. Those plugs are a pain, as they are so large that they can end up covering several sockets on a multiple outlet strip. As it turns out, the amplification is unnecessary; sound boards put out enough power to drive the speakers without amplification.

- Once you've installed a sound board, call the vendor and find out if you've got the most up-to-date drivers. Creative seems to update the Blaster drivers three times per year.

- There is only one place in the Sound Blaster manual that shows you which devices go into what connectors, a diagram on one of the first pages of the manual. The manual's never around when I'm plugging in a microphone or speaker, however, and so I've made up a little legend on a piece of paper that tells me that the top connector is for line input, the middle for microphone, and the bottom is for speaker output. I then tape that paper to the PC, so the information's always close to hand.

Future Developments

There are specialized computers called Digital Signal Processors (DSP). These high speed computers use software, instead of hardware, to generate and interpret signals. Some companies are using them to create modems. With the right software, a DSP can generate voices, be a modem, be a FAX, or be a MIDI controller. In the future, when you buy a modem or sound board, it might be software that runs on the PC's DSP.

Jam Sessions on Your PC

The MIDI (Music Instrument Digital Interface) allows you to be a keyboard artist. Some MPC kits have sound cards with MIDI built into them by including a MIDI controller chip(s) on the sound board. Other MPC kits include separate MIDI and sound cards. Keep in mind that, if your sound board does not have a dedicated MIDI chip, it will not produce very good MIDI output. Unfortunately, MIDI files are manufacturer-specific. Each manufacturer of MIDI instruments assigns different instrument voices (sounds) to the same value. If you play a Roland RT-32 MIDI file on a Yamaha synthesizer, the instruments will be wrong, and the music will sound awful, or perhaps not be audible at all.

Windows actually supports two types of synthesizers—base level, which can play simultaneously up to six notes on three melodic instruments and three notes on three percussion instruments, and extended level, which can play simultaneously up to sixteen notes on nine melodic instruments and sixteen notes on eight percussion instruments. MIDI channels 13 to

16 are used for the base level synthesizer; channels 1 to 10 are used for the extended level synthesizer. Consequently, a Windows MIDI file must actually contain two complete renditions of the composition: one for the base-level synthesizer, the other for the extended- level synthesizer.

To control a MIDI card, a device driver is installed so Windows can communicate with the card. Then you go into Window's control panel and tell Windows which MIDI card you have installed. The Windows 3.1 *User's Guide* devotes several pages to giving a more detailed overview of assigning different voices. If your MIDI card isn't on the list, you can create a custom key map and patch map file.

Installing the Multimedia System

Installing boards and drives—which is what comprise an MPC system—has been covered in a number of chapters in this book that deal with the specific components of such a system, so I will just review some of the important points.

Before even installing an MPC upgrade or sound card, make sure that your computer has a $3^{1}/_{2}$" high-density disk drive. This requirement is in the MPC specification, so most MPC-compatible software comes only on $3^{1}/_{2}$" HD disks.

The MPC standard requires a computer with an AT bus. Therefore, you can use an interrupt above 5 if the lower numbers are already in use. You might also have to adjust the base address if it is being used by another card such as a network card, or other SCSI controller card.

Insist Upon a 30-Day Return Policy and Good Support

I recommend that you buy name brand products with a 30-day return period and good technical support. If the technical support folks don't give you any satisfaction, ship the product back. If your problems can't be resolved now, they probably will not be later, and they might even get worse!

A technical support bulletin board system (BBS) or a CompuServe forum is probably the best technical support a vendor can offer for any system, multimedia or not. This type of system offers a lot of advantages. You can post questions at any time, even at 2 A.M. on Sunday, if other people are having the same problem, you'll know about it, and, when it's time to upgrade, you can download the latest versions of the software you are using.

For multimedia devices, a technical support BBS is even more important. If something is not working correctly, you can quickly find out if the problem is due to the mix of devices you are using, an out-of-date device driver or something you are doing wrong.

Run Diagnostic Software to Map Interrupts

Before you remove the power cord and open your PC, you need to do some homework. First, recheck your system documentation or, less desirably, run a diagnostic program that tells you which boards are installed and their interrupts. Please note that the diagnostic/interrupt checking programs may not be 100% accurate, so it would be better to find that documentation you stuck in a drawer and use *that* information rather than the output of a general-purpose diagnostic program. Since you will be installing the kit or devices in a system with an AT bus, you have several more interrupts available than you would with an XT.

Keep Careful Notes

Because the diagnostic programs to check interrupts are *not* 100% accurate, many people like to place a white label inside the PC case explaining which interrupt is being used by which board. If it's your personal machine, you might want to start keeping a log book of what you have installed. You should also try and keep all the reference manuals in one place. I have both Avery labels and white medical tape in my tool kit for use as label material. Use a permanent ink pen (like a Sharpie) and print neatly. When I've got the computer apart, I use the clear film canisters that

Fuji film comes in to hold small loose parts. Film canisters are available for free from photography stores and one-hour labs.

Read the Manual

You should read the installation manual before doing any installing, or at least skim it. The manual is the only place to find out about how to set the different jumpers. If you don't need to change a jumper, leave it at the factory default. You might also want to write the jumper settings in the manual. Many manuals now supply a place for you to write down this information. *Write it down, now.* Once the thing's up and running, you'll start playing with the demonstration multimedia programs, and you'll forget to write the installation stuff down.

Make Several Emergency Boot Floppies

Installing the sound board, MIDI board or other adapter will require making changes to the CONFIG.SYS file. Before you do this, make three or four emergency boot floppies. And please *try them out before depending on them.* Unless you've got DOS 6.0 and are using the Configuration Manager, you cannot bypass the CONFIG.SYS file at boot-up, and a bad CONFIG.SYS file can hang a PC, making it unbootable. There are times that I have had to use a second boot floppy because I made a bad change to the CONFIG.SYS of the first boot floppy. Since I had the extra backups, I could put the first boot floppy back in and edit its CONFIG.SYS file.

Installing the Kit: The Hardware

When attaching cables, make sure that pin 1 of the connector on the cable goes to pin 1 of the connector on the board. Please look at the board carefully, as the location of pin 1 on one board can be the location of pin 50 on another board. Normally the pin 1 wire has a red stripe on it, but I have seen the cable reversed with pin 34 or 50 having the red stripe. I also label each end of the cable with my handy permanent ink pen. If you need more detailed installation instructions, they can be found in the chapters on the various multimedia components.

Before you put the cover back on the PC, you should also install the software and make sure that everything works. You still have to install the device drivers and other software that controls the boards. Sometimes this is an iterative process which requires the jumpers on the board be changed also.

Installing the Kit: The Software

Software is what really controls the multimedia hardware. If your software does not install properly, or conflicts with other software in your PC, then you will not have multimedia capabilities. Normally, you will let the installation software do a standard or default installation. If you run into conflicts, you might have to adjust some of the switches after installation.

Setting Up the CONFIG.SYS and AUTOEXEC.BAT Files One of the drivers you'll need will be the Microsoft CD-ROM Extensions to DOS, the file MSCDEX.EXE. You should have received a copy of MSCDEX.EXE with your CD-ROM hardware. It seems to be one of those Murphy's Laws, however, that whatever version of MSCDEX.EXE you've got, it's outdated. Contact your vendor before you do anything else, and request the latest MSCDEX.EXE. Chances are that the latest version that they have is newer than what you got in the box with the CD-ROM.

If you are installing version 2.2 of MSCDEX, you will need to use the command SETVER. DOS 5.0 requires version 2.21 of MSCDEX (which is dated 2-04-92 2:21a). Version 2.21 of MSCDEX can be obtained from many sources. Check with another CD-ROM drive owner or download the latest copy from a BBS. Note that as of late 1992, Microsoft no longer supplies MSCDEX.EXE; you've got to get a specific MSCDEX.EXE from your CD-ROM vendor.

You need to install both a device driver for the CD-ROM in the CONFIG.SYS file and MSCDEX.EXE in your AUTOEXEC.BAT file. The device driver makes the CD-ROM visible to your computer, and MSCDEX makes the CD-ROM visible to DOS. You may end up loading *two* device drivers—one for your SCSI adapter and one for your CD-ROM, and then MSCDEX on top of it all. (This stuff can add up to over 70K of RAM; time for a memory manager.)

The device driver is installed like any other device driver as a line in the CONFIG.SYS file. For example, consider a system with *three* CD-ROM drives attached to it. Drives 1 and 3 are Hitachi drives. Drive 2 is a Sony CD-ROM that contains two CD-ROM drives inside it; it counts as one drive because the SCSI system only sees one device. The Hitachi example below is loading support for two different CD-ROM devices on the SCSI chain. The Sony example below is loading support for one CD-ROM device with 2 drives in it.

The syntax is:

```
DEVICE=<filename> /D:<device_name> /N:<number of drives>
```

So this is what it would look like:

```
DEVICE=HITACHI.SYS /D:MSCD001 /D:MSCD002
DEVICE=SONY.SYS   /D:MSCD003 /N:2
```

The MSCDEX.EXE program is put in the AUTOEXEC.BAT file or is run from the DOS command line. MSCDEX.EXE is supplied only by CD-ROM vendors with their CD-ROM drives. MSCDEX.EXE is a CD-ROM "redirector." (It hooks into MS-DOS, just like a network redirector does, for accessing files that are not on local hard or floppy disks.) To DOS, CD-ROM drives look just like network drives.

MSCDEX Command Line Switches This is the command line for MSC-DEX.EXE:

```
MSCDEX.EXE: /D:x /M:n /E /V /L:x /S /K
```

These are what the switches mean.

SWITCH	DEFINITION
/D:<device-name>	Name of device driver. This name must be the same as the one used in the CONFIG.SYS file.
/M:n	Number of sector buffers to use for caching the CD's path table. This should be at least 4 or 5.
/E	Use expanded memory.

SWITCH	DEFINITION
/V	Display memory usage at boot time.
/L:<drive-letter>	Drive letter of the first CD-ROM drive.
/S	On an MS-NET based system, share the CD-ROM drive.
/K	Use Kanji (Japanese) file structures if they are present. (The default file structure is alphanumeric.)

Using a CD-ROM with OS/2

OS/2 2.01 includes support for CD-ROMs, but you may have to help it out a bit. The CONFIG.SYS commands that support a CD-ROM under OS/2 look like this:

DEVICE=C:\OS2\VCDROM.SYS (adds support for CD-ROM under DOS)

BASEDEV=AHA154X.ADD

BASEDEV=OS2SCSI.DMD (supports the SCSI adapter. The AHA154X.ADD is specific to the Adaptec 1542 SCSI. Contact your SCSI vendor for the specific OS/2 driver for your adapter.)

DEVICE=C:\OS2\CDROM_G.SYS (controls your CD-ROM drive; see note below)

IFS=C:\OS2\CDFS.IFS /Q (basically the OS/2 version of MSCDEX)

The only item worth noting is about CDROM_G.SYS. The default OS/2 installation will install a different driver, one called CDROM.SYS. Unless you've got an IBM CD-ROM or a Toshiba CD-ROM, don't use it; use CDROM_G.SYS. Here's why.

OS/2 has built-in support for IBM drives and for SCSI third party drives. The Sony CDU 541 works well. The CDROM.SYS driver, believe it or not, only responds to the CD-ROM if the drive indicates that it is a Toshiba-type drive; Toshiba makes IBM's CD-ROMs. One way to fix that is to patch the vendor ID string into \OS2\CDROM.SYS. Simply replace "TOSHIBA " with "NEC...", i.e. with blank-padding to eight characters. It appears in three places, so if you're spelunking with Norton or debug, keep this in mind. This will only work for drives with SCSI interfaces; the proprietary CD-ROMs are out of luck when it comes to OS/2. If you don't want to patch CDROM.SYS, use CDROM_G.SYS—it's not hard-coded to any drive, and seems to work with many CD-ROMs. The only downside is that you can't play music from the CD-ROM if you've loaded CDROM_G.SYS.

Troubleshooting Tips

If you run into problems, often you need only rearrange the order and location of the DRIVER= lines of the default CONFIG.SYS. Because of all the switches that can be set both in hardware and software, it is important to write down the "before change" and "after change" settings. This makes it easier to see if you made a mistake and makes it easier to reverse changes.

If you've got a problem, this is the time when being able to call technical support or post a question on a bulletin board can save you days of blindly experimenting. Before you call or post a message, write down a complete description of your system and print copies of the CONFIG.SYS and AUTOEXEC.BAT files. This will save both you and the support person time and stress.

One last thing. To prevent problems, before putting the cover back on, check the cables to make sure that they are securely seated and all reconnected. Although it's annoying to dislodge a cable when putting the cover back on, it's even more annoying to have never put on the cable in the first place and notice this after you have reassembled the computer.

Types of Files: Meta versus Bitmap

In the Windows graphics world, there are two different types of files: meta files and bitmaps. A meta file contains high-level commands, such as

"Resolution 300 dots/inch," "Draw Line 1 inch long, start point, angle." A bitmap contains low-level commands, and would contain each point (300 or more) on the line. Meta files can be compressed to reduce storage requirements, but bitmaps generally cannot be compressed. Since sound and graphics files are often very large, storage can be a problem. This is why multimedia is normally delivered on CD-ROM disks.

You will hear the term "lossless compression" being used when people talk about compressing files. *Lossless* means that no data is lost when the file is compressed. This type of compression only works on meta files. If you have a picture (a bitmap file), you might be willing to lose some quality to get it more compressed (*lossey* compression?).

Some Common File Extensions

There is a veritable alphabet soup of file extensions for sound and graphics files. Thank heaven there are external conversion utilities that you can run to convert between the different formats.

The standard Sound Blaster file extension is .VOC. Microsoft uses .WAV as the extension for Window's sound files. (If you have VOC files, Creative Labs offers a conversion to convert between WAV and VOC.) Many graphics files are distributed with the extension .GIF (pronounced "Jif"). This format was developed by CompuServe and is a proprietary format. Microsoft uses the extension .BMP for Window's bitmap files. PC Paintbrush introduced the .PCX extension many years ago. This is less confusing than it looks, and knowing these suffixes will help when you need to know what kind of file you are dealing with.

RIFF and MCI

Microsoft and IBM have tried to create an extensible file format called Resource Interchange File Format (RIFF). According to a Microsoft/IBM announcement:

> RIFF, a tagged file structure, is a general specification upon which many file formats can be defined. The main advantage of RIFF is its extensibility; file formats based on RIFF can be future-proofed, as format changes can be ignored by existing applications.

The Media Control Interface (MCI) is a high-level control mechanism that provides a device-independent interface to multimedia devices and resource files. The Media Control Interface (MCI) provides a command set for playing and recording multimedia devices and resource files. Developers creating multimedia applications are encouraged to use this high-level command interface rather than the low-level functions specific to each platform. The MCI command set acts as a platform-independent layer that sits between multimedia applications and the underlying system software.

The CD-ROM File Structure: High Sierra and ISO-9660

The High Sierra format was the first attempt to create a standard file structure for CDs. It was slightly modified to create the ISO-9660 standard. The ISO-9660 file structure can be placed on any type of media. I even read an electronic message from someone who had put ISO-9660 onto Macintosh floppy disks.

There are two levels of the ISO-9660 standard. Level 1 is designed to be MS-DOS compatible. Level 2 is designed for users of the Unix or Macintosh operating systems. Level 2 ISO-9660 allows longer filenames, up to 32 characters, so Level 2 disks are not usable on some systems (including MS-DOS). If you're interested, High Sierra was chosen as the format's name because the meeting was held at Del Webb's High Sierra Hotel and Casino in Nevada.

Let's look at ISO-9660 in more detail.

- Level one ISO-9660 is similar to an MS-DOS file system.

- All alphabetics are in UPPERCASE.

- Filenames are limited to eight single-case characters, a dot, and a three-character extension (FILENAME.TXT, for example).

- Filenames cannot contain special characters (no hyphens, tildes, equals, or pluses).

- Directory names cannot have the three-digit extension, just eight single-case characters.

- Either the filename or the extension may be empty, but not both ("F." and ".E" are both legal filenames).

- There is a "File Version Number" which can range from 1 to 32,767 and is separated from the extension by a semicolon. (The file version number is ignored on many systems.)

- Subdirectories are allowed to nest up to eight levels deep.

Here are some examples of legal and illegal filenames.

LEGAL	ILLEGAL	WHY
TEST1C.TXT	TEST-1C.TXT	Contains a hyphen
TEST1C.TXT	TEST 1C.TXT	Contains a space
TEST.1C	TEST.1C.TXT	Contains more than one period
README	Readme	Is not single case

Media Life

Though this used to be a very hot topic, this question of CD-ROM longevity seems to have been resolved. The general opinion now is that CD-ROMs will probably last as long as you will. If you were really worried, you could use gold instead of aluminum for the disk. One person has noted that the pits in a CD-ROM could still be read by an electron microscope even if the rest of the disk was destroyed!

Even so, CD-ROM disks should be treated with care. Keep them out of extremes of heat and humidity. Keep them away from direct sunlight and other strong lights. Store them in their jewel boxes or caddies so they do not get dust or fingerprints on them.

Copyrights

Copyrights and multimedia are an area in which the law is just being developed. If you borrow images and music from commercial sources, you can probably play it in an educational or small private setting. In the audiovisual field, companies sell music libraries that you have unlimited reproduction rights to. These are just like software libraries that a programmer buys that the programmer can use in software without paying royalties.

When Xerox chose to use pictures from the New York City marathon, they knew that they might be sued by someone who was able to recognize themselves. (It was impossible to get a signed release from everyone.)

Capturing Images

Your PC does not have eyes, but it can be equipped with vision, using one of several types of add-in boards designed for the purpose. These boards can also be used to capture images from a video source such as videotape or a video camera. Full- motion video at 30 frames per second takes too much storage space if it is uncompressed. There are different levels of image capturing.

- Image capture—these are black-and-white security or monitoring video cameras.
- TV on monitor—these are a TV tuner and present a TV image in a window.
- NTSC video boards—these allow you to capture a video image from the TV, VCR, video camera or other video source.

US televisions display only 525 lines, using a system that has very poor color fidelity. A higher line resolution is only important for computer monitors. The current US color system was designed to be compatible with black and white TVs, which is the reason for much of its limitations. The primary image is black and white, with the color added via a subcarrier band. Though it is currently not available in the United States, once high- definition TV (HDTV) becomes more accessible, television monitors will be more suited for image capturing.

Genlock—Marching to a Common Beat

There are a number of video capture boards available on the market today; some are as inexpensive as $200. Before you buy, however, make sure that the board that you're considering buying has at least one feature—*genlock*.

Inexpensive video capture boards require that an image not move at all in order for these boards to digitize the video output. That means that building digital full-motion videos is impossible with those boards, and capturing any image at all can be troublesome. What these boards lack is the ability to synchronize their capture with the appearance of a frame. You don't see it, but there's lots of time on a video screen when the electron beam has only partially overwritten the previous screen; if you could stop the process at that point—which is what a video capture board without genlock does—then you'd get a screen that showed part of one frame and part of the next frame. You need a board that can say to itself, "Okay, the screen's been entirely painted, and the electron beam hasn't started repainting yet; I'll do the capture now." Genlock allows that.

Like a TV station, an NTSC video capture board requires a common beat for all their equipment to be truly functional. A genlock or a genlock module ties the video image on the capture board to this common heartbeat. By synchronizing all components to each other, the genlock allows for accurate editing, adding sound, and other post-production work.

Keeping Current with Technology

Keeping current is a problem with an area that is evolving as quickly as multimedia is. By the time this book is printed and in your hands, a revolutionary change in multimedia technology may have occurred. This is another area in which bulletin boards come in handy. I used several systems to help me research this chapter. Each has its strengths and weaknesses, but if you use them in combination, they're a good resource for keeping up with the latest technology and user tips. Briefly, here they are:

- Internet—An electronic network linking computers worldwide.

- CompuServe—A broad resource, but messages scroll off in a couple of days. You can download the latest MSCDEX information from CD vendors from CompuServe.

- BIX—Byte Information eXchange. The messages stay around for several years.

- Genie—It has a MIDI area, no multimedia yet. The messages also stay around for several years.

The Internet has a wonderful program called Archie, which is a central card catalog of files and their location on the Internet. These files reside on file server computers. A program called FTP (File Transfer Program) allows you to log into these file servers and retrieve files from them (the syntax is LOGIN: ANONYMOUS PASSWORD: EMAIL_ID). Most sites with Internet access for e-mail also offer FTP and other services that allow you to go out over the Internet. The WELL (Whole Earth eLectronic Link) is one such service, and it can be accessed over the CompuServe network.

CompuServe is a much more polished service for posting messages and getting information back electronically. Unfortunately, Usenet is mostly unmoderated, so some people engage keyboard before engaging brain when someone posts a dumb question. I wish that CompuServe had an Archie-like program. You can search across all the libraries in a Forum but not across Forums.

Genie has a MIDI roundtable, and the messages on it hang around for several years. BIX has multimedia and CD-ROM Conferences, and the messages stay around for several years.

Sources for Disks, Caddies, and More Information

Now that you have all this new information about multimedia, you need a way to put it to use. To this end, Appendix A contains a list of sources around the world of CD-ROM disks, caddies and publications. This is from the "Frequently Asked Questions" (FAQ) monthly posting to alt.cd-rom. (Walnut Creek CDROM compiled and maintains it.) I place a copy in Library 1 of Multimedia on CompuServe every month.

Newsgroups and Mailing Lists

Anyone with electronic mail access to the Internet can get on these mailing lists. To join a newsgroup requires access to the Internet (WELL or other public internet provider). The archive of alt.cd-rom is available via electronic mail.

> **Warning!** The mailing lists can put 64K files in your mailbox on a regular basis.

On the Internet, the best source of information is the newsgroup alt.cd-rom, which is linked to the BITNET list CDROM-L. You can subscribe to CDROM-L by sending the command **SUBSCRIBE CDROM-L** *Your full name* to LISTSERV@UCCVMA.UCOP.EDU.

The Internet newsgroup comp.multimedia is a good source of information on multimedia topics.

CDROMLAN (available on Usenet as *bit.listserv.cdromlan*) covers the use of CD-ROM products on local area or wide area networks. You can join the list by sending the command **SUBSCRIBE CDROMLAN** *Your full name* to LISTSERV@IDBSU.IDBSU.EDU:.

CD-ROMs are in heavy use in libraries and government document repositories, both for access to indexes and for distribution of government data. The relevant lists are PACS-L (*bit.listserv.pacs-l*) and GOVDOC-L (*bit.listserv.govdoc-l*).

Send the command **SUBSCRIBE GOVDOC-L** *Your full name* to LISTSERV@PSUVM.PSU.EDU:.

Send the command **SUBSCRIBE PACS-L** *Your full name* to 2LISTSERV%UHUPVM1.BITNET@VM1.NODAK.EDU. Discussions of music on CD can be found in *rec.music.cd*.

Getting alt.cd-rom via Electronic Mail

I don't know if there is an ftp site anywhere that archives alt.cd-rom, but you can retrieve old articles via e-mail.

For a list of files available, send the message **INDEX CDROM-L** as the first line of your e-mail message to LISTSERV@UCCVMA.BITNET or the Internet address LISTSERV@UCCVMA.UCOP.EDU.

To retrieve an archived message, send the e-mail message **GET CDROM-L LOGyymm** or **SENDME CDROM-L LOGyymm**— as above—where *yymm* is the year and month of the archive wanted, e.g., **LOG9110 = Log of October 91** messages.

Original Copies of the Standards

You can order a copy of the ISO-9660 standard from ANSI and the Green Book from the American CD-I Associations (see Appendix A for the addresses).

Summary

There's a whole new world out there, a world of light, motion, and sound, all waiting to spring forth on your Windows desktop. Just get a sound board and a CD-ROM, and you're on your way. Add a video capture board, a video camera and a few MIDI instruments, and you've got your own studio right on the premises. Best of all, it's not only fun—it can make you more productive, more effective in getting your message across.

APPENDIX

A

Resource Guide

Vendors of Useful Troubleshooting and Maintenance Products

These are the addresses of various products mentioned in the text. Wherever possible, I have included both 800 numbers and non-800 numbers, as I recognize that my non- American readers cannot use 800 numbers.

Products, prices, and addresses change, so you may find that something no longer exists, or does not work as I said it would. I am not endorsing these products, but merely relating that *I* have found them useful.

Altex Electronics
10731 Gulfdale
San Antonio, TX 78216
(800) 531-5369
(512) 366-4081

Altex is a discounter (mail order) that sells power protection products at quite good prices. Look to these folks for Tripplite power conditioners, power supplies from PC Power and Cooling Systems, and other electronic goodies.

The Black Box Corporation
P. O. Box 12800
Pittsburgh, PA 15241
(412)746-5530

Black Box Corp. sells anything you can imagine for data communications. Contact them for their PC Data Communication catalog.

Core International
7171 North Federal Highway
Boca Raton, FL 33487
(407) 997-6055

Core International makes drives and the CORETEST program.

Datashield
500 North Orleans
Chicago, IL 60610
(312) 329-1777
The Datashield 85, $92

Datashield makes a top-quality surge suppressor.

The Edmund Scientific Corporation
101 East Gloucester Pike
Barrington, NJ 08007
(609) 573-6250
Dual function digital lab thermometer, $40, Catalog #E36,987

Edmund has been around for ages selling general scientific equipment. Whether you want a lens to hang on your monitor to make the screen larger, a thermometer as cited above, or a third- hand soldering jig, this is the place to go.

Gibson Research
(800) 736-0637
(714) 830- 2200
SpinRite II, $89

SpinRite II is one of only two programs that can ferret out any troubles with your disk *before* they become a problem. Run SpinRite once or twice a year to find weakening disk parts.

Hall-Comsec, Inc.
2029 Manchester Drive
Fort Collins, CO 80526
(303) 482-9905
WireTap, $42.50

WireTap is a useful and very portable in-line RS232 breakout box.

Kolod Research
1898 Techny Court
Northbrook, IL 60062

(708) 291-1447
hTEST/hFORMAT, $89.95

Kolod makes the "infuriatingly excellent" hTEST/hFORMAT. I describe it that way because, while it is an extremely powerful program, it has what may be the worst user interface of all time, and documentation best suited to rocket scientists. But if you need a "does-it-all" disk utility, this is the one.

Merritt Computer Products, Inc.
5565 Redbird Center Drive, Suite 150
Dallas, TX 75237
(214) 339-0753
SafeSkin, $29.95

Merritt Computer Products makes SafeSkin keyboard covers.

Microbridge Computers International, Inc.
655 Sky Way, Suite 125
San Carlos, CA 94070
(800) 523-8777
(415) 593-8777
(212) 334-1858
CPYAT2PC, $83

CPYAT2PC is one of the only reliable ways to write 360K format data on a 360K diskette with a 1.2-MB drive.

MicroSense
5580 La Jolla Boulevard, Suite 313
La Jolla, CA 92037
(800) 544-4252
(619) 589-1816

If you're having trouble getting an old PC to accept newer-format drives (1.44 MB, 2.88 MB), call MicroSense. They've got all kinds of boards and software to allow your old XT to utilize any floppy drive. Their tech support people are also knowledgeable and friendly.

Microsystems Development
4100 Moorpark Avenue, #104

San Jose, CA 95117
(408) 296-4000
TestDrive floppy drive test program, $25
Dysan alignment disks, $50

Microsystems makes an inexpensive floppy drive workout and test program: TestDrive tests alignment, hysteresis, hub clamping, and more. Contact them for their *free* demonstration test program that is full-featured, but only runs on 360K diskettes.

Multisoft Corporation
15100 S.W. Koll Parkway, Suite L
Beaverton, OR 97006
(503) 644-5644
Super PC-Kwik Cache disk caching software, $70

PC-Kwik is the best cache around in that it is not only fast (lots of cache programs are fast), but also fully Windows-compatible and flexible. It works on any kind of drive.

OnTrack Computer Systems
6200 Bury Drive
Eden Prairie, MN 55346
(800) 752-1333
(612) 937-1107
SuperPROM, $109
Disk Manager, $50
DOSUTILS, $50

OnTrack offers a suite of software and services from Disk Manager (an invaluable tool for low-level formatting of almost any hard drive) to their data recovery service.

PARA Systems, Inc.
1455 LeMay Drive
Carrollton, TX 75007
(800) 238-7272
(214) 446-7363
Power Meter, $90

Want to find out how much power your PC really draws? Get the PARA Systems Power Meter. It acts like an extension cord—plug it into the wall, and plug the PC into the Power Meter, and you'll see how many amps the PC is using. See Chapter 8 for more information on how to use the meter.

> PC Power and Cooling Systems
> 5995 Avenida Encinas
> Carlsbad, CA 92008
> (619) 931-5700

PC Power and Cooling makes better PC power supplies. They also sell reverse-fan power supplies so that a PC in a dusty environment can use a filtered fan; it keeps the dust out of the PC. More recently, they have begun offering a power supply that looks like a normal AT-type power supply, but that is actually a small UPS. At $500, it's a good deal.

> Prime Solutions
> 1940 Garnte Avenue
> San Diego, CA 92109
> (619) 272-5000

This company makes Disk Technician Gold ($99), a disk media testing program. This product and SpinRite are the only complete top-to-bottom media testers.

> Qualitas
> 8314 Thoreau Drive
> Bethesda, MD 20817
> 386 to the Max, $125

Qualitas makes a popular 386 memory manager. It is invaluable for stuffing those device drivers up above 640K.

> Quarterdeck Office Systems
> 150 Pico Boulevard
> Santa Monica, CA 90405
> (310) 392-9851
> QEMM-386, $125

Quarterdeck makes another popular 386 memory manager.

> Sanford J. Zalkovitz
> (714) 894-6808
> TIMEPARK

Call Sanford for information about TIMEPARK, a program that automatically parks the head of the disk.

> SuperSoft
> PO Box 1628
> Champaign, IL 61820
> SuperSoft Service Diagnostics for PCs, $225.

This company manufactures generic PC diagnostic software.

> Tasco Ltd.
> 2875 West Oxford Avenue, #5
> Englewood, CO 80110
> (303) 762-9952
> AC Monitor, $130

Having trouble convincing your boss that surges are a big problem? Plug this into an outlet under his desk. Every surge causes the monitor to buzz in an annoying fashion. It also detects over-and undervoltage, and exactly how many volts the power company is supplying at any given instant.

> The Texwipe Company
> PO Box 575
> Upper Saddle River, NJ 07458
> (201) 327-9100

Texwipe is the best known name in contact cleaner products. As we saw in Chapter 3, one of the most effective troubleshooting techniques for "dead" circuit boards is simply to reseat their socketed chips, and clean their contacts. Texwipe is the place to go to find those cleaning products.

> Touchstone Software
> 909 Electric Avenue
> Seal Beach, CA 97040

(800) 531-0450
(714) 969-7746

Touchstone makes of CheckIt, a popular general-purpose PC diagnostic program.

Ultra-X, Inc.
2118 Walsh Avenue, Suite 210
Santa Clara, CA 95050
RACER, $575

Ultra-X makes plug-in diagnostic boards for PC troubleshooting.

Windsor Technologies, Inc.
130 Alto Street
San Rafael, CA 94901
(415) 456-2200

Windsor Technologies are the makers of the PC-Technician line of professional diagnostic software. Windsor aims their products at the professional PC troubleshooter, so their troubleshooting tools tend to be high quality, but a bit expensive (over $500 for PC-Technician). They also sell a floppy disk alignment tool, and a program to test your printer extensively—the interfaces and the printer itself.

BIOS Upgrade Vendors

These are vendors who sell upgrade BIOS ROMs (usually around $50) to support new hard and floppy drive types, solve some compatibility problem, or add a new feature (such as built- in SETUP).

Alltech Electronics Company
1300 East Edinger, Suite D
Santa Ana, CA 92705
(714) 543-5011

Komputerwerk, Inc.
851 Parkview Boulevard
Pittsburgh, PA 15216
(800) 423-3400
(412) 782-0384

Lolir
2741 Beltline Road, #111
Carrollton, TX 75006
(214) 416-5155

Mentor Electronics
7560 Tyler Boulevard, #E
Mentor, OH 44060
(216) 951-1884

Self-Reliant PC Products
1750 Kalakaua Avenue, #3-133
Honolulu, HI 96826
(808) 946-1808

Upgrades, Etc. 15251 N.E. 90th Street
Redmond, WA 98052
(206)883-0227

Data-Recovery Services

These are firms specializing in recovering data from damaged hard disks.

CNS, Inc.
21 Pine Street

RESOURCE GUIDE

Rockaway, NJ 07866
(201) 625-4056

Data Memory
6130 Variel Avenue
Woodland Hills, CA 91367
(818) 704-9500

Data Retrieval Services
1248 Rogers Street
Clearwater, FL 34616
(813) 461-5900

Disk Drive Repair, Inc.
863 Industry Drive
Seattle, WA 98188
(206) 575-3181

Disktec
4545 South Pinemount
Houston, TX 77041
(713) 460-9650

Drive Service Company
2122 Adams Avenue
San Leandro, CA 94577
(510) 430-0595

Electric Renaissance
109 Aldene Road
Roselle, NJ 07203
(201) 245-2090

FRS, Inc.
1101 National Drive
Sacramento, CA 95834
(916) 928-1107

Hard Drive Associates
3323 S.E. 17th Avenue
Portland, OR 97202
(503) 233-2821

Magnetic Data
6754 Shady Oak Road
Eden Prairie, MN 55344
(800) 634-8355
(612) 942-4500

Micro Max
PO Box 969
Woodland, CA 95695
(916) 668-5637

National Computer Security Association
4401-A Connecticut Avenue N.W., Suite 309
Washington, DC 20015
(202) 364-8252

The National Computer Security Association sells information about viruses and virus protection, and runs a BBS about security-related topics.

OnTrack Data Recovery, Inc.
6321 Shady Oak Road
Eden Prairie, MN 55346
(800) 872-2599

Randomex, Inc.
1100 E. Willow Street
Signal Hill, CA 90806
(310) 595-8301

Resource Dynamics
17304 N. Preston Road
Dallas, TX 75252
(214) 733-6886

Rotating Memory Service
473 Sapena Court, #26
Santa Clara, CA 95054
(408) 988-2334

Scopus
PO Box 1437
Lowell, MA 01853
(508) 454-8033

Valtron Technologies, Inc.
26074 Avenue Hall, Building 23
Valencia, CA 91355
(805) 257-0333

Sources for Disks, Caddies, and More Information

Here are some sources CD-ROM, divided geographically.

North America

Buckmaster Publishing
Route 3, Box 56
Mineral, VA 23117
(703) 894-5777 or (800) 282-5628

A ham radio callbook database and 5000 public domain programs: $50

Bureau of Electronic Publishing
141 New Road
Parsippany, NJ 07054
(800) 828-4766

Publishes lots of CD-ROM titles. Call for a catalog.

CD-ROM INC
1667 Cole Blvd, Suite 400
Golden, CO 80401
(800) 821-5245

Many discs, drives and accessories. Call for a free catalog.

The CD-ROM Source
PO Box 20158
Indianapolis, IN 46220
(317) 251-9833

CDROMS Unlimited
P.O. Box 7476
Fremont, CA 94537-7476
(510) 795-4286. Call for a catalog.

CD-ROM User's Group
Post Office Box 2400

RESOURCE GUIDE

Santa Barbara, CA 93120
(805) 965-0265

Bundle of ten discs for $99.

Compustuff
2759 Medina Rd., Plaza 71
Medina, OH 44258
(216) 725-7729

Computer Man
18546 Sherman Way, Suite B
Reseda, CA 91335
(818) 609-0556

Computers At Large
18728 Cabernet Drive
Saratoga, CA 95070-3561
(408) 255-1081
(408) 255-2388 Fax

Crazy Bob
ERM Electronic Liquidators
37 Washington
St. Melrose, Mass 02176
Order line: (800) 776-5865

Sells mostly outdated or surplus discs at low prices

EBSCO Subscription Services (CD-ROM Handbook)
P.O.Box 325
Topsfield, MA 01983
(508)887-6667
(800) 221- 1826
(508) 887-3923 Fax

EDUCORP
7434 Trade Street
San Diego, CA 92121-2410
(800) 843-9497

Faxon Co., Inc. (Access Faxon)
15 Southwest Park
Westwood, MA 02090
(617) 329-3350
(800) 225-6055
(617) 461-1862 Fax

Knowledge Media
436 Nunneley Rd Suite B
Paradise, CA 95969
(916) 872-3826
(916) 872-3826 Fax
email:pbenson@ecst.csuchico.edu

Graphics software CD-ROM

Mail Boxes Etc.
7657 Winnetka Ave.
Conoga Park, CA 91306
(818) 700-1800

Mr. CD Rom
PO Box 1087
Winter Garden, FL 34777
(800) 444-mrcd
(407) 777-3834 Fax

NASA Space Science Data Center
Code 933.4

NASA Goddard Space Flight Center
Greenbelt, MD USA 20771
Phone (voice) (301) 286-6695

CD-ROMs of data from Voyager, Magellan and Viking for $6 each. If you
have ftp capability, you can sample images from the two currently mounted
CD-ROMS at ames.arc.nasa.gov in the directory SPACE/CDROM.

Nautilus
7001 Discovery Blvd
Dublin, OH 43017-8066
(800) 637-3472

Provides a CD-ROM of the month subscription. 13 CD-ROM's for $138.

Oxford University Press
2001 Evans Rd
Cary, North Carolina 27513
(800) 451-7556

Oxford English Dictionary on CD-ROM

Pacific HiTech, Inc.
4530 Fortuna Way
Salt Lake City, UT 84124
(800) 765-8369
(801) 278-2042
Fax: (801) 278-2666
71175.3152@CompuServe.com.

Info-Mac Sumex-aim Macintosh CDROM
Prime Time Freeware
370 Altair Way, Suite 150
Sunnyvale, CA 94086
(408) 738-4832
(408) 738 2050 Fax
ptf@cfcl.com

UNIX-related source code on CD-ROM

ProComp Computer
12503 Sherman Way
No. Hollywood, CA 91605

Profit Press
2956 N. Campbell Ave.
Tucson, AZ 85719
(602) 577-9624

MEGA-Rom, 600 meg MSDOS, $79
Raynbow Software, Inc.
P. O. Box 327
Rapid City, SD 57709
(605) 394- 8227
louis@ce.ucsc.edu
CompuServe: 70410,413

5000 GIFs on CD-ROM with Search Engine for $55

Reed Reference Publishing
Bowker Electronic Publishing
121 Chanlon Road
New Providence, NJ 07974
(800) 323-3288
(908) 464-6800
(212) 645-9700
(800) 323-3328
info@bowker.com

"Books in Print" on CD-ROM, bi-monthly subscription $1095,
w/reviews $1595

ROM-BO
1300 Mohawk Blvd
Springfield, OR 97477
(800) 536-DISK

Sound Electro Flight
4545 Industrial St. 5N
Simi Valley, CA 93063
(800) 279-4824

Stanford University Press
(415) 723-1593

CD-ROM with authoring system containing four books
illustrating its use: $17

Sterling Software
1404 Ft. Crook Rd. South
Bellevue, NE 68005-2969
(800) 643-NEWS
(402) 291-2108
(402) 291-4362
cdnews@Sterling.COM
uunet!sparky!cdnews, ftp.uu.net:/vendor/sterling

NetNews/CD: Usenet news on CD-ROM

TechCity
17706 Chatsworth St.
Granada Hills, CA 91344

TigerSoftware
800 Douglas Entrance
Executive Tower, 7th FLoor
Coral Gables, Florida 33134
24-hour Fax: (305) 529-2990

Updata Publications, Inc. (CD-ROM Guide)
1736 Westwood Blvd
Los Angeles, CA 90024
(310) 474-5900

(800) 882-2844
(310) 474-4095 Fax

Walnut Creek CDROM
1547 Palos Verdes Mall, Suite 260
Walnut Creek, CA 94596
(800) 786-9907
(510) 947- 5996
(510) 947-1644 Fax

Snapshots of major internet archives on CD-ROM

Wayzata Technology Inc.
P.O. Box 807
Grand Rapids MN 55744
(800) 735-7321 Call for catalog

Europe

Apex Software
PO Box 174
Battle
East Sussex
TN33 9AQ
International: 44-424-830025 (voice or Fax)
44-0424-830025 (voice or Fax)
email: vincea@cix.compulink.co.uk

British Software Licensing
280 (T/L) West Princes Street
Woodlands
Glasgow G4 9EU
United Kingdom
44-41-339-7264
Fax 44-41-334-1675
graham@gimble.demon.co.uk

CD-ROM Jacob
Aarstrasse 98
CH-3005 Bern
Switzerland

CD ROM (UK) Ltd
8 Sheep St, Highworth
Swindon, Wiltshire SN6 7AA
United Kingdom
44-0793-861146
44-0793-765331 Fax

EBSCO Subscription Services
3 Tyers Gate
London SE1 3HX

United Kingdom
44-71-357-7516

Faxon Europe, B.V.
Postbus 197
1000 AD Amsterdam
The Netherlands
31 (20) 91-05-91
31 (20) 91- 17-35 Fax

Micro Haus Limited
P.O. Box 149
Gloucester
GL3 4EF
United Kingdom

Mountain Rose Multi Media
Kikkerveen 331

3205 XC Spijkenisse
The Netherlands
Phone: 31 1880 33083
Fax: 31 1880 41551
Email:sterbbs@sus.eur.nl

STARCOM
International Computer Services
Limburggasse 45
A-9073 Klagenfurt-Viktring
Austria
43 (463) 29 67 22
43 (463) 29 67 24 Fax

WasaWare Oy
Palosaarentie 31
SF-65200 VAASA
Finland
Telephone & Fax: 358 61 173365
Email: hv@uwasa.fi

Asia

Software Studio
Shop 217
Olympia Shopping Center
255 King's Road
North Point
Hong Kong
852 510 7470 Fax

UniForce System Ltd.
903 Kin Tak Fung Comm. Bldg
467-473 Hennessy Road
Hong Kong

Voice: (852)838- 6048
Fax: (852)572-4778

Cache Computer
Shop 29, G/Fl., Golden Shopping Centre
146-152 Fuk Wah St., Shamshuipo
Kowloon
Hong Kong
Voice: (852) 361-9975
Fax: (852) 387-9935

Australia and New Zealand

The Cave MegaBBS
PO Box 2009
Wellington
New Zealand
BBS: 64 4 5643429 V22b
64 4 564-5307 Fax,
clear@cavebbs.gen.nz

CompuCD
GPO Box 1624
Canberra City
ACT 2601
Australia
Fax: 61 06 2319771

Ilb Computing
48 Nebo Drive
Figtree Heights
NSW 2525
Australia
61 42 28 5827

Logicware
1 Riverbank Off. Vil.
Cnr 1st St. & O'Shea Ter.
Katherine, N'rn Terr. 0850
Australia
Fax: 61 89 72 3412

Sources for Caddies

Here are a few sources of caddies—call for the latest prices.

CD-ROM INC
1667 Cole Blvd
Suite 400
Golden, CO 80401
(800) 821-5245

EDUCORP
7434 Trade Street
San Diego, CA 92121-2410
(800) 843-9497

QB Products
1260 Karl Court
Wauconda, IL 60084
(800) 323-6856
(708) 487-3333

Walnut Creek CDROM
1547 Palos Verdes Mall
Suite 260
Walnut Creek, CA 94596
(800) 786-9907
(510) 947-5996
(510) 947-1644 Fax

Periodicals and Publications on CD-ROMs

A catalog describing CD-ROM publications and a newsletter is available from:

>   Future Systems
>   P.O. Box 26
>   Falls Church, VA 22040
>   (800) 323-DISC or 703-241-1799

One of their books contains a list of about 1500 CD-ROM's. CD-ROM Professional is a bi-monthly magazine with product reviews, technical articles, industry news, etc. This is a "must read" for anyone in the CD-ROM business. $39.95/year

>   CD-ROM Professional Magazine
>   462 Danbury Road
>   Wilton, CT 06897
>   (800) 248-8466

"The CD-ROM Directory" is available on either paper or CD-ROM from:

>   UniDisc
>   3941 Cherryvale Avenue,
>   Soquel, CA 95073
>   (408) 464-0707

>   "CD-ROM Collection Builder's Toolkit, 1992 Edition"
>   Paul T. Nicholls
>   Eight Bit Books
>   Weston, CT
>   ISBN: 0-910-96502-1
> $39.95

CD-ROMS IN PRINT 1992
An International Guide to CD-ROM, CD-I, CDTV & Electronic
Book Products
Meckler Publishing
11 Ferry Lane West
Westport, CT 06880

ISO 9660 Standard

ANSI
Attn: Sales
11 West 42nd Street
New York, NY 10036
(212) 642-4900

Cost to US destinations is $50, plus $6 shipping, check or money order.

Red Book, Yellow Book...

You can get the Red Book and Yellow Book from ANSI at this address:

ANSI
Attn: Sales
1430 Broadway
New York, NY 10018
(212) 642-4900
Red Book: CEI IEC 908
Yellow Book: ISO 10149:1989

And the Green Book from

American CD-I Association
11111 Santa Monica, Suite 750
Los Angeles, CA 90025
(213) 444-6619

Panacea

Panacea
24 Orchard View Drive
Londonderry, NH 03053-3376
Phone (603) 437-5022 or (800) 729-7420.

Compact Disc Terminology

"Compact Disc Terminology" by James R. Fricks
Nancy Klocko
Disc Manufacturing Inc.
1409 Foulk Road, Suite 202
Wilmington, DE 19803
(800) 433-DISC (3472)
(302) 479-2514
(302) 479-2527 Fax

B

Short Overview on Reading Hexadecimal

THROUGHOUT this book and in technical publications, you'll see numbers expressed not in *decimal,* the numeric system we're all accustomed to using, but in *hexadecimal,* a somewhat different system. This appendix is a quick guide to what you need to know about hex.

Decimal is based on the number ten as we know it—the number of fingers on most people's hands. *Dec-,* a word root, permeates the English language: *Decathalon* refers to a contest with ten sporting events, *decimate* literally means to kill every tenth person, *December* is the name of what was once the tenth month. We write ten as 10, but that's really only correct if we base the numbering system on ten. Strictly speaking, the number that we write for ten is "one zero," and it means different things in different number systems.

Look at the sequence of how we write the first 11 numbers: 0, 1, 2, 3, 4, 5, 6, 7, 8, 9, 10. Why is ten written with *two* digits, not *one* as are all the numbers before? Because the system is based on ten. So ten is written 10 pretty much by definition once you decide that you're using ten as your number base. Next, look at 10×10, or 100: It's written 100, the first number with three digits. Ditto for the first number with four digits (1,000), which is $10 \times 10 \times 10$. Why did we pick 10 as a basis for a number system? No one knows, but the obvious guess is that ten is, again, the number of fingers most people have.

For reasons that aren't really worth pursuing here, it's easiest to talk about numbers in a computer system (memory or I/O addresses, for example) not in a number system based on ten, but rather on eight or sixteen. A base-8 system is called *octal,* and a base-16 system is called *hexadecimal,* or *hex* for short. PCs tend to use hex, so I'll discuss that here. You don't have to know hex in its entirety, just a few salient points.

Counting in Hex

Recall that a base-10 system uses single-digit numbers up to, but not including, 10. A base-16 system, similarly, has single-digit numbers up to, but not including, 16. They are shown in order in Table B.1.

The next number after F is 10, (which would be 16 in decimal), then 11 (which would be 17 in decimal). With decimal, the two-digit numbers increase up to 99, the last two-digit number. Hex goes up to FF. In hex, 100 isn't 10×10 but 16×16; that is 100 in hex, 256 in decimal.

TABLE B.1:　Hex Digits and Decimal Equivalents

HEX DIGIT	DECIMAL VALUE
0	0
1	1
2	2
3	3
4	4
5	5
6	6
7	7
8	8
9	9
A	10
B	11
C	12
D	13
E	14
F	15

Reading Memory Hex Addresses

You'll recall that the typical PC, when running DOS, can address one megabyte of memory: 640K for user data and programs and 384K of reserved area for video memory, ROMs, and buffers. Let's look at how to read memory addresses in hex.

First, understand that one megabyte is composed of sixteen 64K *segments*. Conveniently, 10,000 in hex equals 64K. 640K is ten 64K segments, so the low 640K is the address range from 00000 to one short of A0000, or 9FFFF. All of the addresses, in 64K increments, are shown in Table B.2.

TABLE B.2: Memory Addresses in Decimal and Hex

DECIMALADDRESS	HEXADECIMALADDRESS	PRECEDING HEXADDRESS
0K	00000	n/a
64K	10000	0FFFF
128K	20000	1FFFF
192K	30000	2FFFF
256K	40000	3FFFF
320K	50000	4FFFF
384K	60000	5FFFF
448K	70000	6FFFF
512K	80000	7FFFF
576K	90000	8FFFF
640K	A0000	9FFFF
704K	B0000	AFFFF

TABLE B.2: Memory Addresses in Decimal and Hex (continued)

DECIMALADDRESS	HEXADECIMALADDRESS	PRECEDING HEXADDRESS
768K	C0000	BFFFF
832K	D0000	CFFFF
896K	E0000	DFFFF
960K	F0000	EFFFF
1024K	100000	FFFFF

So when you see that a VGA puts memory in addresses A0000–BFFFF, you know that the board uses the addresses starting just above 640K and going up to just short of 768K. Or when you see that the BIOS ROM is addressed from FC000 to FFFFF, you know that it's right up against the top of the first megabyte.

You've endured enough theory for the moment. Right now, let's put it to good use. Following are a couple of examples.

Counting in Hex— Determining the Size of a Range

If COM1 uses I/O addresses 3F8 to 3FF, how many I/O addresses does it use?

Count them: 3F8, 3F9, 3FA (remember that A comes after 9), 3FB, 3FC, 3FD, 3FE, 3FF—eight addresses.

Comparing Overlapping ROM Address Ranges

In Chapter 6 about installing new circuit boards, we were discussing where to address a ROM in the ScanJet interface card. I was concerned that the address of the ROM on the ScanJet card should not conflict with the addresses of any other ROMs in the system and said something like this:

> The only thing in the system with ROM is a VGA, but what is its ROM's address? Checking Table 6.4 (earlier in this chapter) gives us C0000–C4FFF. The scanner interface has a factory default of C4000–C7FFF. That would be okay for an EGA, as the EGA's ROM ends at C3FFF, just short of C4000. But note that the VGA's ROM goes all the way up to C6000, which tromps all over the range C4000–C7FFF.

You may have had some trouble following it, so let's review exactly what the quandary was:

1. The factory default address for the ScanJet ROM is C4000–C7FFF. Note that this is a *range* of values: C4001, C4002, and so forth up to C7FFF. There are *lots* of them—16 kilobytes of addresses, in fact.

2. The address range of the EGA ROM (if there is an EGA in the system) is C0000–C3FFF, and that range doesn't conflict with the ScanJet's range. The last value in the EGA range is C3FFF; C4000 comes after C3FFF in hex. You compare numbers in hex just as you do in decimal. If they have the same number of digits, just compare the leftmost one. In this case, they've both got hex digits C in the leftmost position, so there's no difference. If the leftmost digits are the same, look immediately to the right. The number 4 comes after 3, so C4000 is after C3FFF. 3. The address range of the VGA ROM is C0000–C5FFF, and that conflicts with the ScanJet ROM range of C4000–C7FFF. The top of the VGA ROM range is C5FFF. The bottom of the ScanJet ROM range is C4000, which is below C5FFF. Again, how do I know? Compare them: The C in the leftmost position is the same; the 4 and 5 are different. The C5FFF, then, is above C4000 (the starting point for the ScanJet ROM) and so the VGA range overlaps the ScanJet ROM range.

So we've briefly looked at how to use hex when looking at I/O address ranges and memory address ranges. If you'd like to get into the nitty-gritty details, like actually converting hex to decimal and back, read on. But you needn't know any more.

Converting Hex to Decimal

This isn't tough, but you can also live your whole life without having to know it.

First, look back at Table B.1. You'll need to know that F in hex is 15 decimal, 8 in hex is 8 decimal, and so on. Say you have a hex number like C801F. How do you convert it to decimal?

1. **Start at the leftmost digit and convert it to decimal. Multiply it by 16. That's your subtotal so far.** That's C in this case. C hex is 12 decimal, so multiply 12 by 16 to get our subtotal, 192.

2. **If the next digit to the right is the rightmost digit, convert it, add it to the subtotal, and stop. Otherwise, convert it, add it to the subtotal, and multiply the whole subtotal by 16.** The next digit is 8, which isn't the last digit, so add 8 to the subtotal to get 192+8, or 200. Multiply 200 by 16, and you'll get 3200.

3. **If you added the rightmost digit, stop. Otherwise, repeat step 2.** Well, you haven't yet added the rightmost digit, so on to the next one. Rule 2 says "Convert the next digit, add it to the subtotal, and multiply the whole subtotal by 16," so add 0 to 3200 and get 3200. Multiply that by 16 and you'll get 51,200. There are still digits left, so keep going. Next is 1; 1 hex is 1 decimal, so add 1 and the subtotal is now 51,201. Multiply that by 16 and get 819,216. The last digit is F, 15 in decimal. Add it to the subtotal and get 819,231. As it's the last digit, don't multiply by 16, and you're finished. C801F hex equals 819,231 decimal.

Converting Decimal to Hex

This is just about the reverse process. Let's convert 75,000 from decimal to hex.

1. **Divide the decimal number by 16. Convert the remainder to a hex digit and make that the *rightmost* hex digit. That's the first digit in the subtotal.** Seventy-five thousand divided by 16 yields a quotient of 4687 and a remainder of 8, which is just 8 hex, so the rightmost hex digit is 8.

2. **Divide the quotient by 16. Make the remainder the next hex digit; put it to the left of the subtotal.** Dividing 4687 by 16 yields a new quotient of 292 and a remainder of 15. The 15 decimal remainder is F hex, so the next hex digit is F, making the subtotal F8.

3. **If the new quotient is 0, stop. Otherwise, just keep dividing the quotient by 16 and putting the hex remainder to the left of the subtotal.** Two hundred ninety-two divided by 16 yields a new quotient of 18 and a remainder of 4, so 4 goes on the subtotal. It's now 4F8.

   Divide 18 by 16 and you'll get a quotient of 1 with remainder 2, so the subtotal becomes 24F8. Finally, divide 1 by 16 and you get quotient 0, remainder 1, so the subtotal is now the final total—124F8. 124F8 hex equals 75,000 decimal.

APPENDIX

C

Characteristics
of Available
Hard Disk Drives

N otes on Table C.1:

Size	Physical size and form factor
	5F=5¼" full height
	5H=5¼" half height
	3=3½"
Cap	Capacity in megabytes
Cyls	Number of cylinders (tracks) in drive
H	Number of heads (surfaces, sides) in drive
RWC	Reduced Write Current; first cylinder where reduced write current is applied
WPC	Write Precomp Cylinder; cylinder to start write precompensation. (Note for RWC and WPC: If indicated cylinder is greater than or equal to the total number of cylinders, this drive does not need RWC or WPC.)
Enc	Encoding scheme, MFM (M), RLL (R), or ZBR (Z)
Rt	Data transfer rate in MB/second; *B*=buffered, can't directly measure
Seek	Seek time in ms
SPT	Sectors Per Track

TABLE C.1: Drive/Interface, Size, Cap (MB), Cyls, H, RWC, WPC, Enc, Rt, Seek (MS), SPT

DRIVE/ INTERFACE	SIZE	CAP (MB)	CYLS	H	RWC	WPC	Enc	RT	SEEK (MS)	SPT
ALPS ELECTRIC										
ST-506 MFM										
DRND-10A	3	10	615	2	616	616	M	5	60	17
DRND-20A	3	20	615	4	616	616	M	5	60	17
ST-506 RLL										
RPO-20A	3	20	615	2	616	616	R	7.5	60	26
DRPO-20D	3	20	615	2	616	616	R	7.5	60	26
AMPEX										
ST-506										
PYXIS-7	5F	15	320	2	132	132	M	5	90	17
PYXIS-13	5F	10	320	4	132	132	M	5	90	17
PYXIS-20	5F	15	320	6	132	132	M	5	90	17
PYXIS-27	5F	20	320	8	132	132	M	5	90	17
ATASI										
ST-506										
3020		17	645	3	320	320	M	5		17
3033		28	645	5	320	320	M	5		17
3046		39	645	7	320	320	M	5		17
3051		43	704	7	359	350	M	5		17
3053		44	733	7	350		M	5		17
3075		67	1024	8	1025	1025	M	5		17
3085		67	1024	8		512	M	5		17

TABLE C.1: Drive/Interface, Size, Cap (MB), Cyls, H, RWC, WPC, Enc, Rt, Seek (MS), SPT (continued)

DRIVE/ INTERFACE	SIZE	CAP (MB)	CYLS	H	RWC	WPC	Enc	RT	SEEK (MS)	SPT
BASF										
ST-506										
6185		23	440	6	220	220	M	5		17
6186		15	440	4	220	220	M	5		
6187		8	440	2	220	220	M	5		17
BULL										
ST-506										
D-530		25	987	3	988	988	M	5		17
D-550		43	987	5	988	988	M	5		17
D-570		59	987	7	988	988	M	5		17
C. ITOH										
ST-506										
YD-3530		32	731	5	732	732	M	17		
YD-3540	5H	45	731	7	732	732	M	5	26	17
SCSI										
YD-3042	5F	43	788	4	789	789	R	8.5		26
YD-3082	5F	87	788	8	789	789	R	8.5		26
CARDIFF										
ST-506										
F-3053	3	44	1024	5			M	5	20	17
ESDI/SCSI										
F-3080	3	68								26
F-3127	3	68	1024	5			R/N	10	20	35

TABLE C.1: Drive/Interface, Size, Cap (MB), Cyls, H, RWC, WPC, Enc, Rt, Seek (MS), SPT (continued)

DRIVE/ INTERFACE	SIZE	CAP (MB)	CYLS	H	RWC	WPC	Enc	RT	SEEK (MS)	SPT
C D C										
ST-506										
BJ7D5A 77731614	5F	23	670	4	375	375	M	5		17
BJ7D5A 77731608	5F	29	670	5	375	375	M	5		17
94155-21	5F	21	697	3	698	698	M	5	28	17
94155-25		24	697	4	698	128	M	5		17
94155-28		24	697	4	698	128	M	5		17
94155-36	5F	36	697	5	698	698	M	5	28	17
94155-38		31	733	5	734	128	M	5		17
94155-48	5F	40	925	5	926	926	M	5	28	17
94295-51	5F	43	989	5	990	990	M	5	28	17
94155-57	5F	48	925	6	926	926	M	5	28	17
94155-67	5F	56	925	7	926	926	M	5	28	17
94155-77		64	925	8	926	926	M	5		17
94155-85	5F	71	024	8			M	5	28	17
94155-86	5F	72	925	9	926	926	M	5	28	17
94205-51	5H	43	989	5	990	128	M	5	32	17
94335-55	3	46		5			M	5	25	17
94335-100	3	83		9			M	5	25	17
94355-55-SWIFT-2	3	46		5			M	5	16.5	17
94355-100	3	83		9			M	5	16.5	17
ST-506 RLL										
94155-135	5H	115	960	9			R	7.5	28	26
94205-77	5H	63	989	5			R	7.5	28	26

CHARACTERISTICS OF AVAILABLE HARD DISK DRIVES

TABLE C.1: Drive/Interface, Size, Cap (MB), Cyls, H, RWC, WPC, Enc, Rt, Seek (MS), SPT (continued)

DRIVE/ INTERFACE	SIZE	CAP (MB)	CYLS	H	RWC	WPC	Enc	RT	SEEK (MS)	SPT
94355-150	3	128		9			R	7.5	16.5	26
94335-150	3	128	9				R	7.5	25	26
ESDI										
94156-48		40	925	5	926	926	N	5	28	
94156-67		56	925	7	926	926	N	5		
94156-86		72	925	9	926	926	N	5		
94166-101	5F	86	969	5	970	970	N	10	16.5	
94166-141	5F	121	969	7	970	970	N	10	16.5	
94166-182	5F	155	969	9	970	970	N	10	16.5	
94186-383	5F	383	1412	13			R/N	10	8.3	
94186-383H	5F	383	1224	15			R/N	10	14.5	
94186-442	5F	442	1412	15			R/N	10	16	
94216-106	5F	91	969				N	10	16.5	
94356-200-SWIFT 3	3	172		9			R/N	10	16.5	
WREN III	5H	106	969	5				10	18	
SCSI										
94161-86	5F	86	969						16.5	
94161-121	5F	121	969						16.5	
94171-300	5F	300	1365	9			R		16.5	
94171-344	5F	344	1549	9			Z	9-15	17.5	
94181-574	5F	574	1549	15			Z	9-15	16	
94211-91	5F	91	969						16.5	
94221-190	5H	190	1547	5			R	10	18.3	
94351-172-SWIFT 4	3	172		9				10	16.5	

TABLE C.1: Drive/Interface, Size, Cap (MB), Cyls, H, RWC, WPC, Enc, Rt, Seek (MS), SPT (continued)

DRIVE/ INTERFACE	SIZE	CAP (MB)	CYLS	H	RWC	WPC	Enc	RT	SEEK (MS)	SPT
WREN III	5H	106	969	5			R/N	10	18	
SMD										
386 SABRE8"		386		10			1.8	18		
500 SABRE8"		500		10			2.4	18		
736 SABRE8"		741		15			1.8	16		
1230 SABRE8"		1236	1635	15			2.4			
CENTURY DATA										
ESDI										
CAST-10203E	5F	55		3	1051	1051	R/N	10	28	35
CAST-10304	5F	75	1050	4	1051	1051	R/N	10	28	35
CAST-10305	5F	94	1050	5	1051	1051	R/N	1'0	28	35
CAST-14404	5H	114	1590	4	591	1591	R/N	10	25	35
CAST-14405	5H	140	1590	5	1591	1591	R/N	10	25	35
CAST-14406	5H	170	1590	6	1591	1591	R/N	10	25	35
CAST-24509	5F	258	1599	9	1600	1600	R/N	10	18	35
CAST-24611	5F	315	1599	11	1600	1600	R/N	10	18	35
CAST-24713	5F	372	1599	13	1600	1600	R/N	10	18	35
SCSI										
CAST-10203S	5F	55	1050	3	1051	1051	R	10	28	35
CAST-10304S	5F	75	1050	4	1051	1051	R	10	28	35
CAST-10305S	5F	94	1050	5	1051	1051	R	10	28	35
CAST-14404S	5H	114	1590	4	1591	1591	R	10	25	35
CAST-14405S	5H	140	1590	5	1591	1591	R	10	25	35
CAST-14406S	5H	170	1590	6	1591	1591	R	10	25	35
CAST-24509S	5F	258	1599	9	1600	1600	R	10	18	35

TABLE C.1: Drive/Interface, Size, Cap (MB), Cyls, H, RWC, WPC, Enc, Rt, Seek (MS), SPT (continued)

DRIVE/ INTERFACE	SIZE	CAP (MB)	CYLS	H	RWC	WPC	Enc	RT	SEEK (MS)	SPT
CAST-25611S	5F	315	1599	11	1600	1600	R	10	18	35
CAST-24713S	5F	372	1599	13	1600	1600	R	10	18	35
C M I										
ST-506										
3426		20	615	4	616	256	M	5		17
5206		5	306	2	307	256	M	5		17
5205		4	256	2	128	128	M	5		17
5410		8	256	4	128	128	M	5		17
5412		10	306	4	307	128	M	5		17
5616		13	256	6	257	257	M	5		17
5619		15	306	6	307	128	M	5		17
6213		11	640	2	641	256	M	5		17
6426		21	640	4	641	256	M	5		17
6640		33	640	6	641	256	M	5		17
7660		50	960	6	961	450	M	5		17
7880		67	960	8	961	450	M	5		17
COMMODORE										
1000		5					M			
1005		7					M			
1010		14					M			
CONNER PERPHER										
AT-BUS										
CP-342	3	40	805	4			R	7.5	29	

TABLE C.1: Drive/Interface, Size, Cap (MB), Cyls, H, RWC, WPC, Enc, Rt, Seek (MS), SPT (continued)

DRIVE/ INTERFACE	SIZE	CAP (MB)	CYLS	H	RWC	WPC	Enc	RT	SEEK (MS)	SPT
CP-3022	3	21	636	2			R	10	27	
CP-3102	3	104	776	8			R	10		25
SCSI										
CP-340	3	42	788	4			R	7.5	29	
CP-3100	3	104	776	8			R	10		25
CORE INTNL										
ST-506										
AT 32	5H	31	733	5			M	5	21	17
AT 30	5F	31	733	5			M	5	26	17
AT 40	5F	42	988	5			M	5	26	17
AT 63	5F	42	988	5			M	5	26	17
AT 72	5F	107	924	9			M	5	26	17
OPTIMA 30	5H	31	733	5			M	5	21	17
OPTIMA 40	5H	41	963	5			M	5	26	17
OPTIMA 70	5F	71	918	9			M	5	26	17
ST-506 RLL										
AT 32	5H	48	733	5			R	7.5	21	26
AT 30	5F	48	733	5			R	7.5	26	26
AT 40	5F	61	924	5			R	7.5	26	26
AT 63	5F	65	988	5			R	7.5	26	26
AT 72	5F	107	924	9			R	7.5	26	26
OPTIMA 30	5H	48	733	5			R	7.5	21	26
OPTIMA 40	5H	64	963	5			R	7.5	26	26
OPTIMA 70	5F	109	918	9			R	7.5	26	26

TABLE C.1: Drive/Interface, Size, Cap (MB), Cyls, H, RWC, WPC, Enc, Rt, Seek (MS), SPT (continued)

DRIVE/ INTERFACE	SIZE	CAP (MB)	CYLS	H	RWC	WPC	Enc	RT	SEEK (MS)	SPT
ESDI										
HC 40	5F	40	564	4			R/N	10	10	35
HC 90	5H	91	969	5			R/N	10	16	35
HC 150	5F	156	969	9			R/N	10	16	35
HC 260	5F	260	1212	12			R/N	10	25	35
HC 310	5F	311	1582	12			R/N	10	16	35
DISCTRON										
ST-506										
D-503		3	53	2			M	5		17
D-504		4	215	2			M	5		17
D-506		5	153	4			M	5		17
D-507		5	306	2	128	128	M	5		17
D-509		8	215	4	128	128	M	5		17
D-512		11	153	8			M	5		17
D-513		11	215	6	128	128	M	5		17
D-514		11	306	4	128	128	M	5		17
D-518		15	215	8	128	128	M	5		17
D-519		16	306	6	128	128	M	5		17
D-526		21	306	8	128	128	M	5		17
D M A										
ST-506										
306 remov.		11	612	2	612	400	M	5		17
ELCOH										
ST-506										

TABLE C.1: Drive/Interface, Size, Cap (MB), Cyls, H, RWC, WPC, Enc, Rt, Seek (MS), SPT (continued)

DRIVE/ INTERFACE	SIZE	CAP (MB)	CYLS	H	RWC	WPC	Enc	RT	SEEK (MS)	SPT
DISCACHE10		10	320	4	321	321	M	5		17
DISCACHE20		20	320	8	321	321	M	5		17
FUJI										
ST-506 MFM										
FK305-26	3	21	615	4		616	M	5	50	17
FK305-39	3	32	615	4	616	616	M	5	50	17
FK309-26	3	21	615	4		616	M	5	50	17
FK301		10	306	4	307	128	M	5		17
FK302-13		10	612	2	613	307	M	5		17
FK302-26		21	612	4	613	307	M	5		17
FK302-39		32	612	6	613	307	M	5		17
FK303-52	3	40	615	8		616	M	5	50	17
ST-506 RLL										
FK305-39R	3	32	615	4		616	R	7.5	50	26
FK305-58R	3	49	615	6		616	R	7.5	50	26
FK309-39R		32	615	4		616	R	7.5		26
ESDI										
FK308S-58R	3	45	615	6			R	7.5	50	
FK308S-39R	3	32	615	4		616	R	7.5	50	
FK309S-50R	3	41	615	4			R	7.5	50	
FUJITSU										
ST-506										
2230 AS		5	320	2	321	321	M	5		17
2233 AS		10	320	4	321	321	M	5		17
2234 AS		15	320	6	321	321	M	5		17

CHARACTERISTICS OF AVAILABLE HARD DISK DRIVES

TABLE C.1: Drive/Interface, Size, Cap (MB), Cyls, H, RWC, WPC, Enc, Rt, Seek (MS), SPT (continued)

DRIVE/ INTERFACE	SIZE	CAP (MB)	CYLS	H	RWC	WPC	Enc	RT	SEEK (MS)	SPT
2235 AS		20	320	8	321	321	M	5		17
2241 AS		26	754	4	755	755	M	5		17
M2226DS	3	30	615	6			M	5	35	17
M2227D2	3	40	615	8			M	5	3	17
M2242AS2	5F	43	754	7			M	5	30	17
M2243AS2	5F	67	754	11			M	5	30	17
M2243T	5H	68	1186	7			M	5	25	17
ST-506 RLL										
M2225DR	3	32	615	4			R	7.5	35	26
M2226DR	3	49	615	6			R	7.5	35	26
M2227DR	3	65	615	8			R	7.5	35	26
M2243R	5H	110	1186	7			R	7.5	25	26
ESDI										
2244E	5F	73	823	5			R/N	10	25	35
2245E	5F	120	823	7			R/N	10	25	35
M2246E	5F	171	823	10			R/N	10	25	35
ESDI/SCSI										
M2249		389	1243	15			R	10	18	
SCSI										
M244SA		73	823	5			R	B	25	35
M2245SA		120	823	7			R	B	25	35
M2246SA		171	823	10			R	B	25	35
M2344KS		690	624	27			R	B	16	

GITO

ST-506

TABLE C.1: Drive/Interface, Size, Cap (MB), Cyls, H, RWC, WPC, Enc, Rt, Seek (MS), SPT (continued)

DRIVE/ INTERFACE	SIZE	CAP (MB)	CYLS	H	RWC	WPC	Enc	RT	SEEK (MS)	SPT
CG-906	5		306	2	128	128	M	5		
CG-912		11	306	4	128	128	M	5		
PT-912		11	612	2	307	307	M	5		
PT-925		21	612	4	307	307	M	5		
HITACHI										
ST-506										
DK301-1	3	10	306	4			M	5	85	17
DK301-2	3	15	306	6			M	5	85	17
DK511-3	5F	28	699	5			M	5	30	17
DK511-5	5F	40	699	7			M	5	30	17
DK511-8	5F	67	823	10			M	5	23	17
DK521-5	5H	51	823	6			M	5	25	17
ESDI										
DK512-8	5F	67	823	5			R/N	10	23	
DK512-12	5F	94	823	7			R/N	10	23	
DK512-17	5F	134	823	10			R/N	10	23	
DK514-38	5F	330	903	14			R/N	15	16	51
DK522-10	5H	103	823	6			R/N	10	25	36
SCSI										
DK512C-8	5F	67	823	5			R	10	23	
DK512C-12	5F	94	823	7			R	10	23	
DK512C-17	5F	134	819	10			R	10	23	35
DK522C-10	5H	88	819	6			R	10	25	35

CHARACTERISTICS OF AVAILABLE HARD DISK DRIVES

TABLE C.1: Drive/Interface, Size, Cap (MB), Cyls, H, RWC, WPC, Enc, Rt, Seek (MS), SPT (continued)

DRIVE/ INTERFACE	SIZE	CAP (MB)	CYLS	H	RWC	WPC	Enc	RT	SEEK (MS)	SPT
I M I										
ST-506										
5006		5	306	2	307	214	M	5		17
5012		10	306	4	307	214	M	5		17
5018		15	306	6	307	214	M	5		17
J C T										
ST-506										
100	5H	5					M	5	110	17
105	5H	7					M	5	110	17
110	5H	14					M	5	130	17
120	5H	20					M	5	100	17
KALOK CORP										
AT-BUS										
KL343-OCTAGON40		40	644	4	645	645	R	8	25	30
ST-506 MFM										
KL320 OCTAGON20	3	20	615	4	616	300	M	5	48	17
ST-506 RLL										
KL330 OCTAGON30		32	616	4	617	617	R	7.5	48	26
PS/2										
KL332 OCTAGON30		40	615	4			R	8	48	30

TABLE C.1: Drive/Interface, Size, Cap (MB), Cyls, H, RWC, WPC, Enc, Rt, Seek (MS), SPT (continued)

DRIVE/ INTERFACE	SIZE	CAP (MB)	CYLS	H	RWC	WPC	Enc	RT	SEEK (MS)	SPT
SCSI										
KL341 OCTAGON40		40	644	4			R	8	25	30
KYOCERA										
ST-506										
KC20A/B	3	20	616	4			M	5	65	17
ST-506 RLL										
KC30A/B	3	30	615	4			R	7.5	65	26
LAPINE										
ST-506 MFM										
3522		10	306	4	307		M	5		17
LT 10		10	615	2	616		M	5		17
LT 20		20	615	4	616		M	5		17
LT 200		20	614	4	615	300	M	5		17
LT 2000		20	614	4	615		M	5		17
ST-506 RLL										
LT 300		32	614	4	615	300	R	7.5		26
MAXTOR										
ST-506 MFM										
XT-1065	5F	56	918	7	919	919	M	5	28	17
XT-1085	5F	71	1024	8	1025	1025	M	5	28	17
XT-1105	5F	87	918	11	919	919	M	5	27	17
XT-1140	5F	113	918	15	919	919	M	5	27	17
XT-2085	5F	74	1224	7	1225	1225	M	5	30	17

CHARACTERISTICS OF AVAILABLE HARD DISK DRIVES

TABLE C.1: Drive/Interface, Size, Cap (MB), Cyls, H, RWC, WPC, Enc, Rt, Seek (MS), SPT (continued)

DRIVE/ INTERFACE	SIZE	CAP (MB)	CYLS	H	RWC	WPC	Enc	RT	SEEK (MS)	SPT
XT-2140	5F	117	1224	11	1225	1225	M	5	30	17
XT-2190	5F	150	1224	15	1225	1225	M	5	30	17
ST-506 RLL										
XT-1120R	5F	104	1024	8			R	7.5	27	25
XT-1240R	5F	196	1024	15			R	7.5	27	25
ESDI										
XT-4170E	5F	157	1224	7			R/N	10	16	35
XT-4175	5F			7			R/N	10	27	35
XT-4380E	5F	338	1224	15			R/N	10	27	35
XT-8380E	5F	360	1632	8			R/N	15	16	54
XT-8760E	5F	676	1632	15			R/N	15	18	54
SCSI										
XT-3170	5F	146	1224	9				15	30	48
XT-3280	5F		1224	15			R	15	30	
XT-3380	5F			15			R	15	27	
XT-4170S	5F	157	1224	7			R	10	16	36
XT-4280S	5F	338	1224	15			R	10	18	36
XT-8380S	5F	360	1632	8			R	15	16	54
XT-8760S	5F	676	1632	15			R	15	18	54
MEMOREX										
ST-506										
321		5	320	2	321	128	M	5		17
322		10	320	4	321	128	M	5		17
324		20	320	8	321	128	M	5		17
450		10	612	2	321	350	M	5		17

TABLE C.1: Drive/Interface, Size, Cap (MB), Cyls, H, RWC, WPC, Enc, Rt, Seek (MS), SPT (continued)

DRIVE/ INTERFACE	SIZE	CAP (MB)	CYLS	H	RWC	WPC	Enc	RT	SEEK (MS)	SPT
512		25	961	3	321	480	M	5		17
513		41	961	5	321	480	M	5		17
514		58	961	7	321	480	M	5		17
MICROPOLIS										
ST-506										
1302	5F	21	830	3	831	400	M	5		17
1303	5F	36	830	5	831	400	M	5		17
1304	5F	43	830	6	831	400	M	5		17
1323	5F	35	1024	4	1025	1025	M	5	28	17
1323A	5F	44	1024	5	1025	1025	M	5	28	17
1324	5F	53	1024	6	1025	1025	M	5	28	17
1324A	5F	62	1024	7	1025	1025	M	5	28	17
1325	5F	71	1024	8	1025	1025	M	5	28	17
1333A	5F	44	1024	5	1025	1025	M	5	30	17
1334	5F	53	1024	6	1025	1025	M	5	30	17
1335	5F	71	1024	8	1025	1025	M	5	30	17
ESDI										
1353	5F	79	1024	4	1025	1025	R/N	10	23	35
1353A	5F	99	1024	5	1025	1025	R/N	10	23	35
1354	5F	119	1024	6	1025	1025	R/N	10	23	35
1354A	5F	139	1024	7	1025	1025	R/N	10	23	35
1355	5F	159	1024	8	1025	1025	R/N	10	23	35
1556-11	5F	248	1224	11	1225	1225	R/N	10	18	36
1557-12	5F	270	1224	12	1225	1225	R/N	10	18	36

CHARACTERISTICS OF AVAILABLE HARD DISK DRIVES

TABLE C.1: Drive/Interface, Size, Cap (MB), Cyls, H, RWC, WPC, Enc, Rt, Seek (MS), SPT (continued)

DRIVE/ INTERFACE	SIZE	CAP (MB)	CYLS	H	RWC	WPC	Enc	RT	SEEK (MS)	SPT
1557-13	5F	293	1224	13	1225	1225	R/N	10	18	36
1557-14	5F	315	1224	14	1225	1225	R/N	10	18	36
1557-15	5F	338	1224	15	1225	1225	R/N	10	18	36
1566-11	5F	496	1632	11			R/N	15	16	
1567-12	5F	541	1632	12			R/N	15	16	
1567-13	5F	586	1632	13			R/N	15	16	
1568-14	5F	631	1632	14			R/N	15	16	
1568-15	5F	676	1632	15			R/N	15	16	
1653-4	5H	92	1249	4			R/N	10	16	
1653-5	5H	115	1249	5			R/N	10	16	
1654-6	5H	138	1249	6			R/N	10	16	
1654-7	5F	161	1249	7			R/N	10	16	
SCSI										
1373	5F	76	1024	4			B	1.25	23	
1373A	5F	95	1024	5			B	1.25	23	
1374	5F	115	1024	6			B	1.25	23	
1374A	5F	134	1024	7			B	1.25	23	
1375	5F	153	1024	8			B	1.25	23	
1576-11	5F	243	1224	11			B	1.6	18	36
1577-12	5F	266	1224	12			B	1.6	18	36
1577-13	5F	287	1224	13			B	1.6	18	36
1578-14	5F	310	1224	14			B	1.6	18	36
1578-15	5F	332	1224	15			B	1.6	18	36
1673-4	5H	90	1249	4			R	10	16	
1673-5	5H	112	1249	5			R	10	16	

TABLE C.1: Drive/Interface, Size, Cap (MB), Cyls, H, RWC, WPC, Enc, Rt, Seek (MS), SPT (continued)

DRIVE/ INTERFACE	SIZE	CAP (MB)	CYLS	H	RWC	WPC	Enc	RT	SEEK (MS)	SPT
1674-6	5H	135	1249	6			R	10	16	
1674-7	5H	158	1249	7			R	10	16	
1586-11	5F	490	1632	11			R	15	16	
1587-12	5F	535	1632	12			R	15	16	
1587-13	5F	579	1632	13			R	15	16	
1588-14	5F	624	1632	14			R	15	16	
1588-15	5F	668	1632	15			R	15	16	

MICROSCIENCE

ST-506

DRIVE/ INTERFACE	SIZE	CAP (MB)	CYLS	H	RWC	WPC	Enc	RT	SEEK (MS)	SPT
HH-312		10	306	4	307	307	M	5		
HH-315		10	306	4	307	307	M	5		17
HH-325		21	612	4	613	613	M	5	80	17
HH-612		11	306	4	307	307	M	5		17
HH-625		21	612	4	613	613	M	5		17
HH-712	5H	10	612	2	613	613	M	5	105	17
HH-725	5H	21	612	4	613	613	M	5	105	17
HH-825	5H	21	612	4	613	613	M	5	65	17
HH-1050	5H	44	1024	5	1025	1025	M	5	28	17
HH-1075	5H	62	1024	7	1025	1025	M	5	28	17
HH-1090	5H	80	1314	7	1315	1315	M	5	28	17

ST-506 RLL

DRIVE/ INTERFACE	SIZE	CAP (MB)	CYLS	H	RWC	WPC	Enc	RT	SEEK (MS)	SPT
HH-330		32	612	4	613	613	R	7.5		26
HH-738	5H	32	612	4	613	613	R	7.5	105	26
HH-830	5H	32	612	4	613	613	R	7.5	65	26
HH-1060	5H	66	1024	5	1025	1025	R	7.5	28	26

TABLE C.1: Drive/Interface, Size, Cap (MB), Cyls, H, RWC, WPC, Enc, Rt, Seek (MS), SPT (continued)

DRIVE/ INTERFACE	SIZE	CAP (MB)	CYLS	H	RWC	WPC	Enc	RT	SEEK (MS)	SPT
HH-1095	5H	95	1024	7	1025	1025	R		28	26
HH-1120	5H	122	1314	7	1315	1315	R	7.5	28	26
ESDI										
HH-2085							R/N			
HH-2120	5H	121	1024	7			R/N	10	28	
SCSI										
HH-1080							R			
HH-3120	5H	122	1314	7			R	7.5	28	
MINISCRIBE										
8051A	3	42	745	4				8	28	
8425XT	3	21	615	4						
438XT	3	31	615	4						
ST-506 MFM										
1006		5	306	2	153	128	M	5		17
1012		10	306	4	153	128	M	5		17
2006		5	306	2	307	128	M	5		17
2012		11	306	4	307	128	M	5		17
3212	5H	11	612	2	613	128	M	5	85	17
3212 PLUS	5H	11	612	2	613	128	M	5	53	17
3412		11	306	4	307	128	M	5		17
3425	5H	21	612	4	613	128	M	5	85	17
3425 PLUS	5H	21	612	4	613	306	M	5	53	17
3053	5H	44	1024	5	1025	1025	M	5	25	17
3650	5H	42	809	6	810	128	M	5	61	17
4010		8	480	2	481	128	M	5		17

TABLE C.1: Drive/Interface, Size, Cap (MB), Cyls, H, RWC, WPC, Enc, Rt, Seek (MS), SPT (continued)

DRIVE/INTERFACE	SIZE	CAP (MB)	CYLS	H	RWC	WPC	Enc	RT	SEEK (MS)	SPT
628	5F	241	1225	11	1226	1226	R/N	10	10	
638	5F	329	1225	15	1226	1226	R/N	10	20	
SCSI										
717	5F	153	1225	7	1226	1226	R	10	20	
728	5F	241	1225	11	1226	1226	R	10	20	
738	5F	329	1225	15	1226	1226	R	10	20	
PTI										
AT-BUS										
PT-238A	3	32	615	4			R	7.5		35
PT-251A	3	43	820	4			R	7.5		35
PT-357A	3	49	615	6			R	7.5		35
PT-376A	3	65	820	6			R	7.5		35
ST-506 MFM										
PT-255	3	21	615	4			M	5	35	7
PT-234	3	28	820	4			M	5	35	17
PT-351	3	42	820	6			M	5	35	17
ST-506										
PT-238R	3	32	615	4			R	7.5	35	26
PT-251R	3	43	820	4			R	7.5	35	26
PT-357R	3	49	615	6			R	7.5	35	26
PT-376R	3	65	820	6			R	7.5	35	26
PT-4102R	3	87	820	8			R	7.5		26
SCSI										
PT-238S	3	32	615	4			R	7.5		35

CHARACTERISTICS OF AVAILABLE HARD DISK DRIVES

TABLE C.1: Drive/Interface, Size, Cap (MB), Cyls, H, RWC, WPC, Enc, Rt, Seek (MS), SPT (continued)

DRIVE/ INTERFACE	SIZE	CAP (MB)	CYLS	H	RWC	WPC	Enc	RT	SEEK (MS)	SPT
PT-251S	3	43	820	4			R	7.5		35
PT-357S	3	49	615	6			R	7.5		35
PT-376S	3	65	820	6			R	7.5		35
QUANTUM										
AT-BUS										
PRO-40	3	42							19	
PRO-80	3	84							19	
PRO-120	3	120							19	
PRO-170	3	168							19	
ST-506										
Q-510		8	512	2	256	256	M	5		17
Q-520		8	512	4	256	513	M	5		17
Q-530		27	512	6	256	513	M	5		17
Q-540		36	512	8	256	513	M	5		17
ESDI										
PRO-100	3	102							19	
PRO-145	3	145							19	
SCSI										
Q-250	5H	53	823	4			R	10		26
Q-280	5H	80	823	6			R	10		26
Q-160	5H	200		12			R	10		26
RICOH SYS										
ST-506										
RH-5130		10	612	2	613	400	M	5	85	17

TABLE C.1: Drive/Interface, Size, Cap (MB), Cyls, H, RWC, WPC, Enc, Rt, Seek (MS), SPT (continued)

DRIVE/ INTERFACE	SIZE	CAP (MB)	CYLS	H	RWC	WPC	Enc	RT	SEEK (MS)	SPT
RH-5260 remov.		10	615	2			M	5	85	17
SCSI										
RH-5261 remov.		10	612	2			M	5	85	
RODIME										
ST-506										
RO 101	5F	6	192	2	196	192	M	5		17
RO 102	5F	12	192	4	196	192	M	5		17
RO 103	5F	18	192	6	196	192	M	5	55	17
RO 104	5F	24	192	8	196	192	M	5		17
RO 201	5F	5	321	2	132	300	M	5	85	17
RO 201F	5F	11	640	2	264	300	M	5	55	17
RO 202	5H	10	321	4	132	300	M	5	85	17
RO 202E	5F	21	640	4	264	300	M	5	55	17
RO 203	5H	15	321	6	132	300	M	5	85	17
RO 203E	5F	32	640	6	210	210	M	5	55	17
RO 204	5F	21	320	8	132	300	M	5	85	17
RO 204E	5F	43	640	8	264	300	M	5	55	17
RO 251	5H	5	306	2	307	307	M	5	85	17
RO 252	5H	11	306	4	64	128	M	5	85	17
RO 351		5	306	2	307	307	M	5	85	17
RO 352	3	11	306	4	64	128	M	5	85	17
RO 365	3	21	612	4	613	613	M	5		17
RO 3045		37	872	5	873		M	5	28	17

TABLE C.1: Drive/Interface, Size, Cap (MB), Cyls, H, RWC, WPC, Enc, Rt, Seek (MS), SPT (continued)

DRIVE/ INTERFACE	SIZE	CAP (MB)	CYLS	H	RWC	WPC	Enc	RT	SEEK (MS)	SPT
RO 3055		45	872	6	873		M	5	28	17
RO 3065		53	872	7			M	5	28	17
RO 5065	5H	63		5			M	5	28	17
RO 5090	5H	89	1224	7			M	5	28	17
SCSI										
RO 652A		20							85	
RO 652B		20	306	4			R		85	
RO 752A	5H	25							85	
RO 3070S		71						28		
RO 3085S		85	750	7			R	28		
RO 3057S		45	680	5			R	28		
RO 5040		38		3			M	5	28	
RO 5075S	5H	76							28	
RO 5125S	5H	127	1219	5			R	28		
RO 5180S	5H	178	1219	7					28	
SEAGATE										
ST-506										
ST-125	3	21	615	4	616	616	M	5	40/28	17
ST-138	3	32	615	6	616	616	M	5	40/28	17
ST-206	5F	5	306	2	307	128	M	5		17
ST-212	5F	10	306	4	307	128	M	5		17
ST-213	5F	10	615	2	613	307	M	5		17
ST-225	5H	21	615	4	616	307	M	5	65	17
ST-251	5H	42	820	6	821	410	M	5	40	17

TABLE C.1: Drive/Interface, Size, Cap (MB), Cyls, H, RWC, WPC, Enc, Rt, Seek (MS), SPT (continued)

DRIVE/ INTERFACE	SIZE	CAP (MB)	CYLS	H	RWC	WPC	Enc	RT	SEEK (MS)	SPT
MK53FA	5F	43	830	5	831	831	M	5	30	17
MK54FA	5F	60	830	7	831	831	M	5	30	17
MK56FA	5F	86	830	10	831	831	M	5		17
MK134FA	3	44	733	7	734	734	M	5	25	17
ST-506 RLL										
MK53FB	5F	64	830	5	831	831	R	7.5	23	26
MK54FB	5F	90	830	7	831	831	R	7.5	25	26
MK56FB	5F	130	830	10	831	831	R	7.5	25	26
ESDI										
MK153FA	5F	74	830	5	831	831	R/N	10	23	35
MK154FA	5F	104	830	7	831	831	R/N	10	23	35
MK156FB	5F	148	830	10	831	831	R/N	10	23	35
ESDI/SCSI										
MK250F	5F	382	1224	10			R/N	10	18	35
SCSI										
MK153FB	5F	74	830	5	831	831	R	10	23	35
MK154FB	5F	104	830	7	831	831	R	10	23	35
MK156FA	5F	148	830	20	831	831	R	10	23	35
TULIN										
ST-506										
213		10	640	2	656	656	M	5		17
226		22	640	4	656	656	M	5		17
240		33	640	6	656	656	M	5		17
326		22	640	4	641	641	M	5		17
340		33	640	6	641	641	M	5		17

CHARACTERISTICS OF AVAILABLE HARD DISK DRIVES

TABLE C.1: Drive/Interface, Size, Cap (MB), Cyls, H, RWC, WPC, Enc, Rt, Seek (MS), SPT (continued)

DRIVE/ INTERFACE	SIZE	CAP (MB)	CYLS	H	RWC	WPC	Enc	RT	SEEK (MS)	SPT
VERTEX/PRIAM										
ST-506										
V130		26	987	3	988	988	M	5		17
V150		43	987	5	988	988	M	5		17
V170		60	987	7	988	988	M	5		17
WESTERN DIGITAL										
ST-506 MFM										
WD 262		20	615	4	616	616	M	5	80	17
WD 362	3	20	615	4	616	616	M	5	80	17
ST-506 RLL										
WD 344R	3	40	782	4	783	783	R	7.5	40	26
WD 382R/ TM 262R	3	20	782	2	783	783	R	7.5	85	26
WD 384R/ TM 364R	3	20	782	2	783	783	R	7.5	85	26
WD 544R		40	782	4	783	783	R	7.5	40	26
WD 582R		20	782	2	783	783	R	7.5	85	26
WD 584R		40	782	4	783	783	R	7.5	85	26
XEBEC										
SCSI										
OWL II	5H	25		4			M	5	55	
OWL II	5H	38		4			M	5	40	
OWL III	5H	52		4			M	5	38	

INDEX

About This Index: Page numbers shown in **boldface** indicate principal discussions of primary topics and subtopics. Page numbers shown in *italics* denote illustrations.

GETSEC program, 464
.GIF files, 694
gigabytes, 65
Gito hard disk drives, characteristics of, **748–749**
glare screens, 641
GOVDOC-L newsgroup, 700
graphic boards on AT&T computers, 49
GRAPHICS.COM program, 580
graphics coprocessors, **651–653**
Graphics Ultra accelerator board, 666
Green Book CD-ROM standard, 681
ground straps, 148
grounds
   for communications systems, 605
   for power supplies, **314**, **316–317**

H

Haagen-Däzs chocolate ice cream, cleaning off floppies, 539
hair dryers for chip testing, 255
half duplex setting, 601
half-height floppy disk drives, 502–503
   rotation speed of, 527
   in XT computers, 20
handshaking, 619
hard disk drives, **738**
   access time of, **343–345**
   AUTOEXEC.BAT file executed by, **476**
   backups for, **455–457**
   bad areas on, **440–441**
   boot failures, **462–463**
   boot process, **471–475**
   boot records on. *See* boot records
   cables for, 24–25, *24*, 359–360, 364, **419–420**, *421*, 463

caches for, 164, 353–354, **448–449**
controllers for, **10**, 116, *117*, **368–371**
   buffer addresses for, 208
   configuring, **420–427**
   for generic computers, 659
   identifying, 122, *122*
   and interleave factor, 350–351, 370
   removing, 42
   for SCSI, 361
data transfer rates of, **345–346**
drive select jumpers on, **417**, *418*
encoding schemes for, **10**, **354–358**
with FAT damaged, **480–482**
formatting, **433–435**, **439–440**, 451, 483
full-track buffering for, **353–354**
hardcards, 365, 368, **373–374**
hardware structure of, 328, **331–333**, *332–333*
hidden files loaded by, **467–471**
information on, **334–335**
installing, **416–432**
interfaces for, **358–366**
interleave factor for, **345–353**, *346*, *348–350*
IRQs for, 205–206
for multimedia, 675
parking heads for, **446–447**
partition record reading by, **463–466**
partitioning, **435–438**, *436*, 474
on PCMCIA bus, 104
performance of, **342–358**
POST messages for, 178
protecting data on, **451–457**
protecting hardware, 15–16, **444–450**
in PS/2 computers, 39, *41*

J

JCT hard disk drives, characteristics of, **750**
jumper packs, 193, *197*, 417
jumpers. *See also* DIP switches
    for drive select, **417**, *418*
    for floppy disk drives, 511, *512–514*, **515–516**
    for I/O addresses, 202
    for multimedia, 689
    for resource conflicts, **192–193**, *193–194*, *196*
    for ROM addresses, 207

K

K bytes, 78
Kalok Corporation hard disk drives, characteristics of, **750–751**
keeper bars, 20
keyboards, **11**, **110**
    connectors for, 49, 626, *626*
    covers for, 150, 627, 706
    disassembling, **628–629**
    interfaces for, 245, **624–626**
    IRQ for, **205–206**
    maintaining, **627**
    POST for, 172, 174
    replacing, 625, **629–630**
    spills on, **149–150**, 627
    switch design for, **625**
    troubleshooting, **627–629**
keyed cables, 44
keylock connection, 20, 32, 47
kHz (kilohertz), 647
knots in cords for lightning protection, 325
Kyocera hard disk drives, characteristics of, **751**

L

LADDR (Layered Device Driver Architecture) SCSI standard, 401, **405**
LAN (Local Area Network) boards, 120
    buffer addresses for, 208
    configuring, 213, **221–223**
    conflicts in, 207–208, **210–212**
    drivers for, on boot floppy, 4
    grounding problems with, 314
    testing, 227
LAN programs, 164
LANDPRT program, 555
landscape orientation, 558
languages for printers, 580
Lapine hard disk drives, characteristics of, **751**
laptop computers, PCMCIA bus for, **103–106**
laser printers
    circuit board problems in, **591–592**
    corona wires in, **588–589**
    font problems with, **592**
    maintaining, **575–576**
    memory errors with, **591**
    output blotches in, **589–591**, *590*
    paper problems with, **592–593**
    power for, 314
    troubleshooting, **586–593**
LaserJet printers
    features for, **552**, *552–555*
    fonts for, **556–569**
    lines per page with, **556**
    problems with, **591–593**
Layered Device Driver Architecture (LADDR) SCSI standard, 401, **405**
layout of memory chips, **264–267**, *266*, **269–278**

M